UNDERSTANDING

# ISAIAH

# UNDERSTANDING
# ISAIAH

DONALD W. PARRY • JAY A. PARRY • TINA M. PETERSON

DESERET BOOK COMPANY

SALT LAKE CITY, UTAH

**Library of Congress Cataloging-in-Publication Data**

Parry, Donald W.
    Understanding Isaiah / Donald W. Parry, Jay A. Parry, Tina M. Peterson.
        p.    cm.
    Includes bibliographical references and index.
    ISBN 1-57345-361-7 (alk. paper)
    1. Bible. O.T. Isaiah—Commentaries.   2. Christian life—Mormon
authors.   I. Parry, Jay A.   II. Peterson, Tina M., 1965–    .   III. Title.
BS1515.3.P37   1999
224'.1077—dc21                                                      98-15654
                                                                        CIP

Printed in the United States of America                    18961-2883
R. R. Donnelley and Sons, Crawfordsville, IN

10   9   8   7   6   5   4   3   2

# CONTENTS

—⁓—

# ACKNOWLEDGMENTS

We appreciate many individuals who have contributed in a variety of ways to this volume. We gratefully acknowledge the review of portions of the manuscript by dedicated colleagues at Brigham Young University: Robert L. Millet, dean of Religious Education; Stephen D. Ricks, professor of Hebrew and Semitic languages; and Richard D. Draper, Victor L. Ludlow, Joseph Fielding McConkie, and Stephen E. Robinson, professors of ancient scripture. Debra Parker and Melissa Proctor examined portions of an early draft of the manuscript and offered significant and helpful suggestions. We thank Rebecca Chambers, Allison Clinger, Alison Coutts, Vicki Parry, and Shirley Ricks for their proficient editorial work; Susan Southworth and Annaka Parry for typing; Ruth Howard and John Peterson for source checking; and Justin Parry for proofreading the manuscript.

The staff at Deseret Book has done much to turn this work from manuscript into finished book. We're grateful for the leadership of Sheri Dew and Kent Ware and the excellent editorial services of Suzanne Brady and Emily Watts. Others who have brought their considerable professionalism to the task of helping to create a complex book are Ronald O. Stucki, art director; Patricia J. Parkinson, typographer; and Jennifer Pritchett, editorial assistant. Though this work has required the assistance of these and other people, the authors alone are responsible for its content.

# LIST OF ABBREVIATIONS

| | |
|---|---|
| BHS | *Biblia Hebraica Stuttgartensia* |
| DSS | Dead Sea Scrolls |
| GNB | Good News Bible |
| JB | Jerusalem Bible |
| JST | Joseph Smith Translation of the Bible |
| KJV | Holy Bible, Authorized King James Version |
| LB | Living Bible |
| LXX | *Septuaginta* |
| MT | Holy Scriptures according to the Masoretic Text |
| NAB | New American Bible |
| NEB | New English Bible |
| NIV | New International Version of the Holy Bible |
| NKJV | Holy Bible, New King James Version |
| NRSV | Holy Bible, New Revised Standard Version |
| RSV | Holy Bible, Revised Standard Version |

# INTRODUCTION

—◈—

# "GREAT ARE THE WORDS OF ISAIAH"

Most of us as members of the Church know that we have been commanded to diligently search the words of Isaiah. And most of us agree that that is a hard thing to do. Isaiah is indisputably one of the most challenging books in the Bible. We probably wouldn't feel as intimidated if we had been given the special commandment to search Third Nephi or the book of Luke or most of the sections of the Doctrine and Covenants. But Isaiah seems to have been written for another time and place, in a form and language that sometimes seem to defy understanding. In fact, it is common to hear Latter-day Saints say, "I've read First Nephi a dozen times, but I just can't seem to make it through Second Nephi."

What makes Second Nephi so different from First Nephi—or any of the other books in the Book of Mormon? One difference is the Isaiah sections, which Nephi quoted because of their importance and with which we struggle because of their complexity.

## TOOLS FOR UNDERSTANDING

This book provides a set of tools to help remedy that situation. After all, much of the book of Isaiah was written for our time. The following tools are included:

The Book of Mormon and the Joseph Smith Translation have been used to create a more correct, "inspired" version of the King James rendering of Isaiah.

The text of Isaiah has been put back into what may have been Isaiah's original format—a poetic style called parallelism, in which matching phrases repeat the same idea in different words. Seeing Isaiah's words in this form makes them much easier to understand.

The chapters are divided into separate units of thought, to help us make more sense of each part.

Each chapter begins with ideas of how that chapter can be likened unto us and our time.

Helpful background is provided for the many unique words and symbolisms Isaiah used.

A phrase-by-phrase (sometimes word-by-word) commentary is given for the entire book—all sixty-six chapters. This commentary is based principally on the words of the prophets, both ancient and modern.

It is our desire to make Isaiah accessible to members of the Church in many situations and at many educational levels. As you, the reader, apply these tools to your own study, we believe you will begin to understand Isaiah as never before—and will begin to feel for yourself that "great are the words of Isaiah" (3 Ne. 23:1).

## ISAIAH, THE MAN AND HIS WORLD

Isaiah's name means "Jehovah is salvation." How fitting that a man who devoted his life to testifying of the saving power of the Messiah should also have a name that so testified.

Many scholars believe that Isaiah's ministry took place between the years 740 and 700 (or perhaps 699) B.C.—approximately forty years. According to Isaiah 1:1, Isaiah served as a prophet during the reign of several kings in Judah, including Uzziah, Jotham, Ahaz, and Hezekiah. He had personal dealings with at least two of those kings. According to one ancient Jewish source, Isaiah's wife was a daughter of one of the kings of Judah, making Isaiah a member of the royal family by marriage.

Isaiah's wife is called "prophetess" in Isaiah's record (8:3), suggesting that she too had the gift of revelation. Isaiah and his wife had at least two sons who served as signs to Israel, as did Isaiah and his wife themselves. "Behold, I and the children whom the Lord hath given me are for signs and for wonders in Israel from the Lord of hosts" (8:18). As we discuss in the commentary on Isaiah 8, Isaiah stood as a type of God the Father; the prophetess was a type of Mary, the mother of Christ; and one of their sons was a type of Jesus Christ.

According to Josephus, Isaiah was martyred for the faith.[1] King Manasseh, who took rule at the early age of twelve, reportedly put Isaiah in a hollow tree and had him sawed in half[2] (Hebrews 11:37 may be an allusion to this).

What was happening in the political world of Isaiah's time? Assyria, the enemy of Israel, was expanding its borders through whatever means necessary. In 722 and 721 B.C., midway through Isaiah's ministry, Assyria invaded the Northern Kingdom of Israel and carried its inhabitants (the ten tribes of Israel) off into other lands.

In the Southern Kingdom of Judah, where Isaiah ministered, King Uzziah had attempted to burn incense in the temple at Jerusalem without God's authority, and God punished him with leprosy. He died ten years later, in 740 B.C., the same year Isaiah began his ministry. Contrast him with Hezekiah, a righteous king who sought religious reforms.

After conquering the Northern Kingdom of Israel in 721 B.C., Assyria sought to take over the Southern Kingdom of Judah, taking two decades to advance to the city of Jerusalem. Hezekiah and his people were frantic, but Isaiah gave a prophecy of reassurance and comfort: "Therefore thus saith the Lord concerning the king of Assyria, He shall not come into this city, nor shoot an arrow there . . . for I will defend this city to save it for mine own sake. . . . Then the angel of the Lord went forth, and smote in the camp of the Assyrians a hundred and fourscore and five thousand" (37:33–36).

This is an impressive instance of how the Lord spoke through Isaiah and then immediately fulfilled his word. Just as surely, all of the prophecies of Isaiah concerning our day will be fulfilled; not one will fail.

## BLESSINGS FROM STUDYING THE BOOK OF ISAIAH

When we study the writings of Isaiah, we obtain several very important blessings:

We are helped in our efforts to come unto Christ. Nephi wrote, "That I might more fully persuade them to believe in the Lord their Redeemer I did read unto them that which was written by the prophet Isaiah" (1 Ne. 19:23).

We learn truths about ourselves and our circumstances in mortality. "Wherefore, they [Isaiah's words] may be likened unto you, for ye are of the house of Israel" (2 Ne. 6:5); "And now I write some of the words of Isaiah . . . and ye may liken them unto you" (2 Ne. 11:8).

---

[1] *Antiquities of the Jews*, 10.3.1.
[2] Ginzberg, *Legends of the Jews*, 4:279.

We learn about our mission and destiny as members of the house of Israel. The Savior said, "For surely he spake as touching all things concerning my people which are of the house of Israel" (3 Ne. 23:2).

We can learn about the past judgments of God, which we will see repeated in our future. "I have made mention . . . concerning the judgments of God, . . . according to all that which Isaiah hath spoken" (2 Ne. 25:6).

We come to a greater understanding of our future. "And now, behold, I would speak unto you concerning things which are, and which are to come: wherefore, I will read you the words of Isaiah" (2 Ne. 6:4).

We are given cause to rejoice. "And now I write some of the words of Isaiah, that whoso of my people shall see these words may lift up their hearts and rejoice for all men" (2 Ne. 11:8).

Is it any wonder that Nephi said, "Wherefore, they [Isaiah's prophecies] are of worth unto the children of men, . . . for I know that they shall be of great worth unto them in the last days" (2 Ne. 25:8).

## HOW THIS BOOK WILL HELP YOU UNDERSTAND ISAIAH

The Book of Mormon gives four keys to understanding Isaiah, which we must obtain and use for ourselves:

Be righteous—do not do "works of darkness" or "doings of abominations" (2 Ne. 25:2). Righteousness brings the Spirit, which increases understanding.

Be "filled with the spirit of prophecy" (2 Ne. 25:4), which is the spirit of revelation.

Live in the last days, "when they [Isaiah's prophecies] shall come to pass, . . . for in that day shall they understand them" (2 Ne. 25:7, 8).

Make the effort to search, which implies mental and spiritual exertion. Jesus declared twice that we ought to "search these things diligently" (3 Ne. 20:11; 23:1), and Moroni added, "Search the prophecies of Isaiah" (Morm. 8:23).

The Book of Mormon is one of our best commentaries on the book of Isaiah. Nearly a third of the book of Isaiah is quoted in the Book of Mormon, with changes in about half of the verses. In addition, several chapters and verses in the Book of Mormon provide inspired explanations and commentaries of Isaiah's writings. *Understanding Isaiah* brings together all the Book of Mormon insights and changes in the proper context; it also incorporates all the significant changes and insights found in the Joseph Smith Translation of Isaiah.

Nephi taught that we can better understand Isaiah if we understand the "manner of prophesying" among the Jews (2 Ne. 25:1). This manner of prophesying included symbolism and poetic parallelism. *Understanding Isaiah* explains the symbolism Isaiah used in all sixty-six of his chapters, phrase by phrase. And it shows how he used parallelism to teach his divine lessons.

Nephi also suggested that it helps to be familiar with the regions around Jerusalem (2 Ne. 25:6). There are 106 different geographical place-names in the book of Isaiah. *Understanding Isaiah* explains their significance, both literal and symbolic.

Sometimes we tend to read Isaiah's warnings and indictments as having application only (or primarily) to ancient Israel. But when we read by the spirit of prophecy, we suddenly see that they all can be likened to ourselves. We need to remind ourselves constantly that this book is about ancient Israel—and it also is about us.

Elder Bruce R. McConkie plainly taught this principle, saying, "Many prophetic utterances have dual or multiple instances of fulfillment."[3] "As with so many ancient prophecies, these words of Isaiah are subject to the law of dual fulfillment."[4] "The scriptures also provide clear instances of prophecies that may be fulfilled at more than one time," writes Stephen D. Ricks. "The possibility that prophecies may have more than one fulfillment indicates the richness and relevance of the writings of the prophets."[5] Isaiah is filled with multiple meanings—and this volume seeks to explain many of them.

Even several volumes would not provide adequate space for us to say all that we desire about the words of Isaiah. For this volume, we have therefore limited our discussion of historical and cultural perspectives, and we have often not looked at Isaiah's writings from the point of view of his contemporaries. Nevertheless, it has been our goal to present our best possible interpretation of each chapter and verse, even phrases, of this great prophet, focusing on their meaning for our time. We have also sought to be nondogmatic in our views and presentation.

## HOW TO USE THIS BOOK

*Understanding Isaiah* is intended not to be read from beginning to end but to be used as a reference and study aid. The book is organized in chapters following the format of Isaiah, with internal sections breaking the chapters into smaller units. Each

---

[3] *Mortal Messiah,* 2:412 n. 4.
[4] *Doctrinal New Testament Commentary,* 1:368.
[5] "I Have a Question," 28.

section consists of a descriptive heading, an introduction to the section, the text of that passage of Isaiah, and a phrase-by-phrase commentary.

The Isaiah text includes alternate readings from the Book of Mormon, the Joseph Smith Translation, the Dead Sea Scrolls, and the Masoretic text of the Hebrew Bible. It also includes clarifications of archaic words.

The text is arranged in poetic form where possible. Isaiah usually wrote in parallelisms (matching phrases that repeat the same thought in different words). We have marked matching sets of words with italics. If a second parallelism occurs in a set of lines (which is often the case), the parallel words are underlined. For example:

shall be *established* in the top of the <u>mountains</u>,
and shall be *exalted* above the <u>hills</u>;

Brackets in the text indicate a word or phrase that has been added to or altered from the Latter-day Saint edition of the King James Version of the Bible. Brackets are generally accompanied by explanatory footnotes. Scripture citations with only chapter and verse numbers are from Isaiah unless otherwise indicated. Citations such as 1:5a and 1:5b refer, respectively, to the first and second half of the verse cited. Phrases from the verse under discussion appear in italics without quotation marks or a source citation. Full references for the sources in the notes are found in the Bibliography. The transliteration of Hebrew words has been done according to the style guide of Harold Scanlin, *The Dead Sea Scrolls and Modern Translations of the Old Testament.*

It has been our goal to make this a work that combines divine inspiration with human scholarship. Accordingly, we have sought the guidance of the Spirit in coming to our understandings of Isaiah while at the same time seeking insight from inspired statements of prophets and apostles (both ancient and modern) and from the best thinking of scriptural scholars. It has been wonderful for us to read and study the powerful words of the prophet Isaiah. We began as typical students, hoping to find our way to deeper understanding. We bear testimony that that understanding has come, both through diligent effort and through the blessings and grace of the Spirit of the Lord. Because the Lord is just—and because he loves us all—we can bear testimony in confidence that he will help every soul to come to understand the words of his ancient prophet for our day. Those who do will have cause to rejoice, and they will marvel as we do at the greatness of the words of Isaiah.

# ISAIAH 1

### LIKENING ISAIAH 1 UNTO OURSELVES

*The Lord through the prophet Isaiah lists the iniquities of ancient Israel, which include rebelliousness, the commission of social injustices, and the neglect of true temple worship (1:2–15). The Lord then invites Israel to repent and cleanse herself through the power of the Atonement (1:16–20). In our own day the Lord has spoken through the Prophet Joseph Smith and detailed our transgressions, which include social injustices: we "do not impart of [our] substance, as becometh saints, to the poor and afflicted" (D&C 105:3); further, there are "contentions, and envyings, and strifes, and lustful and covetous desires" among us (D&C 101:6; 105). We, like our brothers and sisters of ancient Israel, are invited to repent and become clean through Christ's divine sacrifice: "though your sins be as scarlet, they shall be as white as snow" (1:18).*

*Isaiah 1:24–31 also has direct relevance for us today, for this section speaks of latter-day Zion (that is, us, the latter-day Church), who will be restored, redeemed, and cleansed. Our "dross" and "tin" will be removed; our righteous judges and counselors will be restored.*

## THE VISION OF ISAIAH (1:1)

Isaiah 1:1 presents the name of the prophet (Isaiah), a brief genealogy of Isaiah (son of Amoz), a declaration about the prophecy (the vision of Isaiah), an explanation of the subject (the vision is concerned with Judah and Jerusalem), and the time the vision was given (in the days of the four kings of Judah who ruled during the ministry of Isaiah).

*Isaiah 1:1*

The vision of Isaiah the son of Amoz, which he saw concerning Judah and Jerusalem in the days of Uzziah, Jotham, Ahaz, and Hezekiah, kings of Judah. (1:1)

NOTES AND COMMENTARY

**1:1** *The vision of Isaiah.* Isaiah was a seer and a "prophet" (37:2; 38:1; 39:3). His vision was not a simple, ordinary dream. Joseph Smith, when he spoke of Isaiah and other persons from the Bible, taught that the great visions received by the ancients came after they had received the Second Comforter.[1]

*son of Amoz.* According to the Jewish authority Kimchi, Amoz, not to be confused with the prophet Amos, was "the brother of Amaziah, the father of Uzziah, . . . [which] would make Isaiah of royal lineage and a cousin of Uzziah," king of Judah.[2]

*Judah and Jerusalem.* The vision of Isaiah deals with Judah and Jerusalem, but Isaiah's prophecies also deal with the entire house of Israel, including the lost ten tribes, as the Book of Mormon abundantly testifies. Nephi commands, "Hear ye the words of the prophet [Isaiah], . . . which were written unto all the house of Israel" (1 Ne. 19:24; 2 Ne. 6:5; 3 Ne. 23:2).

*kings of Judah.* These were Uzziah (784–740 B.C.), Jotham (740–735 B.C.), Ahaz (735–715 B.C.), and Hezekiah (715–687 B.C.). Many scholars believe that Isaiah ministered between the years 740 and 700 B.C.

# GOD CHARGES ISRAEL FOR HER SINS (1:2–5A)

This section presents God's charge against Israel. Isaiah's words remind us of a courtroom scene, in which God is both the plaintiff and the judge (3:13: "The Lord standeth up to plead, and standeth to judge the people"; 3:12–15; 5:1–7), the heavens and earth are the witnesses, and Israel is the defendant. The Lord calls his witnesses (1:2a), presents his case and indictment (1:2b–5a, 10–16, 29–31), and pronounces judgment against Israel (1:5b-9). Israel is charged with breaking the covenant[3] and committing great sins.

*Isaiah 1:2–5a*

Hear, O heavens,
    and give ear, O earth

---

[1] *Teachings of the Prophet Joseph Smith,* 151.
[2] Young, *Book of Isaiah,* 1:30–31.
[3] Wildberger, *Isaiah 1–12,* 10; Watts, *Isaiah 1–33,* 15.

For the Lord hath spoken,

*I* have nourished and brought up <u>children</u>,
and <u>they</u> have rebelled against *me*. (1:2)

The *ox* knoweth his <u>owner</u>
and the *ass* his <u>master's</u> [feeding-trough][4]

but *Israel* doth not <u>know</u>,
*my people* doth not [<u>understand</u>].[5] (1:3)

[Woe][6] *sinful* <u>nation</u>,
a <u>people</u> laden with *iniquity,*
a <u>seed</u> of *evildoers,*
<u>children</u> that are *corrupters:*

*they have forsaken* the <u>Lord</u>,
*they have provoked* the <u>Holy One of Israel</u> unto anger, (1:4)
they are gone away backward. (1:4)

Why should *ye be [smitten]*[7] any <u>more</u>?
*ye will revolt* more and <u>more</u>: (1:5a)

## NOTES AND COMMENTARY

**1:2** *Hear/give ear.* This is an injunction to listen intently.

*heavens/earth.* Both the inhabitants of the earth and the angels of heaven stand as witnesses in this formal charge against Israel.[8]

*the Lord hath spoken.* Jehovah is the speaker here.

*I have nourished and brought up children.* God provided ancient Israel with both temporal food (manna; Ex. 16:31–35) and spiritual food (the living bread, which symbolizes the Lord; John 6:31–35), a promised land, the promise of salvation, protection in wars, and prophets; he generally nourished them with constant patience and care, as a parent nourishes a child. God also provides all these things for us.

*rebelled against me.* The term *rebel* here pertains to "the breaking of the covenant."[9] As ancient Israel did, some members of the latter-day Church rebel against the Lord.

---

[4] The Hebrew term *'ebus* reads *feeding-trough* rather than the KJV *crib.* Brown, Driver, and Briggs, *Hebrew and English Lexicon,* 7.

[5] The term *understand* better reflects the Hebrew word *hitebonan,* which is found here.

[6] The term *woe,* used elsewhere in Isaiah (5:18, 20–22), introduces the woe oracle, an accusation form that is usually found in a judgment speech.

[7] The Hebrew root *na kah* used here means "to smite" or "to scourge." Brown, Driver, and Briggs, *Hebrew and English Lexicon,* 645.

[8] Wildberger, *Isaiah 1–12,* 10.

[9] Wildberger, *Isaiah 1–12,* 14.

**1:3** *ox/ass.* These are beasts of burden that need an owner's care and support. The Israelites, like the ox and the ass, must rely on their master (God) for food and must be led to water (Gen. 49:14–15; Hosea 8:8–9; Mosiah 12:5; 21:3). The ox and ass are dumb animals, yet they still obey their master; the children of Israel do not obey their master.

*owner/master.* These symbols refer to the Lord, who is the owner and master of Israel and his people. The Hebrew for *owner* here means someone who has *purchased* an item rather than receiving it through other means such as inheriting it, being given it, or simply finding it. Christ is the purchaser; he purchased us through his atoning sacrifice. This idea is taught by Paul concerning the "church of God, which he [Jesus] hath purchased with his own blood" (Acts 20:28; 1 Cor. 6:20).

**1:4** *sinful, iniquity, evildoers, corrupters.* These words describe the sinful condition of the children of Israel, who have knowingly gone astray from the covenant of the Lord.[10]

*nation/people/seed/children.* These terms speak of the children of Israel and refer directly to the Abrahamic covenant (Abr. 2:9–11). They have great relevance to us today; we too are of the house of Israel and inheritors of the promises given to Abraham.

*Holy One of Israel.* In the Old Testament this title for Jehovah is used almost exclusively by Isaiah, approximately twenty-four times. The term may signify "Temple One of Israel," for in Hebrew the words for *holy* and *temple* derive from the same root.[11] Elsewhere in his book Isaiah uses the same root when he calls God the "Holy One of Jacob" (29:23) and uses *holy* three times in his vision of the Lord sitting on His throne in the heavenly temple, or the celestial kingdom (6:3). We are to emulate the Lord: "Ye shall therefore be holy, for I am holy" (Lev. 11:45).

*unto anger.* The scriptures testify of the indignation of God against the wicked: "I, the Lord, am angry with the wicked" (D&C 63:32); also, "And it shall come to pass, because of the wickedness of the world, that I will take vengeance upon the wicked, for they will not repent; for the cup of mine indignation is full" (D&C 29:17).

**1:5a** *Why should ye be smitten . . . ?* Isaiah asks this rhetorical question to teach us a lesson: Why do you (the house of Israel) continually choose to be smitten by the Lord because of your wickedness? Why will you not learn from the lessons of history recorded in scripture, which tell you that the wicked will be destroyed?

---

[10] Wildberger, *Isaiah 1–12,* 22–23.
[11] Brown, Driver, and Briggs, *Hebrew and English Lexicon,* 871–72; Koehler and Baumgartner, *Lexicon in Veteris Testamenti Libros,* 825–26.

## DESCRIPTION OF ISRAEL'S CONDITION: THE PEOPLE (1:5B–6) AND THE LAND (1:7–9)

Throughout the scriptures, the house of Israel, or church of God, is metaphorically compared to a woman (JST Rev. 12:7; 3 Ne. 22:6), a harlot (Jer. 3:1, 8; Ezek. 16:15–17), a bride (54:1–6; Rev. 21:2, 9; D&C 109:73–74), and a wife (Hosea 1:2–9). Jehovah represents Israel's bridegroom (Matt. 9:15; D&C 33:17–18; 65:3) and eventual husband (54:5; Jer. 31:32).

Similar themes are prominent in Isaiah 1, in which Israel is portrayed as a woman. Isaiah gives us a list of her transgressions, which include apostate temple practices (1:10–16, 29–31), social injustices (1:17, 23), murder (1:21), thievery and bribery (1:23), a lack of true knowledge of God (1:3), and rebellion against God (1:2, 4). In this section Isaiah introduces, through symbolism, a description of this woman (or Israel) in her spiritually diseased state (1:5b-6), and then presents a sketch of Israel's desolate land (1:7–9). We refer to Israel as "Lady Israel."

Much of this section also seems to apply to the time of the Second Coming: references to spiritual sickness, desolation, and burning; enemies coming on Jerusalem, the besieged city; a small surviving remnant; and a destruction that is compared to Sodom and Gomorrah.

*Isaiah 1:5b–9*

> the whole *head* is <u>sick</u>,
> and the whole *heart* [<u>diseased</u>].[12] (1:5b)

> From the sole of the foot even unto the head there is *no soundness* in it;
> but *wounds, and bruises, and putrifying sores:*

> they have not been *closed,*
> neither *bound up,*
> neither *[softened]*[13] with ointment. (1:6)

> Your *country* is <u>desolate</u>,
> your *cities* are <u>burned</u> with fire,

> your *land,* <u>strangers</u> devour it in your presence
> and *it* is desolate, as overthrown by <u>strangers</u>. (1:7)

> And the *daughter of Zion* is left
> as a *cottage* in a <u>vineyard</u>,
> as a [watchman's *hut*][14] in a <u>garden of cucumbers</u>,

---

[12] Brown, Driver, and Briggs, *Hebrew and English Lexicon,* 188.

[13] From Hebrew *rakak,* which means "to soften."

[14] The Hebrew term *melunah* speaks of a "frail, insecure structure." Brown, Driver, and Briggs, *Hebrew and English Lexicon,* 534.

as a besieged *city*. (1:8)

Except the Lord of hosts had left unto us a very small remnant,

*we* should have been as <u>Sodom</u>,
and *we* should have been like unto <u>Gomorrah</u>. (1:9)

## NOTES AND COMMENTARY

**1:5b** *head/heart.* The head of Lady Israel may represent Israel's king and high officials; the heart may represent the common body of Israel. The head and the heart may also refer to a state of complete corruption, both intellectual and spiritual.

*sick/diseased.* These terms refer to the governing body and all the people of Israel who are spiritually ill. Lady Israel's entire body, from the sole of her foot to the crown of her head, is full of bruises and sores—spiritual sicknesses and injuries that came after she (Israel) forsook Jehovah and committed spiritual adultery by seeking foreign deities.

**1:6** *wounds, bruises, sores.* These terms speak of spiritual diseases and injuries and could also represent the social injustices committed by the Israelites.

*ointment.* The term *ointment* may refer to the sacred oil of the temple (Ex. 28:41; Lev. 8:10–12). Isaiah's reference to ointment calls to mind some possible symbolic interpretations. That Lady Israel's wounds and sores were not treated with oil could mean that Israel had forsaken the true temple worship and was involved in apostate temple practices (see commentary on 1:10–16 and 1:29–31). Furthermore, ointment may symbolize the healing power of the blood of the Atonement, meaning that the Israelites failed to make the Atonement effective in their lives by turning to the Lord and repenting. Similarly, all who reject Christ's atonement remain spiritually sick or unhealed.

**1:7** *desolate/burned/devour.* In addition to her illnesses, Lady Israel has suffered the ruin of her once-sacred place of residence (the covenant/promised land) and her cities. They lie desolate, burned with fire and destroyed by strangers. Even the mighty temple city, Jerusalem, now has no more glory or protective spiritual covering (52:1) than a simple cottage or a lowly hut in a garden of cucumbers.

*strangers.* The word is twice mentioned in 1:7, having reference to those who are foreigners (such as the Assyrians and Egyptians) as well as those who live outside the covenant between God and ancient Israel.

**1:8** *daughter of Zion.* This term refers to the city of Jerusalem as well as to its inhabitants (Lam. 1:6–8; 2:10; Zech. 9:9).

*cottage/hut/besieged city.* All that remains in Jerusalem are the cottages and huts. The watchtowers have been removed, and the watchmen (the prophets) have been taken away (Ezek. 3:17–21; 33:1–9). Jerusalem, which once housed the mighty spiritual fortress—God's temple—is now like a cottage.

**1:9** *Lord of hosts.* This title, which may be translated as *Lord of Armies,* is found sixty-two times in Isaiah's writings. The same title is found in the Doctrine and Covenants as "Lord of Sabaoth" (D&C 87:7; 88:2; 95:7). *Sabaoth* ("hosts") should not be confused with *Sabbath.*

The Lord's hosts or armies consist of ancient Israel, which was called "the armies of the living God" (1 Sam. 17:26, 36); the hosts of heaven, also called armies (Dan. 4:35; Rev. 19:14; D&C 88:112); and the latter-day Church, described as being "terrible as an army with banners" (D&C 5:14) and "the army of Israel" (D&C 105:26, 30–31; 109:73). As the Lord's army, we are equipped with the "whole armor of God" (Eph. 6:11–17; D&C 27:15–18), spiritual armor designed to assist us to use light and truth in the battle against the forces of evil.

Jehovah is the "captain" (2 Chr. 13:12), "leader" (55:4), and "man of war" (Ex. 15:3) who will lead us against the armies of evil.

*Sodom/Gomorrah.* These terms represent communities of evil that are recipients of God's divine judgment (Matt. 10:15). Sodom and Gomorrah parallel Israel and Jerusalem here: just as the inhabitants of Sodom and Gomorrah were steeped in sexual sins, through apostasy and false worship Lady Israel has figuratively been unfaithful to her covenant husband, Jehovah.

*remnant.* Although Lady Israel has been destroyed by strangers and her children have been carried away into other lands, the God of Israel, remembering the covenants made with Abraham, permitted a "very small remnant" of Israel to remain upon the earth. If God had not granted this, Lady Israel would have become as the inhabitants of Sodom and Gomorrah and her land as their cities—utterly destroyed. The apostle Paul quoted Isaiah 1:9 and 10:22 (Rom. 9:29 and 27) to demonstrate that God would permit a remnant of Israel to remain on the earth. Joseph Smith, in turn, provided an inspired commentary on these verses of Isaiah and Paul and concluded that "if it were not for the remnant which was left, then might men now be as Sodom and Gomorrah."[15]

---

[15] *Teachings of the Prophet Joseph Smith,* 189.

The remnant mentioned in Isaiah 1:9; 10:21–22; and Romans 9 has reference, in part, to us in this dispensation who have returned to the Lord, hold the priesthood, and honor the Abrahamic covenant.

## CONDEMNATION AGAINST ISRAEL'S APOSTATE TEMPLE PRACTICES (1:10–15)

Isaiah condemns the apostate temple practices and attitudes of Israel. Temple-related terms and phrases include *sacrifices, burnt offerings, fat, blood,* sacrificial animals (*rams, beasts, bullocks, lambs,* and *goats*), temple courtyards (*courts*), *oblations, incense offerings,* temple festivals (*new moons, sabbaths, assemblies, solemn meetings,* and *feasts*), and temple *prayers.* God will not accept temple practices that deviate from those he has ordained: he is "full" of apostate practices and neither "delights" in nor will endure these "abominations"; he "hateth" them and finds them "weary to bear." God hides his eyes from these things and does not hear the prayers of those in the temple.

The Lord is condemning not only apostate religious practices but also insincere obedience to the form of religion. Thus, from this section we learn two lessons: we must not change the form or purpose of the ordinances the Lord gives us, and we must not think that temple worthiness and temple attendance are enough. We also need to love God and serve him with all our hearts.

Again, the theme of covenants between God and Israel plays a prominent role in this scene. The temple and covenant-making are intimately connected, for the temple is the place where covenants are made. This section presents God, represented by several titles and personal pronouns (*Lord,* twice; *me,* four times; *I,* five times; *God; my;* and *mine*), standing in opposition to and accusing the people of Israel (*ye,* four times; *your,* four times; and *you*). In 1:2–5 the Lord makes a formal charge against Israel. Here the Lord further accuses the children of Israel.

*Isaiah 1:10–15*

> *Hear* the <u>word of the Lord</u>, ye rulers of Sodom;
> *give ear* unto the <u>law of our God</u>, ye people of Gomorrah. (1:10)
>
> To what purpose is the multitude of your sacrifices unto me? saith the Lord:
>
> *I am full of* the burnt <u>offerings of rams</u>, and the <u>fat of fed beasts</u>;
> and *I delight not* in the <u>blood of bullocks</u>, or of <u>lambs</u>, or of he <u>goats</u>. (1:11)
>
> When ye come *to appear before me,* who hath required this at your hand,
> *to tread my courts?* (1:12)

Bring no more *vain* oblations;
incense is an *abomination* unto me;

the new moons and sabbaths, the calling of assemblies, *I cannot [endure];*[16]
it is *iniquity,* even the solemn meeting.
Your new moons and your appointed feasts *my soul hateth:* (1:13–14a)

*they* are a trouble unto me;
I am weary to bear *them.* (1:14b)

And when ye *spread forth your hands,* I will hide mine eyes from you;
yea, when ye make many *prayers,* I will not hear:

your hands are full of blood. (1:15)

## NOTES AND COMMENTARY

**1:10** *rulers of Sodom/people of Gomorrah.* These descriptions refer to those who live in the evil community (1:9). That both the rulers and the people are mentioned indicates that the entire populace exists in an apostate condition, as did the inhabitants of Sodom and Gomorrah.

`    *give ear.* To pay spiritual attention to or to listen with your heart (Mosiah 12:27) is to "give ear."

*law of our God.* These are God's commandments and ordinances presented both in the scriptures and in the temple.

**1:11** *sacrifices/burnt offerings.* In this passage Isaiah teaches that although a multitude of sacrifices are being offered, the hearts of the children of Israel are not given with their offerings, and thus their sacrifices are in vain and have no power to draw on the salvation of the Atonement. The emptiness of such offerings, offensive to God, results in condemnation (1 Sam. 15:22). We are under the same condemnation when we observe the forms of our religion without yielding our hearts.

*fat/blood.* The law of Moses provided specific instructions regarding the fat of the sacrificial victim (Lev. 3; 4; 7:23–33; 8:20–26) and its blood (Lev. 4; 8:15, 19, 23–24, 30). The meaning of the sacrifice, which pointed to Christ's atonement, were ignored, misunderstood, or misconstrued in Isaiah's time.

*rams/beasts/bullocks/lambs/goats.* Each of the sacrifices of the Mosaic temple system symbolically pointed to the ministry and atonement of Jesus Christ. Yet because this significance was not understood by the house of Israel, the sacrifices were no longer offered with real intent.

**1:12** *appear before me.* This refers to those who worship God in his temple.[17]

---

[16] The KJV expression *away with* is an archaism, a more modern expression of which is *endure.*

[17] Haran, *Temples and Temple-Service,* 26.

*who hath required this at your hand?* "Who commanded this?"

*courts.* This refers to the courtyards of the temple where temple participants congregated. The three-part temple of Solomon (holy of holies, holy place, and vestibule), the temple of Isaiah's time, had two courtyards attached—an inner and an outer court.

**1:13** *vain oblations.* The sacrifices and offerings of the Israelites were presented to the Lord without the proper attitude or spirit. *Vain* means "empty."

*incense.* Incense, which here refers to the incense offering placed on the altar of incense (Ex. 30:1, 7–8, 34–36), was burned twice daily in the sanctuary. The smoke from these offerings rose to the heavens, symbolizing the prayers of Israel rising to God (Ps. 141:2; Rev. 5:8).

*abomination.* The offerings of Israel were an abomination because the people were wicked, despite their religious observances.

**1:14** *new moons/sabbaths/assemblies/appointed feasts.* These are festive and sacred occasions connected to temple worship. In the Israelite calendar the new moon occurred at the beginning of each month. The sacrificial offerings associated with the new moon included two bullocks, one ram, seven lambs, and one goat. On the Sabbath, two additional lambs were offered. Assemblies and appointed feasts included, among others, Passover (Ex. 12:3–20), Feast of Weeks (Ex. 23:16; 34:22), Day of Blowing of Trumpets (Lev. 23:24; Num. 29:1), Day of Atonement (Lev. 23:26–31), Feast of Tabernacles (Lev. 23:34; Num. 29:12–38), and Purim (Esth. 9). Various sacrificial offerings were presented to the Lord at the appointed feasts. For instance, the sacrifices on the Day of Atonement comprised one bullock, one ram, seven lambs, and one goat.[18]

**1:15** *spread forth your hands.* This divine gesture signifies prayer or supplication. Solomon, for instance, "spread forth his hands toward heaven" (1 Kgs. 8:22) as he uttered the dedicatory prayer of the temple of Solomon. Other references to this temple practice include Psalms 28:2; 63:4; and 134:2.

*hide mine eyes/will not hear.* God will not consider the apostate temple rites and ceremonials to be efficacious, nor is he pleased by correct performances offered by wicked people.

*hands are full of blood.* Here, hands symbolize the whole person, the agent who commits evil deeds (Ps. 7:3; 26:10). Israel spread forth her hands toward God in an act of prayer, but God saw that her hands were *full of blood,* representative of gross

---

[18] *New Bible Dictionary,* 1046.

iniquity (such as murder or bloodshed; Alma 5:22–25). Isaiah employs similar imagery elsewhere in his writings (2:8; 17:8; 37:19; 59:3, 6).

## INVITATION FOR ISRAEL TO REPENT AND CLEANSE THEMSELVES (1:16–20)

Even though the Israelites exist in a spiritually sick condition (1:5b-9) and are found in a state of apostasy (1:10–15), God nevertheless invites them to return to him through repentance, so they can worship the true God of Israel. God then tells them what they must do to become clean and temple worthy once again. God's message requires Israel to become clean through ordinances ("wash ye") and Jesus' atonement (1:18). Emphasis is also placed on having a desire to be clean and on doing good works ("if ye be willing and obedient"), which will allow them to "eat the good of the land" (1:19). Nine imperatives—*wash, make clean, put away, cease, learn, seek, relieve, vindicate,* and *plead*—serve as guidelines that will help Israel return to righteous living. The same imperatives apply to us in this dispensation.

*Isaiah 1:16–20*

Wash [ye],[19]
*make you clean;*

*put away the evil of your doings* from before mine eyes;
*cease to do evil;* (1:16)

Learn to do well;
seek [justice],[20]

*relieve* the oppressed,
*[vindicate]*[21] the fatherless,
*plead* for the widow. (1:17)

Come now, and let us reason together, saith the Lord:

though your sins be as *scarlet,* they shall be as white as snow;
though they be red like *crimson,* they shall be as wool. (1:18)

If ye be *willing and obedient,* ye shall eat the good of the land; (1:19)
But if ye *refuse and rebel,* ye shall be devoured with the sword.

for the mouth of the Lord hath spoken it. (1:20)

---

[19] JST Isa. 1:16 modifies the singular *wash you* to the plural *wash ye.*
[20] The term *justice* adequately fits the description and meaning of the passage and replaces *judgment.* See footnote c to 1:17 in the LDS edition of the Bible.
[21] The term *vindicate* should replace the KJV imperative *judge* used here. Brown, Driver, and Briggs, *Hebrew and English Lexicon,* 1047.

NOTES AND COMMENTARY

**1:16** *Wash.* The term may refer to washing with water the hands and feet of individuals about to enter the temple. It also points to baptism[22] (see also the corrected reading herein of 48:1), which is a ritual cleansing from sins and transgressions. Ultimately, washing with water represents symbolic washing with the blood of Christ to become spiritually clean.

*eyes.* Eyes "are a representation of light and knowledge" (D&C 77:4; 88:67). "God, of course, has all knowledge and is full of light. Thus it is said of him that his eye is an 'all-searching eye' (2 Ne. 9:44) and a 'piercing eye' (Jacob 2:10), meaning there is no place that his eye cannot penetrate and nothing that he does not know. He is omniscient."[23] Thus in 1:16, God is aware of the Israelites' evil doings, and he commands them to cease.

**1:17** *vindicate.* This means to render a just decision for those who have been offended.

*oppressed/fatherless/widow.* These words are symbolic of all individuals—the downtrodden, the oppressed, the unfortunate—who need temporal and spiritual strengthening. The law of Moses required the Israelite community to care for widows, the fatherless, and strangers (Ex. 22:21–22); modern revelation instructs us: "Behold, I say unto you, that ye must visit the poor and the needy and administer to their relief" (D&C 44:6). Again we see a parallel between Sodom and Gomorrah and Jerusalem. Sodom and Gomorrah's inhabitants were destroyed, in part because they failed to care for the needy and oppressed (Ezek. 16:49), and here Jerusalem is warned to care for the downtrodden.

**1:18** *reason together.* The Lord tells the elders of his church in our era that the purpose of reasoning together is "that ye may understand" (D&C 50:10–12; see also D&C 61:13; 45:10). Reasoning together with the Lord is a process that requires prayer and revelation.

*scarlet/crimson.* In this passage scarlet (a bright red) and crimson (a deep red) are both used to symbolize blood, which in turn can signify iniquity. The sins of the children of Israel were both bright and deep-seated, hence this imagery (see *hands are full of blood* in 1:15).

*snow/wool.* The Lord, through Isaiah, contrasts the bloodlike colors scarlet and crimson with two tangible materials, snow and wool, both of which are white. White symbolizes purity, innocence, and light. In addition, wool, as a product from the

---

[22] Smith, *Answers to Gospel Questions,* 1:51.
[23] McConkie and Parry, *Guide to Scriptural Symbols,* 47.

lamb, points to the atonement of Jesus, the "Lamb of God, which taketh away the sin of the world" (John 1:29).

**1:19** *willing and obedient/eat the good of the land.* God made this same promise to us: "The willing and obedient shall eat the good of the land of Zion in these last days. And the rebellious shall be cut off out of the land of Zion, and shall be sent away, and shall not inherit the land" (D&C 64:34–35).[24] These words recall the oft-recurring Book of Mormon statement that "inasmuch as ye shall keep the commandments of God ye shall prosper in the land; and . . . inasmuch as ye will not keep the commandments of God ye shall be cut off from his presence" (Alma 36:30).

**1:20** *ye shall be devoured with the sword.* In the scriptures, the sword symbolizes either warfare (3 Ne. 2:19) or the word of the Lord (1 Ne. 21:2; Alma 31:5; D&C 6:2). Here the sword represents warfare, but note the close connection with the phrase "for the mouth of the Lord hath spoken it." Isaiah presents a graphic image with the word *devoured,* showing that the destruction will be complete.

*mouth.* This organ of speech refers to the whole person.

## LAMENT FOR THE INHABITANTS OF JERUSALEM (1:21–23)

The Lord laments that the inhabitants of Jerusalem have committed gross social injustices and have become like dross and watered-down wine. The opening term *how* is a common introduction to a lament (Lam. 1:1).

*Isaiah 1:21–23*

How is the *faithful city* become an <u>harlot</u>!
*it was full of judgment; righteousness* lodged in it; but now <u>murderers</u>. (1:21)

Thy *silver* is become <u>dross</u>,
thy *wine* mixed with <u>water</u>. (1:22)

Thy princes are *rebellious,*
and *companions of thieves:*

every one *loveth [bribes],*[25]
and *followeth after rewards:*

*They* [vindicate][26] not the <u>fatherless</u>,
neither doth the cause of the <u>widow</u> come unto *them.* (1:23)

---

[24] *Teachings of the Prophet Joseph Smith,* 77.

[25] The Hebrew term *shachad* should read *bribes* rather than *gifts.* Brown, Driver, and Briggs, *Hebrew and English Lexicon,* 1005.

[26] The term *vindicate* should replace the KJV imperative *judge* used here. Brown, Driver, and Briggs, *Hebrew and English Lexicon,* 1047.

NOTES AND COMMENTARY

**1:21** *faithful city.* This signifies Jerusalem, whose inhabitants were once faithful.

*harlot.* In the world of the Bible, cities are considered to be feminine. Here Jerusalem (speaking of her inhabitants) acted as a harlot and was unfaithful to Jehovah (her husband) by pursuing and loving other deities (see commentary on 1:5–9; 23:15–18).

*judgment/righteousness.* This is a word pair used frequently by Isaiah (1:27; 16:5; 28:17; 33:5; 56:1) to describe Jerusalem's inhabitants, who once were just in their dealings and were righteous but who now are "murderers."

*murderers.* This word may refer literally to murder or symbolically to those who guide individuals "away unto destruction" (Alma 36:14; Matt. 10:28); those who cause spiritual destruction are guilty of spiritual murder.

**1:22** *silver/wine.* Individuals who are precious and pure are compared to silver and wine. God is like "a refiner and purifier of silver," and he will in the last days "purify the sons of Levi, and purge them as gold and silver" (Mal. 3:3).

*dross/water.* Dross is the valueless waste material found on the surface of molten metal. Those who were once precious (like silver and wine) but have polluted themselves with the ways of the world are called *dross.* The Lord, through Ezekiel, said that "the house of Israel is to me become dross . . . they are even the dross of silver" (Ezek. 22:18; see Ps. 119:119; Alma 34:29). "Silver can contain some alloy and still be silver, but *silver* which has *become dross* has suffered total degeneration. Similarly, as soon as wine is touched with water no particle of it remains undiluted."[27] Sin corrupts us as water dilutes wine and dross contaminates precious metal.

**1:23** *princes.* This term refers to leaders and chiefs of the city.

*bribes/rewards.* Those who give or receive bribes love money more than righteousness.

*fatherless/widow.* Vindicating the fatherless and pleading for the widow are part of the requirements of repentance given in 1:17. Those who care for the fatherless and the widows are they who practice pure religion (James 1:27).

## ZION TO BE REDEEMED, THE WICKED DESTROYED (1:24–31)

This prophecy speaks of our day. Isaiah prophesies of two separate groups who will live in the last days (the timing of which is made clearer by Joseph Smith):[28]

---

[27] Motyer, *Prophecy of Isaiah,* 49.

[28] *Teachings of the Prophet Joseph Smith,* 93.

those who belong to Zion, and those who belong to the community of wickedness. In the latter days, Zion will be restored, redeemed, and cleansed; her dross and tin will be removed, her righteous judges and counselors will be restored, and once again Zion will be the faithful city—the "city of righteousness." The text makes clear that it is the Lord's atoning sacrifice that will cleanse members of Zion: "I will turn my hand upon thee, and purely purge away thy dross" (1:25). Those who belong to the wicked community will be destroyed, "consumed," "ashamed," "confounded," and burned.

*Isaiah 1:24–31*

Therefore saith the Lord,

the *Lord of hosts,*
the *mighty one of Israel,*

Ah, I will *ease me* of mine <u>adversaries</u>,
and *avenge me* of mine <u>enemies</u>: (1:24)

And I will turn my hand upon thee, and purely *purge away* thy <u>dross</u>,
and *take away* all thy <u>tin</u>: (1:25)

And I will restore thy *judges* as at the <u>first</u>,
and thy *counsellors* as at the <u>beginning</u>:

afterward thou shalt be called, The *city* of <u>righteousness</u>,
the <u>faithful</u> *city.* (1:26)

*Zion* shall be redeemed with [<u>justice</u>],[29]
and her *converts* with <u>righteousness</u>. (1:27)

And the *destruction* of the <u>transgressors</u> and of the <u>sinners</u> shall be together,
and <u>they that forsake the Lord</u> shall be *consumed.* (1:28)

For [ye][30] shall be *ashamed* of the <u>oaks</u> which ye have desired,
and ye shall be *confounded* for the <u>gardens</u> that ye have chosen. (1:29)

For ye shall be as an *oak* whose <u>leaf fadeth</u>,
and as a *garden* that hath <u>no water</u>. (1:30)

And the *strong* shall be as [<u>tinder</u>],[31]
and the *maker* of it as a <u>spark</u>,

and *they* shall both <u>burn</u> together,
and <u>none shall quench</u> *them.* (1:31)

## NOTES AND COMMENTARY

**1:24** *Lord of hosts.* See commentary on 1:9.

---

[29] The term *justice* fits the context better than *judgment.* See footnote *b* to 1:27 in the LDS edition of the Bible.

[30] *Ye* is the correct reading; *they* does not fit the context.

[31] NIV Isa. correctly has *tinder* here.

*mighty one of Israel.* The Lord is called "mighty God" in 9:6 and the "mighty One of Jacob" in 49:26. Such titles describe his great power.

**1:25** *turn my hand upon thee.* This phrase signifies the Lord's great power and ability to keep his promises to his Zion community.

*purge.* This term, which means "to purify and cleanse," clearly points to the atonement of Jesus, by whom we are cleansed from sin (6:7; Ps. 79:9; Heb. 1:3; 9:22). On one occasion Joseph Smith taught that "we need purging, purifying and cleansing."[32]

*dross.* The term applies both to the wicked who are as *dross* and to the wickedness that is within each of us (see commentary on 1:22).

*tin.* In biblical times (as now), metals were graded according to their degree of availability. Gold and silver were the most precious metals; tin, brass, lead, and iron were less precious (Ezek. 22:18–22; Dan. 2:31–42). Tin in this context may represent mediocre individuals who are more righteous than those identified with dross but not as precious as those likened to gold or silver (1:22).

**1:26** *restore thy judges/counsellors.* This verse looks forward to the restoration of officials, authorities, and leaders, or *judges* and *counsellors.* Joseph Smith taught: "One of the most important points in the faith of the Church of the Latter-day Saints, through the fullness of the everlasting Gospel, is the gathering of Israel (of whom the Lamanites constitute a part) that happy time when Jacob shall go up to the house of the Lord, to worship Him in spirit and in truth, to live in holiness; when the Lord will restore His judges as at the first, and His counselors as at the beginning. . . .

". . . In speaking of the gathering, we mean to be understood as speaking of it according to scripture, the gathering of the elect of the Lord out of every nation on earth, and bringing them to the place of the Lord of Hosts, when the city of righteousness shall be built, and where the people shall be of one heart and one mind, when the Savior comes."[33]

*faithful city.* This represents Jerusalem and the New Jerusalem.

**1:27** *Zion . . . redeemed.* The righteous members of the Church have opportunity to become the latter-day Zion, which will be redeemed according to Isaiah's prophecy (D&C 100:13; 105).

*her converts.* Those who dwell in Zion and are pure in heart are the *converts.*[34]

[32] *Teachings of the Prophet Joseph Smith,* 329.
[33] *Teachings of the Prophet Joseph Smith,* 92–93.
[34] *Teachings of the Prophet Joseph Smith,* 76.

**1:28** *transgressors.* Isaiah speaks of Zion and her converts in 1:27 and then speaks of transgressors in 1:28. Joseph Smith also juxtaposes Zion and transgressors when he indicates that those who do not assist in the building of Zion are transgressors.[35]

*consumed.* The scriptures repeatedly affirm that the wicked will be destroyed at the Second Coming by Jesus Christ, who is "a consuming fire" (Heb. 12:29) and "a wall of fire" (Zech. 2:5). Christ will burn the wicked by the light of his glory (D&C 133:41).

**1:29** *oaks.* Oaks are connected to the groves of the Canaanite mother goddess. God commanded Israel to destroy the groves (Ex. 34:13; Deut. 7:5; 2 Kgs. 18:4; Isa. 27:9) because they represented idol worship and apostate temple practices that often took place on high hills (1 Kgs. 14:23; 2 Kgs. 17:10). Such trees and groves are counterfeits of the tree of life, which was associated with the Lord's ancient temples.

*gardens.* Although gardens are typically associated with true temples (Gen. 2:8–16), here the gardens are affiliated with counterfeit temple systems (65:3).[36]

**1:30** *ye shall be as an oak . . . and as a garden.* The two metaphors here (*oak* and *garden*) describe the status of the wicked (Luke 23:31; Alma 5:52; 3 Ne. 14:17–18). Inasmuch as the wicked have chosen to worship idols that are connected to oaks and gardens (1:29), they will in a sense become what they have worshiped—as valueless as an oak tree that is either dying or plagued with disease (*an oak whose leaf fadeth*), or as unfruitful and worthless *as a garden that hath no water.* The oak tree that lacks water (spiritually, Jesus represents the living waters) soon shrivels up and becomes kindling for the fire accompanying the second coming of Jesus that will burn all corruptible things. A dry garden is in a similar state.

*water.* Jesus Christ and the cleansing and purifying power of his atonement are represented by water (33:21; Jer. 2:13; 17:13; John 4:6–14).

**1:31** *tinder/spark.* Tinder (or tow) is composed of short, broken fibers from flax or hemp. These two terms point to the future consumption wherein all the wicked will be burned at the second coming of Christ (Mal. 3; 4; D&C 63:32–34; 101:23–25).

---

[35] *Teachings of the Prophet Joseph Smith,* 254.
[36] Parry, "Garden of Eden," 126–51.

# ISAIAH 2

### LIKENING ISAIAH 2 UNTO OURSELVES

*Isaiah speaks directly to us. Many of us are personally blessed to see the fulfillment of this prophecy as we enter the Lord's temples and are taught therein of "his ways" and walk in "his paths" (2:3). Isaiah's prophecy of the "mountain of the Lord" (2:1–5) is fulfilled as we build temples throughout the world.*

*Isaiah 2:10–22 is one of the greatest prophecies recorded in the standard works of Christ's second coming and his judgments on the proud. Perhaps we, or our children or grandchildren, may witness these events as Jesus Christ comes again to the earth, this time with great power and glory.*

## THE MOUNTAIN (TEMPLE) OF THE LORD (2:1–5)

This prophecy speaks to us in our day. The gathering of Israel, temples, and temple service are the principal themes in this section; we will "flow" upwards to the temple mountain, learn of God's ways (in the temple), and walk in God's paths (in the temple). In addition, temple service and worship (2:2–3) are directly connected to worldwide peace and prosperity (2:4); that is, temple attendance (2:2) results in peace (2:4), a desire to learn of God (2:3), and a willingness to walk in his light (2:5). Micah presents the same prophecy in his writings (Micah 4:1–3).

Joseph Smith summed up the connection between the gathering of Israel and temple service: "The object of gathering the Jews, or the people of God in any age of the world . . . was to build unto the Lord a house whereby He could reveal unto His people the ordinances of His house and the glories of His kingdom, and teach the people the way of salvation."[1]

---

[1] *History of the Church,* 5:423.

*Isaiah 2:1–5*

The word that Isaiah the son of Amoz saw concerning Judah and Jerusalem. And it shall come to pass in the last days, [when][2] the mountain of the Lord's house (2:1–2a)

shall be *established* in the top of the <u>mountains</u>,
and shall be *exalted* above the <u>hills</u>;

and all *nations* <u>shall flow</u> unto it. (2:2b)
And many *people* <u>shall go</u> and say,

*Come* <u>ye</u>,
and let <u>us</u> *go* up

to the *mountain* of the <u>Lord</u>,
to the *house* of the <u>God of Jacob</u>;

and he will *teach us* of <u>his ways</u>,
and *we will walk* in <u>his paths</u>:

for *out of Zion* shall go forth the <u>law</u>,
and the <u>word</u> of the Lord *from Jerusalem*. (2:3)

And he shall *judge* among the <u>nations</u>,
and shall *[settle the case]*[3] for many <u>people</u>:

and they shall beat *their swords* into <u>plowshares</u>,
and *their spears* into <u>pruninghooks</u>:

*nation* shall not lift up <u>sword</u> against *nation*,
neither shall *they* learn <u>war</u> any more. (2:4)

O house of Jacob, *come* ye, and let us <u>walk</u> in the light of the Lord;
[yea, *come,* for ye have all <u>gone</u> astray, every one to his wicked ways].[4] (2:5)

## NOTES AND COMMENTARY

**2:1** *word that Isaiah . . . saw.* Perhaps, like the Prophet Joseph Smith and Sidney Rigdon (D&C 76:11–12, 28), Isaiah actually saw the things described in his prophecies and then recorded them in a scroll or book.

*Judah and Jerusalem.* See commentary on 1:1.

**2:2** *last days.* This expression refers to our day, the dispensation of the fulness of times.

*mountain of the Lord's house.* This term represents the temple of God (56:7; Ex. 15:17). "The whole of America is Zion itself from north to south, and is described by

---

[2] The Book of Mormon replaces the phrase *that the mountain of the Lord's house* with *when the mountain of the Lord's house.* The term *when* implies that the events in 2:2 will come to pass at a specific time.
[3] The Hebrew term *hokiyach* signifies "settle the case" rather than the KJV *judge.*
[4] Both JST Isa. 2:5 and 2 Ne. 12:5 add the phrase *yea, come, for ye have all gone astray, every one to his wicked ways* to the end of 2:5 as an invitation for the wicked to repent and return to the Lord. The added phrase creates a parallelism with *O house of Jacob, come ye, and let us walk in the light of the Lord.*

the prophets, who declare that it is the Zion where the *mountain of the Lord* should be, and that it should be in the center of the land."[5] Jerusalem is also "Zion." The principal features of both Zions will be the temple that will be established in each Zion and the Lord who will sit as king in the throne rooms of the temples (D&C 133:12–13).

*mountains/hills.* Isaiah 2:2 is a prophecy with multiple applications; it refers to the Salt Lake Temple, nestled in the hills and mountains; to the future temple of Jerusalem, established in the mountains of Judea; and to other temples. Joseph Smith learned through revelation that "Zion shall flourish upon the hills and rejoice upon the mountains, and shall be assembled together unto the place which I [God] have appointed" (D&C 49:25).

*shall be exalted.* Spiritually, the temple represents the highest point on earth, which symbolically connects heaven and earth; it is where God's word is revealed to his prophet.

*all nations shall flow.* Joseph Smith taught that "there should be a place where *all nations* shall come up from time to time to receive their endowments."[6] *All nations* (which means some people from all nations) shall come to obey the God of all nations and to build the kingdom of God. For something to "flow," like a river, up a mountain, a power greater than gravity must be at work; this power is the power of God and of the temple.

**2:3** *mountain of the Lord.* See commentary on 2:2.

*house.* The temple is the Lord's house. As with the family home, the temple is a home where people can enjoy the family of God, can delight in peace and quiet away from the world's troubles and concerns, and can offer up their personal prayers to Heavenly Father.

*he will teach us of his ways.* The Lord will teach us through revelation given through his prophets and apostles, through the scriptures, and by way of personal revelation (54:13). Specifically, we will learn of God's ways in his temple.

*walk in his paths.* The "path of the just" (Prov. 4:18) or the "strait and narrow path" (2 Ne. 31:18) leads first through the gates of baptism and then past the portals of the Lord's holy temple. Before being able to walk in God's paths, though, we must first let the Lord teach us his laws and his ways. Jesus Christ, of course, is the path or the way in which we must walk (John 14:6).

---

[5] *Teachings of the Prophet Joseph Smith,* 362; emphasis added; entire statement in italics in original.
[6] *Teachings of the Prophet Joseph Smith,* 367; emphasis added; see also 27.

*out of Zion/from Jerusalem.* These will be the two religious "capitals for the kingdom of God during the millennium."[7] One will be located in Independence, Missouri (D&C 57:3; 84:2–4); the other will be found in old Jerusalem (Ether 13:2–11). Both centers will be called Zion and Jerusalem, and they will possess great temples.

*shall go forth the law.* Regarding this phrase, President Harold B. Lee wrote: "I have often wondered what the expression meant, that out of Zion shall go forth the law. Years ago I went with the brethren to the Idaho Falls Temple, and I heard in that inspired prayer of the First Presidency a definition of the meaning of that term 'out of Zion shall go forth the law.' Note what they said: 'We thank thee that thou hast revealed to us that those who gave us our constitutional form of government were men wise in thy sight and that thou didst raise them up for the very purpose of putting forth that sacred document [as revealed in Doctrine and Covenants section 101]. . . .

"'We pray that kings and rulers and the peoples of all nations under heaven may be persuaded of the blessings enjoyed by the people of this land by reason of their freedom and under thy guidance and be constrained to adopt similar governmental systems, thus to fulfill the ancient prophecy of Isaiah and Micah that " . . . out of Zion shall go forth the law and the word of the Lord from Jerusalem."' (*Improvement Era,* October 1945, p. 564.)"[8]

This prophecy could also mean that the laws of the millennial kingdom will originate in the millennial Zion.

*word of the Lord.* Joseph Smith taught the manner in which the Lord's word would proceed forth: "Moses received the word of the Lord from God Himself; he was the mouth of God to Aaron, and Aaron taught the people, in both civil and ecclesiastical affairs; . . . so will it be when the purposes of God shall be accomplished: when 'the Lord shall be King over the whole earth' and 'Jerusalem His throne.' 'The law shall go forth from Zion, and the *word of the Lord* from Jerusalem.'"[9]

**2:4** *he shall judge/settle the case.* Jesus, under the authority of the Father, will be the judge of the world (John 5:27; Acts 10:42; Heb. 12:23) when he makes his great and dreadful appearance on the earth.

---

[7] Smith, *Doctrines of Salvation,* 3:71.

[8] "Way to Eternal Life," 15.

[9] *Teachings of the Prophet Joseph Smith,* 252; emphasis added.

*swords/spears.* These instruments represent war and destruction (2 Ne. 1:18; 3 Ne. 2:19; D&C 45:33).

*plowshares/pruninghooks.* A plowshare is the cutting blade of a plow; a pruning hook is a tool with a hooked blade that is used for pruning plants. Swords, spears, plowshares, and pruning hooks all have blades; plowshares and pruning hooks are useful and conducive to the work ethic and eventual prosperity, therefore representing instruments of peace and prosperity.[10]

*learn war any more.* Earlier in this verse Isaiah tells us that during the Millennium nations will not participate in war, for they will destroy their weapons and make them into useful implements. Now the prophet informs us that the nations will not even *learn* (study or gain knowledge) of war.

**2:5** *walk.* To walk in God's light demonstrates a spiritual approach to life, righteous living, and a godly attitude. Jesus Christ is the way in which we should walk (John 14:6; 2 Ne. 10:23).

*light of the Lord.* Here the *light of the Lord* is set in the context of the temple. Walking in the light of the Lord has incalculable personal value because the light "enlighteneth [the] eyes" (D&C 88:11), "quickeneth . . . understandings" (D&C 88:11), infuses "joy into [the] soul," and dispels darkness so that the "dark veil of unbelief [is] cast away" (Alma 19:6).

## ISAIAH'S ADDRESS (PRAYER) TO JEHOVAH (2:6–9)

Both the Book of Mormon and the Joseph Smith Translation add the expression "O Lord" at the beginning of this section, which indicates that Isaiah is addressing the Lord in prayer. Isaiah presents a list of sins committed by Israel, including practicing false temple worship (2:6), seeking after earthly riches (2:7), building up arms and weaponry (2:7), worshiping idols (2:8), and indulging in pride (2:9), all of which stand in opposition to the law of Moses. People in our day are also guilty of such sins.

On four occasions Isaiah uses the word *full* or its equivalent (*replenished,* "make full"; 2:6, 7, and 8) to point out that Israel has saturated the land with silver, gold, war vehicles, and idols rather than filling it with righteousness. Isaiah's multiple use of *full* corresponds with the phrase "fully ripe" found in the Book of Mormon (Alma 37:31; 45:16). It might be said of ancient Israel that the "cup of their iniquity [was] *full*" (D&C 101:11), as Jehovah says of our dispensation: "Behold, the day has come, when the cup of the wrath of mine indignation is *full*" (D&C 43:26; 29:17).

---

[10] *Teachings of the Prophet Joseph Smith,* 248.

## Isaiah 2:6–9

Therefore, [O Lord],[11] thou hast forsaken thy people
the house of Jacob, because they be replenished from the east,

and *[hearken unto the]*[12] soothsayers like the Philistines,
and they *[clasp hands]*[13] with the children of strangers. (2:6)

Their land also is *full* of silver and gold,
*neither is there any end* of their treasures;

their land is also *full* of horses,
*neither is there any end* of their chariots: (2:7)

Their land also is full of idols; they worship the *work* of their own hands,
that which their own fingers *have made:* (2:8)

And the *[ordinary]*[14] *man* boweth [not] down,
and the *great man* humbleth himself [not]:[15] therefore forgive them not. (2:9)

### NOTES AND COMMENTARY

**2:6** *thou hast forsaken.* The Lord has forsaken members of the house of Israel because of their wicked condition (2:6–9). The term *forsaken* has the sense of abandoning the house of Israel and leaving them without the Spirit of the Lord, revelation, and God's word through his living prophets.

*replenished . . . east.* To the Israelites, "east is the sacred direction. Holy temples are oriented eastward, . . . Jesus Christ enters his temples from the east (Ezek. 43:1–2; see Ezek. 10:19); and at the time of the Second Coming, the Lord will come from the east (JS–M 1:26; Matt. 24:27; *Teachings,* 287)."[16] In 2:5, the prophet Isaiah commands the house of Israel to "walk in the light of the Lord," which comes from the east. Yet the house of Israel attempted to be spiritually revitalized (*replenished*) through apostate, spurious sources from the east (such as the deities and religious systems of the heathen countries), which constituted mockery unto God.

*soothsayers.* Individuals who pretend to prophesy or predict the future are soothsayers. The law of Moses contained express commands against the Israelites' association with these false prophets (Lev. 18:26; Deut. 18:10–12).

---

[11] Both JST Isa. 2:6 and 2 Ne. 12:6 add the phrase *O Lord* after the conjunctive adverb *therefore,* an addition that identifies the Lord as the referent of the pronouns that follow.

[12] Both JST Isa. 2:6 and 2 Ne. 12:6 add the expression *hearken unto* before the word *soothsayers* to show that the people are not soothsayers themselves but that they listen to the soothsayers.

[13] Hebrew *sepiyqu* means to "clasp hands" rather than the KJV "please themselves."

[14] The KJV *mean* has the present-day meaning of "ordinary."

[15] Both JST Isa. 2:9 and 2 Ne. 12:9 twice insert the term *not* in this passage to show that the ordinary man and the great man do not humble themselves before God.

[16] McConkie and Parry, *Guide to Scriptural Symbols,* 44.

*Philistines.* This was a group of people who occupied southwest Palestine and who often warred against Israel.

*clasp hands . . . children of strangers.* One meaning of this phrase is to participate and make covenants in apostate temple systems with those who are not affiliated with the true Israelite temple. The Hebrew word for *strangers* has reference to characters who are "foreign" or "alien" to the house of Israel.[17] A command from the law of Moses warned the Israelites, "Thou shalt make no covenant with them [strangers; such as the Amorites, Hittites, Perizzites, Canaanites, Hivites, and Jebusites], nor with their gods" (Ex. 23:32). The phrase also refers to God's command that Israelites not intermarry with those who do not belong to covenant Israel (Deut. 7:1–4).

**2:7** *silver/gold/treasures.* When they sought these riches, which are symbolic of worldly materialism (Rev. 17:4; 18:16; 1 Ne. 13:7–8), ancient Israel broke the law of Moses, for they were commanded, "neither shall [you] greatly multiply to [your]self silver and gold" (Deut. 17:17). The Lord's people are ever commanded to seek him rather than the riches of this world.

*horses/chariots.* These represent warfare and military might (31:3; Job 39:19–24; Jer. 46:4; Ezek. 38:4).

**2:8** *idols.* This term refers both to heathen deities constructed of wood and stone and to more abstract things that men become excessively devoted to, including worldly wealth, the honor of men, and things of the flesh. Isaiah speaks of idols in 2:8, 18, 20; 10:10–11; 19:1, 3; and 31:7. The law of Moses speaks clearly against the creation and worship of idols (Ex. 20:3–4).

**2:9** *ordinary/great man.* Both ordinary people, or commoners, and those who have achieved worldly status and position are guilty of pride.

*forgive them not.* Isaiah, whose testimony lists the sins of Israel, stands as a witness against the house of Israel in Jehovah's courtroom (1:2–5; 2:4). Inasmuch as the children of Israel saturate their lives with sins (as Isaiah suggests in the terms *replenished* and *full,* used several times) and fail to hearken to the voice of many prophets by repenting and turning to God, Isaiah can deliver his plea (prayer) before the Lord: *Forgive them not.*

Isaiah has testified against Israel, and now, according to the custom of the court, the judge will deliver his sentence. In this case, the judgment will be delivered by Jesus Christ during the "day of Jehovah" (2:12).

---

[17] Brown, Driver, and Briggs, *Hebrew and English Lexicon,* 648–49.

## THE DAY OF JEHOVAH (2:10–22)

This section features a detailed description of the "day of the Lord," or the Second Coming, which is presented both in symbolic and in plain terms. The repetition found in the passage gives emphasis to specific aspects of the revelation. For example, Isaiah speaks three times concerning the "fear of the Lord" and the "glory of his majesty" (2:10, 19, 21); twice he says that "the Lord alone shall be exalted in that day" (2:11, 17). On two occasions Isaiah uses the phrase "for fear of the Lord [shall come upon them], and the glory of his majesty [shall smite them]" (2:10, 19); twice he notes that the idols of humanity will be destroyed (2:18, 20), and twice he mentions that the loftiness or haughtiness of man would be bowed down or made low (2:11, 17).

This passage also clarifies the great contrast between the exaltation of God and the lowliness of mankind. When the day of the Lord shall come, the wicked will be "humbled," "bowed down," "brought low," and "made low." They will seek low areas of earth (a phrase that recalls hell, the grave, and the underworld), holes, caves, clefts, and rocks that are normally used by dark-seeking creatures like moles and bats. In contrast, the Lord is described as one who causes fear, possesses majesty, is exalted, and has great glory. The events that will accompany the Second Coming will be dreadful for the wicked and the proud and haughty; they will be brought down into the dust through the power, might, and glory of Jesus Christ, and God alone will be exalted.

*Isaiah 2:10–22*

[O ye wicked ones], *enter into the rock,* and *hide [ye] in the dust;*
for the <u>fear of the Lord</u> and the <u>glory of his majesty</u> [shall smite thee].[18] (2:10)

[And it shall come to pass that][19] the *lofty looks of man* shall be <u>humbled,</u>
and the *haughtiness of men* shall be <u>bowed down,</u>

and the Lord alone shall be exalted in that day. (2:11)

For the day of the Lord of hosts [soon cometh *upon* all <u>nations;</u>
yea, *upon* <u>every one;</u>
yea, *upon* the][20] <u>proud and lofty,</u>

---

[18] Both 2 Ne. 12:10 and JST Isa. 2:10 make several changes in this verse. The phrase *O ye wicked ones* explains who will be smitten by God's glory; the phrase *shall smite thee* is added. In JST Isa. 2:10 the term *ye* is changed from *thee,* and the phrase *the glory of* is omitted.

[19] Both JST Isa. 2:11 and 2 Ne. 12:11 add the phrase *and it shall come to pass that,* which suggests a time in the future (subsequent to the time of Isaiah).

[20] The words *soon cometh upon all nations, yea, upon every one; yea, upon the . . .* represent a lengthy insertion found in JST Isa. 2:12 and 2 Ne. 12:12. *Soon cometh* emphasizes the nearness of the day of the Lord, and *upon all nations* accentuates that the judgments of the day of the Lord will be on all peoples.

and *upon* every <u>one that is lifted up</u>; and he shall be brought low: (2:12)
[Yea and the day of the Lord shall come]²¹ *upon* all the <u>cedars of Lebanon,</u>
[for they]²² are high and lifted up,
and *upon* all the <u>oaks of Bashan,</u> (2:13)
And *upon* all the <u>high mountains,</u>
and *upon* all the <u>hills,</u>
[and *upon* all the <u>nations</u> which]²³ are lifted up,
[and *upon* every <u>people</u>.] (2:14)
And *upon* every <u>high tower,</u>
and *upon* every <u>fenced wall,</u> (2:15)
[And *upon* all the <u>ships</u> of the sea],²⁴
and *upon* all the <u>ships</u> of Tarshish,
and *upon* all [<u>luxury ships</u>].²⁵ (2:16)

And the *loftiness of man* shall be <u>bowed down,</u>
and the *haughtiness of men* shall be <u>made low</u>:

and the Lord alone shall be exalted in that day. (2:17)

And the idols he shall utterly abolish. (2:18)
And they shall go into the *holes of the rocks,*
and into the *caves of the earth,*

for *fear of the Lord* [shall <u>come upon them</u>]²⁶
and the *glory of his majesty* [shall <u>smite them</u>]²⁷ when he ariseth to shake terribly
the earth. (2:19)

In that day a man shall cast [away]²⁸ his <u>idols of silver,</u>
and his <u>idols of gold,</u> which [he hath made for himself]²⁹ to worship,

to the *moles*
and to the *bats;* (2:20)

[and]³⁰ go into the *clefts* of the <u>rocks,</u>
and into the *tops* of the ragged <u>rocks,</u>

for *fear* of the <u>Lord,</u>
and for the *glory* of <u>his majesty,</u> when he ariseth to shake terribly the earth. (2:21)

---

²¹ JST Isa. 2:13 and 2 Ne. 12:13 add the phrase *Yea, and the day of the Lord shall come upon,* which continues the poetic flow of the message and emphasizes that the *day* will come on all peoples who are high and
lifted up.
²² The reading is from 2 Ne. 12:13.
²³ The reading is from JST Isa. 2:14 and 2 Ne. 12:14.
²⁴ The reading is from JST Isa. 2:16 and 2 Ne. 12:16.
²⁵ For this reading, see the discussion by Wildberger, *Isaiah 1–12,* 101.
²⁶ JST Isa. 2:19 and 2 Ne. 12:19.
²⁷ A reading from JST Isa. 2:19 and 2 Ne. 12:19. JST Isa. presents the last half of 2:19 as, "and the majesty
of the Lord shall smite them, when he ariseth to shake terribly the earth," while 2 Nephi reads "and the
glory of his majesty shall smite them, when he ariseth to shake terribly the earth." Both of these changes
show that the glory or majesty of the Lord will have a significant effect upon the people.
²⁸ This rendering is from the Hebrew *shlq.*
²⁹ The reading is from JST Isa. 2:20 and 2 Ne. 12:20.
³⁰ The reading is from JB Isa.

[Stop trusting in][31] *man,* whose <u>breath is in his nostrils</u>:
for wherein is *he* to <u>be accounted of</u>? (2:22)

## NOTES AND COMMENTARY

**2:10** *O ye wicked ones.* 2 Nephi 12:10 and JST Isaiah 2:10 clarify the subject of this verse with the addition of this phrase, referring to the wicked of the earth.

*rock/dust.* Revelation 6:15 presents a scenario similar to that found in Isaiah 2:10: "And the kings of the earth, and the great men, and the rich men, and the chief captains, and the mighty men, and every bondman, and every free man, hid themselves in the dens and in the rocks of the mountains" due to their "fear of the Lord."

*for the fear of the Lord.* The Jerusalem Bible reads here, "at the sight of the terror" of the Lord.

*glory of his majesty.* The terms *glory* and *majesty* speak of God's royalty and kingship.

**2:11** *lofty looks/haughtiness.* One of the common themes found in Isaiah pertains to the pride of humanity and God's judgments upon the proud (3:16; 13:11; 25:11–12; 28:1–3; 30:25).

*humbled/bowed down.* All those who do not humble themselves shall be forced into a state of humility by the power and glory of the Lord's coming. It is better for us to humble ourselves than to be "compelled to be humble" (Alma 32:13–15).

**2:12** *day of the Lord.* This phrase often refers to the events connected with Jesus' second coming (2 Ne. 12:12–13; 23:6, 9). The day of the Lord is mentioned five times in this section to emphasize its importance. Throughout Isaiah, the phrases *day of the Lord, in that day, day of visitation, day of his fierce anger,* and *day of the Lord's vengeance* are found more than fifty-five times, underscoring how frequently Isaiah's writings emphasize the last days and the Second Coming. According to modern-day revelation, our era is called "today" until Christ comes: "Behold, now it is called today until the coming of the Son of Man. . . . For after today cometh the burning . . . tomorrow all the proud and they that do wickedly shall be as stubble" (D&C 64:23–24).

*Lord of hosts.* See commentary on 1:9.

*soon cometh.* This phrase parallels the expression "I come quickly," found several times in the Doctrine and Covenants (see, for example, D&C 33:18; 34:12; 49:28). The expressions warn us to be prepared always for the coming of the Lord.

*upon all nations.* The Lord's judgment will be universal.

---

[31] The reading is from NIV Isa.

**2:13** *cedars of Lebanon/oaks of Bashan.* Bashan is a region east of the Jordan River and north of ancient Gilead in Israel; Lebanon is a mountain range in Syria known for its fine cedars. Symbolically, the scriptures consistently use trees to represent men. Green trees are righteous people (Ps. 1:3; D&C 135:6), and dry trees represent the wicked (Luke 23:31; 3 Ne. 14:17–18). In the context of Isaiah 2:11–21, oaks and cedars are like proud people, who, Isaiah informs us, are "high and lifted up," and the "day of the Lord" shall come upon them too.

**2:14** *mountains/hills.* In this context, mountains and hills represent apostate temple systems (14:13; 65:7; Ezek. 6:13) that attempt to imitate the Lord's true temple, the "mountain of the Lord" (2:2–4).

**2:15** *high tower/fenced wall.* Towers (Gen. 11:4; Judg. 9:46–52) and fences (Hosea 8:14) represent humanity's attempts to create protection from enemies and potentially harmful situations; they are mankind's way of relying on the arm of flesh. By contrast, the righteous rely on God for protection because for them God is a "high tower" (2 Sam. 22:3; Ps. 18:2; 144:2) and "wall of fire" (Zech. 2:5).

**2:16** *ships of Tarshish/luxury ships.* Tarshish, whose precise location is unknown, was probably a prosperous and bustling Mediterranean seaport. For instance, it was through Tarshish that Solomon imported such luxury items as gold, silver, ivory, apes, and peacocks (1 Kgs. 10:22). Perhaps because of the city's connection with wealth and affluence, the destruction of Tarshish and its ships symbolizes the Lord's judgment on the proud and arrogant (23:1, 14; Ps. 48:7).

**2:19** *holes of the rocks/caves of the earth.* The earth's proud and wicked attempt to hide in the cavities of the earth (2:10) because they feel more comfortable, as do moles and bats (2:20), in darkness. They try to hide from God and his glory, and they find themselves in Satan's domain, beneath God and his saints' dwelling place (14:15).

*shake . . . the earth.* Many prophets have placed earthquakes in the context of the end of time (Ezek. 38:19–20; JS–M 1:29; Rev. 6:12–17; 16:18).

**2:20** *idols of silver/gold.* These represent any kind of false deity, such as money, illicit sex, and power.

*moles/bats.* Isaiah compares the moles and bats—animals that dwell in the holes of the rocks and the caves—to the proud and the wicked (2:19).

**2:21** *clefts/tops of the ragged rocks.* The proud and the haughty are found in the clefts and tops of rocks (2:19; Jer. 49:16; Obad. 1:3). In times of trouble the wicked choose to flee into the rocks of the earth, rejecting Jehovah, who is the "Rock of Israel" (2 Sam. 23:3) and the "Rock of Heaven" (Moses 7:53). Meanwhile, the righteous build on the rock of Christ and will never fall (Matt. 7:24–27). It is possible that the clefts of the rocks mentioned in Isaiah 2:21 will be produced by the earthquake mentioned in Isaiah 2:19.

**2:22** *man.* Man or mankind comes from the dust (Jacob 2:21; Mosiah 2:25–26; 4:2), is corruptible (Rom. 1:23), and enjoys only brief glory (1 Pet. 1:24). Without Jesus Christ, man remains in this state (see, for instance, 2 Ne. 1:13–23). But with acceptance of Jesus and reliance on his ability to save, man can become like his Maker.

*breath.* God gave man the *breath* of life (42:5; Gen. 2:7), and man is forever reliant on God for all things (D&C 59:21), including air to breathe (Mosiah 2:20–21). King Benjamin reminds us, "Are we not all beggars? Do we not all depend upon the same Being, even God, for all the substance which we have?" (Mosiah 4:19).

# ISAIAH 3

*LIKENING ISAIAH 3 UNTO OURSELVES*

*Things have hardly changed in twenty-five hundred years. As in Isaiah's time (see 3:1–12), today wicked people from all walks of life speak evil things against the Lord and oppress their neighbors and others; even youngsters "behave . . . proudly" and speak out against the elderly (3:5). Many of the leaders are not without guilt, for they cause their people "to err" (3:12).*

*We, the Lord's people of today, are not always innocent of the transgressions listed in Isaiah's words concerning the "daughters of Zion" (3:13–4:1), for we also set our hearts on material goods: designer clothes, luxuries, and wealth.*

## ANARCHY AND RUIN PROPHESIED FOR JERUSALEM AND JUDAH (3:1–12)

Isaiah prophesies that anarchy and ruin will come upon the inhabitants of Jerusalem and Judah because of the sinful nature of their inhabitants, whose speech and actions are against the Lord, and whose sins are likened to the sins committed in Sodom before its destruction (3:8–9). Anarchy may also come because of the Lord's removing the supply of bread and water (famine or drought), or by the loss of righteous leadership in the region, for God, we are told, will remove the region's luminaries (3:2–3), and children, babes, and women will become the rulers (3:4, 12). These prophecies seem to have a double application, referring to judgments against ancient Judah as well as against the wicked in the last days.

## Isaiah 3:1–12

For, behold, the Lord, the Lord of hosts, doth take away from Jerusalem and from Judah

the *[supply]*[1] and the staff,
the whole [staff][2] of bread, and the whole *[supply]* of water, (3:1)

The *mighty man,*
and the *man of war,*
the *judge,*
and the *prophet,*
and the *[one who practices divination]*[3],
and the *[elder]*[4], (3:2)
The *captain of fifty,*
and the *honourable man,*
and the *counsellor,*
and the *[skilled craftsman]*[5] ,
and the *eloquent orator.* (3:3)

And I will give *children* [unto them][6] to be their princes,
and *babes* shall rule over them. (3:4)

And the people shall be oppressed, every *one* by another,
and every *one* by his neighbour:

the *child* shall behave himself proudly against the ancient,
and the *base* against the honourable. (3:5)

When a man shall take hold of his *brother* of the house of his father, [and shall say]:[7]
Thou hast clothing, be thou our ruler, and let [not] this ruin [come][8] under thy hand: (3:6)
In that day shall *he* swear, saying, I will not be a [physician][9];
for in my house [there][10] is neither bread nor clothing: make me not a ruler of the people. (3:7)

For *Jerusalem* is ruined,
and *Judah* is fallen:

---

[1] The reading is from NIV Isa.
[2] The reading is from JST Isa. 3:1 and 2 Ne. 13:1.
[3] Koehler and Baumgartner, *Lexicon in Veteris Testamenti Libros,* 845.
[4] The Hebrew term *zaqen,* as used here, probably refers to an older man and not to an ecclesiastical office.
[5] The reading is from NIV Isa.
[6] JST Isa. 3:4 and 2 Ne. 13:4 add the words *unto them,* clarifying the antecedent.
[7] JST Isa. 3:6 and 2 Ne. 13:6. JST Isa. and the Book of Mormon change the tense from *saying* to *shall say* to indicate a future event.
[8] The changes are from JST Isa. 3:6 and 2 Ne. 13:6.
[9] From the Hebrew root *chobesh,* meaning to "bind" or to "bind up" a wound. Brown, Driver, and Briggs, *Hebrew and English Lexicon,* 290.
[10] JST Isa. 3:7 and 2 Ne. 13:7 add the term *there.*

because their tongue[s][11] and their doings [have been][12] against the Lord,
to provoke the eyes of his glory. (3:8)

The *[show]* of their countenance <u>doth witness</u> against them;
and [<u>doth] declare</u> their sin [to be even] as Sodom, [and *they cannot hide it*].[13]

*Woe* unto <u>their soul</u>!
for they have rewarded *evil* unto <u>themselves</u>. (3:9)

Say [unto] the *righteous* that it [is] <u>well</u> with [them]:[14]
for *they* shall eat the <u>fruit</u> of their doings. (3:10)

Woe unto the wicked! [for they shall perish];[15]
for the reward of his hands shall be given him. (3:11)

[And] my people, *children* are <u>their oppressors</u>,
and *women* <u>rule over them</u>.

O my people, they [who][16] *lead thee* <u>cause thee to err</u>,
and <u>destroy the way</u> of *thy paths*. (3:12)

## NOTES AND COMMENTARY

**3:1** *Jerusalem/Judah.* These refer to the inhabitants of Jerusalem and Judah. In a symbolic sense, these can also refer to an apostate people in the latter days who will be subjected to such judgments as are detailed here.

*bread/water.* These are perhaps representative of all forms of physical nourishment, but they also have spiritual connotations in reference to the Lord, who is metaphorically the bread of life (John 6:33, 48) and the living water (John 4:6–14; 7:37–38). Certainly God removes his presence from us when we become wicked, just as bread and water will be removed from Judah and Jerusalem for their iniquity (3:8–9). Thus, this prophecy foresees both physical and spiritual famine.

**3:2–3** *mighty man . . . orator.* Isaiah lists eleven types of people as a way to represent all who have achieved community honor and status, whether religious (prophets), civic (judges), political (men of war), artistic (craftsmen and orators), or in wisdom (older men). The nation will be left without military might (mighty man, man of war, captain of fifty), spiritual guidance (prophets), wise men (ancients), justice (judges), and artisans (skilled craftsmen). All these will be removed from Jerusalem.

---

[11] JST Isa. 3:8 and 2 Ne. 13:8 present the plural *tongues,* which agrees with the pronominal adjective *their.*
[12] JST Isa. 3:8 and 2 Ne. 13:8 change the KJV *are* to *have been.*
[13] The changes in this verse are from JST Isa. 3:9 and 2 Ne. 13:9.
[14] The changes in this verse are from JST Isa. 3:10 and 2 Ne. 13:10.
[15] From JST Isa. 3:11 and 2 Ne. 13:11. *For they shall perish* carries a stronger connotation of danger than *it shall be ill with him.*
[16] The changes in this verse are from JST Isa. 3:12 and 2 Ne. 13:12.

**3:4** *children/babes.* These terms may refer to the untrained and young who will become rulers because community authority has been taken away by the Lord (3:1–3, 12).

**3:5** *the people shall be oppressed.* The people will trouble and abuse one another because of their lack of love for the Lord and for their neighbors.

*child shall behave himself proudly.* In these days, it may be typical for children to show neither deference nor honor to their elders. This is another evidence of the breakdown of the normal societal and family order.

*base.* The wretched will show no respect for those with integrity.

**3:6** *brother of the house of his father.* This may refer to a brother of blood and lineage, rather than a "brother" who is a countryman or fellow citizen.

*Thou hast clothing, be thou our ruler.* No one will desire to rule the people because of the great ruin that has come upon Judah and Jerusalem. Yet the people will ask the man with clothing to lead them; perhaps his clothing indicates wealth or preparedness.

*ruin.* The context of this section reveals that Judah and Jerusalem will experience political, economic, and spiritual ruin.

**3:7** *physician.* Used here, the term refers to someone who binds up wounds or sores. The same Hebrew root is used in 1:6: the "wounds, and bruises, and putrifying sores" of Israel "have not been closed, neither *bound up,* neither [softened] with ointment."

*neither bread nor clothing.* It is unclear why the man denies having clothing. Perhaps he has insufficient for the group—or maybe he simply does not want the responsibility of leading the others during such troubled times.

**3:8** *tongues/doings. Tongues* refers to the words and *doings* to the actions of the people. The term *for* explains that Jerusalem has stumbled because Israel's works have been against the Lord.

*eyes of his glory.* God, who possesses all glory, has full knowledge of the evil doings of Jerusalem and Judah; he sees them with his *eyes.*

**3:9** *countenance.* One's facial expression, or *countenance,* possesses either the light and spirit of the gospel or the darkness that signifies evil. For instance, an angel's countenance is described as being "as lightning" (D&C 20:6; see also JS–H 1:32), and Jesus' countenance possesses light (3 Ne. 19:25). On the other hand, Cain (Gen. 4:5–6), and at times hypocrites, have a fallen or "sad countenance" (3 Ne. 13:16).

*Sodom.* Sodom and Gomorrah are perfect examples of wicked communities. Their inhabitants committed a variety of sexual sins, and they also failed to care for the needy and oppressed (Ezek. 16:49).

*they cannot hide it.* The wicked cannot hide their wickedness from God because he "knoweth all things, and there is not anything save he knows it" (2 Ne. 9:20); God also "know[s] all their works" (2 Ne. 27:27).

*Woe.* The two *woes* (3:9, 11) indicate the trouble, sorrow, or affliction that will come on the wicked. The term *woe* is found twenty-two times in Isaiah.

*rewarded evil unto themselves.* A better translation is provided by the New International Version: "They have brought disaster upon themselves."

**3:10** *it is well.* This is a statement of approval and blessing (Morm. 7:10; Moro. 7:47; D&C 124:110).

*fruit.* In prophetic language, trees often symbolize people, and their good fruits represent good works. The "fruits of righteousness" (2 Cor. 9:10; Heb. 12:11) come through the atonement of "Jesus Christ, unto the glory and praise of God" (Philip. 1:11). When Isaiah writes that the righteous will "eat the fruit of their doings" (3:10), this may signify that the righteous will enjoy the fruits of the Spirit, which include "love, joy, peace, longsuffering, gentleness, goodness, faith, meekness, [and] temperance" (Gal. 5:22–23; Eph. 5:9, 11). Evil trees, however, will bear rotten fruit, which is representative of the works of the wicked. Christ taught, "by their fruits ye shall know them" (3 Ne. 14:16–20).

**3:12** *children/women rule over them.* See commentary on 3:4.

*they who lead thee cause thee to err/destroy the way of thy paths.* False religious leaders, government officials, and others (3:3) will beguile members of the community, causing them to turn from the path of righteousness.

## JUDGMENT AGAINST THE DAUGHTERS OF ZION (3:13–4:1)

We recall that 1:2–5a and 10–15 feature a courtroom scene, wherein the Lord pronounces a legal decision on the house of Israel. A similar scene, also with Israel as the accused, appears in 3:13–4:1, in which once again the Lord stands as both prosecutor and judge (3:13). Isaiah 3:13–17 describes a heavenly courtroom scene where the Lord stands both to plead and to pronounce a judgment. The reason for the judgment is clear: "The Lord will enter into judgment" because the children of Israel mistreated the poor (3:14b), "beat" God's people (3:15), and were proud and "haughty" (3:16–23). The judgments of God described in 3:17–26 include the following: the

Lord will smite the offenders with a scab on the head (3:17); he will take away their finery and showy materialism (3:18–24); and he will make them bald and cause them to burn, stink, wear rent clothes, fall in war, and become desolate (3:24–26). Isaiah 3:24–26 seems to indicate that the phrase "daughters of Zion" (3:16) speaks not just against women but against all Israel, male and female. Another possible interpretation of the object of God's prophecy is that in 3:14–15, 25, he is talking to males and in 3:16–24 he is talking to females.

*Isaiah 3:13–4:1*

The Lord *standeth* up to plead,
and *standeth* to judge the people. (3:13)

The Lord will enter into judgment with the *[elders]*[17] of his people,
and the *princes* thereof:

for ye have eaten up the *vineyard*
[and][18] the *spoil of the poor* in your houses. (3:14)

What mean ye[?][19] Ye *beat* my people to pieces,
and *grind* the faces of the poor? saith the Lord God of hosts. (3:15)

Moreover, the Lord saith, Because the daughters of Zion are haughty,

and *walk* with stretched forth necks and [flirtatious][20] eyes,
*walking* [along in prancing manner],[21] and [with ornaments jingling on their ankles]:[22] (3:16)

Therefore the *Lord* will smite with a scab the crown of the head of the daughters of Zion,
and the *Lord* will [uncover their forehead].[23] (3:17)

In that day the Lord will take away [their finery:
the bangles and headbands and crescent necklaces, (3:18)
the earrings and bracelets and veils, (3:19)
the headdresses and ankle chains and sashes,
the perfume bottles and charms, (3:20)
the signet rings and nose rings, (3:21)
the fine robes and the capes and cloaks,
the purses (3:22) and mirrors,

---

[17] The Hebrew term *zaqen,* as used here, probably refers to an older man and not to an ecclesiastical office.
[18] JST Isa. 3:14 and 2 Ne. 13:14 insert the word *and* and omit the word *is* found in the KJV between the words *poor* and *in.*
[19] JST Isa. 3:15 and 2 Ne. 13:15 drop the conjunction *and* and divide the statement into two separate questions.
[20] From the Hebrew word *saqar;* see Koehler and Baumgartner, *Lexicon in Veteris Testamenti Libros,* 929.
[21] From the Hebrew terms *haluok* and *tapop.*
[22] The reading is from NIV Isa.
[23] Koehler and Baumgartner, *Lexicon in Veteris Testamenti Libros,* 786.

and the linen garments and tiaras and shawls.][24] (3:23)

And it shall come to pass, instead of *[fragrance]*[25] there shall be <u>stink</u>;
and instead of a [*sash,* a <u>rope</u>]; [26]
and instead of *well set hair,* <u>baldness</u>;
and instead of a [*majestic robe*],[27] a girding of <u>sackcloth</u>;
[<u>humiliation</u>][28] instead of *beauty.*[29] (3:24)

Thy *men* shall fall by the <u>sword</u>
and thy *mighty* in the <u>war</u>. (3:25)

And *her [entrances]*[30] shall <u>lament and mourn</u>;
and *she* [shall be] desolate [and][31] shall <u>sit upon the ground</u>. (3:26)

And in that day, seven women shall take hold of one man, saying: We will eat our own bread, and wear our own apparel; only let us be called by thy name to take away our reproach. (4:1)[32]

## NOTES AND COMMENTARY

**3:13** *The Lord standeth up to plead/judge.* Jesus Christ has two legal roles in the heavenly courts. The first is as an attorney or advocate: "Jesus Christ the righteous" is the "advocate with the Father" (1 Jn. 2:1) who pleads the case of righteous souls. Christ says, "Listen to him who is the advocate with the Father, who is pleading your cause before him—saying: Father, behold the sufferings and death of him who did no sin, in whom thou wast well pleased; behold the blood of thy Son which was shed, the blood of him whom thou gavest that thyself might be glorified; wherefore, Father, spare these my brethren that believe on my name, that they may come unto me and have everlasting life" (D&C 45:3–5; 29:5; 32:3; 62:1).

---

[24] NIV Isa. seems to have translated the Hebrew accurately in this difficult passage. JST Isa. 3:18 and 2 Ne. 13:18 omit the pronoun *their* in three phrases used in the KJV, apparently making a more general statement that all tinkling ornaments, cauls, and round tires will be taken away. Both sources also omit the phrase *about their feet,* which allows for a broader interpretation.

[25] This is from NIV Isa.

[26] Koehler and Baumgartner, *Lexicon in Veteris Testamenti Libros,* 634.

[27] Wildberger, *Isaiah 1–12,* 146.

[28] Wildberger, *Isaiah 1–12,* 146, renders the term *humiliation* after a reading of the Isaiah Scroll in the Dead Sea Scrolls (1QIsaa); hereafter cited as DSS Isa. Scroll.

[29] JST Isa. 3:24 and 2 Ne. 13:24 omit two italicized words, *that* and *and,* in the KJV.

[30] The Hebrew *petacheyah* means "entrances."

[31] In JST Isa. 3:26 and 2 Ne. 13:26, a verb tense change from *being* to *shall be* makes desolation a future condition rather than a present one. Both of these sources also add the word *and* before the phrase *shall sit upon the ground,* which seems to indicate that sitting on the ground is not necessarily a result of being desolate.

[32] JST Isa. includes this verse as part of chapter 3.

Jesus Christ's second role is as the judge in this divine court (Mosiah 3:10; Moro. 10:34; Moses 6:57), who passes judgment on the wicked. *Standing* was important in the ancient Israelite courtroom, where the judge stood to pronounce judgment.

**3:14** *elders/princes.* These terms represent the leadership of the community.

*vineyard.* The house of Israel (5:7; Ps. 80:8–14). The elders and princes have eaten up the vineyard, which means they have consumed "the spoil of the poor," "beat[en] [God's] people to pieces," and ground "the faces of the poor" (see below).

*spoil of the poor.* To spoil the poor means to take forcefully the goods and property of the poor through high taxation, as booty during wartime, or by other means. Social justice for the poor is a constant theme in Isaiah's writings (for example, 10:2; 11:4; 26:6; 32:7; 58:7).

**3:15** *beat my people/grind the faces of the poor.* These phrases may refer to actual physical punishment or to economic hardships due to insufferably high taxes and duties, levies, or assessments imposed on the poor; it may also refer to attitude, for we are also condemned for the state of our hearts.

**3:16** *daughters of Zion.* The plural form *daughters of Zion* is infrequently used in the scriptures (3:16–17; 4:4; Song. 3:11; D&C 124:11). Scholars generally agree that the singular expression *daughter of Zion* refers to the inhabitants of Jerusalem and Judah (Lam. 1:6–8; 2:8–11; Zech. 9:9; 2 Ne. 8:25). What then is the meaning of the plural *daughters of Zion?* There are several possible interpretations. If the phrase *daughter of Zion* represents Jerusalem, then perhaps the plural *daughters* refers to Jerusalem at the time of Isaiah as well as Jerusalem in the last days. The plural *daughters of Zion* may also refer to ancient Jerusalem (and the Southern Kingdom of Judah) and to Samaria (and the Northern Kingdom of Israel). The phrase may be literal, referring to actual women, or it may point to women as symbols of pride and sin in the last days. Note the women's clothing described in 3:18–24 and the actual women that seem to be identified in 4:1. This interpretation parallels Isaiah's condemnation of male pride (2:10–22) and the sick nature of the inhabitants of Jerusalem (1:5–6, 21–23).

*stretched forth necks.* This expression portrays women who look sideways to see if others notice their beauty as they prance along the way or as they look upwards with high heads in a proud manner. For the children of Israel in all eras, the expression denotes a people who pay idolatrous heed to others rather than to God above.

*flirtatious eyes/prancing/ornaments jingling.* Women are casting "seductive glances"[33] at others. The entire picture suggests that the Lord's people have become

---

[33] Wildberger, *Isaiah 1–12,* 149.

harlots, attempting to capture the illicit interest of others. Also, in a spiritual sense, Jerusalem has forsaken her God through transgression and now pursues other deities by committing spiritual adultery with them.

**3:17** *scab/uncover their forehead.* These terms reflect the Lord's judgment on Israel. Baldness is one of God's judgments on the wicked (Jer. 47:4–5; 48:37; Ezek. 7:18), and it may refer to the "humiliating punishment known among the Babylonians" in which the hair of the forehead would be shaved off.[34] In addition, since the Hebrew word for atonement means "covering," an uncovered head may point to one who has lost some of the privileges of the Atonement.

**3:18** *In that day.* This refers to the events connected with our day, or the last days (2:12).

*finery.* The list of apparel in 3:18–23 presents highly visible items of clothing and stands opposite the "plain" garments of Zion mentioned in D&C 42:40.

**3:24** *fragrance . . . beauty.* The entire verse sets forth God's judgments on the daughters of Zion; God will replace prosperity and refinement with humiliation and stink. The *fragrance* may have reference to the expensive balsam oil imported from Raamah and Shebah. It was used as a cosmetic (Esth. 2:12; Song. 4:10, 14) and for religious purposes (Ex. 25:6). It could also refer to the use of perfumes in the last days.

*stink.* The *stink* might possibly be from festering wounds (Ps. 38:5).

*sash/rope.* The wealthy man's *sash,* or expensive belt, will be replaced with a *rope* by which he will be led as a slave.

*baldness/sackcloth.* Self-imposed baldness (3:24), sitting on the ground (3:26), and sackcloth (3:24) are all symbols of mourning, mentioned in connection with the terms *lament* and *mourn* in 3:26. Clearly the context of 3:24–26 is mourning caused by God's judgments on Judah and Jerusalem as well as upon the world in the last days.

**3:25** *sword/war.* This may be a continuation of judgment.

**3:26** *her entrances.* Jerusalem is desolate and no longer has gates but only openings or entrances. Gates may symbolize false security or pride.

*sit upon the ground.* This is a visible symbol of those who mourn.

**4:1** *in that day.* This reminds us again that these events are connected with our day, or the last days.

*seven women.* The headnote to the chapter in the LDS edition of the Bible places this prophecy in the Millennium. Because war has claimed the lives of many of the

---

[34]Wildberger, *Isaiah 1–12,* 149.

men of Jerusalem (identified in 3:25), the ratio of men to women is unequal. Thus *seven women* will take hold of one man. The number *seven* may be literal or symbolic.

*eat our own bread/wear our own apparel.* It is the husband's duty to provide for his bride (Ex. 21:10–11), but in this prophecy Isaiah indicates that the seven women will provide for themselves.

*reproach.* This word means disgrace caused by the barrenness of the womb (Gen. 30:23; Luke 1:25), a result of not having a husband.

---≈≈≈---

# ISAIAH 4

*LIKENING ISAIAH 4 UNTO OURSELVES*

*When Moroni visited Joseph Smith in September 1823, he quoted 4:5–6 and said that this prophecy would soon find fulfillment.[1] Many of the events will take place in our day, and this prophecy has direct relevance for us. For example, the section speaks of temples, temple work, and the Saints' becoming holy through temple worship. It also prophesies of the establishment of Zion in the latter days.*

## THE SURVIVORS: THOSE WHO ESCAPE THE JUDGMENTS OF GOD ARE CLEANSED (4:2–6)

The previous chapter speaks of judgments against the "daughters of Zion." This one deals with those who have survived God's judgments. The survivors are those who are the "escaped of Israel and Judah" and have been "left in Zion," to be "written among the living in Jerusalem." The survivors will love and participate in the ordinances of the Lord's temple, for they will be "called holy" (the term *holy* is generally connected to the temple), their filth and iniquity will be removed, and the same elements (cloud, smoke, fire, glory) that attended and protected the ancient Israelite temples will exist among them in Zion.

The temple theme is also present in the four explicit references to *Zion* or *mount Zion*. The temple, always an integral part of Zion, is located at its center. Further, Zion's inhabitants are pure in heart and worthy to enter the temple and participate in its ordinances.[2] It is significant that the survivors of God's judgments (3:13–4:1) will be a temple-oriented people, for it is their temple orientation that

---

[1] *Messenger and Advocate* 1 (April 1835): 110.
[2] *History of the Church*, 5:423–24.

will help them escape his judgments. Isaiah 4:6 states that the Lord's true servants will find safety and refuge in Zion, an idea repeated in Doctrine and Covenants 45:66–70. The command to us in this dispensation is, "Stand ye in holy places, and be not moved, until the day of the Lord come; for behold, it cometh quickly" (D&C 87:8; 45:32).

## Isaiah 4:2–6

In that day shall the *branch* of the Lord be <u>beautiful and glorious,</u>
and the *fruit* of the earth shall be <u>excellent and comely</u> [to][3] them that are escaped
of Israel [and Judah].[4] (4:2)

And it shall come to pass, [*they* that are][5] <u>left in Zion,</u>
and [<u>remain</u>][6] <u>in Jerusalem</u>, shall be called holy,
even *every one* that is written among the <u>living in Jerusalem</u>: (4:3)

When the Lord shall have *washed away the filth* of the <u>daughters of Zion,</u>
and shall have *purged the blood* of <u>Jerusalem</u> from the midst thereof

by the *spirit* of <u>judgment,</u>
and by the *spirit* of <u>burning</u>. (4:4)

And the Lord will create *upon every dwelling place* of mount Zion,
and *upon her assemblies,*

a cloud and *smoke* by <u>day,</u>
and the shining of a *flaming fire* by <u>night</u>:

for upon all the glory [of Zion][7] *shall be a defence.* (4:5)
And there *shall be a [shelter]*[8]

*for a shadow in the daytime* <u>from the heat,</u>
and *for a place of refuge,*
and *for a covert from storm* and <u>from rain</u>. (4:6)

### NOTES AND COMMENTARY

**4:2** *In that day.* This speaks of our day. The same expression links earlier sections of Isaiah (2:12, 17, 20; 3:7, 18; 4:1) and is a continuation of the day-of-the-Lord theme.

*branch.* This word may have a double meaning. First, the Lord is called *Branch* messianically (Jer. 23:5–6; 33:15–17; Zech. 3:8–10; 6:12–15). Second, an offshoot of the house of Israel is often called "a righteous branch" (Jacob 2:25) or "a branch of

---

[3] The change is from JST Isa. 4:1 and 2 Ne. 14:2.
[4] DSS Isa. Scroll inserts the phrase *and Judah,* which is consistent with the theme of the section.
[5] The change is from JST Isa. 4:2 and 2 Ne. 14:3.
[6] 2 Ne. 14:3 changes the KJV words *he that remaineth* to *remain.*
[7] JST Isa. 4:4 and 2 Ne. 14:5 add the words *of Zion.*
[8] From the Hebrew word *sukah.*

the house of Israel" (1 Ne. 15:12; 2 Ne. 3:5). The context of this section suggests that the *branch* represents a specific remnant, or *branch,* of Israel that remains in Israel after God's judgments, identified in Isaiah 3.

*fruit.* Those who "are escaped of Israel and Judah" will be blessed with the bounties and blessings of the earth. The earth will be fruitful once again because of the presence of temples. "The temple," says John Lundquist, "is associated with abundance and prosperity, indeed is perceived as the giver of these."[9] Again, we are reminded by the promise of Book of Mormon prophets that those who are obedient to God's commands will prosper in the land.

**4:2–3** *escaped of Israel/left in Zion/remain in Jerusalem.* These phrases refer to those who will survive the latter-day judgments of God that will destroy many of the people of the earth (10:20). The *escaped of Israel* will consist of both Jews and other members of the house of Israel (D&C 133:11–13).

*holy.* The Hebrew term translated as "holy" has the root meaning of "temple." Isaiah is saying, in essence, that those who "remain in Jerusalem shall be called a temple people," presumably because they worship in the temple. The group becomes *holy* because of the cleansing/purging process identified by Isaiah as the "spirit of judgment" and the "spirit of burning" (4:4). Also, God is called Holy One (41:14; 1 Jn. 2:20); in the last days, those in Zion will be like God in their holiness.

*written among the living.* The primary object of this phrase seems to be those who are counted among the mortal living. Temporally, those who survived the judgments identified in Isaiah 3 will be *among the living.* The phrase may also refer to the book of life, speaking spiritually of those who are written in the Lamb's book of life and who will go to God's kingdom of heaven (Dan. 12:1; Philip. 4:3; Rev. 20:15).

**4:4** *washed/purged.* The filth of the children of Israel (including us) will be washed away by the ordinance of baptism (1 Ne. 20:1; Alma 7:14) and cleansed by the blood of Jesus (Mal. 3:2–3; Heb. 9:22; Rev. 7:14), a process in which the Holy Ghost plays a prominent role. Joseph Smith taught that "as the Holy Ghost falls upon one of the literal seed of Abraham, it is calm and serene; and his whole soul and body are only exercised by the pure spirit of intelligence; while the effect of the Holy Ghost upon a Gentile, is to purge out the old blood, and make him actually of the seed of Abraham"[10] (see also 3 Ne. 27:20).

*blood/filth.* The blood of humanity often represents iniquity (59:3; Micah 3:10). Paradoxically, Jesus' blood is able to purge and cleanse our souls from iniquity

---

[9] "What Is a Temple?" 97.
[10] *Teachings of the Prophet Joseph Smith,* 149–50.

because of Jesus' innocence, sinlessness, and perfection (Lev. 17:11; John 6:53–54; Moses 6:59–60). In its root sense, the Hebrew word for *filth* has reference to human excrement.[11] The term is used symbolically to emphasize the terrible nature of the sins of Israel and the impurities found within the daughters of Zion.

*daughters of Zion.* See commentary on 3:16.

*spirit of judgment/burning.* Together, God's judgments and his cleansing fires will purge Israel of her sins. God's fire destroys the wicked while at the same time purifying the humble and repentant.

**4:5** *every dwelling place of mount Zion.* Isaiah compares Zion's individual homes to the temple, thus emphasizing the sanctity of Zion and her people in this glorious day.

*cloud and smoke/fire.* These are elements that often accompany a theophany or God's presence in the temple. For instance, God appeared at the Sinai sanctuary (Ex. 15:17) and was accompanied by a cloud, smoke, fire (Ex. 19:9, 18), and similar elements associated with Solomon's temple (1 Kgs. 8:10) and the temple in heaven (6:4; Rev. 15:8). The cloud symbolizes the Lord's glory (D&C 84:2–5). The people of the latter-day Zion will be so righteous that they will all enjoy such blessings.

*shall be a defence.* The word *defence* should read "canopy" or "protective covering."[12] Hence Zion and her inhabitants will be protected by God from spiritual harm in the same way that individuals are protected from physical harm by seeking shelter during the heat of the day or in great storms (4:6).

**4:6** *shelter/refuge/covert.* Similar language is used in a modern-day revelation, in which Zion is called "a city of refuge" and "a place of safety." It will be a "land of peace," and "the terror of the Lord also shall be there, insomuch that the wicked will not come unto it, . . . and it shall be the only people that shall not be at war one with another. And it shall be said among the wicked: Let us not go up to battle against Zion, for the inhabitants of Zion are terrible; wherefore we cannot stand" (D&C 45:66–70; 115:6).[13] Jesus, of course, is our ultimate refuge and shelter from life's battles (25:4).

*storm/rain.* These are symbols for God's judgments on the wicked (Ps. 83:15). The *storms* remove the wicked from their places as chaff is removed from the wheat (Job 21:18; 27:21), while the righteous, like wheat, are gathered into protected units and preserved (in the Lord's temples and other holy places).

---

[11] Brown, Driver, and Briggs, *Hebrew and English Lexicon,* 844.
[12] Brown, Driver, and Briggs, *Hebrew and English Lexicon,* 342.
[13] *Teachings of the Prophet Joseph Smith,* 161.

# ISAIAH 5

*LIKENING ISAIAH 5 UNTO OURSELVES*

*The song of the vineyard is about a caring master (the Lord) who shows great concern
for his vineyard (speaking of the house of Israel, which includes us). Together with our
Israelite ancestors, we are recipients of the Master's concern and love. If we become
like plump, juicy, sweet grapes, it is because the Master has planted us in a fertile hill,
removed stones and weeds, and prepared us for the harvest.*

*The final five verses of this chapter describe the missionary work of our day and
the gathering of the nations around the gospel banner. All members of the Church who
do their part in the great missionary effort of this dispensation are assisting in the fulfillment of this prophecy of Isaiah.*

## THE SONG OF THE VINEYARD (5:1–7)

According to religious scholar J. Alec Motyer, Isaiah 5 naturally divides into
"two sections: the Song of the Vineyard (1–7) and the bitter crop produced (8–30)."[1]
The Song is one of many scriptural parables and allegories used to describe the relationship between the Lord (the owner of the vineyard) and the house of Israel (the
vineyard; see, for example, Rom. 11:17–24; Jacob 5; D&C 101:43–62). The Song
contains two parts: the parable (5:1–6) and its interpretation (5:7). It is also a love
poem (5:1) that features the bridegroom (the Lord)[2] and his bride (the house of Israel).
The Lord, who planted the bride in a "fertile" hill (5:1)[3] and provided for her (5:2),
expected her to "bring forth" good seed or fruit (5:2). But instead she brought forth

---

[1] *Prophecy of Isaiah,* 67.
[2] Watts, *Isaiah 1–33,* 53–54.
[3] For examples from the ancient Near East in which *land* is referred to as a woman, see Wildberger, *Isaiah
1–12,* 182.

bad fruit (5:2, 4), and so the bridegroom let her go to waste, reaping the natural conse-quences of her sowing. The Song shows the great love and attention that the Lord has shown to the house of Israel throughout the ages, including in our own dispensation.

## Isaiah 5:1–7

[And then][4] will I sing to my well-beloved a song of my beloved [about][5] his vine-yard. My well-beloved hath a vineyard in a very [fertile][6] hill: (5:1)

And he [dug up the soil],[7] and gathered out the stones thereof, and planted it with the choicest vine, and built a tower in the midst of it, and also made a winepress therein: and he looked that it should bring forth grapes, and it brought forth [sour][8] grapes. (5:2)

And now, O *inhabitants* of <u>Jerusalem,</u>
and *men* of <u>Judah,</u>

judge, I pray you, [between][9] me and my vineyard. (5:3)

What could have been done more to my vineyard, that I have not done in it? wherefore, when I looked that it should bring forth grapes, [it][10] brought forth [sour] grapes[.] (5:4)

And now go to; I will tell you what I will do to my vineyard:

I will *take away the hedge* thereof, and it shall be [<u>burned</u>];[11]
and [I will][12] *break down the wall* thereof, and it shall <u>be trodden down</u>: (5:5)

And I will lay it waste: it shall not be pruned, nor digged; but there shall come up briers and thorns: I will also command the clouds that they rain no rain upon it. (5:6)

For the *vineyard* of the Lord of hosts is the <u>house of Israel</u>,
and the <u>men of Judah</u> his *pleasant plant:*

and he looked for *judgment*
but behold [<u>bloodshed</u>];[13]
for *righteousness,* but behold a <u>cry</u>. (5:7)

---

[4] The addition of the phrase *and then* (JST Isa. 5:1 and 2 Ne. 15:1) temporally connects the parable of the vineyard to the previous chapter.

[5] This replaces the KJV word *touching.*

[6] This is more descriptive and accurate than *fruitful;* see also JB and NIV Isa.

[7] The Hebrew reads *yerazeqehu,* "he dug up the soil," rather than "fenced it," Brown, Driver, and Briggs, *Hebrew and English Lexicon,* 740.

[8] *Sour* is more descriptive and accurate than *wild.* Brown, Driver, and Briggs, *Hebrew and English Lexicon,* 93.

[9] We have replaced the archaic KJV *betwixt* with *between.*

[10] JST Isa. 5:4 and 2 Ne. 15:4 place the pronoun *it* before *brought* because the second clause is a statement in those sources rather than a question, as in the KJV.

[11] This comes from the Hebrew *leba'er* which means "to be burned" or "consumed." Brown, Driver, and Briggs, *Hebrew and English Lexicon,* 128–29. See also Wildberger, *Isaiah 1–12,* 176.

[12] JST Isa. 5:5 and 2 Ne. 15:5 add *I will,* clarifying the subject and verb.

[13] Most modern English translations have *bloodshed* here instead of *oppression,* as in KJV. Brown, Driver, and Briggs, *Hebrew and English Lexicon,* 705.

NOTES AND COMMENTARY

**5:1** *will I sing.* Isaiah sings a song about the Lord and the house of Israel.

*vineyard.* The house of Israel. This song can appropriately be applied to the Lord's covenant people in all ages.

*well-beloved.* The Lord of Hosts, who is the owner of the vineyard (5:1, 7a).

*fertile hill.* The promised covenant land of Israel where God planted his vineyard, or the house of Israel.

**5:2** *he dug up the soil, and gathered out the stones.* God provided the house of Israel with a choice promised land.

*planted it with the choicest vine.* God made Israel the choicest vine so that she would be fruitful and become a righteous people among the nations.

*tower.* God built a tower in the vineyard so that watchmen (such as the prophets) could watch for impending danger and evil and then warn the children of Israel (Ezek. 3:17; 33:1–7; D&C 101:43–62).

*winepress.* God made a winepress in anticipation of a great harvest. The Song contains powerful images that point to Jesus' atonement: the winepress (63:1–6; D&C 76:107), the fertile hill, and the grapes (John 15:1–7) are all symbols of Jesus' atoning sacrifice.

*grapes.* Plump, juicy, sweet grapes represent the righteous; sour grapes symbolize those who have fallen from the covenant and left God's kingdom.

**5:3** *inhabitants of Jerusalem/men of Judah.* Although the inhabitants of Judah are the immediate audience for the Song presented by Isaiah, the Song may be sung to all Israel throughout all generations.

*I.* Isaiah uses third-person pronouns to refer to the Lord in 5:2 (for example, "he dug up the soil"); in 5:3–6 the Lord is represented by the first-person pronoun, *I.*

**5:4** *What could have been done more to my vineyard?* After doing all things possible to make his vineyard fruitful, the Lord asks, "What could have been done more to my vineyard?" Similarly, the Lord's great compassion is shown in the allegory of the olive tree: "The Lord of the vineyard wept, and said . . . What could I have done more for my vineyard?" (Jacob 5:41).

*my vineyard.* The house of Israel (5:7; Jacob 5; D&C 24:19; 43:28; 101:43–62), which belongs to the Lord (as indicated by the pronoun "my").

*sour grapes.* This passage could read "stinking or worthless grapes."[14] The vineyard was expected to yield good, edible fruit; instead it produced rotten grapes, which

---

[14] Brown, Driver, and Briggs, *Hebrew and English Lexicon,* 93.

symbolize decayed and evil people (Hosea 9:10; Rev. 14:18). Those who are rotten will not partake of the Atonement and abide in Christ (John 15), for if we abide in Christ we will bring forth good fruit. Those who are rotten will be trodden down by the Lord in great fury at the time of his second coming, causing his robe to be red (D&C 133:50–51).

**5:5** *it shall be burned.* This refers to the eventual burning of the wicked of Israel at the Second Coming.

*take away the hedge . . . trodden down.* The wall, hedge, and watchtower (three elements designed to protect a vineyard) signify God's protection of the house of Israel. Nevertheless, God has removed them (5:2) so that wild beasts and invading armies trample the vineyard.

**5:6** *I will lay it waste: it shall not be pruned/digged.* Temporally, the vineyard becomes wasteland because the master of the vineyard determines that he will no longer remove stones, continue to hoe and weed the land, work the soil, or prune the vines. Now briers and thorns overrun the choicest vine, and wild beasts enter the vineyard (because the hedge has been removed) and make it their habitation. Spiritually, the house of Israel (the vineyard) became a wasteland through apostasy and rejection of the kindnesses, love, and care of the Master of the vineyard, who is Jehovah. God would not have laid waste the vineyard had it been fruitful.

*briers and thorns.* Transgressions cause the land that we inhabit to become wasteland covered with *briers and thorns,* representing the fallen condition of the telestial world—and of its inhabitants.

*clouds [will] rain no rain upon it.* Rain represents life, revelation, and the word of God.

**5:7** *Lord of hosts.* The owner of the vineyard.

*vineyard/pleasant plant.* The *vineyard* represents the house of Israel (5:3); the *pleasant plant* refers to the inhabitants of the kingdom of Judah.

*looked for judgment/righteousness.* God wanted his people to be just and righteous, but instead he found bloodshed and cries of distress.[15] Isaiah's use of Hebrew terms in this verse demonstrates his brilliant and elegant literary style. Note the similarity between the Hebrew words for judgment (*mish*ᵉ*pat*) and bloodshed (*mis*ᵉ*pach*), righteousness (*ts*ᵉ*daqah*) and cry (*ts*ᵉ*'aqah*). Hence Isaiah's message is clear: the

---

[15] Motyer, *Prophecy of Isaiah,* 69.

people chose *mis$^e$pach* (bloodshed) instead of *mish$^e$pat* (judgment), *ts$^e$'aqah* (crying) rather than *ts$^e$daqah* (righteousness).

## THE "BITTER CROP": A LISTING OF SINS AND WOES AGAINST THE WICKED (5:8–25)

In the context of the Song of the Vineyard (5:1–7), 5:8–25 presents a series of six woes, all of which demonstrate the low spiritual state of certain groups. The first woe (5:8–10) speaks out against the improper use of land; the second (5:11–17) contains the prophetic word on the manner in which those of the world improperly and with evil intent eat, drink, and make merry; the third (5:18–19) is directed against those who are wicked and mock God and his divine plan; the fourth (5:20) speaks against liars and those who fight against the things of God; the fifth (5:21) deals with conceited individuals who believe themselves to be wise; and the sixth (5:22–23) accuses those who give bribes and belittle the righteous.

*Isaiah 5:8–25*

Woe unto them that join house to house,[16]

till there [can][17] be *no place,*
that they may be *placed alone* in the midst of the earth! (5:8)

In mine ears said the Lord of hosts, Of a truth many houses shall be desolate, [and][18] great and fair, without inhabitant. (5:9)

Yea, *ten acres of vineyard* shall yield one [barrel of wine],[19]
and the *[six bushels of seeds]* shall yield a [bushel of grain].[20] (5:10)

Woe unto them that rise up *early in the morning,* that they may follow strong drink;
[and] that continue *until night,* [and][21] wine inflame them! (5:11)

And the harp, and the [lyre], the [tambourine], and [flute],[22] and wine, are in their feasts:

but they *regard not* the work of the Lord,
*neither consider* the operation of his hands. (5:12)

Therefore my people are gone into captivity, because they have no knowledge:

---

[16] 2 Ne. 15:8 and JST Isa. 5:8 omit the phrase *that lay field to field.*

[17] 2 Ne. 15:8 and JST Isa. 5:8 add the word *can.*

[18] 2 Ne. 15:9 and JST Isa. 5:9 replace *even* with *and.*

[19] This phrase is emended from a combined reading of JB and NIV Isa.

[20] This phrase is emended from a combined reading of JB and NIV Isa.

[21] JST Isa. 5:11 adds two instances of *and.*

[22] For a discussion of the musical items in this verse, see *New Bible Dictionary,* 800–804.

and *their honourable men* are famished,
and *their multitude* dried up with thirst. (5:13)

Therefore hell hath *enlarged herself,*
and *opened her mouth* without measure:

and their glory, and their multitude, and their pomp, and he that rejoiceth, shall
descend into it. (5:14)

And the *[common]*[23] *man* shall be brought down,
and the *mighty man* shall be humbled,
and the *eyes of the lofty* shall be humbled: (5:15)

But the *Lord of hosts* shall be exalted in judgment,
and *God* that is holy shall be sanctified in righteousness. (5:16)

Then shall the *lambs* feed after their manner,
and the waste places of the fat ones shall *[goats]*[24] eat. (5:17)

Woe unto them that draw *iniquity* with cords of vanity,
and *sin* as it were with a cart rope: (5:18)
That say, Let him make speed,[25] *hasten his work,* that we may see it:
and let the counsel of the Holy One of Israel *draw nigh and come,* that we may
know it! (5:19)

Woe unto them that call *evil good,* and good evil;
that put *darkness for light,* and light for darkness;
that put *bitter for sweet,* and sweet for bitter! (5:20)

Woe unto [the][26] *wise* in their own eyes,
and *prudent* in their own sight! (5:21)

Woe unto [the][27] *mighty* to drink wine,
and *men of strength* to mingle strong drink: (5:22)

[Who][28] *justify* the wicked for reward,
and *take away the righteousness* of the righteous from him! (5:23)

Therefore as the *fire* devoureth the stubble,
and the *flame* consumeth the chaff,

their *root* shall be as rottenness,
and their *blossom[s]*[29] shall go up as dust:

because they have *cast away* the law of the Lord of hosts,
and *despised* the word of the Holy One of Israel. (5:24)

Therefore is the *anger of the Lord* kindled against his people,
and *he hath stretched forth his hand* against them, and hath smitten them:

---

[23] *Common* is the modern equivalent of the archaic *mean.*
[24] Hebrew scribe evidently miswrote *gariym,* "strangers," for *gadiym,* "goats." *Goats* parallels *lambs* in this synonymous parallelism.
[25] 2 Ne. 15:19 omits the KJV conjunction *and.*
[26] 2 Ne. 15:21 and JST Isa. 5:21 replace the KJV *them that are* with *the.*
[27] 2 Ne. 15:22 and JST Isa. 5:22 replace the KJV *them that are* with *the.*
[28] 2 Ne. 15:23 replaces the incorrect relative pronoun *which* with the proper *who.*
[29] 2 Ne. 15:24 makes the word *blossom* into the plural *blossoms.*

and the *hills* <u>did tremble</u>,
and their *carcasses* <u>were torn</u> in the midst of the streets.

For all this *his anger* is <u>not turned away</u>,
but *his hand* is <u>stretched out still</u>. (5:25)

## NOTES AND COMMENTARY

**5:8** *Woe.* This means severe anguish and distress resulting from God's judgments, which will come upon the guilty in all ages of the world, including our own.

*house to house.* Perhaps this verse is an accusation against the rich who are covetous and oppress the poor to obtain lands and riches. Or it may speak of anyone who takes advantage of others for material gain.

**5:10** *barrel of wine/bushel of grain.* The judgment against those identified in the first woe is that their houses will become desolate and their land will not bring forth normal amounts of produce, for ten acres of vineyard will produce only one barrel of wine; those who are house-greedy and land-hungry will have neither house nor food.

**5:11** *strong drink/wine.* This indicates revelry and unholy merrymaking among those who spend excessive amounts of time ("early in the morning . . . continue until night") in carnal entertainment. "There shall be many which shall say: Eat, drink, and be merry, for tomorrow we die; and it shall be well with us" (2 Ne. 28:7).

**5:12** *harp/lyre/tambourine/flute.* In this context, these instruments may suggest worldly music and lightmindedness.

*feasts.* In this context *feasts* does not refer to religious feasts and festivals but to bacchanalian revelry.

*regard not the work of the Lord.* The people described here are concerned with their own pleasure and gratification rather than with doing God's will.

**5:13** *captivity.* Because the people "have no knowledge" of the Lord (see below), and because they glory in debauchery and revelry, they are subjected to spiritual and physical *captivity.* They have become "past feeling" because they have misused their agency.

*famished/thirst.* This may refer to literal famine, but it also has an important symbolic meaning. The honorable men (upper class and city dignitaries) and the multitude (commoners) "have no knowledge" of the Lord and his gospel; they lack the words of the Lord; "behold, the days come, saith the Lord God, that I will send a famine in the land, not a famine of bread, nor a thirst for water, but of hearing the words of the Lord" (Amos 8:11). Specifically, the wicked lack an understanding of Jesus Christ and the power of his atonement; they do not partake of the "bread" (John 6:33, 48) and waters (Jer. 2:13; 17:13; 1 Ne. 2:9; Ether 12:28) of life, which refer to

Jesus Christ. Although they partake of "strong drink" and "wine," they experience famine and thirst for spiritual things. By contrast, the righteous have the privilege of feasting on the words of Christ as well as on his love (Jacob 3:2), and of renewing their covenants by the sacrament.

**5:14** *hell hath enlarged herself.* The term *hell* (Hebrew *sheol*) in this verse refers to the world of spirits.[30] Hell opens her mouth wide enough to receive all who are pompous and wicked, as well as their pomp and glory; both the wicked *and* their evil traits will be cast down to hell. This "opened mouth" image that is connected to hell continues the symbolism of feasting ("strong drink," "wine," "feasts") and famine ("famished," "dried up with thirst"). The wicked open their mouths as they eat, drink, and are merry, while at the same time hell opens *her* mouth to swallow *them*. In the end, hell's mouth, not the mouths of the wicked, will be filled.

**5:15** *common man . . . mighty man shall be humbled.* All wicked individuals, regardless of social status, will be humbled when God's judgments come upon them.

*eyes of the lofty shall be humbled.* The eyes of those who covet, lust, and are greedy.

**5:16** *Lord . . . shall be exalted in judgment.* Here *exalted* stands opposite the words in 5:15 that describe the wicked man—*brought down* and *humbled* (twice).

*sanctified in righteousness.* The New International Version presents a better reading of this phrase: "God will show himself holy by his righteousness."

**5:17** *lambs/goats. Lambs* and *goats* roam freely where prosperous people once lived.

*fat ones.* Prosperous people.

**5:18** *draw iniquity with cords of vanity/sin as . . . a cart rope.* The image is of a beast of burden, such as a donkey or ox (representative of a wicked person), pulling a cart of goods (representing sins). The wicked are burdened with sins, which they must drag behind them, just as a beast of burden hauls its load from place to place. The verse also seems to suggest that vanity is the key component from which our cords are made. We commit a sin and then drag it after us because of our vanity and pride. *Vanity* also means uselessness or emptiness, an interesting image. Sin is sometimes as difficult to break as a thick rope that is strong enough to pull a cart, but it is possible to break sin with the help of Christ: "Come unto me, all ye that labour and are heavy laden, and I will give you rest" (Matt. 11:28).

**5:19** *make speed, hasten.* The wicked ask God to quickly reveal his work to them, so that they may know and acknowledge it. Their motive is probably curiosity

---

[30] *Teachings of the Prophet Joseph Smith,* 310.

rather than righteousness, or perhaps they are being sarcastic and mocking. They fail to recognize that God has already revealed a number of truths through his prophets or that his "hand [is] in all things" (D&C 59:21).

**5:20** *call evil good, and good evil.* Wicked ways are often confused with moral values by those who believe they know more than God or his prophets—they are deceived or they seek to justify themselves in their disobedience. Sin is accepted in the world, and evil becomes an acceptable way of life. Moroni 7:14 warns: "Wherefore, take heed, my beloved brethren, that ye do not judge that which is evil to be of God, or that which is good and of God to be of the devil."

**5:21** *wise/prudent in their own sight.* This description refers to those who believe they know more than God or their fellow beings, those who see themselves as being very clever.

**5:22** *mighty to drink wine.* A phrase describing the lifestyle of those who reject God and think that they themselves are gods in the world.

**5:23** *justify the wicked for reward.* Refers to those who claim that the wicked are correct in their deeds, thus committing perjury for a reward (Prov. 17:15).

*take away the righteousness of the righteous.* This phrase describes those who deny impartiality and justice to the innocent. This phrase also speaks of people who mislead or seduce righteous people into sinning or who speak ill of people who are righteous. These people are they who "call evil good, and good evil."

**5:24** *fire/flame.* Filthy people shall "go away into everlasting fire, prepared for them; and their torment is as a lake of fire and brimstone, whose flame ascendeth up forever and ever and has no end" (2 Ne. 9:16). Further, all corruptible beings will burn with fire at the Lord's coming. "Behold, they shall be as stubble; the fire shall burn them" (47:14).

*stubble/chaff.* Symbols of the wicked (Ps. 1:4; Hosea 13:3).

*root/blossoms.* The *root* has reference to one's parentage, and the *blossoms* to offspring. The unrepentant wicked will not enjoy family ties in the eternities (Job 18:16).

*cast away the law of the Lord.* Unrighteous individuals often throw God's law away as if it were no more important or significant than common household garbage. Their reward is to be cast away themselves.

**5:25** *anger . . . kindled.* This idiom, which likens God's anger to fire, is common in Joseph Smith's revelations. The Lord's anger is always directed toward "the wicked and rebellious" (D&C 63:2; 5:8; 82:6).

*stretched forth his hand against them.* This idiom means that God sends forth his power or his judgments against the wicked (Ezek. 6:14; 14:9; Zeph. 1:4).

*hills did tremble.* Both humanity and the earth's elements react to the great glory, majesty, and presence of God. A variety of scriptures explain: "The Lord reigneth; let the people tremble" (Ps. 99:1); "the nations may tremble at thy presence" (64:2); and "let all the inhabitants of the land tremble: for the day of the Lord cometh" (Joel 2:1).

*their carcasses were torn.* Perhaps this phrase describes a result of war.

*his hand is stretched out still.* This poetic refrain, located at 9:12, 17, 21; 10:4, may signify one of two very different things: Although God is angry with his people for their sin and rebellion, he still stretches out his hand in mercy to his children (for this interpretation, see 2 Ne. 28:32); or the Lord's hand is yet stretched out in delivering destruction to the people (for this interpretation, see Ezek. 6:14). The translation of Today's English Version of the Bible in this instance supports the second interpretation: "Yet even so the Lord's anger is not ended; his hand is still stretched out to punish," as does the Jerusalem Bible: "Yet his anger is not spent, still his hand is raised to strike."

## AN ENSIGN TO THE NATIONS: THE GATHERING OF ISRAEL (5:26–30)

This section introduces two divine activities that will attract members of the house of Israel to their gathering places or their lands of promise: God will hold up a flag, or standard, unto all the nations of the earth around which Israel may rally; and God will attract the attention of Israel through a hiss (KJV) or a whistle (Hebrew). A third divine activity is listed in a later section of Isaiah: God will cause a trumpet to be blown, which will serve as a signal for the tribes to gather around the ensign (18:3, 7). These three activities symbolize the manner by which the earth's inhabitants will be called to Zion in the latter days after they accept the gospel of Jesus Christ.

Nothing will impede those who come to Zion. The Saints will not be weary, stumble, or sleep, and their loins will be girded, their shoes will be latched (5:27), and their equipment and vehicles will be ready and prepared (5:28). Those who gather to Zion are compared to a strong and mighty lion in its prime, who roars, catches its prey, and carries it away with no fear (5:29).

*Isaiah 5:26–30*

And he *will lift up an ensign* to the nations from far,

and *will [whistle]*[31] unto them from the end of the earth:

and, behold, they shall come with speed swiftly: (5:26)

*None* shall be weary nor stumble among them;[32]
*none* shall slumber nor sleep;

neither shall the *girdle of their loins* be loosed,
nor the *latchet of their shoes* be broken: (5:27)

Whose *arrows* [shall be][33] sharp,
and all their *bows* bent,

[and][34] *their horses' hoofs* shall be counted like flint,
and *their wheels* like a whirlwind: (5:28)

Their *roaring*[35] like a lion,
they shall *roar* like young lions:

yea, they shall roar, and lay hold of the prey, and shall carry it away safe, and none
shall [rescue][36] it. (5:29)

And in that day they shall roar against them like the roaring of the sea:

and if [they][37] look unto the land, behold *darkness* and sorrow,
and the *light is darkened* in the heavens thereof. (5:30)

## NOTES AND COMMENTARY

**5:26** *he will lift.* The Lord plays an active and personal role in the restoration of
the gospel by lifting the ensign or flag high into the air in view of all nations.

*ensign.* This represents the gospel of Jesus Christ (D&C 45:9; 105:39) and the
light that accompanies it (D&C 115:4–5).[38] The ensign is also the Book of Mormon
(2 Ne. 29:2–3; Moro. 10:27–28).

*whistle.* The whistle or hiss of God signals the gathering of Israel (7:18; Zech.
10:8–10).

*from the end of the earth.* The tribes of Israel were scattered throughout the earth
(Ezek. 12:15; Amos 9:9; 1 Ne. 10:12; 22:3–5) and are gathering in our day; they are
coming from all nations and gathering around the ensign.

*they shall come.* They who accept Jesus Christ as their God and Savior and
believe the Book of Mormon to be the word of God will quickly gather in Zion.

---

[31] Brown, Driver, and Briggs, *Hebrew and English Lexicon,* 1056.
[32] 2 Ne. 15:26 makes this phrase part of v. 26, but KJV makes it part of v. 27.
[33] 2 Ne. 15:28 and JST Isa. 5:28 replace the KJV present tense *are* with the future tense *shall be.*
[34] 2 Ne. 15:28 and JST Isa. 5:28 add the conjunction *and.*
[35] 2 Ne. 15:28 omits the phrase *shall be.* 2 Ne. 15:28 and JST Isa. 5:28 include the phrase *their roaring like a lion* as part of v. 28.
[36] Brown, Driver, and Briggs, *Hebrew and English Lexicon,* 664.
[37] 2 Ne. 15:30 and JST Isa. 5:30 replace *one* with *they* to clarify agreement.
[38] *Teachings of the Prophet Joseph Smith,* 38.

*with speed swiftly.* The scattering of Israel took place over many generations of time, but the gathering of Israel, which began at the beginning of the dispensation of the fulness of times, is presently taking place with great speed. Today, tens of thousands join The Church of Jesus Christ of Latter-day Saints annually.

**5:27** *weary/stumble/slumber/sleep.* Those who rally around God's gospel standard and gather in their lands of inheritance will not weary in accomplishing God's work of gathering.

*girdle of their loins/latchet of their shoes.* Those who come to Zion will do so with so much speed that they will not, symbolically speaking, take the time to remove their clothes or shoes. Like the warriors of old, they will continually be ready to fight and serve as the Lord's soldiers.

**5:28** *arrows/bows.* The bows and arrows of the righteous who gather in Zion symbolize the protection that God will provide for them as they return. Similar imagery was used when God brought ancient Israel out of Egypt (symbolic of the world) into the land of promise (Num. 24:8).

*horses' hoofs . . . like flint/wheels like a whirlwind.* Those who flee from the world and approach Zion in the last days will do so in great haste, as if riding on a whirlwind or traveling on a swift chariot (66:15; Jer. 4:13; Dan. 11:40). Their horses' hooves will not wear out, but will remain durable and strong, tough like flint.

**5:29** *roaring like a lion/young lions.* Those who gather to Zion, or embrace the gospel, will be as fearsome, mighty, and majestic as a great lion in its strength. The lesser animals (or enemies of the righteous) will not impede the Saints' desire to return there (3 Ne. 21:12–13).

*lay hold of the prey.* No enemy will be able to stand against the righteous in latter-day Israel.

**5:30** *roaring of the sea.* The children of Zion, armed with the Spirit and his gifts and possessing great priesthood powers, are mightier than the great roaring of the earth's oceans. The repetition of *roaring* is suggestive of that power.

*land.* The land of the wicked will contain great sin and wickedness to the point of "darkness and sorrow." The spiritual light from heaven will not be found among the unrighteous because it will be centered on Zion's people and their temples.

# ISAIAH 6

*LIKENING ISAIAH 6 UNTO OURSELVES*

*Isaiah 6 details Isaiah's vision of the Lord sitting on his throne. As Latter-day Saints, we too can enjoy the blessings the prophets have envisioned, if our spiritual ears are not "heavy" and our spiritual eyes are not "shut" (6:10). Joseph Smith taught that "God hath not revealed anything to Joseph, but what He will make known unto the Twelve, and even the least Saint may know all things as fast as he is able to bear them."[1] Also, "when any man obtains [the Second Comforter], he will have the personage of Jesus Christ to attend him, or appear unto him from time to time, . . . and the visions of the heavens will be opened unto him."[2]*

## ISAIAH'S VISION OF GOD AND HIS PROPHETIC COMMISSION (6:1–13)

Isaiah's grand vision of the Lord likely took place in 740 B.C. (the year that King Uzziah died). It is told in the first person (Isaiah uses the pronouns "I" and "me") and is similar to other prophetic visions such as those of Moses (Moses 1), Amos (Amos 7:1–9), Ezekiel (Ezek. 1), John (Rev. 1:10–19), and Joseph Smith (D&C 76; 110). Elsewhere we are informed that it was Jesus Christ whom Isaiah envisioned on this great occasion (2 Ne. 11:2–3; John 12:41). The temple identified in this section was the heavenly or celestial temple, or more specifically the throne room or holy of holies.

---

[1] *Teachings of the Prophet Joseph Smith*, 149.
[2] *Teachings of the Prophet Joseph Smith*, 151.

Joseph Smith informs us that Isaiah's vision was connected to the experience wherein his calling and election were made sure and he was given the gift of the Second Comforter, Jesus Christ.[3]

The last three verses of this section (6:11–13) introduce several teachings that concern the scattering of Israel, which is caused by wickedness. These teachings lead into the theme of Isaiah 7, in which Isaiah prophesies that the Lord will not leave Israel in a scattered condition; rather, "a remnant shall return" (Hebrew *sh^e'ar yashub*), a reference to the son of Isaiah.

## Isaiah 6:1–13

In the year that king Uzziah died I saw also the Lord sitting upon a throne, high and lifted up, and [the hems of his robe][4] filled the temple. (6:1)
Above it stood the seraphim:[5] each one had six wings;

*with [two]* he covered his face,
and *with [two]* he covered his feet,
and *with [two]*[6] he did fly. (6:2)

And one cried unto another, and said, Holy, holy, holy, is the Lord of hosts: the whole earth is full of his glory. (6:3)
And the posts of the door moved at the voice of him that cried, and the house was filled with smoke. (6:4)

Then said I, *Woe* is [unto][7] me!
for I am *undone;*

because *I* am a man of unclean lips,
and *I* dwell in the midst of a people of unclean lips:

for mine eyes have seen the King, the Lord of hosts. (6:5)

Then flew one of the seraphim[8] unto me, having a live coal in his hand, which he had taken with the tongs from off the altar: (6:6)

And he *laid it* upon my mouth,
and said, [Behold][9], this hath *touched* thy lips;

and *thine iniquity* is taken away,
and *thy sin* purged. (6:7)

Also I heard the voice of the Lord, saying,

---

[3] *Teachings of the Prophet Joseph Smith,* 150–51.
[4] The reading is from Wildberger, *Isaiah 1–12,* 248. See also Brown, Driver, and Briggs, *Hebrew and English Lexicon,* 1002.
[5] 2 Ne. 16:2 deletes the *s,* which creates a double and redundant plural.
[6] The archaic word *twain* has been replaced three times.
[7] 2 Ne. 16:5 adds the word *unto.*
[8] 2 Ne. 16:6 drops the redundant plural form.
[9] This is from the Hebrew term *hineh.*

*Whom shall I send,* and <u>who will go</u> for us?
Then said I, <u>Here am I</u>; *send me.* (6:8)

And he said, Go, and tell this people,

*Hear ye indeed,* but [they][10] <u>understand not</u>;
and *see ye indeed,* but [they <u>perceived</u>][11] <u>not</u>. (6:9)

Make the *heart* of this people fat, and make their <u>ears</u> heavy, and shut their eyes;
lest they see with their eyes, and hear with their <u>ears</u>, and understand with their
*heart,*

and convert, and be healed. (6:10) Then said I, Lord, how long? And he [said],[12]

Until the *cities* be <u>wasted without inhabitant,</u>
and the *houses* <u>without man,</u>
and the *land* be <u>utterly desolate,</u> (6:11)

And the Lord have removed men far away, [for][13] there be a great forsaking in the
midst of the land. (6:12) But yet [there][14] shall be a tenth, and [they][15] shall return,
and shall be eaten: as a teil tree, and as an oak, whose [stump remains],[16] when
they cast their leaves: so the holy seed shall be the [stump] thereof. (6:13)

## NOTES AND COMMENTARY

**6:1** *the year that king Uzziah died.* Uzziah, king of Judah, died in 740 B.C.
Details regarding his reign are recorded in 2 Kings 15:1–7 (in which his name is rendered *Azariah*) and 2 Chronicles 26. It is evident in this verse that Isaiah wants his
readers to note that he received a vision of the heavenly king in the same year the
earthly king died.

*throne.* Isaiah saw the throne room (the holy of holies) of the temple in heaven.
(For prophetic descriptions of the heavenly throne, see Ezek. 1:26, Rev. 4:2–5, and
D&C 137:3.)

*high and lifted up.* God is greater and more exalted than all creatures. Elsewhere
Isaiah calls God "the high and lofty One that inhabiteth eternity" (57:15).

*hems of his robe.* This speaks of the Lord's flowing temple robes. God is
"clothed with purity, yea, even with the robe of righteousness" (2 Ne. 9:14), as are his

---

[10] 2 Ne. 16:9 and JST Isa. 6:9 add the pronoun *they,* a change that receives support from ancient manu-
scripts. See, for example, Watts, *Isaiah 1–33,* 69.

[11] 2 Ne. 16:9 and JST Isa. 6:9 add *they* and make *perceive* into *perceived.*

[12] 2 Ne. 16:11 and JST Isa. 6:11 replace *answered* with *said.*

[13] 2 Ne. 16:12 and JST Isa. 6:12 replace *and* with *for.*

[14] JST Isa. 6:13 replaces *in it* with *there.*

[15] JST Isa. 6:13 replaces *it* with *they,* clarifying the antecedent.

[16] The Hebrew reads *mitsebet bam.* Brown, Driver, and Briggs, *Hebrew and English Lexicon,* 663. This literally reads *stump in them,* but the corrupted text probably should be read with the term *remains,* as translated in the JB and others.

holy saints. The image of the hems of God's robe filling the temple is used to symbolize the purity, righteousness, and power of the Lord that filled the temple.

*temple.* The temple in heaven was likely accessed through the earthly temple, which in Isaiah's case was located in Jerusalem.

**6:2** *seraphim.* The term *seraphim* comes from the Hebrew root *sarap,* which means "to burn,"[17] and refers to a class of angels who are located in the celestial kingdom. English translations of its plural form may read "burning ones," or "bright shiny ones," both of which describe their glorious condition and location near God's throne. A modern revelation speaks of the "bright, shining seraphs around [God's] throne" who shout "acclamations of praise, singing Hosanna to God and the Lamb!" (D&C 109:79), some of whom are premortal spirits (D&C 38:1).

*six wings.* Each living being seen by Ezekiel (Ezek. 1:9–11) and John (Rev. 4:8) in their visions had wings. The seraphim's wings are probably not literal but may be a "representation of power, to move, to act, etc." (D&C 77:4).

*covered his face/feet.* Perhaps the seraphim covered their faces to protect themselves from the glory of God, which was present in the throne room of the celestial temple.

**6:3** *[Seraphim] cried unto another.* Like the living creatures in Revelation 4–5, the seraphim have the capacity to communicate with God and to worship him, as indicated by their words of praise, "holy, holy, holy," directed to the Lord.

*Holy, holy, holy.* This threefold exclamation plays a significant role in Isaiah's and John the Revelator's visions of the heavenly temple (Rev. 4:8). This cry of "holy, holy, holy" may point to God the Father, the Son, and the Holy Ghost.

*Lord of hosts.* See commentary on 1:9.

**6:4** *posts of the door moved.* Quaking often accompanies God's presence (Ex. 19:18; Hab. 3:3–10), and here the temple posts moved or shook.

*house.* In the ancient Near East it was common to call the sacred temple a *house.*

*smoke.* Presumably smoke originated from the altar of incense, and it represents the prayers of the Saints (Ps. 141:2; Rev. 5:8). Similarly, John the Revelator beheld the temple in heaven in vision and noted that it "was filled with smoke from the glory of God, and from his power" (Rev. 15:8). The smoke may also be connected with the eternal fires found in heaven: "God Almighty Himself dwells in eternal fire; flesh and blood cannot go there, for all corruption is devoured by the fire. 'Our God is a consuming fire.'"[18] At times smoke represents the glory of God (Ex. 19:18; Rev. 15:8).

---

[17] Brown, Driver, and Briggs, *Hebrew and English Lexicon,* 976.
[18] *Teachings of the Prophet Joseph Smith,* 367; see also Deut. 4:24; Heb. 12:29.

**6:5** *Woe.* As Isaiah stood before the "King, the Lord of hosts," he was painfully aware of his frailties and weaknesses as a human and mortal, and thus he exclaimed, "Woe is unto me!" (6:5; 5:18).

*I am undone.* The literal reading is "I am destroyed" or "I am lost." Perhaps Isaiah felt unworthy or overwhelmed to find himself in the presence of the Lord; or, like Moses, he recognized his status in comparison to God's (Moses 1:9–11).

*unclean lips.* Inasmuch as "all [save Jesus Christ] have sinned, and come short of the glory of God" (Rom. 3:23), Isaiah too has "unclean lips" and has to be cleansed (6:6–7). Likewise, Joseph Smith went through a purification process (D&C 29:3; JS–H 1:29).

*mine eyes have seen the King.* Isaiah, like many prophets, saw Jesus Christ. Nephi wrote, "And now I, Nephi, write more of the words of Isaiah, . . . for he verily saw my Redeemer, even as I have seen him. And my brother, Jacob, also has seen him as I have seen him" (2 Ne. 11:2–3).

*King.* Jesus, who is called "King of kings" (Rev. 19:16), sits on the throne in the throne room of the heavenly temple. There is a direct connection between the Lord's temples and kingship.[19] Jesus was the heir to the throne, and we through his atonement may become "joint-heirs with Christ" (Rom. 8:17) and sit on the throne with him and the Father (Rev. 3:21).

**6:6** *live coal.* The burning coal from the altar of sacrifice purified Isaiah so he could enter God's presence (Ezek. 1:13; 10:2; 24:11). The live coal represents the Holy Ghost who purifies and purges us, making it possible for us to enter God's presence.

*altar.* This refers to the altar of sacrifice (Lev. 16:12).

**6:7** *mouth/lips.* Although it was only Isaiah's mouth and lips that are touched, his entire soul was cleansed; he has "been 'atoned'" and can thus "become a tool" for the Lord,[20] using his *mouth* and *lips* in bearing his testimony to the people.

**6:8** *Whom shall I send?* Isaiah, who also answered his prophetic call from the Lord with "here am I," was responding to the Lord following an ancient pattern (Abr. 3:27). In this setting Isaiah also became a type of Christ. *Send* where? Isaiah is sent to the world to bear witness of Christ and to declare his word.

*who will go for us? Go* where? Isaiah is sent to *go* among the people of his day to proclaim God's word of warning and judgment. The plural pronoun *us* suggests that there were others in God's heavenly throne room. In John's vision of the

---

[19] Ricks and Sroka, "King, Coronation, and Temple," 236–71.
[20] Wildberger, *Isaiah 1–12,* 270.

heavenly temple (Rev. 4–5), we read of exalted Saints and others near God's throne in heaven (Gen. 1:26; 3:22; 11:7).

*Here am I.* This saying is often connected to the calling of the Lord's servants (Gen. 22:1; Ex. 3:4; 1 Sam. 3:4–8; Abr. 3:27). It seems to have the meaning of "I am here ready to obey your commandments concerning me."

**6:9** *Hear ye/see ye, but they understand not.* The prophecy was partially fulfilled by the wicked Jews in Jesus' day (Matt. 13:13–15; John 12:37–41; Acts 28:25–28)[21] and has general fulfillment in all those who are so spiritually deaf and blind that they will not understand or accept the words of God given through the prophets. The terms *hear* and *see* refer to physical faculties (eyes and ears) and symbolize spiritual faculties such as understanding and perceptiveness.

**6:10** *heart of this people fat.* The book of Matthew clarifies this passage: "this people's heart is waxed gross" (Matt. 13:15), which means that their hearts have become hardened through their own wickedness, not through the agency of Isaiah or the Lord.

**6:11** *how long?* Isaiah asked the Lord *how long* the inhabitants of the land would choose spiritual blindness. The Lord answered that they would be blind until the houses, cities, and land were destroyed and had become utterly desolate.

*cities be wasted without inhabitant.* Desolation and destruction always attend wickedness. The people are so wicked that they will not repent even though they are being destroyed for not repenting.

**6:12** *Lord have removed men far away.* The Lord exiled his people. It was the custom of Assyrian and Babylonian nations, which served as instruments in God's hand, to deport the peoples whom they conquered (2 Kgs. 17; 24–25). Destruction (6:11) and deportation of the wicked go hand in hand.

**6:13** *tenth.* Only a small remnant of Israel will remain after the destruction spoken of in 6:11–12.

*teil tree/oak.* Israel is likened to trees that are cut down or destroyed and become as stumps.

*holy seed.* This phrase may refer to the remnant or seed (41:8; 45:25; 59:21; 66:22) that will return in the last days and become the new tree (nation of Israel; Jacob 5:2), or to Christ, who is the Holy Seed.

---

[21] *Teachings of the Prophet Joseph Smith,* 95.

# ISAIAH 7

### LIKENING ISAIAH 7 UNTO OURSELVES

*This prophecy has a direct application for us although it was literally fulfilled when Assyria invaded ancient Israel. Assyria is a type and symbol of the warring nations that will exist in the latter days, shortly before the Second Coming. The text provides a number of clues regarding this, including Isaiah's fourfold use of the formula "in that day" (7:18, 20, 21, 23), a phrase that often pertains to our own day. Further, if we accept the Lord's sign of Immanuel (i.e., if we accept Jesus Christ and his atonement), we will be protected during the wars in the last days. The central messages for us in this section are that we should trust the Lord's word that comes through his prophet, rather than rely on the arm of flesh, and Judah's inhabitants should find comfort in knowing that a "remnant of Israel shall return" to Israel, as the Lord has promised.*

## EPHRAIM AND SYRIA WAR AGAINST JUDAH (7:1–9)

The last three verses of the previous section (6:11–13) refer to the deportation of ancient Israel's inhabitants from their homeland and to the ruin of their cities. These somber prophecies deal with the scattering of Israel brought about by her spiritual blindness and hard-heartedness (6:10). This section (7:1–9) nevertheless presents a prophecy intended to bring joy and hope to the people through the presence of a living symbol (8:18) named Shear-jashub, the son of Isaiah and his wife, the prophetess. *Shear-jashub* means "a remnant shall return," and the prophecy is that a remnant of the house of Israel will someday return to their homeland. More is said of Shear-jashub in later prophecies.

An Isaiah scholar explains that the prophecy in this section "was delivered on the occasion of Isaiah's first interview with King Ahaz, after the first alarm had reached Jerusalem that invasion was imminent. The king was apparently supervising the measures being taken to ensure a water-supply for the city in the event of a siege, when the prophet received the command to go with his son Shear-yashub."[1]

Rezin king of Syria and Pekah king of Israel tried to persuade Ahaz king of Judah to ally with them against Assyria, their neighboring superpower. Meanwhile, Isaiah pleaded with Ahaz to trust the Lord for deliverance from the invading armies (7:1–10). Ahaz rejected Isaiah's spiritual counsel and won the support of Tiglath-pileser III, king of Assyria, who in 732 B.C. invaded the Northern Kingdom of Israel and captured many cities (2 Kgs. 15:29; 16:7–9). Because Ahaz rejected Isaiah's (i.e., God's) plan, the armies of Rezin and Pekah invaded Judah, slew one hundred twenty thousand warriors, and carried away some two hundred thousand women and children. Judah was slaughtered, because, in part, of the great sins of her king and her people (2 Kgs. 16:5; 2 Chr. 28:5–8).

The section begins with a historical note that explains the setting and context from which the prophecy originated (7:1–2). Next, the Lord speaks to Isaiah (7:3). Isaiah delivers God's word to Ahaz (7:4), telling him that the two invading kings are but blazing firebrands which will soon be burnt out, and that Syria's plan to rule Judah, dethrone Ahaz, and place a king on Judah's throne will not be successful. Syria, Ephraim, and the son of Remaliah make evil plans (7:5) which the Lord explains will not work (7:7–9).

## Isaiah 7:1–9

And it came to pass in the days of Ahaz the son of Jotham, the son of Uzziah, king of Judah, that Rezin the king of Syria, and Pekah the son of Remaliah, king of Israel, went up toward Jerusalem to war against it, but could not prevail against it. (7:1) And it was told the house of David, saying, Syria is [an ally][2] with Ephraim. And his heart was moved, and the heart of his people, as the trees of the wood are moved with the wind. (7:2) Then said the Lord unto Isaiah, Go forth now to meet Ahaz, thou, and Shear-jashub thy son, at the end of the [aqueduct][3] of the upper pool in the highway of the [washermen's][4] field; (7:3) And say unto him,

Take heed, and be quiet;
fear not, neither be fainthearted

for the *two tails* of these smoking firebrands,
for the fierce anger of *Rezin* with Syria, and of the *son of Remaliah*. (7:4)

Because Syria, Ephraim, and the son of Remaliah, have taken evil counsel against thee, saying, (7:5)

---

[1] Kissane, *Book of Isaiah*, 1:77.
[2] We have replaced the archaic *confederate* with *ally*.
[3] We have replaced the archaic *conduit* with *aqueduct*.
[4] Brown, Driver, and Briggs, *Hebrew and English Lexicon*, 460.

*Let us* go up against Judah, and [cause her sickening dread],[5]
and *let us* [break her down][6] for us,

and set a *king* in the midst of it,

[yea,][7] the *son of Tabeal:* (7:6)

Thus saith the Lord God, *It shall not stand,
neither shall it come to pass.* (7:7)

For the *head of Syria* is <u>Damascus,</u>
and the *head of Damascus,*[8] <u>Rezin</u>;

and within threescore and five years shall *Ephraim* <u>be broken,</u>
that <u>it be not</u> a *people.* (7:8)

And the *head of Ephraim* is <u>Samaria,</u>
and the *head of Samaria* is <u>Remaliah's son.</u>

If *ye* <u>will not believe,</u>
surely *ye* <u>shall not be established.</u> (7:9)

## NOTES AND COMMENTARY

**7:1** *Ahaz.* Ahaz was a king of Judah (735–715 B.C.), the son of Jotham and father of Hezekiah. Ahaz chose to ignore Isaiah's prophetic words and instead followed a path of evil, which included making "molten images for Baalim," offering sacrifices and burning "incense in the high places," and sacrificing his children to false deities (2 Chr. 28:2–4, 23–25; 2 Kgs. 16:2–4, 10–16).

*Rezin.* This king of Syria (2 Kgs. 15:37), together with Pekah, waged an anti-Assyrian campaign. Eventually, Rezin was killed during a battle against Assyria (2 Kgs. 16:7–9).

*Pekah.* Pekah, who was the son of Remaliah, "conspired against" Pekahiah (king of Israel and son of Menahem), assassinated him, and became Israel's eighteenth king. Pekah's reign lasted approximately five years (737–732 B.C.; 2 Kgs. 15:22–26). Pekah, who with Rezin battled against Ahaz king of Judah, was eventually murdered by Hosea (not to be confused with the prophet Hosea), who succeeded him on the throne (2 Kgs. 15:30). It was during King Hosea's reign that the northern tribes of Israel (the ten tribes) were captured and deported by Assyria.

**7:2** *house of David.* This refers to the Davidic dynasty, including Ahaz, who ruled over Judah.

*Syria* (or Aram). The kingdom of Syria, which was north of ancient Israel.

---

[5] Brown, Driver, and Briggs, *Hebrew and English Lexicon,* 881.
[6] Brown, Driver, and Briggs, *Hebrew and English Lexicon,* 132.
[7] JST Isa. 7:6 and 2 Ne. 17:6 replace *even* with *yea.*
[8] 2 Ne. 17:8 replaces *is* with a comma.

*Ephraim.* Here Ephraim represents the Northern Kingdom of Israel, the home of the ten tribes of Israel. Ephraim's boundaries are described in Joshua 16:5–9.

*his heart/heart of his people.* The hearts of Ahaz and the Judahites became afraid because of the anticipated invasion of Syria and Israel's armies into the kingdom of Judah.

**7:3** *Shear-jashub.* Shear-jashub, who was named prophetically (Hebrew, "a remnant shall return"; Hosea 1:6–9), was a son of Isaiah and the prophetess, and the elder brother of Maher-shalal-hash-baz. The Lord commanded Isaiah to take Shear-jashub with him to meet King Ahaz at the upper pool because the boy was to become a living symbol to the Jews (8:18) and a reminder to the Israelites that a remnant would return to their land and their God (6:11–13).

*aqueduct of the upper pool.* The pool was probably located near the Gihon spring in the Valley of Kidron.[9] Ahaz may have been at the pool with his officers to check Jerusalem's water supply for the pending siege. The Lord, who knew Ahaz's location, inspired Isaiah to go there with his son Shear-jashub. This is also the place where Rabshakeh, messenger of the king of Assyria, delivered a message to King Hezekiah (36:2; 2 Kgs. 18:17).

**7:4** *fear not, neither be fainthearted.* King Ahaz had no need to fear the power of the kings of Syria and Israel, for the days of their power were numbered.

*two tails of these smoking firebrands.* A *firebrand* is smoldering wood. The might and majesty of Rezin and Pekah, who were once burning fires with the power to consume, were now nothing more than smoldering embers. The *tails* may symbolize two animals who are retreating from a battle.

*son of Remaliah.* Pekah was Remaliah's son.

**7:5** *evil counsel against thee.* Syria, Ephraim, and the son of Remaliah (Pekah) planned to conquer Judah and set a king over her (7:6).

**7:6** *go up against Judah.* These countries intended to make war against Judah and conquer her.

*cause her sickening dread.* Through intimidation and brutal force, Syria, Ephraim, and the son of Remaliah hoped to strike fear in the hearts of Judah's inhabitants.

*let us break her down.* These forces wished to conquer Judah.

*set a king in the midst of it.* These powers wanted to conquer Judah to expand their own territory and dominion by placing one of their own, a puppet king (the son of Tabeal), over the land.

---

[9] Watts, *Isaiah 1–33,* 91.

*son of Tabeal.* Rezin and Pekah had hoped to install this puppet ruler on Ahaz's throne. The son of Tabeal is considered so insignificant a ruler that his own name is not given in the text.

**7:7** *Thus saith the Lord God.* God is the author of these words.

*It shall not stand, neither shall it come to pass.* God, who is omnipotent and in charge of the affairs of humanity, sees the future. The plans of Syria, Ephraim, and Pekah, the son of Remaliah, will not succeed. Not only does God reveal to his prophets what will happen in the future but he tells them what will not happen, "neither shall it come to pass."

**7:8** *head of Syria is Damascus.* Damascus, located at the foot of Mount Hermon, was the capital (head) of Syria, and Damascus's king (head) was Rezin. Damascus was captured by the Assyrian army, led by Tiglath-pileser (2 Kgs. 16:9).

*threescore and five years.* Isaiah's prophecy that Ephraim would no longer be a kingdom or a nation was fulfilled when Ephraim fell in 721 B.C. King Sargon II of Assyria deported her citizens, the ten tribes of Israel, to the north countries.

**7:9** *head of Ephraim is Samaria.* Samaria was the capital (head) of the Northern Kingdom of Israel, or Ephraim (1 Kgs. 16:23–24, 28), where most of the kings of Israel resided. The king (head) of Samaria was Pekah.

*If ye will not believe.* If Ahaz (and Judah) would not believe in Jehovah and have faith in Isaiah's prophecies, then Ahaz's kingship and kingdom would not remain on the earth.

## THE SIGN TO AHAZ: THE IMMANUEL PROPHECY (7:10–16)

The Lord extended a sign to Ahaz to demonstrate that the events surrounding the plot of Rezin and Pekah would occur precisely as Isaiah had prophesied (7:1–9). The sign was to give Ahaz courage and faith to trust the prophet's word that God's power was far greater than man's armies, and although Ahaz rejected the sign, the Lord provided one anyway. The sign pertained to a specific virgin who would conceive and bring forth a son whose name would be called Immanuel.

The prophecy has a dual application, as shown by a close reading of Isaiah 7:10–16; 8:3–7; and Matthew 1:21. First, the greater fulfillment of the prophecy centers in Jesus Christ, who was Immanuel, the son of the virgin Mary. Matthew recorded this fulfillment: "She shall bring forth a son, and thou shalt call his name Jesus: for he shall save his people from their sins. Now all this was done, that it might be fulfilled which was spoken of the Lord by the prophet [Isaiah], saying, Behold, a virgin shall be with child, and shall bring forth a son, and they shall call his name Emmanuel, which being interpreted is, God with us" (Matt. 1:21–23). Second, because the sign was given, in part, to nurture Ahaz's faith, it would have had some fulfillment in his lifetime. The lesser fulfillment of the Immanuel prophecy thus pertains to Isaiah's wife, the prophetess, who also fulfilled the conditions of Isaiah's prophecy when she brought forth a son. Isaiah, the prophetess, their son, and the conditions surrounding his birth all point to the birth of Jesus Christ. These similarities are shown in Table 1. Isaiah's language in both passages of scripture was deliberate, designed to show that the first fulfillment of the Immanuel prophecy was connected to himself, his wife, and their son, all of whom were signs to Israel (8:18).

## Table 1

| Themes | Isaiah 7:14–17 | Isaiah 8:3–7 |
|---|---|---|
| Mother | Virgin (14) | Prophetess (3) |
| Conception | Shall conceive (14) | She conceived (3) |
| Child is a son | Bear a son (14) | Bare a son (3) |
| Naming of son | Call his name Immanuel (14) | Call his name Maher-shalal-hash-baz |
| Child shall have knowledge | Before the child shall know (16) | Before the child shall have knowledge (4) |
| Child before eight years | To refuse the evil and choose the good (16) | To cry, My father, and my mother (4) |
| Land | Land . . . shall be forsaken (16) | Damascus and . . . Samaria shall be taken away (4) |
| Kings | Both her kings (16) | King of Assyria (4) |
| Role of the Lord | Lord shall bring upon thee (17) | Lord bringeth up upon them (7) |
| Assyrian king | King of Assyria (17) | King of Assyria (7) |

Matthew's account of the fulfillment of this prophecy in the meridian of time also fits the pattern, as shown in Table 2.

## Table 2

| Themes | Isaiah 7:14–17 | Isaiah 8:3–7 | Matthew 1:21 |
|---|---|---|---|
| Mother | Virgin (14) | Prophetess (3) | She (Mary) |
| Conception | Shall conceive (14) | Conceived (3) | Bring forth |
| Child is a son | Bear a son (14) | Bare a son (3) | A son |
| Naming of son | Call his name Immanuel (14) | Call his name Maher-shalal-hash-baz | Call his name Jesus |

### Isaiah 7:10–16

Moreover the *Lord* spake again unto <u>Ahaz</u>, saying, (7:10)
Ask <u>thee</u> a sign of the *Lord* thy God;

ask it either *in the depth,*
or *in the height* above. (7:11)

But Ahaz said, *I will not <u>ask</u>,*
*neither will I* [<u>test</u>][10] the Lord. (7:12)

And [Isaiah] said, Hear ye now, O house of David;

Is it a small thing for you to [*try the patience* of] <u>men</u>,
but will ye [*try the patience* of][11] <u>my God</u> also? (7:13)

Therefore the Lord himself shall give you a sign;

Behold, [the][12] *virgin* shall <u>conceive</u>,
and [shall][13] <u>bear a son</u>,
and shall <u>call his name Immanuel</u>. (7:14)

Butter and honey shall he eat, that *he may know to refuse the evil,* and [to][14] <u>choose the good</u>. (7:15) For before the *child shall know to refuse the evil,* and <u>choose the good</u>,

the land that thou abhorrest shall be forsaken of both her kings. (7:16)

---

[10] Hebrew *naseh.* Brown, Driver, and Briggs, *Hebrew and English Lexicon,* 650.
[11] Hebrew *la'ah.* Brown, Driver, and Briggs, *Hebrew and English Lexicon,* 521.
[12] Many ancient texts make the article definite, that is, *the* virgin in place of *a* virgin; see Wildberger, *Isaiah 1–12,* 282, 285.
[13] JST Isa. 7:14 and 2 Ne. 17:14 insert *shall.*
[14] JST Isa. 7:15 and 2 Ne. 17:15 insert *to.*

## NOTES AND COMMENTARY

**7:10** *the Lord spake again unto Ahaz.* The Lord spoke to King Ahaz through the prophet Isaiah, which is often how God communicates with individuals.

**7:11** *Ask thee a sign.* The sign was a prophecy that received both immediate and later fulfillment (8:3–7). In the Old Testament era, signs were "frequently offered by a prophet so that someone may know that God [was] fulfilling the promises he [had] made"[15] (37:30; 38:7; 1 Sam. 2:34; 10:7–9).

*depth/height.* One could ask for the sign either in the depth (which may refer to the earth) or in heaven itself, for God has the power to reach into the farthest corners of his numberless creations to give any number of signs for his divine purposes. As it was, God indeed gave Ahaz the greatest sign in the universe, one that dealt with the Messiah, who would be called Immanuel (7:14).

**7:12** *test.* Apparently Ahaz was afraid to ask the Lord for a sign. Perhaps he knew that Israel had often been accused of testing the Lord (Ex. 17:2; Num. 14:22; Deut. 6:16; Ps. 95:9), or he was spiritually dead and a nonbeliever, or he was afraid of the sign and what it would mean.

**7:13** *Hear ye now, O house of David.* The sign was not for Ahaz only, for the plural *ye* and the phrase *house of David* indicate that the sign was given to all the people of the kingdom.

**7:14** *virgin.* The term *virgin* describes both one who is physically untouched and one who is pure and undefiled by the world. Isaiah's wife was a virgin in the latter sense, and Mary, Jesus' mother, was a virgin in both senses. The Hebrew word *'al<sup>e</sup>-mah* (despite some arguments to the contrary) does indeed mean "virgin."[16]

The Book of Mormon prophets have identified Mary as "a virgin, and she was exceedingly fair and white" (1 Ne. 11:13); "a virgin, most beautiful and fair above all other virgins" (1 Ne. 11:15); "the virgin . . . the mother of the Son of God" (1 Ne. 11:18); and "a virgin, a precious and chosen vessel" (Alma 7:10).

*son.* The name or title *son* plays a prominent role in defining Jesus' divine mission and atoning sacrifice. Jesus is called "Son" (Moses 5:8), "Son Ahman" (D&C 78:20), "son of Abraham" (Matt. 1:1), "Son of David" (Matt. 9:27), "Son of God" (1 Ne. 10:17), "son of Joseph" (Luke 3:23), "Son of Man" (Moses 6:57), "son of Mary" (Mark 6:3), "Son of Righteousness" (3 Ne. 25:2), "Son of the Eternal Father" (1 Ne. 11:21), "Son of the everlasting God" (1 Ne. 11:32), "Son of the Highest"

---

[15] Watts, *Isaiah 1–33,* 96.
[16] Motyer, *Prophecy of Isaiah,* 84–85.

(Luke 1:32), "Son of the living God" (D&C 14:9), and "Son of the most high God" (1 Ne. 11:6).

*shall call his name Immanuel.* The Hebrew sentence structure makes it clear that the virgin names the child: "the virgin shall . . . call his name Immanuel." The name *Immanuel,* which means "God with us" or "God is with us," indicates that God's love, power, knowledge, grace, and presence are with the righteous. Also, the name indicates that God himself came down from heaven and took upon himself mortality. For these and other reasons, Immanuel is Jesus, the son of David, who is called "King Immanuel" in a modern revelation (D&C 128:22). The names *Immanuel* ("God is with us"), *Maher-shalal-hash-baz* ("to speed, spoil, hasten, plunder"), and *Jesus* ("salvation") are symbolic and have prophetic connotations.

**7:15** *butter and honey.* These are the basics of a pastoral culture (7:21–22).

**7:16** *before the child shall know.* The prophecy explains that before the child is able to make his own moral choices, or arrives at the age of accountability, which is eight years old (D&C 68:25), the kingdoms of Syria and Israel (Northern Kingdom) will be laid waste. This prophecy was fulfilled within a few years, while Maher-shalal-hash-baz was still under the age of eight, when both Syria and Israel fell to Assyria.

*both her kings.* The kings of Syria and the Northern Kingdom of Israel.

## ASSYRIA'S INVASION OF JUDAH (7:17–25)

After providing King Ahaz with a sign (the Immanuel prophecy), Isaiah prophesies that Assyria will invade Israel. Ahaz had been worried about the two kings (Rezin and Pekah) who were threatening to invade his land and kingdom, but, according to Isaiah, Ahaz should have been more concerned with the Assyrian army's impending invasion. Inasmuch as Ahaz had rejected the Lord and lacked faith in him (7:10–14), the Lord set the king of Assyria against Ahaz.

Isaiah prophesies that Assyria's occupation would cover the entire land (7:18–19). Assyria's intent was to humiliate and strip the land's inhabitants of their dignity (7:20), make them poverty-stricken, and deport them from the land (7:21–22). Because of the desolating nature of warfare, the vineyards would become neglected and overrun with thorns and briers (7:23–24), and the farmlands that had once been cultivated (digged with the hoe) would also be abandoned and become a pastureland for cattle and sheep (7:25). Ahaz could have had freedom for his people, but he ignored the Lord's sign.

## Isaiah 7:17–25

The Lord shall bring *upon thee,*
and *upon thy people,*
and *upon thy father's house,*

days that have not come,
from the day that Ephraim departed from Judah; even the king of Assyria. (7:17)

And it shall come to pass in that day,

that the Lord shall [whistle][17] for the *fly* that is in the uttermost part of the rivers of Egypt,
and for the *bee* that is in the land of Assyria. (7:18)

And they shall come, and shall rest all of them *in the desolate valleys,*
and *in the holes of the rocks,*

and *upon all thorns,*
and *upon all bushes.* (7:19)

In the same day shall the Lord shave with a razor that is hired,[18]

*by them* beyond the river,
*by the king* of Assyria,

the *head,* and the *hair of the feet:*
and it shall also consume the *beard.* (7:20)

And it shall come to pass in that day, that a man shall nourish a young cow, and two sheep; (7:21) And it shall come to pass, for the abundance of milk[19] they shall give he shall eat butter: for butter and honey shall every one eat that is left in the land. (7:22)

And it shall come to pass in that day,
[Every place which has a thousand vines worth a thousand pieces of silver
will become *thorns and briers*][20] (7:23)
With arrows and with bows shall men come thither;
because all the land shall become *briers and thorns.* (7:24)
And on all hills that shall be digged with the [hoe],[21]
[you will no longer go there for][22] fear of *briers and thorns:*

but it shall be for the *sending forth of oxen,*
and for the *treading of [sheep].*[23] (7:25)

---

[17] The reading of *whistle* is from the Hebrew.

[18] 2 Ne. 17:20 deletes the term *namely.*

[19] 2 Ne. 17:22 deletes *that.*

[20] Watts, *Isaiah 1–33,* 105. JST Isa. 7:23 and 2 Ne. 17:23 read this verse as "And it shall come to pass in that day, every place shall be, where there were a thousand vines at a thousand silverlings, which shall be for briers and thorns."

[21] Most modern English translations prefer *hoe* to *mattock.*

[22] This translation from the NIV agrees with a number of other modern translations.

[23] Hebrew *seh,* "one of a flock, a sheep; roaming pasture." Brown, Driver, and Briggs, *Hebrew and English Lexicon,* 961–62.

NOTES AND COMMENTARY

**7:17** *Lord shall bring upon thee . . . the king of Assyria.* Inasmuch as Ahaz and most of his people reject the Lord and turn to idolatry and other gross sins, the Lord will use the king of Assyria and his armies to punish King Ahaz, his family (*upon thy father's house*), and his kingdom (*upon thy people*). Note the active role played by God, who will *bring upon [King Ahaz and his kingdom] the king of Assyria.* In 10:5–26, God says he will use the Assyrians as his staff to beat the people.

*days that have not come, from the day that Ephraim departed from Judah.* The disaster that came on the kingdom of Judah is compared to the rebellion of the ten tribes under Jeroboam's leadership (1 Kgs. 12). Israel had not had days so severe since that rebellion.

**7:18** *Lord shall whistle.* The Lord will signal or prompt the Assyrian armies (here referred to as "bees") to come down on Judah. The *Lord shall whistle* to the bees is a symbol built on an actual ancient practice, for Cyrillus of Alexandria (ca. A.D. 400) wrote about beekeepers who whistled to bees to get them to return to their hives.[24]

*fly/bee.* These refer to fighting soldiers (see Deut. 1:44; Ps. 118:12). These symbols are well chosen, for "the flooding of the Nile brought . . . swarms of flies. . . . The hill districts of Assyria were well known for their bees."[25]

*rivers of Egypt/land of Assyria.* Assyria's domination and power would reach as far south as the rivers of Egypt, and Assyria would even rule Egypt for a brief period during the following century.

**7:19** *valleys/rocks, thorns/bushes.* Just as the bee and the fly are able to penetrate every area of the valleys, rocks, thorns, and bushes, so too would the Assyrian soldiers penetrate every area of the kingdom of Judah.

**7:20** *shave with a razor.* The Assyrian king and his armies represent the Lord's hired razor. The symbol of the razor refers to the fact that the Assyrians forced war prisoners to become slaves, humiliating and dishonoring them by shaving them from head to toe. Hence the fly and bee metaphors in 7:18 and the razor metaphor foretell that "no part of the land (7:18–19), no part of the person (7:20) will be free of enemy occupation."[26]

**7:21** *nourish a young cow, and two sheep.* This speaks of the poverty of those who remain in Judah after the Assyrian invasion. Residents who are permitted to

---

[24] Watts, *Isaiah 1–33,* 107.

[25] Motyer, *Prophecy of Isaiah,* 89.

[26] Motyer, *Prophecy of Isaiah,* 89.

remain in the land will be poor in comparison to the prewar years. They will no longer possess large herds of cattle or large vineyards (7:23). They will own only two sheep and a young cow, and they will find it a struggle to nourish their livestock.

**7:22** *abundance of milk.* Ancient Israel was called a land flowing with milk and honey (Ex. 3:8; 13:5) to symbolize its fertile and productive nature, but all that remains now is butter and wild honey. Fresh milk in abundance is gone; only a milk product, butter (which can be stored longer than fresh milk), remains.

*butter/honey.* Those who are not deported by Assyria and thus remain in Israel will eat the very basics of a pastoral culture: butter and honey. Produce (grains, fruits, and other items) will no longer be available because of the war-torn status of the community, economic upheaval, and lack of cultivated lands.

**7:23** *thousand vines.* A vineyard with a thousand vines is very large. The fruits and benefits of horticulture will be lost with Assyria's invasion, the richest vines will become worthless, and briers and thorns will be found in place of the vineyards.

**7:24** *arrows/bows.* Inasmuch as vineyards (7:23) and cultivated lands (7:25) will be gone, hunters, with their bows and arrows, will roam the land to seek their prey.

*land shall become briers and thorns.* The phrase *briers and thorns* occurs three times in this section. Because of the lack of cultivation and care for pasture, the land will become full of briers and thorns.

**7:25** *digged with the hoe.* As the vineyards will be taken over by briers and thorns, so will other cultivated land. Such desolation is symbolic of the judgments the people will receive for their pride and sin.

*oxen/sheep.* Farmlands that were once cultivated (*digged with the hoe*) have now become range for cattle and sheep.

---

# I S A I A H  8

## LIKENING ISAIAH 8 UNTO OURSELVES

*Isaiah presents three images of Jesus Christ that have special meaning for us today—
water, temple, and light. First, Jesus is as essential to our spiritual salvation as water
is to our physical salvation; that is to say, without water we will die physically, and
without Christ we will die spiritually (8:5–10). Second, we will find peace and comfort
in Jesus Christ if we permit him to be our temple (the focus of our worship), our cornerstone (the chief part of the building), and our sure foundation (where we can find
sure footing) (8:11–15). Third, as we walk through mortality, which is like passing in
the shadow or in darkness, we receive great hope, comfort, and joy when we accept
Jesus as our "great light" (8:16–9:2).*

---

## THE IMMANUEL PROPHECY: FIRST FULFILLMENT (8:1–4)

The sign provided to Ahaz was first fulfilled with the union of Isaiah and his wife
and the birth of their son Maher-shalal-hash-baz (see commentary on 7:14–16). At
least nine months would have passed since the conditions of the sign were given to
Ahaz, for the text makes it clear that Isaiah "went unto the prophetess" after the pro-
nouncement of the sign (8:3). Similar language found in 7:14–16 and 8:2–4 makes it
clear that 8:2–4 is the first and immediate fulfillment of the Immanuel prophecy given
in 7:14–16 (see Table 1, page 73). The verses recording the first fulfillment of this
prophecy are written in prose rather than in the poetic parallelistic style.

*Isaiah 8:1–4*

Moreover the [word of the][1] Lord said unto me, Take thee a great [tablet],[2] and

---

[1] JST Isa. 8:1 and 2 Ne. 18:1 insert *word of the*.
[2] Kaiser, *Isaiah 1–12*, 178.

write in it with a man's pen concerning Maher-shalal-hash-baz. (8:1) And I took unto me faithful witnesses to record, Uriah the priest, and Zechariah the son of Jeberechiah. (8:2) And I went unto the prophetess; and she conceived, and bare a son. Then said the Lord to me, Call his name Maher-shalal-hash-baz. (8:3) For [behold,] the child shall [not]³ have knowledge to cry, My father, and my mother, before the riches of Damascus and the spoil of Samaria shall be taken away before the king of Assyria. (8:4)

## NOTES AND COMMENTARY

**8:1** *great tablet.* On a large tablet, Isaiah wrote down the name by which his son would be called, "probably [to] indicat[e] that the inscription was intended for public display."⁴ This action, along with the testimony of the two witnesses, would make the prophecy and fulfillment of the sign to Ahaz public knowledge.

*man's pen.* This was probably a stylus or graver, used to inscribe stone, metal, or clay.

*Maher-shalal-hash-baz.* The son of Isaiah and the prophetess and the younger brother of Shear-jashub. Both Isaiah's sons share prophetic qualities in the book of Isaiah. Maher-shalal-hash-baz may also have been called "Immanuel" (see commentary on 7:14–16 and 8:8, 10). The prophetic nature of the name *Maher-shalal-hash-baz,* which means "to speed, spoil, hasten, plunder," is explained in 8:4: "For before the child shall have knowledge to cry, My father, and my mother, the riches of Damascus and the spoil of Samaria shall be taken away before the king of Assyria." That is, Maher-shalal-hash-baz is a living sign of the great quickness ("speed" or "hasten") with which Assyria would plunder and spoil the Northern Kingdom of Israel (Samaria) and Syria (Damascus). The repetition of *speed* and *hasten* in the son's name emphasizes the swiftness by which the sign will be fulfilled (meaning before the baby Maher-shalal-hash-baz can utter the words *father* or *mother*).

Maher-shalal-hash-baz is a type of Jesus Christ. Both Maher-shalal-hash-baz and Christ possess prophetic names; the name *Maher-shalal-hash-baz* has four parts, similar to the four titles of Jesus found in 9:6. Both were named by revelation from God, and both entered the world during times of political upheaval and warfare. *Maher-shalal-hash-baz* prophesies the manner in which Israel would be speedily destroyed and then plundered; likewise, Jesus Christ will come down to judge the world and speedily destroy those who are wicked. Jewish tradition holds that the prophetess belonged to a royal line. If this is indeed true, then Maher-shalal-hash-baz

---

³ JST Isa. 8:4 and 2 Ne. 18:4 insert the terms *behold* and *not* and move the term *before.*
⁴ Kaiser, *Isaiah 1–12,* 180.

was of royal lineage, as was Jesus Christ. (For other connections between the two, see Table 1 on page 73.)

**8:2** *faithful witnesses . . . Uriah the priest, and Zechariah.* Uriah was a well-known figure who worked as a priest in the Jerusalem temple (2 Kgs. 16:10–16). Little is known of Zechariah, other than that he was the son of Jeberechiah and was considered to be a *faithful witness.* He may have been the same Zechariah who was King Ahaz's father-in-law and the grandfather of King Hezekiah. The fact that Isaiah would have two witnesses, as required by law (Deut. 17:6; 19:15), to the inscription of his son's name on a tablet indicates that he wanted the public to know that the Lord had indeed fulfilled the sign given in 7:14–16. The two witnesses could later testify that Isaiah himself had inscribed the tablet and could confirm the date of inscription.

**8:3** *prophetess.* The prophetess, like her husband, possessed a testimony of Jesus, for "the testimony of Jesus is the spirit of prophecy" (Rev. 19:10). The title *prophetess* "was given to Isaiah's wife because she was literally the bearer of the Lord's word, incarnate in her son."[5] The fulfillment of the sign given to King Ahaz from the Lord came through Isaiah's wife and the birth of her son Maher-shalal-hash-baz (7:14). She typified the virgin Mary (7:14; see also Table 1, page 73).

*son.* Maher-shalal-hash-baz, the son of Isaiah and the prophetess, is a type of Jesus Christ, who is the Son of God (7:14–16).

**8:4** *to cry, My father, and my mother.* Isaiah's prophecy concerning the pending invasion of Assyria will be fulfilled within two or three years. The time element is set forth in the prophecy that Assyria will capture Damascus, Syria, Samaria, and Israel before Maher-shalal-hash-baz is able to say *My father, and my mother.* (Young children are able to say simple phrases such as *my father* or *my mother* near the age of two.) The prophecy was fulfilled in 734–732 B.C. when Tiglath-pileser, king of Assyria, captured the Galilee region, the Jezreel Valley, and Transjordan, and plundered their riches.

*riches of Damascus/spoil of Samaria.* After conquering Syria and Israel, the Assyrian army seized their personal and public wealth. Tiglath-pileser III recorded in his royal chronicle that Israel "with all its inhabitants and its goods, I led to Assyria."[6]

---

[5] Motyer, *Prophecy of Isaiah,* 90.
[6] Watts, *Isaiah 1–33,* 113–14.

## REJECTING JEHOVAH, THE WATERS OF SHILOAH (8:5–10)

Isaiah 7:1–9 recounts King Ahaz's refusal to accept the sign provided by Jehovah; this section deals with the refusal of the people of Israel and Judah to accept Jehovah himself.

Isaiah describes and then contrasts two forms of waters—the soft, rolling waters of Shiloah, located near the temple mount of Jerusalem, and the waters of the Euphrates, a great river that often floods out of control. The waters of Shiloah are controlled and inviting, whereas the Euphrates is dangerous and destructive. The waters of Shiloah bring life to those who drink them; the Euphrates brings death to those who are swept up in its flood. Isaiah's images of the two waters are symbolic: the former represents Jesus, the King of Heaven, who is likened to the waters of life; the latter is the king of Assyria, who leads his great, destructive armies and "cover the earth [like a flood . . . and] destroy the inhabitants thereof" (Jer. 46:8). Inasmuch as the inhabitants of Judah had rejected Jesus, or the waters of Shiloah, the Lord set upon them the king of Assyria, or the strong and mighty waters of the river that would overflow their banks and cover the entire land with its destruction.

*Isaiah 8:5–10*

> The Lord spake also unto me again, saying, (8:5) Forasmuch as this people refuseth the waters of Shiloah that go softly, and rejoice in Rezin and Remaliah's son; (8:6) Now therefore, behold, the Lord bringeth up upon them the waters of the river, strong and many, even the king of Assyria, and all his glory:
>
> and [it] shall *come up over* all [its] channels,
> and *go over* all [its] banks: (8:7)
>
> And *[it] shall pass* through Judah;
> *[it] shall overflow* and go over,
>
> [*it*] shall reach even to the neck;
> and the stretching out of *[its] wings* shall fill the breadth of thy land, O Immanuel. (8:8)
>
> *Associate yourselves,* O ye people, and ye shall be broken in pieces;
> and *give ear,* all ye of far countries:
>
> *gird yourselves,* and ye shall be broken in pieces;
> *gird yourselves,* and ye shall be broken in pieces. (8:9)
>
> *Take counsel together,* and it shall come to [naught];[7]
> *speak the word,* and it shall not stand: for God is with us. (8:10)

---

[7] 2 Ne. 18:10 replaces *nought* with *naught.*

NOTES AND COMMENTARY

**8:5** *Lord spake also unto me.* The Lord is the source of Isaiah's words.

**8:6** *this people.* The people of Israel (1:3; 3:12; 6:9), or any people who refuse the living waters of Christ.

*waters of Shiloah.* This refers to Jesus Christ, who is "the fountain of all righteousness" (Ether 12:28; 8:26; 1 Ne. 2:9) and "the fountain of living waters" (Jer. 2:13; 17:13; Ps. 36:8–9). The image of waters is symbolic of Jesus because he cleanses the righteous who enter the waters of baptism; he also invites us to drink from the waters of salvation, which forever quench the thirst of those who partake.

The waters of Shiloah are located in southeast Jerusalem, possibly belonging to the same body of water as the pool of Siloam of the New Testament. In 8:6, when the people reject the soft rolling waters of Shiloah, they reject Jehovah the King. This rejection results in God's sending against them a great destructive river, representative of the king of Assyria.

*Rezin and Remaliah's son.* Rezin was the king of Syria, and Pekah, the son of Remaliah, was the king of Israel (7:1–9).

**8:7** *waters of the river.* The river spoken of here is the great Euphrates that flowed through Assyria, but Isaiah uses the river as a metaphor for the "king of Assyria" (8:7) and his armies. Other prophets have similarly likened armies to great rivers and floods that "cover the earth" and "destroy the city and the inhabitants thereof" (Jer. 46:8; 47:2; Amos 8:8; Dan. 9:26), just as Noah warned his contemporaries of the worldwide flood that would destroy all creatures save those who found salvation on the ark (Gen. 6:5–17).

*channels/banks.* The waters of the river (the king of Assyria and his armies) will be very destructive when they flood Israel.

**8:8** *neck.* The *neck* is a metaphor for the upper reaches of the land; hence, Assyria's army will destroy the width and breadth of the land.

*stretching out of its wings.* This phrase "could refer to the outward spread of the floodwaters, but it is more vividly seen as a change of metaphor: the Assyrian, like a huge bird of prey, overshadows the whole land, ready to pounce."[8]

*thy land, O Immanuel.* The land is the promised, covenant land that belongs to the Lord (*thy land*). The name *Immanuel* (Hebrew, "God is with us") is mentioned twice in this section (8:8, 10)—once as the transliteration "Immanuel" and again as the translation "God is with us." *Immanuel* serves as a poetic refrain to help the

---

[8] Motyer, *Prophecy of Isaiah,* 92.

reader recall the sign provided to King Ahaz (7:14–16). Immanuel, or Maher-shalal-hash-baz, is a living sign (8:18) to Judah that God (who is "with us") will fulfill his promise to bring security and hope to them as nations come upon them. More importantly, *Immanuel* is the name of Jesus Christ, who brings spiritual salvation to Israel. In the end, the world's nations and alliances fail because the power of Immanuel exceeds theirs.

**8:9** *Associate yourselves.* Isaiah now addresses the invading armies and the "far countries" of the world. He warns them that if they form alliances, they eventually will be "broken in pieces."

*gird yourselves . . . broken in pieces.* Although the inhabitants of the world attempt to protect (*gird*) themselves with temporal weapons, they will be destroyed or *broken in pieces.* The twice-repeated phrase is probably the result of a scribal error. The repetition is not found in the Isaiah Scroll of the Dead Sea Scrolls.

**8:10** *Take counsel together.* Despite the attempt of the world's inhabitants to make war plans and prepare for temporal salvation, their plans will be worthless ("come to naught"); their carefully designed defense "shall not stand."

## JESUS IS LIKE A TEMPLE TO THE RIGHTEOUS (8:11–15)

These verses are an admonition from the Lord to Isaiah and others (second-person plural verbal forms are used here) that they should not follow those evil people who continually conspire and are obsessed with fear of war (8:11–12). Rather, Isaiah and his followers should let the Lord "be [their] fear," for he is as a temple, a cornerstone, and sure foundation for those righteous ones who have placed their trust in him.

*Isaiah 8:11–15*

> For the Lord spake thus to me with a strong hand, and instructed me that I should not walk in the way of this people, saying, (8:11)
>
> *Say* ye not, A [conspiracy],[9]
> to all[10] to whom this people shall *say,* A [conspiracy];
>
> *neither fear* ye their fear,
> *nor be afraid.* (8:12)
>
> *Sanctify the Lord of hosts* himself; and let him be your fear,
> and let him be your dread. (8:13) And *he shall be for a sanctuary;*

---

[9] From Hebrew *gesher.* Brown, Driver, and Briggs, *Hebrew and English Lexicon,* 905.
[10] 2 Ne. 18:12 omits the redundant pronoun *them.*

but for a *stone of stumbling and for a rock of offence* to both the <u>houses of Israel</u>,
for a *[trap]*[11] *and for a snare* to the <u>inhabitants of Jerusalem</u>. (8:14)

And many among them shall *stumble, and fall,*
and *be broken, and be snared, and be taken.* (8:15)

## NOTES AND COMMENTARY

**8:11** *with a strong hand.* This expression means "with power." This phrase is "a
code used to describe the basic experience of a prophet who was receiving a message;
apparently Isaiah is using a formula which had long since come into general use"[12]
(see 1 Kgs. 18:46; Ezek. 3:14; 8:1).

*walk in the way of this people.* To travel in the paths of the wicked.

**8:12** *conspiracy.* The conspiracy may refer to the enemies of Judah who had
hoped to install a puppet ruler (the son of Tabeal) on the throne of Ahaz (7:6).

*neither fear ye their fear.* This refers to the fear of the damned, who carry the
burden of their sins and who succumb to the world's unrighteous and unproductive
influence. The righteous reverence and fear the Lord and thus find peace.

**8:13** *Sanctify the Lord.* The literal translation from the Hebrew reads, "make him
a temple, the Lord of Hosts," meaning let the Lord be your temple, your place of holiness. The same idea is contained in the phrase *shall be for a sanctuary* (8:14). Peter
and Nephi used similar language: "But sanctify the Lord God in your hearts" (1 Pet.
3:15) and "they shall sanctify my name, and sanctify the Holy One of Jacob" (2 Ne.
27:34).

*let him be your fear/dread.* The Israelites should not fear the Assyrian empire's
temporal might and power; instead they should place their attention and fear on the
Lord, who possesses everlasting might. To fear the Lord is to honor, revere, trust, and
obey him.

**8:14** *sanctuary.* Other inspired writers have identified the Lord as a *sanctuary* or
*temple* (Ezek. 11:16; John 2:18–20; Rev. 21:22). In addition, Jesus Christ is both the
temple's "chief corner stone" (Ps. 118:22; Eph. 2:20) and its "sure foundation"
(Jacob 4:16; Hel. 5:12). The veil of the temple represents Christ's flesh (Heb. 9:3).

*stone/rock.* These are two synonymous symbols for the Lord. To the righteous,
Jesus Christ is the elect and precious chief cornerstone (Ps. 118:22; Eph. 2:20) of the
temple "upon which they might build and have safe foundation" (Jacob 4:15), but

---

[11] This word replaces the less familiar *gin.*
[12] Wildberger, *Isaiah 1–12,* 357.

unto "them which stumble at the word," Jesus is "a stone of stumbling, and a rock of offence" (1 Pet. 2:6–8; see also 1 Cor. 1:23).

*both the houses of Israel.* These are the Northern Kingdom of Israel and the Southern Kingdom of Judah.

*trap/snare.* Jehovah lays a snare for the wicked whose values are disordered. He catches them in their sins and eventually he will cast them, still entrapped, into hell.

**8:15** *stumble/fall/be snared.* Many individuals will stumble over the "rock of offence" (Jesus) and fall to the ground. Like an animal, they will be ensnared and taken captive by the devil.

## SEALING THE TESTIMONY AND THE LAW (8:16–9:2)

This section discusses the following:

Isaiah is first instructed to "bind the testimony" and "seal the law" (8:16).

Isaiah and his family are living symbols unto the house of Israel. Their names also are prophetic and serve to instruct the house of Israel according to God's plan (8:18).

Israel wanders lost and alone in the telestial world because of her sins, which have separated her from God (8:21). She does not follow the prophetic word; instead she seeks the word of God through wizards and familiar spirits (8:19).

The world will be walking in darkness, apostasy, and the "shadow of death" when a "great light," Jesus Christ, will make an appearance (8:22; 9:2).

*Isaiah 8:16–9:2*

> Bind up the testimony,
> *seal the law* among my disciples. (8:16)

> And *I will* <u>wait upon the Lord</u>, that hideth his face from the house of Jacob,
> and *I will* <u>look for him</u>. (8:17)

> Behold, *I and the children* whom the <u>Lord</u> hath given me
> are *for signs and for wonders* in Israel from the <u>Lord of hosts</u>, which dwelleth in mount Zion. (8:18)

> And when they shall say unto you:
> *Seek* unto them that have <u>familiar spirits</u>, and unto <u>wizards</u> that peep and[13]
> mutter—
> should not a people *seek* unto their <u>God</u> for the living to [hear from][14] the dead? (8:19)

---

[13] JST Isa. 8:19 and 2 Ne. 18:19 omit *that.*
[14] JST Isa. 8:19 and 2 Ne. 18:19 combine the two questions found in the KJV and add the words *hear from.*

To the law and to the testimony: [and][15] if they speak not according to this word,
it is because there is no light in them (8:20)

And *they* shall [roam through the land],[16] [hard pressed][17] and <u>hungry</u>:
and it shall come to pass, that when *they* shall be <u>hungry</u>,

they shall [*make themselves angry*],[18]
and *curse their king and their God,*

and *look* <u>upward</u>. (8:21)
And they shall *look* <u>unto the earth</u>;

and *behold* <u>trouble and darkness</u>, dimness of anguish;
and they shall be *driven* to <u>darkness</u>. (8:22)

Nevertheless the dimness shall not be such as was in her vexation,

when at the first he *lightly afflicted* the <u>land of Zebulun and the land of Naphtali</u>,
and afterward[s][19] did more *grievously afflict*[20] by the <u>way of the [Red][21] Sea</u>,
<u>beyond Jordan in Galilee of the nations</u>. (9:1)

The *people* that <u>walked in darkness</u> have seen a great light:
*they* that <u>dwell in the land of the shadow of death</u>, upon them hath the light shined.
(9:2)

## NOTES AND COMMENTARY

**8:16** *Bind up the testimony/seal the law.* These actions fit into a divine sequence: the Saints must first receive their endowments, then warn the world's inhabitants of God's coming judgments, which will be followed by the binding up of the testimony and the sealing of the law; finally the judgments of God will come (see D&C 88:84; 109:38, 46; 133:72).[22] After the Lord's people have testified to and warned the nations, they will figuratively "bind," "tie up," or "shut up"[23] their testimonies and "affix [a] seal"[24] to the law of God (the prophetic word).

**8:17** *wait upon the Lord.* To *wait upon the Lord* is to patiently and faithfully await the fulfillment of his promises. Those who wait upon the Lord will receive salvation (Prov. 20:22), physical and spiritual strength (40:31), and eventually the earth for their inheritance (Ps. 37:9, 34).

---

[15] JST Isa. 8:20 and 2 Ne. 18:20 add the conjunction *and.*
[16] The translation is from NIV Isa. and is supported by the Hebrew Bible.
[17] Hebrew *niqisheh,* from the root *qashah.* Brown, Driver, and Briggs, *Hebrew and English Lexicon,* 904.
[18] Brown, Driver, and Briggs, *Hebrew and English Lexicon,* 893.
[19] JST Isa. 9:1 and 2 Ne. 19:1 add the letter *s* to the word *afterward.*
[20] JST Isa. 9:1 and 2 Ne. 19:1 omit the pronoun *her.*
[21] JST Isa. 9:1 and 2 Ne. 19:1 add the word *Red* before *sea.*
[22] *Teachings of the Prophet Joseph Smith,* 92.
[23] Hebrew *tsor.* Brown, Driver, and Briggs, *Hebrew and English Lexicon,* 864.
[24] Hebrew *chatim.* Brown, Driver, and Briggs, *Hebrew and English Lexicon,* 367.

*hideth his face.* This idiom indicates that the Spirit of the Lord has been withdrawn (8:20–22; see also Ezek. 39:29 ) and God's blessings have been removed from the house of Jacob. On the one hand, God hides his face from those who demonstrate a lack of faith and practice evil (Deut. 32:20; Micah 3:4; Deut. 31:17–18); on the other hand, God shows his face to those who are pure in heart (Matt. 5:8; D&C 93:1).

*I will look for him.* The literal translation reads, "I will hope for him." With regard to our hope in Christ, Jacob wrote: "For this intent have we written these things, that they may know that we knew of Christ, and we had a hope of his glory many hundred years before his coming; and not only we ourselves had a hope of his glory, but also all the holy prophets which were before us" (Jacob 4:4).

**8:18** *I and the children . . . are for signs and for wonders.* Isaiah and his two sons were living symbols to the house of Israel (7:3; 8:2–4). Their names are prophetic; *Maher-shalal-hash-baz* speaks of the disaster which would come upon the Israelite people when the Assyrians would "speedily" conquer them and then "plunder" their possessions. *Shear-jashub,* "a remnant shall return," refers to the restoration when "a remnant of Israel will return" to the lands of promise. The name *Isaiah,* "Jehovah is Salvation," prophesies of Jesus Christ and of the salvation that comes through his atonement.

*Lord . . . dwelleth in mount Zion.* In Jerusalem the temple stood on Mount Moriah or Mount Zion. God dwells in his earthly temples that are dedicated and set apart for sacred ordinances.

**8:19** *familiar spirits/wizards.* These two expressions, often used together (Lev. 19:31; Deut. 18:11; 2 Kgs. 21:6), refer to those who seek truth through false means or wish to learn about the future by communicating with spirits. Such will be cut off (Lev. 20:6).

*peep and mutter.* Peeping (or whispering) and muttering are methods the familiar spirits and wizards use to communicate with spirits.

*should not a people seek unto their God for the living to hear from the dead?* Isaiah instructs us that we should seek the truth from God and not from wizards or familiar spirits.

**8:20** *To the law and to the testimony.* Isaiah appears to be swearing a sacred oath by the testimony of God's law and the prophets (8:16, 20).

*no light in them.* The Spirit of the Lord was withdrawn from Israel because her people sought revelation from familiar spirits and wizards (8:19) and rejected the testimonies of the prophets (8:20).

**8:21** *roam through the land.* Here Israel is in her scattered and forsaken condition, lost and without a home.

*hard pressed and hungry.* This may be a literal reference to those who need food and sustenance. It may also symbolize those in exile who suffer because the word of God has been removed (Amos 8:11–12).

**8:21–22** *look upward/look unto the earth.* Those who are driven from their homeland and are hungry for the Lord's word will look upward and earthward for revelation and for the prophetic word, but they will not find it.

*trouble/darkness/dimness of anguish.* Those who lack the prophetic word and the Holy Ghost are in a state of darkness, confusion, and anguish. *Dimness* suggests a darkened mind or gloominess.

*driven to darkness. Darkness* may refer to an actual place on the earth where the gospel is not found, or, more likely, it may refer to people who have chosen darkness (evil) rather than light.

**8:23** *dimness . . . such as in her vexation.* Other versions seem to clarify this phrase: Though in earlier times Israel suffered *vexation,* or trouble, in the end the dimness and anguish will give way to the light that will shine from Christ. As the New International Version says, "There will be no more gloom for those who were in distress."

**9:1** *the land of Zebulun/Naphtali.* These two lands are significant because Jesus dwelt in Capernaum, a city that was located "in the borders of Zabulon and Nephthalim" (Matt. 4:13). Jesus was the "great light" seen by the inhabitants of this area (9:2).

*afflict by the way of the Red Sea.* This expression refers to events surrounding Moses and the Israelites as they fled across the Red Sea from Egyptian bondage.

**9:2** *walked in darkness/dwell in the land of the shadow of death.* The land of the shadow of death is a land peopled by those who do not know Jesus Christ (the "great light") and his gospel; therefore, they walk in darkness.

*great light/light shined.* Jesus was the *great light* that shined upon the inhabitants of Zebulun and Naphtali during his mortal mission. Matthew 4:13–16 contains the fulfillment of the prophecy found in Isaiah 9:1–2.

# ISAIAH 9

### LIKENING ISAIAH 9 UNTO OURSELVES

*Many of us (or perhaps our children or grandchildren) may live to witness the second coming of Jesus Christ, who will destroy the world's kingdoms, become the new king, and reign over the earth during the Millennium. Our joy at that time will be immense (9:3–7).*

*The destruction of the Northern Kingdom of Israel during Isaiah's time, on account of the pride, lack of love, social injustices, and general wickedness of its people (9:9–21), anticipated the devastation that awaits the wicked of our own day; as the Northern Kingdom's inhabitants were destroyed by wars, fire, and burning, so will be the devastation of those who work evil in the last days.*

## THE MESSIAH—THE SON BECOMES THE NEW KING (9:3–7)

Isaiah 9 presents a messianic prophecy that is directly connected to the coronation and enthronement of Jesus (when Jesus is made King of kings). Kingship themes in this section include the victory of Jesus as the new king over oppressive kingdoms (9:4–5); the divine sonship of the new king (see commentary on 9:6; 2 Sam. 7:11–16; Ps. 2); the new king receives the government (9:6); the king receives names fitting for his kingship in a naming ceremony (9:6); the king becomes Father, God, and a member of the royal family, "Prince of Peace" (9:6); the king is given the throne and the kingdom (9:7); and the king rules forever with judgment, peace, and justice (9:7).

Other themes presented in this section are called "Davidic king motifs"; they recall King David and his golden reign over Israel. This prophecy speaks of Jesus Christ, who is the last and greatest king from the house of David. The Davidic king motifs are the dawn of a great light (9:1–2; 2 Sam. 23:4; Ps. 110:3; 118:24, 27), rejoicing (9:3; Ps. 118:15, 24; 132:9, 16), the overthrow of enemies (9:4; Ps. 2:8–9;

72:4; 89:23; 110:1, 5–6; 132:18), burning with fire (9:5; 2 Sam. 23:7; Ps. 21:9; 118:12), and an eternal reign of the Lord (9:7; Ps. 21:4; 61:6–7; 89:3–4, 28–29, 36–37; 132:11–12).[1]

The prophetic setting and context of 9:3–7 primarily point to the millennial reign of Jesus Christ, although subthemes have appropriate applications in other settings. For instance, 9:6 refers to both Jesus' mortal birth and his millennial reign.

Because Jesus Christ has become king, the nation's joy has increased (9:3), the people's yoke and burdens have been lifted and their oppressors removed (9:4), and there is no need for soldiers and other associations with war (9:5); the Prince of Peace (9:6) now reigns.

The four royal names or titles given to Christ at the time of his investiture of authority and kingship—wonderful Counsellor, mighty God, everlasting Father, and Prince of Peace (9:6)—emphasize Jesus' ability to judge in righteousness, his god-hood, his fatherhood, and his royal nature. The four names also recall the four parts inherent in the name of Isaiah's son Maher-shalal-hash-baz. The name *Maher-shalal-hash-baz* speaks of the judgments of God on Israel (8:1–4); the four names of Christ in 9:6 refer to the ultimate victory of the house of Israel because Jesus the Messiah has become King and God.

It is valuable to observe the connections between the Immanuel prophecy (7:14–17), its local fulfillment (8:3–7), and the fulfillment described in this section of Isaiah. All three sections pertain to similar events, including the birth of a son, his naming, oppression and its eventual removal, kings of the world as opposed to the new king, the destruction of the land so that peace may eventually prevail, God's role in mankind's history, and God's presence among the people (Immanuel = "God is with us"). Table 3 demonstrates the connections among the three sections (see the commentary on 7:10–16; see Tables 1 and 2, pages 73 and 74).

---

[1] Motyer, *Prophecy of Isaiah,* 99–100.

## Table 3

| | Immanuel prophecy (7:14–17) | First fulfillment (8:3–7) | Later fulfillment (9:4–6) |
|---|---|---|---|
| Birth of a son | Bear a son (14) | Bare a son (3) | A child is born (6) |
| Ritual of naming | Call his name Immanuel (14) | Call his name Maher-shalal-hash-baz | His name shall be called Wonderful Counsellor, mighty God, everlasting Father, Prince of Peace (6) |
| Oppression/ oppression removed | Assyrians destroy people (17–20) | Assyrians destroy people (7–9) | Broken yoke of their burden, staff of their shoulder, rod of their oppressor/peace there is no end (4, 7) |
| Old kings/new King | King of Assyria (16) | King of Assyria (4) | Prince of Peace, throne of David (6–7) |
| Destruction of land/ peace upon the land | Land shall be for-saken (16) | Damascus and Samaria shall be taken away (4) | Increase of govern-ment, peace upon his kingdom (7) |
| God's control of history | Lord shall bring upon thee, Lord shall hiss (17–18) | Lord bringeth up upon them the king of Assyria (7) | Zeal of the Lord will perform this (7) |
| God is with us | Immanuel (Hebrew "God is with us") (14) | Immanuel twice repeated (8, 10) | Jesus' millennial reign (6–7) |

*Isaiah 9:3–7*

Thou hast *multiplied* the nation,
and[2] *increased* the joy:

[and][3] *they joy* before thee according to the joy in harvest,

---

[2] JST Isa. 19:3 and 2 Ne. 19:3 omit the term *not*.
[3] JST Isa. 19:3 adds the conjunction *and*.

and as *men rejoice* when they <u>divide the spoil</u>. (9:3)

For thou hast broken the *yoke* of <u>[their] burden</u>,
and the *staff* of <u>[their] shoulder</u>,
the *rod* of <u>[their]⁴ oppressor</u>.⁵ (9:4)

For every [*boot* of a soldier that *tramps with a quake*],⁶
and [every *garment*]⁷ *rolled in blood;*

[shall be for *burning*]⁸
and *fuel of fire.* (9:5)

For unto us a *child* <u>is born</u>,
unto us a *son* <u>is given</u>:

and the government shall be upon his shoulder:
and his *name* shall be called
*Wonderful Counsellor,*⁹
The *mighty God,*
The *everlasting Father,*
The *Prince of Peace.* (9:6)

Of the increase of his government and peace there [is]¹⁰ no end,

*upon the throne* of David,
and *upon his kingdom*

to *order* <u>it</u>,
and to *establish* <u>it</u>

with judgment
and *with justice*

from henceforth,
even *for ever.*

The zeal of the Lord of hosts will perform this. (9:7)

## NOTES AND COMMENTARY

**9:3** *multiplied the nation.* This is connected to the Abrahamic covenant, wherein Abraham was promised a great multiplication of his posterity (26:15; Abr. 3:14; Neh. 9:23).

---

⁴The third-person masculine singular pronoun suffix in the Hebrew *his* or *its* probably refers to *nation* in the previous verse. We have used the pronoun *their* (after NIV Isa.) to clarify this concept.

⁵2 Ne. 19:4 omits the phrase *as in the day of Midian.*

⁶From Hebrew *s⁻'on* and *ra'ash.* Brown, Driver, and Briggs, *Hebrew and English Lexicon,* 684, 950. See also JB and NIV Isa.

⁷BHS critical apparatus suggests the phrase *kal simᶜlah,* "every garment."

⁸We have replaced the KJV *this shall be with burning* with the more accurate *shall be for burning.*

⁹Most translations, other than the KJV, do not place a comma between *wonderful* and *counsellor,* thus making the two terms read as one. This practice accords with the Hebrew reading of these terms.

¹⁰JST Isa. 9:7 and 2 Ne. 19:7 replace *shall be* with *is.*

*joy.* How has the joy increased? The answer is found in the threefold repetition of *for* in 9:4–6: there is an increase of joy because the Messiah has broken the rod of the oppressor (9:4); because the soldiers' boots, garments, and other items of war will be burned with fire (9:5); and because a child is born who will establish his righteous government and establish peace among the nations (9:6–7; Luke 2:10–11).

*harvest/divide the spoil.* God's victory over Israel's enemies will bring Israel a joy similar to that experienced by the farmer at the time of harvest when he has an abundant yield, or to victors of war who receive spoils and booty.

**9:4** *yoke/staff/rod.* In biblical times the staff and rod were instruments used by taskmasters on the slaves; a yoke was a wooden frame designed to harness together beasts of burden. These three items—the *yoke, staff,* and *rod*—signify forms of oppression, or the manner in which Israel had been burdened by her neighbors (10:5, 24–27). In particular, the language of this verse recalls the manner in which Egypt oppressed the Israelites before Moses led them out of captivity (for example, see *yoke* in Lev. 26:13; *burden* in Ex. 1:11; 2:11; 5:4–5; 6:6–7; and *taskmasters* in Ex. 3:7; 5:6, 10–14). Just as Moses delivered ancient Israel from the Egyptian yoke of physical bondage, Jesus Christ delivers us from the yoke of spiritual bondage.

**9:5** *boot of a soldier . . . shall be for burning.* Boots, garments, weapons, chariots, and other items used during a holy war were not to become part of the booty or spoil of the victors. Such property was under a ban and had to be burned with fire. (Josh. 7:23–26; 11:6, 9; Ps. 46:9; Ezek. 39:9–10).

*rolled in blood.* This could also mean "stained in blood."

*burning/fire.* Symbolically and prophetically, the boot and garments identified in 9:5 refer to all unclean and corruptible things that will be burned with fire at Jesus Christ's glorious second coming (3 Ne. 25:1; D&C 64:23–24). Specifically, the weapons and chariots of the nations' armies (boot of the soldier) will burn when the Messiah comes to rule. (See also 2:4, which describes weapons being made into agricultural instruments for mankind's benefit.)

**9:6** *For.* This is a transitional word that is connected to the preceding verses (3–5). The joy of the nation has increased, the yoke of the people has been lifted, and oppression and warfare have been removed *for* (or *because*) Jesus has become King and now reigns.

*unto us.* This includes Isaiah and all those who are redeemed through the atonement of Jesus Christ.

*child/son.* Jesus Christ is the *son* and the Holy Child (Moro. 8:3). *Child* refers to Christ's divine ancestry and recalls his divine parentage. *Son* may be an abbreviated form of Son of God (2 Ne. 25:19), Son of Man of Holiness, or Son of the Highest (Luke 1:32).

*Son* may also refer to the concept of divine sonship for all of us through Christ, whereby righteous individuals may become His sons and daughters (Mosiah 5:7; 27:25; Ether 3:14; D&C 25:1). "I will declare the decree: the Lord hath said unto me, Thou art my Son; this day have I begotten thee" (Ps. 2:7; D&C 11:30; 35:2).

*government . . . upon his shoulder.* This phrase points to the vesting rite of a king who, as part of a coronation and enthronement ceremony, places or has placed upon his shoulders the robe of regal authority. In this passage the robe represents both kingly and priestly power (see Rev. 1:13 in which the sacred vestments belong to both the king and the high priest). *Government,* which derives from the same Hebrew root as *prince* (see *Prince of Peace* below), may be read as dominion or rule.[11] The phrase anticipates 22:22: "And the key of the house of David will I lay upon his shoulder." Because Jesus Christ will bear the government on his shoulders, neither that oppressive yoke nor the staff (9:4) will be placed on the shoulders of the faithful after the judgment.

*Wonderful Counsellor.* The Hebrew reading requires these two names to be read together as *Wonderful Counsellor.* The Messiah will be an advisor (counselor) or perhaps one who argues cases in court; "the Lord standeth up to plead, and standeth to judge the people" (3:13). Through his intercessory prayer Jesus serves as our mediator and advocate with the Father (John 17; 3 Ne. 19:19–29).

*mighty God. Mighty* refers to a warrior, and thus the phrase may read "Warrior God," recalling 9:3–5, in which we learn that Jehovah overcomes the nations and all forms of oppression. The title is used again in 10:21.

*everlasting Father.* Jesus Christ is an eternal being who is the Father in a number of senses, as explained in "The Father and the Son: A Doctrinal Exposition by the First Presidency and the Twelve," dated 30 June 1916.[12]

*Prince of Peace.* Christ is part of God's royal family. He is a prince who shares the throne with the Father (Rev. 3:21) and who serves as "King of kings" (Rev. 19:16) over a kingdom of kings and priests, or righteous saints. He is the Prince of Peace and "God of love and peace" (2 Cor. 13:11) who eliminates war and contention and reigns over a peaceful kingdom.

**9:7** *Of the increase.* Christ's kingdoms and peace will increase throughout the eternities (Luke 1:30–33).

---

[11] Brown, Driver, and Briggs, *Hebrew and English Lexicon,* 976, 978.
[12] In Talmage, *Articles of Faith,* 465–73.

*throne of David.* The throne is a metaphor for kingship, dominion, and sovereignty (Gen. 41:40; 2 Sam. 7:16; 1 Kgs. 1:47). Jehovah is crowned, seated on the throne of David, and rules with great glory and justice for eternity.

*to order it.* Christ's society replaces the confusion of the telestial world.

*judgment/justice.* The Messiah will rule his kingdom with perfect justice.

*zeal of the Lord of hosts will perform this.* This expression is also found in 2 Kings 19:31; it "is an assurance that the promise will in fact be fulfilled because [the Lord] will support it with his 'zeal', . . . with all his strength."[13]

## JUDGMENT AGAINST THE NORTHERN KINGDOM OF ISRAEL (9:8–10:4)

The Lord's word, which has application to both ancient and modern Israel, has been given to the house of Israel (9:8) through his prophets, and the Northern Kingdom of Israel will soon suffer destruction (9:9–12). Because the people do not seek the Lord (9:13), are hypocrites, speak follies, and work evil (9:17), he will destroy all levels of society, including its leaders, followers, false prophets, young men, and even those who are usually oppressed, such as the fatherless and widows (9:14–17).

The destruction by fire is described with such terms as *burneth, fire, devour, kindle, roll up high in smoke, land darkened* (perhaps because of the smoke), and *fuel of the fire* (9:18–19). In addition, social chaos will rule and brotherly love will not be found (9:19–20), for family will fight against family and tribe will war against tribe (9:21). Those who make unrighteous and oppressive laws (lawmakers and judges) and who forget the poor, the widows, and the fatherless (10:1–2) will also suffer at the day of judgment and will be among the captives or slain (10:4); they will not be able to flee for help to other sources such as idols or other nations (10:3).

Isaiah 9:8–10:4 is divided into four subsections. The first subsection deals with pride (9:8–12), the second concerns evil leaders (9:13–17), the third decries the lack of love and kindness for others (9:18–21), and the fourth refers to social injustice (10:1–4). The four subsections are part of a single prophecy but are divided structurally with an identical poetic refrain at the end of each section: "For all this his anger is not turned away, but his hand is stretched out still" (9:12, 17, 21; 10:4; see also 5:25).

This prophecy has a dual fulfillment: first, when the ancient kingdom of Israel was destroyed, and second, when the world will be destroyed at the time of the second coming of Christ.

---

[13] Kaiser, *Isaiah 1–12,* 215.

## Isaiah 9:8–10:4

The Lord sent [his][14] *word* [unto][15] Jacob,
and *it* hath [fallen][16] upon Israel. (9:8)

And *all the people* shall know,
even *Ephraim and the inhabitant[s]*[17] *of Samaria,*

that say in the *pride*
and *[haughtiness]*[18] *of heart,* (9:9)

The *bricks are fallen down,* but we will build with hewn stones:
the *sycamores are cut down,* but we will change them into cedars. (9:10)

Therefore the Lord *shall set up* the adversaries of Rezin against him,
and *join* his enemies together; (9:11)

The *Syrians* before,
and the *Philistines* behind; (9:12)

and they shall devour Israel with open mouth.

For all this *his anger* is not turned away,
but *his hand* is stretched out still.

For the *people* turneth not unto him that smiteth them,
neither do *they* seek the Lord of hosts (9:13)

Therefore [will][19] the Lord cut off from Israel *head and tail,*
*branch and [bulrush stem]*[20] in one day. (9:14)

The *[elder],*[21] he is the head;
and the *prophet* that teacheth lies, he is the tail. (9:15)

For the *leaders* of this people cause them to err;
and they that are led of *them* are destroyed. (9:16)

Therefore the Lord shall have *no joy* in their young men,
*neither shall have mercy* on their fatherless and widows:

for *every one* [of them][22] is an hypocrite and an evildoer,
and *every mouth* speaketh folly.

For all this *his anger* is not turned away,
but *his hand* is stretched out still. (9:17)

For wickedness *burneth* as the fire:
*it shall devour* the briers and thorns,

---

[14] JST Isa. 9:8 and 2 Ne. 19:8 replace the indefinite article *a* with the pronoun *his.*

[15] JST Isa. 9:8 and 2 Ne. 19:8 replace *into* with *unto.*

[16] From Hebrew *napalu.* Brown, Driver, and Briggs, *Hebrew and English Lexicon,* 656.

[17] 2 Ne. 19:9 makes the noun *inhabitant* plural.

[18] From the Hebrew term *godel.* Brown, Driver, and Briggs, *Hebrew and English Lexicon,* 152.

[19] 2 Ne. 19:14 places the term *will* before the phrase *the Lord* rather than after it.

[20] Wildberger, *Isaiah 1–12,* 219.

[21] 2 Ne. 19:15 omits the phrase *and honourable.* The term *elder* replaces the KJV *ancient.*

[22] JST Isa. 9:17 and 2 Ne. 19:17 add the expression *of them* to the sentence, showing that the young men, the fatherless, and the widows are the hypocrites and evildoers.

and *shall kindle* in the thickets of the forest[s],[23] [so that it rolled up high in][24] smoke. (9:18)

Through the wrath of the Lord of hosts is the land darkened, and the people shall be as the fuel of the fire: no man shall spare his brother. (9:19)

And he shall *snatch on the right hand,* and be hungry; and he shall *eat on the left hand,* and they shall not be satisfied:

they shall eat every man the flesh of his own arm: (9:20)

Manasseh, Ephraim; and Ephraim, Manasseh:[25] *they together* shall be against Judah.

For all this *his anger* is not turned away, but *his hand* is stretched out still. (9:21)

Woe unto them that *decree* unrighteous decrees, and that *write* grievousness which they have prescribed; (10:1)

*To turn [away]*[26] the needy from judgment, and *to take away* the right from the poor of my people,

that *widows* may be their prey, and that they may rob the *fatherless!* (10:2)

And what will ye do in the *day of visitation,* and in the *desolation* which shall come from far?

*to whom* will ye flee for help? and *where* will ye leave your glory? (10:3)

Without me they shall *bow down* under the prisoners, and they shall *fall* under the slain.

For all this *his anger* is not turned away, but *his hand* is stretched out still. (10:4)

## NOTES AND COMMENTARY

**9:8** *Jacob/Israel.* In this section, God's word is directed to Ephraim or the Northern Kingdom of Israel. It also has application to the covenant people of our day.

**9:9** *all the people shall know.* All will know that the word of the Lord has been delivered to Ephraim.

*Ephraim/Samaria.* Isaiah uses the term *Ephraim* here to refer to Israel's Northern Kingdom (7:2, 5, 8–9; Hosea 5:3; 11:8). Samaria was the capital city of that kingdom.

*haughtiness of heart.* A symbol of pride. In contrast to those with haughty hearts are those who possess "a broken heart and a contrite spirit" (3 Ne. 9:20).

---

[23] 2 Ne. 19:18 makes the noun *forest* into a plural.

[24] Kaiser, *Isaiah 1–12,* 220, supported by Brown, Driver, and Briggs, *Hebrew and English Lexicon,* 5.

[25] 2 Ne. 19:21 omits the conjunction *and.*

[26] 2 Ne. 20:2 replaces *aside* with *away.*

**9:11** *adversaries . . . against him/join his enemies together.* Israel's fiercest enemies during this time period were the Syrians and the Philistines (9:12).

*Rezin.* The king of Damascus.

**9:12** *Syrians/Philistines.* "As history took its course, Israel had to suffer immensely at the hands of both the [Syrians] in the east and the Philistines in the west"[27] (1 Kgs. 20; 22; 2 Kgs. 6:8–7:20; 8:7–12).

**9:13** *devour Israel with open mouth. Devour* and *open mouth* are symbolic of the attack of a lion. The prophets often compare warring nations to lions that mangle and destroy (Num. 23:24; 1 Chr. 12:8; Micah 5:8; 3 Ne. 20:16).

*his hand is stretched out still.* This phrase is repeated three times for emphasis (9:17, 21; 10:4). See commentary on 5:25.

*people turneth not unto him that smiteth them.* To *turn* is to repent. Even though God's judgments come upon Israel, her people still refuse to turn to the Lord who chastises them.

*neither do they seek the Lord.* In the words of a modern revelation, "They *seek not the Lord* to establish his righteousness, but every man walketh in his own way, and after the image of his own god, whose image is in the likeness of the world" (D&C 1:16; emphasis added).

*Lord of hosts.* See commentary on 1:9.

**9:14** *Therefore will the Lord.* The Lord indicates, once again, that God is in charge of the world's affairs, including those of his elect people.

*head/tail.* We learn in 9:15 that *head* represents the elders and old men of the community, and *tail* symbolizes false prophets (Deut. 28:13, 43–44).

*branch and bulrush stem.* The branch is a palm branch, located high up on the tree, representing society's leaders; the bulrush stem, located near the ground, represents the common people.

*in one day.* This phrase means "quickly."

**9:15** *elder.* These are the "head[s]" or leaders of the community.

*prophet that teacheth lies.* The tails are the false prophets who pretend to speak in the Lord's name and utter flattering statements that the people desire to hear. Such prophets, along with the elder and the honorable, lead the people of Israel astray and "cause them to err" (9:16).

**9:16** *leaders . . . cause them to err.* Since the leaders cause the people to stray from truth and justice, and since the people choose to follow, both will be destroyed (9:14).

---

[27] Wildberger, *Isaiah 1–12,* 228.

**9:17** *young men/fatherless/widows*. In the book of Isaiah it is clear that the Lord champions the cause of the widow and the fatherless (1:17, 23; 10:2). In this particular judgment against the Northern Kingdom (9:8–10:4), however, the widows and fatherless are as guilty as their leaders and false prophets, for the Lord does not have joy or mercy even for those who are socially rejected or have temporal needs; "every one [of them] is an hypocrite and an evildoer, and every mouth speaketh folly" (9:17). Certainly the entire nation has been rejected.

*mouth speaketh folly*. The New International Version puts this as "every mouth speaks vileness."

**9:18–19** *wickedness burneth as the fire/devour the briers and thorns . . . thickets/ land darkened/people shall be as the fuel*. Isaiah describes the wicked as undesirable plants, such as briers, thorns, and thickets (10:17, 34). He also says that the judgments for wickedness are like a fire that devours the briers, thorns, and thickets. In other words, the wicked will be like the "fuel of the fire," and the smoke will be so thick that the skies will be darkened. The burning of the wicked here is a type and shadow of the burning that will occur at the Second Coming.

**9:19–20** *no man shall spare his brother, . . . flesh of his own arm*. On many occasions the wicked destroy themselves by warring against their own flesh (Jer. 19:9; Mosiah 9:2).

**9:20** *he shall snatch on the right hand, and be hungry*. During these times of trouble and destruction there will be a great shortage of food so that people will scavenge here and there but will not find enough to satisfy their hunger.

**9:21** *Manasseh/Ephraim*. The Jerusalem Bible reads "Manasseh devours Ephraim, Ephraim [devours] Manasseh," meaning that tribes, families, and even brothers will contend against one another during these times of trouble. Earlier, Isaiah says that "no man shall spare his brother" (9:19) and "they shall eat every man the flesh of his own arm" (9:20).

*they together shall be against Judah*. Manasseh and Ephraim will strive against one another as well as against Judah.

**10:1** *Woe*. In this context, *woe* is severe anguish and distress resulting from God's judgments.

*decree unrighteous decrees*. Unjust laws are made that serve the rich and powerful while preying upon the weak, such as the fatherless and the widows (10:2–3).

*write grievousness which they have prescribed*. A better translation is "those who issue oppressive decrees."[28]

---

[28] Motyer, *Prophecy of Isaiah*, 110.

**10:2** *needy/poor/widows/fatherless.* This refers to all groups or individuals who have special temporal and spiritual needs (1:17), meaning all the inhabitants of the earth. "Are we not all beggars?" asked King Benjamin (Mosiah 4:19). Evil leaders were taking advantage of those who were weak.

**10:3** *ye.* The Lord changes the pronoun from *they* (10:1–2) to *ye* (10:3) for rhetorical purposes. Both pronouns refer to the wicked. *They,* a third-person pronoun, is used impersonally. *Ye,* a second-person pronoun set in two rhetorical questions, is personalized—the Lord is speaking directly to the wicked.

*day of visitation.* A time of the Lord's judgment and indignation (Hosea 9:7; Micah 7:4; D&C 56:1, 16). It is also the time of the Second Coming, when Christ will visit the earth with power and glory (D&C 124:8, 10). The Hebrew term for *visitation* (*pᶜqudah*) also refers to keeping one's promise; hence the *day of visitation* is the day when the Lord will keep his promise to visit the earth with judgment.

*come from far.* This refers both to the Assyrian army that will come from a far country to conquer Israel and to Jehovah, who resides far off and will come to judge the world.

*to whom will ye flee for help?* This is a rhetorical question, showing that during the day of visitation the wicked will have no one to turn to for help. The only one who could assist them is God, and they have turned away from him.

*where will ye leave your glory?* Many translations read, "Where will ye leave your riches?" On the day of judgment, personal wealth will be meaningless and will have no power to save.

**10:4** *bow down under the prisoners/fall under the slain.* During the day of visitation the wicked will fall in the destruction or be taken prisoners.

---❦---

# ISAIAH 10

### LIKENING ISAIAH 10 UNTO OURSELVES

*The ancient nation of Assyria, with its cruel and bloody leaders and well-disciplined, fierce armies, destroyed other equally evil nations. This scenario of Assyria and war anticipates the warring nations of our own day and of the future, contending for land, power, and riches. Those same evils will be present in our own day, and the thirst for blood will also exist. But as Assyria, her leaders, and her armies were soon destroyed according to God's plan, so also will the warring nations of the last days be annihilated at the Second Coming. Isaiah's language—burning of a fire, flame, devour, and consume—applies to both ancient Assyria and the future nations at Christ's coming. Meanwhile, a righteous remnant of Israel will be saved at the last day as they worship in their temples.*

---

## ASSYRIA: INSTRUMENT IN GOD'S HAND (10:5–11)

To fulfill his divine purposes, the Lord sends Assyria's wicked king and his armies to war against Israel. The Lord is actively engaged in this process: "I will send him," he says. The Lord controls all nations and their armies. "Do I not hold the destinies of all the armies of the nations of the earth?" he asks (D&C 117:6.)

Assyria thus represents the Lord's rod of anger, which is used to beat and punish the apostate Israelites. The Lord uses agents to destroy a people who have forsaken the covenant and committed spiritual adultery by worshiping foreign deities. Note that the Lord is speaking in 10:5–7, and the king of Assyria is speaking in 10:8–11 (see also 10:13–14, in which the king of Assyria is quoted).

*Isaiah 10:5–11*

O Assyrian, the *rod* of mine <u>anger</u>,
and the *staff* in their hand is [their][1] <u>indignation</u>. (10:5)

*I will send him* against an [apostate][2] <u>nation</u>,
and against the <u>people of my wrath</u> will *I give him a charge*,

to *take* the <u>spoil</u>,
and to *take* the <u>prey</u>,
and to tread them down like the mire of the streets. (10:6)

[But this is <u>not</u> what *he* <u>intends</u>][3]
<u>neither</u> doth *his heart* <u>think so</u>;

but in his heart [it is][4] to *destroy*
and *cut off* nations not a few. (10:7)

For he saith, Are not my princes altogether kings? (10:8)
*Is not Calno* as *Carchemish*?
*is not Hamath* as *Arpad*?
*is not Samaria* as *Damascus*? (10:9)

As my hand hath found[ed][5] the <u>kingdoms</u> of the *idols*,
and whose *graven images* did excel them of <u>Jerusalem and of Samaria</u>; (10:10)

Shall I not, as I have done unto *Samaria* and <u>her idols</u>,
so do to *Jerusalem* and <u>her idols</u>? (10:11)

## NOTES AND COMMENTARY

**10:5** *Assyrian.* Refers to the king of Assyria as well as his nation. Assyria represents the wicked nations of the last days that will worship idols and false gods and goddesses, war against Israel, and eventually be consumed by the Lord's glory and majesty during the Second Coming.

*rod/staff.* Assyria is the rod and staff that will smite and chasten the people of Israel because they are an "apostate nation" (10:6). Assyria will smite Israel with the staff as a taskmaster smites a slave, and then Assyria will rule over Israel with the rod or scepter.

**10:6** *apostate nation/people of my wrath.* Israel's inhabitants have become like their neighbors, Assyria and Egypt; they are profane, ritually unclean, impure, and

---

[1] 2 Ne. 20:5 changes the pronoun *mine* to *their.*

[2] The Hebrew term *chanep* means "profane, irreligious, [or] apostate." Brown, Driver, and Briggs, *Hebrew and English Lexicon,* 338.

[3] NIV Isa. accurately translates the meaning of the Hebrew.

[4] 2 Ne. 20:7 and JST Isa. 10:7 move the verb *is* from before the phrase *in his heart* and add *it is* after the term *heart.*

[5] 2 Ne. 20:10 and JST Isa. 10:10 write *founded* in place of *found.*

unworthy to worship in God's dwelling place, the temple. They have apostatized from the truth and are the *people of [God's] wrath.*

*to take the spoil/to take the prey.* Spoil and *prey* refer to the prophetic name Maher-shalal-hash-baz, suggesting that Isaiah's earlier prophecy regarding his son (8:1–4) finds at least partial fulfillment in Assyria's capturing and plundering of Israel.

*mire.* Israel's wicked are compared to the deep mud (or mire) in streets trampled under the foot of man and beast.

**10:7** *this is not what he intends.* Assyria's king does not know that he is being used as the Lord's instrument to punish Israel. His intent is to conquer the earth and to gain glory and riches for himself.

*in his heart it is to destroy.* Assyria's king intends to destroy and murder the inhabitants of many nations. It was never his purpose to fulfill the will of the Lord in punishing Israel for their many transgressions.

*cut off nations not a few.* Assyria's goal was to war against and conquer the world.

**10:8** *Are not my princes . . . kings?* The proud Assyrian king believed that he was the king of kings, and that his territorial princes were so mighty that they were as great as the kings of the neighboring nations.

**10:9** *Calno as Carchemish . . . as Damascus.* As the king of Assyria and his armies moved southward, they first destroyed Carchemish, then Calno, then Arpad, and finally conquered Samaria in 721 B.C. The newly conquered cities paid deference, taxes, and tribute to Assyria's king.

**10:10** *my hand hath founded.* The proud king glorifies himself by proclaiming that he has founded a kingdom of people who produce and worship idols that are even superior to those found in Israel (Samaria) and Judah (Jerusalem).

**10:11** *so do to Jerusalem and her idols.* Assyria destroyed the Northern Kingdom of Israel and prepared to destroy Judah, represented here by her capital city, Jerusalem.

## GOD DESTROYS ASSYRIA: A TYPE OF THE DESTRUCTION AT THE SECOND COMING (10:12–19)

After the Lord used Assyria to destroy Israel (10:5–11), he destroyed Assyria, who along with Babylon, Moab, Edom, and Egypt represents all the wicked and proud nations that will inhabit the earth at the time of Christ's second coming. And because all corruptible things must be destroyed, at his coming all the world's nations will be destroyed by fire. Isaiah's language is clear in this regard, using the terms *kindle a burning, burning of a fire, fire, flame, burn and devour,* and *consume.*

## Isaiah 10:12–19

Wherefore it shall come to pass, that when the Lord hath performed his whole work upon Mount Zion and [upon]⁶ Jerusalem,

I will punish the fruit of the stout heart of the king of Assyria, and the glory of his high looks. (10:12)

For he saith, By the *strength of my hand*
[*and by my wisdom* I have done these things];⁷

for I am prudent: and I have [moved the borders]⁸ of the people, and have robbed their treasures, and I have put down the inhabitants like a valiant man: (10:13)

And my hand hath found as a nest the riches of the people:
and as one gathereth eggs that are left,
have I gathered all the earth; and there was none that moved the wing, or opened the mouth, or peeped. (10:14)

Shall the *axe* boast itself against him that heweth therewith?
Shall the *saw* magnify itself against him that [uses]⁹ it?

as if the *rod* should shake itself against them that lift it up,
or as if the *staff* should lift up itself, as if it were no wood! (10:15)

Therefore shall the Lord, the Lord of hosts, send among his fat ones leanness;
and under his glory he shall kindle a burning like the burning of a fire. (10:16)

And the *Light of Israel* shall be for a fire,
and his *Holy One* for a flame:

and ¹⁰shall *burn* and *devour*
his thorns and his briers in one day; (10:17)

And shall *consume* the glory of his forest,
and of his fruitful field, both soul and body: and they shall be as when a
[*sick man wastes away*].¹¹ (10:18)
And the rest of the trees of his forest shall be few, that a child may write them. (10:19)

---

⁶2 Ne. 20:12 and JST Isa. 10:12 replace the preposition *on* with *upon.*
⁷2 Ne. 20:13 and JST Isa. 10:13 reorder the words in the verse and replace the singular pronoun *it* with *these things.*
⁸2 Ne. 20:13 and JST Isa. 10:13 replace the phrase *removed the bounds* with *moved the borders.*
⁹We have replaced the incorrect *shaketh* with *uses.*
¹⁰2 Ne. 20:17 omits the pronoun *it.*
¹¹The translation is of the Hebrew *kimᶜsos noses.* Brown, Driver, and Briggs, *Hebrew and English Lexicon,* 651.

## NOTES AND COMMENTARY

**10:12** *performed his whole work.* After the Lord performs his work on Mount Zion and Jerusalem, he will destroy Assyria with fire. In a latter-day context, that work may be the saving of the people of Israel at the Second Coming (Zech. 14:1–11) and the resurrection of the righteous (D&C 133:56), after which the world will be destroyed.

*Mount Zion.* This name refers to the temple of Jerusalem and the mount upon which it stood.

*punish the fruit.* The *fruit* represents works, hence the intent of the Lord here may be to punish the king of Assyria because of his evil works (Jer. 21:14). Partial fulfillment of this promise of punishment came when an "angel of the Lord went out, and smote in the camp of the Assyrians" and destroyed one hundred eighty-five thousand people (2 Kgs. 19:35).

*stout heart/high looks.* The words describe pride and haughtiness (46:12; Ps. 18:27; 76:5). The king's boastful, proud manner comes through in this statement, "With the multitude of my chariots I am come up to the height of the mountains, to the sides of Lebanon, and will cut down the tall cedar trees thereof, and the choice fir trees thereof" (2 Kgs. 19:23).

**10:13** *strength of my hand/by my wisdom.* The king believed that it was his own power and wisdom that enabled him to conquer the world's kingdoms and nations. He failed to recognize that the Lord's "hand [is found] in all things" (D&C 59:21).

*I am prudent.* This phrase should read, "I have understanding."

*moved the borders.* As the king conquered nations and kingdoms, he removed their political borders and joined their lands with his own kingdom.

*robbed their treasures.* The Lord prophesied, "I will send [the king of Assyria] against an apostate nation, . . . I will give him a charge, to take the spoil" (10:6). The prophecy was fulfilled with exactness when the king robbed the people of their properties, goods, and treasures.

**10:14** *nest/eggs/wing/peeped.* Israel is compared to a bird's nest, eggs, wings, and capacity to peep (3 Ne. 10:4–6; D&C 10:65; 29:1–2). The eggs in the nest represent Israel's riches (10:13). The fact that Israel was not able to move her wings or to make a peep signifies that she, like a little chick, was helpless before Assyria's ravenous armies.

**10:15** *axe/saw.* These are tools used to cut down trees of the forest, mentioned in 10:18–19. Here the *axe* or *saw* represents Assyria in the Lord's hand. Assyria and her king are proud enough to believe that they are greater than God, who holds the tools in his hands and uses them for his divine purposes.

*rod/staff.* Isaiah makes it clear that the *rod* or *staff*—symbols of Assyria (10:5)—are as fragile as pieces of wood when compared to the might and power of God.

**10:16** *fat ones leanness. Fatness* represents temporal prosperity, goodness, and earthly blessings (Gen. 45:18; Deut. 31:20; Neh. 9:25; Prov. 13:4); *leanness* represents a lack of temporal or spiritual prosperity and earthly blessings and is caused by wickedness and slothfulness (17:4–5; Gen. 41:2–20). Thus in the passage cited above, the Lord replaces the world's fatness with leanness.

*his glory.* The expressions *his thorns, his briers, his forest,* and *his fruitful field* (10:16–19) refer to the king of Assyria in all *his glory.*

**10:17** *Light of Israel/Holy One for a flame.* These names for the God of Israel are appropriate in this context because it is Jehovah's light and glory that consumed ancient Assyria and will consume the wicked at his coming.

**10:16–18** *kindle a burning/burning of a fire/fire/flame/burn and devour/consume.* Isaiah 10:16–18 describes the manner in which the forests and trees (representative of people, and here specifically of ancient Assyria as well as the wicked world of the last days) will be destroyed when Jesus comes with fire and burning. The forest-fire imagery parallels the section of Isaiah (10:33–34) in which God, as the forester, cuts down the forest of Assyria with his mighty ax.

*thorns/briers.* Isaiah, who uses these parallel terms elsewhere (5:6; 7:23–25; 9:18; 27:4), identifies the wicked as *thorns* and *briers,* meaning thorny, prickly, and often dry plants that are not only valueless but tormenting, the cause of afflictions to both man and beast.

**10:18** *forest/fruitful field.* Scripturally, the *forest* represents people (Jer. 21:14; Ezek. 20:45–47; Zech. 11:1–2), and the *field* symbolizes the world (1 Ne. 8:20; D&C 86:1–2). The destruction of the forest (uninhibited natural growth) and the fruitful field (ordered cultivation) expresses totality of destruction.[12] The forest will be destroyed by the Lord's ax, saw (10:15), and fires.

*soul and body.* Assyria, or the modern world, will be completely consumed and destroyed.

*sick man wastes away.* Isaiah likens those who will be destroyed by God's burning fires to an individual whose body is decayed and wasting away.

**10:19** *trees . . . shall be few.* Dry, dead trees (the wicked; Luke 23:31; 3 Ne. 14:17–18; D&C 135:6) will be consumed by the Lord's glory, and the green trees

---

[12] Motyer, *Prophecy of Isaiah,* 116.

(the righteous; Ps. 1:3; Zech. 4:8–14; D&C 135:6) will survive, though they may be singed. The trees (righteous people) that remain will be so few that even a little child will be able to count and list them.

## REMNANT OF ISRAEL SHALL RETURN (10:20–27)

Three major players are featured in this section: the God of Israel, the remnant of Israel, and the enemy of Israel (the Assyrian empire). The events of this section took place when the Assyrian empire was destroyed through God's divine acts and a remnant of the house of Israel returned to the land of promise. There are clues that these events will occur once more during our day. The remnant of Israel will be those members of the house of Israel who survive latter-day wars and destructions caused by modern-day Assyria, which "has become a code name for the world power [meaning the earth's wicked]."[13]

The remnant of Israel will return to their lands of promise, rebuild their temples, and renew their covenant status with God. God in turn will fight their battles against Assyria with power similar to that displayed when he overcame Egypt in Moses' day. Isaiah 10:20–21 indicates that the remnant includes those who repent and have faith in the Lord. "The remnant shall return" (10:21) recalls the prophetic name of Isaiah's son Shear-jashub (7:3).

*Isaiah 10:20–27*

And it shall come to pass in that day,

that the *remnant of Israel,*
and such as are *escaped of the house of Jacob,*

shall no more again *[lean]*[14] upon <u>him that smote them;</u>
but shall *[lean]* upon the <u>Lord, the Holy One of Israel,</u> in truth. (10:20)

The *remnant* shall return,
[yea,]¹⁵ the *remnant of Jacob,* unto the mighty God. (10:21)

For though thy people Israel be as the sand of the sea, yet a remnant of them shall return:
the [complete destruction]¹⁶ decreed shall overflow with righteousness. (10:22)

---

[13] Kaiser, *Isaiah 1–12,* 244.
[14] From the Hebrew word *nishᵉ'an.* Brown, Driver, and Briggs, *Hebrew and English Lexicon,* 1043. The term also means "to support oneself."
[15] 2 Ne. 20:21 and JST Isa. 10:21 replace *even* with the emphatic *yea.*
[16] Hebrew *kilayon.* Brown, Driver, and Briggs, *Hebrew and English Lexicon,* 478.

For the Lord God of hosts shall make a [complete destruction],[17] even determined in[18] all the land. (10:23)

Therefore thus saith the Lord God of hosts, O my people that dwellest in Zion, be not afraid of the Assyrian:

he *shall smite* thee with a <u>rod</u>,
and *shall lift up* his <u>staff</u> against thee, after the manner of Egypt. (10:24)

For yet a very little while, and the *indignation* shall cease,
and mine *anger* in their destruction. (10:25)

And the *Lord of hosts shall [lash them with a whip]*,[19] <u>according to the slaughter of Midian</u> at the rock of Oreb:
and as his rod was upon the sea, so *shall he lift it up* <u>after the manner of Egypt</u>. (10:26)

And it shall come to pass in that day,

that his *burden* shall be taken away from <u>off thy shoulder</u>,
and his *yoke* from <u>off thy neck</u>, and the yoke shall be destroyed because of the [oil].[20] (10:27)

## NOTES AND COMMENTARY

**10:20** *that day.* This is our day, or the last days (2:12).

*remnant of Israel/escaped of . . . Jacob.* Those who escape God's judgments (because of their righteousness) at the last days (4:2).

*lean/him that smote them.* The remnant of Israel will no longer lean on the rod (Assyria) that smote them (2 Kgs. 16:7), but they will lean on or trust the rod (Jehovah) that enabled them to flee safely from Egypt of old.

**10:21** *remnant shall return.* In Hebrew, this phrase is the name *Shear-jashub,* Isaiah's son who was a sign unto the house of Israel (8:18). The word *return* (Hebrew *shub*) has two connected meanings: "to return" and "to repent." The remnant of Israel who survive the destructions shall return "unto the mighty God" (10:21) through repentance and shall go back to their land of promise. The Old Testament formula for an apostate people's return to God is found in 2 Chronicles 30:6–9, which speaks of their return to the promised land, to God through repentance, and to true temple worship.

**10:22** *as the sand of the sea.* This expression recalls the Abrahamic covenant (Gen. 22:17; Abr. 3:14). Although the number of the children of Israel will be exceedingly high, only a remnant of them will return.

---

[17] Brown, Driver, and Briggs, *Hebrew and English Lexicon,* 478.
[18] 2 Ne. 20:23 and JST Isa. 10:23 omit the KJV phrase *the midst of.*
[19] Motyer, *Prophecy of Isaiah,* 118.
[20] Hebrew *shamen,* meaning "oil" or "fat." Brown, Driver, and Briggs, *Hebrew and English Lexicon,* 1032.

*destruction decreed.* God, through his prophets, decreed destruction that has application for our day. Joseph Smith wrote, "The Saints have not too much time to save and redeem their dead, and gather together their living relatives, that they may be saved also, before the earth will be smitten, and the *consumption decreed* falls upon the world."[21]

*overflow with righteousness.* The destruction, which will originate with the Lord (10:23), will be a just and righteous act on his part.

**10:23** *Lord God of hosts.* This title, or *Lord God of armies,* is appropriate, considering the section's holy war context (1:9).

*even determined in all the land.* Through the mouth of his prophets, the Lord decreed a destruction upon the land's inhabitants, just as he has upon all the earth at the last day.

**10:24** *people . . . in Zion.* The concept of *Zion* is always attached to a promised land, temple worship, and a covenant people who possess pure hearts (note the connection to the Abrahamic covenant in 10:22).

*Assyrian/Egypt.* These are two of Israel's chief enemies in biblical times. They are also symbolic of the worldly powers that will fight against Zion in the last days. Isaiah tells those who dwell in Zion to trust God and *be not afraid of the Assyrian,* for his power will be temporary and limited. Eventually God will destroy the Assyrian and save the remnant of Israel.

*rod/staff.* Assyria will smite Israel with a rod, similar to the manner in which Egypt of old forced the children of Israel to become slaves ("after the manner of Egypt"; Ex. 1:11, 14). The term *staff* may also be rendered scepter, representing dominion; thus Assyria will smite the Israelites with the rod and then rule over them.

**10:25** *indignation/anger.* Israel was scattered because of her transgressions against God. But in due time ("yet a very little while"), he will remember his covenant people once more, and his indignation and anger will cease.

**10:26** *lash them with a whip.* After Assyria serves the Lord's purposes by smiting and bruising the kingdoms of Israel and Judah, the Lord will lash the Assyrians with a whip, meaning he will punish them for their pride and wickedness.

*slaughter of Midian/manner of Egypt.* Just as God delivered Moses and the Israelites from Pharaoh's armies (Ex. 14:30–31), and saved Gideon and the children of Israel from the Midianites' destructive hand (Judg. 6–7), he will once again use a rod and a whip against Assyria to save members of the house of Israel (or the children of Zion).

---

[21] *Teachings of the Prophet Joseph Smith,* 330; emphasis added.

*rod . . . upon the sea.* Assyria was like a taskmaster's *rod;* it afflicted the children of Israel (10:5). Jehovah's rod, however—the same power by which Moses divided the Red Sea and enabled Israel to flee from the armies of Egypt—will save Israel once again. The rod of Jehovah will overcome the rod of wickedness, or Assyria.

**10:27** *burden/yoke.* Through the Lord's power, Assyria's burdens will be removed from Israel's shoulders (9:4).

*oil.* This may refer to the Messiah (Hebrew "anointed one"), who was anointed with olive oil and the Holy Ghost (Acts 10:38). In addition, 10:26–27 contains symbols that represent Jesus the Messiah, including rock, rod, and the removal of the yoke and burden (Matt. 11:28–29).

## ASSYRIA MARCHES TO JERUSALEM (10:28–34)

The mighty Assyrian army marches southward toward Jerusalem, destroying and sacking all towns and villages in its path. Isaiah identifies several cities whose inhabitants cry out with fear as they flee from the Assyrians: Aiath, Migron, Michmash, Geba, Ramah, Gibeah, Gallim, Laish, Anathoth, Madmenah, Gebim, and Nob. The army lays up supplies at Michmash and stops at Nob to rest. Finally the angry army halts before Jerusalem and makes a threatening gesture toward the sacred mount of Judah, the temple mount.

Many scholars believe Isaiah's prophecy was fulfilled when King Sennacherib invaded Judah in 701 B.C. (37:36–37); others believe it was King Sargon's invasion of 715 B.C. that fulfilled the prophecy. The section may also refer to a future campaign against Israel when some of the world's nations war against her. This is quite possible, because the prophecies in Isaiah 11 will be fulfilled in the last days (JS–H 1:40).

Isaiah's prophecy takes a different turn in the final two verses when Jehovah, as the great forester, uses his mighty iron ax to fell Assyria's armies as they approach the gates of Zion. (Isaiah employs similar imagery elsewhere; 2:12–18; 10:18–19.) Jehovah's use of the ax to cut down the earth's nations and mighty men (both represented by the trees) allows for the shoot or sprig (meaning the Messiah) to branch out of the tree stump of Judah, which is identified in 11:1–5. Because of the work of the forester, the Assyrians are not successful in capturing Jerusalem.

Historically, Isaiah tells us that an angel (who acts for the forester) destroyed one hundred eighty-five thousand of the Assyrians who were camped at Zion's gate: "Then the angel of the Lord went forth, and smote in the camp of the Assyrians a hundred and fourscore and five thousand" (37:36–37). Similar events may take place in the future.

### Isaiah 10:28–34

> *He is come* to Aiath, *he is passed* to Migron; at Michmash he hath laid up his [supplies]:[22] (10:28)
> *They are gone* over the passage: they have taken up their lodging at Geba;
> *Ramah* is <u>afraid</u>;
> *Gibeah* of <u>Saul is fled</u>. (10:29)
>
> *Lift up thy voice,* O <u>daughter of Gallim</u>:
> *cause it to be heard* unto Laish, O <u>poor Anathoth</u>. (10:30)
>
> *Madmenah* is <u>removed</u>;
> the *inhabitants of Gebim* gather themselves to <u>flee</u>. (10:31)
>
> As yet shall he remain at Nob that day: he shall shake his hand against the mount of the daughter of Zion, the hill of Jerusalem. (10:32)
>
> Behold, the Lord, the Lord of hosts, *shall lop* <u>the bough</u> with terror:
> and <u>the high ones</u> of stature *shall be hewn down,*
> and the <u>haughty</u> *shall be humbled.* (10:33)
>
> And he *shall cut down* the <u>thickets of the forest</u> with iron,
> and <u>Lebanon</u> *shall fall* by a mighty one. (10:34)

### NOTES AND COMMENTARY

**10:28** *Aiath/Migron/Michmash.* The Assyrian army captures Aiath, Migron, and Michmash on its way to Jerusalem. At Michmash, the army stores its equipment and supplies (KJV, "laid up his carriages"), perhaps so it will not be burdened as it approaches Jerusalem.

**10:29** *They are gone over the passage.* This phrase describes the advance of the Assyrian army as it crosses over an unnamed mountain pass on its way to Jerusalem.

*they have taken up their lodging at Geba.* The Assyrian army temporarily halts its advance to rest at Geba.

*Ramah is afraid/Gibeah . . . is fled.* As the Assyrian army approaches, Jerusalem's fearful inhabitants flee. *Gibeah of Saul* is so named because it was the place of Saul's birth and his residence while he was king (1 Sam. 10:26; 13–15).

**10:30** *daughter of Gallim/poor Anathoth.* Gallim and Anathoth's inhabitants raise up their voices in fear because of the impending devastation by the Assyrians. It was common for the prophets to refer to Near Eastern cities as *daughter,* such as

---

[22] We have replaced the archaic *carriages* with *supplies.*

*daughter of Gallim* ("daughter of Jerusalem," 37:22, and "daughter of Babylon," 47:1).

**10:31** *Madmenah is removed/inhabitants of Gebim . . . flee.* Madmenah and Gebim's inhabitants also flee from imminent destruction at the hands of the Assyrian army.

**10:32** *shall he remain at Nob that day.* The Assyrians will pause at the city of Nob, which is near Jerusalem, perhaps to rest, devise plans, and prepare for their attack against Jerusalem.

*shake his hand against the mount of the daughter of Zion.* Assyria might be shaking "his hand in threat against Jerusalem,"[23] directing particular attention to the temple mount and the house of the Lord, thus making a mockery of ancient Israel's chief religious symbol.

**10:33** *Lord of hosts.* Jehovah, the mighty forester who wields a great ax, enters into the scene and prevents Assyria from destroying all his children.

*lop the bough.* As elsewhere in the scriptures, Assyria the nation is compared to a mighty tree (Jer. 11:16; Hosea 14:6; Rom. 11:17–24; Jacob 5). Similarly, Ezekiel wrote that "the Assyrian was a cedar in Lebanon with fair branches, and with a shadowing shroud, and of an high stature; and his top was among the thick boughs" (Ezek. 31:3). Jehovah, the forester, chops down the tree with an ax.

*high ones of stature shall be hewn down.* The forester will also cut down Assyria's proud and haughty people.

**10:34** *cut down . . . with iron.* The term *iron* here refers to an iron ax.

*thickets of the forest.* After Jehovah, the forester, chops down the mighty cedars of Lebanon and the great Assyrians, he will clean up the underbrush so that the tree of Jesse, or the tree of the Messiah (identified in the following section), can flourish.

*mighty one.* Jehovah.

---

[23] Young, *Book of Isaiah,* 1:376.

# ISAIAH 11

### LIKENING ISAIAH 11 UNTO OURSELVES

*The prophecies recorded in Isaiah 11 are principally for us. Joseph Smith, when he recalled the angel Moroni's visit on the night of 21 September 1823, wrote that Moroni "quoted the eleventh chapter of Isaiah, saying that it was about to be fulfilled" (JS–H 1:40). These prophecies foretell that Jesus the Messiah will smite the earth and slay the wicked at his coming, preparing the way for the glorious Millennium, when he will rule with justice and righteousness.*

*The final six verses of this chapter (11:11–16) also deal with us and are being fulfilled right now. The gospel ensign has been raised and Israel's exiles are gathering around it, events that constitute "a marvelous work and a wonder" (2 Ne. 25:17).*

---

## THE STEM OF JESSE (JESUS CHRIST) PROPHECY (11:1–5)

The discussion of the tree (stump, shoot, branch, and roots) in Isaiah 11:1 is a continuation of the prophecy regarding the cutting down of the forest ("lop the bough," "high ones . . . shall be hewn down," "cut down the thickets of the forest") from the previous two verses (10:33–34). The Lord, or forester, carefully trims the boughs and cuts down the trees (the power and glory of the foreign leaders and their nations) and in this manner cleans out the forest's evil trees to prepare the way for the new shoot, the stump of Jesse, to flourish. As Hans Wildberger writes, "Out of the stump, from roots of what has been cut down, a new ruler will come forth."[1] Otto Kaiser adds, "the Davidic dynasty is compared with a tree, all that is left of which is a

---

[1] Wildberger, *Isaiah 1–12*, 467.

stump. Just as this can again send forth shoots, so too the royal family will renew itself from a further group of descendants of Jesse, the father of King David."[2]

The Book of Mormon (2 Ne. 30:9 especially) and the Doctrine and Covenants (113) reinforce the fact that Jesus Christ is the main character in Isaiah 11. He is the Messiah who will have the "spirit of the Lord," the "spirit of wisdom and understanding," "counsel and might," "knowledge," and "fear of the Lord" (11:2); he is the Messiah who will serve as the righteous judge (11:3); and he will be the advocate of the poor and the meek and will settle their case (11:4). In the end, the Messiah will smite the wicked of the earth with his great power at the Second Coming, resulting in the glorious conditions of the Millennium (11:6–10).

## Isaiah 11:1–5

And there shall come forth a [*shoot*][3] out of the [*stump*][4] of Jesse,
and a *Branch* shall grow out of his roots: (11:1)

And the *spirit* of the Lord shall rest upon him,
the *spirit* of wisdom and understanding,
the *spirit* of counsel and might,
the *spirit* of knowledge and of the fear of the Lord; (11:2)

And shall make him of quick understanding in the fear of the Lord:

and he shall *not judge* after the sight of his eyes,
*neither reprove* after the hearing of his ears: (11:3)

But with righteousness shall [the Lord God][5] *judge* the poor,
and [*settle the case*] with equity for the meek of the earth:

And he shall *smite the earth* with the rod of his mouth,
and with the breath of his lips shall he *slay the wicked.* (11:4)

And *righteousness* shall be the girdle of his loins,
and *faithfulness* the [sash around his waist].[6] (11:5)

NOTES AND COMMENTARY

**11:1** *shoot* (KJV, *rod*). "What is the rod spoken of in the first verse of the 11th chapter of Isaiah, that should come of the Stem of Jesse? Behold, thus saith the Lord: It is a servant in the hands of Christ, who is partly a descendant of Jesse as well as of Ephraim, or of the house of Joseph, on whom there is laid much power" (D&C 113:3–4). Sidney Sperry suggested that the *rod* or "servant in the hands of Christ"

[2] Kaiser, *Isaiah 1–12,* 255.
[3] Hebrew *choter.* Brown, Driver, and Briggs, *Hebrew and English Lexicon,* 310.
[4] Hebrew *geza'.* Brown, Driver, and Briggs, *Hebrew and English Lexicon,* 160.
[5] 2 Ne. 30:9 replaces the pronoun *he* with the expression *the Lord God.*
[6] NIV Isa.; see also Brown, Driver, and Briggs, *Hebrew and English Lexicon,* 323.

referred to the Prophet Joseph Smith.[7] It may also refer to another latter-day prophet yet to come forth.

*stump of Jesse* (KJV, *stem of Jesse*). The *stump of Jesse* is Christ. The Doctrine and Covenants is explicit: "Who is the Stem of Jesse spoken of in the 1st, 2d, 3d, 4th, and 5th verses of the 11th chapter of Isaiah? Verily thus saith the Lord: It is Christ" (113:1–2).

*Branch.* Elder Bruce R. McConkie explained that the Branch is Christ: "As to the identity of the Stem of Jesse, the revealed word says: 'Verily thus saith the Lord: It is Christ.' (D&C 113:1–2.) This also means that the Branch is Christ"[8] (Jer. 23:3–6; Zech. 3:8).

**11:2** *the spirit of the Lord shall rest upon him.* According to Doctrine and Covenants 113:1–2, Christ is the recipient of this great blessing. The Spirit of the Lord is connected to the anointing of kings (1 Sam. 16:13; 2 Sam. 23:2–3), including the Messiah (42:1; 59:21; 61:1). The Spirit of the Lord magnifies persons for special tasks (63:10–11; Ex. 31:2–3; Num. 11:17; 27:18; Judg. 6:34; 1 Sam. 16:13).

*wisdom and understanding.* These two qualities are attributed to the Messiah and generally to kings (2 Sam. 14:17; 1 Kgs. 3:5, 9); however, the king of Assyria only *claimed* to possess them (10:13).

*counsel and might.* These additional qualities are attributed to the Messiah (D&C 113:1–2). The two terms recall two of Jehovah's throne names identified by Isaiah in 9:6: "Wonderful Counsellor" and "mighty God."

*spirit of knowledge.* The Messiah will be blessed with great knowledge.

*fear of the Lord.* To have reverence for God (Gen. 20:11; Ex. 20:20) is to be obedient and behave in a certain manner (Neh. 5:9, 15); it is connected with worship (Ps. 5:7) and is the mark of the true believer.

**11:3** *not judge after the sight of his eyes.* The Messiah will not judge an individual solely by the testimony received from witnesses, nor from outward appearances; rather, he is able to see into the very heart of an individual and therefore judges righteously (1 Sam. 16:7).

**11:4** *with righteousness shall the Lord God judge the poor.* When the Lord judges the world, he will repair (with righteousness and equity) all the injustices of mortality, including the deprivations and disadvantages experienced by the poor and the meek.

---

[7] Sperry, *Old Testament Prophets,* 41.
[8] *Promised Messiah,* 192.

*smite the earth.* The Lord will destroy all corruptible things at his second coming. Isaiah 11:4–5 is cited in 2 Nephi 30:9, 11. The Nephite record adds the following words between Isaiah's prophecy regarding the Lord smiting the earth with the rod and the prophecy of the Lord's millennial reign: "For the time speedily cometh that the Lord God shall cause a great division among the people, and the wicked will he destroy; and he will spare his people, yea, even if it so be that he must destroy the wicked by fire" (2 Ne. 30:10). The Lord will destroy the wicked with fire but will spare the righteous.

*rod of his mouth/breath of his lips.* Jesus will destroy the wicked with his word of truth, uttering judgments against evil (Rev. 19:15, 21). Other prophets have used similar phraseology in their teachings (2 Thes. 2:8; D&C 19:15).[9]

**11:5** *girdle of his loins.* The Lord is clothed in righteousness and faithfulness; these two qualities represent his very existence. Righteous individuals should imitate Christ: "every man should take *righteousness* in his hands and *faithfulness* upon his *loins,* and lift a warning voice unto the inhabitants of the earth; and declare both by word and by flight that desolation shall come upon the wicked" (D&C 63:37; emphasis added; Eph. 6:14). The Lord girds his loins with righteousness as he prepares to do his important work. The loins symbolize the creative powers (Gen. 35:11; 1 Kgs. 8:19; Acts 2:30). These items of clothing, the girdle of the loins and the sash around the waist, are also suggestive of temple ordinances.

## GLORIOUS CONDITIONS OF THE MILLENNIUM (11:6–10)

The millennial reign can take place because the Messiah comes forth with the Spirit of the Lord (11:2) to judge the earth's people and destroy the wicked (11:4). The branch or stem recalls Eden's tree of life; the motifs of the wolf, lamb, leopard, and kid dwelling together (11:6) and the lion eating straw (11:7) are also reminiscent of the wonderful setting of Eden (Gen. 1:29–30). The child harmlessly playing near the snake's lair (11:8) and the lack of hurt or destruction in all the earth (11:9) set forth the new Eden, the terrestrial Millennium.

Isaiah 11:6–7 shows that old enemies and hostile conditions will no longer exist, signaling a change in the order of things. Isaiah 11:8 recalls the curse between the serpent and the seed of the woman (Gen. 3:15), which is now removed. Further, conditions during the Millennium (11:9) mirror the Edenic state of peaceful bliss, and knowledge of the Lord (11:9) comes as the result of the Lord's removal of wickedness

---

[9] *Teachings of the Prophet Joseph Smith,* 36.

(11:4). The control of the little child over the animals recalls the dominion over the animals found in the Eden story (Gen. 1:28).[10]

## Isaiah 11:6–10

[And then shall the *wolf*][11] dwell with the lamb,
and the *leopard* shall lie down with the kid;
and the *calf* and the *young lion* and the *fatling together*; and a little child shall lead them. (11:6)

And the cow and the bear shall feed; their young ones shall lie down together: and the lion shall eat straw like the ox. (11:7)

And the *sucking child* shall play on the hole of the asp,
and the *weaned child* shall put his hand on the cockatrice' den. (11:8)

They shall not hurt nor destroy in all my holy mountain:
for the earth shall be full of the knowledge of the Lord,
as the waters cover the sea. (11:9)

And in that day there shall be a root of Jesse, which shall stand for an ensign of the people; to [him][12] shall the Gentiles seek: and his rest shall be glorious. (11:10)

NOTES AND COMMENTARY

**11:6** *wolf/leopard/lion/lamb/kid/calf.* Six animals are listed (not counting the fatling, see below); three are wild carnivores (*wolf, leopard, lion*) that feed on the three tame animals (*lamb, kid, calf*). The wild animals, which are ferocious, aggressive, and vicious, are a threat to mankind; the tame animals are docile, submissive, and useful to man. This passage may be taken literally; or the wolf, leopard, and lion may represent those who foment war and murder; the lamb, kid, and calf may symbolize meek and peaceful people.

*fatling.* The King James Version translation of *fatling* is probably incorrect. The Jerusalem Bible suggests "calf and lion cub feed together," replacing *fatling* with the verb *feed.*

*little child shall lead them.* Small children will not only feel safe among the ferocious beasts but will have control over them and lead them.

**11:7** *cow/bear/lion/ox.* Isaiah continues to compare wild, carnivorous animals (*bear* and *lion*) with tame animals (*cow* and *ox*). His prophecy that the lion will pasture like the ox suggests that there will be no shedding of blood during the

---

[10] *Teachings of the Prophet Joseph Smith,* 71; see also 316.
[11] 2 Ne. 30:12 clarifies that the conditions of the Millennium will occur after the events of Isa. 11:1–5.
[12] This emendation is based upon NIV Isa.

Millennium by man or beast. During the Millennium, "the enmity of man, and the enmity of beasts, yea, the enmity of all flesh, shall cease from before my face" (D&C 101:26).

*their young ones.* This refers to the offspring of the cow and the bear and indicates that the subsequent generations of beasts will have no hostilities toward one another. This peaceful state of affairs, wherein no blood is shed, will endure.

**11:8** *sucking child/weaned child/asp/cockatrice.* Both the nursing infant and the weaned toddler are completely helpless in the face of danger, but during the Millennium, both will be able to play at the asp (possibly the cobra) and the cockatrice's (possibly the viper's) dens, for poisonous snakes that once harmed and destroyed will be harmless. The curse between the seed of the woman (the child) and the serpent (Gen. 3:15) will be gone. The serpents here call to mind "that old serpent, called the Devil, and Satan" (Rev. 12:9), whose intent it is to harm and destroy the souls of mankind. Satan, however, will be bound during the Millennium, with all of his angels, so that peaceful conditions can hold sway.

**11:9** *They shall not hurt nor destroy in all my holy mountain.* Enmity will be removed from the earth, and peace, love, and kindness will be the rule. *Holy mountain* may refer to the entire earth in its temple-like condition.

*earth shall be full of the knowledge of the Lord.* Joseph Smith quoted this statement, but he added that it will be "sacred knowledge" that will fill the earth.[13] Nephi, after quoting Isaiah's statement that "the earth shall be full of the knowledge of the Lord," explained that "the things of all nations shall be made known; yea, all things shall be made known unto the children of men. There is nothing which is secret save it shall be revealed; there is no work of darkness save it shall be made manifest in the light; and there is nothing which is sealed upon the earth save it shall be loosed. Wherefore, all things which have been revealed unto the children of men shall at that day be revealed" (2 Ne. 30:15–18).

*as the waters cover the sea.* The sacred knowledge of God and his gospel will be as extensive as the waters that cover much of the earth's surface.

**11:10** *root of Jesse.* "What is the root of Jesse spoken of in the 10th verse of the 11th chapter? Behold, thus saith the Lord, it is a descendant of Jesse, as well as of Joseph, unto whom rightly belongs the priesthood, and the keys of the kingdom, for an ensign, and for the gathering of my people in the last days" (D&C 113:5–6; Rom. 15:12). Latter-day Saint scholars[14] generally agree that the *root of Jesse* refers to the

---

[13] *Teachings of the Prophet Joseph Smith,* 93.
[14] See, for example, Sperry, *Voice of Israel's Prophets,* 34–38; Ludlow, *Isaiah,* 170–74; and Nyman, "Abinadi's Commentary on Isaiah," 73–74.

Prophet Joseph Smith. He is a descendant of both Jesse and Joseph; he held the priesthood; he possessed the keys of the kingdom; he played a primary role in the lifting of the ensign upon the tops of the mountains; and the keys of the gathering of Israel were committed into his hands (D&C 110:11). This prophecy may also be fulfilled by another prophet yet to come, who shall also have the characteristics Isaiah saw.

*an ensign of the people; to [him] shall the Gentiles seek.* A modern revelation explains that God's everlasting covenant is a standard or *ensign* that the *Gentiles* shall *seek* (D&C 45:9). In another revelation Zion "shall be an ensign unto the people, and there shall come unto her out of every nation under heaven" (D&C 64:42). Here Isaiah suggests that the *root of Jesse* is also *an ensign* and *to him shall the Gentiles seek.*

*rest.* This prophet's rest in the presence of God will be glorious. The meaning of *rest* is presented in the scriptures (JST Ex. 34:2; Alma 40:12; D&C 84:23–24).

## AN ENSIGN SHALL GATHER ISRAEL (11:11–16)

This prophecy is being fulfilled in our day. Isaiah prophesies that the Lord will use his power ("set his hand") to gather his people from all the nations of the earth (11:11–12). God will first send a signal to the nations of the earth (he will erect the banner or ensign). Israel will gather around the ensign (11:12), resulting in the unification of the kingdom of Israel (11:13). The gentiles will assist in the gathering (11:14), and the Lord will use his almighty power to provide a way for the exiles to return (11:15–16). All these divine activities constitute "a marvelous work and a wonder among the children of men" (2 Ne. 25:17).

The language of the prophecy recalls the Israelite exodus from Egypt under the leadership of Moses: "the Lord shall utterly destroy the tongue of the Egyptian sea" (11:15); "like as it was to Israel in the day that he came up out of the land of Egypt" (11:16). The gathering in our own day, then, will be conducted through the power of God under the leadership of prophets who possess the same authority as Moses.

*Isaiah 11:11–16*

And it shall come to pass in that day,
that the Lord shall set his hand again the second time to recover the remnant of his people,
which shall be left, from *Assyria,* and from *Egypt,* and from *Pathros,* and from *Cush,*

and from *Elam,* and from *Shinar,* and from *Hamath,* and from the *islands of the sea.* (11:11)

And he shall set up an ensign for the nations,

and shall *assemble* the outcasts of Israel,
and *gather together* the dispersed of Judah from the four corners of the earth. (11:12)

The *envy also of Ephraim* shall depart,
and the *adversaries of Judah* shall be cut off:

*Ephraim* shall not envy Judah,
and *Judah* shall not vex Ephraim. (11:13)

But *they shall fly* upon the shoulders of the Philistines toward the west;
*they shall spoil* them of the east together:

*they* shall lay their hand upon Edom and Moab;
and the children of Ammon shall obey *them.* (11:14)

And the *Lord shall utterly destroy* the tongue of the Egyptian sea;
and with his mighty wind shall *he shake his hand* over the river,

and shall smite it in the seven streams, and make men go over dryshod. (11:15)

And there shall be an *highway* for the remnant of his people, which shall be left, from Assyria;
*like as it was* to Israel in the day that he came up out of the land of Egypt. (11:16)

## NOTES AND COMMENTARY

**11:11** *in that day.* This is our day, or the last days (2:12).

*Lord shall set his hand again the second time.* This prophecy is being fulfilled right now, in our day. The first time the Lord set his hand to gather his people was when he "led Israel out of Egyptian bondage and captivity"[15] (Ex. 3:19–20; 13:3; Deut. 6:21). The restoration of the gospel, which began with Joseph Smith's ministry, signaled the *second time* God began recovering the remnants of Israel from the nations of the world. Joseph Smith taught that "The time has at last arrived when the God of Abraham, of Isaac, and of Jacob, has set his hand again the second time to recover the remnants of his people."[16] The Book of Mormon adds to our knowledge of this prophecy (2 Ne. 6:14; Jacob 6:2).

*recover the remnant.* In Hebrew this phrase means to purchase or acquire *the remnant.* God will bring back his people through redemption and the Atonement (1 Ne. 10:14; 3 Ne. 20:13). The *remnant* or remnants are members of the house of Israel "who are scattered abroad upon all the face of the earth" (3 Ne. 5:24). These include the Nephites and Lamanites (Book of Mormon Title Page; 1 Ne. 13:34; Alma

---

[15] Richards, *Marvelous Work and a Wonder,* 202.
[16] *Teachings of the Prophet Joseph Smith,* 14.

46:23; 3 Ne. 20:10), members of the Church (D&C 52:2), and others of the house of Israel. They will be gathered in "from the four quarters of the earth" (3 Ne. 5:24; 20:13) and be "converted from their wild and savage condition to the fulness of the everlasting gospel" (D&C 109:65) by their accepting Christ and the Book of Mormon (1 Ne. 10:14; 3 Ne. 20:13; Morm. 5:12; 7:1).

*Assyria/Egypt/Pathros/Cush/Elam/Shinar/Hamath/islands.* Isaiah lists many of the nations that surrounded ancient Israel.[17] The list represents the entire world and anticipates similar phraseology in the following verse—*nations, outcasts, dispersed, four corners of the earth.* God will gather the covenant people from all the nations of the earth to his covenant lands.

**11:12** *ensign.* A flag or banner will be raised on a high mountain for all of Israel's outcasts to see, prompting them to gather around it. The *ensign* represents the gospel of Jesus Christ (D&C 45:9) and the light that accompanies it (D&C 115:4-5;[18] see also commentary on 5:26-30).

*assemble the outcasts/gather . . . dispersed.* The outcasts of Judah and Israel will see the ensign, recognize it as a divine signal from God, and then gather to Zion. The gathering is centered on temples and temple work, as Joseph Smith instructed the early saints.[19]

*four corners of the earth.* All the house of Israel, including the ten lost tribes and members of the house of Judah, have been scattered throughout the world, as the scriptures clearly testify: "shalt be removed into all the kingdoms of the earth" (Deut. 28:25); "the Lord shall scatter thee among all people, from the one end of the earth even unto the other" (Deut. 28:64); "removed to all the kingdoms of the earth . . . among all the nations" (Jer. 29:18); "scatter them among the nations, and disperse them in the countries" (Ezek. 12:15); "my flock was scattered upon all the face of the earth" (Ezek. 34:6); "I scattered them among the heathen, and they were dispersed through the countries" (Ezek. 36:19); "I will sift the house of Israel among all nations, like as corn is sifted in a sieve" (Amos 9:9); "I scattered them with a whirl-wind among all the nations" (Zech. 7:14); "the house of Israel . . . should be scattered upon all the face of the earth" (1 Ne. 10:12); "the house of Israel, sooner or later, will be scattered upon all the face of the earth, and also among all nations . . . Yea, the more part of all the tribes have been led away; and they are scattered to and fro upon the isles of the sea" (1 Ne. 22:3-5); "scattered abroad upon the face of the earth"

---

[17] *Teachings of the Prophet Joseph Smith,* 14.
[18] *Teachings of the Prophet Joseph Smith,* 38.
[19] *History of the Church,* 5:423-24.

(3 Ne. 20:13); and "this people shall be . . . scattered among all nations" (D&C 45:19). It stands to reason that members of the house of Israel will be gathered from the *four corners of the earth* (11:12).

**11:13** *envy also of Ephraim/adversaries of Judah shall be cut off.* The entire verse recalls the tensions and hostilities that existed between Ephraim (the Northern Kingdom) and Judah (the Southern Kingdom), beginning with Jeroboam's break with Rehoboam (1 Kgs. 11–12). God's latter-day gathering will result in the uniting of the kingdoms of Judah and Israel, made possible because the gospel teaches peace and love and because the Messiah, who is the true king of Israel and Judah, rules with justice and righteousness (11:1–5). The Book of Mormon also plays a prominent role in reuniting Ephraim and Judah (Ezek. 37:15–28).

**11:14** *fly upon the shoulders . . . and the children of Ammon shall obey them.* Compare the translation in the New International Version: "They will swoop down on the slopes of Philistia." As Israel gathers to God's signal (ensign) and possesses righteousness, the priesthood, and the power received in the temple, then Israel's former enemies, the Philistines, Edomites, Moabites, and Ammonites—symbols for the nations of our day—will be subject to them.

**11:15** *tongue of the Egyptian sea.* The word *tongue* should be translated "gulf." This phrase recalls the occasion when Moses and the Israelites crossed the Red Sea on dry ground (Ex. 14:21–22), an event that anticipates the gathering in the last days, when no powerful nation, mortal tyrant, or army will stop the promised events of the gathering of the saints around God's standard.

*with his mighty wind shall he shake his hand over the river . . . and make men go over dryshod.* Three elements in this passage, *mighty wind, hand,* and *go over dry-shod,* recall the Israelites' crossing of the Red Sea. "Moses stretched out his *hand* over the sea; and the Lord caused the sea to go back by a *strong east wind* all that night, and made the sea dry land . . . And the children of Israel went into the midst of the sea upon the *dry ground*" (Ex. 14:21–22; emphasis added). The same powers that guided the ancient Israelites out of Egypt will guide modern Israel out of symbolic Egypt (the world) to their gathering places.

*seven streams.* The Living Bible translation provides a possible interpretation: "The Lord will . . . wave his hand over the Euphrates, sending a mighty wind to divide it into seven streams that can easily be crossed."

**11:16** *highway . . . from Assyria.* The *highway* may be an actual road or path for members of the house of Israel to travel on as they return to the land of promise. The fact that "unclean" people, lions, or ravenous beasts (35:8–10; 51:10–11) will not pass over the highway indicates its connection with the straight and narrow path. For this meaning of *highway,* see 40:3; 42:16; 49:11; 57:14; 62:10.

*which shall be left.* This phrase speaks concerning the remnant of His people, *which shall be left,* identified in 11:11.

*like as it was to Israel in the day that he came up out of the land of Egypt.* Once again the prophet reminds us that the Lord's almighty power saved Moses and the Israelites from Pharaoh and his army. In doing so, Isaiah gives us confidence that the Lord will prevent all worldly powers from halting our latter-day gathering.

# ISAIAH 12

*LIKENING ISAIAH 12 UNTO OURSELVES*

*Isaiah 12 is Israel's "Songs of Salvation" that we will sing in the future, perhaps at Christ's coming or during the Millennium. The first hymn has been individualized with the frequent use of the first person pronouns I and me—each of us will praise the Lord with these sacred words. The second hymn will also be sung by us ("thou inhabitant of Zion"). It is not evident where we will sing these hymns: perhaps in the temple, at the gathering at Adam-ondi-Ahman, at general conference, or in other sacred settings.*

## ISRAEL'S SONGS OF SALVATION (12:1–6)

This section presents the two hymns that we will sing to the Lord in the future, both of which are introduced with similar statements: "And in that day thou shalt say" and "And in that day shall ye say." Both hymns center on the Lord; the first uses the titles *Lord* (twice), *God, Lord Jehovah,* and a number of metaphors and terms that identify the Lord as our salvation, strength, and song. The second hymn uses the titles *Lord* and *Holy One of Israel.* The two hymns also refer to those who are singing them. The first hymn is filled with first-person singular pronouns such as *I* (twice), *me* (twice), and *my* (four times); the second simply refers to the "inhabitant of Zion." Hence, the hymns juxtapose two essential elements: God and those who worship him.

The principal theme of the first hymn is the salvation of the members of the house of Israel: three times salvation is mentioned, twice affirming that the Lord is "my salvation" and once referring to the righteous who "draw water out of the wells of salvation." The chief theme of the second hymn pertains to the singer or worshiper who rejoices in the Lord's greatness. The hymn features a number of command verbal forms, such as *praise, call upon, declare, make mention, sing, cry out,* and *shout,* all of which recognize and honor the Lord's exalted name, his excellent works, and his greatness for dwelling in the midst of Israel.

## Isaiah 12:1–6

And in that day thou shalt say,

O Lord, I will praise thee:
though thou wast angry with me,
thine anger is turned away,
and thou comfortest me. (12:1)
Behold, God is my salvation;
I will trust, and not be afraid:
for the Lord Jehovah is my strength and my song;
he also [has]¹ become my salvation. (12:2)
Therefore with joy shall ye draw water out of the wells of salvation. (12:3)

And in that day shall ye say,

*Praise* the Lord,
*call upon* his name,
*declare* his doings among the people,
*make mention* that his name is exalted. (12:4)
*Sing unto the* Lord; for he hath done excellent things:
this is known in all the earth. (12:5)
*Cry out and shout,* thou inhabitant of Zion:
for great is the Holy One of Israel in the midst of thee. (12:6)

## NOTES AND COMMENTARY

**12:1** *in that day.* This phrase, which is twice repeated in this chapter (12:1, 4), provides a link with 11:10–11. *In that day* refers to the events connected with our day (2:12).

*thou wast angry.* Similar language is found in the Doctrine and Covenants, wherein the Lord exclaims, "I . . . was angry with you [Israel] yesterday, but today mine anger is turned away" (D&C 61:20).

*thou comfortest.* God comforts his children with the Holy Ghost (John 15:26), but when read in the context of both of the hymns, this phrase may refer to Jesus Christ, who is called the Second Comforter.²

**12:2** *God is my salvation.* Salvation is spoken of twice in this verse for emphasis. *Lectures on Faith* defines *salvation* as follows: "Salvation consists in [gaining] the glory, authority, majesty, power and dominion which Jehovah possesses and in nothing else; and no being can possess it but himself or one like him."³

---

¹ 2 Ne. 22:2 replaces *is* with *has.*
² *Teachings of the Prophet Joseph Smith,* 149–51.
³ *Lectures on Faith,* 76.

*Lord Jehovah is my strength.* God is "the Strength of Israel" (1 Sam. 15:29; 1 Ne. 21:5; 2 Ne. 22:2), a name that sets forth the Lord's ability to save Israel both temporally and spiritually.

*Lord Jehovah is . . . my song.* God is the central focus of our song and music.

**12:3** *draw water/wells of salvation.* A better translation for *wells of salvation* is "springs of salvation," which depicts living, flowing water. Christ represents the *waters* of salvation (Jer. 2:13; 17:13; Ether 8:26; 12:28). The parallel between literal water and the waters of salvation is evident—the first is essential for physical life, the second for eternal life. In part, the expression *wells of salvation* refers to the great privilege the righteous have to partake of the blessings connected with the First and Second Comforters (John 7:38–39; 14:16–26);[4] but more fully the expression pertains to those who will receive exaltation in the celestial kingdom and will drink eternally from the wells of salvation (Rev. 21:6).

**12:4** *declare his doings. His doings* refers to all God's works that bring salvation to mankind during the history of the world, including his restoring priesthood keys, revealing his word, and establishing Zion among his people.

*his name is exalted.* The names *Jehovah, Jesus Christ, Son of God,* and others belonging to the Lord are the highest, most honorable, and most magnificent of all names.

**12:4–6** *praise/call upon/declare/make mention/sing/cry out/shout.* These terms are indicative of those who worship the Lord through song, prayer, or praise. We recall a modern-day revelation that promises, "The song of the righteous is a prayer unto me, and it shall be answered with a blessing upon their heads" (D&C 25:12).

*he hath done excellent things.* The Lord has done a multitude of wondrous things that men are unable to do for themselves; most notably, Jesus Christ wrought the infinite atonement.

**12:6** *inhabitant of Zion.* The terms *cry out, shout, inhabitant,* and *thee* are feminine forms in the Hebrew and personify Christ's bride who is ready to be received by the Holy One of Israel. Zion is depicted as the bride elsewhere (54:1–6; Rev. 21:2, 9; D&C 109:73–74), and Jehovah is portrayed as the husband (54:5). Zion's inhabitants are the pure in heart (D&C 97:21).

*Holy One of Israel in the midst of thee.* Christ, the Holy One of Israel, will reign over the Saints during the Millennium.

---

[4] *Teachings of the Prophet Joseph Smith,* 149–51.

# ISAIAH 13

## LIKENING ISAIAH 13 UNTO OURSELVES

*Beginning with Joseph Smith and continuing through the administration of all the latter-day prophets, the Lord has been preparing his Saints to become a Zion people, a righteous army to battle against modern-day Babylon and its evil forces (13:1–5).*

*Meanwhile, we benefit from studying Isaiah's prophecy of ancient Babylon's wickedness and ultimate destruction (13:6–22) because these historical events serve as shadows of the evil that we are presently witnessing upon the earth. Soon we will see the destruction of modern-day Babylon by Jesus Christ at his coming.*

## THE LORD OF ARMIES CALLS FORTH HIS HOSTS (13:1–5)

The events listed in this prophecy are being fulfilled by us (members of the Church) right now in our own day. Isaiah 13:2–5 (an interlude in the larger scene of the judgment of Babylon; see 13:1, 6–22) comprises the Lord's command to us to gather Israel by hoisting a banner or ensign on a mountain; calling with a voice; and beckoning with the hand (13:2). When these three signals are given, the earth cannot doubt the veracity of the invitation to join the Saints in Zion.

Those who gather will come from all parts of the earth (13:5), will be sanctified in the temple (13:3), and will become part of the Lord's army to serve in the holy war against evil (13:4–5), all of which will occur in preparation for the Lord's coming when he will destroy modern Babylon as he destroyed ancient Babylon. As the Lord invites his people to gather to Zion and the temple, Satan simultaneously entices people to become part of Babylon (14:4–20).

*Isaiah 13:1–5*

The burden of Babylon, which Isaiah the son of Amoz did see. (13:1)

*Lift ye up* [my][1] banner upon the high mountain,
*exalt* the voice unto them,

[wave][2] the hand, that they may go into the gates of the nobles. (13:2)

I have *commanded* my sanctified ones,
I have also *called* my mighty ones,

for mine anger [is not upon them][3] that rejoice in my highness. (13:3)

The *noise* of [the][4] multitude in the mountains like as of a great people,
a tumultuous *noise* of the kingdoms of nations gathered together,

the Lord of Hosts mustereth the hosts of the battle. (13:4)

They come *from* a far country,
*from* the end of heaven,

[yea,][5] the Lord, and the weapons of his indignation, to destroy the whole land. (13:5)

## NOTES AND COMMENTARY

**13:1** *burden.* A *burden* is a prophecy of doom or judgment against a people. The Hebrew root (*masa'*) literally means "lifting" or "a lifting up," perhaps indicating that the prophecy or judgment is lifted up by the voice of the prophet against the people.[6] Isaiah's prophetic calling included uttering a prophecy of doom against many peoples or nations, including Moab (15:1), Damascus (17:1), Egypt (19:1), the desert of the sea (21:1), Dumah (21:11), Arabia (21:13), the valley of vision (22:1), Tyre (23:1), and the beasts of the south (30:6). Similarly, the *burden* of the word of the Lord also came to Nahum (1:1), Habakkuk (1:1), Zechariah (12:1), and Malachi (1:1).

The same Hebrew root is also used in connection with the lifting of the ensign (5:26; 11:12; 13:2) upon a high mountain. Hence, the Lord will "lift up" judgment against the wicked and will "lift up" an ensign to the righteous.

*Babylon.* A symbol of the world and wickedness: "Go ye out from among the nations, even from Babylon, from the midst of wickedness, which is spiritual Babylon" (D&C 133:14).

---

[1] JST Isa. 13:2 adds the personal pronoun *my,* showing that the banner belongs to the Lord.
[2] From Hebrew *nup.* Brown, Driver, and Briggs, *Hebrew and English Lexicon,* 631.
[3] 2 Ne. 23:3 adds this explanatory phrase.
[4] JST Isa. 13:4 and 2 Ne. 23:4 change the indefinite article to the definite.
[5] JST Isa. 13:5 and 2 Ne. 23:5 replace *even* with *yea.*
[6] "A lifting up of the voice, hence an utterance or oracle." Kissane, *Book of Isaiah,* 1:160.

*Isaiah . . . did see.* The revelations came to Isaiah as visions wherein he saw the future (1:1).

**13:2** *banner.* The *banner* also means "ensign," which is found earlier in 5:26 and 11:10. Anciently, Israel's families and clans gathered with their own banner around the temple of Jehovah (Num. 2:2; Mosiah 2:5–6). Similarly, members of God's kingdom of this dispensation will figuratively lift up the gospel banner upon the mountain (18:3; 30:17), which symbolizes the temple, and the nations of the earth will seek after it.

*high mountain.* A symbolic reference to the temple.[7]

*exalt the voice unto them.* This is the "voice of warning" that shall be raised "unto all people, by the mouths of [the Lord's] disciples" (D&C 1:4). Also, "And let your preaching be the warning voice, every man to his neighbor" (D&C 38:41).

*wave the hand.* To *wave the hand* is to beckon or extend an invitation to another.

*gates of the nobles.* Possibly a symbolic reference to the entrances into Zion or to the temple's portals.

**13:3** *my sanctified ones.* Jehovah's *sanctified ones* (Josh. 3:5) are those who are temple worthy, who actually attend the temple, and who are made holy by Christ's power. In ancient Israel the soldiers prepared for the holy war by participating in holy rituals connected with the temple (Deut. 23:10–15). In this dispensation, Jesus Christ's soldiers (members of the Church) prepare for the battle against Babylon by participating in temple rituals.

*my mighty ones.* This phrase can read "my warriors." The saints are warriors who battle against evil forces under Jehovah's direction, using his weapons (13:5).

*mine anger.* See commentary on 13:13.

*rejoice in my highness.* Jesus is the "Son of the Highest" (Luke 1:32), and God is "the highest of all" (D&C 76:70). *Highness* refers to the Lord's exaltation.

**13:4** *noise of the multitude . . . nations gathered together.* The word *noise* in this verse may also be translated "voice," such as in "the voice of many people in the mountains." Elsewhere Isaiah likens the noise of a great multitude of people to the "noise of the seas" (17:12) and "the rushing of mighty waters" (17:12). The saints, or *multitude,* will gather together from the world's nations and kingdoms with the intent of building Zion (Matt. 24:30–31; D&C 29:7–11; 45:66–71; 103:22–25).

*in the mountains like as of a great people.* This has reference to gathering of the Saints in the Rocky Mountains. On 6 August 1842, Joseph Smith prophesied that

---

[7] McConkie and Parry, *Guide to Scriptural Symbols,* 84.

some of the Saints would "live to go and assist in making settlements and build cities and see the saints become *a mighty people in the midst of the Rocky Mountains.*"[8]

*Lord of Hosts mustereth the hosts of the battle.* See commentary on 1:9.

**13:5** *They come from a far country, from the end of heaven.* Those who join the Lord's army will be gathered from all the nations of the earth. "Yea, verily I say unto you again, the time has come when the voice of the Lord is unto you: Go ye out of Babylon; gather ye out from among the nations, from the four winds, from one *end of heaven* to the other" (D&C 133:7; JS–M 1:37; emphasis added). *The end of heaven* may simply suggest the farthest reaches of the earth.

*weapons of his indignation.* These represent the Lord's heavenly powers. Compare Jeremiah's words, "The Lord hath opened his armory, and hath brought forth the weapons of his indignation" (Jer. 50:25).

*to destroy the whole land.* Isaiah seems to be saying here that the Lord's valiant servants will successfully battle evil during this time period. A modern revelation adds light to this phrase of Isaiah: "Wherefore, I [the Lord] call upon the weak things of the world, those who are unlearned and despised, to thrash the nations by the power of my Spirit; And their arm shall be my arm, and I will be their shield and their buckler; and I will gird up their loins, and they shall fight manfully for me; and their enemies shall be under their feet; and I will let fall the sword in their behalf, and by the fire of mine indignation will I preserve them" (D&C 35:13–14; 133:58–59).

## JUDGMENT ON BABYLON: DAY OF THE LORD COMETH (13:6–10)

The ancient city of Babylon, with all its pomp, arrogance, and worldliness, is symbolic of the world in the last days (D&C 1:16). The day of the Lord (the last days and the Second Coming) will be a time of great destruction and desolation on the land, when all sinners and every corruptible thing will be destroyed. Great signs in the heavens will play a prominent role in these events; Isaiah mentions the stars and constellations of heaven, the sun, and the moon. The wicked will possess great fear and will "howl," their hands will "be faint," their "heart[s] shall melt," they will be filled with "pangs and sorrows," and their faces will be "as flames." During these terrible events we will be protected by God and we shall not fear (13:22).

---

[8] *Teachings of the Prophet Joseph Smith,* 255; emphasis added; see also *Discourses of Wilford Woodruff,* 30.

*Isaiah 13:6–10*

> Howl ye; for the *day* of the <u>Lord</u> is at hand;
> *it* shall come as a destruction from the <u>Almighty</u>. (13:6)

> Therefore shall all *hands* be <u>faint</u>,
> every man's *heart* shall <u>melt</u>; (13:7)

> And *they* shall be <u>afraid</u>;
> <u>pangs and sorrows</u> shall take hold of *them;*[9]

> they shall be amazed one at another;
> their faces shall be as flames. (13:8)

> Behold, the day of the Lord cometh, cruel both with wrath and fierce anger,

> to lay the *land* <u>desolate</u>;
> and he shall <u>destroy the sinners</u> thereof out of *it*. (13:9)

> For the *stars* of heaven and the constellations thereof shall <u>not give their light</u>;
> the *sun* shall be <u>darkened</u> in his going forth,
> and the *moon* shall <u>not cause her light to shine</u>. (13:10)

## NOTES AND COMMENTARY

**13:6** *Howl ye.* This recurring expression of Isaiah (16:7; 23:1, 6, 14; 65:14) implies that the wicked (those who belong to Babylon) are like dogs[10] and wolves who howl while under distress. During this destruction, God's servants "shall sing for joy of heart," but the wicked "shall cry for sorrow of heart, and shall howl for vexation of spirit" (65:14). "O ye ought to begin to howl and mourn, because of the great destruction which at this time doth await you, except ye shall repent" (Hel. 9:22).

*day of the Lord.* This refers to our day, or the last days (2:12).

*at hand.* The phrase means "near" or "soon."

*destruction from the Almighty.* Christ will destroy the wicked when he comes again.

**13:7** *hands be faint/every man's heart shall melt.* The two idiomatic expressions here denote fear, as explained in the phrase "and they shall be afraid" (13:8; Josh. 2:11).

**13:8** *pangs and sorrows.* A *pang* is a sudden, sharp, and brief physical pain; it can also be emotional or spiritual, such as pangs of conscience. *Sorrow* usually denotes a long, deep, emotional distress. Hence the wicked who experience the day of the Lord will suffer both physical pain and emotional distress.

---

[9] 2 Ne. 23:8 omits the phrase *they shall be in pain as a woman that travaileth.*
[10] For dogs as symbols of wicked persons, see McConkie and Parry, *Guide to Scriptural Symbols,* 40.

*amazed one at another.* The New International Version reading is more descriptive: "They will look aghast at each other," because of the terrible happenings.

*faces shall be as flames.* In the immediate context, this speaks of the bright red shame and guilt that evil persons are experiencing. This may also speak of the Second Coming when the wicked will burn with fire. Meanwhile, the righteous will "shine forth in the kingdom of God" (Alma 40:25; D&C 115:5).

**13:9** *cruel both with wrath and fierce anger.* God is capable of *wrath* and *anger.* The day is a cruel day for those who are not prepared.

*land desolate.* The desolation of the land is a prominent theme in Isaiah (1:7; 6:11; 13:9; 49:19; 62:4) and is the result of the inhabitants' wickedness.

*destroy the sinners.* Jesus will destroy all corruptible things at his glorious coming, including the wicked.

**13:10** *stars/constellations/sun/moon/not give their light/darkened.* Isaiah lists some of the "signs and wonders" that will be "shown forth in the heavens above" (D&C 45:40) before the great day of the Second Coming. Many other prophets have prophesied of the same events, including Joseph Smith (D&C 34:9; 45:42; 88:87).[11]

## JUDGMENT ON BABYLON: THE WICKED ARE PUNISHED AT THE SECOND COMING (13:11-22)

The Medes identified in 13:17 indicate that this prophecy of Isaiah (13:11-22) was fulfilled when the Medes, under the leadership of "Darius the Median" (Dan. 5:31) and in alliance with the Persians led by Cyrus (Dan. 6:28), destroyed Babylon in approximately 539 B.C. The destruction of ancient Babylon served as a shadow of what will happen to the sinful inhabitants of the world during the judgments in the last days, for Babylon is a symbol of the world (D&C 1:16). The wicked will flee destructions with fear, only to find destruction in their own country; their young men and women and children will suffer terrible deaths at the hands of others; and their homes and palaces will be made desolate, inhabited by frightful creatures—all within a short period of time.

*Isaiah 13:11-22*

> And I will punish the *world* for <u>evil</u>,
> and the *wicked* for their <u>iniquity</u>;

---

[11] *Teachings of the Prophet Joseph Smith,* 71.

I will cause the *arrogancy* of the proud to cease,
and will lay down the *haughtiness* of the terrible. (13:11)

I will make a *man* more precious than fine gold;
even a *man* than the golden wedge of Ophir. (13:12)

Therefore, I will *shake* the heavens,
and the earth shall *remove* out of her place,

in the *wrath* of the Lord of Hosts,
and in the day of his fierce *anger.* (13:13)

And [he][12] shall be as the [hunted *deer*],[13]
and as a *sheep* that no man taketh up;

and they shall *every man* turn to his own people,
and flee *every one* into his own land. (13:14)

*Every one* that [is proud] shall be thrust through;
yea, and *every one* that is joined [to the wicked][14] shall fall by the sword. (13:15)

*Their children* also shall be dashed to pieces before their eyes;
*their houses* shall be spoiled and their *wives* ravished. (13:16)

Behold, I will stir up the Medes against them,
which shall not regard silver and gold,
nor shall they delight in it. (13:17)

*Their bows shall also dash* the young men to pieces,
and *they shall have no pity* on the fruit of the womb;
*their eyes shall not spare* children. (13:18)

And Babylon, the *glory* of kingdoms,
the *beauty* of the Chaldees' excellency,

shall be as when God overthrew Sodom and Gomorrah. (13:19)

*It shall* never be inhabited,
neither *shall it* be dwelt in from generation to generation:

neither shall the *Arabian* pitch tent there;
neither shall the *shepherds* make their fold there. (13:20)

But *wild beasts* of the desert shall lie there;
and their houses shall be full of *doleful creatures;*

and *owls* shall dwell there,
and [he-goats][15] shall dance there. (13:21)

And the *wild beasts* of the islands shall cry in their desolate houses,
and [jackals][16] in their pleasant palaces;

and *her time* is near to come,

---

[12] Hebrew *hayah* can read *it* or *he.* The latter fits the context better, speaking of the wicked.

[13] Hebrew *mudach,* "hunted." Brown, Driver, and Briggs, *Hebrew and English Lexicon,* 623, and Hebrew *tsᵉbiy.* Brown, Driver, and Briggs, *Hebrew and English Lexicon,* 840.

[14] The bracketed expressions in this verse are from JST Isa. 13:15 and 2 Ne. 23:15 and clarify the meaning of the verse.

[15] Hebrew *sᵉ'iyriym.* Brown, Driver, and Briggs, *Hebrew and English Lexicon,* 972.

[16] Hebrew *taniym.* Brown, Driver, and Briggs, *Hebrew and English Lexicon,* 1072.

and *her [day]*[17] shall <u>not be prolonged</u>.

[For I will destroy her speedily;
yea, for I will be merciful unto my people, but the wicked shall perish].[18] (13:22)

## NOTES AND COMMENTARY

**13:11** *I will punish the world for evil/wicked for their iniquity.* The *world* is synonymous with wickedness (John 1:10–11; 15:18–19; JS–M 1:4). God is the agent of the destruction mentioned here, the wicked are the recipients of the destruction, and iniquity is the cause of the judgments.

*arrogancy of the proud/haughtiness of the terrible.* Arrogancy, haughtiness, and pride are often connected in the scriptures (2:11; 16:6; 1 Sam. 2:3; Prov. 8:13; Jer. 48:29). President Ezra Taft Benson taught that "pride is characterized by 'What do I want out of life?' rather than by 'What would God have me do with my life?' It is self-will as opposed to God's will. It is the fear of man over the fear of God."[19] The *terrible* are those who are ruthless or tyrannical in dealing with others.

**13:12** *man more precious than fine gold/golden wedge of Ophir.* *Fine* gold (2 Chr. 3:8; Lam. 4:2) is a grade of a higher quality than metal simply referred to as *gold,* and the gold of Ophir (1 Kgs. 9:28; 22:48; Job 28:16) was prized in the ancient Near East because it was a grade of gold of the highest quality. The statement here that man will be *more precious than fine gold* calls to mind two things: a great number of people will be slaughtered during the destructions identified in this section, so that those who remain on the earth will be more scarce than a precious metal like gold; and those who remain after the decreed desolations and survive the furnace of affliction will be purified like gold; they will no longer possess dross (sin).

**13:13** *shake the heavens/earth shall remove out of her place.* This prophecy, first recorded in Isaiah's writings, has since been repeated by many prophets and placed in the context of Christ's second coming (Joel 3:16; D&C 43:18; 45:48; 49:23; 84:118; Moses 7:61).[20] Both Haggai (Hag. 2:6–8, 21–23) and Paul (Heb. 12:26–29) explained this prophecy.

*wrath of the Lord of Hosts/day of his fierce anger.* *Wrath* and *fierce anger* are terms found in 13:9 (66:15; 2 Thes. 1:8; D&C 29:12; 133:41). It was God's fierce anger that caused the destruction of the people during Noah's time (Moses 7:34).

**13:14** *as the hunted deer/as a sheep that no man taketh up.* Isaiah compares a wicked person during the judgments of the last days to deer and sheep. A hunted deer

[17] 2 Ne. 23:22 reads *day* rather than the KJV *days.*
[18] The entire phrase represents an addition to the text from both JST Isa. 13:22 and 2 Ne. 23:22.
[19] "Cleansing the Inner Vessel," 6–7.
[20] *Teachings of the Prophet Joseph Smith,* 29.

is endangered when hunters are present, and sheep are endangered when shepherds are absent. The imagery implies that the wicked will be like a hunted deer; they will flee for their lives during this time (there will be wars—Matt. 24:6), and they will be like unprotected sheep, meaning those who have not accepted Jesus as their shepherd may not receive his protection.

*every man turn to his own people/flee every one into his own land.* During God's judgments, the wicked will flee (because of fear; Jer. 50:16) to their lands and homes in Babylon (meaning the world), perhaps looking for safety among their own political and economic institutions. The righteous will flee from Babylon and its carnal preoccupations to Zion and its temples (spiritual concerns; Jer. 50:28; D&C 133:12–13). The Israelite exodus from Egypt under Moses' direction and the Lehite exodus from Jerusalem under Lehi's direction serve as examples of people who flee from the world (1 Ne. 3:18) under direction of living prophets to promised lands and the Lord's temple.

**13:15** *wicked shall fall by the sword.* The *sword* represents war and its instruments (2 Ne. 1:18; 3 Ne. 2:19; D&C 45:33). In the last days, the wicked will destroy themselves during the many wars and battles of which the prophets have testified.

**13:16** *children . . . dashed to pieces before their eyes/houses . . . spoiled/wives ravished.* The symbolic hunted deer and shepherdless sheep will be pursued (13:14) and destroyed by the sword (13:15), and their children and wives will find no mercy from the destructive armies. The murder of children and the ravishing of wives is not new to history but represents here both an increase of the hideous crimes against nature and man's savage inclination. Meanwhile, righteous men, with their wives and children gathered around them, will reside in "a land of peace, a city of refuge, a place of safety for the saints of the Most High God. . . . And it shall come to pass among the wicked, that every man that will not take his sword against his neighbor must needs flee unto Zion for safety . . . and it shall be the only people that shall not be at war one with another" (D&C 45:66–69).

**13:17** *stir up the Medes against them, which shall not regard silver and gold.* God used Assyria as a rod to destroy many ancient Near East peoples; now he uses the wickedness of the Medes to kill each other (the Medes were located in the mountainous region north and east of Babylon). God is in control of history at every stage, in every moment, and he knows the beginning from the end.

Historically, the Medes, having formed an alliance with the Persians under Cyrus the Great's leadership, conquered the great Babylonian empire by damming the Euphrates River, marching through its riverbed, going under the city walls, and subsequently capturing Babylon. This event took place more than one hundred sixty years after Isaiah's prophecy. The phrase *shall not regard silver and gold* indicates that the Medes did not go into battle to obtain plunder (silver and gold); instead, their motivation was to kill, and gain power and control. Perhaps ancient Media points forward to all nations of the last days who have the same wicked designs.

**13:18** *bows shall also dash the young men to pieces.* The archer's bow symbolizes war and its various instruments. Soldiers and warriors are merciless; they slay young men during the war. The Revised Standard Version translates the phrase: "their bows will slaughter the young men."

*no pity on the fruit of the womb.* The cruel and unfeeling soldiers will also slay *the fruit of the womb,* a common biblical idiom for children (Gen. 30:2; Deut. 7:13; Ps. 127:3). The phrase also suggests the slaying of pregnant women and their unborn children.

*eyes shall not spare children.* No one will be spared during the wars. Invading armies will look for even small children to murder so that future generations will not arise in rebellion to avenge their parents' deaths.

**13:19** *Babylon, the glory of kingdoms.* Babylon, with its riches, glorious gardens, magnificent temples, fortressed walls, and high towers, was famous in the ancient world. It was the most glorious of the world's kingdoms. As noted elsewhere, Babylon is a symbol of the world in the last days.

*beauty of the Chaldees' excellency.* *Chaldean* is often "used as a synonym for Babylonian"[21] (13:19; 47:1, 5; 48:14, 20). "The *Chaldeans* were a group of tribes in the lower delta of the twin rivers below the most southerly Babylonian cities"[22] who "had gained a leading position within Babylonia by the time of Isaiah; Merodach-baladan and Nebuchadrezzar were both Chaldeans. It was under Nebuchadrezzar (605–562 B.C.) that Babylonia reached its zenith of power, pomp and splendour, but his empire fell only a generation after his death."[23]

*shall be as when God overthrew Sodom and Gomorrah.* Sodom (Hebrew "bituminous area") and *Gomorrah* (Hebrew "ruined heap"), two biblical cities that were destroyed when God rained fire and brimstone upon them (Gen. 19:24–25), are typical of any wicked city that will be destroyed by God's judgments (Matt. 10:15; Rom. 9:29). According to Jude, Sodom and Gomorrah are "set forth for an example" of God's divine judgment on all those who are evil (Jude 1:7). In the centuries following

---

[21] *New Bible Dictionary,* 203.
[22] Watts, *Isaiah 1–33,* 199.
[23] *New Layman's Bible Commentary,* 781.

Isaiah's prophecy, Babylon was sacked and destroyed by a number of invading armies and became a heap of ruins. Similarly, the world's great cities will be destroyed at Christ's coming.

**13:20** *shall never be inhabited.* Just as Sodom and Gomorrah became desolate and uninhabited, so will Babylon never be inhabited again.

*from generation to generation.* This idiomatic expression refers generally to a lengthy period of time (34:10; 51:8; Ex. 17:16; Lam. 5:19). Contrary to the wicked who will be removed from Babylon and will not inhabit it *from generation to generation,* the righteous will be planted, well-rooted, and "shall grow up on the land of Zion, to possess it *from generation to generation,* forever and ever" (D&C 69:8; emphasis added).

*neither shall the Arabian pitch tent there/shepherds make their fold there.* So desolate will Babylon be after its destruction that even visitors will not set up camp among its ruins.

**13:21** *wild beasts/doleful creatures/owls/he-goats/jackals.* Isaiah identifies creatures of the night that are ritually impure and are not domesticated. Such creatures will inhabit desolate Babylon (34:13–14; Jer. 50:39), even taking over the abandoned houses. John the Revelator wrote that "Babylon the great is fallen, is fallen, and is become the habitation of devils, and the hold of every foul spirit, and a cage of every unclean and hateful bird" (Rev. 18:2).

**13:22** *palaces.* The fact that palaces will be inhabited by creatures indicates that even wealthy, upper-class groups will not be exempt from God's destructions and judgments.

*her time is near to come . . . for I will destroy her speedily.* Babylon, referred to here, was first destroyed by the Assyrians in 689 B.C. After Babylon's leaders rebuilt her, Cyrus marched against the city in 539 B.C., and Darius Hystapes finally destroyed Babylon in 518 B.C. Similarly, the Second Coming is near at hand; Babylon (the world) will possess worldly honor for only a moment and will then be quickly destroyed.

*I will be merciful unto my people.* While the wicked are experiencing pangs and sorrows, death and destruction, God will give the righteous mercy and peace.

*the wicked shall perish.* The prophets' words have always been that the wicked "*shall perish;* and they perish because they cast out the prophets, and the saints, and stone them, and slay them" (2 Ne. 26:3; Ps. 37:20; 68:2; Prov. 11:10; 2 Ne. 13:11).

# ISAIAH 14

*LIKENING ISAIAH 14 UNTO OURSELVES*

*Isaiah's prophecy that we (Israel) will be gathered to our lands of promise is now being fulfilled as we become members of the Church, build temples, and accept God's covenants; the prophecy has direct application to us (14:1–3).*

*Much of Isaiah 14 pertains to Lucifer, his evil plans for humanity, and his attempt to gain control from God. Today, as in days of old, Lucifer is persuading us to commit sins so that he may drag us down to hell.*

*Isaiah 14:24–27 provides us comfort in the knowledge that God controls the destiny of all the nations of the earth; he controlled humanity's affairs in the past, he directs the present, and he commands the future. Knowing of his power over the nations enables us to trust him and the prophets who speak his words.*

## ISRAEL WILL BE GATHERED, CHOSEN OF GOD, AND REST FROM SORROW (14:1–3)

Following a lengthy prophecy concerning Babylon's fall (13:11–22), Isaiah extends hope to us (the house of Israel) that we will be gathered to our promised lands and eventually rest from sorrow. Certainly our (Israel's) return to our covenantal lands is a prominent sign of the times. After we have gathered to our promised lands, we will eventually "exercise dominion domestically (*menservants and maidservants*), militarily (*take . . . captives*), and politically (*rule over/*'dominate')" (14:2).[1] We who follow Christ and make his atonement effective in our lives will, in the end, rest from sorrow, fear, and hard bondage (14:3).

---

[1] Motyer, *Prophecy of Isaiah*, 142.

Cyrus's invitation (Ezra 1:1–4) for the Jews to return to Israel to rebuild the city and temple is but a small shadow of things to come in our own day, for we will also build temples unto the Lord.

## Isaiah 14:1–3

For the Lord will *have mercy on* Jacob,
and will yet *choose* Israel,

and set them in their own land;

and the [*foreigners*][2] shall be joined with them,
and *they* shall cleave to the house of Jacob. (14:1)

And the people shall *take them and bring them* to their place;
[yea, from far unto the ends of the earth; and *they shall return* to their lands of promise.][3]

And the *house of Israel* shall possess them,
and the *land of the Lord* shall be for servants and handmaids;

and *they shall take them captives* unto whom they were captives;
and *they shall rule over* their oppressors. (14:2)

And it shall come to pass in [that][4] day that the Lord shall give thee rest from thy sorrow, and from thy fear, and from the hard bondage wherein thou wast made to serve. (14:3)

## NOTES AND COMMENTARY

**14:1** *mercy on Jacob.* The Lord promises mercy to members of the house of Israel, which includes the Saints of the latter days. Jehovah also used the term *mercy* when he brought Israel out of Egypt (Ex. 34:6; Deut. 4:31; Ps. 78:38; Joel 2:13).

*choose Israel.* Isaiah repeatedly declares that Jehovah has chosen the Israelites (including all who come unto Christ by covenant and obedience) to be his people (44:1–2; 49:7). Christ said to the house of Israel, "You only have I known of all the families of the earth" (Amos 3:2).

*their own land.* Israel and America are the lands belonging to the house of Israel (14:2 below). The possession of land recalls the Abrahamic covenant.

*foreigners shall be joined with them/cleave to the house of Jacob.* In ancient Israel, foreigners enjoyed a special status (Deut. 14:21, 29; 16:11). The verbs *joined* and *cleave,* which indicate more than a temporary, earthly union, may refer to the non-Israelites (45:14–25; 60) who, in the latter days, will flee to "Zion for safety"

---

[2]The KJV reads *strangers.* The Hebrew reads *nilevah,* and "foreigners" is a better translation.
[3]This lengthy addition is from JST Isa. 14:2 and 2 Ne. 24:2.
[4]This addition is from JST Isa. 14:3 and 2 Ne. 24:3.

(D&C 45:68). Elsewhere Isaiah prophesies that the foreigners and their kings will join Israel or Zion and serve her (60:1–14).

**14:2** *people shall take them . . . to their place.* The Gentiles will help members of the house of Israel return to their lands of promise (1 Ne. 22:6–8; 2 Ne. 10:9).

*from far unto the ends of the earth.* Inasmuch as the members of the house of Israel have been scattered throughout the centuries to every nation and country of the world (11:12), they will gather from the *ends of the earth* to their lands of promise.

*they shall return to their lands of promise.* America and the Holy Land are Israel's lands of promise and are prepared by God (1 Ne. 2:20; Ether 13:2). Each of the two promised lands is "the place for the city of Zion" (D&C 57:2), a place for the temple of the Lord (D&C 124:38), a place of refuge against the forces of the world (2 Ne. 1:3–5), and each stands as an antithesis to the place of "bondage and captivity" (Alma 36:28). Symbolically, these lands are a type and shadow of heaven, which is "a far better land of promise" (Alma 37:45). If the inhabitants of the land are wicked, they will be swept off (Ether 2:8–9), an occurrence that is well attested in history for both lands of promise.

*land of the Lord.* The lands of promise belong to the Lord.

*take them captives unto whom they were captives.* Those who oppressed members of the house of Israel will become their captives. The verse should not be taken literally; instead it likely signifies that the house of Israel will be eternal rulers in God's kingdom.

**14:3** *in that day.* This means the day of the Lord (13:6, 9, 13) and refers to God's judgments on the nations and Jesus' second coming (2:12).

*Lord shall give thee rest from thy sorrow, . . . fear, and . . . hard bondage.* Temporal rest from fear and hard bondage came to the house of Israel under the leadership of King David (David received "rest round about from all his enemies," 2 Sam. 7:1) and King Solomon (1 Kgs. 8:56), both of whom were types and shadows of the King of kings, Jesus Christ, who will give the house of Israel eternal rest. The expression *hard bondage* recalls the time the Israelites spent in Egypt as slaves of the Egyptian taskmasters.

## FALL OF THE KING OF BABYLON (14:4–11)

Isaiah 14 contains two parallel texts that should be closely compared and contrasted. The first text speaks of the king of Babylon (14:4–11); the second deals with Lucifer (14:12–20). The rule of the king of Babylon reminds us of Lucifer's reign, and Lucifer's wicked desires remind us of those of the Babylonian king. Although the King and Lucifer are separate individuals, they share similar characteristics—they both are evil, they have both ruled with horror and destruction, both have weakened the nations with their evil ways, and both will eventually be sent down to hell. The fall of ancient Babylon's king recalls Lucifer's fall from heaven and anticipates a future time when Lucifer will be cast down, bound in hell, and become powerless. Isaiah 14:4–11 speaks of an unnamed king of Babylon who served Lucifer and became like him; 14:12–20 refers to Lucifer, *the* king of Babylon—worldliness and sin.

The demise of the king of Babylon is accompanied by the destruction of the wicked with their golden city Babylon—a perfect example of an evil place. It is through God's power that the king, his followers, and their city are destroyed. Although the inhabitants of the earth suffered during the king's evil reign, all God's creations sing and rejoice when their tormentor is exiled and sent to hell. Meanwhile, former kings and rulers will say to the fallen king of Babylon, "You are now as weak as we are, lacking power and pomp and worldly glory, and similar to us, the maggots and worms destroy your body" (14:11). This prophecy will have a dual fulfillment, first with the destruction of ancient Babylon, and then with the destruction of the wicked world at the second coming of Christ.

The Hebrew *sheol,* translated as "hell" in 14:9 and as "grave" in 14:11, refers to the world of spirits.[5] Isaiah 14:9–11 provides several insights about the world of the spirits: it is perceived (perhaps symbolically) to be a place that is physically lower than heaven or earth (14:9; 5:14); there is life after death there (14:9–10); there individuals are recognized (14:10); it is a place where kings, rulers, and others go (14:9); verbal communication exists there (14:10); it is where many of the dead become weak (14:10), perhaps because their spirits have been separated from their bodies (14:11) but also because they cannot rely on their earthly wealth and glory; and it is where mankind's pomp (14:11) and earthly glory end (5:14).

*Isaiah 14:4–11*

[And it shall come to pass in that day,][6] that thou shalt take up this proverb against the king of Babylon, and say:

How hath the *oppressor* ceased,
the *golden city* ceased! (14:4)

---

[5] *History of the Church,* 5:425.
[6] This addition is from JST Isa. 14:4 and 2 Ne. 24:4.

The Lord hath broken the *staff* of the <u>wicked</u>,
the *scepters* of the <u>rulers</u>. (14:5)

*He who smote the people* <u>in wrath with [unceasing blows]</u>,[7]
*he that ruled the nations* <u>in anger [with relentless aggression]</u>[8] (14:6)

*The whole earth* is <u>at rest, and is quiet</u>;
*they* <u>break forth into singing</u>. (14:7)

Yea, the *fir-trees* <u>rejoice</u> at thee,
<u>and [also]</u>[9] the *cedars of Lebanon,* saying:

Since thou art laid down no [woodsman][10] is come up against us. (14:8)

*Hell from beneath* <u>is moved</u> for thee to meet thee at thy coming;
<u>it stirreth up</u> *the dead* for thee,

even all the *chief ones of the earth;*
it hath raised up from their thrones *all the kings of the nations.* (14:9)

All they shall speak and say unto thee:

*Art thou* also <u>become weak as we</u>?
*Art thou* <u>become like unto us</u>? (14:10)

Thy *pomp* is <u>brought down to the grave</u>;
the *noise of thy viols* is <u>not heard</u>;

the *worm* is <u>spread under thee</u>,
and the *worms* <u>cover thee</u>. (14:11)

## NOTES AND COMMENTARY

**14:4** *in that day.* Refers to our day, or the last days (2:12).

*proverb against the king of Babylon.* A proverb is "an object-lesson from which others may learn appropriate lessons."[11] Here the king of Babylon is the object lesson from whom all of us may learn (Ezek. 16:44; Hab. 2:6).

*oppressor ceased/golden city ceased.* Egypt was once the oppressor of Israel, God's chosen people (Ex. 3:7; 5:2), but the oppressor mentioned here is Babylon (the world) and her king (Satan). Babylon is the *golden city,* "that great city that was clothed in fine linen, and purple, and scarlet, and decked with *gold* and precious stones, and pearls" (Rev. 18:16; emphasis added). Babylon attempts to imitate, in its wicked and corruptible manner, the true city of God, with its streets of "pure *gold* as it were transparent glass" (Rev. 21:21; emphasis added). The golden city will cease to exist because God will destroy it, as prophets have revealed.

---

[7] The translation is from Motyer, *Prophecy of Isaiah,* 143.
[8] From NIV Isa.
[9] JST Isa. 14:8 and 2 Ne. 24:8.
[10] KJV has the archaic *feller.*
[11] *New Bible Dictionary,* s.v. "proverb."

**14:5** *broken the staff of the wicked/scepters of the rulers.* Kingship in its true and divine sense belongs to God, but very early in the history of the world, the wicked gained power from Satan, the king of hell and the prince of the world. When Jesus, the King of kings (Rev. 19:16), comes in clouds of glory at the Second Coming, he will judge those who have possessed the staff and the scepters, and he will reign with glory and truth.

**14:6** *He who smote the people in wrath with unceasing blows.* Babylon's king was cruel and murderous; also Satan and his followers apparently do not sleep or rest, but they continuously attack and strike out at mortals with unceasing blows.

*that ruled the nations in anger with relentless aggression.* The king of Babylon's (as well as Satan's) very essence is anger, aggression, and the desire to rule (14:13–14).

**14:7** *whole earth is at rest, and is quiet.* The earth will rest and become quiet once the king of Babylon, or Satan, is cast down to hell (14:7–8). Enoch asked the Lord, "When shall the earth rest?" (Moses 7:58), to which the Lord responded, "for the space of a thousand years the earth shall rest" (Moses 7:64), referring to the Millennium, when Satan is bound and powerless.

**14:7–8** *fir-trees/cedars of Lebanon/rejoice at thee.* The verse recalls other scriptures in which God's creations (the trees, forest, mountains, earth, and heavens) "break forth into singing" when the Lord redeems Jacob (44:23), comforts his people, and has mercy on the afflicted (49:13; D&C 128:22). The trees, representative of people (Judg. 9:15; Ezek. 31:8; Hosea 14:8; Zech. 11:2), now rejoice and sing because Satan has been cast down to hell.

*no woodsman is come up against us.* This implies that the king of Babylon had cut down some of the trees, or murdered the people. Thus the king was seeking to become like God, who has authority to end life. We recall also that Jehovah is the great forester identified in 10:33–34, and hence the king of Babylon attempts to imitate God's ability to cut down nations and peoples. Yet, as J. Alec Motyer observes, "With exact justice the arrogant woodsman [the king of Babylon] has 'had the chop!'"[12] Satan, similarly, attempts to make people suffer the second death.

**14:9** *Hell from beneath is moved for thee to meet thee at thy coming.* Those in hell know that the king of Babylon will imminently join them.

*it stirreth up the dead for thee.* The New International Version reading here is instructive; it says that hell "rouses the spirits of the departed to greet you—all those who were leaders in the world, it makes them rise from their thrones."

---

[12] Motyer, *Prophecy of Isaiah,* 143.

*chief ones of the earth/kings of the nations.* These will marvel that the mighty king of Babylon has been cut down and become like them (14:10).

**14:10** *Art thou also become weak as we?* During mortality the king of Babylon ruled with glory and power and possessed great wealth and importance. After death, while in the spirit prison, other spirits asked him, "Have you now become like us, without glory and wealth? Have you now become weak like us?"

**14:11** *Thy pomp is brought down to the grave.* The king's glory and worldly pomp no longer exist once his body is placed in the grave.

*worm is spread under thee, and the worms cover thee.* Although the king of Babylon may have enjoyed luxury and wealth during mortality, his dead body, like that of all the deceased, will lie in the dust, and worms will eat his flesh (Job 21:26). *Spread* or *cover* suggests a bed, since the king, who sat on his throne in temporal glory, now sleeps in a cold bed in hell; he leaves his pomp on earth, and his body becomes like that of all sinful people who preceded him.

## FALL OF LUCIFER (14:12–23)

Lucifer's statement (14:13–14) about his goals demonstrates his extreme self-centeredness. He begins all five lines with the personal pronoun *I*, which shows that he is interested in his own goals and in glorifying himself. Lucifer had a fivefold plan: He wanted to enter heaven (without following God's laws), to be greater than other souls, to become part of the assembly of gods, to be exalted above other authorities and powers, and to become like God himself (14:13–14). In contrast, God's Saints are taught to lose themselves in the service of others (Matt. 16:25; Luke 9:24) not by looking after self but by seeking out the widows, the poor, the fatherless, and those with spiritual and temporal needs.

Isaiah's treatment of the archdevil and enemy of all humanity, Lucifer, sets forth terms and phrases that on one hand demonstrate Lucifer's attempt to imitate God's exalted state, and on the other present Lucifer's true degradation. Note the language connected with Lucifer's attempts at exaltation: *ascend, heaven, exalt, above, stars, mount,* and *north* (14:13); and *ascend, above, heights, clouds,* and *Most High* (14:14). Contrast that with the language that deals with Lucifer's actual lowliness: *fallen, cut down, to the ground* (14:12); *brought down to hell, pit* (14:15); and *cast out of thy grave, go down, pit,* and *trodden under* (14:19).

The section has two applications: Lucifer's fall from heaven during the premortal existence, and the time when Lucifer will be cast down to hell, after the Millennium.

In the end, Babylon will be completely destroyed because it housed Lucifer and his followers (14:21–23).

## Isaiah 14:12–23

How *art thou* <u>fallen from heaven</u>, O Lucifer, son of the morning!
*Art thou* <u>cut down to the ground</u>, which did weaken the nations! (14:12)

For thou hast said in thy heart:

*I will ascend* <u>into heaven</u>,
*I will exalt my throne* <u>above the stars of God</u>;
*I will sit* also <u>upon the [mountain of the assembly of the gods]</u>[13] in the [farthest][14]
north; (14:13)
*I will ascend* <u>above the heights of the clouds</u>;
*I will be like* the <u>Most High</u>. (14:14)

Yet thou shalt be brought down to hell, to the [depth] of the pit. (14:15)

They that see thee shall [stare][15] at thee,
and [shall] consider thee, [and shall say:][16]

Is this the man that *made the earth* <u>to tremble</u>,
that <u>did shake</u> *kingdoms?* (14:16)

[And] made *the world* <u>as a wilderness</u>,
and <u>destroyed</u> *the cities thereof,* [and][17] opened not the house of his prisoners?
(14:17)

All the kings of the nations, [yea],[18] all of them, lie in glory, every one of them in
his own house. (14:18)

But thou art cast out of thy grave like an abominable branch, and [the remnant][19]
of those that are slain, thrust through with a sword, that go down to the stones of
the pit; as a carcase trodden under feet. (14:19)

Thou shalt not be joined with them in burial, because thou hast destroyed thy
land, and slain thy people: the seed of evildoers shall never be renowned. (14:20)

Prepare slaughter for his children for the [iniquities][20] of their fathers, that they do
not rise, nor possess the land, nor fill the face of the world with cities. (14:21)

For *I will rise up against them,* <u>saith the Lord of Hosts</u>,
and *cut off from Babylon the name, and remnant, and son, and nephew,* <u>saith the
Lord</u>. (14:22)

---

[13] Keil and Delitzsch, *Commentary,* 7:1:312, reads "assembly of gods." Brown, Driver, and Briggs, *Hebrew
and English Lexicon,* 417, has "assembly (of the gods)," and Watts, *Isaiah 1–33,* 207, reads "the mountain
where the gods assemble."
[14] Watts, *Isaiah 1–33,* 206. *Sides of the north* is an archaic way of saying *farthest.*
[15] *Stare* is Motyer's reading, *Prophecy of Isaiah,* 145.
[16] The changes in this line are from JST Isa. 14:16 and 2 Ne. 24:16.
[17] JST Isa. 14:17 and 2 Ne. 24:17 replace the KJV *that* with *and.*
[18] JST Isa. 14:18 and 2 Ne. 24:18 replace the KJV *even* with *yea.*
[19] JST Isa. 14:19 and 2 Ne. 24:19 read *the remnant* rather than the KJV *as the raiment.*
[20] 2 Ne. 24:21 reads the plural *iniquities* rather than *iniquity.*

*I will also make it* a <u>possession for the bittern</u>, and pools of water; and *I will* sweep *it* with the [broom][21] <u>of destruction</u>, saith the Lord of Hosts. (14:23)

## NOTES AND COMMENTARY

**14:12** *fallen from heaven/cut down to the ground.* The first phrase implies that Lucifer was a star that lost its heavenly prominence by falling (Rev. 8:10; 9:1; 2 Ne. 2:17). The second phrase suggests that Lucifer was a mighty tree that was *cut down* by God the forester (10:33–34). Both the star and the tree commonly symbolize an individual, and both show how Lucifer was once mighty.

*Lucifer.* "And was called Perdition, for the heavens wept over him—he was Lucifer, a son of the morning" (D&C 76:26).

The name Lucifer (Hebrew *helel*) means "shining one."[22] If the name is given different vowels (*helal*), it signifies the crescent of the moon, having a possible meaning that Lucifer had less light (symbolically) than the full moon, or Lucifer's light waned as does the light of the moon during its cycle. Further, Lucifer's light was far less than the light of Jesus Christ, whose light is the sun (Ps. 84:11; D&C 88:7–9). Isaiah may also be using a play on words, for Lucifer's name (*helel*) sounds like a word Isaiah uses in 13:6 where he commands those of Babylon to "Howl!" (Hebrew *helili*).

*son of the morning.* In Hebrew this means "son of the dawning light." Doctrine and Covenants 76:26 recalls Isaiah's words: "And was called Perdition, for the heavens wept over him—he was Lucifer, a son of the morning." The title *son of the morning* recalls the phrase *morning stars* (Job 38:7; D&C 128:23) and refers to eminent persons from the premortal existence. Christ, we recall, is the "bright and morning star" (Rev. 22:16) and the "morning star" (Rev. 2:28), the most eminent of all stars.

*which did weaken the nations.* Satan's work among the nations has brought dishonor, corruption, perversion, anarchy, immorality, exploitation, war, greed, and a myriad of other evils to every nation and people since the beginning: "And the children of men were numerous upon all the face of the land. And in those days Satan had great dominion among men, and raged in their hearts; and from thenceforth came wars and bloodshed; and a man's hand was against his own brother, in administering death" (Moses 6:15).

**14:13** *thou hast said in thy heart.* Lucifer was (and is) a self-centered individual who secretly makes his own plans without seeking God's assistance.

---

[21] Brown, Driver, and Briggs, *Hebrew and English Lexicon,* 370.
[22] Brown, Driver, and Briggs, *Hebrew and English Lexicon,* 237.

*I will ascend into heaven.* Although Lucifer was an eminent figure in the premortal world (14:12), he did not enjoy the status of God, who lived in heaven. Lucifer also said to God, "Give me thine honor, which is my power," which resulted in "a third part of the hosts of heaven turn[ing] away from [Christ] because of their agency" (D&C 29:36).

*I will exalt my throne above the stars of God.* Lucifer sins and errs because of his desires. First, he believes that he is able to exalt himself. Yet, the scriptures inform us that no one can become exalted without Jesus Christ and his atonement; Jesus is the way to heaven (John 14:6). Second, Lucifer speaks concerning his throne. Yet no one can possess a heavenly throne without overcoming the world and receiving God's permission and blessing. "To him that overcometh will I grant to sit with me in my throne, even as I also overcame, and am set down with my Father in his throne" (Rev. 3:21).

*The stars of God* refers to righteous people who belong to God (Job 38:7; D&C 128:23; Gen. 37:9). Satan wants to possess a throne that is higher than those of God's other children.

*I will sit also upon the mountain of the assembly of the gods in the farthest north.* The *mountain of the assembly of the gods* refers to the general assembly of the exalted where decisions have been made or are being made concerning the creation of the worlds and other eternal events. Lucifer desires to become part of the assembly, which would give him equal power and authority with the gods. The expression *farthest north* (Ps. 48:2) is an allusion to heaven, meaning a place far away from the habitations of humanity.

**14:14** *I will ascend above the heights of the clouds.* Lucifer wanted to dwell in heaven, which is *above the clouds,* but no soul is able to ascend into heaven without following the proper prescriptions set forth by God, including being baptized, receiving the Holy Ghost, and attaining a godly character. Lucifer, therefore, will never enter heaven. The irony here is that Lucifer received the opposite of his desire—instead of *ascending* into heaven, he fell, or was "cut down to the ground" (14:12).

*I will be like the Most High.* The title *Most High* indicates a vertical hierarchy: God is higher than all; he is the Most High. Lucifer desired to be like the Most High, but he has been cast down to hell (14:9, 11, 12, 15).

**14:15** *Yet thou shalt be brought down to hell, to the depth of the pit.* Similar language is used in 14:19 (Ps. 28:1; 38:18; 143:7), which says that Lucifer will be cast "to the stones of the pit." The *pit,* which is another term for hell, expresses hell's conditions; it is dark, narrow, restrictive, and extremely uncomfortable for its inhabitants.

Satan sought a high position in heaven (14:13–14); in response to Satan's machina-
tions, God, whose justice is exact and faultless, sent him to the place farthest from
heaven.

**14:16** *They that see thee shall stare at thee.* Hell's inhabitants will be amazed
that Lucifer, who shook kingdoms with his evil intent, has been brought down to the
depths.

*Is this the man that made the earth to tremble, that did shake kingdoms?* On seeing Lucifer in hell, the inquiry will come, Is this the man who caused such great dis-
turbances upon the earth ("made the earth to tremble, . . . destroyed the cities";
14:16–17), and now he is like "an abominable branch," like "a carcase" that others
trample on (14:19)? By calling him *man,* Isaiah emphasizes here that Lucifer is by no
means a god.

**14:17** *made the world as a wilderness.* The Lord's creative effort made the world
into a place that was called "good" (Gen. 1:10–31), but Lucifer's work had an opposite effect, for he *made the world as a wilderness.*

*destroyed the cities.* Lucifer is the destroyer; he destroys both cities and souls.

*opened not the house of his prisoners.* The New International Version reads that
Lucifer "would not let his captives go home," which is a possible reference to the fact
that Lucifer does not want his spiritual captives, or those bound by sin, to be released.
Lucifer's goal, of course, stands in direct opposition to Jesus Christ's righteous and
perfect desire, which is to release from sin all those who come unto him.

**14:18** *kings of the nations . . . lie in glory.* The kings who rule over the telestial
earth are buried in magnificent tombs decorated with marble. The once powerful
tyrant (king of Babylon or Lucifer) is not treated with honor but is cast away with
great disgrace.

**14:19** *cast out of thy grave like an abominable branch.* The grave of Nebuchadnezzar, Babylon's king, has never been discovered, and Lucifer will never have a
grave or a monument because he never received a body. The imagery of *cast out of
the grave* stands opposite Jesus and his tomb (53:9), where Jesus arose from the dead
and possessed "life in himself" (John 5:26); he used his own power to arise and exit
the tomb. Lucifer, the *abominable branch,* can be contrasted to the useful "Branch"
that will "grow out of" the roots of Jesse (11:1; D&C 113:1–2). John D. Watts, an
Isaiah scholar, summarizes this section of Isaiah by writing of Nebuchadnezzar: "The
body has not been buried, but abandoned like garbage (v. 19). He shares the fate of
the dead among the poorest people: like the *aborted fetus,* like *the clothes of one*

*stabbed* in a brawl, one killed in a *fall,* one *trampled* by a mob or on a battle-field, he is simply dumped in a pit and left to the birds and animals."[23]

*the remnant of those that are slain.* Isaiah's imagery here likens Lucifer to the corpse of one who was killed by the sword, the sword wounds visible on the body. According to the law of Moses, any individual who touches the corpse (representative here of Lucifer) becomes ritually unclean and impure (Num. 19:11). Those who remain unclean, having forsaken Christ and his atoning sacrifice, cannot enter the celestial temple, or heaven (Alma 11:37).

*that go down to the stones of the pit.* See commentary on 14:15.

*as a carcase trodden under feet.* Lucifer is likened to a carcass that has not received a proper burial; instead it has been left on the ground to be trampled by man or animals. This analogy is more meaningful when considered in light of Joseph Smith's words: "The place where a man is buried is sacred; . . . one of the greatest curses the ancient prophets could put on any man, was that he should go without a burial."[24]

**14:20** *Thou shalt not be joined with them in burial.* See commentary on 14:19. Lucifer, because of his destructive and murderous acts, will not join the "kings of the nations" (14:18) who receive monumental tombs. Lucifer, of course, never received a body and therefore will never be buried.

*thou hast destroyed thy land.* Lucifer's code has always been war and destruction against both humanity and nature.

*slain thy people.* Lucifer uses men as instruments by tempting them to murder their fellow beings; Lucifer also leads people "away unto destruction" (Matt. 10:28; Alma 36:14). In a sense, he slays their souls so they will suffer spiritual death.

*the seed of evildoers shall never be renowned.* Lucifer, or the king of Babylon, and others like them will not be honored or acclaimed in the eternities.

**14:21** *Prepare slaughter for his children for the iniquities of their fathers.* The children of evildoers will perish because they heeded their wicked fathers' sayings.

*that they do not rise, nor possess the land, nor fill the face of the world with cities.* The righteous will possess the lands of promise (14:1–2) and build cities of Zion for the pure in heart. The wicked, however, will not be blessed to inherit such cities of Zion.

**14:22** *I will rise up against them.* The Lord will destroy all things connected to Babylon.

[23] Watts, *Isaiah 1–33,* 211.
[24] *History of the Church,* 5:361.

*Lord of Hosts.* See commentary on 1:9.

*cut off from Babylon the name, and remnant, and son, and nephew.* The term *cut off* is the same as excommunication (Ex. 12:15, 19). Hence, those in Babylon who are cut off will be excommunicated from God and his saints, and they will not have any part of God's covenants. The reference to *son* and *nephew* here indicates that the line of inheritance will be cut off to make room for the new King Messiah to reign.

*saith the Lord.* Jehovah is the origin and authority of the revelation.

**14:23** *I will also make it a possession for the bittern, and pools of water.* Babylon's destruction will be so complete that bittern (variously translated as owl, hedgehog, and waterfowl) will inhabit it, and "there will be no regular irrigation or cultivation of the soil, and the place will become a swamp."[25]

*I will sweep it with the broom of destruction.* Just as one sweeps his or her house to eliminate dust and dirt, so will God sweep Babylon of her foul matter so that none remains.

## GOD IS IN CONTROL OF ALL NATIONS (14:24–27)

The Lord's plans, designs, and purposes will come to pass according to his desires. This fact is emphasized here twice—first in the words of the Lord: "Surely as I have thought, so shall it come to pass; and as I have purposed, so shall it stand" (14:24), and again in Isaiah's explanation of the Lord's power to carry out his plans: "For the Lord of hosts hath purposed, and who shall disannul it? and his hand is stretched out, and who shall turn it back?" (14:27). God has always been in control of humanity's affairs; he is in charge of the present, and he holds the future in his hands. The Assyrians, for instance, were in God's control. They served his purposes by smiting the wayward Israelites, but then God in turn destroyed the Assyrians.

*Isaiah 14:24–27*

The Lord of Hosts hath sworn, saying:

Surely as *I have thought,* <u>so shall it come to pass;</u>
and as *I have purposed,* <u>so shall it stand</u>—(14:24)

That I will bring the Assyrian in my land, and upon my mountains tread him under foot;

then shall *his yoke* <u>depart from off them,</u>
and *his burden* <u>depart from off their shoulders.</u> (14:25)

---

[25] Kissane, *Book of Isaiah,* 1:174.

*This is the purpose that is purposed <u>upon the whole earth</u>;*
and *this is the hand that is stretched out <u>upon all nations</u>.* (14:26)

For the *Lord of Hosts hath purposed,* and <u>who shall disannul</u>?
And *his hand is stretched out,* and <u>who shall turn it back</u>? (14:27)

## NOTES AND COMMENTARY

**14:24** *Lord of Hosts hath sworn, saying.* The Lord makes a promise to his children that his word will be fulfilled. Elsewhere the Lord has said, "Though the heavens and the earth pass away, my word shall not pass away, but shall all be fulfilled" (D&C 1:38). See commentary on 45:23.

*Surely as I have thought, so shall it come to pass.* Unlike the plans or goals of the Assyrian king (10:5–11), the Syrian king (7:5–7), or others (29:8, 15; 30:1), the Lord's purposes are certain and will be fulfilled exactly as he plans them.

**14:25** *I will bring the Assyrian in my land.* The fulfillment of this prophecy is chronicled in Isaiah 36 when the Assyrians enter Palestine.

*upon my mountains tread him under foot.* God's mountains are the Judean mountains in Palestine, the hill country that extends north and south some thirty-five miles and is approximately fifteen miles wide. After the Assyrians have fulfilled the Lord's purposes, he will trample on them as if they were dust.

*then shall his yoke depart from off them.* This phrase recalls 10:27, wherein the Lord promises the Israelites that the Assyrian "yoke shall be destroyed." The Assyrian burden was removed from Israel a few years after the prophecy was given. Symbolically, the yoke of Assyria (the world) is removed from covenant Israel as they accept Jesus Christ and forsake their sins.

**14:26** *purpose that is purposed upon the whole earth.* This is the Lord's decision and it will certainly come to pass.

*hand that is stretched out upon all nations.* Assyria wanted to conquer all nations (10:14), but the Lord's purposes are greater. He is in control of all nations and has power over all the earth.

**14:27** *the Lord of Hosts hath purposed, and who shall disannul.* When God devises a divine plan, no being has the power to obstruct or hinder.

## JUDGMENT AGAINST THE PHILISTINES (14:28–32)

This revelation given to Isaiah is yet another prophecy directed to one of the world's kingdoms. It shows that the Lord's prophets do not serve the house of Israel alone. The Philistines are warned against rejoicing over the temporary defeat of the

Assyrian forces because Assyria eventually regroups, wars against Philistia, and destroys her. Meanwhile, the Lord has established Zion, and all who wish to become a part of her will find rest and peace.

### Isaiah 14:28–32

In the year that king Ahaz died was this burden. (14:28)

Rejoice not thou, whole Palestina, because the rod of him that smote thee is broken;

for out of the *serpent's root* shall come forth a <u>cockatrice</u>, and *his fruit* shall be a fiery <u>flying serpent</u>. (14:29)

And the *first-born of the poor* <u>shall feed</u>, and the *needy* <u>shall lie down in safety</u>;

and I *will kill* <u>thy root</u> with famine, and [I]²⁶ *shall slay* <u>thy remnant</u>. (14:30)

*Howl,* <u>O gate</u>; *cry,* <u>O city</u>;

thou, whole Palestina, art dissolved; for there shall come from the north a smoke, and none shall be alone in his appointed times. (14:31)

What shall then answer the messengers of the nations? That the Lord hath founded Zion, and the poor of his people shall trust in it. (14:32)

### NOTES AND COMMENTARY

**14:28** *In the year that king Ahaz died.* Isaiah dated an earlier vision by the death of King Uzziah (6:1). The date of Ahaz's death was probably between 740 and 714 B.C.

*burden.* This is a prophecy of desolation and destruction on a wicked nation.

**14:29** *Rejoice not thou, whole Palestina, because the rod of him that smote thee is broken.* Palestine, or Philistia, which consists of five kingdoms—Gaza, Ekron, Gath, Ashdod, and Ashkalon—is warned not to celebrate Assyria's (the "serpent's") lost power, because the Assyrians will regain their strength (the serpent's seed will produce a cockatrice, another poisonous serpent) and once again smite the Philistines.

*his fruit shall be a fiery flying serpent.* Isaiah again uses imagery to describe how the poisonous snake (Assyria) will produce offspring that will war against the Philistines. The serpent is called fiery probably because of its terrible burning venom; it is called flying probably because of the speed with which it strikes (30:6; Num. 21:6).

---

²⁶DSS Isa. Scroll restores the correct pronoun (*I* instead of *he*) to the Hebrew Bible.

**14:30** *first-born of the poor shall feed.* Those who are humble and who suffer (the poor and needy) will join Zion, which was founded by Jehovah (14:32). The New International Version suggests that the *first-born of the poor* are the poorest of the poor.

*I will kill thy root with famine.* God will create a famine in Philistia, or Palestine, that will destroy its remaining inhabitants after the wars with Assyria have ended. The *root* may refer to the Philistines who are yet producing children, those who are about to bring forth another generation.

**14:31** *Howl, O gate/cry, O city.* The inhabitants of all Philistine cities will wail and moan once the Assyrians begin their destructive advances.

*come from the north a smoke.* *Smoke* represents the burning cities the Assyrians destroyed by fire as they advanced southward toward Philistia.

*none shall be alone in his appointed times.* The Jerusalem Bible reads "there are no deserters in those battalions," which means that all enlisted men who belong to the Assyrian army are mighty warriors; there are no cowards or deserters among them.

**14:32** *What shall then answer the messengers of the nations?* When envoys from various nations ask how they may be saved from Assyria's destructive forces, they will find comfort in knowing that "the Lord hath founded Zion" (2 Ne. 24:32).

*Lord hath founded Zion.* The Lord himself has established a place for the pure in heart to dwell. Indeed he is the very foundation of it; he is our "safe foundation" and our "sure foundation" (Jacob 4:15, 17; Hel. 5:12).

*poor of his people shall trust in it.* The poor will find both temporal and spiritual salvation in Zion.

# ISAIAH 15

*LIKENING ISAIAH 15 UNTO OURSELVES*

*Moab's inhabitants were enemies of Israel and constantly warred against them (Num. 22–25; Judg. 3:12–30). As such, they serve as a type and a shadow of the wicked today who are Zion's enemies. Also, as ancient Moab was "laid waste" and her inhabitants were "brought to silence," so will the wicked of our day be destroyed at the Lord's coming.*

## A PROPHECY OF JUDGMENT AGAINST MOAB (15:1–9)

Moab, which was named after the firstborn son of Lot's eldest daughter (Gen. 19:37), was the nation that bordered the Dead Sea on the east. The prophet warns the Moabites that they will be destroyed, despite the fact that they are prosperous in trading and commerce. The listing of sixteen cities and places in this section, which are located in both the northern and southern regions of Moab, indicates that all of Moab will be affected by the devastation.

Moabites will mourn and lament their destruction. They will mourn by weeping, howling, shaving their heads, cutting off their beards (15:2), girding with sackcloth, howling on housetops and in the streets (15:3), and crying out to the point that the voice is heard from distant places ("even unto Jahaz"); even "soldiers of Moab shall cry out" (15:4).

*Isaiah 15:1–9*

> The burden of Moab.
>
> Because *in the night Ar of Moab is laid waste,* and *brought to silence*;
> because *in the night Kir of Moab is laid waste,* and *brought to silence*; (15:1)

He is gone up to Bajith, and to Dibon, the high places, to *weep*:
Moab shall *howl* over Nebo, and over Medeba:

on *all their heads* shall be baldness,
and *every beard* cut off. (15:2)

*In their streets* they shall gird themselves with sackcloth:
*on the tops of their houses, and in their streets,* every one shall howl, weeping
abundantly. (15:3)

And *Heshbon* shall cry, and *Elealeh:*
*their voice* shall be heard even unto Jahaz:

therefore the *armed soldiers* of Moab shall cry out;
*his life* shall be grievous unto him. (15:4)

My heart shall cry out for Moab; his fugitives shall flee unto Zoar, an heifer of
three years old:

*for by the mounting up of Luhith* with weeping shall they go it up;
*for in the way of Horonaim* they shall raise up a cry of destruction. (15:5)

For the *waters of Nimrim shall be desolate:* for the hay is withered away,
the grass faileth, *there is no green thing.* (15:6)

Therefore the *abundance* they have gotten,
and *that* which they have laid up,

shall they carry away to the brook of the willows. (15:7)

For the *cry* is gone round about the borders of Moab;
the *howling* thereof unto Eglaim,
and the *howling* thereof unto Beer-elim. (15:8)

For the waters of Dimon shall be full of blood:
for I will bring more upon Dimon,

lions upon him that escapeth of Moab,
and upon the remnant of the land. (15:9)

## NOTES AND COMMENTARY

**15:1** *burden of Moab.* This refers to a prophecy of destruction upon a wicked
people.

*in the night Ar of Moab/Kir of Moab is laid waste, and brought to silence.* Ar and
Kir are two cities of Moab that will be destroyed. The phrase *in the night* may mean
that Moab's cities will be destroyed with such great force and speed, it will be as if
the destruction took place without warning in a single night. The expression *brought
to silence* indicates that the devastation was so complete that no inhabitants remained
in the cities, meaning no conversations among adults, no children playing in the
streets, and no bustling noise in the marketplaces.

**15:2** *He is gone up to Bajith, and to Dibon, the high places, to weep.* The inhabitants of Moab go to their temples (Hebrew *Byth,* "temple") and high places to mourn and lament because of the destruction.

*Moab shall howl over Nebo, and over Medeba.* The nation will also mourn for the destruction of Nebo and Medeba, two of Moab's notable cities.

*on all their heads shall be baldness/every beard cut off.* It was customary for males to demonstrate their sorrow by shaving their heads and beards (22:12; Micah 1:16). The once proud inhabitants of Moab are now reduced to humility and shame.

**15:3** *In their streets/on the tops of their houses.* In the ancient Middle East, extreme mourning was done in public places so that all could see.

*they shall gird themselves with sackcloth.* Mourning (2 Sam. 3:31) was often accompanied by rending the garments, weeping, fasting, praying, and sitting in ashes and wearing sackcloth.

*every one shall howl.* Every citizen has been affected by the destruction, and perhaps all have lost a loved one in the destruction.

*weeping abundantly.* This expression shows the deep anguish the people felt.

*Heshbon shall cry, and Elealeh/Jahaz.* These are cities in Moab's north region. The phrase *even unto Jahaz* indicates that the people who dwell in even the farthest regions of the land, the border cities of Moab, will lament because of the destruction.

**15:4** *the armed soldiers of Moab shall cry out.* Even the hardened men of war will feel sorrow and will cry out.

*his life shall be grievous unto him.* The life of each armed soldier will be painful and distressful because of the devastation of his homeland.

**15:5** *My heart shall cry out for Moab.* The pronoun *my* refers either to God or to Isaiah; both are experiencing great emotional pain because of the destruction of Moab's inhabitants.

*his fugitives shall flee unto Zoar.* Zoar is located near the southern end of the Dead Sea; the fugitives are fleeing south, away from the heat of the battle.

*heifer of three years old.* A *heifer of three years old* is "in her strength," or full of vigor. Zoar was strong but soon would be destroyed when Sennacherib, king of Assyria, invaded.

*for by the mounting up of Luhith with weeping.* As the fugitives flee from the battles and destruction toward Luhith, a Moabite city in the south near Zoar, they will weep.

*for in the way of Horonaim they shall raise up a cry of destruction.* The inhabitants of Horonaim, a Moabite city near Zoar, will wail for the loss of their homeland.

**15:6** *waters of Nimrim shall be desolate.* This site in southern Moab will suffer because of the national disaster. Perhaps drought will be added to the other troubles.

*for the hay is withered away/grass faileth.* Cultivated lands, pastures, and green plants wither because of the lack of water in Nimrim and the lack of care by local farmers.

**15:7** *shall they carry away to the brook of the willows.* Refugees grab their personal belongings and treasures as they flee from the invading army. *Brook of the willows* may be Wadi Zered, which is located in the southern end of Moab (Num. 21:12; Deut. 2:13).

**15:8** *the howling thereof unto Eglaim/Beer-elim.* The devastation is nationwide, with the howling of the country's residents echoing as far away as Eglaim and Beer-elim, cities on the northern and southern borders of Moab.

**15:9** *For the waters of Dimon shall be full of blood.* So great will be the blood-bath in Dimon that its waters will run with the blood of the slain.

*for I will bring more upon Dimon.* The destruction is not yet over.

*lions upon him that escapeth of Moab.* Armies, like lions, will pursue the refugees and those who attempt to flee from the carnage, with the intent of destroying them. This prophecy may also have a literal fulfillment, with lions sent upon the land as a further judgment by the Lord.

# ISAIAH 16

### LIKENING ISAIAH 16 UNTO OURSELVES

*The desolation of historical Moab (chapter 15) anticipates the destruction of the modern nations that work evil and worship false gods; the mourning and lamentation of Moab's inhabitants after her destruction (16:6–14) foretells the anguish that will be experienced by earth's inhabitants during and after the latter-day wars; and Moab's refugees who sought protection in Judah (16:1–5) parallel those in the last days who will flee unto Zion from the warring nations (D&C 45:68–69).*

## MOAB SEEKS REFUGE IN JUDAH (16:1–5)

After the destruction of historical Moab, which is a type of all nations that will be destroyed for their wickedness, many Moabite refugees seek refuge in Judah (16:1–5); they wander around the fords of Arnon like a nestling who was cast out of her nest (16:2). Possibly following royal protocol, the refugees send a lamb to pay tribute to the king of Judah (16:1); they seek advice and protection from Judah: "Advise us what to do" (JB 16:2), and "protect and hide us from our enemies" (JB 16:3–4).

Ultimately, this section is a prophecy of Jesus Christ. "Once the oppression is over, and the destroyer is no more" (JB 16:4), the throne and kingdom of David will be set up once again (16:5). Jesus Christ is the king who will sit upon the throne in his temple ("tabernacle of David"), which recalls the throne in Solomon's temple and the Tabernacle of Moses.

*Isaiah 16:1–5*

> Send ye the lamb to the ruler of the land from Sela to the wilderness, unto the mount of the daughter of Zion. (16:1)

For it shall be, that, as a wandering bird cast out of the nest, so the daughters of Moab shall be at the fords of Arnon. (16:2)

Take counsel, execute judgment; make thy shadow as the night in the midst of the noonday; hide the outcasts; bewray not him that wandereth. (16:3)

Let mine <u>outcasts [of Moab]</u>[1] *dwell with thee;*
*be thou a covert* to <u>them</u> from the face of the spoiler

for the *extortioner* <u>is at an end,</u>
the *spoiler* <u>ceaseth,</u>
the *oppressors* <u>are consumed</u> out of the land. (16:4)

And *in mercy* shall the <u>throne</u> be established:
and he shall sit upon <u>it</u> *in truth* in the tabernacle of David,

judging, and seeking judgment, and hasting righteousness. (16:5)

## NOTES AND COMMENTARY

**16:1** *lamb to the ruler.* As a tribute, and following the formalities of the period, the Moabite refugees sent a lamb to the ruler in Judah. This recalls 2 Kings 3:4, which describes Mesha, king of Moab, giving a tribute to the king of Judah of one hundred thousand lambs and one hundred thousand rams with their wool.

*Sela. Sela* may refer to cliffs and caves where the refugees of Moab fled for safety; to Petra, the capital of Edom; or to an unidentified site in Moab.

*mount of the daughter of Zion.* This is a possible reference to the temple mount in Jerusalem, which is called *the daughter of Zion.*

**16:2** *wandering bird cast out of the nest.* The Moabites (or "daughters of Moab") who survive the destruction (chapter 15) wander through the land like a nestling who has lost its nest.

*fords of Arnon.* Many Moabites gather at the fords of Arnon, perhaps because there is water there to take care of their needs. Arnon, now called Wadi el-Mujib, is Moab's chief river. It flows into the Dead Sea.

**16:3** *Take counsel, execute judgment.* The Jerusalem Bible reads "advise us what to do, decide for us." The Moabites (likened to nestlings without a nest in 16:2) request that the ruler of Judah provide them political refuge. They seek protection under his wings ("make thy shadow"), as a chick is sheltered from the noonday sun ("midst of the noonday") by the hen.

**16:4** *mine outcasts [of Moab] dwell with thee.* The appeal of the Moabites continues.

---

[1] Following the New American Bible.

*extortioner is at an end/spoiler ceaseth/oppressors are consumed.* Isaiah 16:4–5 is a messianic prophecy. The newly restored kingdom of David removes oppression and destruction; the Messiah sits on the throne (16:5), a symbol of kingship.

**16:5** *mercy/truth/judging, and seeking judgment, and hasting righteousness.* These qualities belong to Jesus the Messiah, who will reign from his throne.

*tabernacle of David.* The *tabernacle* refers to the temples of heaven, Jerusalem, and New Jerusalem. The Messiah, like David of old, will rule over the united tribes of Israel (Ezek. 37:21–28).

## LAMENT FOR MOAB (16:6–14)

In Isaiah 15 the prophet gives a prophecy of Moab's destruction followed by a description of her refugees' flight for safety (16:1–5). In 16:6–11 Isaiah's prophecy is in the form of a lamentation, bewailing Moab's destruction. The lamentative terms of the section include *howl* (used twice), *mourn* (16:7), *bewail with weeping, water with tears* (16:9); we find no gladness or joy, no singing or joyful shouting, and especially none of the rejoicing that would occur at harvest time (16:10), so that even the heart (KJV, "bowels") and soul (KJV, "inward parts") mourn for Moab's destruction (16:11).

Interwoven into the prophecy are images of Moab's grape industry, including the terms *vine, wine, vineyards, plants,* and *harvest.* Isaiah's prophecy of the destruction of Moab and her agricultural industry should be taken literally, but it appears that Isaiah also uses the grapes and plants to refer to her inhabitants.

The prayers of Moab's inhabitants (16:12–13) to their gods will not stop the decreed destruction, which will occur within three years (16:14) from the time the prophecy is uttered. Isaiah 16:6 explains that Moab is destroyed because of her *pride, haughtiness, lies,* and *evil works.*

*Isaiah 16:6–14*

> We have heard of the *pride of Moab;* of his <u>haughtiness</u>
> and *his pride,* [for][2] he is very <u>proud</u>;
>
> and his wrath, his lies,
> [and all his evil works].[3] (16:6)
>
> Therefore shall *Moab* <u>howl</u> for Moab,
> *every one* <u>shall howl</u>:

---

[2] JST Isa. 16:6 adds the preposition *for* and reorders the phrase *he is very proud* in the verse.
[3] JST Isa. 16:6 adds this phrase and omits the KJV phrase *but his lies shall not be so.*

for the *foundations* of Kir-hareseth <u>shall ye mourn</u>;
surely *they* <u>are stricken</u>. (16:7)

For the *fields of Heshbon* languish,
and the *vine of Sibmah:*

the lords of the heathen have broken down the principal plants thereof, they are come even unto Jazer, they wandered through the wilderness:

*her branches* are <u>stretched out</u>,
*they* are <u>gone over the sea</u>. (16:8)

Therefore I will bewail with the *weeping* of Jazer the vine of Sibmah:
I will water thee with my *tears,* O Heshbon, and Elealeh:

for the shouting for thy summer fruits and for thy harvest is fallen. (16:9)

And *gladness* is <u>taken away</u>,
and *joy* <u>out</u> of the plentiful field;

and in the vineyards there shall be <u>no singing</u>,
<u>neither</u> shall there be <u>shouting</u>:

the treaders shall tread out no wine in their presses;
I have made their vintage shouting to cease. (16:10)

Wherefore *my bowels* shall sound like an harp <u>for Moab</u>,
and *mine inward parts* <u>for Kir-haresh</u>. (16:11)

And it shall come to pass, when it is seen that Moab is weary on the high place, that he shall come to his sanctuary to pray; but he shall not prevail. (16:12)

This is the word that the Lord hath spoken concerning Moab since that time. (16:13)

But now the Lord hath spoken, saying, Within three years, as the years of an hireling, and the glory of Moab shall [cease to command respect],[4] with all that great multitude; and the remnant shall be very small and feeble. (16:14)

## NOTES AND COMMENTARY

**16:6** *pride of Moab.* Isaiah gives several reasons for Moab's destruction by God—pride (mentioned three times), haughtiness, wrath, lies, and evil works. Our own world, following Moab as a type, has the same sins.

**16:7** *Moab howl for Moab.* Moab's inhabitants will lament and howl because of the destruction of their homeland.

*foundations of Kir-hareseth shall ye mourn.* Kir-hareseth is the modern Kerak, located seventeen miles south of the fords of Arnon (16:2) and some eleven miles east of the Dead Sea. Kir-hareseth's economy was founded on its wine industry. Verses 7–10 contain references to this famous industry that existed in ancient Moab. They include *fields of Heshbon, vine of Sibmah, principal plants, branches, vine of*

---

[4]We prefer the reading of the JB over the archaic KJV reading of *contemned.*

*Sibmah, summer fruits, harvest, plentiful field, vineyards, wine,* and *vintage.* Moab's inhabitants will mourn because its economic mainstay, in which it placed so much trust, will be lost.

Some translators read "raisin cakes of Kir-hareseth" rather than "foundations of Kir-hareseth." Such a reading fits well into the context of this section of Isaiah, for raisin cakes, used in apostate religious practices (Hosea 3:1), were made of dried and compressed grapes (2 Sam. 6:19; 1 Chr. 16:3).

**16:8–11** *Heshbon, Sibmah, Jazer, Elealeh, and Kir-haresh.* These are principal Moabite cities connected with the wine industry and are mentioned here to indicate the industry's breadth. Isaiah also recounts that "her branches are stretched out, they are gone over the sea," which indicates that Moab's wine export business was regionally and perhaps even internationally known.

**16:9** *I will bewail/weeping/tears.* This may be the mourning of the Moabites over their lost grape industry or, more importantly, over the Moabites who are slain in the destruction. Or it may refer to the mourning of the Lord or his prophet that the people had to be destroyed.

**16:10** *gladness/joy is taken away.* The lamentation continues, and the happiness shown in the gladness, joy, singing, and shouting normally connected with harvest, blessings, and peaceful conditions is gone.

*in the vineyards there shall be no singing, neither . . . shouting.* The customary singing and joyful shouting that accompany the grape treaders are gone; lamenting replaces them.

*treaders shall tread out no wine in their presses.* Workers will cease their laboring and the normal economy will be disrupted.

*I have made their vintage shouting to cease.* The joy that attends the bounteous harvest is replaced with mourning, because of the judgments of the Lord.

**16:11** *mine inward parts/my bowels shall sound like an harp for Moab.* The pronouns *my* and *mine* may refer to the Lord or to Isaiah, who groans and mourns because of Moab's destruction, or to individual inhabitants of Moab who mourn the loss of their homeland.

**16:12** *he shall come to his sanctuary.* Worshipers shall seek comfort from their idols at their temples, but the Lord's word will be fulfilled; Moab's devastation will be complete.

**16:13** *Lord hath spoken.* Jehovah is the source of this prophecy.

**16:14** *But now the Lord hath spoken.* A new revelation from Jehovah concerning Moab.

*Within three years.* The destruction of Moab will be complete within three years.

*all that great multitude.* Despite the number of its inhabitants, Moab will be destroyed.

*remnant shall be very small and feeble.* Few will remain in Moab, perhaps chiefly the elderly and the sick or injured.

# ISAIAH 17

*LIKENING ISAIAH 17 UNTO OURSELVES*

*The prophecy of Isaiah in this chapter may be likened unto our own generation. The idolatrous practices of the ancient countries of Syria and Israel resulted in their downfall and destruction (17:1–11). People and nations in the last days who put their trust in idols, such as riches, power, false security, or illicit sex, will similarly be destroyed.*

## A PROPHECY OF JUDGMENT AGAINST DAMASCUS AND ISRAEL (17:1–11)

Damascus and other Syrian cities will be destroyed and depopulated (17:1–3), and Israel will experience similar judgments (17:4–5). Isaiah compares Israel's destruction and depopulation to an individual who was healthy but has become emaciated by disease. Similarly, those who remain after Israel's destruction will be as sparse as the remaining stalks of wheat after the reaping or as the olives after the olive trees have been stripped (17:4–6).

Isaiah 17:7–8 seems to be parenthetical; this passage promises that some will turn from idolatry and focus their eyes on the Holy One of Israel.

Isaiah 17:9–11 is a continuation of the judgments against Syria and Israel (recorded in 17:1–6) because of their idolatries. Isaiah continues his comparison of idolatrous Israel to a man who planted his vineyard with inferior plants, and, though he cultivated and cared for the vines, his harvest was poor. The man's disappointment was great; "the harvest shall be a heap in the day of grief and of desperate sorrow" (17:11). The effect of God's judgments on Syria and Israel will bring about Israel's return to God when his people no longer trust in their self-created idols (17:7–8).

## Isaiah 17:1–11

The burden of Damascus.

Behold, *Damascus* is <u>taken away from being a city,</u>
and *it* shall be a <u>ruinous heap.</u> (17:1)

The cities of Aroer are forsaken: they shall be for flocks, which shall lie down, and none shall make them afraid. (17:2)

The *fortress* also shall cease from *Ephraim,*
and the *kingdom* from *Damascus,* and the remnant of Syria: they shall be as the glory of the children of Israel, saith the Lord of hosts. (17:3)

And in that day it shall come to pass,

that the *glory of Jacob* shall be <u>made thin,</u>
and the *fatness of his flesh* shall <u>wax lean.</u> (17:4)

And it shall be as when the *harvestman* <u>gathereth the corn,</u>
and <u>reapeth the ears</u> with *his arm;*
and it shall be as *he* that <u>gathereth ears</u> in the valley of Rephaim. (17:5)

Yet gleaning grapes shall be left in it, as the shaking of an olive tree, two or three berries in the top of the uppermost bough, four or five in the outmost fruitful branches thereof, saith the Lord God of Israel. (17:6)

At that day shall a *man look* to his <u>Maker,</u>
and *his eyes* shall have respect to the <u>Holy One of Israel.</u> (17:7)

And he shall not look to the *altars,* the <u>work of his hands,</u>
neither shall respect that which his <u>fingers have made,</u> either the *groves,* or the *images.* (17:8)

In that day shall his strong cities be [like the deserted places of the Hivites and the Amorites, which they deserted][1] because of the children of Israel: and there shall be desolation. (17:9)

Because thou hast *forgotten* the <u>God of thy salvation,</u>
and hast *not been mindful* of the <u>rock of thy strength,</u>

therefore shalt thou *plant* <u>pleasant plants,</u>
and shalt *set it* with <u>strange slips:</u> (17:10)

*In the day* shalt thou make <u>thy plant to grow,</u>
and *in the morning* shalt thou make <u>thy seed to flourish:</u>

but the harvest shall be a heap in the day of grief and of desperate sorrow. (17:11)

## NOTES AND COMMENTARY

**17:1** *burden of Damascus.* A prophecy of judgment against Damascus, capital of Syria and other Syrian cities (17:2).

*Damascus . . . shall be a ruinous heap.* Damascus will be destroyed and become a heap of rubble.

---

[1] The reading is according to the NRSV.

**17:2** *cities of Aroer are forsaken: they shall be for flocks.* Other Syrian cities, along with Damascus, will be destroyed and abandoned. Their destruction will be so complete that flocks of sheep will pasture where they once stood.

**17:3** *fortress also shall cease from Ephraim.* With the fall of Damascus, Ephraim (Israel's Northern Kingdom) would lose her powerful ally and hence its protection (meaning "fortress"). Ephraim was destroyed in 721 B.C.

*the kingdom [shall cease] from Damascus.* With the fall of Syria's capital city and other municipal centers, the kingdom ceased to exist.

*the remnant of Syria . . . shall be as the glory of the children of Israel.* Those who remain in Syria after it becomes a heap of ruins will have little glory, similar to the "thin" glory Israel will have after it becomes desolate (17:4).

*saith the Lord of hosts.* Jehovah is the source of this prophecy.

**17:4** *glory of Jacob shall be made thin.* The nation of Israel (Jacob) is likened to a man whose body has become weak and thin. Similar to Syria in its destruction ("in that day it shall come to pass"), Israel, in all its glory and prosperity, will become as a shadow—thin and afflicted. Unlike Syria, however, which would be afflicted both body and soul (annihilated from the earth), Israel's spirit would be left intact, eventually enabling a remnant to return to God with full strength.

**17:5** *harvestman gathereth the corn . . . in the valley of Rephaim.* The valley of Rephaim (2 Sam. 5:18), southwest of Jerusalem, was a fertile agricultural area. Isaiah compares the harvest and subsequent emptiness of the valley to Israel's destruction and the few inhabitants that will remain. As the corn is harvested and removed from Rephaim, so will Israel's inhabitants be removed from the land; only a few will remain.

**17:6** *Yet gleaning grapes shall be left in it.* In ancient Israel, the landless poor were permitted to glean any grains and produce that remained after the harvest (Deut. 24:19–22; Ruth 2:2–23). The olives (KJV reads "grapes") that the gleaners could not reach with their hands were knocked from the upper branches with a stick, or they were shaken from the tree (24:13; Deut. 24:20). Isaiah continues the comparison between the valley of Rephaim's harvest and Israel's destruction by likening her few remaining inhabitants to the four or five olives that remain in the tree's uppermost bough (2 Kgs. 24:14; 25:12).

**17:7** *At that day shall a man look to his Maker.* After the troubles, disasters, and depopulation of the land, at least some of those who remain will repent of their sins and return to God, looking to him with new "respect."

*Maker.* Isaiah contrasts *man* and *Maker;* man is weak, frail, and dependent compared to the Maker, who is the Creator, Omnipotent, and Lord of all. Verse 8 continues the contrast when Isaiah reproves mankind for vainly creating idols with his own tools ("the work of his hands") rather than relying upon God (the *Maker*), who created him.

**17:8** *he shall not look to the altars . . . or the images. Altars, groves,* and *images* refer to the Canaanite religion and its temples (Ex. 34:13). The groves were poles or trees or stone pillars erected near the Canaanite temple's altar in honor of Ashera, a Canaanite female deity, and Baal, a Canaanite male deity. Some of the Israelites who survive the prophesied calamities will turn from their idols and return to God.

**17:9** *In that day shall his strong cities be like.* Israel's cities will be like the cities of the Hivites and Amorites after Israel conquered them (Deut. 7:1)—empty and desolate.

**17:10** *forgotten the God of thy salvation.* Israel had forgotten God, who was both their temporal and their spiritual salvation.

*plant pleasant plants . . . strange slips.* Israel was indulging in the false worship of fertility gods or goddesses (17:11; Jer. 2:21).

**17:11** *in the morning shalt thou make thy seed to flourish.* The Israelites are eager and quick (*in the day* and *in the morning*) to plant their plants to the fertility gods, but at the time of harvest, the plants will be useless, becoming heaps of rotten produce. The plants and sprigs that Israel plants represent none other than Israel herself in her apostate condition.

*harvest shall be a heap in the day of grief and of desperate sorrow.* Israel should be a choice vine that relies upon Jesus Christ for life and power (John 15); its fruits should be plump and nourishing. Instead, Israel has become a wild, inferior, and unfruitful vine. The harvest of rotten produce, therefore, will be cast into a great *heap.* This is why God should be the planter and the keeper of the vineyard (Jacob 5–6): if the people of Israel had permitted God to become the focus of their lives, they would have produced good fruits (3 Ne. 14:17–18).

## PORTRAYAL OF THE DOWNFALL OF THE NATIONS THAT OPPRESS ISRAEL (17:12–14)

The reason for the woe in 17:12 is not given explicitly, but 17:14 suggests that the oracle is directed toward all nations or peoples who rob or plunder members of the house of Israel (represented by the pronoun *us,* which is used twice). Three key phrases point out the disaster that awaits the multitudes who "spoil us" and "rob us": They are "God shall rebuke them," "they shall flee far off," and "they shall be chased" (17:13).

## Isaiah 17:12–14

Woe to the multitude of *many people,* which <u>make a noise like the noise of the seas;</u>
and to the rushing of *nations,* that <u>make a rushing like the rushing of mighty waters!</u> (17:12)

The nations shall rush like the rushing of many waters: but God shall rebuke them,
and they shall flee far off,
and shall be chased

*as the chaff* of the mountains <u>before the wind,</u>
and *like a rolling thing* <u>before the whirlwind.</u> (17:13)

And behold at *eveningtide* <u>trouble;</u>
and before the *morning* <u>he is not.</u>

This is the *portion* of them <u>that spoil us,</u>
and the *lot* of them <u>that rob us.</u> (17:14)

## NOTES AND COMMENTARY

**17:12** *Woe to the multitude of many people.* This refers to the world, or all nations (for example, ancient Assyria, Egypt, and Syria) who do not seek God.

*make a noise like the noise of the seas/mighty waters.* Great multitudes and nations are often compared to waters (see 8:7; Jer. 47:2; Rev. 17:1, 15).

**17:13** *God shall rebuke them.* God will chasten the worldly nations and cause them to scatter and flee as the useless chaff is scattered by the four winds during harvest. Chaff is worthless and easily removed from the precious kernels of grain.

*they shall flee.* Worldly nations will flee from God's wrath and terrible rebuke.

*chaff . . . before the wind/rolling thing before the whirlwind.* God will carry off and scatter the nations to the four corners of the world as easily as a tumbleweed is carried off by the whirlwind, or as effortlessly as the wind blows the chaff through the air.

**17:14** *at eveningtide trouble . . . before the morning he is not.* God's judgment will come swiftly (*before the morning*) upon the wicked.

*the portion of them that spoil us . . . that rob us.* The eventual lot of those who plunder and harm members of the house of Israel is destruction.

# ISAIAH 18

## LIKENING ISAIAH 18 UNTO OURSELVES

*In this chapter Isaiah is speaking directly to us. He prophesies of the gospel ensign that has been raised at the beginning of this dispensation, to which people from many nations are gathering. Isaiah also speaks of our missionaries who are sent forth to proclaim the gospel to the nations of the earth.*

## THE LORD'S MESSENGERS TAKE THE GOSPEL TO THE WORLD (18:1–7)

President Joseph Fielding Smith wrote: "This chapter is clearly a reference to the sending forth of the missionaries to the nations of the earth to gather again this people who are scattered and peeled. The ensign has been lifted upon the mountains, and the work of gathering has been going on for over one hundred years. No one understands this chapter, but the Latter-day Saints, and we can see how it is being fulfilled."[1]

*Isaiah 18:1–7*

Woe to the land shadowing with wings, which is beyond the rivers of Ethiopia:
(18:1). That sendeth ambassadors by the sea, even in vessels of bulrushes upon
the waters, saying, Go, ye swift messengers, to a nation scattered and peeled, to a
people terrible from their beginning hitherto; a nation meted out and trodden
down, whose land the rivers have spoiled! (18:2)

All ye *inhabitants* <u>of the world,</u>
and *dwellers* <u>on the earth,</u>

*see ye,* when <u>he lifteth up an ensign</u> on the mountains;
and when <u>he bloweth a trumpet,</u> *hear ye.* (18:3)

---

[1] *Signs of the Times,* 54–55.

For so the Lord said unto me, I will take my rest, and I will consider in my dwelling place like a clear heat upon herbs, and like a cloud of dew in the heat of harvest. (18:4)

For afore the harvest, when the bud is perfect, and the sour grape is ripening in the flower,

he shall both *cut off* the <u>sprigs</u> with pruning hooks,
and take away and *cut down* the <u>branches</u>. (18:5)

They shall be left together unto the *fowls* of the <u>mountains,</u>
and to the *beasts* of the <u>earth</u>:

and the *fowls* shall <u>summer upon them,</u>
and all the *beasts* of the earth shall <u>winter upon them</u>. (18:6)

In that time shall the present be brought unto the Lord of hosts

of a people scattered and peeled,
and from a people terrible from their beginning hitherto;
a nation meted out and trodden under foot, whose land the rivers have spoiled, to the place of the name of the Lord of hosts, the mount Zion. (18:7)

## NOTES AND COMMENTARY

**18:1** *Woe to the land shadowing with wings, which is beyond the rivers of Ethiopia.* This expression refers to America, which is "in the shape of wings."[2] Joseph Fielding Smith wrote: "America . . . is the land 'shadowing with wings' spoken of by Isaiah that today is sending ambassadors by the sea to a nation scattered and peeled."[3] Hyrum Smith spoke of the gathering of Israel to America by saying that "the gathering will be from the nations to North and South America, which is the land of Zion. North and South America, are the symbols of the wings."[4]

Apparently the woe does not belong in the introduction to 18:1. "The chapter shows clearly that no woe was intended, but rather a greeting. . . . A correct translation would be, 'Hail to the land in the shape of wings.'"[5]

**18:2** *That sendeth ambassadors by the sea, even in vessels.* The *ambassadors* and "swift messengers" (D&C 124:26) are our "elders of Israel," our "messengers of the kingdom,"[6] or the Lord's servants who are working to establish Zion in the last days. They travel swiftly in a variety of vehicles, represented here with the phrase *vessels of bulrushes,* which means "vessels of speed," according to Joseph Fielding Smith.[7]

---

[2] Smith, *Signs of the Times,* 51.
[3] Conference Report, 14; see also McConkie, *Millennial Messiah,* 94–95.
[4] *History of the Church,* 6:322.
[5] Smith, *Signs of the Times,* 51.
[6] McConkie, *New Witness for the Articles of Faith,* 536.
[7] Smith, *Signs of the Times,* 51.

*a nation scattered and peeled, to a people terrible from their beginning hitherto.* President Joseph Fielding Smith asked, "Do you know of any land like that? Terrible in the beginning and later meted out and scattered, peeled and a curse upon the land? That land is Palestine."[8]

**18:3** *All ye inhabitants of the world.* The focus of the prophecy turns to all the inhabitants of the earth.

*see ye . . . hear ye.* The inhabitants of the earth are commanded to *see* God's ensign and *hear* the blowing of the trumpet; they should hearken to the gospel message as declared by the Lord's messengers.

*when he lifteth up an ensign on the mountains.* The *ensign* (a flag or banner) will be raised upon a high mountain for all of Israel's outcasts to see and be prompted to gather around it. The ensign represents the gospel of Jesus Christ (D&C 45:9; 105:39) and the light that accompanies it (D&C 115:4–5).[9] The ensign, regularly mentioned in Isaiah (5:26; 11:10–12; 18:3; 30:17; 31:9; 49:22), was raised "here in America, and the Lord calls upon all the world to take notice when this ensign is lifted upon the mountains."[10]

*when he bloweth a trumpet.* The trumpet, with the ensign mentioned above, beckons the world's inhabitants to gather to Zion and its temples (27:13; Matt. 24:31). Every missionary of our dispensation is instructed that "at all times, and in all places, he shall open his mouth and declare my gospel as with the voice of a trump" (D&C 24:12) so the earth's inhabitants will hear the gospel's message. Thus the Lord's trumpet is the voice of his missionaries.

**18:4** *For so the Lord said unto me.* The Lord spoke to Isaiah.

*I will take my rest, and I will consider in my dwelling place.* God's place of *rest* and his *dwelling place* is his heavenly temple (celestial kingdom). God is considering events pertaining to the earth's inhabitants, and at the right moment he will carry out his designs.

*like a clear heat upon herbs, and like a cloud of dew in the heat of harvest.* Victor Ludlow writes: "Verse 4 explains that, as the gospel goes forth, the Lord will calmly remain in his dwelling place like a 'clear heat' or a 'dewy mist' during the harvest season. . . . Like the delicate balance of warmth and moisture needed to fully ripen the grapes, God attends to the harvest of souls by providing the proper

---

[8] *Signs of the Times,* 52.
[9] See also *Teachings of the Prophet Joseph Smith,* 38.
[10] Smith, *Signs of the Times,* 54.

light (truth) and water (cleansing powers) to ensure the full development of each person."[11]

**18:5** *For afore the harvest.* Before the sweet, ripe grapes are plucked from the vine.

*he shall both cut off the sprigs with pruning hooks.* Just before the grapes are ripe for plucking, the Great Pruner (the Lord) will take his pruning hook and prune the vine of its unwanted sprigs and branches, here representing unrighteous people or wicked nations.

**18:6** *They shall be left together unto the fowls of the mountains.* After the Lord has destroyed the wicked (or permitted their destruction), so many human corpses will be scattered on the face of the land that fowls and beasts will feed on the carnage: "And it shall come to pass that the beasts of the forest and the fowls of the air shall devour them up" (D&C 29:20; see also Deut. 28:26; Ps. 79:2; Jer. 7:33; 16:4; Ezek. 32:4).

*fowls shall summer upon them, and all the beasts of the earth shall winter upon them.* There will be so many bodies that the vultures and beasts will feast for one year (see Ezek. 39:12, which states that it will take seven months to bury the bodies of Gog).

**18:7** *In that time.* This is the time of the events identified in the previous six verses.

*shall the present be brought unto the Lord of hosts.* These are the gifts of homage that Israel will bring to the Lord after her restoration. The gifts may be no less than the state of purity and righteousness of the Saints who have made the Atonement effective in their lives.

*a people scattered and peeled . . . whose land the rivers have spoiled.* The words in 18:2 are repeated here for emphasis but with the added phrase *to the place of the name of the Lord of hosts, the mount Zion,* a reference to the temple.

---

[11] Ludlow, *Isaiah,* 208.

# ISAIAH 19

*LIKENING ISAIAH 19 UNTO OURSELVES*

*This entire prophecy pertains to Egypt and its people, as indicated by the frequent reference to* Egypt *(seventeen times),* Egyptian(s) *(six times), and* land of Egypt *(three times). The time frame for the prophecy, at least with regard to 19:16–25, is the last days, as indicated by the expression* in that day *(19:16, 18, 19, 21, 23). Thus those of us who are permitted to live in the final decades before the coming of the Savior may witness the events of this chapter. Egypt as referred to herein may be the literal nation in Africa, or may symbolize one or more unidentified latter-day nations.*

## A PROPHECY CONCERNING EGYPT'S DEVASTATION AND ULTIMATE RETURN TO THE LORD (19:1–25)

The prophecy, which appears to have a latter-day application, consists of two parts. The first part consists of the judgments against Egypt's people, leaders, and deities (19:1–18). Egypt will experience internal confusion, perhaps civil war, and eventually the rule of an external tyrant (19:1–4). Egypt will also encounter economic upheaval when the Nile and irrigation ditches dry up, negatively affecting the farmers and the fishing, flax, and weaving industries. Egypt's inhabitants will suffer (19:5–10).

The second part of this prophecy (19:19–25) deals with the Egyptians' turning to the Lord, with evidence that the gospel will exist among them. The prophecy speaks of prayer ("they shall cry unto the Lord," 19:20; and "he shall be intreated of them," 19:22); a Savior and deliverance (19:20); and a people that "shall know the Lord" (19:21). In addition, spiritual healing will come through God's power (this aspect of the prophecy is emphasized when it is twice repeated, 19:22); repentance and conversion ("they shall return even to the Lord," 19:22); oneness among the nations (19:23–24); blessings unto the people (19:25); and a temple of the Lord ("shall there be an altar," 19:19); sacrifices and vows (19:21).

The two parts of the prophecy may be summarized in two words, *smite* and *heal*, both occurring twice in 19:22. The first section, the smiting of Egypt, refers to the turmoil and confusion that Egypt experiences by not knowing God (19:1–18); the second section deals with the healing that will occur when Egypt's people turn to God (19:19–25). Notice how Isaiah compares the two parts: civil war and internal confusion (19:2) are replaced with one language (19:18); the idols and false gods (19:3) are replaced with the Lord and Savior (19:20); the fierce and evil king (19:4) is replaced with the Lord who heals Egypt (19:22); and the drying up of the river (19:5) is replaced with the highway and the Lord's blessing (19:22–23).

Isaiah teaches that it is God who has governed and will continue to govern Egypt's affairs—as he does with all nations. This truth is emphasized by including the term *Lord* (Jehovah) ten times, *Lord of Hosts* (Jehovah of Hosts) seven times, and *Lord* (Adonai), *saviour,* and *great one* once. Specific phrases that identify God as the chief moving force behind certain events that have or will take place in Egypt include: "let them know what the Lord of hosts hath purposed upon Egypt" (19:12), "the Lord hath mingled a perverse spirit in the midst thereof" (19:14), "because of the counsel of the Lord of hosts, which he hath determined against it" (19:17), "the Lord . . . shall send them a saviour, and a great one, and he shall deliver them" (19:20), "Lord shall smite Egypt: he shall smite and heal it" (19:22).

This chapter may be interpreted on at least two different levels. It is possible that Isaiah saw these events occurring in the literal latter-day Egypt. But it may be that these things refer to another nation (or many nations) that will repent and turn to God after suffering great judgments and punishments for their sins.

*Isaiah 19:1–25*

> The burden of Egypt. Behold, the Lord rideth upon a swift cloud, and shall come into Egypt:
>
> and the *idols of Egypt* shall be moved at his presence,
> and the *heart of Egypt* shall melt in the midst of it. (19:1)
>
> And I will set the *Egyptians* against the Egyptians:
> and they shall fight *every one* against his brother,
> and *every one* against his neighbour;
> *city* against city,
> and *kingdom* against kingdom. (19:2)

And the spirit of Egypt shall fail in the midst thereof; and I will destroy the counsel thereof:

and they shall seek to the *idols,*
and to the *charmers,*
and to *them that have familiar spirits,*
and to the *wizards.* (19:3)

And the *Egyptians will I give over* into the hand of a <u>cruel lord</u>;
and a <u>fierce king</u> *shall rule over them,*

saith the *Lord,*
the *Lord of hosts.* (19:4)

And the *waters* <u>shall fail</u> from the sea,
and the *river* <u>shall be wasted and dried up.</u> (19:5)

And *they shall turn* the <u>rivers</u> *far away;*
and the <u>brooks</u> of defence shall be *emptied and dried up:*

the *reeds and flags* <u>shall wither.</u> (19:6)
The *paper reeds* by the brooks, by the mouth of the brooks, and every thing sown by the brooks, <u>shall wither,</u> be driven away, and be no more. (19:7)

The *fishers* also <u>shall mourn,</u>
and all *they that cast angle* into the brooks <u>shall lament,</u>
and *they that spread nets* upon the waters <u>shall languish.</u> (19:8)

Moreover *they* that <u>work in fine flax,</u>
and *they* that <u>weave networks,</u> shall be confounded. (19:9)

And they shall be broken in the purposes thereof, all that make sluices and ponds for fish. (19:10)

Surely the *princes of Zoan* are <u>fools,</u>
the counsel of the *wise counselors of Pharaoh* is become <u>brutish</u>:

how say ye unto Pharaoh, I am the *son* <u>of the wise,</u>
the *son* <u>of ancient kings</u>? (19:11)

*Where* are <u>they</u>?
*where* are thy <u>wise men</u>?

and let them tell thee now, and let them know what the Lord of hosts hath purposed upon Egypt. (19:12)

The *princes of Zoan* are become <u>fools,</u>
the *princes of Noph* are <u>deceived</u>;

*they* have also seduced <u>Egypt,</u>
even *they* that are the stay of the <u>tribes thereof.</u> (19:13)

The Lord hath mingled a *perverse spirit* in the <u>midst thereof</u>: and they have caused <u>Egypt</u> to *err* in every work thereof, as a drunken man staggereth in his vomit. (19:14)

Neither shall there be any work for Egypt, which the head or tail, branch or rush, may do. (19:15)

In that day shall Egypt be like unto women: and it shall be afraid and fear

because of the *shaking of the hand* of the <u>Lord of hosts,</u>
which <u>he</u> *shaketh* over it. (19:16)

And the *land of Judah* shall be a <u>terror</u> unto Egypt,
every one that maketh mention *thereof* shall be <u>afraid</u> in himself,

because of the counsel of the Lord of hosts, which he hath determined against it.
(19:17)

In that day shall five cities in the land of Egypt speak the language of Canaan, and
swear to the Lord of hosts; one shall be called, The city of the Sun.[1] (19:18)

In that day shall there be an *altar* <u>to the Lord</u> *in the midst of* the land of Egypt,
and a *pillar at the border thereof* <u>to the Lord.</u> (19:19)

And it shall be for a sign and for a witness unto the Lord of hosts in the land of
Egypt: for they shall cry unto the Lord because of the oppressors,

and *he* <u>shall send</u> <u>them</u> a saviour, and a great one,
and *he* <u>shall deliver them.</u> (19:20)

And the *Lord shall be known* <u>to Egypt,</u>
and the <u>Egyptians</u> *shall know* the *Lord* in that day,

and shall *do sacrifice* and oblation;
yea, they shall *vow a vow* unto the Lord,
and *perform* it. (19:21)

And the *Lord* shall <u>smite Egypt:</u>
*he* shall <u>smite and heal it:</u>

and *they shall return* even to the <u>Lord,</u>
and <u>he</u> shall *be intreated of them,* and shall heal them. (19:22)

In that day shall there be a highway out of Egypt to Assyria, and the Assyrian
shall come into Egypt, and the Egyptian into Assyria, and the Egyptians shall
serve with the Assyrians. (19:23)

In that day shall Israel be the third with Egypt and with Assyria, even a blessing in
the midst of the land: (19:24)

Whom the Lord of hosts shall bless, saying,

Blessed be *Egypt* <u>my people,</u>
and *Assyria* <u>the work of my hands,</u>
and *Israel* <u>mine inheritance.</u> (19:25)

## NOTES AND COMMENTARY

**19:1** *burden of Egypt.* This statement is a prophecy of judgment against Egypt.

*the Lord rideth upon a swift cloud.* Jehovah has the power to move through the
heavens at his will and pleasure (2 Sam. 22:11). He also rides upon his cherub (Ps.
18:10); he "maketh the clouds his chariot" (Ps. 104:3). The *cloud* represents the
Lord's glory (D&C 84:5).

---

[1] DSS Isa. Scroll corrects *City of Destruction* to *City of the Sun.*

*shall come into Egypt.* The Lord will visit Egypt with destruction, as outlined in the following verses.

*idols of Egypt shall be moved at his presence.* This expression indicates that Jehovah is more powerful than the creations of man.

*heart of Egypt shall melt.* The Egyptians shall fear because of the Lord's devastating works (13:7; Josh. 2:11; Ezek. 21:7).

**19:2** *I will set the Egyptians against the Egyptians.* This statement speaks of a fractured society that is involved in civil war or perhaps even broken families. Isaiah carefully orders his words; he begins with the basic unit of society (family) and progresses in size from neighborhood to city and finally to kingdom. Such an approach may indicate that the demise of any society begins with the demise of the family.

**19:3** *spirit of Egypt shall fail.* The Egyptians will be demoralized because of the civil wars and broken families identified in 19:2.

*I will destroy the counsel thereof.* The Lord will destroy the plans and designs of various Egyptian entities, perhaps including government offices and economic and religious groups.

*they shall seek to the idols/charmers/familiar spirits/wizards.* A confused and godless society turns to false deities, wizards, and false prophets. Members of such a society, feeling helpless and desperate, grasp for help, often from the wrong sources. *Charmers* are those who pretend to understand their gods' desires, *them that have familiar spirits* are those who pretend to communicate with spirits of the departed, and *wizards* are male witches.

**19:4** *fierce king shall rule over them.* An evil dictator will rule Egypt for a period of time. The fulfillment of this prophecy "may have been the 'Ethiopian' Pharaoh Piankhi (715), the conquests of Sargon II (*cf.* 20:1ff.) or Sennacherib, or the invasion and conquest of Egypt by Esarhaddon (680), Ashurbanipal (668), or the Persian Artaxerxes III Ochus (343)."[2] Its fulfillment might also come in the future.

*Lord of hosts.* See commentary on 1:9.

**19:5** *river shall be wasted and dried up.* Egypt's economic structure was connected to the great Nile River. Isaiah may be speaking symbolically here and in the following five verses, referring to the economic collapse Egypt will suffer, or the prophecy might refer to an actual drought that will cause economic disintegration in Egypt.

---

[2] Motyer, *Prophecy of Isaiah,* 165.

**19:6** *they shall turn the rivers far away.* This passage includes Egypt's various waterways and rivers. The phrase *they shall turn the rivers far away* may refer to the Aswan Dam built during the 1960s and the waterways connected to it.[3]

**19:7** *every thing sown by the brooks, shall wither.* Vegetation shall cease.

**19:8** *fishers also shall mourn.* Isaiah 19:8–9 speaks of three of Egypt's industries: fishing (casting the net and casting the hook), flax growing, and weaving. The demise of these three industries points to national economic disaster.

**19:9** *they that work in fine flax . . . shall be confounded.* See commentary on 19:8.

**19:10** *they shall be broken in the purposes thereof.* The Jerusalem Bible reads: "The weavers will be dismayed and all the workmen dejected." Workers at all levels will experience anxiety and economic distress.

**19:11** *princes of Zoan are fools/counsel of the wise counselors of Pharaoh is become brutish. Zoan* (Tanis), in the northern delta, was Egypt's capital from approximately 1100 to 660 B.C. and the location from which Moses sent forth the plagues of Egypt. The administrative qualities of the government officials (princes), legislative/judicial leaders (counselors), and other public servants had degenerated to the point that their leadership was no more than foolishness (brutish), which brought Egypt to disaster.

*how say ye unto Pharaoh, I am the son of the wise/the son of ancient kings.* "The wisdom of Egypt, which was renowned among the ancients . . . , was the hereditary possession of the priestly caste, and from the same class were descended the kings. Pharaoh's counsellors could therefore boast that they were descended from wise men and from the ancient kings."[4] Neither their heritage nor their boasting could prevent Egypt's wise men from becoming fools.

**19:12** *where are thy wise men?* This rhetorical question is followed by a statement that the Lord is in charge of Egypt and has full knowledge of his plan concerning it.

**19:13** *princes of Zoan are become fools.* Officers and leaders of Zoan (19:11) and Noph (or Memphis, once Egypt's capital during the Old Kingdom), have lost their ability to lead. They act more like fools than true leaders, perhaps due to self-deception.

*they have also seduced Egypt.* The thoughtless leaders and governors of Egypt's provinces lead the citizens astray with their wickedness and deceptions.

---

[3] Ludlow, *Isaiah,* 214–16.
[4] Kissane, *Book of Isaiah,* 1:217.

**19:14** *The Lord hath mingled a perverse spirit in the midst thereof: and they have caused Egypt to err in every work thereof.* This verse offers two reasons why Egypt's once wise government leaders and royalty have lost their status and become fools: Jehovah has "poured into them a spirit of dizziness" (NIV), so much that Isaiah likens Egypt's inhabitants to "a drunken man [who] staggereth in his vomit"; and the corrupt leaders have caused the people of the land to work evil in all they do.

**19:15** *Neither shall there be any work for Egypt, which the head or tail, branch or rush, may do.* The *head* (Egypt's leaders, identified above) and *tail* (the followers) will be unable to be productive in either the quality or the quantity of their work.

**19:16** *In that day.* This expression is found six times in this section (19:16, 18, 19, 21, 23, 24). The time frame for the prophecy belongs to an unknown era in the history of Egypt or to the last days and Jesus' second coming (2:12)—or perhaps to both ancient and future times.

*Egypt be like unto women: and it shall be afraid and fear.* Isaiah's imagery presents a clear picture as he compares the fears of the Egyptians to a woman who demonstrates concern for her children during impending danger.

*the shaking of the hand of the Lord of hosts.* Once again (19:14) Isaiah confirms that Jehovah is a moving cause behind some of Egypt's actions when He shakes his hand over it. The *shaking* of Jehovah's hand refers to his power (see 5:25; 9:12).

**19:17** *land of Judah shall be a terror unto Egypt, every one that maketh mention thereof shall be afraid in himself.* Those who hear mention of Judah in Egypt are fearful because of the plans Judah's God has against Egypt. It may be also that the Egyptians are fearful of Judah because of Jehovah's powerful demonstration in days of old when he battled against Ramses, an Egyptian Pharaoh, and sent plagues of various kinds upon the Egyptians. In this prophecy Jehovah again makes plans against Egypt ("the counsel of the Lord . . . which he hath determined against" Egypt), causing its inhabitants to fear.

**19:18** *In that day shall five cities in the land of Egypt speak the language of Canaan, and swear to the Lord of hosts.* The language of Canaan is Hebrew, as John N. Oswalt notes: "Egypt's turn to God will be so complete that some cities will go so far as to adopt even the language of Judah."[5] A portion of Egypt (represented by "five cities") will "swear" or make sacred covenants with the Lord of Hosts.

*The city of the Sun.* One of the five cities may have been called the City of the Sun, perhaps meaning that the city belongs to Jesus Christ, who is the Sun (Ps. 84:11; Mal. 4:2).

---

[5] *Book of Isaiah,* 377.

**19:19** *an altar to the Lord in the midst of the land of Egypt.* The altar is representative of a temple that will be built and dedicated to Jehovah in the land of Egypt.

*a pillar at the border thereof to the Lord.* A sign or a monument dedicated to the Lord.

**19:20** *it shall be for a sign and for a witness unto the Lord.* The pillar will serve as both a sign and witness of the Lord throughout Egypt.

*they shall cry unto the Lord . . . he shall send them a saviour . . . he shall deliver them.* The words *cry unto the Lord, oppressors,* and *he shall deliver them* recall the period of the judges when Israel, oppressed by her enemies, cried unto the Lord and was sent deliverers (Judges 3:9, 15; 6:7–14; 10:10). Now it is Egypt that will cry unto the Lord and receive a *saviour* who will *deliver them.*

**19:21** *Egyptians shall know the Lord in that day.* The Egyptians will have true knowledge concerning Jehovah.

*shall do sacrifice and oblation; yea, they shall vow a vow unto the Lord.* Sacrifices, oblations, and vows pertain to temple worship and also to Sabbath worship (D&C 59:9–12). That the Egyptians will make sacrifices to Jehovah indicates the presence of a temple dedicated to Jehovah in Egypt.

**19:22** *Lord shall smite Egypt . . . and heal it.* "The Lord's blows will be for healing, not destruction (Hosea 6:1). And Egypt may know his healing at any point, just as Israel may."[6]

*they shall return even to the Lord.* To *return* (Hebrew *shub*) is to repent. The phrase indicates that many Egyptians will repent of their sins and worship Jehovah.

*he shall be intreated of them.* Egyptians will pray to Jehovah.

*Lord . . . shall heal them.* This statement indicates that Jehovah will heal the Egyptians of their spiritual diseases and sicknesses.

**19:23** *a highway out of Egypt to Assyria, and the Assyrian shall come into Egypt.* Christ's gospel brings peace to formerly warring nations. The highway is the way of holiness on which the righteous tread as they return to God (11:16).

**19:24** *shall Israel be the third with Egypt and with Assyria.* Israel, Egypt, and Assyria will share the gospel's blessings equally; one will not be favored over the others.

*even a blessing in the midst of the land.* The presence of members of the house of Israel will be a blessing to all the earth's inhabitants.

---

[6] Oswalt, *Book of Isaiah,* 380.

**19:25** *Blessed be Egypt my people, and Assyria the work of my hands.* The phrases *my people* and *work of my hands* regularly refer to Israel, but Isaiah prophesies of the time when the Lord will bless Egypt and Assyria and will call them his people.

# ISAIAH 20

*The chapter has a dual meaning for us. First, it shows that Isaiah was a prophet not to Judah alone but to all the known world, in that Isaiah warned Egypt and Ethiopia of impending doom. Likewise, the president of The Church of Jesus Christ of Latter-day Saints is the prophet for the entire world. Second, the prophecy served to warn Judah not to place her trust in Egypt and Ethiopia, nor to make them her allies. Similarly, as individuals and as members of the Church, we should never place our trust in armed forces or powerful countries. Our trust should be in Jesus Christ.*

## Conquest of Ethiopia and Egypt: Isaiah's Dramatization (20:1–6)

Isaiah dramatizes this prophecy, which pertains to three major countries: Egypt (identified four times in the section), Ethiopia, and Assyria (each mentioned three times). The Lord instructs the prophet three times to remove his sackcloth and sandals and walk "naked and barefoot," which he does for three years. Isaiah's symbolic and prophetic actions (explained in 20:3–4) are a "sign and wonder" to Egypt and Ethiopia. Note the comparative language: *"Like as* my servant Isaiah hath walked naked and barefoot . . . *so shall"* (20:3–4) the Egyptians and Ethiopians walk naked and barefoot as slaves to the Assyrian conquerors. Isaiah's dramatization prophesies that Assyria will capture and enslave the Egyptians and Ethiopians.

This section is written in prose rather than in the poetic parallelistic style.

## Isaiah 20:1–6

In the year that Tartan came unto Ashdod, (when Sargon the king of Assyria sent him) and fought against Ashdod, and took it; (20:1) At the same time spake the Lord by Isaiah the son of Amoz, saying, Go and loose the sackcloth from off thy loins, and put off thy shoe from thy foot. And he did so, walking naked and barefoot. (20:2) And the Lord said, Like as my servant Isaiah hath walked naked and barefoot three years for a sign and wonder upon Egypt and upon Ethiopia; (20:3) So shall the king of Assyria lead away the Egyptians prisoners, and the Ethiopians captives, young and old, naked and barefoot, even with their buttocks uncovered, to the shame of Egypt. (20:4) And they shall be afraid and ashamed of Ethiopia their expectation, and of Egypt their glory. (20:5) And the inhabitant of this isle shall say in that day, Behold, such is our expectation, whither we flee for help to be delivered from the king of Assyria: and how shall we escape? (20:6)

### NOTES AND COMMENTARY

**20:1** *In the year.* In 711 B.C. Tartan came to Ashdod, a Philistine port city.

*Tartan.* Cupbearer and servant of King Sargon and later chief captain of King Sennacherib (2 Kgs. 18:17).

*Sargon.* Sargon II was an Assyrian king who ruled from 722–705 B.C.

**20:2** *spake the Lord by Isaiah.* The Lord is the source of Isaiah's prophecy.

*loose the sackcloth.* Often made of goats' hair, the sackcloth worn by Isaiah may have been similar to Elijah's hairy clothing (2 Kgs. 1:8) or to John the Baptist's camel-hair garment (Matt. 3:4). Symbolically, sackcloth represented repentance, mourning, or humility (Ps. 35:13; Matt. 11:21). That Isaiah had to be told to remove his sackcloth perhaps indicates that he was not permitted to mourn the forthcoming disaster that would befall Ethiopia and Egypt.

*he did so.* This was not a parable; it was an actual prophecy that was acted out by the prophet in view of his contemporaries, including perhaps his family, friends, and neighbors.

*naked and barefoot.* This phrase, mentioned three times in the section, emphasizes the Lord's command to Isaiah to remove his clothing. It is probable that Isaiah removed only his upper garment, which would have made only the upper portion of his body bare.[1]

The Assyrians forced their captives to march naked and barefoot to humiliate them, and the *naked and barefoot* Isaiah prophesied of the time when Egypt and Ethiopia, as Assyria's captives, would be forced to walk naked.

---

[1] Keil and Delitzsch, *Commentary,* 7:1:372.

In a spiritual sense, *naked and barefoot* represents the way we stand without the Atonement, "uncovered" before the Lord, for the Hebrew term for atonement (*kapar*) signifies a covering.[2]

**20:3** *Lord said.* After Isaiah dramatized the prophecy, the Lord spoke again and explained its meaning.

*sign and wonder.* This word pair often expresses a great sign from God (Deut. 28:46; 3 Ne. 2:1; Hel. 14:6). Here, Isaiah's action symbolizes the great sign from God that prophesied the captivity of Egypt and Ethiopia.

*Ethiopia.* Ethiopia is located below Egypt and is part of the kingdom of Nubia that was settled by the descendants of Cush (Gen. 10:6).

**20:4** *So shall the king of Assyria lead away the Egyptians prisoners.* The symbolism of Isaiah's dramatization is explained here. Just as Isaiah walked naked and barefoot, so will the Egyptians and Ethiopians walk naked and barefoot while prisoners of war.

**20:5** *they shall be . . . ashamed.* People who looked to Ethiopia and Egypt for power and glory, who imagined that these countries' chariots and weapons would save them, will be ashamed for trusting these worldly nations.

**20:6** *inhabitant of this isle.* This phrase refers to the Philistines.

*how shall we escape.* If the powerful nations of Egypt and Ethiopia, with their military might, have been overthrown, how can we, the inhabitants of Philistia, escape bondage?

---

[2] Koehler and Baumgartner, *Lexicon in Veteris Testamenti Libros,* 450.

# ISAIAH 21

LIKENING ISAIAH 21 UNTO OURSELVES

*This prophecy speaks not only of Babylon (and Duman and Arabia) of old but also of modern Babylon, which is the world (Rev. 14:8; 18:2; D&C 1:16). Ancient Babylon was destroyed as quickly as a whirlwind passes through the desert, and so will modern Babylon be devastated. "And again, verily I say unto you, the coming of the Lord draweth nigh, and it overtaketh the world as a thief in the night." For us, the command is, "gird up your loins, that you may be the children of light, and that day shall not overtake you as a thief" (D&C 106:4–5).*

## A PROPHECY OF JUDGMENT AGAINST BABYLON (21:1–10)

Disaster upon Babylon will be as quick and destructive as the whirlwinds that sweep over the Negev, and the destruction will advance from the direction of a "terrible land" (21:1), identified in 21:2 as the nations of Elam and Media. The vision is so clear to Isaiah that he hears the military leader shout the command to the Elamite and Mede armies to attack Babylon: "Go up [attack], O Elam, besiege, O Media" (21:2). As Elam and Media prepare to attack, the people of Babylon feast and celebrate, vainly relying on their watchmen to warn them of impending danger (21:5).

Isaiah finds the vision in this section painful and disturbing. He calls it a "grievous vision" (21:2); he is physically pained—his "loins [are] filled with pain"—and experiences sharp pangs likened to a woman in labor; he is "bowed down," and his "heart panted" after hearing and seeing things in the vision. He also experiences emotional pain and a loss of sleep (21:3–4). The pain probably came from the horror of the scene that he witnessed.

## Isaiah 21:1–10

The burden of the desert of the sea. As whirlwinds in the south pass through; so it cometh from the desert, from [the] terrible land. (21:1)

A grievous vision is declared unto me;

the *treacherous dealer* dealeth treacherously,
and the *spoiler* spoileth.

*Go up,* O Elam:
*besiege,* O Media;

all the sighing thereof have I made to cease. (21:2)

Therefore are *my loins* filled with pain:
pangs have taken hold upon *me,* as the pangs of a woman that travaileth:

*I was bowed* down at the hearing of it;
*I was dismayed* at the seeing of it. (21:3)

My *heart panted, fearfulness* affrighted me: the night of my pleasure hath he turned into *fear* unto me. (21:4)

Prepare the table, watch in the watchtower, eat, drink: arise, ye princes, and anoint the shield. (21:5)

For thus hath the Lord said unto me, Go, set a watchman, let him declare what he seeth. (21:6)

And he saw [chariotry, horsemen in pairs, riders on donkeys, riders on camels];[1] and he hearkened diligently with much heed: (21:7)

And [the watchman][2] cried, My lord,

*I stand continually* upon the watchtower in the daytime,
and *I am set* in my ward whole nights: (21:8)

And, behold, here cometh a chariot of men, with a couple of horsemen. And he answered and said, Babylon is fallen, is fallen; and all the graven images of her gods he hath broken unto the ground. (21:9)

O my threshing, and the corn of my floor: that which I have heard of the Lord of hosts, the God of Israel, have I declared unto you. (21:10)

## NOTES AND COMMENTARY

**21:1** *burden.* A prophecy of judgment against Babylon, meaning both the ancient kingdom and, symbolically, the latter-day world of wickedness.

*desert of the sea.* This image refers to Babylon. That city sat on a hot and dusty plain in the Euphrates valley, but anciently, before flood-control dams were built, the

---

[1] This translation from Oswalt, *Book of Isaiah,* replaces the unclear translation in the KJV.
[2] The KJV reading of "a lion" is corrupt, as indicated by the Masoretic text. DSS Isa. Scroll preserves the reading *ra'ah,* "one who sees" or "watchman"; compare Motyer, *Prophecy of Isaiah,* 175.

whole plain was flooded each spring during the high-water runoff of the Euphrates. Thus, Babylon sat both in a desert and on a sea.[3]

*whirlwinds in the south.* Destruction will come upon Babylon with a speed and force comparable to the whirlwinds that arise in the desert area known as the Negev.

*terrible land.* Isaiah calls Elam and Media the *terrible land* because of the extremely cruel nature of their leaders and armies. Isaiah 13:17–18 describes the Medes as people who love warfare for the sake of warring and killing, rather than for the rich booty it brings.

**21:2** *grievous vision is declared unto me.* The vision was painful, perhaps because it revealed explicit scenes of bloodshed and horror that will come with Babylon's destruction. Certainly the statement reveals Isaiah's great compassion for his people.

*treacherous dealer dealeth treacherously/spoiler spoileth.* This phrase sums up the vision's contents. Babylon is destroyed and plundered by destructive forces— warring nations who love to murder and cause havoc.

*Go up, O Elam: besiege, O Media.* Elam (the western portion of ancient Persia) was famous for its archers (Jer. 25:25; 49:34–39). "Media was the ancient name for NW Iran, southwest of the Caspian Sea and north of the Zagros Mountains."[4] Under King Cyrus's leadership, Elam and Media captured Babylon in 538 B.C.

Isaiah may have envisioned some of the actual bloodshed and warfare connected to this historical event, but he presents here a simple war cry uttered by a military leader (or perhaps by one of the warriors): "Go up, O Elam; besiege, O Media." Jeremiah received a portion of this same vision (Jer. 51:11, 28).

**21:3** *my loins filled with pain.* The vision brought Isaiah physical distress. He experienced pangs that resembled the sharp pains a woman experiences during labor.

**21:4** *night of my pleasure hath he turned into fear unto me.* The phrase may mean that the vision came and disturbed the prophet in the night, or Isaiah looked forward to the night when he could sleep and gain relief from the pain of the vision, but even then he found no relief. Job experienced similar struggles (Job 6:4).

**21:5** *watch in the watchtower, eat, drink: arise, ye princes, and anoint the shield.* Babylon's leaders and revelers feast and celebrate while the watchman looks for invaders. Trusting in their own man-made security and defense (*watchtower*), the people of Babylon (the worldly) prepare a banquet ("prepare the table") and then eat and drink, unaware of their imminent destruction. The phrase *anoint the shield*

---

[3] Keil and Delitzsch, *Commentary,* 7:1:377.
[4] *New Bible Dictionary,* s.v. "Medes, Media."

speaks of warriors who prepare for war, because shields were oiled to make them slick so that arrows would be diverted.

**21:6** *the Lord said unto me.* The Lord told Isaiah to "Go, set a watchman."

*Go, set a watchman.* The *watchman* may be Isaiah himself (21:11), all the true prophets of all ages (Jer. 6:17; Ezek. 3:17), or all of God's true witnesses who warn their neighbors and cities of approaching invaders or impending danger; "And in that day all who are found upon the watch-tower, or in other words, all mine Israel, shall be saved" (D&C 101:12).

**21:7** *he saw chariotry, horsemen in pairs, riders on donkeys, riders on camels.* The watchman sees the army that will soon destroy Babylon.

**21:8** *I stand continually upon the watchtower.* The watchman is diligent in keeping watch.

**21:9** *here cometh a chariot of men, with a couple of horsemen.* Now the watchman sees the army that has destroyed Babylon and he hears the declaration, "Babylon is fallen."

*Babylon is fallen.* The prophecy does not actually identify Babylon by name until now. The phrase *Babylon is fallen* is an expression that was also revealed to John (Rev. 14:8; 18:2) and Joseph Smith (D&C 1:16).

*graven images of her gods he hath broken.* Conquerors often made their captives' humiliation complete and their new kingdom secure by destroying the deities of the conquered people. They did this to show that *their* deities and kingdom were greater and more powerful than those of the fallen empire. When Jehovah destroys the kingdoms of the world (Babylon) at his second coming and before his millennial reign, he will destroy the people's images and gods.

**21:10** *that which I have heard . . . have I declared unto you.* Isaiah declared this vision to his audience after he received it.

## A PROPHECY OF JUDGMENT AGAINST DUMAH (21:11–12)

The prophecy is a dialogue between Isaiah and an unnamed man of Seir. It goes as follows:

> *Man of Seir:* "Watchman, how much of the night remains? Watchman, how much of the night remains?"

*Isaiah, the watchman:* "The morning is coming, but then the night will come again. If you wish to inquire again, return to your home and come again to me later."

In the greater context of Isaiah's prophecies of judgment against the nations, the prophecy appears to be about a man who, weary from living in the apostate world (Seir = Edom = world), asks Isaiah, "Watchman, how much of the night [sin, darkness, apostasy] remains? Watchman, how much of the night remains?" Isaiah responds with, "The morning [truth, light, the gospel] is coming, but the night [sin, darkness, apostasy] will return once more. If you wish to inquire again, return to your home and come again to me." Those who read Isaiah must remember that the prophecy is concerned with Dumah, although there may be a number of appropriate applications.

## Isaiah 21:11–12

The burden of Dumah. He calleth to me out of Seir,

*Watchman, <u>what of the night</u>?*
*Watchman, <u>what of the night</u>?* (21:11)

The watchman said,

The *morning* cometh,
and also the *night:*

if *ye* will *inquire,*
*inquire ye:*

return,
come. (21:12)

## NOTES AND COMMENTARY

**21:11** *burden.* See commentary on 21:1.

*Dumah. Dumah* was the son of Ishmael (Gen. 25:13–14; 1 Chr. 1:29–30) and founder of an Arab community. These descendants gave their name to Dumah, capital of a district known as Jawf, about halfway across northern Arabia between Palestine and southern Babylonia.[5] A second possible application for *Dumah* may indicate the silence that follows destruction, for the Hebrew word means "silence."

*He calleth to me out of Seir.* One of Seir's inhabitants called to Isaiah, "Watchman, what of the night?" *Seir* refers to Edom's land and people and is a symbol of worldliness (D&C 1:36).

---

[5] *New Bible Dictionary,* s.v. "Dumah."

*Watchman, what of the night?* This phrase is repeated for emphasis. An individual asks of the watchman (Isaiah), "What remains of the night [apostasy and darkness] before the morning light [truth, gospel] arises?" Isaiah responds with, "In the morning you will receive light followed by further darkness [night]." Isaiah is the watchman in this context, but compare with 21:6.

**21:12** *if ye will inquire.* Isaiah encourages inquiries pertaining to spiritual things.

*return, come.* Isaiah says, "Go home and return to me and inquire again at a later time."

# A PROPHECY OF JUDGMENT AGAINST ARABIA (21:13–17)

This section contains a single prophecy directed to three groups: the Dedanite caravans, Tema's inhabitants, and Kedar's nomads. Isaiah prophesies that within a year many of Kedar's people will be destroyed (21:16–17). Refugees will flee the swords and bows of the conquering nation and escape the "grievousness of war" (21:15); Isaiah calls upon the inhabitants of Dedanim and Tema to provide water and food (21:13–14) for these fugitives from Kedar (21:15–16). No mention is made of who it is that will war against the nomads of Kedar.

*Isaiah 21:13–17*

> The burden upon Arabia. In the forest in Arabia shall ye lodge, O ye travelling companies of Dedanim. (21:13)
>
> The inhabitants of the land of Tema brought water to him that was thirsty, they prevented with their bread him that fled. (21:14)
>
> For they fled from the swords, from the drawn sword, and from the bent bow, and from the grievousness of war. (21:15)
>
> For thus *hath the Lord said* unto me,
> Within a year, according to the years of an hireling, and all the *glory of Kedar* shall fail: (21:16)
> And the residue of the number of archers, the *mighty men of the children of Kedar,* shall be diminished:
> for the *Lord God of Israel hath spoken* it. (21:17)

## NOTES AND COMMENTARY

**21:13** *burden upon Arabia.* This expression refers to a judgment against Arabia.

*forest in Arabia shall ye lodge.* The Dedanite caravans (traveling companies) are camping in the Arabian forest. Dedan, which was named after a son of Cush (Gen.

10:7), was a "city and people of Northwest Arabia famous for its role in the caravan trade."[6]

**21:14** *inhabitants of the land of Tema.* Tema, which was named after one of the sons of Ishmael (Gen. 25:15), was an oasis and an important caravan stop. It was located on an ancient trade route on the Arabian peninsula some two hundred fifty miles southeast of Aqaba.

*brought water to him that was thirsty.* Tema's inhabitants supplied Kedar's refugees with water and food.

**21:15** *fled from the swords/drawn sword/bent bow.* The battle was raging when the refugees fled, as indicated by the phrases *drawn sword* and *bent bow,* weapons in use at that time. This verse provides the reason why the people *fled:* it was to escape the bloodshed and horrors of war.

**21:16** *Lord said unto me.* The Lord is the source of Isaiah's prophecy.

*Within a year.* The time frame of Isaiah's prophecy is explicit: Kedar will fall within a year.

*glory of Kedar shall fail.* Kedar's prosperity will come to an end because of the war.

*Kedar.* A son of Ishmael and grandson of Abraham (Gen. 25:13; 1 Chr. 1:29), whose descendants lived in tents in the Syro-Arabian desert and raised goats, sheep, and camels (60:7).

**21:17** *mighty men of the children of Kedar shall be diminished.* Only a few of Kedar's warriors will survive the destruction.

*Lord God of Israel hath spoken it.* God is the source of Isaiah's words.

---

[6] *New Bible Dictionary,* s.v. "Dedan."

# ISAIAH 22

### LIKENING ISAIAH 22 UNTO OURSELVES

*Isaiah's prophecy to Jerusalem (22:1–14) applies to all communities in all time periods: When war is imminent, do not rely on your weapons inventory and your fortified walls for salvation; rather, trust in the Lord and his ability to protect and save.*

*Isaiah's prophecy of Shebna and Eliakim (22:15–25) speaks of two types of people found in our own society. Shebna is the proud, wicked person who looks after his own welfare before seeking the good of others. Eliakim is the priestly minister whose concern is others, such as the widow and the fatherless. In the end, Shebna does not obtain a monumental grave but dies in shame; Eliakim takes his rightful place in his Father's kingdom and receives glory.*

## A PROPHECY OF JUDGMENT AGAINST THE VALLEY OF VISION (JERUSALEM) (22:1–14)

The people of Jerusalem are the subject of this section, as can be seen by Isaiah's use of feminine pronouns (apparent in the Hebrew only) to modify Jerusalem. Other expressions indicate that Jerusalem is the focus, including *city,* which is repeated three times (22:2, 9); in 22:10, Jerusalem is explicitly identified. Jerusalem mourns the loss of her inhabitants. She was once full of joy and activities, but now her children are gone, taken captive and moved to distant lands (22:1–3). Therefore, she weeps bitterly and refuses to be comforted by the Lord (22:4).

For Jerusalem, this is a "day of trouble, and of treading down" and of "breaking down the walls" (22:5), referring to her impending destruction by invading armies. Elam and Kir are the enemies prepared to battle against Jerusalem; they will fill the nearby valleys with chariots and horsemen and even approach the city's gates

(22:6–7). Jerusalem had prepared for this possibly lengthy war by building up a weapons inventory, fortifying the walls, and preparing the water supply (22:8–11). It is unfortunate, however, that Jerusalem relied for security on her weapons and preparations for war rather than on her Maker, the God of Israel, who created her long ago (22:11). All along, God desired that Jerusalem repent ("weeping," "mourning," "girding with sackcloth"; 22:12), but instead she chose riotous living, indulgences, feasting, and drunkenness (22:13–14). Therefore, Jerusalem will die in her sins (22:14).

## Isaiah 22:1–14

The burden of the valley of vision.
What aileth thee now, that thou art wholly gone up to the housetops? (22:1)

Thou that art *full of stirs*,
a *tumultuous* city,
a joyous city:

thy *slain men* are not slain *with the sword,*
nor *dead in battle.* (22:2)

All thy rulers are *fled* together, they are bound by the archers:
all that are found in thee are bound together, which have *fled* from far. (22:3)

Therefore said I, Look away from me; I will weep bitterly, labour not to comfort me, because of the spoiling of the daughter of my people. (22:4)

For it is a day of trouble, and of treading down, and of perplexity by the Lord God of hosts in the valley of vision, breaking down the walls, and of crying to the mountains. (22:5)

And *Elam* bare the quiver with chariots of men and horsemen,
and *Kir* uncovered the shield. (22:6)

And it shall come to pass, that thy choicest *valleys* shall be full of chariots,
and the horsemen shall set themselves in array at the *gate.* (22:7)

And he discovered the covering of Judah, and thou didst look in that day to the armour of the house of the forest. (22:8)

Ye have seen also the breaches of the city of David, that they are many: and ye gathered together the waters of the lower pool. (22:9)

And ye have numbered the houses of Jerusalem, and the houses have ye broken down to fortify the wall. (22:10)

Ye made also a ditch between the two walls for the water of the old pool:

but ye have *not looked* unto the Maker thereof,
*neither had respect* unto him that fashioned it long ago. (22:11)

And in that day did the Lord God of hosts call to *weeping,*
and to *mourning,*
and to *baldness,*
and to *girding with sackcloth:* (22:12)

And behold *joy*
and *gladness,*

*slaying* oxen,
and *killing* sheep,

*eating* flesh,
and *drinking* wine:

let us eat and drink; for to morrow we shall die. (22:13)

And it was revealed in mine ears by the Lord of hosts, Surely this iniquity shall not be purged from you till ye die, saith the Lord God of hosts. (22:14)

## NOTES AND COMMENTARY

**22:1** *burden of the valley of vision.* This prophecy is of judgment that will come against Jerusalem, the city where Isaiah and many of the prophets received divine visions.

*What aileth thee now.* What is wrong with you that you are climbing to the housetops?

*thou art wholly gone up to the housetops.* Jerusalem climbed upon the rooftop to mourn (a custom in ancient Israel; 15:3; Jer. 48:38) the loss of her children, who had been carried away into captivity.

**22:2** *Thou that art full of stirs, a tumultuous city, a joyous city.* Jerusalem, normally a city full of joy, now mourns the loss of her children.

*thy slain men are not slain with the sword.* Jerusalem's dead did not perish in a battle, but in captivity.

**22:3** *rulers are fled together, they are bound by the archers.* While the enemy was approaching Jerusalem, her leaders fled the city in cowardice and fear. Nevertheless, they were captured and bound by the archers and sent into captivity. After the captives were taken into exile, "none remained, save the poorest sort of the people of the land" (2 Kgs. 24:14).

**22:4** *Therefore said I, Look away from me; I will weep bitterly.* The personal pronoun *I* now replaces *you* and *your,* which are used in the first three verses to refer to Jerusalem. *I* refers to Isaiah, who weeps bitterly and demonstrates great emotion as he witnesses this vision of destruction (21:3–4).

*daughter of my people. Daughter* is another name for Jerusalem (Lam. 1:6–8; 2:8–11; Zech. 9:9; 2 Ne. 8:25), and *my people* often refers to Jerusalem and Judah's inhabitants.

**22:5** *For it is a day of trouble, and of treading down.* The language here refers to the pending destruction of Jerusalem and parallels the language used when prophets speak of the Second Coming. Joel, for instance, called it "a day of darkness and of gloominess, a day of clouds and of thick darkness" (Joel 2:2).

*by the Lord God of hosts.* The Lord permitted the destruction of Jerusalem and Judah.

*the valley of vision.* See commentary on 22:1.

*breaking down the walls.* The high walls that surround Jerusalem and are designed to defend her will be broken and destroyed by those who attack the city.

**22:6** *Elam bare the quiver with chariots of men and horsemen.* In this passage, Elam's famed archers (Jer. 49:34–39) pull their arrows from their quivers and set them in their bows, ready to battle against Jerusalem. Earlier, Isaiah heard the war cry of an army captain commanding Elam to go to battle against Babylon (21:2).

*Kir uncovered the shield. Kir* was a Mesopotamian city situated east of the Tigris River on the main highway that ran from Elam to Babylon. A leather covering protected a warrior's shield when it was not in use, and the phrase *uncovered the shield* indicates that Kir's warriors held their shields in readiness; it parallels the anticipation of Elam's soldiers who had their arrows removed from the quivers, ready for an impending battle.

**22:7** *thy choicest valleys shall be full of chariots.* The enemy has surrounded Jerusalem, fully armored, ready for the battle. The army is composed of chariots that serve as war vehicles and horsemen who have "set themselves in array at the gate[s]" of Jerusalem. The valleys mentioned here may be those immediately next to Jerusalem—Kidron, Hinnom, and Tyropoeon—or other valleys in the region.

**22:8** *he discovered the covering of Judah.* Jerusalem and Judah's defense was not adequate, and the invaders removed Jerusalem's fortifications.

*armour of the house of the forest.* This phrase refers to a building constructed under Solomon's direction on the temple mount, which formed part of Solomon's palace complex. The structure was called *house of the forest* because it was constructed of cedar columns and beams, and it housed armor and other items (1 Kgs. 7:2–5; 10:17–21). Isaiah's inspired words show irony in the situation: the Jews prepared for the coming war by trusting in their armories, including the house of the forest, but they ignored the most significant building on the very same mount: Solomon's temple—the only place from which both temporal and spiritual salvation could have come.

**22:9** *Ye have seen also the breaches of the city of David.* The Jews prepared for the war by repairing weaknesses in Jerusalem's walls.

*gathered together the waters of the lower pool.* The *pool* refers to Hezekiah's Tunnel, an engineering marvel that was created to permit Jerusalem's inhabitants to safely obtain outside water through the city's walls during a siege. Isaiah selects his terms well; Judah relied on the waters that originated from the ground (Hezekiah's Tunnel) but rejected Jehovah, the "waters of Shiloah that go softly" (8:6) and the "fountain of living waters" (Jer. 2:13; 17:13; Isa. 33:21).

**22:10** *numbered the houses of Jerusalem.* The Jerusalemites took a census to determine how many men of fighting age were available to defend the city.

*houses have ye broken down to fortify the wall.* Jerusalem's inhabitants prepared for the battle by destroying a number of their own homes so they could obtain building materials such as cut stones to repair and reinforce the wall's strength (22:9).

**22:11** *Ye made also a ditch.* Jerusalem's inhabitants created a channel to move water from outside the city to the inside so water could be obtained during a siege (22:9).

*but ye have not looked unto the Maker thereof.* This clause is a pivotal point. The people of Judah prepared for the battle by adding to their weapons supply, repairing the city's walls, and so on (22:8–10), but they had not looked to nor had respect for Jehovah, the God of Israel. Judah should have been fasting, praying, worshiping in the temple, and seeking God's word through the mouths of the prophets. Note the terminology Isaiah uses as he explains Judah's reliance on worldly might instead of heavenly powers: during this period of impending battle, Jerusalem's inhabitants did *look* at their armories (22:8), and they *have seen* that their water supply was in order (22:9), but they *have not looked* unto Jehovah, their Maker (22:11).

*Maker.* According to Isaiah's imagery, Jehovah was the Maker (D&C 30:2; Hosea 8:14) of Jerusalem, the great Architect who "fashioned it long ago." Again Isaiah's words are instructive and show contrasts between those who attempted to build Jerusalem through repairs, fortifications, and water channels (22:8–11), and God, who was the city's original builder (22:11).

**22:12** *in that day did the Lord God of hosts call to weeping.* Weeping, mourning, baldness, and sackcloth symbolize repentance and sorrow. Jehovah wanted the people to repent with their hearts, but instead they chose revelry (22:13).

**22:13** *let us eat and drink; for to morrow we shall die.* The Jerusalemites failed to turn to Jehovah at this critical time. Their attitude was to seek pleasure and *eat and drink; for tomorrow we die* (see also 2 Ne. 28:8; 1 Cor. 15:32), which is the attitude held by those who do not believe in God or in a postmortal existence.[1]

---

[1] *Teachings of the Prophet Joseph Smith,* 56.

**22:14** *revealed in mine ears by the Lord of hosts.* Isaiah witnesses that the Lord revealed the prophecy found in Isaiah 22:1–14.

*Surely this iniquity shall not be purged from you till ye die.* The New International Version reads, "'Til your dying day this sin will not be atoned for.'" In very strong language Isaiah testifies that Judah has gone beyond the point of repentance and will not receive forgiveness in this life for her sins. His revelation closes with the affirmation that it is the Lord who has spoken, "saith the Lord God of hosts."

## JUDGMENT UPON SHEBNA AND BLESSINGS UPON ELIAKIM (22:15–25)

This prophecy rests on the heads of two historical characters, Shebna and Eliakim, who were Isaiah's contemporaries and likely acquainted with him. The section consists of two parts. First, Isaiah 22:15–19 sets forth certain details pertaining to Shebna, an important and influential government official or treasurer (22:15; 37:2) who served in the court of Hezekiah, king of Judah. Shebna, a proud man of wealth, is rebuked by the Lord through Isaiah for his haughtiness and attempt to build for himself a monumental tomb. Therefore, Isaiah prophesies that a judgment will fall upon his head (22:17–19): Shebna will lose his important position in the kingdom of Judah; he will be violently captured and carried into captivity; his glory will become shame, and he will die in exile.

Shebna symbolizes all wicked people of his day and ours. He is an example of what many individuals have become: "He was, therefore, individually what the nation was collectively: wedded to present satisfactions and self-confident in the face of the future."[2]

Second, Isaiah 22:20–25 pertains to the righteousness and blessing of Eliakim, who was a priest and official in Hezekiah's house (36:3; 37:2). This section is of great import to the reader because Eliakim's life and ministry parallels Jesus Christ's.[3] Eliakim serves as a type of Jesus in several ways: as Eliakim replaced an evil ruler of Judah (Shebna), so Christ will replace all of the temporal rulers of Judah and Israel when he takes his rightful place as King of kings; Eliakim's name is prophetic ("may God raise") and points to Christ's power to lift us from both sin and death as a priest, Eliakim points to Jesus' role as the priest (Heb. 7:17); and similar to Eliakim's

[2] Motyer, *Prophecy of Isaiah,* 186.
[3] That this prophecy is messianic is indicated in the *Times and Seasons* 5 (1844): 748.

ministry "over the house" of Hezekiah, king of Judah, Christ possesses eternal power over the house of Judah or Israel.

Other prophetic elements of this section about Eliakim point to Jesus' divine mission: Eliakim's call (22:20); his participation in a vesting rite (22:21); his reception of the government (22:21; 9:6–7); his fatherhood (22:21); and his reception of the "key of the house of David" (22:22). All refer to Jesus Christ's divine call and election, his investiture, coronation, and enthronement in the temple setting, his reception of God's true government, his divine and everlasting fatherhood (9:6), and his possession of great priesthood authority (keys). Further, the concept that "they shall hang upon him all the glory of his father's house" (22:24) may refer to an enthronement ceremony; the "nail" (22:23, 25) speaks of Jesus' crucifixion, the "throne" refers to his kingship (22:23), and the subject of offspring (22:24) may refer to his spiritual children.

*Isaiah 22:15–25*

Thus saith the Lord God of hosts, Go, get thee unto this treasurer, even unto Shebna, which is over the house, and say, (22:15)

*What* hast thou <u>here</u>?
and *whom* hast thou <u>here</u>,

that thou hast *hewed* thee out a <u>sepulchre</u> here,
as he that *heweth* him out a <u>sepulchre</u> on high,
and that *graveth* an <u>habitation</u> for himself in a rock? (22:16)

Behold, the *Lord* will [certainly <u>grab you</u>][4] and [<u>hurl you</u> away, O mighty man][5] (22:17)
*He* will surely violently <u>turn and toss thee</u> like a ball into a large country:

there shalt thou die, and there the chariots of thy glory shall be the shame of thy lord's house. (22:18)

And I will *drive thee* <u>from thy station</u>,
and <u>from thy state</u> shall he *pull thee down*. (22:19)

And it shall come to pass in that day, that I will call my servant Eliakim the son of Hilkiah: (22:20)

And I will *clothe him* with <u>thy robe</u>,
and *strengthen him* with <u>thy girdle</u>,

and I will commit thy government into his hand:
and he shall be a father to the inhabitants of Jerusalem, and to the house of Judah. (22:21)

And the key of the house of David will I lay upon his shoulder;

---

[4] Brown, Driver, and Briggs, *Hebrew and English Lexicon,* 742.
[5] Brown, Driver, and Briggs, *Hebrew and English Lexicon,* 376.

so he shall *open,* and none shall shut;
and he shall *shut,* and none shall open. (22:22)

And I will fasten him as a nail in a sure place; and he shall be for a glorious throne to his father's house. (22:23)

And they shall hang upon him all the glory of his father's house, the offspring and the issue, all vessels of small quantity, from the vessels of cups, even to all the vessels of flagons. (22:24)

In that day, saith the Lord of hosts, shall the nail that is fastened in the sure place be removed, and be cut down, and fall; and the burden that was upon it shall be cut off: for the Lord hath spoken it. (22:25)

## NOTES AND COMMENTARY

**22:15** *Thus saith the Lord.* The Lord is the source of Isaiah's prophecy.

*treasurer, even . . . Shebna.* Shebna held the prominent position of a royal treasurer (perhaps over the temple treasury) in the kingdom of Judah.

**22:16** *What hast thou here/whom hast thou here.* Isaiah asks Shebna, "Who do you think you are, that you make a great sepulchre for yourself, that you are trying to exalt yourself?"

*thou hast hewed thee out a sepulchre.* Shebna tries to imitate God and God's glory with permanence (*sepulchre*) and self-exaltation (*on high*). The location of Shebna's sepulchre is unknown, although some scholars place it with other tombs carved in rock in the valley of Kidron, east of Jerusalem.

**22:17** *the Lord will . . . [hurl you away].* Shebna will be hurled away, or taken into captivity, by the Lord's power.

**22:18** *He will surely violently turn and toss thee like a ball into a large country.* This is a continuation of the prophecy concerning eventual exile that is formulated in Isaiah 22:17: Shebna/Judah, *like a ball,* will be *violently* kicked and bounced about on their way to exile.

*there shalt thou die.* Shebna and many of Judah's inhabitants will die while in captivity. How, then, did Shebna end up in his tomb (22:16), if he died in exile? Either his body was returned from his exiled land to Jerusalem for burial, or, more likely, Shebna was a symbol of all wicked people.

*the chariots of thy glory.* Chariots represent the self-reliance, self-might, and glory of the wicked as they look to war and weaponry for temporal salvation. Meanwhile, the righteous view God as both their temporal and spiritual salvation; he is their refuge and place of safety.

**22:19** *I will drive thee from thy station.* Because of Shebna's pride and attempt at self-exaltation, he is removed from his important station (treasurer) in the kingdom.

*from thy state shall he pull thee down.* Shebna will be pulled down from his position of honor in Hezekiah's courts.

**22:20** *it shall come to pass in that day.* Refers to the day when Shebna is destroyed. This statement indicates a transition from a prophecy about Shebna to one about Eliakim.

*I will call my servant Eliakim.* Eliakim, the priest, receives a call and replaces Shebna as the servant. Now he typifies Jesus Christ, who is also called "servant" (42:1; Matt. 12:18) and who serves Heavenly Father (Ps. 40:8; John 8:29).

**22:21** *I will clothe him with thy robe/girdle.* Eliakim (or Christ) receives the garments of priesthood authority, kingship, and righteousness. The *robe* and *girdle* refer to the temple's sacred vestments (see commentary on 9:6).

*I will commit thy government into his hand.* This pertains to Eliakim, but it is also a messianic statement about Jesus, who received "the throne of David," a "kingdom," and "the government . . . upon his shoulder" (9:6–7). *Hand* represents power or authority.

*he shall be a father.* Jesus is the spiritual father (9:6).

**22:22** *the key of the house of David will I lay upon his shoulder.* The key, which represents authority and power (Matt. 16:19; Rev. 3:7), opens the door to the heavenly temple.

*he shall open, and none shall shut/he shall shut, and none shall open.* Only Christ has the power to open and close the door of the heavenly temple. The words in this phrase are repeated in Revelation 3:7.

**22:23** *I will fasten him as a nail in a sure place.* This image pertains to Christ's crucifixion. "'The nail fastened in a sure place,' remains a mystery to the world, and will, but the wise understand."[6]

*he shall be for a glorious throne to his father's house.* The *throne* represents kingship; Christ will sit upon his Father's throne (Rev. 3) and rule and reign with great glory.

**22:24** *they shall hang upon him all the glory of his father's house.* The prophet may be presenting a word play; inasmuch as Christ *hung* on the cross to atone for the sins of mankind, even so will God "*hang* upon him all the glory" of his Father's kingdom. The phrase *hang upon him all the glory* may represent the robe of righteousness that will hang on Christ's shoulder, or the key of the house of David that will (symbolically) hang around his neck. One recalls similar expressions from Isaiah, such as

---

[6] *Times and Seasons* 5 (1844): 748.

"and the government shall be upon his shoulder" (9:6; 22:21–22) and the "key . . . will I lay upon his shoulder" (22:22).

*offspring and the issue.* This phrase pertains to Jesus Christ.[7] Those who become part of Christ's spiritual family through his atonement will be his *offspring.* See 22:21 above, concerning Christ as the Father.

*vessels of small quantity/cups/flagons.* The varying sizes of vessels may be metaphors for members of Christ's spiritual family. A flagon is a large vessel, often with a handle and a lid.

**22:25** *In that day.* This refers to the last days and Christ's second coming.

*saith the Lord of hosts.* The Lord is the source of Isaiah's prophecy.

*nail that is fastened in the sure place be removed, and be cut down, and fall.* "If any man believes that the 25th verse is true translation and explanation of the 'nail,' he is welcome to his opinion; he knows nothing of the key of David, and little about the keys of the kingdom."[8] This is a reference to the crucifixion and the Atonement. One possible meaning: the nail prints will remain in Christ's body even after the resurrection, until every person has witnessed them, acknowledged that he is the Savior, and accepted judgment. All persons will be judged in proportion to their acceptance of him and his tokens. This passage, then, may refer to the completion of Jesus Christ's divine work and the judgments against the wicked, when justice has been eternally served.

*Lord hath spoken it.* The Lord is the source of Isaiah's prophecy.

---

[7] *Times and Seasons* 5 (1844): 748.
[8] *Times and Seasons* 5 (1844): 748.

# ISAIAH 23

## LIKENING ISAIAH 23 UNTO OURSELVES

*Tyre was a famous Phoenician city noted for her commercial enterprises, great wealth, and materialism. Tyre was so well-known that she was called a "market place of nations" (23:3), and her traders and merchants were so celebrated that they were equated with the princes and the "honorable of the earth" (23:8).*

*The Lord spoke against Tyre (and her inhabitants), decrying her pride by calling her a harlot. He also warned her inhabitants to repent, lest she become a desolate city. Tyre's inhabitants did not listen to the prophet and were thus destroyed.*

*Tyre may be like many of the large cities in our world today, whose inhabitants' primary interest is obtaining material wealth. Such cities—if their inhabitants are proud, if they glory in wickedness, and if they sell themselves to the ways of the world— will be destroyed when the Lord returns to the earth with great glory, just as Tyre was destroyed so long ago. Tyre, then, serves as a warning to us of the pitfalls of pride and materialism and the resultant destruction.*

## THE SONG OF THE DESTRUCTION OF TYRE AND SIDON (23:1–14)

Isaiah 23 is the last of nine prophetic warnings against the heathen nations surrounding Israel. Isaiah began this series of pronouncements in chapter 13 with a prophecy against Babylon; he concludes it in this chapter with a prophecy against Tyre. These two cities symbolize worldliness—Tyre was the center of commerce and a leading sea power; Babylon was the center of politics and a leading land power. Both were condemned for pride (13:11; 23:9) and referred to as harlots (23:15–17; D&C 86:3). The prophecy against Babylon attacks worldliness; the prophecy against Tyre strikes at materialism. Both are types of the world in our day.

Isaiah prophesies that the merchants of Tyre will learn of the destruction of their homeland and mourn (23:1). He uses colorful descriptions of Tyre's glory—it is like a "market place of nations" (23:3), a "joyous city" (23:7), a "crowning city," full of "princes" and the "honorable of the earth" (23:8). As a contrast, Isaiah describes the destruction of Tyre—a defiled woman (23:9), who is weak (23:10), shamed (without children; 23:4), and a ruin (23:13). The Lord is responsible for planning Tyre's devastation (23:9), using Assyria's armies to accomplish his plan (23:13). The destruction of Tyre is a type of the destruction of the wicked—and their wealth—at the time of the Lord's return.

## Isaiah 23:1–14

The burden of Tyre.
Howl, ye ships of Tarshish; for it is laid waste,
so that there is no house, no [harbor]:[1]
from the land of Chittim it is revealed to them. (23:1)

Be still, ye inhabitants of the isle;
thou whom the merchants of Zidon, that pass over the sea, have replenished. (23:2)

And by *great waters* the seed of Sihor,
the harvest of the *river,* is her revenue;
and she is a [market place][2] of nations. (23:3)

Be thou ashamed, O Zidon:
for *the sea* hath spoken,
even *the strength of the sea,* saying,

I *travail* not,
nor *bring forth children,*

neither do I *nourish up* young men,
nor *bring up* virgins. (23:4)

[When] the *report [comes to] Egypt,*
[they will be] sorely pained at the *report [from] Tyre.* (23:5)[3]

Pass ye over to Tarshish; howl, ye inhabitants of the isle. (23:6)

Is this your joyous city, whose antiquity is of ancient days?
her own feet shall carry her afar off to sojourn. (23:7)

Who hath taken this counsel against Tyre, the crowning city,
*whose merchants* are princes,
*whose [traders]*[4] are the honorable of the earth? (23:8)

---

[1] NIV Isa. 23:1.
[2] The word *mart* can be better rendered as *marketplace* or *fair.*
[3] All bracketed changes are from NIV Isa. 23:5.
[4] The word *traffickers* can be better rendered as *traders.*

The Lord of hosts hath purposed it, to *[defile]*[5] *the pride* of <u>all glory,</u>
and to *bring into contempt* <u>all the honorable of the earth</u>. (23:9)

[Cultivate][6] thy land as [along the Nile],[7] O daughter of Tarshish:
there is no more strength [in thee].[8] (23:10)

He *stretched out his hand* <u>over the sea,</u>
he shook the kingdoms:
the Lord hath *given a commandment* <u>against [Phoenicia]</u>,[9]
to destroy the strong holds thereof. (23:11)

And he said, Thou shalt *no more rejoice,* O thou <u>oppressed virgin,</u>
<u>daughter of Zidon</u>: arise, pass over to Chittim;
there also shalt thou *have no rest.* (23:12)

Behold the land of the Chaldeans; this people [did not exist],[10]
till the Assyrian founded it for them that dwell in the wilderness:

they *set up* the <u>towers</u> thereof,
they *raised up* the <u>palaces</u> thereof,
he brought it to a <u>ruin</u>. (23:13)

Howl, ye ships of Tarshish: for your [fortress][11] is laid waste. (23:14)

## NOTES AND COMMENTARY

**23:1–2** *burden.* See commentary on 13:1.

*Tyre/Zidon (Sidon).* Tyre and Sidon, Phoenicia's chief cities, are a symbol for the whole land of Phoenicia; like Babylon, they symbolize the world that will be judged by God (D&C 1:16).

*Howl.* The ships of Tarshish are commanded to cry out in anguish (*howl*) over the many deaths and mourn the loss of their city, Tyre.

*ships of Tarshish.* The location of Tarshish is unknown. The *ships of Tarshish* symbolize Tyre's people, and especially the merchants who, because of their wealth and prestige, represent the world's pride and arrogance (see commentary on Isaiah 2:16).

*it is laid waste.* Tyre will soon be destroyed.

*Chittim (Kittim).* Early name for Cyprus, an island colonized and controlled by Tyre. Since Tyre will be laid waste, so that there will be no house or harbor for people

---

[5] The KJV *stain* comes from Hebrew *chalal* meaning to "pollute, defile, [or] profane." Brown, Driver, and Briggs, *Hebrew and English Lexicon,* 320.
[6] DSS Isa. Scroll 23:10 reads *'abediy,* to "work," rendered here as "cultivate"; see Watts, *Isaiah 1–33,* 303.
[7] NIV Isa. 23:10 reads *along the Nile,* replacing the KJV *a river.*
[8] JST Isa. 23:10 adds *in thee.*
[9] The Hebrew reads *Canaan.* Brown, Driver, and Briggs, *Hebrew and English Lexicon,* 488.
[10] We prefer the reading of *did not exist.* Brown, Driver, and Briggs, *Hebrew and English Lexicon,* 226.
[11] NIV Isa. 23:14.

or ships to rest in, *Chittim* is an ideal location for Tyre's refugees, who will bring news of the destruction to Tyre's merchants who are traveling away from home.

**23:2** *Be still, ye inhabitants of the isle.* Be still (Hebrew *damam*) carries two meanings associated with stillness, "motionless" and "silent."[12] *Isle* specifically refers to the island of Tyre. In contrast to *howl* in 23:1, the Lord commands the inhabitants of Tyre to *be still.* The once bustling city of Tyre will be silenced by the destruction of her houses, port, and inhabitants.

*merchants . . . replenished.* Sidon's merchants carried corn, dyed cloth, grain, wine, metal, horses, wood, and oil as they voyaged on the seas. Tyre and Cyprus were supported (*replenished*) by Sidon's trading (see commentary on 2:6).

**23:3** *seed of Sihor/harvest of the river.* Seed and harvest refer to the grain produced near Sihor (Josh. 13:3) and the Nile River and shipped by the Phoenicians over great waters to other nations, thereby providing Phoenicia with revenue.

*market place of nations.* During Isaiah's time, Tyre and Sidon were the Mediterranean's most powerful commercial cities; the Mediterranean nations all traded with Phoenicia.

**23:4** *ashamed.* According to Israelite tradition, shame fell on the woman who was barren or violated, or who lost all her children through death. Tyre and Sidon, portrayed as women, will be humbled and shamed. Tyre, referred to as the "strength of the sea," will be virtually depopulated, her people killed, enslaved, or made refugees, and therefore unable to raise up a new generation of young men and virgins to populate the island.

*strength of the sea.* This phrase, which speaks of Tyre, can be translated as "stronghold" or "fortress of the sea."[13]

*I travail not, nor bring forth children, neither do I nourish up.* Tyre, presented as a barren or vanquished woman, speaks of the shame she will feel when she becomes childless through the loss of sons and daughters in battle. It will be as if Tyre had never been populated and the sea had never been a major shipping lane.

*young men/virgins.* The lack of young men and virgins implies the loss of honor and life, symbolizing Tyre's destruction and the enslavement of her inhabitants. So will it be with the wicked in the last days.

**23:5** *Egypt . . . will be sorely pained at the report.* Egypt's inhabitants, who rely heavily on trade with Tyre, will be hurt by Tyre's destruction.

---

[12] Motyer, *Prophecy of Isaiah,* 190.
[13] Motyer, *Prophecy of Isaiah,* 191.

**23:6** *Pass ye over to Tarshish.* Those who survive or escape the destruction of Tyre are instructed to flee to Tarshish, which had once brought them great profit.

*howl, ye inhabitants.* Tyre's inhabitants will mourn the loss of Tyre as they flee to Tarshish (23:1).

**23:7** *joyous city, whose antiquity is of ancient days.* Tyre took pride and joy in her prosperity and antiquity, and Isaiah mocks her inhabitants with a question that essentially asks, "Where is your joyous, bustling city now?" (22:2; 32:13).

*her own feet shall carry her afar off to sojourn.* After the destruction of their city, Tyre's refugees will migrate to distant places.

**23:8–9** *Who hath taken this counsel against Tyre.* Isaiah answers his own question: The Lord, who made this plan against Tyre, *hath taken this counsel.* The Hebrew word *ya'ats,*[14] translated as both "counsel" (23:8) and "purposed" (23:9), speaks both of the plans made and of the determination to follow through. Elsewhere in Isaiah the Lord plans the destruction of Babylon (14:24, 27) and Egypt (19:12).

**23:8** *crowning city.* This description represents Tyre's splendor and glory—her pride. Despite her worldly greatness, the Lord of Hosts is about to bring her low (see Isa. 23:1).

*merchants are princes/traders are the honorable of the earth.* Tyre's merchants are so well-respected and famous, it is as if they were princes, or sons of kings. The *honorable of the earth* can be understood as those who receive the honors of men rather than those of God (see commentary on 47:15; see also 3:3–4). The scriptures make it clear that the honors of men are worthless in eternity because only those honors conferred by God will persist (Alma 60:36).

**23:9** *defile the pride/bring into contempt.* The Lord determines to bring down the proud of Tyre, causing her glory to cease; instead, she will be defiled. This same fate will fall upon the proud in the last days (see commentary on 2:12–17; Lev. 26:19; Prov. 16:18).

**23:10** *Cultivate thy land as along the Nile.* Because Tyre's inhabitants have lost their domination of the trading market and been pressed into servitude by a foreign nation, they must resort to cultivating their land, as was the practice along the Nile River in Egypt.[15] The occupation of merchant was preferred to farming—but the people of Tyre will be forced back to the land.

*daughter of Tarshish.* Tyre is essentially dependent on Tarshish ships for her strength and livelihood (see commentary on 23:1).

---

[14] Brown, Driver, and Briggs, *Hebrew and English Lexicon,* 419.
[15] Watts, *Isaiah 1–33,* 303.

**23:11** *stretched out his hand.* This foresees the time when the Lord stretches forth his hand in punishment (see commentary on Isaiah 5:25).

*he shook the kingdoms.* In an action as simple as stretching out his hand, God destroys nations and kingdoms.

*commandment against Phoenicia.* God commands Assyria (23:13) to destroy Phoenicia's strongholds.

**23:12** *Thou shalt no more rejoice.* Because of her destruction, Sidon cannot rejoice.

*oppressed virgin.* Sidon is portrayed as a woman, as is customary for cities referred to by Isaiah.

*daughter of Zidon (Sidon).* It was customary for Isaiah to call cities *daughter* (23:10; 37:22; 47:1).

*arise, pass over to Chittim.* Sidon's refugees are told to flee to Chittim, or Cyprus (compare 23:6).

*there also shalt thou have no rest.* In Cyprus, the refugees from Sidon will experience troubles, perhaps warfare, as they did in Sidon.

**23:13** *this people did not exist.* The Chaldeans were Semitic nomads who came to be known as Babylonians. They inhabited the wilderness areas of the Fertile Crescent where Babylon was built. They had little significance (*did not exist*) among the earth's nations until the Assyrians came and built cities and fortifications ("founded it") in their land, thus making the city of Babylon powerful.

*set up the towers.* The Assyrian army set up siege towers as they surrounded Tyre.

*they stripped its palaces.* The Assyrians stripped Sidon's palaces of their ornaments, wealth, and leaders; they even pulled down Tyre's walls.

*he brought it to a ruin.* The subject here is the Lord, who brought about Tyre's harsh and swift ruin through Assyria (25:2).

**23:14** *Howl, ye ships of Tarshish: for your fortress is laid waste.* Isaiah reiterates the command to the Tarshish ships to *howl* (23:1). Again, this prophecy symbolizes the great destruction of the proud and the wicked at the end of the world; they will have ample cause to howl and mourn.

## TYRE AND SIDON RESTORED FOR THE PURPOSES OF THE LORD (23:15–18)

Contrasting the message of doom of the previous section, the Lord now reveals a message of restoration: After seventy years, Tyre will begin to rebuild her trading industry (23:16–17) and will sing "the song of the harlot" (23:15).

*Isaiah 23:15–18*

And it shall come to pass in that day, that Tyre shall be forgotten seventy years, according to the days of one king: after the end of seventy years, [it shall be unto Tyre as the song of the harlot].[16] (23:15)

Take an harp, go about the city,
thou harlot that hast been forgotten;
make sweet melody, sing many songs,
that thou mayest be remembered. (23:16)

And it shall come to pass after the end of seventy years, that the Lord will visit Tyre, and
she shall turn to her hire, and shall commit fornication with all the kingdoms of the world upon the face of the earth. (23:17)

And *her merchandise* and her hire shall be holiness to the Lord: it shall not be [hoarded][17] nor laid up; for *her merchandise* shall be for them that dwell before the Lord, to eat sufficiently, and for [choice][18] clothing. (23:18)

### NOTES AND COMMENTARY

**23:15** *forgotten seventy years/days of one king.* The decline of the Assyrian empire permitted Tyre to regain commercial domination (23:17) approximately seventy years after her destruction (see commentary on Isaiah 23:1). The *days of one king* are said to be seventy years.

*as the song of the harlot.* This may be a street song heard in seaport towns, directed to a forgotten harlot who tries to revitalize her image and former occupation. The harlot is encouraged to take up her harp and sing "about the city" to gain attention. Isaiah uses this song to refer to Tyre and her profitable trade, which could be compared to prostitution because Tyre sought to satisfy the carnal desires of men by selling them all manner of wares.

---

[16] The KJV *shall Tyre sing as an harlot* can also be read as *it shall be unto Tyre as the song of the harlot,* making an easier transition to verse 16.

[17] From the Hebrew root *'atsar,* meaning "to lay up, store up, or hoard." Brown, Driver, and Briggs, *Hebrew and English Lexicon,* 70.

[18] From Hebrew *'atiyq,* meaning "eminent, surpassing, choice." Brown, Driver, and Briggs, *Hebrew and English Lexicon,* 801.

**23:16** *go about the city/sing many songs, that thou mayest be remembered.* The forgotten harlot (Tyre) must go about her *city* (the world's marketplaces) to solicit men's attention (Prov. 7:10–19) with alluring cries (*songs*) in the hope of somehow regaining her former status among the nations.

**23:17** *the Lord will visit Tyre.* Tyre was previously visited in judgment by the Lord (23:9, 11), but after the completion of the seventy-year sentence, the Lord will again visit Tyre, this time to restore her to her former status. But she will again find success in trading with the world's nations and return to her harlotry.

*Tyre . . . shall commit fornication.* This perhaps speaks of the immoral practices, greed, or idolatry that Tyre will sell to the world's kingdoms.

*kingdoms of the world.* Tyre's influence will again extend throughout the known world.

**23:18** *her hire shall be holiness to the Lord.* This may refer to an ancient custom by which the wealth of a city designated for destruction was consecrated to the Lord (Josh. 6:17, 19; Micah 4:13). Or perhaps the time of which Isaiah speaks is yet to come, and Tyre is a symbol of the wealthy nations of the world who, in the last days, will bring gifts, money, and honor to the Lord and his people (60:5–7; Ps. 45:12; Hag. 2:8).

*it shall not be hoarded.* Tyre possessed treasuries, and her inhabitants "heaped up silver as the dust, and fine gold as the mire of the streets" (Zech. 9:3). Isaiah prophesies that Tyre will not hoard her treasures, but "her merchandise shall be for them that dwell before the Lord" (23:18).

# ISAIAH 24

## LIKENING ISAIAH 24 UNTO OURSELVES

*When any of us transgress the laws of God, "seek not the Lord," do not "establish his righteousness," or walk in our "own way" (D&C 1:16), we join to a greater or lesser degree the earth's inhabitants who "have transgressed the laws, changed the ordinance, [and] broken the everlasting covenant" (24:5). We should instead strive to obey the laws of God, seek the Lord, establish his righteousness, and walk in his way. If we do so, we will "glorify . . . the Lord in the region of light, even the name of the Lord God of Israel in the isles of the sea" (24:15).*

## THE WORLD CHANGES THE ORDINANCE AND BREAKS THE COVENANT (24:1–12)

Isaiah teaches us of the great apostasy, when earth's inhabitants made three major errors: they "transgressed the laws, changed the ordinance, [and broke] the everlasting covenant" (24:5). Because of this great apostasy from God's truth and his plan of happiness, God has wasted, turned upside down, emptied, and utterly spoiled the earth. Furthermore, the earth mourns, fades away, languishes, is defiled, and a curse devours it (24:1–6); because of the apostasy, God has scattered and burned the earth's inhabitants so that the few who remain do not experience happiness—"all joy is darkened" (24:11).

Although this prophecy of Isaiah speaks of many apostasies that have occurred during the history of the earth, it speaks especially of the period preceding the restoration of the gospel—an apostasy that continues to this day among most of the world's people. In a revelation to the Prophet Joseph Smith, the Lord quoted Isaiah 24:5: "For they have strayed from mine ordinances, and have broken mine everlasting covenant."

The Lord then explained, "They seek not the Lord to establish his righteousness, but every man walketh in his own way, and after the image of his own god." Because of these things, and "knowing the calamity which should come upon the inhabitants of the earth," the Lord "called upon . . . Joseph Smith, Jun., and spake unto him from heaven, and gave him commandments" (D&C 1:15–17). The calamity to which the Lord refers comprises the second half of this section. The great cause of the destruction preceding the Second Coming is the wickedness that grows from apostasy.

## Isaiah 24:1–12

Behold, the Lord *maketh the earth empty,*
and *maketh it waste,*
and *turneth it upside down*
and *scattereth abroad the inhabitants* thereof. (24:1)

And it shall be, *as with the people,* so with the priest;
*as with the servant,* so with his master;
*as with the maid,* so with her mistress;
*as with the buyer,* so with the seller;
*as with the lender,* so with the borrower;
*as with the [creditor],* so with the [debtor].[1] (24:2)

The land shall be [*completely laid waste*],[2]
and [*completely plundered*]:[3]
for the Lord hath spoken this word. (24:3)

The *earth mourneth* and [withereth][4] away,
*the world languisheth*[5] and [withereth][6] away,
*the haughty people* of the earth do languish. (24:4)

The earth also is defiled under the inhabitants thereof;
because they have *transgressed* the laws,
*changed* the ordinance,
*broken* the everlasting covenant. (24:5)

Therefore hath the *curse devoured* the earth,
and they that dwell therein are [*held guilty*]:[7]

---

[1] Bracketed words in this verse come from the Hebrew root *nasha'*, meaning "to lend." Brown, Driver, and Briggs, *Hebrew and English Lexicon,* 674.

[2] From Hebrew *baqaq,* meaning to "empty [or] lay waste." Brown, Driver, and Briggs, *Hebrew and English Lexicon,* 132, replacing the KJV *utterly emptied.*

[3] The word *plundered* is from Hebrew *bazaz,* meaning to "spoil [or] plunder." Brown, Driver, and Briggs, *Hebrew and English Lexicon,* 102, replacing the KJV *utterly spoiled.*

[4] From Hebrew *nabal,* meaning to "sink or drop down, languish, wither and fall, fade" (as in *devastated*). Brown, Driver, and Briggs, *Hebrew and English Lexicon,* 615, replacing the KJV *fadeth away.*

[5] From the Hebrew *'amal* meaning to "be weak . . . [or] feeble, languish." Brown, Driver, and Briggs, *Hebrew and English Lexicon,* 51.

[6] See note 4.

[7] The Hebrew *'asham,* "to offend, be guilty," in this form can be translated as *to be held guilty or to bear punishment.* Brown, Driver, and Briggs, *Hebrew and English Lexicon,* 79.

therefore <u>the inhabitants of the earth</u> are *burned,*
and <u>few men</u> left; (24:6)

The *new wine* <u>mourneth,</u>
the *vine* <u>languisheth,</u>[8]
*all the merryhearted* <u>do sigh</u>. (24:7)

*The mirth of [timbrel]*[9] <u>ceaseth,</u>
*the noise of them that rejoice* <u>endeth,</u>
*the joy of the harp* <u>ceaseth</u>. (24:8)

They shall <u>not</u> *drink wine* <u>with a song</u>;
*strong drink* <u>shall be bitter</u> to them that drink it. (24:9)

The *city of confusion* is <u>broken down:</u>
*every house* is <u>shut up</u>, that *no man* may <u>come in</u>. (24:10)

There is a *crying for wine in the streets;*
all joy is darkened,
the *mirth of the land is [removed]*.[10] (24:11)

*In the city,* <u>desolation</u> [remains],[11]
and *the gate* is [crushed to <u>ruins</u>].[12] (24:12)

## NOTES AND COMMENTARY

**24:1** *Lord maketh the earth empty.* This refers to the destruction of the earth's inhabitants at the Second Coming. A modern revelation uses similar language: "For a desolating scourge shall go forth among the inhabitants of the earth, and shall continue to be poured out from time to time, if they repent not, until *the earth is empty, and the inhabitants thereof are consumed away and utterly destroyed* by the brightness of my coming" (D&C 5:19).

*maketh it waste.* The judgments that precede the second coming of Christ will turn the earth into a wasteland (Rev. 8:7–12).

*turneth it upside down.* Similar imagery was used in the Lord's declaration, "I will wipe Jerusalem as a man wipeth a dish, wiping it, and *turning it upside down*" (2 Kgs. 21:13). The Lord will cleanse the earth of the wicked as one turns a bowl upside down and empties, or pours out, the filth.

---

[8] See note 5. Perhaps a better translation here would be *droops.*
[9] From Hebrew *tupiym* meaning "timbrel" or "tambourine." Brown, Driver, and Briggs, *Hebrew and English Lexicon,* 1074, replacing the KJV *tabrets.*
[10] From Hebrew *galah,* meaning "uncover [or] remove; [to] become clear." Brown, Driver, and Briggs, *Hebrew and English Lexicon,* 162, replacing the KJV *gone.*
[11] *Desolation remains* is a clearer rendering than the KJV *left desolation.*
[12] Brown, Driver, and Briggs, *Hebrew and English Lexicon,* 510, renders this phrase as *crushed to ruins,* replacing the KJV *smitten with destruction.*

*scattereth abroad the inhabitants.* The Lord scatters the world's inhabitants (Gen. 11:8–9) as punishment for wickedness (Ps. 92:9).

**24:2** *as with the people, so with the priest; as with the servant, so with his master.* Isaiah lists twelve groups (people, priests, servants, masters, and others) who represent all levels of society. The inhabitants of the land will be scattered, regardless of their status or position.

**24:3** *completely laid waste.* The term *completely* emphasizes the totality of destruction and shows that the devastation promised in verse 1 will be complete.

*the Lord hath spoken this word.* Isaiah speaks by the authority of Jehovah.

**24:4** *earth mourneth and withereth away.* The repetition of *withereth,* in conjunction with *languisheth,* emphasizes the earth's depleted and droughtlike condition. With her strength gone, the earth is no longer able to bring forth fruit as she once had, a curse that has been associated with sin since the world's beginning (Gen. 3:17–19). This in turn affects all who dwell on the earth—human beings, animals, and vegetables (24:7; 40:7–8; Hosea 4:3; JST Isa. 64:6). The earth mourns and withers both from judgment and from apostasy.

*the haughty people of the earth do languish.* In the last days, the proud will languish, or droop, under the weight of their sins (10:33; 13:11; Prov. 16:18).

**24:5** *earth also is defiled under the inhabitants.* To *defile* (Hebrew *chanap*) means "to pollute, profane or make godless."[13] Earth's inhabitants have polluted her by transgressing laws, changing ordinances, and breaking the everlasting covenant.

*transgressed the laws.* People have disregarded the revealed word of God by transgressing the laws given to them by the prophets. *Law* (Hebrew *torah*), used here in a rare plural form (Gen. 26:5; Ex. 16:28; Ps. 105:45), indicates that all God's laws have been transgressed; this by itself is enough to bring a curse upon the people (Dan. 9:10–11).

*changed the ordinance.* Ordinance (Hebrew *choq*)[14] comes from the root word *chaqaq,* which means "to carve or engrave." God's ordinances were essentially carved in stone and were not meant to be changed; rather, they were to be engraved on the hearts of the children of God. When the ordinances such as baptism (JST Gen. 17:3–6; Moroni 8:14, 16) are changed, their power to save is lost.

*broken the everlasting covenant.* The everlasting covenant is the gospel with its covenants and ordinances. Because the ordinances had been perverted or lost, the Lord revealed for the last time through the Prophet Joseph Smith the everlasting

[13] Brown, Driver, and Briggs, *Hebrew and English Lexicon,* 337–38.
[14] Brown, Driver, and Briggs, *Hebrew and English Lexicon,* 349.

covenant for the earth, "lest all of the earth be smitten with a curse" (D&C 1:12–16, 22; D&C 29:8–10).

**24:6** *curse devoured the earth.* The Lord pronounces blessings for faithfulness (Mosiah 2:41) and cursings for rebellion (Deut. 28:15–68). War, slavery, pestilence, plague, disease, famine, poverty, and death are all curses sent from God for not keeping the commandments (Deut. 27–30). All these curses will be poured out on the earth in the last days (D&C 112:23–24).

*they that dwell therein are held guilty.* The term *guilty* (Hebrew *'asham*)[15] refers to the guilt that requires restitution and cleansing ordinances before it can be removed. Those who continue to be *held guilty* (i.e., do not repent) must bear the punishment of their sins.

*the inhabitants of the earth are burned.* When the Lord comes to cleanse his vineyard, the earth's wicked inhabitants will be burned because they have strayed from the ordinances and broken the everlasting covenant (9:18; Mal. 4:1–3; 3 Ne. 25:1–3; JS–H 1:37). It was because of this pending calamity that the Lord gave the Prophet Joseph Smith the necessary saving principles and ordinances to prepare the righteous remnant who will remain after the destruction of the wicked (24:5).

*few men left.* So few will remain after the destruction of the wicked that a child will be able to number them (10:19), individuals will be accounted more precious than fine gold (13:12), and "many houses shall be desolate, even great and fair, without inhabitant" (5:9; 6:11–12). Elder Bruce R. McConkie wrote: "In the coming day when the vineyard of the Lord is burned, some few will abide the day, but the masses of men will be destroyed. Only those who are quickened, as were Shadrach, Meshach, and Abednego in the furnace of Nebuchadnezzar, shall be able to abide the day of burning."[16]

**24:7** *new wine mourneth/vine languisheth.* These statements may speak of the drought that occurs when the physical earth reacts to wickedness and destruction (24:4–5).

*the merryhearted do sigh.* The merryhearted sigh, or groan, because of the destruction and wickedness that precede the Second Coming.

**24:8** *mirth/noise/joy.* Isaiah 24:7–11 draws a strong correlation between the sounds of gaiety and the free abundance of wine. The party lifestyle of the world, which so often depends on alcohol, will cease to exist; instead of the sounds of

---

[15] Brown, Driver, and Briggs, *Hebrew and English Lexicon,* 79.
[16] *New Witness for the Articles of Faith,* 645.

laughter, groans of discontent will prevail. The dependency on artificial stimulants for happiness indicates the pitiful state of the earth's inhabitants.

*timbrel/harp.* Instruments that accompany the sounds of merriment and revelry have also stopped their joyous sounds. Babylon is to be thrown down, "and the voice of harpers, and musicians, and of pipers, and trumpeters, shall be heard no more at all" (Rev. 18:22). Apparently, earth's inhabitants can no longer find joy or entertainment in their music.

**24:9** *They shall not drink wine with a song/strong drink shall be bitter.* Isaiah emphasizes the mourning and sighing that will exist. There may also be a spiritual meaning here: The wicked will partake not of wine and strong drink but of the cup of the Lord's wrath when they experience his judgments.

**24:10** *city of confusion is broken down.* This reference is not to a particular city but to all cities that are full of *confusion* and chaos because of inequality and destruction.

*every house is shut up.* The wicked will shut their doors out of fear of the coming judgments, while the righteous will close their doors in obedience to this counsel: "Come, my people, enter thou into thy chambers, and shut thy doors about thee: hide thyself as it were for a little moment, until the indignation pass over" (26:20).

**24:11** *There is a crying for wine in the streets.* This may be literal, or it may speak of the loss of joy during this time.

*joy is darkened/mirth is removed.* In the time of judgment the people will no longer find enjoyment or mirth in their sinful ways. Worldly joy will be replaced with despair.

**24:12** *In the city, remains desolation/gate is crushed to ruins.* This image refers to the "city of confusion" (24:10), whose streets are empty, whose houses are shut, whose defenses are gone, and whose social interaction has vanished (1:7; 5:9).

## A RIGHTEOUS REMNANT REJOICES (24:13–16A)

In the midst of the apostasy and destruction described in the section above, the Lord will gather us (i.e., those who are members of the Church) from among the wicked, as one seeks the few remaining olives on the trees after the harvest. We are the remnant that is being gathered from the nations. According to Isaiah, we are "lift[ing our] voice," "cry[ing] aloud for the majesty of the Lord," sharing the gospel message from Zion ("the region of light"), and glorifying his name throughout the entire world.

*Isaiah 24:13–16a*

When thus it shall be *in the midst of the land*
*among the people*,
there shall be as [when an olive tree is beaten,
or as when gleanings are left over after the grape harvest][17] is done. (24:13)
*They* shall lift up their voice,
*they* shall [cry aloud][18] for the majesty of the Lord,
*they* shall [cry shrilly][19] from the sea. (24:14)
Wherefore *glorify ye the Lord* in the [region of light],[20]
*even the name of the Lord God of Israel* in the isles of the sea. (24:15)
From the uttermost part of the earth have we heard songs, even [*'Glory to the righteous one'*].[21] (24:16a)

## NOTES AND COMMENTARY

**24:13** *When thus it shall be in the midst of the land.* Isaiah establishes the time reference for the next three verses. The prophecies contained in them will take place during or after the destruction identified in Isaiah 23 and 24:1–15.

*when an olive tree is beaten.* A few olives always remain on the olive trees after the completion of the harvest, especially on the upper branches, and a stick is usually used to beat these olives from the branches. These remaining olives represent the righteous who will remain after the destruction of the wicked, represented by the harvesting of an olive tree. On many occasions the prophets compare the harvest to the destruction of the wicked (Matt. 13:39; D&C 86:4–7).

*gleanings are left over after the grape harvest.* Only a few individuals will remain after the harvest or destruction of the world.

**24:14** *They shall lift up their voice/cry shrilly.* The righteous who remain will *lift up their voice*—a phrase often associated with prayer (Gen. 21:16) and song (42:11). When the Lord comes, all "who remain, even from the least unto the greatest . . . shall be filled with the knowledge of the Lord, and shall see eye to eye, and shall lift up their voice, and with the voice together sing this new song" (D&C 84:98). The words to the song are found in D&C 84:99–102.

*they shall cry aloud.* This pertains to the preaching of the gospel. Joseph Smith counseled the elders of the Church: "Oh, ye elders of Israel, hearken to my voice; and

---

[17] NIV Isa. 24:13.
[18] Brown, Driver, and Briggs, *Hebrew and English Lexicon,* 943, replacing the KJV *sing.*
[19] Brown, Driver, and Briggs, *Hebrew and English Lexicon,* 843, replacing the KJV *cry aloud.*
[20] From Hebrew *'uriym,* meaning "region of light" or the "East." Brown, Driver, and Briggs, *Hebrew and English Lexicon,* 22, replacing the KJV *fires.*
[21] NIV Isa. 24:16.

when you are sent into the world to preach, tell those things you are sent to tell; preach and cry aloud, 'Repent ye, for the kingdom of heaven is at hand; repent and believe the Gospel.'"[22]

*they shall cry . . . from the sea.* The Lord's servants cry across the sea to all other nations, inviting them to become part of the gospel.

**24:15** *region of light.* The gathered remnant, or the Saints, glorify the Lord in the region of light, or the place where the Spirit of God is abundant.

**24:16a** *From the uttermost part.* The songs that glorify and honor the Lord will be heard from the ends of the earth (24:14), for he is the righteous one (53:11).

*Glory to the righteous one.* These appear to be some of the actual words of one of the songs that will be sung by the righteous remnant.

## EARTH REACTS TO HER INHABITANTS' INIQUITIES (24:16B–23)

Here Isaiah's soul mourns for the wicked: "I waste away, I waste away, woe unto me!" He then continues the theme introduced in Isaiah 24:1–12 concerning human relationships and the earth's reaction to her inhabitants' transgressions. While the righteous remnant will "glorify . . . the Lord in the region of light, even the name of the Lord God of Israel in the isles of the sea" (24:15), the transgressors will find that "fear, and the pit, and the snare, are upon" them (24:17).

*Isaiah 24:16b–23*

> But I said, [I waste away, I waste away],[23] woe unto me!
> *the treacherous dealers* have <u>dealt treacherously</u>;
> yea, [with treachery have *the treacherous dealers* <u>dealt very treacherously</u>.][24]
> (24:16b)
>
> Fear, and the pit, and the snare, are upon thee, O inhabitant of the earth. (24:17)
>
> And it shall come to pass, that he who *fleeth* from the noise of the <u>fear</u>,
> shall *fall* into the <u>pit</u>; and he that cometh up out of the midst of the pit
> shall be *taken* in the <u>snare</u>:
> for the *windows from on high* are <u>open</u>,
> and the *foundations of the earth* do <u>shake</u>. (24:18)
>
> The *earth* is utterly <u>broken down</u>,

---

[22] *Teachings of the Prophet Joseph Smith,* 292.

[23] From NIV Isa. 24:16, replacing the KJV *My leanness, my leanness.*

[24] See Brown, Driver, and Briggs, *Hebrew and English Lexicon,* 93, replacing the KJV *the treacherous dealers have dealt very treacherously.*

the *earth* is <u>clean dissolved,</u>
the *earth* is <u>moved</u> exceedingly. (24:19)

The earth shall *reel to and fro* <u>like a</u> <u>drunkard,</u>
and shall be *removed* <u>like a cottage;</u>

and the transgression thereof shall be heavy upon it;
and it shall fall, and not rise again. (24:20)

And it shall come to pass in that day,
that the Lord shall punish the host of the *high ones* that are <u>on high,</u>
*and the kings of the earth* <u>upon the earth.</u> (24:21)

And they shall be gathered together, as prisoners are gathered in the pit, and shall
be shut up in the prison, and after many days shall they be visited. (24:22)

Then the *moon* shall be <u>confounded,</u>
and the *sun* <u>ashamed,</u>

when the Lord of hosts shall reign in mount Zion, and in Jerusalem,
and before his ancients gloriously. (24:23)

## Notes and Commentary

**24:16b** *I waste away, woe unto me.* Isaiah expresses the pain and sorrow he feels
over the sins and destruction of earth's inhabitants (21:3–4; 22:4). His exclamation
*Woe is me* was uttered earlier when, in God's presence, he was conscious of his own
sins (6:5). He now feels the pain of others' condemnation as deeply as he felt his
own.

*treacherous dealers.* Isaiah's heartfelt sorrow is caused by the world's wickedness. The wicked have been treacherous in their hearts and have dealt treacherously
with the innocent (21:2; 33:1). They have preyed on the weak, have sworn falsely
both to their neighbors and to God (48:1), and have broken the everlasting covenant
(24:5).

**24:17** *the pit, and the snare, are upon thee.* Just as an animal flees from the
hunter only to be caught in a pit or a snare, so do the wicked flee destruction. When
the judgment comes, they will try to escape it, but they will be caught in the snare of
their own wickedness (Alma 30:60).

**24:18–20** *who fleeth from the noise of the fear.* Those who work iniquity fear the
Lord's judgments and attempt to hide in the rocks and dust; they "fear . . . the Lord,
and . . . the glory of his majesty" (2:19). This is in striking contrast to the command
given to the Saints to "fear not, for the kingdom is yours" (D&C 38:15).

*fall into the pit.* While trying to flee the judgments of the Lord, the wicked will
"fall into the pit," which is a reference to hell.

*windows from on high are open.* The Lord will open the windows of heaven and
send forth blessings (Mal. 3:10) or judgments (Gen. 7:11–12). For instance, at the

time of Noah the windows of heaven were opened, and floods burst forth from both the heavens and the foundations of the earth to cleanse the earth of her wicked.

*foundations of the earth do shake.* Joseph Smith stated that the "earth groans under the weight of its iniquity" (D&C 123:7); Isaiah taught that "the earth mourneth" (33:9); and Moses recorded that when "Enoch heard the earth mourn, he wept, and cried unto the Lord, saying: O Lord, wilt thou not have compassion upon the earth?" (Moses 7:49). Here in Isaiah 24:18–20, Isaiah makes seven statements to portray the earth's reaction to the transgressions of humanity that are "heavy upon it": "the foundations of the earth do shake," "the earth is utterly broken down," "the earth is clean dissolved," "the earth is moved exceedingly," "the earth shall reel to and fro like a drunkard," the earth "shall be removed like a cottage," and the earth "shall fall, and not rise again." These expressions may refer to great earthquakes that will occur in the last days when God's judgments come upon a wicked world (see D&C 43:25; 88:89). They may particularly refer to the last great earthquake that will occur at the time of the coming of the Lord (see Rev. 16:18–20).

Isaiah's expression is very poetic. He portrays the earth staggering about like a man whose sense of balance has been affected by strong drink; he also compares the movement of the earth to a cottage—a frail, temporary structure that shakes during a strong wind.

**24:21** *host of the high ones/kings of the earth.* The proud and mighty of the world will be subject to God's judgments and punishments.

**24:22** *gathered together, as prisoners.* The high ones and kings will be gathered together in spirit prison after their earthly probation ends. There they will wait, with full remembrance of their sins and without the knowledge necessary to free themselves from those sins until they are visited by the Lord's messengers, who can teach them the principles needed for their salvation.

*pit/prison.* These terms refer to spirit prison (14:15, 19; Rev. 19:19–20:3).

*shall they be visited.* Isaiah assures us that the dead who have been gathered together as prisoners in a pit will be visited after many days. Just as Christ's ministers visited those in spirit prison to "proclaim liberty to the captives, and the opening of the prison to them that are bound" (61:1; John 5:25), and to "bring out the prisoners from the prison, and them that sit in darkness out of the prison house" (42:7), so too will "we find that God will deal with all the human family equally, and . . . those characters referred to by Isaiah [will] have their time of visitation and deliverance; after having been many days in prison."[25] Elder Orson Pratt taught that they will have

---

[25] *Teachings of the Prophet Joseph Smith,* 219.

the opportunity to be redeemed from their prison through the preaching of the gospel in the spirit world and through the performance of vicarious ordinances in mortality.[26]

**24:23** *the moon shall be confounded, and the sun ashamed.* In comparison with the glory and brilliance that will surround the Lord when he "reign[s] in mount Zion," the light of the sun and the moon will pale and be *confounded* and *ashamed.* It will be the glory of the Lord that will light the city of Zion (60:19; Rev. 21:23).

*The Lord of hosts shall reign in mount Zion, and in Jerusalem.* "Two separate Jerusalems, the old and the new, will serve as headquarters of the millennial kingdom of God from which Jesus will rule. Old Jerusalem will be built up by Judah. The New Jerusalem, also to be known as Zion (D&C 45:66–67), will be built up in Jackson County, Missouri, by Ephraim."[27] Temples will be located at the centers of these two capital cities.

*before his ancients gloriously.* The New International Version reads "The Lord Almighty will reign on Mount Zion and in Jerusalem, and before its elders, gloriously."

---

[26] *Journal of Discourses,* 7:87 (28 August 1859).
[27] Ogden, "Jerusalem," 723.

# ISAIAH 25

*LIKENING ISAIAH 25 UNTO OURSELVES*

*Latter-day Saints love to worship the Lord through singing hymns, and we do so on many occasions, such as at sacrament meetings, general conference, and baptisms. Isaiah, some seven hundred years before Christ, provided the words of a hymn (25:1–5) that the righteous will sing after Jesus Christ destroys wickedness and corruption from off the face of the earth at his second coming. The words of the hymn should give us hope for the future as well as build our faith in him.*

*The second part of this chapter introduces us to a great sacred feast that will be prepared by the Lord (25:6–12). This feast is the supper of the Lord, or the Bridegroom, which will be attended by all the righteous.*

## A HYMN OF PRAISE: TRIUMPH OVER THE WICKED (25:1–5)

Those who survive the judgments and the destructions upon the earth, as set forth in Isaiah 24, will praise the Lord, perhaps in prayer or song. Isaiah preserves the words of a hymn of praise in these verses. The hymn includes words that bring us great comfort: Jehovah is our "strength" and our "refuge from the storm"; he is our "shadow from the heat." He is always there when we need him, whether for spiritual protection or physical safety.

*Isaiah 25:1–5*

O Lord, thou art my God; *I will* exalt thee,
*I will* praise thy name;

*for thou hast done* wonderful things;
*thy counsels of old* are faithfulness and truth. (25:1)

For thou hast made[1] of a *city* an <u>heap</u>;
of a defenced *city* a <u>ruin</u>:
a *palace of strangers* to <u>be no city</u>;
it shall never be built. (25:2)

Therefore shall the *strong people* <u>glorify thee</u>,
the *city of the terrible* nations shall <u>fear thee</u>. (25:3)

For thou hast been *a strength* to <u>the poor</u>,
*a strength* to <u>the needy in his distress</u>,

*a refuge* from <u>the storm</u>,
*a shadow* from <u>the heat</u>,
when the blast of the terrible ones is as a storm against the wall. (25:4)

Thou shalt *bring down the noise* of <u>strangers</u>,
as the heat in a dry place; even the heat with the shadow of a cloud:
the [*song*][2] of <u>the terrible ones</u> shall *be brought low.* (25:5)

## NOTES AND COMMENTARY

**25:1** *O Lord, thou art my God.* After addressing the Lord *(O Lord),* the one who utters this prayer bears testimony that Jehovah is God, a personal God.

*I will exalt thee, I will praise thy name.* Isaiah explains why we will praise God's name: He has "done wonderful things," and his "counsels of old are faithfulness and truth."

*thou hast done wonderful things.* The word *wonderful* (Hebrew *pele'*) means something of an extraordinary nature. Jehovah has done extraordinary things for us, including abolishing death and wickedness and promising eternal life for the faithful. We recall that Jesus is called "Wonderful Counsellor" in 9:6. The Psalmist praised the Lord: "Thou art the God that doest wonders: thou hast declared thy strength among the people. Thou hast with thine arm redeemed thy people, the sons of Jacob and Joseph" (Ps. 77:14–15).

*counsels of old.* Counsels (Hebrew *ya'ats*) speaks both of the plans that were made and of the determination to follow through with the plans (23:8–9). The words *of old* hark back to the premortal existence, when great ones made plans for the earth and her inhabitants.

**25:2** *thou hast made of a city an heap.* City here refers to all cities wherein wickedness reigns. It is found in the singular form, perhaps recalling the ancient city of Babylon, which represents worldliness (D&C 1:16). Here Isaiah tells us that God will

---

[1] *Sam'at min* means literally "constitute from," thus "transform."
[2] Brown, Driver, and Briggs, *Hebrew and English Lexicon,* 274, replacing the KJV *branch.*

make a city into a heap of stones and rubble, and a fortified city into a ruin. This is one of the reasons why we will praise God's name.

**25:3** *strong people glorify thee.* This refers to the Lord's righteous people (Job 17:9), both the house of Israel (Gen. 25:23) and the Gentiles who serve the Lord. In the last days, they will glorify (praise) the name of the Lord because of his mighty work of cleansing the earth of the wicked and redeeming the righteous.

*city of the terrible nations shall fear thee.* The New International Version reads "cities of ruthless nations will revere you." This may speak of the people who will remain after the destruction at Christ's coming and then become converted and worship the Lord (Ps. 86:9; Zech. 14:16).

**25:4** *thou hast been a strength to the poor.* The Hebrew word for *strength* may be translated as "stronghold" (23:4), aptly describing how "God is our refuge and strength, a very present help in trouble" (Ps. 46:1). The poor and needy described here are not simply financially bereft; they include the poor in spirit and the meek who are willing to submit to God's will and who will inherit the earth and the kingdom of heaven (3 Ne. 12:5; D&C 56:18–19). The Lord's strength makes these poor and needy into "strong people," standing in contrast to the strength of the rich and their "strong city" (Prov. 10:15), which will be brought down by the Lord (25:5).

*thou hast been . . . a refuge from the storm.* Jehovah is our refuge from the storm, our protection from both physical and spiritual danger. He is also our "sanctuary" (8:14) and our "tabernacle for a shadow in the daytime from the heat, and for a place of refuge" (4:6).

*a shadow from the heat.* The Lord protects us from the blast, or judgments, against the wicked.

*blast of the terrible ones . . . storm.* The *blast* may refer to the Lord's judgments upon the wicked, or *terrible ones;* it may also refer to the battle that will be waged between Israel and the nations of the world, when the nations of the world will come close to overtaking Jerusalem. Their fury will pound against the walls of the city until the Lord comes to defend his people.

**25:5** *Thou shalt bring down the noise of strangers/song of the terrible ones.* The Lord at his second coming will silence the strangers (foreigners, or those not of the covenant) and the terrible ones; their clamorous atmosphere and noise of battle will be brought low and no longer exist.

*heat in a dry place . . . shadow of a cloud.* The New International Version reads, "You [Lord] silence the uproar of foreigners; as heat is reduced by the shadow of a cloud."

## THE LORD PREPARES A FEAST FOR THE RIGHTEOUS (25:6–12)

Jehovah plays a very active role in the events of the earth, including those that will occur during these last days and at his second coming, as set forth in this section. He will make a feast for all people (although only the meek and humble of the earth will attend), "destroy . . . the veil that is spread over all nations," he will "swallow up death in victory," "wipe away tears from off all faces," and take away the "rebuke of his people."

After we have partaken of the Lord's feast, and after he has wiped away our tears, we will worship him with these words (25:9):

> Lo, this is our God;
> we have waited for him,
> and he will save us:
> this is the Lord;
> we have waited for him,
> we will be glad and rejoice in his salvation.

Note that with these words we will twice testify "this is our God/Lord," twice affirm "we have waited for him," and twice speak of his salvation ("save us"/"salvation").

### Isaiah 25:6–12

And in this mountain shall the Lord of hosts make unto all people
*a feast of fat things,* <u>a feast of wines</u> on the lees,
of *fat things full of marrow,* of <u>wines on the lees well refined</u>. (25:6)

And he will destroy in this mountain the *face* of the <u>covering cast over all people</u>,
and the *veil* that is <u>spread over all nations</u>. (25:7)

*He* will <u>swallow up death</u> in victory;
and the *Lord God* will <u>wipe away tears</u> from off all faces;
and the rebuke of his people shall he take away from off all the earth:
for the Lord hath spoken it. (25:8)

And it shall be said in that day, Lo, this is our *God;* <u>we have waited</u> for him,
and he will *save us:*
this is the *Lord;* <u>we have waited</u> for him,
we will be glad and rejoice in his *salvation.* (25:9)

For in this mountain shall the hand of the Lord rest, (25:10a)

And *Moab shall be trodden down* under him,
even as *straw is trodden down* for the dunghill. (25:10b)

And he shall *spread forth his hands* in the midst of them,
as he that swimmeth *spreadeth forth his hands* to swim:

and he shall *bring down* their pride together with the spoils of their hands. (25:11)
And the fortress of the high fort of thy walls *shall he bring down*, lay low,
*and bring to the ground*, even to the dust. (25:12)

## NOTES AND COMMENTARY

**25:6** *this mountain.* This phrase refers to Isaiah 24:23 and also to "Mount Zion," or the New Jerusalem (D&C 84:2). Thus the great feast identified in this section will take place in the New Jerusalem.

*feast of fat things, a feast of wines.* By teaching the gospel to the earth's inhabitants, our missionaries invite people to come to this feast, also called "the supper of the Lord" (D&C 58:11), the "supper of the house of the Lord" (D&C 58:9), and the "marriage supper of the Lamb" (Rev. 19:9). "All nations" are invited—"first, the rich and the learned, the wise and the noble"—but when these reject the invitation to the feast, the Lord's representatives will invite the poor and the humble. Only those who have received the ordinances of the temple and who are truly the humble followers of Christ will be able to partake of the feast. This feast will take place at or near the time of the Second Coming (D&C 58:9–11; Rev. 19:7–8; Matt. 22:2–14; Luke 14:16–24).

*fat things full of marrow.* The feast, like the sacramental emblems, reminds us of Christ's atonement, for *fat things* and wines recall sacrificial offerings (Lev. 3:3–16); these things also imply abundance and bounty. The phrase *wines on the lees well refined* speaks of "wine that remains upon its settlings until it is well matured. It is then poured off and strained to provide the best wine possible,"[3] since only the very best will be served at the Lord's feast.

**25:7** *he will destroy in this mountain the face of the covering.* This covering, or veil, that is "cast over all people" or "all nations" may speak of the dark veil of ignorance or unbelief (Alma 19:6; 2 Cor. 3:14–16; Ether 4:15) that covers the hearts and minds of all people. The Lord has promised, "The day soon cometh that ye shall see me, and know that I am; for the veil of darkness shall soon be rent, and he that is not purified shall not abide the day" (D&C 38:8; 2 Ne. 30:16–18).

**25:8** *He will swallow up death in victory.* Christ victoriously overcame death at his resurrection and made it possible for us also to swallow up death in victory. Paul quoted this passage: "So when this corruptible shall have put on incorruption, and this mortal shall have put on immortality, then shall be brought to pass the saying that

---

[3] Hailey, *Commentary on Isaiah,* 206.

is written, Death is swallowed up in victory. . . . Thanks be to God, which giveth us the victory through our Lord Jesus Christ" (1 Cor. 15:54–57; see also Hel. 14:14–18).

*Lord God will wipe away tears.* Tears come from the pain and sorrow associated with mortality, affliction, pain, death, and personal sin. When he dwells with us after his coming, Jesus Christ, who is well acquainted with grief (53:3), will remove the pains of our mortality (Rev. 7:17; 21:4; D&C 101:29).

*for the Lord hath spoken it.* God is the source of this revelation, and it will therefore surely come to pass.

**25:9** *in that day.* The time frame for this chapter is the same as for chapters 24–25: the time of the Lord's second coming (24:21).

*we have waited for him.* When the Lord wipes away our tears from our faces, we will rejoice.

*save us/rejoice in his salvation. Save* is the verb counterpart of the noun *salvation; Savior* is one of the titles of Jesus Christ. Jesus saves us from death ("he will swallow up death in victory") and from sin ("God will wipe away tears from off all faces").

**25:10** *in this mountain.* See commentary on 25:6.

*hand of the Lord rest.* The *hand of the Lord,* which previously was stretched out against his people, now rests.

*Moab shall be trodden down.* Moab symbolizes the wicked, proud, and arrogant (16:6; Jer. 48:27–32), who will be completely destroyed (15 and 16). In contrast to the Lord's hand, which rests with his people, his feet will tread on Moab as easily as one treads upon the straw mixed with the dung on the dunghill. Isaiah's imagery expresses the great degradation of the world (Moab), which is as corrupt and polluted as filthy dung.

**25:11** *he shall spread forth his hands.* In divine judgment the Lord will *spread forth his hands* and destroy Moab, or the wicked. With the same ease of a swimmer who puts forth his arms to pass through water, the Lord's judgments will pass through the midst of Moab until she has been brought down.

**25:11–12** *he shall bring down their pride.* The pride of the wicked will be brought down (Prov. 16:18), along with the spoil of their hands, which speaks of things gained by their treacherous deeds. To emphasize their complete destruction, Isaiah uses repetitive language: "bring down" (twice), "lay low," "bring down to the ground," and "to the dust."

# ISAIAH 26

## LIKENING ISAIAH 26 UNTO OURSELVES

*Isaiah, through revelation, composed a song for us to sing in "the land of Judah." The words of the song are about the city of Jerusalem, described as a "strong city" that is protected by God himself. Unlike the cities of the biblical world, Zion will not have regular walls that surround and protect it, because God himself will be her protection (26:1–6).*

*Isaiah 26:7–18 is a prayer about the way the Lord sends judgments upon the wicked. The prayer is perhaps uttered by Israel, our ancestors, or ourselves in the near future. The Lord responds to this prayer in Isaiah 26:19–21, promising the righteous that they will be safe during the destruction of the wicked and gives a promise of the resurrection. These words bring us great comfort in a world with so many negative occurrences and influences in our lives and in our communities.*

## A SONG ABOUT A "STRONG CITY" AND THE "LOFTY CITY" (26:1–6)

This song, which will be sung by "the righteous nation which keepeth the truth" at the time of the Second Coming, is about a "strong city" and the "lofty city." The strong city is Zion, or Jerusalem. She has gates that only the righteous may enter. Her strength does not come from walls and bulwarks made of mortar and stone but from God's salvation. His power and everlasting strength will protect the city's inhabitants, who will enjoy perfect peace.

By contrast, Jehovah will bring down those who dwell in the lofty city, where the wicked and proud are found. In fact, Jehovah will bring down this city "even to the dust," and the feet of the poor and the needy will "tread it down."

## Isaiah 26:1–6

In that day shall this song be sung in the land of Judah;
We have a strong city;
salvation will God appoint for walls and [ramparts].[1] (26:1)

Open ye [your gates],[2]
that the righteous nation which keepeth the truth may enter in. (26:2)

Thou wilt keep him in perfect peace,
*whose mind [rests]*[3] on thee:
because *he trusteth* in thee. (26:3)

*Trust* ye in the Lord for ever:
for in the Lord Jehovah is everlasting *strength:* (26:4)

For *he bringeth down* them that dwell on high;
the lofty city, *he layeth it low;*

*he layeth it low,* even to the ground;
*he bringeth it* even to the dust. (26:5)

The foot shall tread it down,
even the *feet* of the poor,
and the *steps* of the needy. (26:6)

## NOTES AND COMMENTARY

**26:1** *In that day.* The time frame for chapter 26 is the same as for chapters 24 and 25: the day of the Lord, or the time of the Lord's second coming (2:12; 24:21).

*song.* Isaiah provides the actual words of the song here. The song will probably be sung by the Jews, as indicated by the phrase *in the land of Judah.*

*the land of Judah.* This expression refers to the land of the Jews.

*We have a strong city.* The *strong city* is Jerusalem, although the New Jerusalem has also been appointed as a strong city, or a refuge (D&C 124:36). The Lord has promised both these cities: "For I, saith the Lord, will be unto her a wall of fire round about, and will be the glory in the midst of her" (Zech. 2:5). In contrast, the cities of the world will be destroyed (25:2, 10–12).

*salvation . . . for walls and ramparts. Salvation* is one of the names of Jehovah. No ordinary walls, towers, or ramparts (Ps. 91:9; Jer. 17:5) will guard Zion: rather the Lord and the power of his atonement will defend his Zion communities (Ps. 125:2; Zech. 2:9).

---

[1] From the Hebrew *cheyl,* meaning "rampart [or] fortress." Brown, Driver, and Briggs, *Hebrew and English Lexicon,* 298, replacing the KJV *bulwarks.*

[2] DSS Isa. Scroll 26:2 reads *your gates* as opposed to the KJV *the gates.*

[3] From the Hebrew *samak,* meaning to "lean, lay, rest, [or] support." Brown, Driver, and Briggs, *Hebrew and English Lexicon,* 701, replacing the KJV *is stayed.*

**26:2** *Open ye your gates.* The righteous will sing out to God, asking for entrance to the holy city: "Open to me the gates of righteousness: I will go into them, [and] I will praise the Lord: This gate of the Lord, into which the righteous shall enter" (13:2; Ps. 118:19–20).

*righteous nation which keepeth the truth.* These are the Lord's covenant people. The truths they keep are the laws and covenants of God, and their obedience will give them the right to enter the gates (33:14–16; 35:8–10).

**26:3** *perfect peace.* The literal reading is *peace, peace.* Those of the strong city will have *perfect peace* if their mind rests on Jehovah and if they trust in him. Isaiah calls the Lord the Prince of Peace (9:6).

*whose mind [rests] on thee.* In our day the Lord has said, "Look unto me in every thought" (D&C 6:36). Those whose thoughts are upon the Lord continually are blessed with perfect peace.

**26:4** *Trust ye in the Lord for ever.* Those singing here are not calling for a single act of faith, but faith that lasts an eternity.

*everlasting strength.* The Hebrew word for *strength* has the same root as the word for *rock.* Isaiah reminds us that the Lord is our sure foundation (17:10; 28:16; Hel. 5:12)—our eternal rock.

**26:5** *he bringeth down them that dwell on high.* These are the proud and haughty who will be laid low (24:4).

*the lofty city.* This refers to Babylon, the city of worldliness. See also Isaiah's reference to the "crowning city" (23:8) and the "city of confusion" (24:10).

*he bringeth it even to the dust.* Isaiah emphasizes the humbling of the wicked with the phrases *he bringeth down, he layeth it low* (twice), *even to the ground, he bringeth it to the dust.* Also, the feet of the poor and needy will tread upon the lofty city. The words *dust* and *ground* recall the mortal nature of the proud, who were created from the dust.

**26:6** *the feet of the poor.* "For the dwellers on high to be trampled under foot is indeed humiliation. The humiliation is seen to be even greater when we read that the feet that do the trampling are those of the ones who themselves had been oppressed. They are the needy and poor, who formerly had suffered from those who dwelt in the high city. Isaiah's figure shows the complete defeat of the enemies of God's kingdom and the full exaltation of those who in the eyes of the world were regarded as insignificant and poor, and who had suffered at the hands of unjust oppressors."[4]

---

[4]Young, *Book of Isaiah,* 2:211.

*poor/needy.* These words may be taken literally; or they may speak of them who can rely only on the Lord for strength (25:4).

## A PRAYER ABOUT THE LORD'S JUDGMENTS (26:7–18)

In this prayer Israel addresses God as "O Lord," "Lord," or "O Lord our God" seven times. The prayer is uttered by more than one person, as indicated by the frequent use of the plural *we,* although 26:9 twice uses the singular *I.* The theme of the prayer is the justice of the Lord, for the term *judgments* appears often; it is found in such expressions as "the way of thy judgments" and "thy judgments are in the earth." Other expressions are less explicit: "thy hand is lifted up" and "thy chastening was upon them."

The Lord's justice works two ways: the wicked suffer shame ("they shall see, and be ashamed") and destruction ("fire . . . shall devour them") as the result of the judgments, while the righteous experience peace ("Lord, thou wilt ordain peace for us"), an increase of Zion's numbers, and an expansion of Zion's borders (26:15).

When will this prayer be uttered? This prayer or one like it has been offered by the righteous since the beginning of the world, for it sets forth their desires for God's judgments. The prayer should also represent our desires.

*Isaiah 26:7–18*

> The *way of the just* is <u>uprightness</u>:
> thou, <u>most upright</u>, dost [make level][5] the *path of the just.* (26:7)
>
> Yea, in the way of thy judgments, <u>O Lord</u>, have we *waited for thee;*
> the *desire of our soul* is to <u>thy name</u>, and to the remembrance of thee. (26:8)
>
> *With my soul* have <u>I desired thee in the night;</u>
> yea, *with my spirit within me* will <u>I seek thee early</u>:
>
> for when thy *judgments* are in the <u>earth,</u>
> the <u>inhabitants of the world</u> will learn *righteousness.* (26:9)
>
> Let favor be [shown][6] to the wicked,
> yet will he not learn righteousness:
> in the land of uprightness will he deal unjustly,
> and will not behold the majesty of the Lord. (26:10)
>
> Lord, when thy hand is lifted up,
> they will not see:

---

[5] From *palas,* meaning to "weigh [or] make level." Brown, Driver, and Briggs, *Hebrew and English Lexicon,* 814, replacing the KJV *weigh.*
[6] We have replaced the archaic *shewed* with *shown.*

but they shall see,
and be ashamed for their envy at the people;
yea, the fire of thine enemies shall devour them. (26:11)

Lord, thou wilt ordain peace for us:
for thou also hast wrought all our works in us. (26:12)

O Lord our God,
other lords beside thee have had dominion over us:
but by thee only will we make mention of thy name. (26:13)

*They are dead,* they shall not live;
*they are deceased,* they shall not rise:

therefore hast thou visited and *destroyed* them,
and *made* all their memory *to perish.* (26:14)

*Thou hast increased* the nation, *O Lord,*
*thou hast increased* the nation: thou art glorified:
*thou hast [extended]* all the boundaries of the land].[7] (26:15)

Lord, in *trouble* have they visited thee,
they poured out a prayer when *thy chastening* was upon them. (26:16)

Like *as a woman with child,* that draweth near the time of her delivery, is in pain,
and crieth out in her pangs; so have *we* been in thy sight, O Lord. (26:17)

*We have been* with child,
*we have been* in pain,
*we have as it were* brought forth wind;

we have not wrought any *deliverance* in the earth;
neither have the inhabitants of the world *fallen.* (26:18)

## NOTES AND COMMENTARY

**26:7** *way of the just/path of the just.* The *way* or *path* leads back to the presence of God; it represents life's journey taken by the *just.* The path is the straight and narrow path; Jesus is the way back to our Father's presence (John 14:6).

*most upright, dost make level.* Jesus Christ is the *most upright,* or the most righteous of all, who *makes level* the path of the just. To make level in the physical sense is to clear the path of bumps, boulders, and large holes so that the traveler can journey thereon. In the spiritual sense, Jesus Christ, through his atonement, provides a clear path for all who will make their way back to the Father (Ps. 25:8; 2 Ne. 31:16).

**26:8** *way of thy judgments . . . waited for thee.* The righteous remain faithful to their covenants and wait patiently until God manifests his judgment (33:2).

---

[7] From the Hebrew *richaq'at.* Brown, Driver, and Briggs, *Hebrew and English Lexicon,* 935. This phrase replaces the KJV *moved it far unto all the ends of the earth.*

*desire of our soul is to thy name.* The deepest desire of the righteous is to bear the name of the Lord and gain the salvation that comes only through that name (2 Ne. 31:13, 21).

**26:9** *With my soul have I desired thee in the night; yea, with my spirit.* Both the body and the spirit yearn for the Lord and his presence continually; *night* and *early* express this thought.

*when thy judgments are in the earth, the inhabitants . . . learn righteousness.* When the judgments of the Lord "are withheld and men seem to prosper, they tend to forget God. On the other hand, when times of adversity come and the judgments of God are felt, at that time men do learn God's righteousness."[8]

**26:10** *Let favor be shown to the wicked, yet will he not learn righteousness.* Although God sends blessings or judgments to give the wicked man opportunity to repent, he will not *learn righteousness.* Rather, Isaiah says he will deal unjustly in the land of uprightness.

*land of uprightness . . . unjustly.* Even in a land where others obey God's laws, the wicked will still do wickedly.

*not behold the majesty of the Lord.* The wicked will not behold the Lord's majesty, but will be destroyed by the fire of his second coming (24:6).

**26:11** *Lord, when thy hand is lifted up, they will not see.* Transgressors do not perceive God's power in the judgments that are sent to the earth in every generation; they "confess not his hand in all things" (D&C 59:21).

*but they shall see, and be ashamed for their envy at the people.* The Jerusalem Bible has a much different reading: "Let them see your jealous love for this people and be ashamed, let the fire prepared for your enemies consume them." The shame that the wicked will experience pertains to the loss of the glory or honor that they would have received as God's worthy children. The fire mentioned here is an actual fire that will consume the wicked.

**26:12** *Lord, thou wilt ordain peace for us.* Jehovah has established peace for us—a blessing that arises from a covenant relationship with him and membership in a strong city (26:3).

*wrought all our works.* The New International Version reads, "all that we have accomplished you have done for us."

**26:13** *O Lord our God, other lords beside thee have had dominion over us.* "Two views are held regarding the term *other lords.* One is that they were foreign rulers who, at various times beginning with the period of the judges, had held sway over

---

[8]Young, *Book of Isaiah,* 2:214–15.

Israel. . . . The second view is that the prophet is referring to the idol-gods which the people had served repeatedly throughout their history (cf. Isa. 2:8; [2 Kgs. 18:4–6;] Amos 5:25–26)."[9]

*by thee only will we make mention of thy name.* We have a responsibility to bear record of the name of the Lord to the world, and the Spirit and power accompany his name only.

**26:14** *They are dead, they shall not live . . . hast thou visited and destroyed them.* The foreign lords or false gods who once ruled the people of Israel no longer live; the Lord has visited them with destruction (23:17). He has "made all their memory to perish." Indeed, how many of us can name any of the gods of the Amorites, Hittites, or Moabites?

**26:15** *Thou hast increased the nation.* The phrase is repeated twice for emphasis. In contrast to the destruction of wicked nations, the Lord's nation has been increased. The Lord, by means of scattering Israel and bringing the gospel to the Gentiles, has brought about an increase of his people.

*thou art glorified.* The fulfillment of the Abrahamic covenant brings glory to the Lord.

*thou hast extended all the boundaries.* This image speaks of the growth of Zion and her stakes in our day. Isaiah presents a full discussion of these things in Isaiah 54:1–3, where he instructs us to enlarge our tent and stretch forth our habitations; we will do this to accommodate our numbers because there will be so many members of Israel who will "break forth on the right hand and on the left" and even make "the desolate cities to be inhabited."

**26:16** *in trouble have they visited thee.* This idea is more clearly expressed in Doctrine and Covenants 101:8: "In the day of their peace they esteemed lightly my counsel; but, in the day of their trouble, of necessity they feel after me."

*thy chastening was upon them.* This message is also for us, who are part of Zion: "I, the Lord, will contend with Zion . . . and chasten her until she overcomes and is clean before me" (D&C 90:36); also, "My people must needs be chastened until they learn obedience" (D&C 105:6).

**26:17–18** *Like as a woman with child.* Israel is like a pregnant woman who has carried her child for nine months and then suffers the great pains that are associated with delivering a child. She does not, however, bring forth a child but rather brings forth "wind," perhaps symbolizing her destruction.

---

[9] Hailey, *Commentary on Isaiah,* 213.

Israel was responsible for bringing forth the fruit that the Lord intended, such as the gospel with its saving ordinances. She (Israel) did not provide that deliverance or life to the world (Isaiah says, "We have not wrought any deliverance in the earth"), neither have the inhabitants of the world "fallen from the womb" (Hebrew *napal*)[10] or become born of God. Instead, Israel brought forth nothing but wind, and the pain associated with her delivery (such as God's chastisements, exile, etc.) was for naught.

## THE LORD RESPONDS TO ISRAEL'S PRAYER AND PROMISES THE RESURRECTION (26:19–21)

Israel offered a prayer to the Lord in the previous section, contemplating different aspects of God's judgments upon the wicked (26:7–18). Here the Lord responds to that prayer with a promise of the resurrection and of safety from devastation.

Isaiah presents clear prophetic statements about the resurrection of Jehovah and humanity. The words "Thy dead men shall live, together with my dead body shall they arise" are straightforward, so as not to be misunderstood. Jehovah has arisen from the dead, along with many of the Saints, in partial fulfillment of Isaiah's words, for many have witnessed his resurrection, including the Nephites at the temple in Bountiful (3 Ne. 11). Others have witnessed the resurrection of the Saints (Matt. 27:52–53); other resurrections are yet to come.

Isaiah provides information vital to us for surviving God's judgments upon the earth: "Enter into [our] chambers . . . until the indignation pass over" (26:20).

*Isaiah 26:19–21*

Thy *dead men* shall live,
together with my *dead body* shall they arise.

Awake and sing, ye that dwell in dust:
for thy dew is as the dew of [the morning],[11]
and the earth shall cast out the dead. (26:19)

Come, my people, enter thou into thy chambers,
and shut thy doors [behind][12] thee:
hide thyself as it were for a little moment,
until the indignation [pass over].[13] (26:20)

---

[10] Brown, Driver, and Briggs, *Hebrew and English Lexicon,* 658.
[11] Following NIV Isa.
[12] NIV Isa. 26:20, replacing the KJV *about.*
[13] Hebrew *'abar,* meaning to "pass over, through, by, pass on." Brown, Driver, and Briggs, *Hebrew and English Lexicon,* 716.

For, behold, the Lord cometh out of his place to punish the inhabitants of the earth
for their iniquity:
the earth also shall *disclose* her blood,
and *shall no more cover* her slain. (26:21)

## NOTES AND COMMENTARY

**26:19** *Thy dead men shall live.* This is a promise of the resurrection.

*together with my dead body shall they arise.* The dead body referred to is that of
Jesus Christ. This prophecy was fulfilled at Jesus' resurrection. Matthew recorded
that after Jesus arose from the dead, "the graves were opened; and many bodies of the
saints which slept arose" (Matt. 27:52–53).

*Awake and sing, ye that dwell in dust.* The call is made for those who are dead to
awake from the sleep of death and sing praises to the Lord who made the resurrection
possible. Joseph Smith also prophesied, "And the graves of the saints shall be
opened; and they shall come forth and stand on the right hand of the Lamb, when he
shall stand upon Mount Zion, and upon the holy city, the New Jerusalem; and they
shall sing the song of the Lamb, day and night forever and ever" (D&C 133:56; D&C
128:22).

*for thy dew is as the dew of the morning.* The literal reading of the phrase *dew of
the morning* is "dew of lights." Isaiah compares resurrected bodies to the dew of the
morning because of dew's association with life. "*Dew* is a very important element in
Palestine's ecosystem. During the long dry months it is the only moisture the vegetation receives. It became a symbol for life. Light is also an important symbol of life
and well-being."[14] Interestingly, dew is also associated with the manna given to the
Israelites to save their lives during the exodus (Ex. 16:13–15; Num. 11:9).

*earth shall cast out the dead.* This is another reference to the resurrection.

**26:20** *Come, my people, enter thou into thy chambers.* The Lord invites us to
enter our chambers while he destroys the wicked ("until the indignation pass over").
*Chambers* may refer to our homes and inner chambers, where we offer our prayers to
our Father (Matt. 6:6); it may refer to the Lord's temples, where the righteous seek
refuge from the world, or *chambers* may refer to the Lord himself, who is our "refuge
from the storm" (25:4).

*shut thy doors behind thee.* Contrasting the open gates of verse two, before the
appearance of the Lord, Isaiah counsels the Lord's people to shut their doors. The
shut doors recall the Passover, when the people of Israel remained within their homes

---

[14] Watts, *Isaiah 1–33,* 342.

while the angel destroyed Egypt's firstborn (Ex. 12:21–27); they also recall Noah's family, shut in the ark until the destructive floods had passed (Gen. 7:1, 16).

*indignation.* God's great judgment, which will cleanse or purify the earth.

**26:21** *Lord cometh out of his place.* The Lord will come forth from his heavenly temple to cleanse the world of sin.

*earth also shall disclose her blood.* The blood of the innocent, speaking figuratively, has long called out from the earth for vengeance (Gen. 4:10; Job 16:18; Ezek. 24:7–8).

# ISAIAH 27

*LIKENING ISAIAH 27 UNTO OURSELVES*

*The marvelous prophecies of this chapter are being fulfilled in our dispensation by elders and sisters who are serving full-time missions and by the Saints who are letting their light shine before their neighbors and friends. We are teaching individuals the gospel, and one by one they are coming unto Christ. We are "the weak things of the earth," "thrash[ing] the nations by the power of the Spirit" (D&C 133:59). We are also witnessing the fulfillment of Isaiah's prophecy concerning temple work (27:13).*

## ISRAEL WILL BE GATHERED IN THE LAST DAYS (27:1–13)

This entire chapter deals directly with us as members of the Church; it shows the great love and care that the Lord has for us and outlines the many blessings that can be ours:

With his great sword, the Lord punishes Satan (27:1);

He provides us (the vineyard) with water every moment (27:3);

He watches over us (the vineyard) night and day (27:3);

He protects us from our enemies (briers and thorns) (27:4);

He provides us with peace (27:5);

Because of him, we will "fill the face of the world with fruit" (27:6); and

He will thresh the nations and gather us from the world one by one (27:12).

The words in this chapter imply a covenantal relationship. In return for the many blessings bestowed on us by the Lord, we will share the gospel in all the world (27:6, 12) and worship him at his holy temple (27:13).

*Isaiah 27:1–13*

In that day the Lord with his [hard][1] and great and strong sword
*shall punish* leviathan the [fleeing][2] serpent, even leviathan that crooked serpent;
and he *shall slay* the dragon that is in the sea. (27:1)

In that day sing ye [about],[3] A vineyard of [delight].[4] (27:2)

*I the Lord* do keep it;
*I* will water it every moment:
lest any hurt it, *I* will [guard][5] it night and day. (27:3)

Fury is not in me:
who would set the briers and thorns against me in battle?
*I would go through* them,
*I would burn* them together. (27:4)

Or let him take hold of my strength,
that *he may make* peace with me;
and *he shall make* peace with me. (27:5)

[In days to come *Jacob* will][6] take root:
*Israel* shall blossom and bud,
and fill the face of the world with fruit. (27:6)

*Hath he smitten him,* as he smote those that smote him?
or *is he slain* according to the slaughter of them that are slain by him? (27:7)

[By warfare and exile you contend with him],[7]
he stayeth his rough wind in the day of the east wind. (27:8)

By this therefore shall the *iniquity of Jacob* be purged;
and this is all the fruit to take away *his sin;*

when he maketh all the *stones of the altar* as chalkstones that are beaten in sunder,
the *groves and images* shall not stand up. (27:9)

Yet the *defenced city* shall be desolate,
and the *habitation* forsaken,
and left like a *wilderness:*

*there shall* the calf feed,
and *there shall* he lie down,
and consume the branches thereof. (27:10)

---

[1] From Hebrew *qashah,* meaning to be "hard, severe [or] . . . fierce." Brown, Driver, and Briggs, *Hebrew and English Lexicon,* 904, replacing the KJV *sore.*

[2] From the Hebrew *barach,* meaning to "go through [or] flee." Brown, Driver, and Briggs, *Hebrew and English Lexicon,* 137, replacing the KJV *piercing.*

[3] The preposition *'al* in Hebrew can be translated as "to, for, in regard to, about."

[4] From the Hebrew *chemed,* meaning "desire, delight." Brown, Driver, and Briggs, *Hebrew and English Lexicon,* 326; cf. Amos 5:10. This replaces the KJV *red wine.*

[5] From Hebrew *natsar,* meaning to "watch, guard." Brown, Driver, and Briggs, *Hebrew and English Lexicon,* 665, replacing the KJV *keep.*

[6] NIV Isa. 27:6 replacing the KJV *he shall cause them that come of Jacob to.*

[7] This reading from NIV Isa. better reflects the reading of the Hebrew Bible.

When the *boughs* thereof <u>are withered,</u>
*they* <u>shall be broken off:</u>
the women come, and <u>set</u> *them* <u>on fire:</u>

for it is a people of no understanding:
therefore *he that made them* <u>will not have mercy on them,</u>
and *he that formed them* <u>will [show]</u>[8] <u>them no favor.</u> (27:11)

And it shall come to pass in that day,
that the Lord shall beat off from the *channel of the river*[9]
unto *the stream of Egypt,*
and ye shall be gathered one by one, O ye children of Israel. (27:12)

And it shall come to pass in that day, that the great trumpet shall be blown,
and they shall come which were *ready to perish* in the <u>land of Assyria,</u>
and *the outcasts* in the <u>land of Egypt,</u>
and shall worship the Lord in the holy mount at Jerusalem. (27:13)

## NOTES AND COMMENTARY

**27:1** *In that day.* In the day of the Lord, meaning the time of the Lord's second coming (see 2:12).

*great and strong sword.* At his second coming, Jesus Christ will use his sword to wage war against Satan (see commentary on 34:5).

*leviathan/fleeing serpent/crooked serpent/dragon.* These terms refer to Satan. The meaning of *leviathan* is uncertain. Elsewhere Satan is identified as "serpent" and "dragon" (51:9; 2 Ne. 2:18)—terms that describe his nature. *Fleeing* may also be understood as swift, while *crooked* suggests deception or treachery. Both are valid descriptions of the adversary, who must be conquered in order for the Lord's vineyard to be safe and for Zion to be fully established. The Lord will accomplish this at the beginning of his millennial reign (Rev. 20:1–2).

*sea.* The "destroyer rideth upon the face" of the waters (D&C 61:19).

**27:2** *sing ye.* Verses 2–6 recall the song of the vineyard introduced in Isaiah 5. The song in chapter 5 addresses the vineyard's destruction; these verses here speak of the vineyard's redemption.

*vineyard of delight.* The house of Israel, meaning the covenant people of the Lord. In contrast to the wild grapes of Isaiah 5:2, 4 and the languishing vineyards of Isaiah 24:9–11, Israel will become a *vineyard of delight.* For this reason the Lord will take great care of it by keeping and watering it every moment and guarding it night and day.

---

[8] We have replaced the archaic KJV *shew.*
[9] The river here is the Euphrates.

**27:3** *I the Lord do keep it.* The Lord himself is the caretaker and the guardian of the vineyard. This is a contrast to Isaiah 5:5, in which he no longer protects Israel because of her nonproductivity, or wickedness.

*I will water it every moment.* For the meaning of *water* here, see Isaiah 8:6. The expression *every moment* indicates that the Lord will give divine attention to the vineyard.

*lest any hurt it.* The Lord will not permit his enemies to destroy the vineyard.

*I will guard it night and day.* A destroyer continually waits to attack, so Jehovah will watch over his vineyard constantly. Similarly, "He that keepeth Israel shall neither slumber nor sleep. The Lord is thy keeper: the Lord is thy shade upon thy right hand. The sun shall not smite thee by day, nor the moon by night. The Lord shall preserve thee from all evil: he shall preserve thy soul" (Ps. 121:4–7; Isa. 25:4–5).

**27:4** *Fury is not in me.* The wrath of the Lord, which once hung over the unrighteous of his covenant people, has been lifted, and now he seeks to defend his vineyard (contrast Isa. 5:5–7, 25).

*briers/thorns.* The enemies of the Lord's people. As briers and thorns hamper the growth of the vineyard, so Israel's enemies attempt to halt the growth of the Lord's vineyard (7:23–25). Briers and thorns were previously allowed to grow in the vineyard (5:6; 32:13), but now they are removed.

*I would burn them.* The Lord at his coming will act against the wicked, overcoming all who oppose him by destroying them with fire (10:17; 26:11); this destruction will be as simple as burning the briers and thorns in a vineyard.

**27:5** *let him take hold of my strength.* This statement is made concerning the briers and thorns in the vineyard, or the enemies of the kingdom, indicating that membership in the vineyard is granted to any who will turn to the Lord. We can *take hold* of God's strength by making covenants.

*he may make peace with me.* The blessing and reward of a covenant relationship with God is peace.

**27:6** *Jacob/Israel.* The covenant people of the Lord (Ether 13:10–11).

*Jacob will take root.* The vineyard *(Jacob)* will take root, or will become firmly established, in the promised land; after the vineyard matures (blossoms and buds), it will fill "the world with fruit," which may speak of literal offspring (2 Ne. 3:4; Gen. 30:2) or possibly righteous deeds (Jer. 17:7–8; see also commentary on 35:1).

**27:7** *Hath he smitten him.* The verse is difficult without the grammatical subjects and objects, so we supply them here in brackets: "Hath he [God] smitten him [Israel], as he [God] smote those [Israel's oppressors] that smote him [Israel]? or is he [Israel] slain according to the slaughter of them [Israel's oppressors] that are slain by him [God]?" The two rhetorical questions show that even in Israel's gross wickedness, the Lord did not completely destroy Israel as he did her oppressors (Assyria and Babylon). Rather, the Lord has scattered Israel as a chastisement to bring about a repentant people.

**27:8** *By warfare and exile you contend with him.* The Lord punishes Israel by sending armies to war against her and by sending her into exile.

*he stayeth his rough wind in the day of the east wind.* The east wind is God's destructive wind, symbolizing his judgments.

**27:9** *By this . . . shall the iniquity of Jacob be purged.* "Warfare" and "exile"—God's chastisements upon Israel—will purge Israel from her iniquity: "I, the Lord, will contend with Zion . . . and chasten her until she overcomes and is clean before me" (D&C 90:36).

*this is all the fruit to take away his sin.* The *fruit* (result) of the purging of Israel, which will remove the blemish of sin, is the destruction of all forms of false worship.

*he maketh all the stones of the altar as chalkstones.* Chalkstone, a soft stone that crumbles easily and quickly dissolves in rain, symbolizes the complete destruction of the altars of idolatry. When Israel's inhabitants destroy all forms of idolatry and false worship from their land and hearts, as if making all the stones of the altars into chalkstone, then will their iniquity be purged.

*the groves.* See commentary on 1:29; 17:8.

**27:10** *the defenced city shall be desolate.* Before the nation of Israel obtains redemption, her great, walled cities will be destroyed and the people carried away captive. This will leave both city and house empty and open to any wandering animal (6:11–12).

*wilderness.* "Diametrically opposite to the promised land, the Garden of Eden, and Zion stands the wilderness or desert (Isa. 51:3; Joel 2:3; Isa. 35:6–7). Scriptural expressions set forth the desolate state of the wilderness—it is a 'land of darkness' (Jer. 2:31), a 'parched ground,' a 'thirsty land,' and a 'habitation of dragons' (Isa. 35:6–7). Further, 'the wilderness' is a 'land of deserts and of pits, . . . a land of drought, and of the shadow of death, . . . a land that no man passed through, and where no man dwelt' (Jer. 2:6). Divine curses and judgments transform rich lands and fruitful territories into deserts, due to the wickedness and abominations of the people which inhabit such areas (Joel 3:19; Jer. 17:5–6; 50:12–13)."[10]

---

[10] McConkie and Parry, *Guide to Scriptural Symbols,* 107.

*there shall the calf feed.* With the inhabitants of the cities gone, cattle will roam the land, eating what they can find and sleeping wherever they wish (5:5; 7:25). In the process they will strip bare the branches of the vineyards and the trees, so that there will be nothing of value left, except withered wood for fire (27:11).

**27:11** *women come, and set them on fire.* Withered wood will be all that remains of value once the homes and cities are destroyed; women will seek for wood, using it as fuel for cooking and warmth. There is a spiritual meaning here: After the destruction of idolatry (27:9) and the desolation of cities and homes (27:10) in the last days, all that will remain will be the burning, representing the burning at the Second Coming.

*people of no understanding.* This same accusation is made in 1:3. The people of the Lord do not understand who their God is or their covenantal relationship with him. Therefore, the Lord "that made them will not have mercy on them."

**27:12** *that day.* Isaiah now prophesies of the last days.

*the Lord shall beat off from the channel of the river unto the stream of Egypt.* The New International Version reads, "The Lord will thresh from the flowing Euphrates to the Wadi of Egypt." We, the house of Israel, are God's threshing (21:10). Jehovah himself will take an active role in the gathering of Israel in the last days; he will thresh the entire world (from the Euphrates to the Nile, because these were the original boundaries of the realm of David; see Gen. 15:18; 1 Kgs. 4:21; 8:65), seeking the precious kernels of wheat (see the parable of the farmer in 28:23–29). As representatives of the Lord, we are assisting in the gathering of Israel through missionary work and through being a light upon a hill (Matt. 5:14–16). We are "the weak things of the world, those who are unlearned and despised"—those whom God has called upon "to thrash the nations by the power of [his] Spirit" (D&C 35:13).

*ye shall be gathered one by one.* Ye refers to the children of Israel. In our day the elders of Israel are commanded to assist in the gathering of Israel: "And ye are called to bring to pass the gathering of mine elect" (D&C 29:7). Members of the house of Israel do not usually join the Church in large groups; instead, they gather one by one as they hearken to the truth.

**27:13** *the great trumpet shall be blown.* The Lord calls upon the nations to gather to the gospel "by the mouth of [his] servants, and by the ministering of angels, and by [his] own voice . . . and by the great sound of a trump" (D&C 43:25; Matt. 24:31; D&C 49:23).

*they shall come which were ready to perish in the land of Assyria, and the outcasts in the land of Egypt.* The scattered children of Israel, at the point of perishing spiritually, will hearken to the trumpet and gather to the gospel banner. Assyria and Egypt, two of Israel's former enemies, serve here as symbols of wickedness.

*shall worship the Lord in the holy mount.* The *holy mount* refers to the temples of the Lord. "The object of gathering the Jews, or the people of God in any age of the world . . . was to build unto the Lord a house whereby He could reveal unto His people the ordinances of His house."[11]

---

[11] *History of the Church,* 5:423.

# ISAIAH 28

### LIKENING ISAIAH 28 UNTO OURSELVES

*We are often reminded of the pride and wickedness of ancient Babylon, but we some-
times forget that our Israelite ancestors, including the tribes of Ephraim and
Manasseh, were also proud and wicked. The Lord first warned our ancestors through
the voice of many prophets, each of whom in turn warned, testified, and prophesied of
impending destruction; afterward, the Lord permitted the fierce armies of Assyria to
capture and kill these people.*

*Much may be learned from these lessons in history. We, modern Israel, should
always follow the voice of our prophets, who, like Isaiah and other ancient prophets,
declare the word of the Lord. We should also look into our own lives to determine how
much pride we possess, or how often we sin against the Lord.*

## ISAIAH PROPHESIES OF THE DESTRUCTION OF EPHRAIM (28:1–8)

The Northern Kingdom of Israel, under the leadership of the tribe of Ephraim,
will fall under condemnation because of pride and wickedness (28:1). As a result, a
mighty and strong nation (Assyria; 28:2) has been commissioned to accomplish
eagerly and swiftly the judgments of the Lord (28:3–4).

In the last days, the "residue" of the children of Israel will consider the Lord to be
"a crown of glory" and "a diadem of beauty" (28:5); they will find wisdom and
strength in their association with him (28:6).

*Isaiah 28:1–8*

Woe to the crown of pride, to the drunkards of Ephraim,
whose glorious beauty is a fading flower,
which are on the head of the fat valleys:
of them that are overcome with wine! (28:1)

Behold, the Lord hath a mighty and strong one,
which as a *tempest of hail* and a *destroying storm,*
as a *flood of mighty waters* overflowing,
shall cast down to the earth with the hand. (28:2)

The crown of pride,
the drunkards of Ephraim,
shall be trodden under feet: (28:3)

And the glorious beauty,
which is on the head of the fat valley,
shall be a fading flower,
and as the [early ripe fig][1] before the summer;
which when he that looketh upon it seeth,
while it is yet in his hand he eateth it up. (28:4)

In that day shall the Lord of hosts be for a *crown* of glory,
and for a *diadem* of beauty, unto the residue of his people, (28:5)

And for a *spirit of judgment* to him that sitteth in judgment,
and for *strength* to them that turn the battle to the gate. (28:6)

But they also have *erred* through wine,
and through strong drink are *out of the way;*
the priest and the prophet have *erred* through strong drink,
they are *swallowed up* of wine,
they are *out of the way* through strong drink;

they *err* in vision,
they *stumble* in judgment. (28:7)

[Indeed][2] all tables are full of vomit and filthiness, so that there is no place clean. (28:8)

## NOTES AND COMMENTARY

**28:1** *Woe.* The *woe* referred to here is the severe anguish and distress pronounced upon Ephraim resulting from God's judgments. Six woes are pronounced in chapters 28 through 33 (28:1; 29:1, 15; 30:1; 31:1; 33:1).

*crown of pride.* The crown is Samaria, the capital of Ephraim, which is in the Northern Kingdom of Israel. Its walled city stood on a hill, perhaps presenting the

---

[1] From the Hebrew word *bikurah,* meaning "first ripe fig, early fig." Brown, Driver, and Briggs, *Hebrew and English Lexicon,* 114, replacing the KJV *hasty fruit.*

[2] *Kiy* may also be read *indeed,* which replaces the KJV *for.* Brown, Driver, and Briggs, *Hebrew and English Lexicon,* 471–72.

image of a crown, and its people were full of pride (see Isa. 9:9). As President Ezra Taft Benson said in our own generation, pride continues to be a great sin on the earth.[3]

*drunkards of Ephraim.* Ephraim is the name for the Northern Kingdom of Israel, headed by the tribe of Ephraim. Drunkenness is also an accusation made by Isaiah against Samaria (28:1, 3), and Ephraim is singled out for drunkenness in Hosea 7:5, 14. It is not simply literal drunkenness that is being condemned here, however, but spiritual "drunkenness" through sin and apostasy.

*whose glorious beauty is a fading flower.* Samaria had been a flourishing and glorious community, but its time of glory was about to pass away.

*head of the fat valleys.* The New International Version reads that Samaria was "set on the head of a fertile valley."

**28:2** *mighty and strong one.* This is the nation of Assyria, which besieged Samaria in 724 B.C. under Shalmaneser, and three years later took her people away into captivity under Sargon II (10:3–11; 2 Kgs. 17:3–6). Interestingly, the Lord said he would raise up "one mighty and strong" in the last days (D&C 85:7).

*which as a tempest of hail.* Assyria demolished the Northern Kingdom as easily as *a tempest of hail* or a destroying storm destroys a flower, or as a flood of mighty waters overcomes the banks of a river.

**28:3** *crown of pride.* The city of Samaria, the pride of the kingdom of Israel (28:1).

*drunkards of Ephraim.* Sin and apostasy (28:1).

*shall be trodden under feet.* Assyria will capture the inhabitants of the Northern Kingdom. *Under feet* speaks of subjugation and enslavement (1 Cor. 15:24–25; D&C 49:6; 76:61, 106).

**28:4** *glorious beauty.* See commentary on 28:1.

*shall be a fading flower.* See commentary on 28:1.

*as the early ripe fig.* As easily as an *early ripe fig* is singled out, picked, and eaten by a passerby (Nahum 3:12), so will Assyria consume Samaria.

**28:5** *In that day.* Isaiah 28:5–6 is parenthetical and prophesies of the last days, when a remnant of Israel will consider the Lord to be a crown of beauty.

*shall the Lord . . . be for a crown of glory/diadem of beauty.* In contrast to the crown of pride in 28:1 and 3, the Lord—the true king—is both beautiful and glorious to his people (2:11; 4:2). This passage also alludes to the temple and the promise that the Lord's saints may receive a *crown of glory* at his right hand (D&C 104:7).

---

[3] See "Cleansing the Inner Vessel," 6–7.

*residue of his people.* The remnant of Israel, which will be gathered in the last days (24:13; 27:12–13).

**28:6** *spirit of judgment to him that sitteth in judgment.* The Lord gives his appointed judges (such as bishops; D&C 58:17–18) the spirit of judgment to enable them to judge with equity (1:26).

*turn the battle to the gate.* The Lord will give strength to those who guard Zion's city gates so they can turn back those who attack, both physically and spiritually.

**28:7** *the priest and the prophet have erred through strong drink.* Isaiah, a prophet of the Southern Kingdom of Judah, turns his attention to the corrupt priests and prophets of the Northern Kingdom. This may also refer to apostate priests and prophets of the last days. He mentions the wine of the priest and prophet twice and their *strong drink* three times; they have *erred* twice, they are "out of the way" twice, and "swallowed up" once. But inasmuch as Isaiah is using metaphors, he presents the meaning behind his words: "they err in vision" and "they stumble in judgment." In short, they are drunk with wickedness to the point of spiritual staggering.

*they err in vision, they stumble in judgment.* It was the prophets' privilege to receive visions on behalf of the people, but they erred in vision; and it was the priests' privilege to represent the nation before God and to pronounce just judgments for the nation (Mal. 2:7), but they stumbled in judgment. The lives of the priests and prophets should have reflected the teachings of Jehovah, but they had become so immersed in the intoxication of sin that they had completely disassociated themselves from him. This verse refers also to the false religious leaders of Joseph Smith's day—and perhaps of ours.[4]

**28:8** *tables are full of vomit and filthiness.* Apostate prophets and priests are incapable of providing their congregations with the necessary spiritual food because their tables are full of vomit and filthiness, or iniquities—"there [was] no place clean."

## INDIVIDUALS LEARN DOCTRINE LINE UPON LINE (28:9–13)

Second Nephi 28:30 summarizes the meaning of Isaiah 28:9–13: "For behold, thus saith the Lord God: I will give unto the children of men line upon line, precept upon precept, here a little and there a little; and blessed are those who hearken unto my precepts, and lend an ear unto my counsel, for they shall learn wisdom; for unto

---

[4] McConkie, *Millennial Messiah,* 76.

him that receiveth I will give more; and from them that shall say, We have enough, from them shall be taken away even that which they have."

## Isaiah 28:9–13

*Whom* shall he <u>teach knowledge</u>?
and *whom* shall he <u>make to understand doctrine</u>?

them that are *weaned* from <u>the milk</u>,
and *drawn* from <u>the breasts</u>. (28:9)

For *precept must be upon precept,*
precept upon precept;

line upon line,
line upon line;

here a little,
and *there a little:* (28:10)

For with *stammering* <u>lips</u> and
*another* <u>tongue</u> will he speak to this people. (28:11)

To whom he said,
*This* is the <u>rest</u> wherewith ye may cause the weary to rest;
and *this* is the <u>refreshing</u>: yet they would not hear. (28:12)

But the word of the Lord was unto them *precept upon precept,*
precept upon precept;

line upon line,
line upon line;

here a little,
and *there a little;*

that they might go,
and <u>fall backward,</u>
and <u>be broken,</u>
and <u>snared,</u>
and <u>taken</u>. (28:13)

## NOTES AND COMMENTARY

**28:9** *Whom shall he teach knowledge.* After declaring the apostasy of the Northern Kingdom's inhabitants, especially of their priests and prophets (28:1–8), Isaiah asks, "[To] whom shall [the Lord] teach knowledge" and "make to understand [his] doctrine?" Certainly not the drunken priests and prophets, but those who qualify themselves through humility and righteousness.

*weaned from the milk/drawn from the breasts.* Isaiah likens milk to the basic principles of the gospel—faith, repentance, and baptism—that are the basis for further learning. Paul built upon this imagery: "For every one that useth milk is unskilful in the word of righteousness: for he is a babe. But strong meat belongeth to them that are of full age, even those who by reason of use have their senses exercised to discern both good and evil" (Heb. 5:13–14; JST 1 Cor. 3:2; Alma 12:9; D&C 19:21–22).

**28:10** *For precept must be upon precept . . . line upon line.* Joseph Smith taught this same principle to the Latter-day Saints: "When you climb up a ladder, you must begin at the bottom, and ascend step by step, until you arrive at the top; and so it is with the principles of the Gospel—you must begin with the first, and go on until you learn all the principles of exaltation."[5]

**28:11** *with stammering lips and another tongue will he speak to this people.* Inasmuch as the people of the Northern Kingdom refused to believe and obey the words of the Lord, they were scattered among foreign nations that spoke languages other than their native Hebrew. Paul referred to this verse in one of his letters to the Corinthians in connection with the gift of tongues (1 Cor. 14:20–22). This passage may have an alternate reading. Perhaps the Lord announces here that he will speak to his people through weak mortal lips and slow speech—and perhaps even through a messenger from another land.

*this people.* The inhabitants of Ephraim, the Northern Kingdom. In a broader sense, this can apply to the covenant people in all ages.

**28:12** *This is the rest/this is the refreshing. Rest* and *refreshing* may refer to the Sabbath day, a sign of Israel's covenant relationship with the Lord (Ex. 31:16–17). It is through this covenant relationship that the obedient and weary find the rest and refreshing that come from the gospel (30:15). The Lord tried to tell the leaders of the people how to find this rest, but "they would not hear." Their gradual falling away from the word of the Lord led to both physical and spiritual captivity. *Rest* and *refreshing* may also refer to the peace of the gospel—the peace that Christ gives us (John 14:27).

**28:13** *precept upon precept.* See commentary on 28:10.

*fall backward, and be broken, and snared, and taken.* Because Ephraim disregarded the words of the Lord, they lost the blessings associated with obedience. They fell away from the truth and the Lord and eventually were *broken, and snared, and taken* captive by their sins (24:18).

---

[5] *Teachings of the Prophet Joseph Smith,* 348; emphasis omitted.

## THE OVERFLOWING SCOURGE (28:14–22)

Isaiah now turns his attention from the inhabitants of the Northern Kingdom to those of the Southern Kingdom. Because the people of Judah refused to trust in the Lord and instead entered into a "covenant with death" (28:15; 31:1–3), the Lord decreed an overflowing scourge (28:18). This scourge symbolizes a greater scourge that will cover the entire earth before Jesus' second coming. To prepare a righteous remnant for this terrible event, the Lord established a precious cornerstone (Jesus Christ) as the beginning of the foundation of Zion. Those who build upon the cornerstone will find safety.

*Isaiah 28:14–22*

Wherefore hear the word of the Lord,
ye scornful men, that rule this people which is in Jerusalem. (28:14)

Because ye have said, *We have made a covenant* with death,
and with hell are *we at agreement;*

when the overflowing scourge shall pass through,
it shall not come unto us:

for we have made *lies* our refuge,
and under *falsehood* have we hid ourselves: (28:15)

Therefore thus saith the Lord God,
Behold, I lay in Zion for *a foundation a stone,* a tried stone,
a precious corner stone, *a sure foundation:*
he that believeth shall not make haste. (28:16)

*Judgment* also will I lay to the line,
and *righteousness* to the plummet:

and the *hail* shall sweep away the refuge of lies,
and the *waters* shall overflow the hiding place. (28:17)

And your *covenant with death* shall be disannulled,
and your *agreement with hell* shall not stand;

when the *overflowing scourge shall pass through,* then ye shall be trodden down
by it. (28:18)
From the time that *it goeth forth* it shall take you:

for *morning by morning* shall it pass over,
by *day and by night:*
and it shall be a vexation only to understand the report. (28:19)

For the *bed is shorter* than that a man can stretch himself on it:
and the *covering narrower* than that he can wrap himself in it. (28:20)

For the *Lord shall rise up* as in mount Perazim,
*he shall be wroth* as in the valley of Gibeon,

that he may *do his work,* his strange work;
and *bring to pass his act,* his strange act. (28:21)

Now therefore be ye not mockers, lest your bands be made strong:
for I have heard from the Lord God of hosts a consumption,
even determined upon the whole earth. (28:22)

## NOTES AND COMMENTARY

**28:14** *hear the word of the Lord.* This counsel was directed to Jerusalem's wicked leaders, who represented the inhabitants of the kingdom of Judah. The Lord calls the leaders "scornful men."

*this people.* The Lord's covenant people, the inhabitants of the kingdom of Judah.

**28:15** *We have made a covenant with death/hell.* Judah's leaders, against the Lord's counsel, made a covenant with Egypt to fight Assyria in hopes that they (Judah) might free themselves from Assyria's rule (30:1; 31:1). Judah's stand against Assyria and her trust in Egypt's might and power jeopardized the lives of the people of Judah, because they did not rely on the Lord; hence, Judah was signing her own death warrant, called by Isaiah a *covenant with death.*

In the last days, many leaders will sin by not hearkening to the Lord's counsels or trusting in his might and power, relying rather on human strength for survival. Theirs is an agreement with hell rather than heaven. In another sense, many will make covenant with Satan, or with the forces of evil, hoping thereby to perpetuate their power.

*overflowing scourge.* The Assyrian army and its brutal, destructive ways are called an *overflowing scourge.* Isaiah combines two images here: *Overflowing* refers to a flood, bringing to mind the picture of one drowning in violent waters. This image was also used to describe the destruction of Judah in Isaiah 8:6–8. One meaning of *scourge* was a whip used to flog people and inflict upon them great pain. The figure of a scourge was also used in Isaiah 10:26 to portray the cruel Assyrians. Judah's inhabitants were aware of the Assyrians but erroneously believed that their alliances would protect them; the "overflowing scourge . . . shall not come unto us," they said (30:1; 31:1).

A great scourge sufficient to cleanse the world has been decreed for the last days (D&C 84:96–97). The Lord prophesied through Joseph Smith: "For a desolating scourge shall go forth among the inhabitants of the earth, and shall continue to be poured out from time to time, if they repent not, until the earth is empty, and the inhabitants thereof are consumed away and utterly destroyed by the brightness of my coming" (D&C 5:19). The inhabitants of Zion will be protected from the overflowing scourge. Joseph Smith declared, "Repent ye, repent ye, and embrace the everlasting covenant, and flee to Zion, before the overflowing scourge overtake you."[6] Also, "'the ransomed of the Lord shall return, and come to Zion with songs and everlasting joy upon their heads' [35:10]; and then they will be delivered from the overflowing scourge that shall pass through the land.'"[7]

*we have made lies our refuge.* The leaders of Judah deceived themselves into believing that Egypt would protect them from Assyria's armies, creating a false security or refuge.

**28:16** *I lay in Zion for a foundation a stone.* This is a prophecy of Jesus Christ, in which he is called a *stone,* a *tried stone* (or a stone tested for strength), and a *precious corner stone.* A cornerstone adds permanence and strength to the foundation of a building. Here the building is the latter-day Zion, and "he that believeth" may have a "sure foundation" on which to build (1 Pet. 2:6–8).

*he that believeth shall not make haste.* Peter's quotation of Isaiah here reads, "He that believeth on him shall not be confounded" (1 Pet. 2:6), and Paul's quotation reads, "shall not be ashamed" (Rom. 9:33; 10:11). The meaning of this phrase, then, is: "Whosoever believes on him [Christ, the stone] shall not be [confounded or] ashamed."

**28:17** *Judgment . . . will I lay to the line, and righteousness to the plummet.* The verse is directly related to 28:16, wherein Isaiah uses imagery related to building practices. Stonemasons use a measuring line and plumb bob (plummet) to ensure a proper fit in the structure. Here Isaiah likens these tools to *judgment* and *righteousness,* and by these the Lord will evaluate and measure his people. If the stones do not measure up to these standards, they will be set aside (1:21). A firmly established building with righteous dwellers will survive sweeping hail and overflowing waters.

Joseph Smith referred to this verse: "The world has had a fair trial for six thousand years; the Lord will try the seventh thousand Himself; 'He whose right it is, will possess the kingdom, and reign until He has put all things under His feet'; iniquity will hide its hoary head, Satan will be bound, and the works of darkness destroyed; righteousness will be put to the line, and judgment to the plummet, and 'he that fears the Lord will alone be exalted in that day.'"[8]

---

[6] *Teachings of the Prophet Joseph Smith,* 18; cf. D&C 45:31.
[7] *Teachings of the Prophet Joseph Smith,* 17.
[8] *Teachings of the Prophet Joseph Smith,* 252.

*hail shall sweep away the refuge of lies.* Hail and waters are used here as figures of divine judgment (28:2; Mosiah 12:6), which will sweep away the refuge and hiding place of the wicked. The same judgments, however, will not harm the righteous, for they have been carefully built with a measuring line and plumb bob.

**28:18** *your covenant with death shall be disannulled.* Judah's covenant with Egypt, or death (28:15), will not stand but will be broken, as will the covenant of those in the last days with the mortal arm of flesh.

*overflowing scourge.* See commentary on 28:15.

*trodden down by it.* The overflowing scourge that trod upon Judah was the Assyrian army (5:5; 7:25; 10:6).

**28:19** *by day and by night.* Once the scourge (Assyrian army) had been unleashed, there was no escaping it. It overcame the inhabitants of Judah. Similarly, in the last days, "vengeance cometh speedily upon the ungodly as the whirlwind; and who shall escape it? The Lord's scourge shall pass over by night and by day, and the report thereof shall vex all people; yea, it shall not be stayed until the Lord come; For the indignation of the Lord is kindled against their abominations and all their wicked works. Nevertheless, Zion shall escape if she observe to do all things whatsoever I have commanded her. But if she observe not to do whatsoever I have commanded her, I will visit her according to all her works, with sore affliction, with pestilence, with plague, with sword, with vengeance, with devouring fire" (D&C 97:22–26).

*vexation only to understand the report.* When reports of the overflowing scourge reach the ears of the people, this will cause fear and trembling. Similarly, the report of the scourge of the last days "shall vex all people" (D&C 97:23).

**28:20** *bed is shorter than that a man can stretch himself on it.* In the same way that a small bed is too short for a tall person or a small blanket does not adequately provide warmth and comfort to an adult, the protection the wicked have sought to gain will be wholly inadequate.

**28:21** *the Lord shall rise up as in mount Perazim/the valley of Gibeon.* The Lord will rise up in his wrath to accomplish his judgments against the wicked, as he did anciently at Mount Perazim against the Philistines (2 Sam. 5:17–20) and in the valley of Gibeon against the Amorites (Josh. 10:6–14).

*he may do his work, his strange work/strange act.* God's *strange act,* mentioned in Doctrine and Covenants 95:4; 101:95, is the establishment of Zion and his millennial kingdom. *Strange* may also be translated *foreign* or *alien,* meaning that the Lord's work will be alien to the people of the world. The laying of the "precious corner stone" is the beginning of Zion (28:16).

**28:22** *be ye not mockers.* Because judgment is inevitable, Isaiah advises the people of Judah to heed rather than mock the prophecies. The same counsel applies to us in the last days.

*lest your bands be made strong.* Isaiah returns to the image of imprisonment, introduced in 24:17–18, to refer to the consequences of sin and mockery.

*consumption, even determined upon the whole earth.* Although the Lord sends scourges upon various peoples throughout the history of the earth, in the last days his judgments will consume *all* the wicked of the world.

## PARABLE OF THE FARMER (28:23–29)

Isaiah's parable explains how the Lord uses an established plan as he works with his people, who are his "threshing, and the corn of [his] floor" (21:10). The lesson presented here is based on the work of the farmer, who plows, plants, and harvests each item in its own way and according to its own time. The Lord has scattered his people at different times in various places; the Lord will gather and thresh his people in order to bring an increase to himself according to appointed times. "God's strategy for history, like his strategy for agriculture, is wonderful and achieves success. Thus his instruction should be sought by [all the earth's inhabitants], as it is sought and followed by farmers. And his strategy is to be trusted with patient faith."[9]

*Isaiah 28:23–29*

> *Give ye ear,* and <u>hear my voice</u>;
> *hearken,* and <u>hear my speech</u>. (28:23)

> Doth the *plowman* <u>plow</u> all day to sow?
> doth *he* <u>open and break the clods of his ground</u>? (28:24)
> When *he* hath <u>made plain the face</u> thereof,

> doth he not *cast abroad* the <u>fitches</u>,
> and *scatter* the <u>cummin</u>,
> and *cast* in the principal <u>wheat</u> and the appointed
> <u>barley</u> and <u>rye</u> in their place? (28:25)

> For his God doth *instruct* him to discretion,
> and doth *teach* him. (28:26)

> For the *fitches* are not <u>threshed with a threshing instrument</u>,
> neither is a <u>cart wheel turned about</u> upon the cummin;

> but the *fitches* are beaten out with a <u>staff</u>,
> and the *cummin* with a <u>rod</u>. (28:27)

---

[9] Watts, *Isaiah 1–33*, 375–76.

Bread corn is *bruised;*
because he will not ever be *threshing it,*

nor *break it* <u>with the wheel of his cart,</u>
nor *bruise it* <u>with his horsemen</u>. (28:28)

This also cometh forth from the Lord of hosts,
which is *wonderful* in <u>counsel</u>,
and *excellent* in <u>working</u>. (28:29)

## NOTES AND COMMENTARY

**28:23** *Give ye ear/hearken.* Listen closely to the prophet's words.

**28:24** *Doth the plowman plow all day to sow.* The Lord is the plowman who, like the farmer, performs all his work in its proper order and has specific results in mind. Through a rhetorical question Isaiah explains that a plowman does not plow continually (literally all day and every day). If so, the growing season would be over before the seeds were ever planted. The farmer must move on to other duties if the plants are to be fully grown at harvest time. Similarly, the Lord follows a precise pattern as he deals with his people.

**28:25** *fitches/cummin/wheat/barley/rye.* Once the soil is prepared, the seeds must be sown, each in its proper place. Fitches (caraway?) and cumin are seeds that can be sown anywhere, because they do not require any special attention to ensure their germination, nor are they as valuable as wheat or other staple grains. On the other hand, wheat, a staple food item, is carefully sown in rows so it can easily be covered with soil and thus properly germinate. Barley is sown in well-plowed areas, and rye, a low-yield, coarse-grained crop, is sown around the edges of the field where the earth is not as well cultivated.[10] As the farmer plants many seeds in different conditions, so does the Lord "plant" different individuals and groups in different mortal circumstances.

**28:26** *God doth instruct him.* The Lord has instructed the farmer in the proper order in the cultivation process, the planting of various types of seeds, the harvesting, and nature's patterns. Isaiah is trying to show us that if the Lord provides order for the farmer and his crops, his own actions also have a specific order, even if we are unable to discern it.

**28:27** *fitches are not threshed with a threshing instrument.* A threshing instrument, drawn by an ass or oxen, was "dragged over the grain to separate kernels of grain from the husks."[11] Fitches and cumin bear small, delicate seeds. If a threshing

---

[10] Keil and Delitzsch, *Commentary,* 7:2:14-17.
[11] Watts, *Isaiah 1–33,* 376.

machine or cart wheel were used to thresh them, they would be completely destroyed or lost. Therefore, the "fitches are beaten out with a staff, and the cummin with a rod" to loosen and separate the seeds. Isaiah's message seems to be this: The Lord uses different means to punish or chastise the unrighteous. Some he crushes with a threshing instrument or cart wheel; others he beats with a rod or staff.

**28:28** *Bread corn is bruised.* Bread corn is any variety of grain such as wheat, barley, or rye used to make bread; it must be treated more roughly than fitches and cumin in order to separate the kernels from the chaff. Anciently, after the bread corn was spread upon the threshing floor, a threshing instrument or cart wheel was rolled over it, bruising but not crushing the kernels. The farmer did not spend too much time threshing ("he will not ever be threshing"), lest the wheel of the cart or the horsemen crush the kernels.

**28:29** *This also cometh from the Lord of Hosts.* All of these principles of farming and the harvest come from the Lord.

# ISAIAH 29

*LIKENING ISAIAH 29 UNTO OURSELVES*

*Very few words of Isaiah are quoted more often than are those from this chapter, which contains detailed prophecies of the Book of Mormon. We frequently hear the words "a marvelous work and a wonder," "a book that is sealed," and "three witnesses" in Sunday School classes or from the pulpit. All of these phrases are from Isaiah 29 (JST, KJV). This chapter provides many details about the book of scripture that is the keystone of our religion. Isaiah 29 was written some twenty-seven hundred years ago for us as a witness of the Book of Mormon.*

## JERUSALEM TO BE BROUGHT DOWN BY THE LORD (29:1–10)

Ariel, a prophetic name for Jerusalem, will be destroyed by a "multitude of all the nations" (29:7–8) that will "distress," "camp against," "lay siege" to, and "raise forts against" her (29:2–3). This destruction will occur because Jerusalem's inhabitants have rejected the Lord's prophets and seers (29:10). Historically, Jerusalem was destroyed by the Babylonians, Romans, and other nations. Prophetically, a "multitude of all the nations" will yet "lay siege against" Jerusalem before the second coming of Jesus (Zech. 14:2, 16).

Nephi paraphrased a few of Isaiah's words, as recorded in Isaiah 29:2–4, likening the people of Jerusalem to his own people and their destruction (2 Ne. 26:15). The Nephite nation was indeed destroyed according to the words of Nephi in a manner similar to the destruction of Jerusalem.

When Joseph Smith translated the Bible, he made a number of notable changes in this section of Isaiah 29. The King James Version second-person forms, *thou, thee,* and *thy,* which refer to Jerusalem, are changed to the third-person singular forms *her*

[ 259 ]

and *she* in eight instances in verses 3–5 of the Joseph Smith Translation. The Joseph Smith Translation also replaces *thou* with *they* in verse 6, changing the referent from Jerusalem to her enemies.

## Isaiah 29:1–10

Woe to Ariel, to Ariel, the city where David dwelt!
add ye year to year; let them kill sacrifices. (29:1)

Yet I will distress Ariel, and there shall be heaviness and sorrow:
[for thus hath the Lord said unto me], It shall be unto[1] Ariel. (29:2)

[That] *I [the Lord] will camp* against [her] round about,
and *will lay siege* against [her] with a mount,
and *I will raise forts* against [her].[2] (29:3)

And [she] shalt be brought down, and [shall] *speak* out of the ground,
and [her] *speech* shall be low out of the dust,
and [her] *voice* shall be, as of one that hath a familiar spirit, out of the ground,
and [her][3] *speech* shall whisper out of the dust. (29:4)

Moreover the *multitude of [her]*[4] *strangers* shall be like small dust,
and the *multitude of the terrible ones* shall be as chaff
that passeth away: yea, it shall be at an instant suddenly. (29:5)

[For they shall][5] be visited of the Lord of Hosts,
with *thunder,* and with *earthquake,* and [with] a *great noise,*
and with *storm,* and [with] *tempest,* and [with][6] the *flame of devouring fire.* (29:6)

And the multitude of all the nations that *fight* against Ariel,[7]
even all that *fight* against *her* and her munition,[8]
and that *distress her,* shall be as a dream of a night vision. (29:7)

[Yea,] it shall [be unto them even as unto a] *hungry man [who] dreameth,*
and, behold, he eateth,
but he *awaketh,* and his soul is empty:
or [like unto] a *thirsty man [who] dreameth,* and, behold, he drinketh;
but he *awaketh,* and, behold, he is faint, and his soul hath appetite:
[Yea, even][9] so shall the multitude of all the nations be, that fight against mount Zion. (29:8)

---

[1] The bracketed changes are from JST Isa. 29:2.
[2] The bracketed changes are from JST Isa. 29:3.
[3] The bracketed changes are from JST Isa. 29:4.
[4] The bracketed changes are from JST Isa. 29:5.
[5] The KJV reads *Thou shalt be visited;* JST Isa. 29:6 reads *For they shall be visited;* 2 Ne. 27:2 reads *And when that day shall come they shall be visited.*
[6] The bracketed changes are from 2 Ne. 27:2.
[7] The 2 Ne. 27:3 reading of this verse has *Zion* in place of *Ariel.* Also, Nephi's record deletes *the multitude of* in this line.
[8] The entire line *even . . . munition* is not found in the 2 Ne. 27:3 reading of Isa. 29:7.
[9] The bracketed changes are from JST Isa. 29:8 and 2 Ne. 27:3. JST Isa. 29:8 reads *who dreameth;* 2 Ne. 27:3 reads *which dreameth.*

[For behold, all ye that doeth iniquity], *stay yourselves,* and <u>wonder</u>;
[for ye shall] *cry out,* and <u>cry</u>;
[yea, ye shall be] *drunken,* but <u>not with wine</u>;
[ye shall]¹⁰ *stagger,* but <u>not with strong drink</u>. (29:9)

For [behold,] the Lord *hath poured out upon you the spirit of deep sleep.*
[For behold, ye *have] closed your eyes,*
[and ye have rejected] the <u>prophets</u> and your <u>rulers</u>;
[and] the *seers* hath he covered [because of your iniquity].¹¹ (29:10)

## NOTES AND COMMENTARY

**29:1** *Woe.* Isaiah pronounces distress upon Jerusalem, resulting from God's judgments.

*Ariel.* The city of Jerusalem. *Ariel* appears five times in the Old Testament, all in Isaiah 29. The word is commonly translated as "lion of God," "lioness of God," or "altar-hearth" of God.¹² The lion is a symbol of Judah (Gen. 49:9).

*add year to year/kill sacrifices.* Elder Orson Pratt explained, "After the Messiah came and was sacrificed for the sins of the world, the Jews continued to 'kill sacrifices,' when they should have been done away; they added 'year to year' to the laws of Moses."¹³

**29:2** *I will distress Ariel.* The pronoun *I,* referring to the Lord, is used three times in verses 2–3. One meaning of *distress* is to overcome by pain and suffering.

**29:3** *I the Lord will camp against her.* This verse describes an army preparing to battle against Jerusalem. *Camp, mount,* and *forts* refer to the soldiers who will pitch their tents around Jerusalem's outer walls as they prepare to lay siege against her. The phrase *I the Lord will camp against her* indicates that the Lord will lead the enemies of Jerusalem in destroying her. Nephi likened this verse unto his own people and their destruction (2 Ne. 26:15).

**29:4** *she shalt be brought down.* Jerusalem (and the Nephite nation) will be destroyed.

*her speech shall be low out of the dust.* "Ariel, after being besieged, descends into the land of the dead, becoming like a ghost."¹⁴ In the same way, like Jerusalem and her people, the Jaredite and Nephite nations were destroyed and their peoples

---

¹⁰The bracketed changes are from JST Isa. 29:9 and 2 Ne. 27:4; the JST Isa. passage changes the Book of Mormon phrase *doeth* to *do.*

¹¹The bracketed changes are from JST Isa. 29:10 and 2 Ne. 27:5; the Book of Mormon passage includes the phrase *because of your iniquity* at the end of the verse whereas the JST Isa. passage does not.

¹²Brown, Driver, and Briggs, *Hebrew and English Lexicon,* 72.

¹³*Orson Pratt's Works,* 270.

¹⁴Watts, *Isaiah 1–33,* 382.

became part of the dust of the earth.[15] As Jerusalem shall cry to us out of the dust through her records, so shall the Jaredites and Nephites speak to us through the Book of Mormon (2 Ne. 3:19; 26:16; 33:13; Morm. 8:23; Moro. 10:27).

*familiar spirit.* This phrase refers to a ghost or spirit.[16] Jews will bear testimony of their offenses and the resulting punishment, as will the Jaredites and Nephites, who speak "out of the ground," as it were, through their written records. "Here Nephi applies Isaiah's words to the departed of his own people who, through the Book of Mormon, speak to those of the last days from the grave with a voice of warning."[17]

**29:5** *multitude of her strangers shall be like small dust.* The multitude, mentioned twice in this verse, refers to the nations that destroyed Jerusalem in the past (including Babylon, Rome, and all others who laid siege against her; 29:3) or who will fight against Jerusalem in the future. These once-mighty nations will suffer the judgments of God and become like the fine dust of the earth.

*it shall be at an instant suddenly.* Nephi wrote: "Wherefore, as those who have been destroyed have been destroyed speedily; and the multitude of their terrible ones shall be as chaff that passeth away—yea, thus saith the Lord God: It shall be at an instant, suddenly" (2 Ne. 26:18).

**29:6** *visited of the Lord of Hosts.* The Lord controls the nations of the earth, and his judgments come upon them for their role in destroying Jerusalem and her inhabitants.

*thunder/earthquake/great noise/storm/tempest/devouring fire.* The judgments of God were sent when the Nephite nation was destroyed (2 Ne. 26:4–6). They will occur again "in the last days, or in the days of the Gentiles," when "all the nations of the Gentiles and also the Jews . . . will be drunken with iniquity and all manner of abominations—and when that day shall come they shall be visited of the Lord of Hosts, with thunder and with earthquake, and with a great noise, and with storm, and with tempest, and with the flame of devouring fire" (2 Ne. 27:1–2). These judgments will come upon the wicked after they have rejected the testimonies of the Church's prophets and missionaries (D&C 43:24–25; 88:88–90).

**29:7** *nations that fight against Ariel . . . shall be as a dream of a night vision.* The Babylonians, Romans, and all the *nations that fight against Ariel,* after their day of might and dominion, will fade away *as a dream* vanishes during the night.

---

[15] On this interpretation, see McConkie, *New Witness for the Articles of Faith,* 432–33; Pratt, *Orson Pratt's Works,* 270–71.

[16] Brown, Driver, and Briggs, *Hebrew and English Lexicon,* 15.

[17] McConkie and Millet, *Doctrinal Commentary on the Book of Mormon,* 1:306.

**29:8** *as unto a hungry man who dreameth.* The nations that fight against Jerusalem and Zion will, in the end, have no more lasting satisfaction than does a hungry person who only dreams of eating.

**29:9** *ye that doeth iniquity . . . shall be drunken, but not with wine.* The wicked (including those who have rejected the Lord's prophets and seers; 29:10) are likened to those who are drunk with strong drink, but the wicked stagger because they walk in darkness and apostasy and have lost their spiritual faculties.

**29:10** *the Lord hath poured out upon you the spirit of deep sleep.* The *spirit of deep sleep* describes the apostate condition of those who reject the Lord's prophets and words. The Lord pours out this spirit upon the people because they have closed their spiritual eyes, rejected the prophets, and committed iniquities.

*closed your eyes.* Jerusalem's inhabitants have *closed [their] eyes* and are spiritually in a deep sleep. This will also be the condition of the world in the last days.

*seers hath he covered because of your iniquities.* God took away his prophets and seers because of the wickedness of Jerusalem's inhabitants.

## THE BOOK OF MORMON: A MARVELOUS WORK AND A WONDER (JST 29:11–26 = KJV 29:11–14)

Isaiah envisioned the coming forth of the Book of Mormon and his prophecy presents specific events related to our keystone scripture. Isaiah's prophecy of the coming forth of the Book of Mormon describes the Prophet Joseph Smith; the three witnesses of the Book of Mormon; other witnesses; and Martin Harris's visit to Professor Anthon of New York, an acknowledged expert in ancient languages, even giving the exact words Anthon would utter.

Isaiah uses the word *book* twenty times in this section to refer to the gold plates. This book contains "revelation from God" and is a record of the Jaredite and Nephite nations, those "who have slumbered in the dust" (JST 29:14). It is a "sealed book," parts of which are kept from the wicked but which will come forth in the Lord's time to be read "by the power of Christ" (JST 29:16). After Joseph Smith has completed his translation of a portion of the sealed book, he will return it to God, who will "preserve" the record until he sees fit to bring it forth (JST 29:24).

The following verses of Isaiah 29 are cited in the Book of Mormon:[18]

Isaiah 29:3–5 = 2 Nephi 26:15–16, 18;

---

[18] For a discussion of Isa. 29 as used in the Book of Mormon, see Cloward, "Isaiah 29 and the Book of Mormon," 191–247.

Isaiah 29:11 = 2 Nephi 27:15–18;
Isaiah 29:6 = 2 Nephi 6:15;
Isaiah 29:6–10 = 2 Nephi 27:2–5;
Isaiah 29:13b, 15 = 2 Nephi 28:9;
Isaiah 29:13–24 = 2 Nephi 27:25–35;
Isaiah 29:14 = 1 Nephi 14:7;
Isaiah 29:14; 11:11 = 2 Nephi 29:1 (see also 25:11);
Isaiah 29:21 = 2 Nephi 28:16a.

Evidently, Nephi's citations of Isaiah were from the brass plates. Isaiah's prophecy as set forth in the Book of Mormon and the Joseph Smith Translation is much longer than the corresponding text in the King James Version. For this reason we have marked the verses of this section according to the Joseph Smith Translation.

## JST Isaiah 29:11–26 = KJV Isaiah 29:11–14

[And it shall come to pass, that the Lord God shall bring forth unto you the words of a book;
and they shall be the words of them which have slumbered. (JST 29:11)

And behold, the book shall be sealed;
and in the book shall be revelation from God,
from the beginning of the world to the end thereof. (JST 29:12)

Wherefore because of the things which are sealed up, the things which are sealed shall not be delivered in the day of wickedness and abomination of the people. Wherefore, the book shall be kept from them. (JST 29:13)

But the book shall be delivered unto a man, and he shall deliver the words of the book, which are the words of those who have slumbered in the dust;
and he shall deliver these words unto another, but the words that are sealed he shall not deliver, neither shall he deliver the book. (JST 29:14)

For the book shall be sealed by the power of God, and the revelation which was sealed shall be kept in the book until the own due time of the Lord, that they may come forth; for, behold, they reveal all things from the foundation of the world unto the end thereof. (JST 29:15)

And the day cometh, that the words of the book which are sealed shall be read upon the housetops; and they shall be read by the power of Christ; and all things shall be revealed unto the children of men which ever have been among the children of men, and which ever will be, even unto the end of the earth. (JST 29:16)

Wherefore, at that day when the book shall be delivered unto the man of whom I have spoken, the book shall be hid from the eyes of the world, that the eyes of none shall behold it, save it be that three witnesses shall behold it by the power of God, besides him to whom the book shall be delivered: and they shall testify to the truth of the book and the things therein. (JST 29:17)

And there is none other which shall view it, save it be a few according to the will of God, to bear testimony of his word unto the children of men; for the Lord God hath said, that the words of the faithful should speak as it were from the dead. (JST 29:18)

Wherefore, the Lord God will proceed to bring forth the words of the book; and in the mouth of as many witnesses as seemeth him good will he establish his word; and woe be unto him that rejecteth the word of God].[19] (JST 29:19)

[But behold, it shall come to pass that the Lord God shall say unto him to whom he shall deliver the book: Take these words which are not sealed and deliver them to another, that he may show them unto the][20] learned, saying, Read this, I pray thee. (JST 29:20 = KJV 29:11)

[And the learned shall say: Bring hither the book, and I will read them. And now, because of the glory of the world and to get gain will they say this, and not for the glory of God. And the man shall say: I cannot bring the book,] for it is sealed. [Then shall the learned say:] I cannot [read it].[21] (JST 29:21 = KJV 29:11)

[Wherefore it shall come to pass, that the Lord God will] deliver [again] the book [and the words thereof] to him that is not learned [and the man that is not learned shall say,] I am not learned. [Then shall the Lord God say unto him: The learned shall not read them, for they have rejected them, and I am able to do mine own work; wherefore thou shalt read the words which I shall give unto thee].[22] (JST 29:22 = KJV 29:12)

[Touch not the things which are sealed, for I will bring them forth in mine own due time; for I will show unto the children of men that I am able to do mine own work].[23] (JST 29:23)

[Wherefore, when thou hast read the words which I have commanded thee, and obtained the witnesses which I have promised unto thee, then shalt thou seal up the book again, and hide it up unto me, that I may preserve the words which thou hast not read, until I shall see fit in mine own wisdom to reveal all things unto the children of men].[24] (JST 29:24)

[For behold, I am God; and I am a God of miracles; and I will show unto the world that I am the same yesterday, today, and forever; and I work not among the children of men save it be according to their faith].[25] (JST 29:25)

[And again it shall come to pass that]
the Lord [shall say unto him that shall read the words that shall be delivered him]
Forasmuch as this people *draw near [unto] me* <u>with their mouth</u>,
and <u>with their lips</u> do *honor me,* but have removed their heart[s] far from me,
and their fear toward me is taught by the precept of men—

Therefore, I will proceed to do a marvelous work among this people;
[yea], a marvelous work and a wonder:
for the *wisdom of their wise* [and learned][26] shall <u>perish</u>,

---

[19] This lengthy addition is from JST Isa. 29:11–19; the versification is from the JST.
[20] The bracketed changes are from JST Isa. 29:20 and 2 Ne. 27:15.
[21] The bracketed changes are from JST Isa. 29:21 and 2 Ne. 27:15–18.
[22] The bracketed changes are from JST Isa. 29:22 and 2 Ne. 27:19–20.
[23] The bracketed changes are from JST Isa. 29:23 and 2 Ne. 27:21.
[24] The bracketed changes are from JST Isa. 29:24 and 2 Ne. 27:22.
[25] The bracketed changes are from JST Isa. 29:25 and 2 Ne. 27:23.
[26] The bracketed changes are from JST Isa. 29:26 and 2 Ne. 27:24–26.

and the *understanding of their prudent* shall be <u>hid</u>. (JST 29:26 = KJV 29:13–14)

## NOTES AND COMMENTARY

**JST 29:11** *words of a book.* The Book of Mormon.

*them which have slumbered.* The Nephites and Jaredites.

**JST 29:12** *book . . . sealed.* This phrase seems to refer to the portion of the golden plates that was sealed. Sacred records have been sealed up many times in religious history (Dan. 12:1, 4; Rev. 5:1–14; 1 Ne. 14:26; Ether 3:21–22).

*revelation . . . from the beginning of the world to the end thereof.* Isaiah emphasizes that the sealed portion of the book contains the *revelation from God,* for the words *revelation* or *revealed* are used five times in this section (29:12, 15, 16, 24). He emphasizes the contents of the sealed portion by repeating three times that it contains God's revelation: "from the beginning of the world to the end thereof" (JST 29:12); "from the foundation of the world unto the end thereof" (JST 29:15); "all things . . . which ever have been among the children of men, and which ever will be, even unto the end of the earth" (JST 29:16).

**JST 29:13** *things which are sealed shall not be delivered in the day of wickedness.* The sealed portion of the plates will be revealed in the Lord's own time, but not in the day of wickedness.

**JST 29:14** *book shall be delivered unto a man.* The Prophet Joseph Smith received the plates of gold from the angel Moroni. Joseph Smith's history states that the "heavenly messenger delivered [the plates] up to me" (JS–H 1:59).

*those who have slumbered in the dust.* The Jaredites and Nephites *have slumbered in the dust,* or have died, and their bodies have returned to the dust.

*he shall deliver these words unto another.* "The Book itself was not to be delivered to the learned, but only 'the words of a Book;' this was literally fulfilled . . . as clearly testified of, not only by the 'plain looking countryman,' namely Martin Harris, but by the learned professor, Anthon himself."[27]

*words that are sealed he shall not deliver.* Joseph Smith did not permit the plates themselves to pass to others, according to Moroni's instructions (JS–H 1:42). Neither did he translate the sealed portion to give to others.

**JST 29:15** *sealed by the power of God.* God's *power* is central—the book is *sealed by the power of God;* the time would come when the sealed book would "be read by the power of Christ" (JST 29:16); and three witnesses would see the plates "by the power of God" (JST 29:17).

---

[27] Pratt, *Divine Authenticity of the Book of Mormon,* 88–89.

*kept . . . until the own due time of the Lord.* Isaiah emphasizes that the Lord is in charge of the calendar, for the revelations of the sealed book will not come forth *until the own due time of the Lord* (JST 29:15): "I will bring them forth in mine own due time" (JST 29:23), "until I shall see fit in mine own wisdom to reveal" these things (JST 29:24).

**JST 29:16** *words of the book . . . shall be read upon the housetops.* The time will come when the sealed portion of the plates will be revealed to many.

**JST 29:17** *book shall be hid from the eyes of the world.* Joseph Smith and a select group of faithful Saints saw the plates, but no others were permitted to see them.

*three witnesses shall behold it.* Both Isaiah and Moroni prophesied that the plates would be shown "unto three . . . by the power of God" (Ether 5:2–3). The three witnesses, Oliver Cowdery, David Whitmer, and Martin Harris, declared, "We . . . testify that we have seen the engravings which are upon the plates; and they have been shown unto us by the power of God" (Testimony of Three Witnesses).

*they shall testify to the truth of the book.* The three witnesses testified, "Be it known unto all nations, kindreds, tongues, and people, . . . : That we, through the grace of God the Father, and our Lord Jesus Christ, have seen the plates which contain this record. . . . And we also know that they have been translated by the gift and power of God . . . ; wherefore we know of a surety that the work is true" (Testimony of Three Witnesses).

**JST 29:18** *none other . . . shall view it, save it be a few.* A few individuals in addition to the Three Witnesses saw the gold plates, including Christian Whitmer, Jacob Whitmer, Peter Whitmer Jr., John Whitmer, Hiram Page, Joseph Smith Sr., Hyrum Smith, and Samuel H. Smith.

*words of the faithful . . . speak as it were from the dead.* The faithful here include Nephi, Alma, Samuel, Mormon, Moroni, and many others.

**JST 29:19** *in the mouth of as many witnesses as seemeth him good will he establish his word.* There will be several witnesses to the gold plates so that God's word will be established (2 Cor. 13:1).

*woe be unto him that rejecteth the word of God.* Those who "reject the words of the prophets" will "stand with shame and awful guilt before the bar of God. . . . And according to the power of justice, . . . [they] must go away into that lake of fire and brimstone" (Jacob 6:8–10). Individuals reject God's word because of "the fear of persecution and the cares of the world" (D&C 40:2), as well as because of gross wickedness (Hel. 6:2).

**JST 29:20** *deliver them to another/show them unto the learned.* Martin Harris "presented the characters which had been translated, with the translation thereof, to Professor Charles Anthon, a gentleman celebrated for his literary attainments" and to Dr. Mitchell (JS–H 1:64–65), both of whom were "learned."

**JST 29:21** *because of the glory of the world.* The Lord gave the world's "learned" an opportunity to accept or reject the words of the book. He knew their motivation would be not "for the glory of God" but for "the glory of the world and to get gain." Therefore, the Lord said, "The learned shall not read them, for they have rejected them, and I am able to do mine own work" (2 Ne. 27:20).

*I cannot read it.* During the meeting between Martin Harris and Charles Anthon, Anthon asked Harris to deliver the gold plates to him so that he could translate them. Harris replied that "part of the plates were sealed, and that [he] was forbidden to bring them," to which Anthon responded, "I cannot read a sealed book" (JS–H 1:65).

**JST 29:22** *I am not learned.* Elder Orson Pratt explained that "this was fulfilled when the angel of the Lord delivered the Book into the hands of Mr. Smith; though unlearned in every language, but his own mother tongue, yet he was commanded to read or translate the Book. Feeling his own incapability to read such a Book, he said to the Lord, in the words of Isaiah, 'I am not learned.' When he made this excuse, the Lord answered him in the words of Isaiah, next verses [Isaiah 29:13–14]. . . . What could be more marvellous and wonderful, than for the Lord to cause an unlearned youth to read or translate a Book which the wisdom of the most wise and learned could not read?"[28]

**JST 29:23** *Touch not the things which are sealed.* Joseph Smith was commanded not to touch the sealed portion of the plates, that is, not to translate it.

**JST 29:24** *seal up the book again, and hide it up.* After the translation of the Book of Mormon, the angel Moroni took the plates from the Prophet (JS–H 1:59).

**JST 29:25** *I am a God of miracles/I am the same yesterday, today, and forever.* The coming forth of the Book of Mormon—the creation of the "plates of ore" by Nephi (1 Ne. 19:1), the engraving of the plates by ancient prophets, the hiding of the plates by the power of God, the angel's delivering the plates to the young Prophet, Joseph Smith's translating the plates into English, the subsequent translation of the English text into scores of languages, and the great spirit that attends the Book of Mormon and transforms the lives of millions—indicates that the Lord is a God of

---

[28] *Divine Authenticity of the Book of Mormon,* 88–89. Joseph Smith said of himself, "I am not learned but the Lord had prepared spectacles for [me] to read the Book therefore I commenced translating the characters and thus the Prop[h]icy of Is[ai]ah was fulfilled." Jessee, *Papers of Joseph Smith,* 1:9.

miracles. There is an antithetical relationship between the followers of Christ, who believe in a God of miracles who is the "same yesterday, today, and forever," and nonbelievers, who "have imagined up unto [them]selves a god who doth vary, and in whom there is shadow of changing, then have [they] imagined up unto [them]selves a god who is not a God of miracles" (Morm. 9:10).

*I work . . . according to their faith.* Mormon explained that "it is by faith that miracles are wrought," such as the coming forth of the Book of Mormon, "and it is by faith that angels appear and minister unto men," such as the appearance of Moroni to Joseph Smith (Moro. 7:37).

**JST 29:26** *this people. This people* refers to the hypocrites and wicked persons of Jesus' day (Matt. 15:7–8; Mark 7:5–7), those of Joseph Smith's day (JS–H 1:17–19), and those of any other time period who worship the Lord "with their mouth" but their hearts are far from him.

*draw near unto me with their mouth . . . but have removed their hearts far from me.* Isaiah's words were recited by Christ himself to Joseph Smith during the First Vision (JS–H 1:19). Ezekiel used similar words: "They hear [God's] words, but they will not do them: for with their mouth they shew much love, but their heart goeth after their covetousness" (Ezek. 33:31).

*their fear toward me is taught by the precept of men.* "Their fear" means their attitude in worship. It should be founded on a divinely inspired awe, deep respect of the Holy One. But it has become . . . 'a human command' which can be taught and recited without involving the will."[29]

*marvelous work and a wonder.* The Restoration in its entirety, including temple worship, priesthood keys and powers, gospel ordinances, and the Book of Mormon and other scriptural records and revelations, composes the marvelous work and a wonder foretold by Isaiah. Elder Bruce R. McConkie summarized, "Many latter-day revelations identify the marvelous work here named as the restored gospel."[30]

Isaiah was the first prophet to use the phrase "marvelous work and a wonder," but during this dispensation the phrase is used frequently (for example, D&C 4:1; 6:1; 11:1; 12:1; 14:1) to remind the Saints of the marvelous work of the Restoration.

*wisdom of their wise . . . shall perish.* The teachings and precepts of the world's wisest and greatest scholars are foolishness to God, and their wisdom will perish. Paul recalled Isaiah's words: "The preaching of the cross is to them that perish foolishness; but unto us which are saved it is the power of God. For it is written, I will

---

29 Watts, *Isaiah 1–33,* 386.
30 McConkie, *Millennial Messiah,* 107.

destroy the wisdom of the wise, and will bring to nothing the understanding of the prudent" (1 Cor. 1:18–19; see also D&C 76:9).

## THE MEEK REJOICE IN THE BOOK OF MORMON
## (JST 29:27–32 = KJV 29:15–24)

Isaiah's prophecy of the coming forth of the Book of Mormon continues. The conjunction *and,* at the beginning of this section, connects it with the preceding section. Once again, Isaiah identifies the Book of Mormon simply as "the book" (JST 29:30), implying that it will come forth during a time when people seek and work iniquity and attempt to hide their dark acts from the Lord. He utters a "woe" unto such individuals. This prophecy of woe is countered with the promise that the Book of Mormon will bring light and joy to those who were previously spiritually blind and deaf. The same book will assist in sanctifying the Saints and will teach the true doctrines of the gospel to those who "erred in spirit" (29:24).

*JST Isaiah 29:27–32 = KJV Isaiah 29:15–24*

[And]³¹ woe unto them that seek deep to *hide their counsel from the Lord.*
[And] their *works are in the dark;*
and they say, Who <u>seeth us</u>
and who <u>knoweth us</u>? [And they also say:]

Surely your turning of things upside down shall be esteemed as the potter's clay: (JST 29:27 = KJV 29:15–16a)

[But behold, I will show unto them, saith the Lord of Hosts, that I know all their works.]³²

For shall the *work say of him that made it,* <u>He made me not?</u>
or shall the *thing framed* say *of him that framed it,* <u>He had no understanding?</u> (JST 29:28 = KJV 29:16b)

[But behold, saith the Lord of hosts: I will show unto the children of men, that it is not]³³ yet a very little while, and Lebanon shall be turned into a fruitful field, and the fruitful field shall be esteemed as a forest. (JST 29:29 = KJV 29:17)

And in that day shall the *deaf hear* the words of the book,
and the eyes of the *blind shall see* out of <u>obscurity,</u> and out of <u>darkness.</u>

---

³¹ The bracketed changes are from JST Isa. 29:27 and 2 Ne. 27:27.
³² The bracketed changes are from JST Isa. 29:28.
³³ The bracketed changes are from JST Isa. 29:29 and 2 Ne. 27:28. The Book of Mormon omits the word *not* in this phrase.

[And][34] the *meek* also shall increase, [and] their joy [shall be] in the Lord,
and the *poor* among men shall rejoice in the Holy One of Israel. (JST 29:30 =
KJV 29:18–19)

[For, assuredly as the Lord liveth, they shall see that][35] the *terrible one* is brought
to nought,
and the *scorner* is consumed,
and *all that watch for iniquity* are cut off,

[And they][36] that *make a man an offender* for a word,
and *lay a snare* for him that reproveth in the gate,
and *turn aside* the just for a thing of naught. (JST 29:31 = KJV 29:20–21)

Therefore, thus saith the Lord,
who redeemed Abraham,
concerning the house of Jacob, *Jacob shall not* now be ashamed,
*neither shall his face* now wax pale.

But when he seeth *his children,*
the *work of [my]*[37] *hands,* in the midst of him,

they shall *sanctify* my name,
and *sanctify* the Holy One of Jacob,
and shall *fear* the God of Israel.

*They also that erred in spirit* shall come to understanding,
and *they that murmured* shall learn doctrine. (JST 29:32 = KJV 29:23–24)

## NOTES AND COMMENTARY

**JST 29:27** *woe.* A prophecy of trouble, sorrow, and affliction.

*seek deep to hide their counsel.* The wicked work hard to hide their plans from
the Lord and others (2 Ne. 28:9).

*works are in the dark.* Acts of wickedness are conducted secretly, without the
knowledge of others.

*Who seeth us?* The wicked believe that their sinful deeds go unnoticed, but the
Lord informs them: "I will show unto them . . . that I know all their works" (JST
29:28).

*turning of things upside down/potter's clay.* Unrighteous individuals accuse
God's people of "stirring up the hearts and minds of people, disturbing the traditions
of the fathers (Jeremiah 16:19–21)."[38] Such was the case in the New Testament era
(Acts 17:6), and so it appears to be the case in our own dispensation. Unrighteous

---

[34] The bracketed changes are from JST Isa. 29:30 and 2 Ne. 27:30.
[35] The bracketed changes are from JST Isa. 29:31a and 2 Ne. 27:31.
[36] The bracketed changes are from JST Isa. 29:31b and 2 Ne. 27:32.
[37] The bracketed changes are from JST Isa. 29:32b and 2 Ne. 27:34.
[38] McConkie and Millet, *Doctrinal Commentary on the Book of Mormon,* 1:326.

individuals believe, falsely, that the work of God's people has no lasting significance, that it has the same permanence as potter's clay, which is easily broken.

**JST 29:28** *I know all their works.* Other prophets also witness that "God . . . knoweth all things, and there is not anything save he knows it" (2 Ne. 9:20); and "he knows all the thoughts and intents of the heart" (Alma 18:32).

*work say of him that made it, He made me not?* We, the creations of God, should not deny that he created us, neither should we attempt to counsel him and declare that he has no understanding. Elsewhere Isaiah warns, "Woe unto him that striveth with his Maker! . . . Shall the clay say to him that fashioneth it, What makest thou?" (45:9). Rather, let us acknowledge, "O Lord, thou art our father; we are the clay, and thou our potter; and we all are the work of thy hand" (64:8).

**JST 29:29** *I will show unto the children of men.* The turning of Lebanon into a fruitful field seems to be a sign (*I will show unto the children of men*) for the earth's inhabitants that the Book of Mormon has come forth.

*Lebanon/fruitful field.* These terms may refer to the reforestation and the agricultural development of Lebanon, or Palestine, at the time of the coming forth of the Book of Mormon. Elder Mark E. Petersen explained: "Isaiah indicated that Palestine, long languishing in the grip of the desert, was destined to be turned into a fruitful field in connection with the gathering of the Jews to their homeland. . . . A sacred book was to come forth before that time. . . . Not only did the prophets predict its appearance, but Isaiah set a limit on the time of its publication. That time limit was related to the period when fertility would return to Palestine. Isaiah said that the book would come forth first, and then added that in 'a very little while . . . Lebanon shall be turned into a fruitful field'" (29:17).[39]

This verse also has a symbolic meaning—the forest represents the people of God, and the fruitful field represents their works; see commentary on 35:1 and 32:15.

**JST 29:30** *deaf hear the words of the book.* At the time that Lebanon becomes a fruitful field, the Book of Mormon will empower the spiritually blind to see the truth and the spiritually deaf to hear the word of God—if they will so choose. That is possible because a strong spiritual force accompanies the book.

*blind shall see out of obscurity.* The Book of Mormon removes darkness from our minds and hearts, permitting us to draw closer to God. "There is a power in the book which will begin to flow into your lives the moment you begin a serious study of the book. You will find greater power to resist temptation. You will find the

---

[39] Conference Report, October 1965, 61.

power to avoid deception. You will find the power to stay on the strait and narrow path."[40]

*the meek also shall increase.* The terms *meek* and *poor* seem to refer to disciples of Christ (see Matt. 5:3, "poor in spirit" and Matt. 5:5, "meek"). The number of true disciples of Christ (*meek* and *poor*) increases through acceptance and study of the Book of Mormon.

**JST 29:31** *terrible one is brought to nought.* The meek and the poor will witness the destruction of the wicked, identified by Isaiah as the *terrible one* (29:5), *scorner, all that watch for iniquity, they that make a man an offender for a word,* they who *lay a snare* for others, and they who *turn aside* righteous things as if they were nothing. The terrible ones in verse 5 were Jerusalem's enemies; here the *terrible one* may refer to Satan himself.

*all that watch for iniquity.* This description refers to those who pursue evil and to those who find fault with others, whether justified or unjustified.[41]

*that make a man an offender for a word . . . and turn aside the just.* The translation of this phrase in the New International Version is instructive: "Those who with a word make a man out to be guilty, who ensnare the defender in court and with false testimony deprive the innocent of justice." Joseph Smith likened Isaiah's words to himself and the early Saints: "We refer you to Isaiah, who considers those who make a man an offender for a word, and lay a snare for him that reproveth in the gate. . . . We have reproved in the gate, and men have laid snares for us. We have spoken words, and men have made us offenders."[42]

**JST 29:32** *redeemed Abraham . . . Jacob shall not now be ashamed.* Redemption that came to father Abraham now comes to Israel when she accepts Jesus Christ and draws closer to God through studying the Book of Mormon and living righteously.

*the work of my hands.* This phrase recalls the mention of clay in 29:27–28 in the Joseph Smith Translation. God is the divine sculptor who forms and molds his people into true disciples; we are the work of his hands.

*they shall sanctify my name.* God's children will hallow his name in worship.

*fear the God of Israel.* In this context *fear* means to stand in awe of the Lord.

*They also that erred in spirit shall come to understanding/shall learn doctrine.* By making "known the plain and precious things which have been taken away" (1 Ne. 13:40) and by the "confounding of false doctrines and laying down of contentions, and

---

[40] Benson, "The Book of Mormon—Keystone of Our Religion," 7.
[41] *Teachings of the Prophet Joseph Smith,* 91, 315.
[42] *Teachings of the Prophet Joseph Smith,* 124.

establishing peace" (2 Ne. 3:12), the Book of Mormon will teach true doctrine to those who have *erred in spirit.* Elder Orson Pratt taught: "Oh, how precious must be the contents of a book which shall deliver us from all the errors taught by the precepts of uninspired men! Oh, how gratifying to poor, ignorant, erring mortals who have murmured because of the multiplicity of contradictory doctrines that have perplexed and distracted their minds, to read the plain, pure and most precious word of God, revealed in the Book of Mormon!"[43]

---

[43] *Orson Pratt's Works,* 278–79.

# ISAIAH 30

*LIKENING ISAIAH 30 UNTO OURSELVES*

*Many of us who dwell in Zion repeat the transgressions of some of our ancient Israelite ancestors: We reject our living prophets, or we accept only a portion of their counsel; we forget to pray to our Father, or we pray insincerely or irregularly; we trust in our arms and armies for protection rather than in our God, as our ancestors trusted anciently in Egypt's horses, chariots, and armies; and we despise God's word, or find the gospel too hard to accept (30:1–17).*

*Others of us who dwell in Zion experience the great fulfillment of Isaiah's prophecies: The Lord hears and answers our prayers, the Holy Ghost provides us with constant guidance, and we enjoy the bounties of the land (30:18–26).*

## JUDAH REJECTS HER PROPHETS AND WALKS WITH EGYPT (30:1–17)

Isaiah addresses the issue of trusting in man rather than in God. Judah's leaders sought an alliance with Egypt against Assyria, contrary to the counsel of the Lord (30:1–2). Now Isaiah promises that their reliance on Egypt will be unfruitful and will cause their downfall (30:3). Because of Judah's wickedness and her rebellion against God, her destruction will come "suddenly at an instant" (30:13). Her sins are many: she does not take counsel from the Lord (30:1); she does not pray to the Lord (30:2); she trusts Egypt and its horses rather than the Lord (30:2, 16); she carries her riches there (30:6); she rejects her prophets and seers and desires them to prophesy "smooth things" and lies (30:10); and she despises God's word (30:12). Note the Lord's command to Isaiah to record this prophecy in a book so that future generations, including our own, will learn that Judah was "a rebellious people" (30:8–9).

*Isaiah 30:1–17*

Woe to the rebellious children, saith the Lord, that *take counsel,* but not of me;
and that *poured out a libation,*[1] but not of my spirit, that they may add sin to sin:
(30:1)

That *walk to go down* into Egypt, and have not asked at my mouth;
to *strengthen* themselves in the strength of Pharaoh,
and to *trust in* the shadow of Egypt! (30:2)

Therefore shall the *strength of Pharaoh* be your shame,
and the *trust in the shadow of Egypt* your confusion. (30:3)

For his *princes* were at Zoan,
and his *ambassadors* came to Hanes. (30:4)

*They were all ashamed* of a people that could not profit them,
nor be an help nor profit, but a *shame, and also a reproach.* (30:5)

The burden of the beasts of the south: into the land of trouble and anguish,
from whence come the young and old lion,
the viper and fiery flying serpent,

they will carry their *riches* upon the shoulders of young asses,
and their *treasures* upon the bunches of camels, to a people that shall not profit
them. (30:6)

For the Egyptians shall help in vain, and to no purpose:
therefore have I cried concerning this, Their strength is to sit still. (30:7)

Now go, *write* it before them in a table,
and *note* it in a book,
that it may be for the time to come for ever and ever: (30:8)

That this is a *rebellious* people, *lying* children,
children *that will not hear the law of the Lord:* (30:9)

Which say to the *seers,* See not;
and to the *prophets,* Prophesy not unto us right things,

*speak* unto us smooth things,
*prophesy* deceits: (30:10)

*Get* you out of the way,
*turn aside* out of the path,
*cause the Holy One of Israel* to cease from before us. (30:11)

Wherefore thus saith the Holy One of Israel,
Because ye *despise* this word,
and *trust* in *oppression* and perverseness,
and *stay* thereon: (30:12)

Therefore this iniquity shall be to you as a *breach* ready to fall,
*swelling out* in a high wall,
whose *breaking* cometh suddenly at an instant. (30:13)

---

[1] From the Hebrew *masekah,* meaning "to pour out as libation." Brown, Driver, and Briggs, *Hebrew and English Lexicon,* 650–51.

And *he shall break it* as the breaking of the potters' vessel that is broken in pieces;
*he shall not spare:* so that there shall not be found in the bursting of it a sherd

to *take fire* from the hearth,
or to *take water* withal out of the pit. (30:14)

For thus saith the Lord God, the Holy One of Israel;
In *returning and rest* shall ye be saved;
in *quietness and in confidence* shall be your strength:

and *ye* would not. (30:15)
But *ye said,* No;

for *we* will flee upon horses;
therefore shall *ye* flee:

and, *We* will ride upon the swift;
therefore shall *they* that pursue you be swift. (30:16)

*One thousand shall flee* at the rebuke of one;
at the rebuke of five shall *ye flee:*

till ye be left as a *beacon* upon the top of a mountain,
and as an *ensign* on an hill. (30:17)

## NOTES AND COMMENTARY

**30:1** *Woe.* This message of judgment against Judah (5:8) is also against "the rebellious children" in all ages.

*rebellious children.* This describes the inhabitants of Judah and the rebellious children in all ages (1:2).

*take counsel, but not of me.* Judah ignored the word of the Lord received through the prophets and sought counsel from such foreign nations as Egypt, as well as from false gods. In our day, many do the same, listening to guidance and counsel from many sources, while rejecting the true prophets and the Holy Spirit of God.

*poured out a libation, but not of my spirit.* Judah made offerings to false gods and offerings that were not directed or approved by the Lord.

*add sin to sin.* Judah refused to follow the counsel of the Lord concerning her relationship with Assyria, which brought Judah under Assyrian vassalage. Judah's people then sought to free themselves from the shadow of Assyria by forming an alliance with Egypt, again ignoring the Lord's counsel, thus adding "sin to sin" (Jer. 2:18). Likewise, we add sin to sin by first rejecting the voice of the Lord and then walking in our own way contrary to his.

**30:2–3** *walk . . . down into Egypt.* Instead of walking on the Lord's paths, the leaders chose to follow a path of rebellion leading to Egypt, where Israel was once in bondage. We ourselves walk down into bondage in Egypt symbolically when we walk the path of sin.

*have not asked at my mouth.* Judah's wicked leaders were not praying to the Lord or seeking the Lord's counsel through his prophets.

*strengthen themselves in the strength of Pharaoh.* Jerusalem's leaders sought to strengthen themselves by establishing an alliance with Egypt, ruled by Pharaoh Psamtik I, who seemed to offer strength and protection. The consequence of Judah's alliance with Egypt was the eventual enslavement and deportation of the people by the Assyrians, to their shame and confusion. It is always a sin to trust in the arm of flesh rather than the power of God.

*trust in the shadow of Egypt.* Judah trusted in Egypt's military might and political strength. Isaiah's reference to *shadow of Egypt* indicates that the might and strength of Egypt are as a mere shadow—fleeting, dark, and insubstantial—when compared to the power of God.

**30:4** *For his princes were at Zoan, and his ambassadors came to Hanes.* Zoan (also known as Tanis) and Hanes were cities in Egypt where the princes and ambassadors of Egypt met with Judah's representatives to discuss a possible alliance.

**30:5** *They were all ashamed.* Judah's ambassadors were ashamed of their alliance with Egypt, for it did not profit them—Egypt was not strong enough to stand against Assyria.

**30:6** *burden of the beasts of the south.* A *burden* is a prophecy of doom or judgment against a people. This prophecy, strangely enough, is pronounced on the beasts, the camels and asses belonging to Judah's leaders, who are using them to transport their gifts and bribes to Egypt. Ironically, the children of Israel once escaped bondage through the Negev (*south*) carrying Egypt's treasures with them (Ex. 11:2), but now they return with the treasures of Jerusalem to purchase an alliance, another form of bondage. The beasts may represent Judah's leaders.

*young and old lion/viper/fiery flying serpent.* These same creatures plagued the Israelites as they escaped Egypt's pharaoh and armies (Num. 21:4–6; Deut. 8:15; see the discussion of *fiery flying serpent* in commentary on 14:29).

*they will carry their riches upon . . . young asses.* Judah's leaders will carry gifts to Egypt, a people that shall not profit them. Similarly, we sometimes devote our time, energy, or resources (our riches) to purposes or causes that are contrary to God's will. In the end, all such activities will not profit us.

**30:7** *Egyptians shall help in vain.* The Egyptians' help will not profit Judah (30:5). Whenever we seek help from the world, apart from God, it will be in vain.

*Their strength is to sit still.* Isaiah has cried out to Judah that she should sit still, for her strength lies not in taking action against Assyria but rather in trusting the Lord.

**30:8** *write . . . in a table/note it in a book.* The Lord commands Isaiah to record this testimony against Judah as a witness to future generations (for the time to come for ever and ever) that Judah is a rebellious people, that is, children who will not hear the law of the Lord.

**30:9** *this is a rebellious people.* Isaiah lists in a book the iniquities of the people of Judah—they are rebellious, lying children, who will not hear the law of the Lord. They refuse to hearken to their prophets and seers but tell them to "See not; . . . Prophesy not . . . , speak . . . smooth things, . . . get . . . out of the way, . . . cause the Holy One of Israel to cease from before us" (30:10–11).

**30:10** *Prophesy not unto us right things/speak . . . smooth things/prophesy deceits.* "If a prophet come among you and declareth unto you the word of the Lord, which testifieth of your sins and iniquities, ye are angry with him, and cast him out. . . . But behold, if a man shall come among you and shall say: Do this, and there is no iniquity; do that and ye shall not suffer; . . . do whatsoever your heart desireth— . . . because he speaketh flattering words unto you, and he saith that all is well, then ye will not find fault with him" (Hel. 13:26–28).

**30:11** *Get you out of the way.* See commentary on 26:7.

*cause the Holy One of Israel to cease from before us.* Inasmuch as "the guilty taketh the truth to be hard, for it cutteth them to the very center" (1 Ne. 16:2), they do not want religion and they do not want God in their lives.

**30:12** *despise this word.* The phrase *this word* refers to Isaiah's revelation concerning the futility of an alliance with Egypt, a prophecy Judah refused to heed.

*trust in oppression and perverseness, and stay thereon.* The Jerusalem Bible reads, "you . . . prefer to trust in wile and guile and rely on these." Judah chose to trust in the might of the pharaoh of Egypt, a man of wile and guile, rather than in the Lord.

**30:13** *breach ready to fall, swelling out in a high wall.* Isaiah compares Judah's iniquity to a large crack in the outside wall that protects Jerusalem. The crack expands, weakening the wall until it suddenly crumbles. Similarly, Judah's inhabitants have been weakened through sin; their iniquity increases like the crack in the wall until the nation is destroyed because its enemies are able to enter through the breach. This excellent description illustrates the effect of sin on all of us. Even a little sin, not repented of, can be like a crack in a wall, which can grow larger and larger until it leads to our spiritual destruction.

**30:14** *he shall break it as the breaking of the potters' vessel.* Isaiah likens the fall of Judah to a shattered clay vessel that can no longer serve its original purpose. Not a single shard (a fragment of the shattered vessel) is large enough to serve as a scoop "to take fire from the hearth" or "to take water" from a pool of water. Similarly, Judah's inhabitants are not suitable to serve as God's holy people.

**30:15** *In returning and rest shall ye be saved.* The New International Version reads, "In repentance and rest is your salvation." The people of Judah would have found salvation from God and deliverance from Assyria through repentance, but they said "No!" (30:16).

**30:16** *for we will flee upon horses.* In direct opposition to the will of the Lord (Deut. 17:16), Judah's leaders placed their confidence in Egypt's horses and chariots (31:1), believing they would be able to flee from the Assyrian armies. The Lord, however, warns Judah that these plans will not work, for her pursuers will be swift (Amos 2:14–15; Deut. 28:49).

**30:17** *One thousand shall flee at the rebuke of one.* The Jerusalem Bible reads, "A thousand will flee at the threat of one." The Lord had earlier promised Israel that five of them would chase one hundred enemies and that one hundred of them would put ten thousand to flight (Lev. 26:8) because the Lord would be with them. But that promise was no longer in effect, and now Judah would be put to flight because she abandoned God.

*till ye be left as a beacon . . . and as an ensign.* Where there had once been a multitude living in a city, only a small remnant would be left. Although only a few of Judah's population would remain, they will still act as an *ensign* and *beacon,* or light to the world.

## Zion Is Restored in Jerusalem (30:18–26)

Wonderful blessings await the Lord's people who will "dwell in Zion at Jerusalem" (30:19): They will no longer weep; Jehovah promises to answer their prayers; they will be blessed to see their "Teacher," he who taught them the law and the gospel; the Holy Ghost will give them guidance; they will renounce all their false gods; and they will receive the bounties of the land.

## Isaiah 30:18–26

And therefore will the *Lord wait,* that he may <u>be gracious</u> unto you,
and therefore will *he be exalted,* that he may <u>have mercy</u> upon you:

for the Lord is a God of judgment:
blessed are all they that wait for him. (30:18)

For the people shall dwell in Zion at Jerusalem: thou shalt weep no more:

*he will be very gracious unto thee* at the <u>voice of thy cry</u>;
when he shall hear <u>it,</u> *he will answer thee.* (30:19)

And though the Lord give you the *bread* of <u>adversity,</u>
and the *water* of <u>affliction,</u>

yet shall <u>not</u> thy *teachers* be <u>removed</u> into a corner any more,
but thine eyes shall <u>see</u> thy *teachers:* (30:20)

And thine ears shall hear a word behind thee, saying,
This is the way, walk ye in it,

when ye *turn* to the <u>right hand,</u>
and when ye *turn* to the <u>left.</u> (30:21)

Ye shall defile also the *covering* of thy <u>graven images of silver,</u>
and the *ornament* of thy <u>molten images of gold:</u>

*thou shalt* <u>cast them away</u> as a menstruous cloth;
*thou shalt* say unto it, <u>Get thee hence.</u> (30:22)

Then shall he give the rain of thy seed, that thou shalt sow the ground withal;
and bread of the increase of the earth, and it shall be fat and plenteous:

in that day shall thy *cattle* <u>feed</u> in large pastures. (30:23)
The *oxen* likewise and the *young asses* that ear the ground <u>shall eat</u> clean provender,
which hath been winnowed with the shovel and with the fan. (30:24)

And there shall be *upon every high mountain,*
and *upon every high hill,*
rivers and streams of waters in the day of the great slaughter,
when the towers fall. (30:25)

Moreover the *light of the moon* shall be <u>as the light of the sun,</u>
and the *light of the sun* shall be sevenfold, <u>as the light of seven days,</u>

in the day that the Lord *bindeth up* the <u>breach</u> of his people,
and *healeth* the stroke of their <u>wound.</u> (30:26)

## NOTES AND COMMENTARY

**30:18** *therefore will the Lord wait.* The Hebrew reading of this verse indicates that the Lord is waiting to be gracious and show mercy on Israel, but his blessings must wait until justice has been served.

*therefore will he be exalted.* This phrase should more properly read "therefore will he rise."

*blessed are all they that wait for him.* Note the reciprocal relationship shown in the double usage of the verb *wait* in this verse: The Lord waits (longs) to be gracious to the righteous, and those who wait, or long, for the Lord, will be blessed.

**30:19** *weep no more.* Once the Jews have been restored to their homeland and the Lord comes to reign, he will wipe away their tears. The same promise was made in 25:7–8 to those in New Jerusalem.

*he will be very gracious unto thee.* The Lord will pour forth the blessings of the Atonement and the bountiful gifts of his Spirit on all who dwell in Zion.

*at the voice of thy cry.* When Israel cries to the Lord in prayer, the Lord will answer her prayers.

**30:20** *bread of adversity/water of affliction.* Though our trials be as common as our daily bread and water, yet the Lord promises us that "all things wherewith you have been afflicted shall work together for your good, and to my name's glory" (D&C 98:3; 122:7).

*thine eyes shall see thy teachers.* The phrase *thy teachers* should read the singular, *thy teacher,* because it refers to the Lord, who was Israel's great teacher and eternal lawgiver. When this prophecy is fulfilled, the Lord will not "be removed into a corner"; he will no longer need to withdraw himself from his people because they will no longer be idolatrous or rebellious. Rather, their eyes shall see their teacher when he comes in glory to Israel as a whole and to her people individually.

**30:21** *thine ears shall hear a word behind thee, saying, This is the way.* The Lord guides his people with a quiet, unseen voice, the voice of the Holy Ghost. He prevents them from straying *to the right hand* or *to the left.*

**30:22** *Ye shall defile also the covering of thy graven images.* Rather than idols and graven images defiling individual members of Israel, as had happened many times throughout history, Israel will now cast away her idols as one throws away a menstruous cloth. According to the law of Moses, a menstruous cloth defiled anyone who touched it, making him or her ritually unclean (Lev. 15:19–30); similarly, anyone who touched an idol was religiously unclean. Israel will tell her idols, *Get thee hence.*

**30:23** *rain/increase of the earth.* Wickedness is often associated with drought and the earth's infertility (24:4; Deut. 11:17), whereas righteousness brings blessings and plenty. With Israel's full dedication to the Lord comes the promise of beneficial rains, fertile ground, and the Lord's bounty in all areas (*fat and plenteous* and *large* *pastures).* The blessing of *rain* and *bread* promised here contrasts with the *water of affliction* and the *bread of adversity* given to Israel's rebellious people (30:20).

**30:24** *oxen likewise and the young asses that ear the ground.* These animals were used to *ear the ground,* or to plow the fields and work the soil. These, like the cattle mentioned in verse 23, will be well fed and blessed because of the righteousness of Israel.

**30:25** *there shall be upon every high mountain, and upon every high hill, rivers and streams.* The rain promised in 30:23 will lead to an abundance of water on every hill and mountain (41:18). The implication is that we, the house of Israel, will receive great spiritual blessings, an abundance of the "living waters" of Christ.

*the day of the great slaughter/towers fall.* The blessings mentioned in 30:23–25 will come to the Lord's people at the same time that a great slaughter assails the wicked, when battles and warfare destroy fortifications and *towers fall.* This slaughter may refer to God's judgments on the wicked in the last days, perhaps in the form of nations fighting amongst themselves.

**30:26** *light of the moon shall be as the light of the sun.* This passage may be understood in several ways: The magnification of the sun "sevenfold, as the light of seven days" may be symbolic of the seventh thousand-year period of the earth, the Millennium, when Christ and his much greater light will be on the earth. In 24:23, these same heavenly bodies symbolically participated in a great event associated with Jehovah, so the moon and the sun are linked to the time when the Lord "bindeth up the breach of his people, and healeth the stroke of their wound." Moreover, the moon and sun's increase in brightness may indicate the increase in the light of Christ, Holy Ghost, and gifts of the Spirit that will be present among the people after their wounds are healed. Heavenly spheres have often been mentioned in prophecies in a literal manner; perhaps this prophecy will have a literal fulfillment.

*Lord bindeth up the breach.* The Lord will remove the "breach in the wall" caused by Israel's wickedness (30:13). This primary function of the atonement of Jesus Christ makes us "at one" with God.

*Lord . . . healeth the stroke of their wound.* Through the power of the Atonement, Jehovah, the great physician, heals Israel's spiritual wounds.

# THE LORD BURNS THE WICKED AT HIS SECOND COMING (30:27–33)

Isaiah describes the destruction of Assyria, meaning the wicked and their wickedness, to take place at Jesus Christ's second coming. He speaks of *burning, devouring fire, flame of a devouring fire, scattering, tempest, hailstones,* and *brimstone.* Isaiah assures those who dwell in Zion (the pure in heart who become one with their fellows) that they will be protected during these events and promises that they will sing songs to the Lord, worship at his temple, and experience a gladness of heart.

*Isaiah 30:27–33*

Behold, the name of the Lord cometh from far,
burning with his anger,
and the burden thereof is heavy:

*his lips* are full of indignation,
and *his tongue* as a devouring fire: (30:27)
And his *breath,* as an overflowing stream,

shall reach to the midst of the neck, to sift the nations with the sieve of vanity:
and there shall be a bridle in the jaws of the people, causing them to err. (30:28)

Ye shall have a *song,* as in the night when a holy solemnity is kept;
and *gladness of heart,* as when one goeth with a pipe to come into the mountain of the Lord,
to the mighty One of Israel. (30:29)

And the *Lord shall cause* his glorious voice to be heard,
and *shall [show]²* the lighting down of his arm,

*with* the indignation of his anger,
and *with* the flame of a devouring fire,
*with* scattering, and tempest, and hailstones. (30:30)

For through the voice of the Lord shall the Assyrian be beaten down,
which smote with a rod. (30:31)

And in every place where the grounded staff shall pass, which the Lord shall lay upon him,
it shall be with tabrets and harps: and in battles of shaking will he fight with it. (30:32)

For Tophet is ordained of old; yea, for the king it is prepared;
he hath made it deep and large:
the pile thereof is fire and much wood;
the breath of the Lord, like a stream of brimstone, doth kindle it. (30:33)

---

² We have replaced the archaic KJV *shew* with *show.*

## Notes and Commentary

**30:27** *name of the Lord cometh from far.* The Lord will come from the distant heavens to cleanse the earth of the wicked.

*burning with his anger/his lips are full of indignation, and his tongue as a devouring fire.* These descriptive phrases speak of the destruction that will occur when the Lord comes to punish the wicked. The Hebrew word translated here as "anger" may also be translated "nose." Thus Isaiah describes God's countenance with the four terms *nose, lips, tongue,* and *breath,* connecting each with his anger and power to destroy.

**30:28** *midst of the neck.* See commentary on 8:8, in which the same language is used in a similar context.

*sift the nations with the sieve of vanity.* In the last days the Lord will sift the nations, removing the tares from the wheat with the *sieve of vanity* or "the sieve of destruction."[3] Compare Amos 9:9, in which God uses the same "sieve" to "sift the house of Israel, . . . yet shall not the least grain fall upon the earth."

*bridle in the jaws of the people.* As a beast of burden is held in its path by the *bridle* it wears, so will the wicked be restrained, unable to escape God's judgments.

**30:29** *Ye shall have a song . . . and gladness of heart.* Perhaps for our benefit, so that we will not become depressed or unduly anxious as we read about the destructions that will befall transgressors, Isaiah interjects here a parenthetical statement. During the judgments of the last days, the Lord's people will focus on praising him with song, and they will experience *gladness of heart.* Our gladness will be similar to that experienced when a "holy solemnity is kept," perhaps a reference to a sacred temple occasion such as a festival or a solemn assembly. Our gladness will be similar to the joyous ancient processions to the house (mountain) of the Lord when one would approach the mighty One of Israel accompanied by the music of an instrument such as a flute (2 Sam. 6:5–6).

*mighty One of Israel.* This is a name for Jehovah.

**30:30** *voice to be heard.* The Lord's voice will be heard as he destroys the wicked. "And he shall utter his voice out of Zion, and he shall speak from Jerusalem, and his *voice shall be heard* among all people" (D&C 133:21–22).

*lighting down of his arm.* The New International Version reads, "his arm coming down." When the Lord's arm comes down (that is, in judgment), "the flame of a devouring fire, with scattering, and tempest, and hailstones" will destroy the wicked.

---

[3] Brown, Driver, and Briggs, *Hebrew and English Lexicon,* 996.

The Lord revealed to Joseph Smith, "But before the arm of the Lord shall fall, an angel shall sound his trump, and the saints that have slept shall come forth to meet me in the cloud. . . . Then shall the arm of the Lord fall upon the nations . . . and the nations of the earth shall mourn. . . . And calamity shall cover the mocker, and the scorner shall be consumed; and they that have watched for iniquity shall be hewn down and cast into the fire" (D&C 45:45–50).

**30:31** *For through the voice of the Lord shall the Assyrian be beaten down.* When the Lord speaks, the Assyrians (those who are wicked) will be destroyed. Concerning Assyria's rod, see commentary on 10:24.

**30:32** *staff . . . which the Lord shall lay upon him.* The New International Version presents this verse quite differently: "Every stroke the Lord lays on them with his punishing rod will be to the music of tambourines and harps, as he fights them in battle with the blows of his arm." The Lord's arm was spoken of in verse 30; his *staff* replaces Assyria's rod mentioned in 30:31.

*tabrets and harps.* Apparently, as the Lord battles the wicked, the righteous continue their joyous praise of the Lord with tambourines and harps; in verse 29 they approach the temple with pipes (or flutes). This continuing music contrasts sharply with the cessation of joy, when the wicked no longer play the tabrets and harps (24:8).

**30:33** *Tophet is ordained of old.* This phrase may also be read "Tophet was prepared of old." Tophet is an area south of Jerusalem where humans were sacrificed to Molech, a fire god. Molech's worshipers dug a large, deep pit, filled it with wood, ignited the fire, and then sacrificed humans there. Unfortunately, Molech was worshiped by apostate Israelites at various times (LDS Bible Dictionary, "Molech"). Now, however, justice is served because the Lord symbolically uses the deep pit and the wood to burn the wicked at his second coming, and "the breath of the Lord, like a stream of brimstone, doth kindle it."

# ISAIAH 31

*LIKENING ISAIAH 31 UNTO OURSELVES*

*Isaiah's message to ancient Judah is the same one we have received from our modern prophets: "Man should not . . . trust in the arm of flesh" (D&C 1:19). Judah's trusting in Egypt's horses, chariots, and armies for deliverance and temporal salvation is no different from our trusting in tanks, warplanes, or personal weapons—or money and temporal security. We can and should learn from history's lessons. If we trust in the Lord's power to protect us, both spiritually and physically, he will "defend" us, "deliver" us, and "preserve" us (31:5).*

## DIVINE PROTECTION FOR ZION AND JERUSALEM (31:1–9)

Isaiah 31 may be divided into two parts. Part one, 31:1–3, prophesies woe unto all who rely on the arm of flesh rather than on God. Specifically, Judah had relied on Egypt's military powers for deliverance rather than trusting in God, but the woe applies to us if we rely on our armies, weapons of war, or other means of temporal deliverance, or security, rather than on our God.

Part two, 31:4–9, speaks mainly to us today. If we, who are part of Zion, will cast away our wickedness as one casts away false gods, then the Lord will defend Zion. He will be like a mighty lion, "roaring on his prey" (31:4), or like a bird, flying protectively over her nestlings to preserve them; he will use his mighty sword to protect Zion.

*Isaiah 31:1–9*

> Woe to them that go down to <u>Egypt</u> for *help;*
> and *stay* on <u>horses,</u>

and *trust* in <u>chariots</u>, because they are many;
and in <u>horsemen</u>, because they are very strong;

but they *look* not unto the <u>Holy One of Israel</u>,
neither *seek* the <u>Lord</u>! (31:1)

Yet he also is wise, and will *bring evil*,
and will *not call back his words:*

but will arise *against the house* of the <u>evildoers</u>,
and *against the help* of <u>them that work iniquity</u>. (31:2)

Now the *Egyptians* are <u>men</u>, and not God;
and *their horses* <u>flesh</u>, and not spirit.

When the Lord shall stretch out his hand,
both *he that helpeth* <u>shall fall</u>,
and *he that is [helped]*[1] <u>shall fall down</u>,
and *they all* <u>shall fail</u> together. (31:3)

For thus hath the Lord spoken unto me,
Like as the lion and the young lion roaring on his prey,
when a multitude of shepherds is called forth against him,

he will not *be afraid* of <u>their voice</u>,
nor *abase himself* for the <u>noise of them</u>:

so shall the *Lord of hosts* come down to fight <u>for mount Zion</u>,
and <u>for the hill</u> thereof. (31:4)

As birds flying, so will the *Lord of hosts* <u>defend Jerusalem</u>;
defending also *he* <u>will deliver it</u>;
and passing over *he* <u>will preserve it</u>. (31:5)

Turn ye unto him from whom the children of Israel have deeply revolted. (31:6)

For in that day every man shall cast away his *idols* of <u>silver</u>,
and his *idols* of <u>gold</u>, which your own hands have made unto you for a sin. (31:7)

Then shall the Assyrian fall with *the sword*, <u>not of a mighty man</u>;
and *the sword*, <u>not of a mean man</u>, shall devour him:

but *he* shall <u>flee from the sword</u>,
and *his young men* shall <u>be discomfited</u>. (31:8)

And *he* shall pass over to his strong hold for <u>fear</u>,
and *his princes* shall <u>be afraid</u> of the ensign,

saith the Lord, whose *fire* is in <u>Zion</u>,
and his *furnace* in <u>Jerusalem</u>. (31:9)

## Notes and Commentary

**31:1** *Woe.* This represents the severe anguish and distress pronounced upon Judah, or Israel, who has her trust in Egypt.

---

[1] The KJV *holpen* is an older form of *helped.*

*trust in chariots.* Judah put her trust in Egypt's army with its great number of horses and chariots rather than looking to the Lord, the Holy One of Israel, for divine protection. Egypt symbolizes the world and her manmade weapons of war, including tanks, bombs, artillery, and soldiers—in which we too often put our trust.

*Holy One of Israel.* See commentary on 1:4.

**31:2** *he . . . is wise.* The Lord, who knows all things, gave wise counsel to Judah in 30:1–17.

*bring evil/not call back his words.* Because of Judah's wickedness and rebellion, the Lord has commissioned Assyria and Babylon to *bring evil* (or misfortune) to Jerusalem. God will *not call back his words*—"What I the Lord have spoken, I have spoken, and I excuse not myself; and though the heavens and the earth pass away, my word shall not pass away, but shall all be fulfilled" (D&C 1:38).

*house of the evildoers/help of them.* The *house of the evildoers* is the house, or tribe, of Judah—or any group who choose not to follow the Lord's will; the phrase *help of them* refers to Egypt, who was the *help* of Judah. Isaiah includes Egypt in his prophecy of destruction.

**31:3** *Egyptians are men, and not God; and their horses flesh, and not spirit.* Isaiah points out the simple truth that Egypt and her horses cannot compare to God's power. Judah should trust in the strength of her God rather than in Egypt's military might.

*Lord shall stretch out his hand.* The Lord stretches forth his hand to punish (see commentary on 5:25).

*both he that helpeth shall fall, and he that is helped.* Reiterating the prophecy in 31:2, Isaiah says that both Judah and Egypt will be punished.

**31:4** *Like as the lion and the young lion roaring on his prey.* As mentioned in the introduction to this section, verses 4 through 9 change the subject of verses 1 through 3. Like the self-assured lion who defends his prey, unafraid of the shouts and clamor of the shepherds, the Lord will not be deterred ("abase himself") from his objective.

*fight for mount Zion.* The Lord will fight on behalf of Zion with the strength of a lion. Zion is called *Mount* Zion to underscore the central importance of Zion and the temple thereof (temples are represented by mountains).

*for the hill thereof.* The Lord will also fight in behalf of Zion's temple, here identified as the *hill.*

**31:5** *As birds flying, so will the Lord of hosts defend Jerusalem.* The Lord, like a mother bird that hovers over her chicks to protect them from predators, will do three things for Zion—*defend, deliver,* and *preserve*—but only after his people have cast away their idols (31:7; 30:22). The words *passing over* remind us of the Lord's Passover, when he preserved Israel by passing over them while destroying the firstborn of Egypt (Ex. 12:11–13).

**31:6** *Turn ye unto him.* Isaiah pleads with the people of Judah (the Southern Kingdom) to learn from the folly of the people of Israel (the Northern Kingdom), who had "deeply revolted" from the ways of the Lord. He urges them to end their rebellion and *turn* back to the Lord. *Turn* in Hebrew also means "repent."

**31:7** *every man shall cast away his idols.* Isaiah prophesies once again that one day the people of Israel will cease their worship of false gods (see commentary on 30:22).

**31:8** *Assyrian fall with the sword.* The Lord promises that if his people will cast away their idols, he will destroy Assyria. The *sword* here belongs to the Lord (see commentary on 27:1; 34:5).

*mighty man/mean man.* Neither the *mighty man* nor the *mean* (ordinary) *man* will cause Assyria's fall. Rather the Lord of Hosts will accomplish it, as he did during Hezekiah's reign (37:36), and Assyria's young (*strong*) men will lose their power (*be discomfited*). This prophecy also applies to the day of the Lord's second coming, when he will destroy Assyria (the world of sin) and establish Zion.

**31:9** *he shall pass over to his strong hold for fear.* The Assyrians (the wicked) will flee to their own fortresses because of their fear of the Lord and his power to destroy.

*princes shall be afraid of the ensign.* Even the mighty leaders of Assyria, or the world, will flee before the ensign, or Zion's banner. This ensign identifies the Lord's army, the inhabitants of Zion. A modern revelation confirms that "the glory of the Lord" shall be in Zion, and "the terror of the Lord also shall be there, insomuch that the wicked will not come unto it. . . . And it shall be said among the wicked: Let us not go up to battle against Zion, for the inhabitants of Zion are terrible; wherefore we cannot stand" (D&C 45:67–70).

*whose fire is in Zion, and his furnace in Jerusalem.* Zion and Jerusalem are the centers of the Lord's reign during the Millennium (24:23). The phrases *fire is in Zion* and *furnace in Jerusalem* find a counterpart in 33:14, where it is written that the righteous will *dwell with the devouring fire* and *everlasting burnings,* which are references to Christ. The two phrases in this verse also seem to parallel Doctrine and Covenants 45:66–67, which speaks of the "glory of the Lord" and the "terror of the Lord" that will be in Zion, protecting the righteous from the wicked.

# ISAIAH 32

### LIKENING ISAIAH 32 UNTO OURSELVES

*Isaiah 32 contains prophecies concerning the last days and the millennial reign of Jesus Christ, which we or our posterity will be privileged to witness. When the Lord becomes our ruler, he will remove evil people from our society, including those who use obscene language, are hypocritical, and attempt to destroy the faith of others.*

*Already we see the Spirit of the Lord being poured out upon us, the result being a great increase in the fruits and produce of the earth. More important, we may experience greater personal peace and righteousness because of our acceptance of Jesus Christ and his commandments and because of the gifts and powers of the Holy Ghost.*

## THE RESULTS OF THE REIGN OF JESUS, OUR KING (32:1–8)

After the destruction of the wicked, described by Isaiah in previous chapters, Jesus Christ will reign on the earth in righteousness. As king he will protect his people, both physically and spiritually, from their enemies and will bring relief from the tempests and droughts that have caused suffering. During his rule and establishment of justice people will no longer speak obscenity, "work iniquity," "practice hypocrisy," or destroy the faith of others.

*Isaiah 32:1–8*

> Behold, a *king* shall <u>reign in righteousness</u>,
> and *princes* shall <u>rule in judgment</u>. (32:1)

> And a *man* shall be as an *hiding place* from the <u>wind</u>,
> and a *covert* from the <u>tempest</u>;
> as *rivers of water* in a <u>dry place</u>,
> as the *shadow of a great rock* in a <u>weary land</u>. (32:2)

And the *eyes of them* that see shall not be dim,
and the *ears of them* that hear shall hearken. (32:3)

The *heart* also of the rash shall understand knowledge,
and the *tongue* of the stammerers shall be ready to speak plainly. (32:4)

The *vile person* shall be no more called [noble],[1]
nor the *churl* said to be bountiful. (32:5)

For the *vile person* will speak villainy,
and *his heart* will work iniquity,

*to practice* hypocrisy,
and *to utter* error against the Lord,

to make empty the soul *of the hungry,*
and he will cause the drink *of the thirsty* to fail. (32:6)

The *instruments* also of the churl are *evil:*
he deviseth *wicked devices*

to destroy the *poor* with lying words,
even when the *needy* speaketh right. (32:7)

But the [noble][2] deviseth [noble] *things;*
and by [noble] *things* shall *he* stand. (32:8)

## NOTES AND COMMENTARY

**32:1** *king shall reign in righteousness.* Jesus Christ, the king, shall reign in righteousness during the Millennium (see 11:4). Jeremiah prophesied similarly to Isaiah, naming the king "the Lord our Righteousness" (Jer. 23:6).

*princes shall rule in judgment.* The princes who serve under the king are those who receive exaltation and become part of the family of Christ. These will *rule in judgment,* or judge righteously.

**32:2** *a man shall be as an hiding place from the wind. Man* refers to the king mentioned above, or Jesus Christ. Isaiah provides four metaphors to indicate the Lord's eternal preservation of the Saints: *hiding place* (or shelter), *covert, rivers of water,* and *shadow of a great rock;* these correspond with *wind, tempest, dry place,* and *weary land,* words that cause us to recall this telestial existence with all of its tribulation and hardships.

**32:3** *eyes of them that see shall not be dim.* Those who choose to see and hear the truth will be blessed with continuing clear spiritual sight and understanding.

---

[1] From the Hebrew *nadiyb,* meaning "inclined, generous, noble." Brown, Driver, and Briggs, *Hebrew and English Lexicon,* 622.

[2] NIV Isa. 32:8.

**32:4** *heart also of the rash shall understand knowledge.* The *rash* are those who proceed with haste, without understanding. The Lord will open their hearts to knowledge.

*tongue of the stammerers.* Those who formerly had difficulty communicating will now be able to speak the truth plainly.

**32:5** *vile person shall be no more called noble.* When the Lord reigns in truth and righteousness on the earth, vile persons will no longer be viewed as noble or generous but will be recognized for what they are.

*nor the churl said to be bountiful.* The LDS Bible footnote reads "miser" for *churl,* which makes sense with the term *bountiful* in the same context. Also, the Jerusalem Bible reads, "nor the villain be styled honorable."

**32:6** *vile person.* Isaiah defines the *vile person* mentioned in 32:5. He or she *speak[s] villainy* (obscenity), *work[s] iniquity, practices hypocrisy,* and *utter[s] error against the Lord.* These actions deprive others' souls of spiritual things, making them hungry and thirsty. In other words, the vile person destroys the faith of others.

**32:7** *churl . . . deviseth wicked devices.* Isaiah defines the *churl* spoken of in 32:5. He is one who devises wicked plans to further his power and prosperity. Frequently his victims are the poor and needy, whom he *destroy[s] . . . with lying words.* For a man such as this to be called *bountiful* (32:5) requires a warped morality and an eye blind to truth.

**32:8** *noble.* Standing opposite the vile person and the churl are the *noble,* those who make honorable plans and possess integrity.

## DESTRUCTION FOR THE WICKED, PEACE FOR THE RIGHTEOUS (32:9–20)

The troubles and sorrows allotted to Israel, or Judah (32:9–14), will continue until the restoration of the gospel in the last days, when the Lord pours out his Spirit on his people. At this time the Lord will remove the curse from the earth (D&C 61:17), so that wildernesses and deserts will become fruitful fields, or bounteous sources of food. Also accompanying the outpouring of the Spirit will be increased spirituality among the inhabitants of Zion—Isaiah specifically mentions righteousness and peace.

We should be comforted by Isaiah's prophecy that as the crops and homes of the wicked are being flattened, Zion's inhabitants will dwell securely in peace.

*Isaiah 32:9–20*

Rise up, *ye women that are at ease;* hear my voice,
*ye careless daughters;* give ear unto my speech. (32:9)

Many days and years shall ye be troubled, ye careless women:
for the *vintage* shall fail,
the *gathering* shall not come. (32:10)

*Tremble,* ye women that are at ease;
*be troubled,* ye careless ones:

strip *you,*
and make *you* bare,

and gird sackcloth upon *your loins.* (32:11)
[Beat upon *your breasts*]³

for the *pleasant fields,*
for the *fruitful vine.* (32:12)

Upon the land of my people shall come up thorns and briers;
yea, upon all the houses of joy in the joyous city: (32:13)

Because the *palaces* shall be forsaken;
the *multitude of the city* shall be *left* [desolate];⁴
the *forts and towers* shall be for *dens* for ever,

a *joy* of wild asses,
a *pasture* of flocks; (32:14)

Until the spirit be poured upon us from on high,

and the *wilderness* be a fruitful field,
and the fruitful field be counted for a *forest.* (32:15)

Then *judgment* shall dwell in the wilderness,
and *righteousness* remain in the fruitful field. (32:16)

And the *work of righteousness* shall be peace;
and the *effect of righteousness* quietness and assurance for ever. (32:17)

And my people shall dwell in a *peaceable* habitation,
and in *sure* dwellings,
and in *quiet* resting places; (32:18)

When it shall hail, coming down on the forest;
and the city shall be low in a low place. (32:19)

Blessed are ye that sow beside all waters,
that send forth thither the feet of the ox and the ass. (32:20)

## NOTES AND COMMENTARY

**32:9** *women that are at ease/careless daughters.* The women who continue in
their daily activities without concern for the calamity about to befall them represent

---

³ The Hebrew actually reads *mourning upon the breasts,* meaning "lament with beating upon your breasts."
⁴ From JST Isa. 32:14.

the inhabitants of the Israelite or Judean cities, male and female, who are *at ease* and ignore the prophets' warnings of impending doom (compare commentary on 3:16).

*hear my voice/give ear unto my speech.* This is a summons to listen carefully to the words of the prophet.

**32:10** *Many days and years.* This idiom means a long time.

*the vintage shall fail/the gathering shall not come.* Israel's crops will fail.

**32:11** *Tremble, ye women that are at ease; be troubled.* Isaiah commands the *women that are at ease* to fear the coming destruction.

*strip you, and make you bare.* These phrases represent enslavement and captivity (see 20:2–3). By the use of symbols Isaiah warns Israel of what the future holds for them.

*gird sackcloth upon your loins. Sackcloth* represents the mourning typically associated with death, disaster, or heartfelt repentance. Isaiah prophesies that after Israel is carried away captive, she will mourn the loss of freedom, family, friends, home, and temple.

**32:12** *Beat upon your breasts.* This action is also an expression of mourning (Nahum 2:7).

*pleasant fields/fruitful vine.* The fields and vineyards that once produced an abundance of grain and fruit will become barren, symbolic of the spiritual state of the people themselves.

**32:13** *land of my people.* This term is a synonym for Israel, the land of God's covenant people.

*thorns and briers.* This phrase refers to the curse that comes upon the earth because of wickedness (Moses 4:23–24). *Thorns and briers* also represent Israel's enemies (see commentary on 27:4).

*houses of joy/joyous city.* Everyone, from the individual *(house)* to the community *(city),* is caught up in this sense of "all is well." They are unable to believe that their cities will fall, but the Lord has decreed that Israel's enemies will overrun her.

**32:14** *palaces shall be forsaken.* The rich are not exempt from the calamity; even the palaces will be forsaken. All of Jerusalem's inhabitants will flee, and the once-crowded city will be abandoned. The fortifications will become dwelling places for animals.

**32:15** *Until the spirit be poured upon us from on high.* The word *until* is significant here—the "women that are at ease" (32:9, 14) will experience calamity and mourn over the loss of their freedom and their land *until the spirit* of the Lord is poured out upon them. The Spirit was previously rejected by Israel (see 31:3).

This phrase also applies to the Restoration (Joel 2:28–29; JS–H 1:41). During the last days, the Lord will prune his vineyard one last time, "that I may bring to pass my strange act, that I may *pour out my Spirit upon all flesh*" (D&C 95:4). This phrase reminds us that the Lord had formerly poured out upon the people "the spirit of deep sleep" in 29:10 (see commentary on 29:10).

*wilderness be a fruitful field, and the fruitful field be counted for a forest.* The desolation and scattering of the people will continue until the Lord's Spirit is poured out and the people (*forest*) are restored to spiritual fruitfulness. This phrase recalls 29:17, which reads *Lebanon* instead of *wilderness:* "Lebanon shall be turned into a fruitful field, and the fruitful field shall be esteemed as a forest." This verse pertains to the Restoration, after the coming forth of the Book of Mormon (see commentary on 29:29; 35:1).

**32:16** *judgment shall dwell in the wilderness.* "Judgment" may read "justice" here (see footnotes in LDS edition of the Bible to Deut. 32:4; Job 19:7; Ps. 33:5; 37:28; Isa. 1:17, 21, 27). When the Lord pours out his Spirit on the earth, *justice* and *righteousness* will be an integral part of Zion—even in areas that formerly were dry and unfruitful—because the people belong to the Messiah (see 11:2–4; 32:1).

**32:17** *work of righteousness shall be peace.* Isaiah explains that the results of righteousness are *peace, quietness,* and *assurance* (confidence); these three will abound in Zion.

**32:18** *my people shall dwell in a peaceable habitation.* Zion is a place of "peaceful dwelling places," "secure homes," and "undisturbed places of rest" (NIV). This verse reminds us of a modern revelation in which Zion is called "a land of peace, a city of refuge, a place of safety for the saints of the Most High God" (D&C 45:66). Elder Orson Pratt applied 32:17–19 to the Saints when they sought in the Rocky Mountains relief from persecution.[5]

**32:19–20** *When it shall hail. . . . Blessed are ye.* The New International Version reads, "Though hail flattens the forest and the city is leveled completely, how blessed you will be, sowing your seed by every stream, and letting your cattle and donkeys range free." *Hail,* one of the Lord's judgments upon the wicked in the last days (D&C 29:16–17), here represents all his judgments. The "forest" and the "city" refer to the "proud and the wicked" (footnote *b* to 32:19). See commentary on 32:15. These verses mean that although the homes and crops of the wicked are destroyed, Zion will enjoy peace and security, planting crops in an almost carefree manner and letting cattle graze without fear.

---

[5] *Journal of Discourses,* 18:148–49.

# ISAIAH 33

*LIKENING ISAIAH 33 UNTO OURSELVES*

*The Lord is the constant support of the righteous—we pray "be thou [our] arm every morning" (33:2). But the wicked have no such promise, and they will be destroyed by burning at the last day. In contrast to the fire of destruction, Isaiah sets forth six statements that describe the fire of holiness. If we are holy, we will not burn at Christ's coming but will dwell with him in "everlasting burnings."*

## A WOE ORACLE AGAINST SENNACHERIB (33:1)

The destroyer to whom Isaiah refers in this woe oracle is often identified as Sennacherib, the king of Assyria who attacked Jerusalem in 701 B.C. These prophecies also apply to transgressors of any age who "destroy" and "deal treacherously." The Lord destroyed Sennacherib and his armies and will continue to destroy all others who follow Sennacherib's pattern of evil.

*Isaiah 33:1*

> Woe to thee that [*destroy*], and thou <u>wast not [destroyed]</u>;
> and *dealest treacherously,* and they <u>dealt not treacherously</u> with thee!
>
> when thou shalt *cease [destroying],*
> thou shalt <u>be [destroyed]</u>;[1]
> and when thou shalt *make an end to deal treacherously,*
> they shall <u>deal treacherously</u> with thee. (33:1)

---

[1] These four words translated in the KJV as *spoil* come from the Hebrew root *shadad,* meaning "to deal violently with, despoil, devastate, ruin." Brown, Driver, and Briggs, *Hebrew and English Lexicon,* 994.

NOTES AND COMMENTARY

**33:1** *Woe.* This word invokes severe anguish and distress upon those who *destroy* and *deal treacherously* with others.

*destroy/dealest treacherously.* A woe pronounced upon those who destroy and who deal evil unto others. The phrases apply historically to the Assyrian king Sennacherib, who had offered to spare the lives of the inhabitants of Jerusalem if they agreed to pay him tribute (2 Kgs. 18:13–16). At great cost they paid him tribute, but he *treacherously* continued his attack against them, seeking to *destroy* them. These phrases also apply to the wicked of any age who deal treacherously with others.

*when thou shalt cease destroying, thou shalt be destroyed.* Isaiah's prophecy was fulfilled. The Lord destroyed 185,000 men in a single night, and the king abandoned his camp and fled to Nineveh, where he was murdered by his sons (see commentary on 37:38).

## THE RIGHTEOUS PRAISE THE LORD IN PRAYER (33:2–6)

This wonderful prayer or hymn presents an example of how we may praise and worship the Lord. It appears to be the prayer of those who dwell in Zion, or at least those who desire and anticipate the building of Zion. It sets forth the attributes of God, including his graciousness, strength, salvation, exaltation, justice, and righteousness.

*Isaiah 33:2–6*

> O *Lord,* be gracious unto <u>us</u>;
> <u>we</u> have waited for *thee:*
>
> be thou [our][2] *arm* every <u>morning</u>,
> our *salvation* also in the <u>time of trouble</u>. (33:2)
>
> At the *noise of the [tumult]*[3] the <u>people</u> fled;
> at the *lifting up of thyself* the <u>nations</u> were scattered. (33:3)
>
> And your spoil shall be gathered *like the gathering* of the <u>caterpillar</u>:
> *as the running to and fro* of <u>locusts</u> shall he run upon them. (33:4)
>
> The *Lord* is <u>exalted</u>;
> for *he* <u>dwelleth on high</u>:
> he hath filled Zion with judgment and righteousness. (33:5)

---

[2] Most versions read *our* instead of *their.*

[3] From Hebrew *hamon,* meaning "sound, murmur, roar, crowd, abundance," especially "sound made by a crowd of people, murmur, roar." This word may also be translated as "rumbling from earthquakes, thunder or chariots." Brown, Driver, and Briggs, *Hebrew and English Lexicon,* 242.

[He will be the sure foundation for your times,
a rich store of salvation and wisdom and knowledge][4]
the fear of the Lord is his treasure. (33:6)

## NOTES AND COMMENTARY

**33:2** *O Lord.* This expression indicates that the words that follow are a prayer or a hymn.

*be gracious unto us.* The text could also read, "Show favor to us."

*we have waited for thee.* The Hebrew reads, "we hope for you."

*be thou our arm every morning.* We seek the Lord's protective care *every morning.* We seek protection from our enemies, from danger, and from evil.

*our salvation . . . in the time of trouble.* We ask the Lord to deliver us from trouble.

**33:3** *noise of the tumult.* The New International Version reads, "At the thunder of your voice the peoples flee." The Lord's voice brings judgment, causing the wicked to flee (30:30).

*lifting up of thyself.* When the Lord rises to defend his people, the nations scatter.

**33:4** *your spoil shall be gathered like the gathering of the caterpillar. Spoil* generally refers to goods taken from an enemy during war. In this context it may refer to spiritual benefits (peace, joy, love) the righteous receive as they partake of the Lord's victory over sin and death.

**33:5** *Lord is exalted.* Jehovah possesses eternal life and has "all power" (D&C 132:20). The phrase *he dwelleth on high* speaks of heaven.

*he hath filled Zion with judgment and righteousness.* Elsewhere Isaiah taught that "Zion shall be redeemed with judgment [justice] and her converts with righteousness" (1:27). The Psalmist wrote, "Righteousness and judgment [justice] are the habitation of [God's] throne" (Ps. 97:2).

**33:6** *He will be the sure foundation.* Jesus is "the great, and the last, and the only sure foundation" (Jacob 4:16) upon which we can build. He is our "safe foundation" (Jacob 4:15; see Isa. 28:16).

*rich store of salvation and wisdom and knowledge.* Isaiah creates a metaphor—Jehovah is a treasury or storehouse of riches to the righteous. The riches include *salvation, wisdom,* and *knowledge.*

*fear of the Lord is his treasure.* Worshipful reverence of God (Ps. 5:7) is a treasure to the righteous because it results in wisdom, knowledge, and salvation.

---

[4] NIV Isa. 33:6.

## THE WICKED ARE BURNED AT CHRIST'S SECOND COMING (33:7–14)

During these last days we are witnessing many of the events set forth in Isaiah's prophecy. We see individuals who lack integrity, and break covenants and agreements with others. We notice that people have little regard for others (33:8). In families as well as among cities and nations there is a great lack of love. For these and a host of other reasons, the Lord is going to come forth and for the last time burn all evil from the face of the earth.

Isaiah's language is most descriptive—he compares transgressors to women who become pregnant, but not with precious children; rather they "conceive chaff," and "bring forth stubble" (33:11). Such people will be burned as though they were thorns and briers in intensely hot fires (33:12). Those who secretly sin and are hypocrites should fear these things (33:14).

*Isaiah 33:7–14*

Behold, their *valiant ones* <u>shall cry</u> without:
the *ambassadors* of peace <u>shall weep</u> bitterly. (33:7)

The highways lie waste,
the wayfaring man ceaseth:

*he* hath <u>broken the covenant</u>,
*he* hath <u>despised the cities</u>,
*he* <u>regardeth no man</u>. (33:8)

The *earth* <u>mourneth</u> <u>and languisheth</u>:
*Lebanon* is <u>ashamed</u> <u>and hewn down</u>:

*Sharon* is like a <u>wilderness</u>;
and *Bashan and Carmel* <u>shake off their fruits</u>. (33:9)

*Now will I* <u>rise</u>, saith the Lord;
*now will I* <u>be exalted</u>;
*now will I* <u>lift up myself</u>. (33:10)

*Ye* shall <u>conceive chaff</u>,
*ye* shall <u>bring forth stubble</u>:
*your breath*, as fire, shall <u>devour you</u>. (33:11)

And the *people* shall be as the <u>burnings of lime</u>:
as *thorns* cut up shall they be <u>burned in the fire</u>. (33:12)

*Hear*, <u>ye that are far off</u>, *what I have done;*
and, <u>ye that are near</u>, *acknowledge my might.* (33:13)

The *sinners* in Zion are <u>afraid</u>;
[<u>trembling</u>][5] hath [seized][6] the *hypocrites.* (33:14)

## NOTES AND COMMENTARY

**33:7** *valiant ones shall cry/ambassadors of peace shall weep.* All will weep when the world is destroyed, including warriors (*valiant ones*) and peacemakers (*ambassadors of peace*).

**33:8** *highways lie waste, the wayfaring man ceaseth.* These phrases speak of a time when battles and wars rage in the land, when civilians avoid the highways for fear of their safety, or perhaps the highways have been destroyed by armies and their artillery. All business and travel between cities ceases because no one dares to venture forth.

*he hath broken the covenant, he hath despised the cities, he regardeth no man.* Some scholars believe that *cities* should read "witnesses" here, meaning prophets or missionaries. The pronoun *he* in these three phrases is impersonal, and can read "they" or "people," as in "people have broken covenants," etc. The Jerusalem Bible reads, "Treaties are broken, witnesses despised, there is respect for no one." The intent is to portray the general lack of integrity and love that will exist in the last days, toward both God and man.

**33:9** *earth mourneth and languisheth.* The earth mourns and languishes as a reaction to the wickedness of her peoples. To languish is to become weak or feeble. This language is also used by Isaiah in 24:4.

*Lebanon is ashamed and hewn down.* Isaiah uses symbolic language to express the destruction of fruitful fields and productive forests (32:15), symbolizing the proud and the wealthy, who will be *ashamed* and *hewn down* at the last day. It is apparent from 10:33–34 that Jehovah is the forester who hews down Lebanon (2:12–13).

**33:10** *Now will I rise, saith the Lord.* The Lord uses three parallel phrases: *Now will I rise, Now will I be exalted, now will I lift up myself.* In the last days, the Lord will come into view, or show himself, to enact his decrees of justice, coming in his glory to purge the world of the wicked, thereby exalting himself in righteousness.

**33:11** *Ye shall conceive chaff.* You (plural, referring to the wicked) will conceive (become pregnant with) chaff, or useless husks of grain. This harsh statement to the wicked tells them that their lives and plans will founder and are in vain.

---

[5] From Hebrew *r'adah,* "trembling" a noun paralleling fear, the subject of the verb *seized.* Brown, Driver, and Briggs, *Hebrew and English Lexicon,* 944.
[6] From Hebrew verb *achazah,* meaning "grasp, take hold, take possession." Brown, Driver, and Briggs, *Hebrew and English Lexicon,* 28.

*ye shall bring forth stubble.* Your pregnancy has come to completion, and you (plural, referring to the wicked) will now bring forth stubble, rather than useful grains of wheat. In other words, the lives and evil designs of the wicked will be worthy only to be burned, as chaff and stubble are burned. This passage clearly refers to the judgment and great burning of the wicked that will occur at the Second Coming.

*your breath, as fire, shall devour you.* The Jerusalem Bible reads, "my breath shall devour you like fire." This reading accords with Isaiah's earlier images of the Lord burning the wicked (see 30:27–28).

**33:12** *people shall be as the burnings of lime.* This may refer to the intense heat that is necessary to extract the lime from bones (Amos 2:1). Thus it would symbolize the complete destruction of the wicked at the Lord's coming.

*as thorns cut up shall they be burned in the fire.* Thorns and weeds are burned to prevent them from overcoming useful plants. When they are cut down and placed in a pile, the fire becomes fiercer and hotter, and they burn more easily. Such will be the burning of the wicked at Christ's second coming: Sinners will burn as easily as thorns are consumed in a fire.

**33:14** *sinners in Zion are afraid.* Members of Zion will be aware of the destruction that the rising up of the Lord brings to the wicked, and Zion's *sinners* will be equally aware and *afraid* of the Lord's coming because of their own sins. The knowledge of their hypocrisy will cause them to fear and tremble.

## RIGHTEOUS DWELL IN EVERLASTING BURNINGS (33:14–17)

One common link between the previous section and this one is *fire*—the wicked will be destroyed by fire at Jesus' second coming, while the righteous will come to dwell in the "everlasting burnings" of the celestial world. The section begins with two parallel rhetorical questions asking who can dwell with God in his fire (33:14); these are followed by a response to the questions, detailing the attributes of one who is able to dwell with God (33:15), which in turn is succeeded by a description of the blessings of those who will be privileged to dwell with God (33:16–17). This passage has the same structure as two psalms that give the requirements for entrance into the temple (Ps. 15, 24), both of which have two rhetorical questions, a response to the questions, and a description of the blessings. The psalms, however, deal with the earthly temple, in contrast to this section of Isaiah, which asks, "Who is worthy to enter God's temple in heaven, or the celestial kingdom?"

## Isaiah 33:14–17

> *Who among us shall dwell with* the <u>devouring fire?</u>
> *who among us shall dwell with* <u>everlasting burnings?</u> (33:14)

> He that *walketh* <u>righteously,</u>
> and *speaketh* <u>uprightly;</u>

> he that *despiseth* the <u>gain of oppressions,</u>
> that *shaketh* his *hands* <u>from holding of bribes,</u>

> that *stoppeth* his <u>ears</u> from hearing of blood,
> and *shutteth* his <u>eyes</u> from seeing evil; (33:15)

> He shall *dwell* on *high:*
> his *place of defence* shall be the [<u>stronghold</u>][7] <u>of rocks:</u>

> *bread* shall <u>be given</u> him;
> his *waters* shall <u>be sure.</u> (33:16)

> Thine *eyes shall see* the <u>king in his beauty:</u>
> *they shall behold* the <u>land that is very far off.</u> (33:17)

### NOTES AND COMMENTARY

**33:14** *Who among us shall dwell with the devouring fire/everlasting burnings.* Joseph Smith taught that "God dwells in everlasting burnings,"[8] and "flesh and blood cannot go there, for all corruption is devoured by the fire."[9]

Isaiah's two rhetorical questions ask who will be able to abide the devouring fire of the Lord's glory. He answers these questions in 33:15.

**33:15** *He that walketh righteously*—Isaiah sets forth six statements to describe the qualities of one who will inherit and endure the glories of the celestial kingdom:

*he that walketh righteously*—one who moves forward in the Lord's paths of righteousness and obedience.

*speaketh uprightly*—one who speaks the truth, does not bear false witness against another, or use profanity, and so forth.

*he that despiseth the gain of oppressions*—one who refuses to gain power or wealth, or other things by oppressing another. Footnote *b* to 33:15 in the LDS edition of the Bible says, "profit by extortion."

*shaketh his hands from holding of bribes*—one who refuses to bribe or to be bribed, on any level of society, in any situation.

---

[7] From Hebrew *m'tsadot,* meaning "stronghold." Brown, Driver, and Briggs, *Hebrew and English Lexicon,* 844.
[8] *Teachings of the Prophet Joseph Smith,* 361.
[9] *Teachings of the Prophet Joseph Smith,* 367.

*stoppeth his ears from hearing of blood*—according to the Jerusalem Bible, one who "shuts suggestions of murder [or violence] out of his ears."

*shutteth his eyes from seeing evil*—one who does not participate in or condone evil actions or works.

**33:16–17** *He shall dwell on high.* Isaiah sets forth six statements to describe the blessings of those who will inherit the celestial kingdom:

*he shall dwell on high*—he or she will dwell in heaven, which is "on high."

*his place of defence shall be the stronghold of rocks*—as a rock stronghold provides protection from earthly enemies, God will eternally defend and protect the righteous.

*bread shall be given him*—this phrase reminds us of the sacrament. Christ is the Bread of Life (John 6:48) and the source of eternal life for those who inherit the celestial kingdom.

*his waters shall be sure*—this phrase also reminds us of the sacrament. Christ will give the waters of eternal life to exalted souls, for he is the "fountain of living waters" (Jer. 17:13).

*thine eyes shall see the king in his beauty*—exalted souls will be privileged to behold God in all of his glory.

*they shall behold the land that is very far off*—exalted souls will be privileged and blessed to see (and dwell in) God's celestial kingdom, the land that is very far off.

## THE RESTORATION OF ZION (33:18–24)

When the Lord comes in his glory, his people will see with their own eyes their righteous King, Lawgiver, Judge, and Savior in all his glory (33:17, 22; 32:1). Zion's stakes will be perfected, and the Lord's temples will never again be threatened by destruction (33:20). The people of the Lord will no longer be threatened by foreign invasion (33:18–19), and the inhabitants of Zion will be healed physically and spiritually by the Lord's healing power (33:24).

*Isaiah 33:18–24*

Thine heart shall meditate terror.
*Where* is the <u>scribe?</u>
*where* is the <u>receiver?</u>
*where* is he that <u>counted the towers?</u> (33:18)

Thou shalt not see a fierce people,
a people of a *deeper speech* than thou canst <u>perceive</u>;
of a *stammering tongue,* that thou canst not <u>understand</u>. (33:19)

*Look* upon <u>Zion</u>, the city of our solemnities:
thine *eyes shall see* <u>Jerusalem</u> a quiet habitation,

a *tabernacle* that shall <u>not be taken down</u>;
<u>not one</u> of the *stakes* thereof shall ever be <u>removed</u>,
<u>neither</u> shall <u>any</u> of the *cords* thereof <u>be broken</u>. (33:20)

But there the glorious Lord will be unto us a place of broad rivers and streams;
wherein shall *go no* <u>galley with oars</u>,
*neither shall* <u>gallant ship</u> *pass* thereby. (33:21)

For the *Lord* is our <u>judge</u>,
the *Lord* is our <u>lawgiver</u>,
the *Lord* is our <u>king</u>;
*he* will <u>save us</u>. (33:22)

Thy *tacklings* are <u>loosed</u>;
they could <u>not well strengthen</u> their *mast*,
they could <u>not spread</u> the *sail:*

then is the *prey* of a great spoil <u>divided</u>;
the lame <u>take</u> the *prey*. (33:23)

And the *inhabitant* <u>shall not say, I am sick</u>:
the *people that dwell* therein <u>shall be forgiven their iniquity</u>. (33:24)

## NOTES AND COMMENTARY

**33:18** *Thine heart shall meditate terror.* The Jerusalem Bible reads, "Your heart will look back on its fears." When the Lord reigns in Zion, we will look back on mortality and recall our fears of evil, enemies, and death.

*Where is the scribe/receiver/he that counted the towers.* The New International Version reads, "Where is the chief officer? Where is the one who took the revenue? Where is the officer in charge of the towers?" As we recall our mortal fears, we will remember many uncomfortable aspects of mortality, represented by these three rhetorical questions.

**33:19** *Thou shalt not see a fierce people.* We will no longer be threatened by fierce foreign enemies, because the Lord will be our defender (33:16).

**33:20** *Look upon Zion, the city of our solemnities.* Zion will be a city of solemnities, or, perhaps, solemn assemblies.

*Jerusalem a quiet habitation.* Jerusalem, a city that has witnessed many wars and much bloodshed, will be a peaceful city (see 32:17) when the Lord reigns as "our king" (33:22).

*a tabernacle . . . shall not be taken down.* This refers to the tabernacle of Moses, a portable temple that was a large tent with stakes and cords. The stakes were sticks or posts driven into the ground; cords or ropes connected the tabernacle to the stakes. Both the stakes and cords supported the tabernacle.

The entire verse speaks about latter-day Zion and informs us that the temples of the Lord will be surrounded and upheld by the stakes of Zion, which are gathering places of the Lord's people. As the stakes and cords of a tent serve to uphold it during a storm, so the stakes of Zion are "for a defense, and for a refuge from the storm, and from wrath when it shall be poured out without mixture upon the whole earth" (D&C 115:6). The phrase "a tabernacle . . . shall not be taken down" contrasts with Moses' portable tabernacle that had to be repeatedly put up and "taken down"—Jerusalem at the Second Coming will be a permanent, everlasting place.

**33:21** *Lord will be unto us a place of broad rivers/streams. Rivers* and *streams* are metaphors for the Lord, who provides us with the "waters of life" (see commentary on 8:6). Notice the abundance of water—*broad rivers and streams*—available to those who wish to partake.

*wherein shall go no galley with oars, neither shall gallant ship pass.* In ancient times large warships transported armies. These galleys were often powered by slaves, and on return trips to the homeland the galleys were often loaded with spoils and captives. Isaiah states that such ships will not pass over the broad rivers and streams, indicating that the Lord will protect those who have access to him. The New International Version translates *gallant ship* as *mighty ship.*

**33:22** *the Lord is our judge.* In this verse Isaiah explains why Zion will be such a marvelous place to live. "The Lord is our judge, the Lord is our lawgiver, the Lord is our king; he will save us." Surely no one can conceive of a better justice of the peace, lawmaker, ruler, and protector than the Lord himself.

**33:23** *tacklings/mast/sail.* Isaiah returns to the subject of warships, spoken of in 33:21, and emphasizes that the once-feared ships will no longer be able to function because the masts are not secure and their tackle hangs loose. This condition symbolizes the way in which the wicked will lose their power in the final judgments.

*then is the prey of a great spoil divided; the lame take the prey.* Because the armies of the wicked are completely destroyed by the Lord, even the lame will gather and divide the spoils left behind by their enemies (33:4; 26:5–6).

**33:24** *the inhabitant shall not say, I am sick.* The physical bodies of those who remain in Zion after the destruction of the wicked will be changed and thereafter never experience sickness.

*shall be forgiven their iniquity.* The truly celestial inhabitants of Zion, those who have yielded their hearts to God, will have repented and will be cleansed and forgiven of their sins.

# ISAIAH 34

## LIKENING ISAIAH 34 UNTO OURSELVES

*Isaiah 34 applies directly to our time, the last days, because the prophecies in that chapter will occur when the Lord comes in his glory to the earth. Some of our generation may witness the slaughter of the wicked, as described in 34:1–8, or we may see the burning of the earth, as set forth in 34:9–15; 34:16–17 alludes to the blessings of eternal marriage.*

## A DAY OF WRATH UPON EDOM (THE WORLD) (34:1–8)

Isaiah prophesies to all the peoples of the earth, as signaled by his use of the words *nations, people, the earth,* and *the world* in 34:1. His message is plain: the Lord is angry with the nations of the earth and their armies; therefore, he is going to destroy them at his second coming. Isaiah's words regarding the destruction are vivid and descriptive—*utterly destroyed, slaughter, slain, carcases, blood, filled with blood, sacrifice,* and *soaked with blood.* In addition, Isaiah's terminology recalls animal sacrifice at the Lord's temple: *slaughter, blood, fat, blood of lambs and goats,* and *fat of the kidneys of rams.* The Lord is going to destroy the nations as if they were sacrificial animals.

Isaiah's symbolism is clear to us: those who accept the Savior's atoning sacrifice will be delivered from destruction, but those who reject his atonement will be slaughtered, as were the sacrificial animals of his temple. During all this slaughter, Jehovah will "uphold Zion's cause" (NIV 34:8) and protect his Saints.

*Isaiah 34:1–8*

> Come near, *ye nations,* to <u>hear</u>;
> and <u>hearken</u>, *ye people:*

let the *earth* hear, and <u>all that is therein</u>;
the *world,* and <u>all things that come forth of it</u>. (34:1)

For the [*wrath*][1] *of the Lord* is upon all <u>nations,</u>
and *his fury* upon all their <u>armies</u>:

*he* hath utterly <u>destroyed them,</u>
*he* hath <u>delivered them to the slaughter.</u> (34:2)

*Their slain* also shall <u>be cast out,</u>
and *their stink* shall <u>come up out</u> of their carcases,

and the *mountains* shall be <u>melted</u> with their blood. (34:3)
And all the *host of heaven* shall be <u>dissolved,</u>

and the *heavens* shall be <u>rolled together</u> as a scroll:

and all their host shall <u>fall down,</u>
as the *leaf* <u>falleth</u> off from the vine,
and as a <u>falling</u> *fig* from the fig tree. (34:4)

For my sword shall be bathed in heaven:
behold, it shall come down *upon Idumea,*
and *upon the people of my curse,* to judgment. (34:5)

The sword of the Lord is filled with *blood,* it is made <u>fat with fatness,</u>
and with the *blood* of lambs and goats, with the *<u>fat of the kidneys</u>* of rams:

For the Lord hath a *sacrifice* in <u>Bozrah,</u>
and a great *slaughter* in the land of <u>Idumea</u>. (34:6)

And the [*wild oxen*][2] shall come down with <u>them,</u>
and the *bullocks* with the [<u>mighty ones</u>];[3]

and *their land* shall be soaked <u>with blood,</u>
and *their dust* made fat <u>with fatness.</u> (34:7)

For it is the *day* of the Lord's <u>vengeance,</u>
and the *year* of <u>recompenses</u> for the controversy of Zion. (34:8)

## NOTES AND COMMENTARY

**34:1** *nations/people.* The voice of warning is to all *nations, people,* the entire *earth,* and the *world,* which encompasses all societies, peoples, and governments.

**34:2** *wrath/fury.* The Lord's wrath and fury will be expressed in the last days by the destruction of the wicked (13:13).

*the slaughter.* The Lord will destroy the nations as if they were animals led to slaughter.

---

[1] From Hebrew *qetsep,* meaning "wrath" or sore anger. Brown, Driver, and Briggs, *Hebrew and English Lexicon,* 893.

[2] From Hebrew *r'emiym,* referring to a "wild ox" or "unicorns, and (oftener) rhinoceros." Brown, Driver, and Briggs, *Hebrew and English Lexicon,* 910.

[3] From Hebrew *'abiyriym,* meaning "strong" or "mighty"; *'byr "the Strong,* old name for God (poet)." Brown, Driver, and Briggs, *Hebrew and English Lexicon,* 7.

**34:3–4** *Their slain.* Isaiah depicts the scene of destruction and death: The carcasses of the slain will stink, and "the mountains will be soaked with their blood" (NIV).

*mountains shall be melted with their blood.* This passage may be translated as "the mountains shall be soaked with their blood," referring to the slain and the carcasses spoken of earlier in the verse.

*And all the host of heaven shall be dissolved.* This event will occur at the Second Coming and speaks of the passing away of "the heavens and the earth" (3 Ne. 26:3).

*rolled together as a scroll.* A scroll is rolled up before it is put away. This phrase is difficult to understand but seems to refer to the events connected with the passing away of the heavens and the earth, which will occur at Christ's second coming: "Behold, will ye believe in the day of your visitation—behold, when the Lord shall come, yea, even that great day when the earth shall be rolled together as a scroll, and the elements shall melt with fervent heat, yea, in that great day when ye shall be brought to stand before the Lamb of God—then will ye say that there is not God?" (Morm. 9:2).

*their host shall fall down . . . as a falling fig from the fig tree.* A modern-day revelation explains, "For not many days hence and the earth shall tremble and reel to and fro as a drunken man; and the sun shall hide his face, and shall refuse to give light; and the moon shall be bathed in blood; and the stars shall become exceedingly angry, and shall cast themselves down as a fig that falleth from off a fig-tree" (D&C 88:87). As shriveled fruit or dry leaves fall from the tree, so shall the stars (Mark 13:25; D&C 45:42; Rev. 8:10) fall from the heavens (D&C 88:87; Rev. 6:13–14; 8:10).

**34:5** *sword.* Symbolically, the Lord's sword exacts judgment and destruction on Earth's inhabitants (see commentary on 27:1).

*bathed in heaven.* Jehovah's sword is prepared to destroy the wicked.

*it shall come down upon Idumea.* The Lord's sword will come down upon Idumea, or Edom, which also refers to the wicked world (D&C 1:36).

*people of my curse.* The wicked.

*to judgment.* Part of the Lord's judgment upon the wicked is their destruction.

**34:6** *sword of the Lord is filled with blood.* The destruction of the wicked is so great that the sword of the Lord is covered with blood.

*blood/fatness/kidneys.* In the Mosaic law of sacrifice, the blood and fat of a sacrificed animal are reserved for the Lord (Lev. 3:15–17). By using these three words in the context of the slaughter of the wicked, Isaiah emphasizes the Lord's right to exact the penalty for iniquity. It is noteworthy that blood and kidneys, with other internal organs, regulate the life of humans and beasts. The Lord's slaughter will be complete, claiming the very life force of the wicked.

*lambs, goats, rams.* These sacrificial animals were used for sin and trespass offerings to symbolically cleanse the repentant offerer from both willful and inadvertent sins. In this context, it may suggest that the wicked will have to die for their own sins because they would not partake of the blessings of the sacrifice of Christ.

*sacrifice/slaughter.* These are parallel terms. Those who did not accept Jesus' atoning sacrifice will be slaughtered as are the sacrificial animals in the temple (Jer. 46:10; Rev. 19:17–18).

*Bozrah/Idumea.* Bozrah (perhaps modern Busra) is the capital of Edom, here called Idumea. Both Bozrah and Idumea represent the world (D&C 1:36) and will be destroyed by the Lord (Ezek. 25:14).

**34:7** *wild oxen/bullocks.* Known for their great strength, oxen and bullocks represent mighty people that will be destroyed.

*mighty ones.* This term may refer to the politically and socially important people of the world.

*soaked with blood.* The destruction will be so great that the land will be soaked with the blood of the wicked.

**34:8** *day of the Lord's vengeance/year of recompenses.* The day of vengeance, which falls upon the wicked (D&C 97:26), is also referred to as the day of the Lord (2:12). The implication is that the Lord's vengeance will be brief (*day*) in comparison to the time of recompense (*year*) The *year of recompenses* is the same as the *year of my redeemed* identified in 63:4 (see commentary there; see also D&C 133:51–52).

*controversy of Zion.* The New International Version reads "to uphold Zion's cause." At the same time the Lord destroys the wicked, he will support Zion's cause.

## EDOM (THE WORLD) TO BE BURNED (34:9–15)

Isaiah continues his prophecy concerning the destruction of Edom, or the world (34:1–8). Isaiah's portrayal of the "burning pitch" that fills the land of Edom and the billowing smoke that arises "for ever" is reminiscent of the destruction of Sodom and Gomorrah by fire and brimstone. It presents a picture of terror for the wicked, who will be consumed by the great power of Christ's glory at his second coming.

## Isaiah 34:9–15

And the *streams* thereof shall be turned into pitch,
and the *dust* thereof into brimstone,
and the *land* thereof shall become burning pitch. (34:9)

It shall *not* be *quenched* night nor day;
the *smoke* thereof shall go up for ever:

from *generation to generation* it shall lie waste;
none shall pass through it *for ever and ever.* (34:10)

But the *cormorant and the bittern* shall possess it;
the *owl also and the raven* shall dwell in it:

and he shall stretch out upon it the *line* of [desolation],[4]
and the [*plummet*][5] of emptiness. (34:11)

They shall call the *nobles* thereof to the kingdom, but none shall be there,
and all her *princes* shall be nothing. (34:12)

And *thorns* shall come up in her palaces,
*nettles and brambles* in the fortresses thereof:

and it shall be an *habitation* of [jackals],[6]
and an [*enclosure*][7] for owls. (34:13)

The *wild beasts* of the desert shall also meet with the wild beasts of the island,
and the *satyr* shall cry to his fellow;

the *screech owl* also shall rest there,
and find for *herself* a place of rest. (34:14)

There shall the great *owl* make her nest, and lay, and hatch, and gather under her shadow:
there shall the *vultures* also be gathered, every one with her mate. (34:15)

## NOTES AND COMMENTARY

**34:9** *pitch/brimstone/burning pitch.* The world, like Sodom and Gomorrah, will be destroyed because of great wickedness (Gen. 19:1–29; also D&C 29:21). Destruction will be the result of pitch and brimstone, flammable materials that will cover the land.

**34:10** *smoke thereof shall go up for ever.* The phrases *it shall not be quenched night nor day* and *smoke . . . shall go up forever* remind one of hell.

---

[4] From Hebrew *tohu,* meaning "formlessness, confusion, unreality, emptiness, . . . nothingness, waste." Brown, Driver, and Briggs, *Hebrew and English Lexicon,* 1062.
[5] From Hebrew *'ab'ney,* meaning "stones." Brown, Driver, and Briggs, *Hebrew and English Lexicon,* 6.
[6] From Hebrew *taniym.* Brown, Driver, and Briggs, *Hebrew and English Lexicon,* 1072.
[7] From Hebrew *chatsiyr,* meaning "enclosure [or] courtyard." Brown, Driver, and Briggs, *Hebrew and English Lexicon,* 346.

*generation to generation/lie waste.* When Christ comes to destroy the world (Edom) at his second coming, the effects of this destruction will last "for ever and ever," for the world will be renewed and become a paradisiacal sphere during the Millennium. "None shall pass through it for ever and ever" for the same reason—that state of the earth will no longer exist.

**34:11** *cormorant/bittern/owl/raven.* These (and the others listed) are unclean creatures that inhabit lands made desolate by God (13:21–22; Jer. 50:39). (Some translate *cormorant* as "desert owl" and *bittern* as "screech owl.") These creatures inhabited ancient Edom after its destruction. They and their desolate dwelling places symbolize telestial domains. Their existence in Edom reveals the completeness of its ruin and desolation. Similarly, at the Second Coming, the world (Edom) will be destroyed, and all corruptible things will be consumed.

*line/plummet.* The land is being surveyed and assigned to destruction (28:17).

*desolation/emptiness.* Edom will become "desolation" and "emptiness," two terms which described the earth before God organized the elements (these two terms are used in Gen. 1:2 in the Hebrew).

**34:12** *nobles, princes.* The nobles and princes of Edom (the world) will never again exercise power or order government. They will not exist. The government will be in the Lord's hands.

**34:13–14** *thorns, brambles.* Edom's mansions become wasteland.

*jackals/owls/wild beasts/satyr/screech owl.* The satyr is probably a wild goat. See commentary on 34:11.

**34:15** *There shall the great owl make her nest.* This verse emphasizes both the extent of the desolation (owls and vultures will gather where man once lived) and its length (owls and vultures will live there long enough to make nests, lay and hatch eggs, and care for their young).

## THOSE WHOSE NAMES ARE WRITTEN IN THE BOOK OF THE LORD RECEIVE THE LAND (34:16–17)

The land of the wicked has been made desolate and assigned to chaos by means of the Lord's "line" and "plummet." The Lord will also use these devices to assign the glorified earth to the righteous, whose names are recorded in the book of the Lord (34:17; see also D&C 103:7). These will have an eternal inheritance with the Lord (34:16); thus, they will always remain with their spouses and have an eternal increase

(34:16; see also D&C 132:30–31). There are a number of parallel word choices between this and previous sections, especially between 34:10–11 and 34:17.

## Isaiah 34:16–17

> Seek ye out of the book of the Lord,
> and read [the names written therein]:[8]
>
> *no one* of these shall <u>fail</u>,
> *none* shall [<u>lack</u>][9] [their] <u>mate</u>:
>
> for *my mouth* it hath <u>commanded</u>,
> and [*my*][10] *spirit* it hath <u>gathered</u> them. (34:16)
>
> And [*I have*] *cast* the lot for <u>them</u>,
> and [*I have*] *divided* it unto <u>them</u> by line:
>
> they shall *possess* it <u>for ever</u>,
> from <u>generation to generation</u> [they shall][11] *dwell* therein. (34:17)

## NOTES AND COMMENTARY

**34:16** *book of the Lord.* During the day of the Lord, those whose names are found in the book of the Lord will be delivered from the "time of trouble" (Dan. 12:1), and they will inherit the celestial city (Rev. 21:22–27). This book of the Lord may be the "book of life" identified more than a dozen times in the scriptures (Dan. 12:1; Rev. 3:5; 20:12; D&C 76:68; 128:7).

*none shall lack their mate.* Those whose names are written in the book will have their spouses through eternity. This is a rare Old Testament reference to eternal marriage. Note the parallel in 34:15, in which Isaiah states that creatures would have their mates after the destruction of Edom—meaning, they would propagate their species at least for a few generations. Here, Isaiah promises that after the destruction of the world, those whose names are written in the book of the Lord will also have their mates.

*my spirit . . . gathered them.* This passage speaks of the role of the Holy Ghost in gathering individuals to the gospel of Jesus Christ.

**34:17** *cast the lot.* Those in the Lamb's book are chosen as the Lord's servants.

*divided . . . by line.* By a godly decree the land once known as Edom is surveyed and apportioned to those whose names are in the Lord's book (Rev. 21:27). The earth,

---

[8] JST Isa. 34:16.

[9] From Hebrew *n'drh,* from the root '*dr,* meaning to "be lacking." Brown, Driver, and Briggs, *Hebrew and English Lexicon,* 727.

[10] All bracketed changes in this verse are from JST Isa. 34:16.

[11] All bracketed changes in this verse are from JST Isa. 34:17.

once a telestial world inhabited by telestial beings, will become a celestial kingdom, inhabited by celestial beings.

*for ever/generation to generation.* The righteous will inhabit the earth eternally.

# ISAIAH 35

### LIKENING ISAIAH 35 UNTO OURSELVES

*Chapter 35 presents a glorious picture of Zion in the latter-days. Those of us who attain to Zion will "be glad," "rejoice," and "rejoice even with joy and singing"; there will be "songs and everlasting joy upon" our heads. We will "obtain joy and gladness," and "sorrow and sighing" shall "flee away" from us. Most important, as we are obedient and worthy, we will "see the glory of the Lord, and the excellency of our God."*

## LATTER-DAY ISRAEL REJOICES AND BLOSSOMS AS A ROSE (35:1–10)

With the restoration of the gospel, the righteous of latter-day Israel, which includes the Lamanites, is no longer comparable to a wilderness or desert but is like the garden of God, or Eden (see commentary on 27:10; see also D&C 33:5). Zion "blossom[s] abundantly" (35:2), thanks to the abundance of "waters," "streams," and "springs of water" (35:6–7)—all of which refer symbolically to Jesus Christ and the great life-giving blessings associated with him and his gospel.

Modern revelation adds light to this chapter of Isaiah: "But before the great day of the Lord shall come, Jacob shall flourish in the wilderness, and the Lamanites shall blossom as the rose. Zion shall flourish upon the hills and rejoice upon the mountains" (D&C 49:24–25). The revelation places Jacob in the "wilderness," a term also used in Isaiah 35, and we learn that Jacob and Zion shall "flourish" and the Lamanites shall "blossom." The words *flourish* and *blossom* suggest that Jacob, Zion, and the Lamanites are like plants or flowers.

Doctrine and Covenants 49 presents a host of teachings about what Zion will be like in the last days:

It will be a place of rejoicing, joy, gladness, singing, and glory (D&C 49:1–2, 10);

Inhabitants of Zion will "see the glory of the Lord" (D&C 49:2);

Inhabitants of Zion will strengthen one another spiritually (D&C 49:3–4);

God will open the eyes of the blind and the ears of the deaf (D&C 49:5);

The waters of life will flow abundantly (D&C 49:6–7);

The "way of holiness" will be in Zion (D&C 49:8);

The "way of holiness" will be off limits to the "unclean" and enemies of Zion (D&C 49:8–9);

The "way of holiness" will be for the "redeemed" and "ransomed of the Lord" (D&C 49:9–10);

Those who "come to Zion" will experience "everlasting joy," and "sorrow and sighing shall flee away" (D&C 49:10).

We also read some, but not all, of Isaiah's statements literally, seeing in our time the deserts of both Utah and Israel responding to the Lord's blessing the land. The great irrigation systems and man-made water systems enable places that were once wastelands to become farming communities; hence, the desert and the wilderness are blossoming as a rose.

## Isaiah 35:1–10

The *wilderness* and the *solitary place* shall <u>be glad</u> for them;
and the *desert* shall <u>rejoice,</u> and <u>blossom</u> as the rose. (35:1)

It shall *blossom* <u>abundantly,</u>
and *rejoice* even with <u>joy and singing</u>:

the *glory* of <u>Lebanon</u> shall be given unto it,
the *excellency* of <u>Carmel</u> and <u>Sharon,</u>

they shall see the *glory* of the <u>Lord,</u>
and the *excellency* of our <u>God</u>. (35:2)

*Strengthen* ye the <u>weak hands,</u>
and *confirm* the <u>feeble knees</u>. (35:3)

Say to them that are of a fearful heart,
Be strong, fear not:

behold, your *God will come* with <u>vengeance,</u>
*even God* with a <u>recompence</u>;
*he will come* and save you. (35:4)

Then the *eyes of the blind* shall be <u>opened,</u>
and the *ears of the deaf* shall be <u>unstopped</u>. (35:5)

Then shall the *lame* man <u>leap</u> as an hart,
and the tongue of the *dumb* <u>sing</u>:

for in the *wilderness* shall <u>waters</u> break out,
and <u>streams</u> in the *desert*. (35:6)

And the *parched ground* shall become a <u>pool</u>,
and the *thirsty land* <u>springs of water</u>:

in the [resort of jackals],[1] where each lay,
shall be grass with reeds and rushes. (35:7)

And [a] *highway* <u>shall be there</u>;
[for] a *way* [<u>shall be cast up</u>] and it shall be called The *way of holiness;*

[T]he *unclean* shall not <u>pass over it</u>;
but it <u>shall be [cast up]</u> for those [who are *clean,*
and]* the wayfaring men, though [they are accounted][2] fools, shall *not err therein.*
(35:8)

No *lion* shall <u>be there</u>,
nor any *ravenous beast* shall <u>go up thereon</u>,
*it* shall <u>not be found there</u>;
but the redeemed shall walk there: (35:9)

And the ransomed of the Lord shall *return,*
and *come* to Zion with songs and <u>everlasting joy</u> upon their heads:
they shall obtain <u>joy and gladness</u>, and sorrow and sighing shall flee away. (35:10)

## NOTES AND COMMENTARY

**35:1** *desert shall . . . blossom as the rose.* Isaiah equates the desert to Israel, an important point to understanding this chapter; here he prophesies that the desert shall blossom, just as earlier he had prophesied that Israel shall blossom (see commentary on 27:6, 10). For Isaiah's prophetic world, the words *desert* and *wilderness* relate not only to a barren and desolate land but to a people or nation (1:30) who lack the living waters of Jesus Christ. When Isaiah prophesies that the desert shall blossom as the rose, he refers to the restoration of the gospel: "Israel shall blossom and bud, and fill the face of the world with fruit" (27:6), "Jacob shall flourish in the wilderness" (D&C 49:24), and the full blessings of the temple shall again be made available.

After the death of Jesus and his apostles, the Church was driven "into the wilderness" (D&C 86:3), but with the restoration of the gospel we have witnessed "the coming forth of [the Lord's] church out of the wilderness" (D&C 5:14). We, the house of Israel, are no longer a desert but are flourishing and filling "the face of the world with fruit" (27:6). We drink deeply of the waters of Christ (58:11).

---

[1] Hebrew *taniym.* Brown, Driver, and Briggs, *Hebrew and English Lexicon,* 1072.
[2] All bracketed changes in v. 8 are found in JST Isa. 35:8.

**35:2** *It shall blossom abundantly.* The house of Israel will not simply blossom but will blossom abundantly.

*joy and singing.* We will rejoice for the founding of Zion and for the Lord's glory (51:3).

*glory of Lebanon shall be given unto it, the excellency of Carmel and Sharon.* Isaiah likens us, latter-day Israel, to the lush forests of Lebanon, the fertile fields of Carmel, and the beauty and flowers of Sharon (2:13; 33:9; 60:13).

*they shall see the glory of the Lord.* As we witness the flourishing of the Church in the last days, we will see the hand of God. With the restoration of the priesthood and its ordinances, the privilege of the obedient and worthy to behold God is now on the earth.

**35:3** *weak hands/feeble knees.* In the last days we are commanded to "succor the weak, lift up the hands which hang down, and strengthen the feeble knees" (D&C 81:5) so that all will remain faithful until the Lord's coming.

**35:4** *Be strong, fear not.* All of us are commanded to strengthen the weak by saying, "Be strong, fear not" and remind them that God will come and save us.

*vengeance/recompence.* Christ will exact vengeance on the wicked for their iniquities (Morm. 3:15) and recompense those who are part of his kingdom (see commentary on 34:8).

**35:5** *eyes of the blind shall be opened.* This statement has a literal, physical application (D&C 84:69–70), but it also refers to those who are spiritually blind, deaf, and dumb, who will be made whole through their conversion to the restored gospel.

**35:6–7** *waters/streams/pool/springs of water.* This image has a dual application: desolate wastelands become gardens in the last days; through the power of Christ, "Israel shall blossom and bud, and fill the face of the world with fruit" (27:6) and "Jacob shall flourish in the wilderness" (D&C 49:24). The waters point to Christ and his salvation. Earlier Isaiah wrote that the "Lord will be unto us a place of broad rivers and streams" (33:21).

**35:7** *grass with reeds and rushes.* Reeds and rushes require ample water and cannot grow in the harsh wilderness. These plants also represent righteous individuals who partake of the waters of life.

**35:8** *highway.* This word may also be read "exalted path"[3] (or "way that is high"—highway). This highway, called "the way of holiness" (11:16; 35:8), is our path to God. It brings us out of bondage and into the promised land. It leads us

---

[3] Brown, Driver, and Briggs, *Hebrew and English Lexicon,* 699–700.

through the gates of baptism and to the temple, or the presence of God (Jer. 31:21; see also Isa. 51:10–11). That the way is a "way of holiness" for the "redeemed" but not for the "unclean" emphasizes the connection with temples and temple ordinances.

*unclean shall not pass over.* Those who have chosen not to avail themselves of the Lord's atonement and enter into covenants with him will not pass over the way of holiness.

*wayfaring men.* The traveler on this particular highway is the searcher for truth. The sincere disciple of truth eventually finds the path of the Lord, and, though many account such to be a fool for his conversion to the gospel of the Lord, he will not err by walking this highway.[4]

**35:9** *lion/ravenous beast.* These creatures represent the Lord's enemies, who desire to harm those on the highway of holiness, but they will not succeed.

*redeemed.* Those who have taken upon them the name of the Lord and his covenants and applied the Atonement in their lives are thus redeemed and ransomed by the Lord.

**35:10** *ransomed of the Lord shall return.* Those who accept the restored gospel and its covenants are the ransomed of the Lord. These people will return (*return* in Hebrew also means "repent") from centuries of scattering and exile in various lands and will "come to Zion" (D&C 45:71).

*with songs . . . upon their heads.* Our pioneer ancestors literally sang as they traveled, but this passage also refers to our worship services today. Sacred songs have always been part of true worship among the Saints.

*they shall obtain joy.* Joy accompanies sacred music, obedience, and temple attendance.

---

[4] See *Teachings of the Prophet Joseph Smith*, 95, 370.

# ISAIAH 36

## LIKENING ISAIAH 36 UNTO OURSELVES

*King Hezekiah set a wonderful example for us to follow. When faced with tremendous challenges, including the approach of the Assyrian armies, he turned to the Lord in prayer and sought counsel from the Lord's prophet; then he trusted the Lord to deliver him and his people. So should we do when we are faced with trials, challenges, and threats to our lives. The Lord stands ready to help us—but we must ask him and be obedient to his will if we hope to receive his blessing.*

---

## THE INVASION OF SENNACHERIB (36:1–21)

While Hezekiah is king over Judah, Sennacherib, the king of Assyria, and his armies capture most of the fortified cities of Judah (36:1). Then Sennacherib sends his armies, led by Rabshakeh, to Jerusalem (36:2) to demand gifts and to inform Judah of the terms of surrender, which include the deportation of the people of Jerusalem (36:8, 16–17). Rabshakeh emphasizes that the inhabitants of Jerusalem should not rely on Egypt (36:4–6) or their God (36:7, 10, 15, 18–20) for deliverance.

Hezekiah, in exchange for what he hopes will be Sennacherib's mercy and consequent departure from Judea in peace, pays Sennacherib three hundred talents of silver and thirty talents of gold (2 Kgs. 18:14–16). Sennacherib, however, treacherously sends his armies to destroy Jerusalem.

*Isaiah 36:1–21*

> Now it came to pass in the fourteenth year of king Hezekiah, that Sennacherib king of Assyria came up against all the defenced cities of Judah, and took them. (36:1) And the king of Assyria sent Rabshakeh from Lachish to Jerusalem unto king Hezekiah with a great army. And he stood by the conduit of the upper pool in

the highway of the fuller's field. (36:2) Then came forth unto him Eliakim, Hilkiah's son, which was over the house, and Shebna the scribe, and Joah, Asaph's son, the recorder. (36:3)

And Rabshakeh said unto them, Say ye now to Hezekiah, Thus saith the great king, the king of Assyria, What confidence is this wherein thou trustest? (36:4) I say, [thy] words are but vain [when thou sayest,][1] I have counsel and strength for war: now on whom dost thou trust, that thou rebellest against me? (36:5) Lo, thou trustest in the staff of this broken reed, on Egypt; whereon if a man lean, it will go into his hand, and pierce it: so is Pharaoh king of Egypt to all that trust in him. (36:6) But if thou say to me, We trust in the Lord our God: is it not he, whose high places and whose altars Hezekiah hath taken away, and said to Judah and to Jerusalem, Ye shall worship before this altar? (36:7) Now therefore give pledges, I pray thee, to my master the king of Assyria, and I will give thee two thousand horses, if thou be able on thy part to set riders upon them. (36:8) How then wilt thou turn away the face of one captain of the least of my master's servants, and put thy trust on Egypt for chariots and for horsemen? (36:9) And am I now come up without the Lord against this land to destroy it? the Lord said unto me, Go up against this land, and destroy it. (36:10)

Then said Eliakim and Shebna and Joah unto Rabshakeh, Speak, I pray thee, unto thy servants in the Syrian language; for we understand it: and speak not to us in the Jews' language, in the ears of the people that are on the wall. (36:11) But Rabshakeh said, Hath my master sent me to thy master and to thee to speak these words? hath he not sent me to the men that sit upon the wall, that they may eat their own dung, and drink their own piss with you? (36:12)

Then Rabshakeh stood, and cried with a loud voice in the Jews' language, and said, Hear ye the words of the great king, the king of Assyria. (36:13) Thus saith the king, Let not Hezekiah deceive you: for he shall not be able to deliver you. (36:14) Neither let Hezekiah make you trust in the Lord, saying, The Lord will surely deliver us: this city shall not be delivered into the hand of the king of Assyria. (36:15) Hearken not to Hezekiah: for thus saith the king of Assyria, Make an agreement with me by a present, and come out to me: and eat ye every one of his vine, and every one of his fig tree, and drink ye every one the waters of his own cistern; (36:16) Until I come and take you away to a land like your own land, a land of corn and wine, a land of bread and vineyards. (36:17) Beware lest Hezekiah persuade you, saying, The Lord will deliver us. Hath any of the gods of the nations delivered his land out of the hand of the king of Assyria? (36:18) Where are the gods of Hamath and Arphad? where are the gods of Sepharvaim? and have they delivered Samaria out of my hand? (36:19) Who are they among all the gods of these lands, that have delivered their land out of my hand, that the Lord should deliver Jerusalem out of my hand? (36:20)

But they held their peace, and answered him not a word: for the king's commandment was, saying, Answer him not. (36:21)

## NOTES AND COMMENTARY

**36:1** *fourteenth year of king Hezekiah.* Approximately 701 B.C.

---

[1] Bracketed changes are from JST Isa. 36:5.

*Sennacherib.* King of Assyria (704–681 B.C.).

**36:2** *Rabshakeh.* A trusted officer of Sennacherib's army, he was sent from Lachish with his own large army to deal with Hezekiah.

*Lachish.* This fortified city guarded the highway to Jerusalem from the south.

*upper pool/highway.* The *upper pool* is the Spring of Gihon; adjoining the pool was a *highway* that ran through a valley called the Fuller's Field.

**36:3** *Eliakim/Shebna/Joah.* Hezekiah sends three of his high officials to meet Rabshakeh.

**36:4** *wherein thou trustest.* Rabshakeh asks from what source Hezekiah has received the confidence to raise a rebellion against Assyria when Egypt was unable to support him.

**36:5** *thy words are but vain.* The field commander mocks Hezekiah's plans to wage war against Assyria (30:2–7; 31:1–3).

**36:6** *staff of this broken reed.* Rabshakeh compares Hezekiah's placing his trust in Egypt to a man who trusts in a reed for support as he walks; when the reed snaps, it is driven into his hand (Ezek. 29:6).

**36:7** *trust in the Lord.* Rabshakeh attacks Judah's trust in God by attacking Hezekiah's recently established religious policies.

*high places/altars Hezekiah hath taken away.* In an attempt to stop the worship of false gods, Hezekiah has Judah's high places and altars destroyed (2 Kgs. 18:1–7). Rabshakeh attempts to undermine the trust people have in Hezekiah's relationship with the Lord by implying that Hezekiah has angered the Lord by destroying the high places.

**36:8** *pledges.* Rabshakeh asks Jerusalem to pledge her services and devotion to Assyria.

*two thousand horses.* Rabshakeh implies that the army of Judah is of no consequence—he promises horses if Hezekiah can muster enough men to use them.

**36:10** *the Lord said unto me, Go up against this land.* Rabshakeh claims that Jehovah commissioned Assyria to destroy Jerusalem (Isa. 30; 31).

**36:11** *Speak . . . in the Syrian language.* Hezekiah's officials desire Rabshakeh to speak Syriac (or Aramaic), the common tongue of the Assyrians, so that the onlooking Jews cannot understand the negotiations. Rabshakeh, however, wishing to intimidate the onlookers, chooses to address Hezekiah's envoys in Hebrew.

**36:12** *eat their own dung.* Rabshakeh plays on the people's fears by creating a picture of famine and destitution caused by Assyria's seizure of the land; the only thing available for consumption would be human refuse.

**36:13** *Rabshakeh . . . cried with a loud voice.* Rabshakeh not only refuses to speak Syriac (36:11) but shouts his words to the people on the walls.

**36:14** *he shall not . . . deliver you.* Rabshakeh attempts to create fear by boasting that neither Hezekiah nor his God could deliver Jerusalem from the mighty Assyrian power.

**36:16** *Make an agreement . . . by a present.* Rabshakeh asks for the people to pay tribute in exchange for their freedom.

**36:17** *take you away to a land.* It was Assyrian practice to deport captured peoples from their homelands, a tactic that was part of a larger strategy of humiliation.

*corn/wine/bread/vineyards.* To soften the blow of deportation, Rabshakeh promises that the inhabitants of Judah will be sent to lands of produce and plenty.

**36:19** *Hamath/Arphad/Sepharvaim/Samaria.* These cities were conquered by Sennacherib during his military campaigns before he reached Jerusalem. Rabshakeh notes that the gods of these cities (which of course were false gods) could not defend their inhabitants from Assyrian conquest.

**36:20** *Who . . . among all the gods of these lands.* Rabshakeh asks, "What makes you think that the Lord will deliver you, when other gods have failed their worshippers?" This blasphemy brought the Lord's wrath on the Assyrians (37:29–38).

**36:21** *answered him not.* Hezekiah has ordered his officials to listen to Rabshakeh but not to respond.

# ISAIAH 37

### LIKENING ISAIAH 37 UNTO OURSELVES

*All of us may go to the temple with our cares and challenges, whether small or great, and seek God's help through prayer. That is exactly what Hezekiah does. With thousands of enemy soldiers camped outside Jerusalem's gates, waiting to destroy the inhabitants, Hezekiah petitions the Lord through prayer in the house of the Lord. The Lord hears his prayer and sends an angel, who destroys 185,000 men in the Assyrian camp, thus saving Hezekiah and his people from destruction (37:36).*

*The Assyrian wars constitute a "day of trouble" for Israel (37:3), anticipating our own day when the warring nations of the earth cause fear in the hearts of many. It would be well if, like Hezekiah of old, the various leaders of the world sought the Lord's counsel and the counsel of his prophets.*

## HEZEKIAH SEEKS ISAIAH'S COUNSEL AND PRAYS TO THE LORD (36:22–37:20)

Hezekiah responds to Rabshakeh's blasphemy against God (36:1–21) with grief and humility (37:1) by seeking Isaiah's counsel (37:2–5) and by praying to the Lord in his temple (37:14–20).

*Isaiah 36:22–37:20*

> Then came Eliakim, the son of Hilkiah, that was over the household, and Shebna the scribe, and Joah, the son of Asaph, the recorder, to Hezekiah with their clothes rent, and told him the words of Rabshakeh. (36:22) And it came to pass, when king Hezekiah heard it, that he rent his clothes, and covered himself with sackcloth, and went into the house of the Lord. (37:1) And he sent Eliakim, who was over the household, and Shebna the scribe, and the elders of the priests covered with sackcloth, unto Isaiah the prophet the son of Amoz. (37:2)

And they said unto him, Thus saith Hezekiah, This day is a day of trouble, and of rebuke, and of blasphemy: for the children are come to the birth, and there is not strength to bring forth. (37:3) It may be the Lord thy God will hear the words of Rabshakeh, whom the king of Assyria his master hath sent to reproach the living God, and will reprove the words which the Lord thy God hath heard: wherefore lift up thy prayer for [those found in this city].[1] (37:4)

So the servants of king Hezekiah came to Isaiah. (37:5) And Isaiah said unto them, Thus shall ye say unto your master, Thus saith the Lord, Be not afraid of the words that thou hast heard, wherewith the servants of the king of Assyria have blasphemed me. (37:6) Behold, I will send a [spirit][2] upon him, and he shall hear a rumor, and return to his own land; and I will cause him to fall by the sword in his own land. (37:7)

So Rabshakeh returned, and found the king of Assyria warring against Libnah: for he had heard that he was departed from Lachish. (37:8) And he heard say concerning Tirhakah king of Ethiopia, He is come forth to make war with thee. And when he heard it, he sent messengers to Hezekiah, saying, (37:9)

Thus shall ye speak to Hezekiah king of Judah, saying, Let not thy God, in whom thou trustest, deceive thee, saying, Jerusalem shall not be given into the hand of the king of Assyria. (37:10) Behold, thou hast heard what the kings of Assyria have done to all lands by destroying them utterly; and shalt thou be delivered? (37:11) Have the gods of the nations delivered them which my fathers have destroyed, as Gozan, and Haran, and Rezeph, and the children of Eden which were in Telassar? (37:12) Where is the king of Hamath, and the king of Arphad, and the king of the city of Sepharvaim, Hena, and Ivah? (37:13)

And Hezekiah received the letter from the hand of the messengers, and read it: and Hezekiah went up unto the house of the Lord, and spread it before the Lord. (37:14) And Hezekiah prayed unto the Lord, saying, (37:15)

O Lord of hosts, God of Israel, that dwellest between the cherubims, thou art the God, even thou alone, of all the kingdoms of the earth: thou hast made heaven and earth. (37:16) Incline thine ear, O Lord, and hear; open thine eyes, O Lord, and see: and hear all the words of Sennacherib, which [he][3] hath sent to reproach the living God. (37:17) Of a truth, Lord, the kings of Assyria have laid waste all the nations, and their countries, (37:18)

And have cast their gods into the fire: for they were no gods, but the work of men's hands, wood and stone: therefore they have destroyed them. (37:19) Now therefore, O Lord our God, save us from his hand, that all the kingdoms of the earth may know that thou art the Lord, even thou only. (37:20)

## NOTES AND COMMENTARY

**37:1** *rent his clothes.* Hezekiah rends his clothing and covers himself with sackcloth to express his profound grief (Gen. 37:34; 2 Sam. 3:31) and humility (Ps. 35:13).

---

[1] DSS Isa. Scroll 37; see Watts, *Isaiah 34–66*, 32.
[2] Hebrew *ruach* meaning "breath, wind [or] spirit." Brown, Driver, and Briggs, *Hebrew and English Lexicon*, 924–25.
[3] JST Isa. 37:17.

*house of the Lord.* After humbling himself, Hezekiah goes to the temple to call upon the Lord for assistance.

**37:2** *Isaiah the prophet.* Hezekiah sends his officials to Isaiah, seeking his counsel regarding the Assyrian army.

**37:3** *day of trouble.* Hezekiah faces a time of such trouble that the Lord must intervene if Jerusalem is to survive.

*children are come to the birth, and there is not strength to bring forth.* If a woman in labor lacks strength to bring forth her baby, both mother and child are in danger of death. The day of reckoning has arrived for Hezekiah and his armies, and he realizes they don't have strength in themselves to be victorious over their enemies.

**37:4** *lift up thy prayer.* Hezekiah asks Isaiah to pray for those who remain in Jerusalem.

**37:7** *send a spirit.* The Lord will cause Sennacherib's mind to be filled with confusion and fear, clouding his judgment and causing him to withdraw (19:14; 1 Kgs. 22:21–23).

*hear a rumor.* Sennacherib hears a rumor that causes him to return home.

*I will cause him to fall by the sword.* Sennacherib remains near Nineveh until his sons kill him with the sword, fulfilling Isaiah's prophecy (37:7, 38).

**37:9** *Tirhakah king of Ethiopia.* Because the king of Ethiopia is coming to battle against him, Sennacherib wants to end his standoff with Hezekiah to avoid fighting on two fronts.

**37:11** *kings of Assyria.* Rabshakeh reminds Hezekiah that Assyrian kings and armies conquered all lands, so why should Hezekiah believe that Judah will be saved?

**37:13** *Hamath/Arphad/Sepharvaim/Hena/Ivah.* The kings of these lands received no support from their gods and were removed from their thrones by Assyria's kings.

**37:14–15** *received the letter . . . prayed.* When Hezekiah receives Sennacherib's threatening and blasphemous letter, he takes it to the temple and exercises his faith in prayer.

**37:16** *between the cherubims.* This phrase is a reference to the ark of the covenant (1 Sam. 4:4) and to the Lord's throne, which was situated between the cherubim on top of the ark (Ex. 25:18–22).

*thou art the God.* Hezekiah recognizes that Jehovah is God, the Creator.

**37:17** *Incline thine ear/open thine eyes.* Hezekiah pleads with the living God in prayer.

**37:20** *save us from his hand, that all . . . may know that thou art the Lord.* Hezekiah prays not for his own glory but for God's, so that all the earth's kingdoms might know that the God of Hezekiah and his people is the true God. The Lord answers Hezekiah's prayer.

## ISAIAH'S RESPONSE FROM THE LORD (37:21–38)

In response to Hezekiah's humble prayer in the temple, the Lord sends his prophet Isaiah to the king, promising deliverance from the Assyrians. Isaiah assures Hezekiah that Jerusalem's inhabitants need not fear, for the Lord will not permit the Assyrians to enter the city of Jerusalem (37:34). As for Sennacherib himself, the Assyrian king will return to his own land and there be slain "by the sword" (37:7; compare 37:38).

*Isaiah 37:21–38*

Then Isaiah the son of Amoz sent unto Hezekiah, saying, Thus saith the Lord God of Israel, Whereas thou hast prayed to me against Sennacherib king of Assyria: (37:21)

This is the word which the Lord hath spoken concerning him;
The *virgin,* the *daughter of Zion,*
hath <u>despised</u> thee, and <u>laughed thee to scorn</u>;
the *daughter of Jerusalem* hath <u>shaken her head at thee</u>. (37:22)

*Whom* hast thou <u>reproached</u> and <u>blasphemed</u>?
and against *whom* hast thou <u>exalted thy voice,</u>
and <u>lifted up thine eyes on high</u>?
even against the *Holy One of Israel.* (37:23)

By thy servants hast thou reproached the Lord, and hast said,
By the multitude of my chariots am
I come up to the *height of the mountains,*
to the *sides of Lebanon;*
and I will cut down the tall <u>cedars</u> thereof,
and the choice <u>fir trees</u> thereof:
and I will enter into the *height of his border,*
and the <u>forest</u> of his Carmel. (37:24)

I have digged, and drunk water; and with the sole of my feet have I dried up all the [Nile][4] of [Egypt].[5] (37:25)

Hast thou not heard *long ago,* how <u>I have done it</u>;
and of *ancient times,* that <u>I have formed it</u>?

---

[4] Hebrew *yᵉ'orey* meaning the "stream of the Nile." Brown, Driver, and Briggs, *Hebrew and English Lexicon,* 384.
[5] NIV Isa. 37:25.

now have I brought it to pass, that thou shouldest be to lay waste defenced cities into ruinous heaps. (37:26)

Therefore their inhabitants were of small power, they were dismayed and confounded: they were as the grass of the field, and as the green herb, as the grass on the housetops, and as corn blasted before the [east winds].[6] (37:27)

But I know *thy* [rising up],[7]
and *thy* going out,
and *thy* coming in,
and *thy* rage against me. (37:28)

Because thy *rage* against me,
and thy *tumult,* is come up into mine ears,

therefore will I put *my hook* in thy nose,
and *my bridle* in thy lips,
and I will turn thee back by the way by which thou camest. (37:29)

And this shall be a sign unto thee,
Ye shall eat *this year* such as groweth of itself;
and *the second year* that which springeth of the same:
and in *the third year* sow ye, and reap, and plant vineyards, and eat the fruit thereof. (37:30)

And the remnant that is escaped of the house of Judah shall again
*take* root downward,
and *bear* fruit upward: (37:31)

For *out of Jerusalem* shall go forth a remnant,
and they that escape *out of* [*Jerusalem* shall come up upon][8] mount Zion:
the zeal of the Lord of hosts shall do this. (37:32)

Therefore thus saith the Lord concerning the king of Assyria,
He shall *not come* into this city,
*nor shoot an arrow* there
*nor come* before it with shields,
*nor cast a bank* against it. (37:33)

*By the way* that he came,
*by the same* shall he return,
and shall not come into this city, saith the Lord. (37:34)

For I will defend this city to save it for *mine own* sake, and for *my servant David's* sake. (37:35)

Then the angel of the Lord went forth, and smote in the camp of the Assyrians a hundred and four-score and five thousand: and when they [who were left][9] arose early in the morning, behold, they were all dead corpses. (37:36) So Sennacherib king of Assyria departed, and went and returned, and dwelt at Nineveh. (37:37) And it came to pass, as he was worshiping in the house of Nisroch his god, that

---

[6] DSS Isa. Scroll 37:27 (see also Gen. 41:6, 23, 27); see Watts, *Isaiah 34–66,* 41.
[7] DSS Isa. Scroll 37:28; see Watts, *Isaiah 34–66,* 41.
[8] JST Isa. 37:32. Clarifying the escaped as being from Jerusalem, not Mt. Zion; the escaped then proceed to Mt. Zion.
[9] JST Isa. 37:36.

Adrammelech and Sharezer his sons smote him with the sword; and they escaped into the land of Armenia: and Esar-haddon his son reigned in his stead. (37:38)

## NOTES AND COMMENTARY

**37:22** *virgin . . . daughter of Zion.* These are metaphors for Jerusalem (1:8; 3:16).

*shaken her head at thee.* Jerusalem scorned Assyria.

**37:23** *reproached/blasphemed.* Sennacherib and Assyria were guilty of blasphemy (36:14–15; 37:10–13).

*lifted up thine eyes on high.* Sennacherib, proud and arrogant, thought he was greater than Israel's God (Num. 15:30–31).

*Holy One of Israel.* See commentary on 1:4.

**37:24** *By thy servants.* Sennacherib had blasphemed the Lord through his servants (36:4–10).

*height of the mountains/sides of Lebanon/height of his border/Carmel.* These represent the great and prosperous peoples and lands that Assyria has conquered (2:13; 10:34; 33:9). The cedars, fir trees, and forest also represent the peoples of these lands.

**37:25** *I have digged, and drunk water/I dried up all the Nile of Egypt.* Sennacherib boasts of his power to produce water—or to dry it up, symbolizing his confidence in his ability to conquer Egypt. As one commentator notes, "The king's foot is equal to blocking even the Nile itself!"[10]

**37:26** *long ago.* In this verse, the Lord seems to cease repeating Sennacherib's boasts and, instead, now speaks of and for himself. Sennacherib has no right to boast, the Lord says, because he, the Lord, planned Assyria's rise to power long before this time. It is the Lord who has "brought it [Assyria's supremacy] to pass."

**37:27** *they were as the grass of the field/green herb.* The cities Assyria destroyed were as weak as fragile herbs before the scorching desert wind, or as the grass on the housetops that cannot find root (see also Ps. 37:2; 90:5–6; Isa. 40:6–8).

**37:28** *I know thy . . . going out, and thy coming in.* The Lord knows all the details of Sennacherib's life, from the moment he rises and leaves his house to the time he returns (Deut. 28:6).

**37:29** *hook in thy nose/bridle in thy lips.* Because of Sennacherib's rage against the Lord, the Lord will restrain him with a hook or ring in his nose (as one restrains an ox) or with a bridle in his lips (as one restrains a horse).

---

[10] Motyer, *Prophecy of Isaiah*, 283.

**37:30** *sign.* The Lord, who had directed his speech to Sennacherib in the previous verses, now speaks to Jerusalem's inhabitants. A sign was given to the people of Jerusalem to provide hope and to confirm to subsequent generations that the Lord fulfills his promises. The sign was this: Because of the Assyrian threat, the people could not farm for two years ("this year . . . and the second year"), but they would eat whatever "groweth of itself." In the third and subsequent years, though, the people would be able to plow, plant, and eat the fruit of their labors.

**37:31** *remnant that is escaped.* Those from Judah who fled during the Assyrian wars will return and once again establish themselves (*take root*) and prosper (*bear fruit*).

**37:32** *mount Zion.* This phrase refers to the temple of Jerusalem (see commentary on 8:18; 10:12).

*the zeal of the Lord.* The Lord's power of salvation assures the outcome of the sign given in 37:30 (9:7).

**37:33** *king of Assyria . . . shall not come.* The Lord promises Hezekiah and his people that neither Sennacherib nor his armies will build an embankment to cross Jerusalem's walls or so much as shoot an arrow over them. Rather, the king will return to his homeland by the same route he took to reach Palestine (37:29).

**37:35** *for mine own sake/David's.* The Lord will defend Jerusalem to honor his word (37:20) and to keep the covenant he made with David to establish his kingdom forever (2 Sam. 7:12–16).

**37:36** *angel of the Lord.* The angel of the Lord destroys 185,000 Assyrian soldiers, and Sennacherib, abandoning his intent to destroy Jerusalem, returns to Nineveh. These events fulfill prophecies uttered by Isaiah (14:25; 30:31; 31:8).

**37:38** *as he was worshiping.* As Sennacherib worships his god Nisroch in his temple in Nineveh, he is murdered by two of his sons, Adrammelech and Sharezer. His god failed to protect him—an ironic contrast to Hezekiah's prayer at the temple (37:15–20) and subsequent deliverance from his enemies (not to mention the irony of Sennacherib's message to Hezekiah in Isaiah 36:14–20 not to rely on the Lord because the Lord would not save him).

*Esar-haddon.* Esarhaddon, Sennacherib's youngest son, inherits his father's throne in 681 B.C.

# ISAIAH 38

## LIKENING ISAIAH 38 UNTO OURSELVES

*Hezekiah sets a righteous example for us in the latter days. Sick nigh unto death, he "prayed unto the Lord" (38:2); after he is healed, he writes a psalm praising and giving thanks to the Lord for the blessings of healing and deliverance from sin (38:17). Like Hezekiah, we should praise God in prayer after we are healed from sickness and disease, both spiritual and physical; and we, like this great king, should teach our children of God's truth (38:19).*

## THE SICKNESS OF KING HEZEKIAH (38:1–8)

This section contains a fulfillment of yet another prophecy given by Isaiah that occurs during the time of the Assyrian threat in Palestine. Hezekiah, who is sick and near to death during Sennacherib's campaign, is promised fifteen more years of life (38:5) because of his faith and for the sake of the covenant that the Lord made with David.

*Isaiah 38:1–8*

In those days was Hezekiah sick unto death. And Isaiah the prophet the son of Amoz came unto him, and said unto him, Thus saith the Lord, Set thine house in order: for thou shalt die, and not live. (38:1)

Then Hezekiah turned his face toward the wall, and prayed unto the Lord, (38:2) And said, Remember now, O Lord, I beseech thee, how I have walked before thee in truth and with a perfect heart, and have done that which is good in thy sight. And Hezekiah wept sore. (38:3)

Then[1] came the word of the Lord to Isaiah, saying, (38:4) Go, and say to Hezekiah, Thus saith the Lord, the God of David thy father, I have heard thy prayer, I have seen thy tears: behold,[2] I will add unto thy days fifteen years. (38:5) And I will deliver thee and this city out of the hand of the king of Assyria: and I will defend this city.[3] (38:6) And this shall be a sign unto thee from the Lord, that the Lord will do this thing that he hath spoken; (38:7) Behold I will bring again the shadow of the degrees, which is gone down in the sun dial of Ahaz, ten degrees backward. So the sun returned ten degrees, by which degrees it was gone down. (38:8)

## NOTES AND COMMENTARY

**38:1** *In those days.* During the Assyrian siege.

*sick unto death.* Hezekiah's life-threatening illness apparently included boils (38:21). Although they are not fatal by themselves, they may be symptoms of a greater ailment.

*Set thine house in order.* Isaiah counsels Hezekiah to arrange for the royal succession, for his death seemed imminent. This issue is of significant concern for Hezekiah, because at this time he has no male heir to whom he could pass the kingship.

**38:2** *turned his face toward the wall, and prayed.* Hezekiah's illness made him ritually unclean, preventing him from entering the temple, so he turned his face toward the temple wall to pray. Before his illness, Hezekiah prayed in the temple (37:14–15).

**38:3** *I have walked before thee.* Hezekiah reaffirms that he has been faithful to the Lord.

**38:5** *David thy father.* The reference to King David reassures Hezekiah that the royal line will continue (37:35).

*heard thy prayer.* The Lord answers Hezekiah's prayer by extending his life fifteen years, leaving him sufficient time to prepare a son for kingship. Manasseh was born approximately two years after these events and ascended the throne at age twelve or thirteen when Hezekiah died.

**38:7** *a sign.* The Lord's sign to Hezekiah, assuring him that his life will be extended, contradicts the ordinary course of nature. The Lord causes the sun's

---

[1] 2 Kgs. 20:4 includes a longer text here: *afore Isaiah was gone out into the middle court.* The phrase implies an immediate response to Hezekiah's prayer.

[2] 2 Kgs. 20:5 includes the following: *I will heal thee: on the third day thou shalt go up unto the house of the Lord.*

[3] 2 Kgs. 20:6 and DSS Isa. Scroll add *for mine own sake and for my servant David's sake* (cf. 37:35).

shadow to move "ten degrees backward" (38:8), indicating that time had been added to the day (Hel. 12:14). This was a sign for Hezekiah, who has time added to his life.

## KING HEZEKIAH'S PSALM (38:9–22)

After Hezekiah, who is sick and near unto death (38:1–8), learns that the Lord will postpone his death, he writes a psalm portraying his humility, meekness, and reliance upon the Lord (38:9–20).

*Isaiah 38:9–22*

> The writing of Hezekiah king of Judah, when he had been sick, and was recovered of his sickness: (38:9) I said in the [midst][4] of my days, I shall go to the gates of the grave: I am deprived of the residue of my years. (38:10)
>
> I said, I shall *not see* the Lord, even the Lord, in the <u>land of the living</u>: I shall *behold* man *no more* with the <u>inhabitants of the world</u>. (38:11)
>
> *Mine age* is departed, and is <u>removed</u> from me as a shepherd's tent: I have <u>cut off</u> like a weaver *my life:* he will <u>cut</u> *me* <u>off</u> with pining sickness:
>
> from *day even to night* wilt thou <u>make an end of me</u>. (38:12) I reckoned till *morning,* that, as a lion, so will he <u>break all my bones</u>: from *day even to night* wilt thou <u>make an end of me</u>. (38:13)
>
> *Like a crane or a swallow,* so did I <u>chatter</u>: <u>I did mourn</u> *as a dove:*
>
> mine eyes fail with looking upward: O Lord, I am oppressed; undertake for me. (38:14)
>
> What shall I say? he hath both spoken unto me, and himself hath [healed me]. I shall go softly all my years, [that I may not walk][5] in the bitterness of my soul. (38:15) [Oh] Lord, [thou who art the life of my spirit, in whom I live]; so wilt thou recover me, and make me to live; [and in all these things I will praise thee].[6] (38:16) Behold, [I had great bitterness instead of peace,] but thou hast in love to my soul [saved me][7] from the pit of corruption, for thou hast cast all my sins behind thy back. (38:17)
>
> For the *grave* cannot <u>praise thee,</u> *death* cannot <u>celebrate thee</u>: they that go down into *the pit* cannot <u>hope for thy truth</u>. (38:18)
>
> The *living, the living,* he shall <u>praise thee,</u> as I do this day: the *father to the children* shall <u>make known thy truth</u>. (38:19)

---

[4] Brown, Driver, and Briggs, *Hebrew and English Lexicon,* 198.
[5] Bracketed changes are from JST Isa. 38:15.
[6] Bracketed changes are from JST Isa. 38:16.
[7] Bracketed changes are from JST Isa. 38:17.

The Lord was ready to save me: therefore we will sing my songs to the stringed instruments all the days of our life in the house of the Lord. (38:20) For Isaiah had said, Let them take a lump of figs, and lay it for a plaister upon the boil, and he shall recover. (38:21) Hezekiah also had said, What is the sign that I shall go up to the house of the Lord? (38:22)

NOTES AND COMMENTARY

**38:9** *The writing of Hezekiah.* After Hezekiah recovers from his illness, he records his feelings and appreciation for the Lord.

**38:10** *midst of my days . . . gates of the grave.* Even though Hezekiah is in the middle of his life, he stands at the threshold of death, about to enter the grave.

**38:11** *I shall not see the Lord/I shall behold man no more.* Hezekiah mourns lost opportunities for worship and association with other people because his life is about to end.

**38:12** *Mine age.* Hezekiah's future, his time of old age, is taken from him.

*as a shepherd's tent/like a weaver.* Hezekiah's life ends as easily as a shepherd dismantles his tent or as quickly as a weaver cuts and gathers the finished fabric from the loom.

*day even to night.* In a single day, Hezekiah's anticipation of a long life changes to an anticipation of death.

**38:13** *lion . . . break all my bones.* Hezekiah anticipates complete destruction, such as that carried out by a beast that overcomes and devours its prey (Jer. 50:17).

**38:14** *Like a crane or a swallow/dove.* Hezekiah's pleadings with the Lord are at times loud, as a crane's cry, at other times as soft as a swallow's chirp, and on occasion mournful, as a dove's cooing.

*mine eyes fail.* Hezekiah pleads so long that his eyes become weak from looking heavenward, symbolizing his great efforts in petitioning the Lord for his life.

*I am oppressed.* Hezekiah, feeling the pressure a debtor feels from a creditor (Matt. 18:28–30), asks the Lord to take the responsibility for the debt ("undertake for me"), that is, to free him from immediate death.

**38:15** *What shall I say?* The climax of the psalm is the point at which Hezekiah learns that his life has been extended: He is more or less speechless (*What shall I say?*).

*go softly.* Hezekiah commits himself to walk humbly (softly) in the Lord's paths.

**38:16** *life of my spirit.* Hezekiah testifies that the Lord is the sustaining force of life (cf. D&C 10:70; 50:27; 88:11–13).

**38:17** *bitterness instead of peace.* Hezekiah had felt anguish of soul at the prospect of death, but with his healing, he now feels clean and wholly at peace.

*pit of corruption.* Hell.

*cast all my sins behind thy back.* Being healed by the Lord is often associated with being forgiven of sins (Matt. 9:6; James 5:15).

**38:18** *grave cannot praise thee.* The opportunity of praising and celebrating the Lord's name in his presence is not given to those who are consigned to the pit (hell); they have no hope of basking in the truth and light of the Lord (D&C 76:81–87; 121:19–24).

**38:19** *the living.* The living, those who are spiritually alive and have avoided the fate of those consigned to the pit (38:18), praise the Lord.

*father to the children.* It is the obligation of parents to teach their children God's truths (D&C 68:25).

**38:20** *we will sing . . . all the days of our life.* Hezekiah determines to sing praises to the Lord in the temple all the days of his life.

**38:21** *lump of figs . . . boil.* Isaiah tells Hezekiah to apply to his boils a paste made of figs. Hezekiah obeys, and "he recovered" (2 Kgs. 20:7).

**38:22** *go up to the house of the Lord.* After an illness that had kept one from entering the temple was cured, it was customary to wash and go before the priests to be pronounced clean.

# ISAIAH 39

*LIKENING ISAIAH 39 UNTO OURSELVES*

*Isaiah deals personally with at least two of the kings of Judah: Ahaz and Hezekiah. In chapter 39, Isaiah converses briefly with King Hezekiah and utters a prophecy upon his head. The king responds, "Good is the word of the Lord which thou hast spoken." Certainly our lives would be greatly blessed if the leaders of the nations of the world consulted often with the living prophet, and then, after receiving direction, responded with "Good is the word of the Lord."*

## ISAIAH'S PROPHECY OF BABYLONIAN CAPTIVITY (39:1–8)

Prince Merodach-baladan, the son of the king of Babylon, visits Jerusalem. He views the temple treasury and the armory and sees other precious things belonging to the kingdom of Judah. Isaiah uses this occasion to prophesy to Hezekiah, king of Judah, that the time will come when the Babylonians will conquer Judah and carry off the very things that Merodach-baladan has seen—"nothing shall be left, saith the Lord" (39:6). More important, the Babylonians will carry off Hezekiah's sons and make them eunuchs in the king's palace at Babylon. Hence, Hezekiah's political activities (39:2–4) appear to have initiated a chain of events that combine with the wickedness of the people of Judah to lead to Jerusalem's destruction and to the captivity of Judah (39:5–7).

*Isaiah 39:1–8*

> At that time Merodach-baladan, the son of Baladan, king of Babylon, sent letters and a present to Hezekiah: for he had heard that he had been sick, and was recovered. (39:1) And Hezekiah was glad of them, and [showed] them the house of his precious things, the silver, and the gold, and the spices, and the precious ointment,

and all the house of his [armor], and all that was found in his treasures: there was nothing in his house, nor in all his dominion, that Hezekiah [showed][1] them not. (39:2)

Then came Isaiah the prophet unto king Hezekiah, and said unto him, What said these men? and from whence came they unto thee? And Hezekiah said, They are come from a far country unto me, even from Babylon. (39:3) Then said he, What have they seen in thine house? And Hezekiah answered, All that is in mine house have they seen: there is nothing among my treasures that I have not [showed][2] them. (39:4)

Then said Isaiah to Hezekiah, Hear the word of the Lord of hosts: (39:5) Behold, the days come, that all that is in thine house, and that which thy fathers have laid up in store until this day, shall be carried to Babylon: nothing shall be left, saith the Lord. (39:6) And of thy sons that shall issue from thee, which thou shalt beget, shall they take away; and they shall be eunuchs in the palace of the king of Babylon. (39:7) Then said Hezekiah to Isaiah, Good is the word of the Lord which thou hast spoken. He said moreover, For there shall be peace and truth in my days. (39:8)

## NOTES AND COMMENTARY

**39:1** *At that time.* The events in this section occur after Hezekiah recovers from his illness (Isa. 38).

*Merodach-baladan. Merodach-baladan* conquered Babylon in 703 B.C. In an effort to solicit Hezekiah's support against Assyria, he sent letters, a gift, and then a delegation to Hezekiah, using Hezekiah's recovery as an excuse for a visit.

**39:2** *Hezekiah was glad.* Hezekiah is happy to receive the envoys of such a strong, potential ally as the Babylonians.

*precious things.* Hezekiah proudly shows off his wealth and armaments to impress the Babylonian delegates.

**39:3** *What said these men?* Hezekiah answers Isaiah's questions, perhaps knowing that Isaiah came as a prophet to deliver a message of judgment.

**39:6** *carried to Babylon.* Judah's accumulated wealth and Hezekiah's posterity, Jehoiakim and his family, were carried away to Babylon in 598 B.C. by Nebuchadnezzar.

**39:7** *eunuchs.* Eunuchs were emasculated men who served in the courts of kings as officials and as guardians of the harem. Hezekiah's descendants, specifically Jehoiakim's family and other Judean princes, were forced to serve in the courts of the kings of Babylon (Dan. 1:1–6).

---

[1] Bracketed changes are from JST Isa. 39:2.
[2] We have replaced the archaic KJV *shewed.*

**39:8** *Good is the word of the Lord.* Hezekiah humbly accepts the message as a righteous judgment from the Lord. Though the message promises ill fortune for his descendants, he values the implication of peace during his reign.

# ISAIAH 40

*LIKENING ISAIAH 40 UNTO OURSELVES*

*Many of us apply the words "prepare ye the way of the Lord, make straight in the desert a highway for our God" exclusively to John the Baptist. Yet, a revelation to Joseph Smith reveals that these words apply to all of us as full-time or member missionaries of the Church. The revelation reads, in part, "Yea, open your mouths and they shall be filled, saying: Repent, repent, and prepare ye the way of the Lord, and make his paths straight" (D&C 33:10). After the word has gone forth, the Lord will come "with a strong hand" (40:10). Those who are righteous will receive him, and "he shall gather the lambs with his arm, and carry them in his bosom" (40:11).*

---

## THE LORD'S MESSAGE OF COMFORT TO JERUSALEM (40:1–8)

On the heels of a message of national disaster (39:5–7) come words of comfort and forgiveness to Jerusalem's inhabitants. Although the national disaster took place centuries before Jesus' birth and ministry, the prophecy of comfort to Jerusalem will not find fulfillment until the last days and the second coming of Christ. At that time the iniquity of Jerusalem will be pardoned, and "the glory of the Lord shall be revealed" (40:5).

This section contains a commandment for all of us as members of the Church: "Prepare ye the way of the Lord, make straight in the desert a highway for our God" (40:3).

*Isaiah 40:1–8*

Comfort ye, comfort ye my people, saith your God. (40:1)
*Speak* ye comfortably to <u>Jerusalem</u>,
and *cry* unto <u>her</u>,

that her *warfare* is <u>accomplished</u>,
that her *iniquity* is <u>pardoned</u>:
for she hath received of the Lord's hand double for all her sins. (40:2)

The voice of him that crieth in the wilderness,
*Prepare* ye the <u>way</u> <u>of the Lord</u>,
*make straight* in the desert a <u>highway</u> <u>for our God</u>. (40:3)

Every *valley* shall be <u>exalted</u>,
and every *mountain* and *hill* shall be made <u>low</u>:
and the *crooked* shall be made <u>straight</u>,
and the *rough* places <u>plain</u>: (40:4)

And the *glory of the Lord* shall be <u>revealed</u>,
and all flesh shall <u>see</u> *it* together:
for the mouth of the Lord hath spoken it. (40:5)

The voice said, Cry. And he said, What shall I cry?
All *flesh* is <u>grass</u>,
and all the *goodliness thereof* is as the <u>flower of the field</u>: (40:6)

The *grass* <u>withereth</u>,
the *flower* <u>fadeth</u>:
because the spirit of the Lord bloweth upon it:
surely the people is grass. (40:7)

The *grass* <u>withereth</u>,
the *flower* <u>fadeth</u>:
but the word of our God shall stand for ever. (40:8)

## NOTES AND COMMENTARY

**40:1** *comfort ye my people.* These opening words are meant to comfort the people of Jerusalem. (Of course, in a broader sense, *my people* refers to all of the Lord's covenant people.) *Comfort ye* is repeated for emphasis, because Jerusalem's warfare will soon be over. Elder Orson Hyde was told by the Spirit, "Go ye forth . . . and declare these words unto Judah, and say, . . . 'assemble yourselves, and let us go into the defensed cities. . . . Speak ye comfortably to Jerusalem, and cry unto her, that her warfare is accomplished—that her iniquity is pardoned, for she hath received of the Lord's hand doubly for all her sins.'"[1]

**40:2** *Jerusalem.* This word refers both to the city as well as its inhabitants, that is, the Jews (and, again, in a broader sense, all the covenant people of the Lord).

*warfare is accomplished/iniquity is pardoned. Warfare* (Hebrew *ts$^e$ba'ah*) should be translated as "hard service."[2] This possibly refers to the hardships, persecution, and burdens that the Jewish nation had to endure as a result of their sins against God.

---

[1] *History of the Church,* 4:376.

[2] Brown, Driver, and Briggs, *Hebrew and English Lexicon,* 839.

This term of service will be completed near the time in which "the voice . . . crieth in the wilderness," when "every valley shall be exalted," and "the glory of the Lord shall be revealed" (40:3–5).

*double for all her sins.* The word *double* recalls the law of Moses, which required double payment as restitution for theft (Ex. 22:4, 7) or breach of trust (Ex. 22:9). It indicates that the full measure of debt has been paid for the nation's sins (Jer. 16:18).

**40:3** *voice . . . crieth in the wilderness.* This passage has several fulfillments:

John the Baptist, during his mortal ministry (JST John 1:6–24; Mark 1:1–8; Luke 1:76–79) and also his appearance to Joseph Smith to restore the keys of the Aaronic Priesthood, thus commencing the preparation for the Lord's coming (D&C 13).

Joseph Smith, who "laid the foundation for the kingdom of God . . . that the world might be prepared for the coming of the Lord."[3]

Priesthood leaders and missionaries, who are told to cry repentance and "prepare ye the way of the Lord, and make his paths straight" (D&C 33:10).

Angelic messengers, who helped restore the gospel (D&C 128:20) to prepare a righteous people for the Lord's coming.

The Lord's Spirit, which "is as the voice of one crying in the wilderness—in the wilderness, because you cannot see him" (D&C 88:66).

*Prepare ye the way of the Lord.* This statement is a commission to prepare for the coming of the Lord by crying repentance and gathering a people sufficiently prepared by covenant and ordinance to receive him (Mal. 3:1; JST Luke 3:4–10; D&C 84:28).

*make straight in the desert a highway for our God.* This phrase means "prepare the way of the Lord," or prepare for the Second Coming by making the Saints' path back to God's presence level or smooth (that is, remove all obstacles out of the way so that others can be obedient to the laws and ordinances of the gospel).[4] The modern equivalent to Isaiah's phrase *make straight in the desert a highway for our God* is "make his paths straight" (D&C 33:10; 65:1; 45:2). The desert symbolizes the world of sin. The *highway* here is "the way of holiness" (19:19–25; 35:8).

**40:4** *valley . . . exalted/mountain . . . made low.* This passage may refer to the great earthquake that will accompany the Lord's return (Rev. 16:18–20). Symbolically, it suggests that the humble will be exalted and the proud brought low (see also D&C 49:23; 109:74; 133:22).

---

[3] Smith, *Doctrines of Salvation,* 1:195.
[4] Brown, Driver, and Briggs, *Hebrew and English Lexicon,* 448–49.

*crooked shall be made straight, and the rough places plain.* These statements are similar in meaning to "make straight in the desert a highway" (40:3). *Crooked* also means "deceitful" or "sly," so the phrase could read, the "deceitful shall be made upright."

**40:5** *the glory of the Lord . . . revealed.* This passage refers to the coming of the Lord in his glory (see commentary on 24:23).

*all flesh shall see it together.* When the Lord comes in his glory, all the world will see him (D&C 88:95–98; 101:23).

**40:6** *The voice said, Cry.* The voice of the Lord, his Spirit, or perhaps an angel commands Isaiah to cry, to which he asks, "What shall I cry?" Isaiah is commanded to cry out, "All flesh is grass, . . . surely the people is grass."

*All flesh is grass.* Grass and flowers swiftly dry up and wither away when the hot desert winds blow on them. The Spirit of the Lord blows, in the form of judgments, upon men and causes them to wither away and die like grass (Ps. 102:11). The glory of man is temporary, like that of the flower (James 1:10; 1 Pet. 1:24; D&C 124:7).

**40:8** *word of our God shall stand for ever.* In contrast to mankind's transitory nature, the word of God—his judgments and decrees—stands forever.

## The Lord Comes like a Shepherd (40:9–11)

Isaiah calls out to Zion and Jerusalem to prepare for the coming of their Lord in strength and judgment to rule on the earth and reward her inhabitants according to their works. He will be a shepherd who will care for, protect, and lead his followers.

*Isaiah 40:9–11*

> O *Zion,* that bringest good tidings, get thee up into the high mountain;
> O *Jerusalem,* that bringest good tidings, lift up thy voice with strength;
>
> *lift it up, be not afraid;*
> *say unto the cities of Judah,* Behold your God! (40:9)
>
> Behold, *the Lord God* will come with strong hand,
> and his arm shall rule for *him:*
>
> behold, his *reward* is with him,
> and his *work* before him. (40:10)
>
> He shall *feed* his flock like a shepherd:
> he shall *gather* the lambs with his arm,
>
> and *carry* them in his bosom,
> and shall gently *lead* those that are with young.[5] (40:11)

---

[5] Those "giving suck." Brown, Driver, and Briggs, *Hebrew and English Lexicon,* 732.

NOTES AND COMMENTARY

**40:9** *Zion . . . get thee up into the high mountain.* Before Zion's people take the gospel (*good tidings*) to the world, they are commanded to go up to the high mountain, or God's temple. Isaiah's words apply to us: We are "sent forth . . . to teach the children of men the things which I have put into your hands by the power of my Spirit; and ye are to be taught from on high. Sanctify yourselves and ye shall be endowed with power" (D&C 43:15–16; 110:9).

*good tidings.* This is the restored gospel, which is to be preached to the entire world.

*Jerusalem . . . lift up thy voice.* The Lord will come in glory to Jerusalem to reign on the earth (24:23). The good news of the Lord's reign will then go forth from Jerusalem to the cities of Judah, or to all of the lands where the children of Judah dwell, to call them to come and "Behold your God!" In a broader sense, Jerusalem stands as a symbol for the covenant people of God.

**40:10** *God will come with strong hand/arm. Hand* and *arm* represent power. The same arm that has been stretched out in judgment now establishes the Lord's reign.

*his reward is with him.* Judgment accompanies Jesus at his coming, whereby everyone will be rewarded for his works (Rev. 22:12).

**40:11** *flock/lambs.* This is a metaphor for the followers of Christ.

*like a shepherd.* Christ is the shepherd who protects, feeds, and provides water for his flock (Ps. 23; 28:9; Jer. 23:3); he gathers the lambs and carries them "in his bosom," or the fold of the shepherd's robe, a symbol of intimate, loving care.

# WHO IS LIKE UNTO THE LORD? (40:12–25)

Isaiah contrasts the greatness of the Lord with the nothingness of mankind. The Lord has power to create the heavens (40:12), possesses all knowledge, wisdom, and understanding, and no man can instruct him (40:14); he is greater than all his creations and has no equal (40:20). When contrasted with God, the nations of the earth are as insignificant as a single drop of water in a bucket, a few particles of dust (40:15–17), or small grasshoppers. Even the great princes and judges of the earth are nothing (40:23) compared to God, who has power to add to his creations as easily as a person opens the curtains in his home (40:22). Isaiah uses ten rhetorical questions as a teaching tool in this section; five of them begin with the words *who* or *whom.*

## Isaiah 40:12–25

Who hath *measured the waters* [of the sea]⁶ in the hollow of his hand,
and *meted out heaven* with the span,
and *comprehended the dust* of the earth in a measure,
and *weighed the mountains* in scales,
and *the hills* in a balance? (40:12)

Who hath *directed* the Spirit of the Lord,
or being his counselor hath *taught* him? (40:13)

*With whom* took he counsel,
*and who* instructed him,

and *taught* him in the path of judgment,
and *taught* him knowledge,
and [*showed*]⁷ to him the way of understanding? (40:14)

Behold, the *nations* are as a drop of a bucket,
and are counted as the small dust of the balance:
behold, he taketh up the *isles* as a very little thing. (40:15)

And *Lebanon* is not sufficient to burn,
nor *the beasts thereof* sufficient for a burnt offering. (40:16)

All *nations* before him are as nothing;
and *they* are counted to him less than nothing, and vanity. (40:17)

To whom then will ye *liken* God?
or what *likeness* will ye *compare unto* him? (40:18)

The *workman* melteth a graven image,
and the *goldsmith* spreadeth it over with gold, and casteth silver chains. (40:19)

He that is so impoverished that he hath no oblation *chooseth a tree* that will not
rot;
he seeketh unto him a cunning workman to prepare a *graven image,* that shall not
be moved. (40:20)

Have *ye* not known?
have *ye* not heard?
hath it not been told *you* from the beginning?
have *ye* not understood from the foundations of the earth? (40:21)

It is he that sitteth upon the circle of the earth,
and the inhabitants thereof are as grasshoppers;

that *stretcheth out* the heavens as a curtain,
and *spreadeth* them out as a tent to dwell in: (40:22)

That *bringeth* the princes to nothing;
he *maketh* the judges of the earth as vanity. (40:23)

Yea, *they* shall not be planted;
yea, *they* shall not be sown:
yea, *their* stock shall not take root in the earth:

---

⁶DSS Isa. Scroll 40:12.
⁷We have replaced the archaic KJV *shewed.*

and he shall also *blow upon them,* and they shall <u>wither</u>,
and the *whirlwind* shall take them away as <u>stubble</u>. (40:24)

To whom then will ye *liken* me, or shall I *be equal?* saith the Holy One. (40:25)

## NOTES AND COMMENTARY

**40:12** *measured the waters . . . in the hollow of his hand.* God created Earth's great oceans as easily as a man cups his hand and fills it with water. He created "heaven with the span" as easily as a man measures a household object with a ruler. All of creation, formed by him with exactness (*measured*), is held *in the hollow of his hand,* meaning he is aware of and protective of all.

*comprehended the dust of the earth in a measure.* This phrase emphasizes that the Lord knows everything from the largest of his creations to the smallest (Mosiah 4:9).

**40:13** *Who hath directed the Spirit of the Lord.* No one is able to teach or counsel God, who controls and comprehends all things (see commentary on 55:9; Rom. 11:33–34; Alma 26:35).

**40:14** *taught . . . judgment/knowledge/understanding.* No one needed to instruct the Lord in matters of judgment, knowledge, or discernment (11:2–5).

**40:15** *nations are as a drop of a bucket.* The great nations of the world are insignificant when compared to the vast and marvelous creations of the Lord and his immense power and knowledge (Hel. 12:7–8). To Joseph Smith the Lord said, "Have I not made the earth? Do I not hold the destinies of all the armies of the nations of the earth?" (D&C 117:6).

**40:16** *Lebanon is not sufficient to burn.* Lebanon, known for its immense forests (2:13; 60:13), could not provide enough wood or animals to support a sacrifice worthy of God.

**40:17** *nations before him are as nothing.* Though the nations of the earth consider themselves to be world powers, they are nothing compared to the Lord.

**40:18** *To whom then will ye liken God?* Since God is much more powerful than man can comprehend, how can he try to create a likeness of him or worship anyone or anything else?

**40:19** *workman melteth a graven image.* Though God is too magnificent for any to understand fully, many foolishly seek to make representations of him by fashioning images and idols overlaid and decorated with precious metal (44:10–17).

**40:20** *impoverished . . . chooseth a tree that will not rot.* Those who could not afford ostentatious displays of worship sought cheaper methods (wood) by which to display their gods for worship. They carefully selected wood that would not rot, for a rotting or decaying god would have seemed powerless to help itself or its worshipers.

*graven image, that shall not be moved.* Once an idol was created, it was nailed or anchored to keep it from tipping over (41:7). Ironically, the anchoring of the idol emphasizes its powerlessness (Judg. 6:25–31). The Lord, however, could never be restrained.

**40:21** *Have ye not known?* The four rhetorical questions of this verse indicate that humanity has been taught the truth about God from the beginning of the world, but because of wickedness, they have not heard it (6:9–10).

**40:22** *sitteth upon the circle of the earth.* This statement emphasizes the magnitude of the Lord (40:12–15), whose greatness is such that the earth is as a footstool to him (66:1).

*inhabitants . . . as grasshoppers.* The people of the earth are great in number and have devastated the land, yet compared to God, they are small and insignificant.

*stretcheth out the heavens as a curtain/tent.* The Lord created the heavens as easily as we open or close the curtains in our home.

**40:23** *judges of the earth as vanity.* The earth's powerful and wise inhabitants are weak fools compared to God, the Omnipotent (Job 12:21).

**40:24** *they shall not be planted.* The powerful people of the earth, here likened to plants, will not have a place or thrive in the Lord's kingdom because of their rebellion and wickedness (40:6–8). They will be destroyed as quickly as a whirlwind carries away the stumps of grain (stubble) that are left after the harvest.

**40:25** *To whom . . . shall I be equal.* This statement is a reminder that man-made things are powerless and only God can accomplish these events.

## THE LORD SUSTAINS HIS PEOPLE WITH HIS POWER (40:26–31)

The Lord is the Creator of all that the eye can see and the orchestrator of every movement in the heavens. Nothing slips by him unseen, and nothing that his Spirit sustains ever fails; therefore, Isaiah promises that those who trust and rely on him will be replenished by his sustaining strength.

*Isaiah 40:26–31*

> Lift up your eyes on high, and behold *who hath created* these things,
> *that bringeth* out their host by number:
> *he calleth* them all by names by the greatness of his might,

for that he is strong in power; not one faileth. (40:26)

Why *sayest* thou, O <u>Jacob</u>,
and *speakest*, O <u>Israel</u>,

*My way* is <u>hid</u> <u>from the Lord</u>,
and *my judgment* is <u>passed over</u> <u>from my God</u>? (40:27)

Hast *thou* not <u>known</u>?
hast *thou* not <u>heard</u>,

that the *everlasting God*,
the *Lord*, the *Creator* of the ends of the earth,
<u>fainteth not</u>, <u>neither is weary</u>?
there is no searching of his understanding. (40:28)

He *giveth power* to the <u>faint</u>;
and to them that have <u>no might</u> he *increaseth strength*. (40:29)

Even the *youths* shall faint and be <u>weary</u>,
and the *young men* shall <u>utterly fall</u>: (40:30)

But they that wait upon the Lord shall renew their strength;
they shall mount up with wings as eagles;

they shall *run*, and not be <u>weary</u>;
and they shall *walk*, and not <u>faint</u>. (40:31)

## NOTES AND COMMENTARY

**40:26** *Lift up your eyes on high.* Isaiah summons the Lord's people to look at the heavens as an example of the Lord's might. He who created all the stars and heavenly bodies directs all of their movements and knows each by name (Ps. 147:4); not one ceases to act according to God's direction ("not one faileth").

**40:27** *Jacob/Israel.* The recipient of this revelation is identified. *Jacob* and *Israel* are symbolic names for the Lord's people in any age, from the days of Jacob to the present.

*My way is hid from the Lord.* Some of us may have an incorrect belief that the Lord is not aware of all our actions or that he will disregard unforgiven sin in the Day of Judgment.

**40:28** *Hast thou not known?* The prophets have taught of God and his ways since the beginning (40:21).

*the Creator . . . fainteth not.* The Lord does not tire or sleep.

*no searching of his understanding.* So great is the Lord's wisdom that it is impossible for mankind to comprehend his knowledge (Rom. 11:33).

**40:29** *He giveth power to the faint.* God has given all of us the breath of life, and he "is preserving [us] from day to day, by lending [us] breath, . . . and even supporting [us] from one moment to another" (Mosiah 2:21). Without his power we would be nothing; we would not exist. Even the "youths" and "young men," those who are in the prime of life, "shall utterly fall" without God's power upholding them (40:30).

**40:31** *they that wait upon the Lord.* Those who seek righteousness will be upheld by God's power (D&C 24:12).

*run, and not be weary.* Those who *wait upon the Lord* will receive the spiritual blessing of magnification. This promise certainly pertains to the physical body (D&C 89:20), and it also anticipates the immortal body.

# ISAIAH 41

*LIKENING ISAIAH 41 UNTO OURSELVES*

*Isaiah addresses a number of issues that concern us as members of The Church of Jesus Christ of Latter-day Saints. We need to be reminded often that we are the Lord's "chosen" people so that we will order our lives accordingly. We need to know, at a young age, that God will direct each one of us through life; he will hold our right hand and assure each of us, "Fear not; I will help thee" (41:13). And if we are ever thirsty, physically or spiritually, our small, empty cups will never suffice, for God desires to give us a great river full of water to fill our needs.*

## ISRAEL IS THE LORD'S SERVANT (41:1–20)

Isaiah's prophetic promises to Israel are wonderful, and they have application to us, of whom the Lord has said, "ye are the children of Israel" (D&C 103:17). Isaiah tells us that, as part of Israel,

We are God's servants (41:8–9);

We are his chosen people (41:8–9);

God has called us from the chief men of the earth (41:9);

We are to fear not, for God will strengthen, help, and uphold us (41:10);

Those who are against us will be ashamed and confounded and will perish (41:11);

They who war against us will be "as nothing, and as a thing of nought" (41:12);

While holding our right hand, God will say, "Fear not; I will help thee" (41:13);

God will mold us into powerful, unique instruments, enabling us to perform our work (41:15–16);

When our poor and needy (speaking of all of us) seek water, God will provide more than enough for us. He says, "I will open rivers . . . and fountains . . . and . . . springs of water" (41:18). Such are the great promises unto us, who are of the house of Israel.

*Isaiah 41:1–20*

Keep silence before me, O islands;
and let the people renew their strength:
let them come near; then let them speak:
let us come near together to judgment. (41:1)

Who *raised* up the righteous <u>man</u> from the east,
*called* <u>him</u> to his foot,
*gave the nations* before <u>him,</u>
and *made* <u>him</u> *rule* over kings?

he gave them as the *dust* to his <u>sword,</u>
and as *driven stubble* to his <u>bow.</u> (41:2)

He pursued them, and passed safely;
even by the way that he had not gone with his feet. (41:3)

Who hath wrought and done it, calling the generations from the beginning?

*I the Lord,* the <u>first,</u>
and with the <u>last</u>; *I am he.* (41:4)

The *isles* saw it, and <u>feared</u>;
the *ends of the earth* were <u>afraid,</u>

*drew near,*
and *came.* (41:5)

They *helped* <u>every one his neighbor</u>;
and <u>every one said to his brother,</u> *Be of good courage.* (41:6)

So the *carpenter* encouraged the <u>goldsmith,</u>
and *he that smootheth* with the hammer <u>him that smote the anvil,</u> saying,

It is ready for the sodering:
and he fastened it with nails, that it should not be moved. (41:7)

But thou, *Israel,* art my <u>servant,</u>
*Jacob* whom I have <u>chosen,</u>
the *seed of Abraham* my <u>friend.</u> (41:8)

Thou whom I have *taken* from the <u>ends of the earth,</u>
and *called* thee from the <u>chief men thereof,</u>

and said unto thee,
Thou art my servant;
I have chosen thee,
and not cast thee away. (41:9)

*Fear thou not;* for <u>I am with thee</u>:
*be not dismayed;* for <u>I am thy God</u>:

*I will* strengthen thee;
yea, *I will* help thee;
yea, *I will* uphold thee with the right hand of my righteousness. (41:10)

Behold, all *they* that were incensed against thee shall be ashamed and confounded:
*they* shall be as nothing;
and *they* that strive with thee shall perish. (41:11)

*Thou shalt* seek them,
*and shalt not* find them,

even *them* that contended with thee:
*they* that war against thee

shall be as nothing,
and as a thing of nought. (41:12)

For I the Lord thy God will hold thy right hand, saying unto thee,

*Fear not;* I will help thee. (41:13)
*Fear not,* thou worm Jacob, and ye men of Israel; I will help thee,

saith the Lord, and thy redeemer, the Holy One of Israel. (41:14)

Behold, I will make thee a new sharp threshing instrument having teeth:
thou shalt *thresh* the mountains, and *beat* them small, and shalt make the hills as
*chaff.* (41:15)

*Thou* shalt fan them,
and the *wind* shall carry them away,
and the *whirlwind* shall scatter them:

and thou shalt *rejoice* in the Lord,
and shalt *glory* in the Holy One of Israel. (41:16)

When the *poor and needy* seek water,
and there is none, and *their tongue* faileth for thirst,

I the *Lord* will hear them,
I the *God of Israel* will not forsake them. (41:17)

I will open *rivers* in high places,
and *fountains* in the midst of the valleys:

I will make the wilderness a *pool of water,*
and the dry land *springs of water.* (41:18)

I will *plant in the wilderness* the cedar, the shittah tree, and the myrtle, and the oil
tree;
I will *set in the desert* the fir tree, and the pine, and the box tree together: (41:19)

That they may *see,* and *know,* and *consider,* and *understand* together,

that the hand of the *Lord* hath done this,
and the *Holy One of Israel* hath created it. (41:20)

NOTES AND COMMENTARY

**41:1** *Keep silence before me, O islands.* This command is issued to all the nations of the earth. To *keep silence* is perhaps to acknowledge the Lord's supremacy.

*let the people renew their strength.* The promise of renewed strength was made previously to those who rely on the Lord (40:31); the Lord now extends a call to all the peoples of the earth to find renewal in him.

*let us come near together to judgment.* The Lord invites the people of the earth to come, speak, and gather at the "place of judgment" (NIV). This gathering is held so the Lord can tell the nations about the "righteous man from the east" and about God's righteous acts (41:2–5). After telling the nations, they "feared" and "drew near, and came" (41:5). The "speaking" may be the nations' defense of their actions before the judgment.

**41:2** *righteous man from the east.* Jesus Christ, who is righteous, will come from the east at his second coming and will rule over kings and nations. This passage also refers to Cyrus, the king who conquered much of the world and ruled over kings (44:24–45:5).

*called him to his foot.* This idiom means "called him to serve."

*rule over kings.* This phrase refers to both Jesus and Cyrus.

*dust to his sword/stubble to his bow.* A sword passes through dust easily, as does an arrow shot through airborne (driven) stubble. These metaphors indicate the ease with which both Jesus (at his coming in glory) and Cyrus will conquer the nations.

**41:3** *He pursued them, and passed safely.* The Lord provides the means for Cyrus to pass safely, perhaps referring to his personal safety while leading his armies.

*had not gone with his feet.* This phrase may indicate the use of horses for travel by Cyrus.

**41:4** *Who hath . . . done it.* The Lord paves the way for Cyrus's rise to power.

*calling the generations from the beginning.* The Lord has controlled the forces of history from the beginning of time.

*the first/last.* These titles describe Christ's eternal nature and role as the "author and finisher of our faith" (Heb. 12:2; Rev. 1:8–11).

*I am he.* Jesus Christ's self-affirmation and testimony.

**41:5** *isles saw it, and feared.* The nations of the known world (see commentary on 41:1) see the coming destruction of Cyrus's armies and fear what will happen to them. At the Second Coming, the nations will possess great fear at the appearance of Jesus Christ.

**41:6** *They helped every one his neighbor.* The fearful nations attempt to comfort each other, and then they turn to their gods to find comfort and to incur their favor.

**41:7** *carpenter/goldsmith.* These craftsmen are those who fashion false gods. As the nations perceive the oncoming destruction, they seek to please their gods by making elaborate representations of them (see commentary on 40:19–20).

*fastened it with nails, that it should not be moved.* The people may have nailed down or soldered their images to keep them from tipping over.

**41:8** *Israel/Jacob/seed of Abraham.* The Lord, who has been speaking to the nations, now addresses his covenant people.

*I have chosen.* The people of Israel were chosen to serve the Lord (Deut. 7:6; 26:18) and make his name known to all the world (66:19; 1 Kgs. 8:43).

*my friend.* Abraham was called "Friend of God" (James 2:23) because of his faith and obedience.

**41:9** *taken from the ends of the earth . . . from the chief men.* Israel was chosen from among all the earth, a nation of simple people selected from among the great and powerful of the world.

*I have . . . not cast thee away.* However greatly Israel may deserve to be cast away by the Lord as if they were impure metal, the Lord promises not to take such an action. Rather he will send them through a refiner's fire to purify them until they learn to obey him.

**41:10** *I am with thee.* The Lord makes five statements directly to us, Israel, to quiet our fear and dismay: *I am with thee, I am thy God, I will strengthen thee, I will help thee, I will uphold thee.* This verse is echoed in the comforting Latter-day Saint hymn "How Firm a Foundation."[1]

*right hand of my righteousness.* The Lord upholds us with his right hand, his covenant hand.

**41:11** *they that strive with thee shall perish.* The Lord gives us a wonderful promise that those who contend with us, the house of Israel, will be *ashamed* and *confounded,* will *be as nothing,* will *perish,* and will be *as a thing of nought* (41:12). Though Israel will look around for her enemies, they will not be found ("Thou shalt seek them, and shalt not find them"; 41:12), for they will have been destroyed.

**41:13** *I . . . will hold thy right hand.* The *right hand* is the covenant hand. This phrase reminds us of the covenant relationship we have with the Lord, as his "servant" and "chosen" (41:8–9). It suggests that the Lord will hold up our hand, meaning he will sustain us as we seek in righteousness to keep our covenants. It also

---

[1] *Hymns,* no. 85.

suggests that the Lord will hold our hand as an expression of comfort and support (42:6).

**41:14** *thou worm Jacob.* As our enemies will be as "nothing" before us (41:11–12), so are we as nothing before the Lord. Yet, despite our mortal and spiritual weakness, the Lord will support and sustain us; he will protect and defend us. Twice he states, "I will help thee" and twice he commands, "Fear not" (41:13–14).

*redeemer.* The Lord, Jesus Christ. A *redeemer* had a legal meaning in ancient Israel: he was responsible to take a helpless relative's obligations on his own shoulders (Lev. 25:25; Num. 5:8), to avenge a murder (Num. 35:12; Deut. 19:6), to care for a dead relative's widow (Ruth 3–4), or to purchase one's release from debtor's prison. Such is the relationship of the Lord with us (Gen. 48:16): he will care for our needs, avenge us, and release us from bondage, especially the bondage of our sins.

*Holy One of Israel.* See commentary on 1:4.

**41:15** *I will make thee a new sharp threshing instrument.* To help us, the house of Israel, fulfill our mission, the Lord will make us into a new threshing instrument. Most threshing instruments work best on level ground, but this special threshing tool, because it is created by the Lord, is capable of threshing hills and mountains, a seemingly impossible task. That means that we, the house of Israel, are capable of performing impossible works through the power of God, who created us. Part of our goal, through harvesting the white fields (D&C 4), is to seek out the honest in heart. Eventually the gathering will separate the righteous from the wicked, just as wheat is separated from the tares.

**41:16** *Thou shalt fan them.* This statement refers to the separation of the chaff from the kernels after the threshing is complete. The chaff represents the wicked.

*whirlwind shall scatter them.* The Lord's judgments will destroy the wicked as a whirlwind carries away and scatters chaff.

*thou shalt rejoice in the Lord.* We will rejoice in the Lord for his work among us.

**41:17** *poor/needy.* All of us are poor and need the waters of life that only the Lord can provide. When we seek water, God provides an abundance. He says, "I will open rivers . . . fountains . . . and . . . springs of water" for you (41:18).

**41:18** *rivers/fountains/pool/springs.* Christ is the living waters that will satisfy our thirst. In the last days there will be an outpouring of this living water to our spirits as well as an increase of water in the wilderness (35:1, 7; see also D&C 117:7; 133:29).

*dry land.* Nations or peoples that lack the gospel or Church members who lack the Spirit.

**41:19** *plant in the wilderness the cedar.* Isaiah's list of seven trees represents righteous people (Ps. 1:1–3). As indicated in 41:20, these "trees" see, know, consider, and understand together. Seven is a symbolic number that denotes wholeness or completion. These trees represent the variety of individuals that will drink deeply from the living water of 41:18. Note the Lord's interest in the trees and his active role with them: I *will plant* and I *will set* the trees in the wilderness.

**41:20** *hand of the Lord hath done this.* This statement summarizes Isaiah's point: the Lord knows the outcome of everything in history, and it is he who gives us power to partake of his blessings.

## GRAVEN IMAGES ARE CONFUSION (41:21–29)

The Lord challenges the false gods and graven images that the people have created for themselves to prophesy and foretell the future. He asks the false gods to relate a few historical facts, and he invites them to perform any kind of act—a good act or even an evil act. The Lord issues these challenges so that the people who created these graven images may see if their images are indeed gods, possessing powers and life within themselves. The false gods, of course, are unable to respond, because they are nothing more than "wind and confusion." Whoever makes a graven image is an "abomination" and "vanity."

*Isaiah 41:21–29*

> *Produce your cause,* <u>saith the Lord</u>;
> *bring forth your strong reasons,* <u>saith the King of Jacob</u>. (41:21)

> Let them bring them forth,
> and [*show*][2] us <u>what shall happen</u>:
> let them [*show*] <u>the former things</u>, what they be,

> that we may *consider* them, and *know* <u>the latter end of them</u>;
> or *declare* us <u>things for to come</u>. (41:22)

> [*Show*] the <u>things that are to come hereafter</u>,
> that we may know that ye are gods:
> yea, do good, or do evil, that we may be dismayed, and behold it together. (41:23)

> Behold, *ye* are <u>of nothing</u>,[3]
> and *your work* <u>of nought</u>:
> an abomination is he that chooseth you. (41:24)

---

[2] We have replaced the archaic KJV *shew.*
[3] Literally "from nothing." Brown, Driver, and Briggs, *Hebrew and English Lexicon,* 34.

I have raised up one from the north,
and he shall come: from the rising of the sun shall he call upon my name:
and *he* shall [tread][4] upon princes as upon mortar,
and as the *potter* treadeth clay. (41:25)

Who hath declared from the *beginning,* that we may know?
and *beforetime,* that we may say, He is righteous?

yea, *there is none* that [showeth],[5]
yea, *there is none* that declareth,
yea, *there is none* that heareth your words. (41:26)

The first *shall say* to Zion, Behold, behold them:
and I *will give* to Jerusalem one that bringeth good tidings. (41:27)

For I beheld, and *there was no* man; even among [men],[6]
and *there was no* counselor, that, when I asked of them, could answer a word.
(41:28)

Behold, *they* are all vanity;
*their works* are nothing:
their *molten images* are wind and confusion. (41:29)

## NOTES AND COMMENTARY

**41:21** *Produce your cause/bring forth your strong reasons.* The Lord challenges the false gods to bring forth their case and arguments (D&C 71:8) to attempt to prove they are more powerful than he.

**41:22** *Let them . . . show us what shall happen.* For emphasis, Isaiah twice rephrases this statement as *declare us things for to come* and *show the things that are to come hereafter* (41:23). The Lord challenges the false gods to prophesy, to tell what will happen in the future, an act that only God can do, often through his prophets.

*let them show the former things.* The false gods are not even able to tell things that have already happened, because they are not living. Even men are able to relate historical facts.

**41:23** *do good, or do evil, that we may be dismayed.* When the Lord's challenge to the pagan gods to disclose the future is met only by silence, he challenges them to *do good, or do evil* or anything at all, so that the people *may know that ye are gods.*

**41:24** *ye are nothing/your work of nought.* Inasmuch as silence meets the Lord's challenge, the natural conclusion is that these gods are incapable of answering. These

---

[4] Brown, Driver, and Briggs, *Hebrew and English Lexicon,* 100.
[5] We have replaced the archaic KJV *sheweth.*
[6] JST Isa. 41:28.

gods are not gods; they are nothing, and the works attributed to them are nothing but falsehoods.

*abomination.* Those who worship idols are an abomination (2 Ne. 9:37).

**41:25** *raised up one.* The Lord will raise up a conqueror (see commentary on 41:2) *from the north,* speaking of Cyrus. Though Cyrus was from the east (see commentary on 41:2), he would conquer from the north.

*shall he call upon my name.* At the beginning of his reign, Cyrus claimed to believe in all Middle Eastern gods, but once the prophecies of Isaiah were brought to his attention, he turned to Jehovah at least to a degree (see commentary on 45:5).

*upon princes as upon mortar.* Cyrus "tramples on rulers as if they were mud, like a potter trampling clay" (GNB). Cyrus' enemies will provide no obstacles for him (41:2–3).

**41:26** *Who hath declared from the beginning.* The Lord asks those who worship the false gods, "Which god has been able to prophesy?" Then he answers his own question with "there is no false god that is able to give you visions [*showeth*], to speak to you [*declareth*], or who can answer your prayers [*heareth your words*]."

*He is righteous.* The gods are challenged to prove they are worthy of worship by foretelling events by which the people can establish the gods' existence.

**41:27** *The first shall say.* The Lord is the *first.*

*behold them.* "Look at the false gods that cannot speak or act; I am going to send a God who can bring good tidings."

*one that bringeth good tidings.* Jesus Christ brought good tidings, or the gospel, to Jerusalem.

**41:28** *there was no man . . . could answer a word.* No one could be found who could speak the mind of these gods.

**41:29** *they are all vanity.* The Lord concludes by condemning those who worship false gods as vain and the false gods themselves as wind and confusion.

# ISAIAH 42

*LIKENING ISAIAH 42 UNTO OURSELVES*

*Isaiah had a great understanding of the Savior and his mission. He knew that Jesus'*
*mission would include serving the house of Israel, the Gentiles, those in spirit prison,*
*and those who are spiritually and physically weak; he knew that Christ would not fail*
*his mission (42:1–9). Isaiah also understood that Jesus is a mighty God, who will per-*
*sonally destroy all wickedness from off the face of the earth (42:10–17). As members of*
*the Lord's church, we can understand these truths and receive a testimony of them.*
*Knowledge of Jesus Christ and his gospel is not reserved for the prophets alone; it is*
*also available to all who will seek.*

## A PROPHECY OF JESUS CHRIST'S MISSION AND MINISTRY (42:1–9)

The heading of chapter 42 in the LDS edition of the Bible reads, "Isaiah speaks Messianically." Biblical scholars C. F. Keil and F. Delitzsch write that this section speaks of the "future Christ."[1] Jesus is God's "servant," who will serve the physically and the spiritually weak (42:3); he will not fail in his mission, nor will he become discouraged (42:4). His mission is to serve Israel, the Gentiles, and the dead who are in spirit prison (42:1, 4, 7; 49:9); indeed, he will be "a light of the Gentiles" (42:6).

*Isaiah 42:1–9*

> Behold *my servant,* whom I uphold;
> *mine elect,* in whom my soul delighteth;

---

[1] Keil and Delitzsch, *Commentary,* 7:174.

I have <u>put my spirit upon</u> *him:*
he shall bring forth judgment to the Gentiles. (42:1)

He shall not *cry,* nor *lift up,* nor *cause his voice to be heard* in the street. (42:2)

A *bruised reed* shall he not <u>break,</u>
and the *smoking flax* shall he not <u>quench:</u>
he shall bring forth judgment unto truth. (42:3)

He shall not fail nor be discouraged,
till he have set *judgment* in the <u>earth:</u>
and the <u>isles</u> shall wait for his *law.* (42:4)

Thus saith God the Lord,
he that *created* the <u>heavens,</u>
and *stretched* <u>them</u> out;

he that *spread forth* the <u>earth,</u>
and *that* which cometh out of <u>it;</u>

he that giveth *breath* unto the <u>people</u> upon it,
and *spirit* to <u>them that walk</u> therein: (42:5)

I the Lord
have *called* <u>thee</u> in righteousness,
and will *hold* <u>thine hand,</u>
and will *keep* <u>thee,</u>
and *give* <u>thee</u>

for *a covenant* of the <u>people,</u>
for *a light* of the <u>Gentiles;</u> (42:6)

To *open* the <u>blind eyes,</u>
to *bring out* the <u>prisoners</u> from the prison,
and <u>them that sit in darkness</u> out of the prison house. (42:7)

I am the Lord: that is my name:
and *my glory* will I not give <u>to another,</u>
neither *my praise to* <u>graven images.</u> (42:8)

Behold, the *former things* are <u>come to pass,</u>
and *new things* <u>do I declare:</u>
before *they spring forth* <u>I tell you</u> of them. (42:9)

## NOTES AND COMMENTARY

**42:1** *my servant/mine elect.* The prophecy finds fulfillment in Jesus Christ (Matt. 12:17–21). God the Father calls Jesus *my servant, mine elect* (chosen), and says, *my soul delighteth* in him; also, the statement "I have put my spirit upon him" was fulfilled, in part, at Jesus' baptism (Matt. 3:16–17); the phrase in Isaiah, *he shall bring forth judgment to the Gentiles,* another reference to Jesus, indicates that he will deal justly with the Gentiles by providing a way for them to enter into a covenant relationship with God.

**42:2** *He shall not cry . . . nor cause his voice to be heard in the street.* Biblical commentators Keil and Delitzsch write concerning this phrase: "Although [the Lord] is certain of His divine call, and brings to the nations the highest and best, His manner of appearing is nevertheless quiet, gentle, and humble; the very opposite of those lying teachers, who endeavored to exalt themselves by noisy demonstrations. He does not seek His own, and therefore denies Himself; He brings what commends itself, and therefore requires no forced trumpeting."[2]

**42:3** *A bruised reed shall he not break . . . smoking flax shall he not quench.* A reed is a marsh plant with tall, hollow stems. A bruised reed is one that is cracked, and therefore is weak. Symbolically, a *bruised reed* may be a mortal with physical weaknesses or bodily afflictions. A *smoking flax* is a wick made from flax for an oil lamp, whose flame wavers, about to go out. This may signify someone who is spiritually weak, whose light flickers and does not burn brightly. Jesus healed and cared for the physically infirm (bruised reed), and he taught and guided the spiritually weak (smoking flax). A reed requires much water for it to grow properly; a flax or wick burns brightly when it has sufficient oil. Symbolically, Jesus Christ (as the waters of life) provides water to the reed, and (as the Anointed One) provides oil to the wick.

*judgment unto truth.* The New International Version reads: "In faithfulness he will bring forth justice." The passage is difficult in this context, but it may refer to the Day of Judgment (see Matt. 12:20), when the Lord will be victorious and establish truth in his kingdom on the earth (D&C 52:11).

**42:4** *He shall not fail nor be discouraged.* Jesus Christ will not fail his mission, nor will he become discouraged, but he will *set judgment in the earth.*

*wait for his law.* The New International Version provides a better reading: "In his law the islands will put their hope." This means that some people in the farthest reaches of the earth will believe in Jesus and hearken to his laws and commandments.

**42:5** *created the heavens . . . spread forth the earth.* Jesus Christ, who would serve among mortals (42:1–4), is the same who created the heavens and the earth, and all things *which cometh out* of the earth (see also D&C 104:14). The Jerusalem Bible indicates that it was the heavens, not the earth, that were spread: "he who created the heavens and spread them out, who gave shape to the earth and what comes from it."

*breath/spirit.* The crowning achievement of creation is mankind, given the breath of life from the Lord. The Lord continues to support and give life to all creation by the power of his Spirit (D&C 88:5–13).

---

[2] Keil and Delitzsch, 7:2:175.

**42:6** *called thee in righteousness.* The verse makes five statements about Jesus Christ's mission: he was *called . . . in righteousness,* God will guide Jesus (*hold [his] hand*), God will protect him (*keep [him]*), Jesus will be *a covenant of the people* ("i.e., the means through whom people will come into a covenant relation with the Lord"[3]), and he will be *a light of the Gentiles* (see also 49:8–9; D&C 45:9). This prophecy has some interesting parallels with that found in 49:1–10; see commentary there.

**42:7** *blind eyes.* This phrase represents those unable to see or comprehend spiritual truths (6:9–10). During his mortal ministry, Christ opened the eyes of those who were physically and spiritually blind (Matt. 11:5; Ps. 146:8).

*bring out the prisoners.* The prisoners are those who dwell in spirit prison (1 Pet. 3:19–20; D&C 76:73–74). Christ opened the way for the prisoners to be taught and provided them with the opportunity to be freed from prison. Joseph Smith said, "It is very evident from this that He [Jesus] not only went to preach to them [those in the spirit world], but to deliver, or bring them out of the prison house."[4]

**42:8** *I am the Lord.* The Lord bears testimony that he exists, that he is God.

*my glory will I not give to another.* No one else (whether Satan, or mortals, or idols) deserves the glory due the Lord, because no other has accomplished such a marvelous plan or work for his people nor has any other offered such a sacrifice as Christ has.

*neither my praise to graven images.* The Lord acknowledges the existence of idols but he does not praise them or work through them.

**42:9** *former things are come to pass, and new things do I declare.* All former prophecies given through the Lord's servants came to pass in their own time (1 Ne. 20:3), and all other prophecies will yet be fulfilled in the future: *before they spring forth I tell you of them.*

## A HYMN TO JEHOVAH THE REDEEMER (42:10–17)

Isaiah 42:10–12 is a command for all the earth's inhabitants and creatures to praise the Lord with a new song. The phrases "end of the earth," "the sea," "the isles," "the wilderness," "the cities," "the villages," "the rock," "the mountains," and "the islands" indicate that the earth's inhabitants are universally invited to sing praises to the Lord. Isaiah 42:13–17 describes God as a mighty warrior who will destroy the

---

[3] Motyer, *Prophecy of Isaiah,* 322.
[4] *Teachings of the Prophet Joseph Smith,* 219.

wicked, especially those who pronounce to their graven images that "ye are our gods." Note the active role God plays in their destruction, for the personal pronoun *I*, referring to the Lord, is found eleven times. Isaiah 42:16 is an interjection about the spiritually blind. We, the house of Israel, are the blind (JST 42:19–23) whom God leads down paths, and out of darkness into the light.

## Isaiah 42:10–17

Sing unto the Lord a new song,
and his praise from the end of the earth,

ye that go down to the *sea,* and all that is therein;
the *isles,* and the inhabitants thereof. (42:10)

Let the *wilderness* and the cities thereof lift up their voice,
the *villages* that Kedar doth inhabit:

let the *inhabitants* of the rock sing,
let *them* shout from the top of the mountains. (42:11)

Let them *give glory* unto the Lord,
and *declare* his *praise* in the islands. (42:12)

*The Lord* shall go forth as a mighty man,
*he* shall stir up jealousy like a man of war:
*he* shall cry, yea, roar;
*he* shall prevail against his enemies. (42:13)

*I* have long time[5] [held] my peace;
*I* have been still, and refrained myself:

now will *I* cry like a travailing woman;
*I* will destroy and devour at once. (42:14)

I will *make waste mountains and hills,* and dry up all their herbs;
and I *will make the rivers islands,* and I will dry up the pools. (42:15)

And I will *bring* the blind by a way that they knew not;
I will *lead* them in paths that they have not known:

*I* will make darkness light before them, and crooked things straight.
These things will *I* do unto them, and not forsake them. (42:16)

*They* shall be turned back,
*they* shall be greatly ashamed,

*that trust* in graven images,
*that say* to the molten images,
Ye are our gods. (42:17)

---

[5] DSS Isa. Scroll inserts *truly* before *long time.*

NOTES AND COMMENTARY

**42:10** *Sing unto the Lord a new song.* Singing a new song unto the Lord is mentioned ten times in the scriptures (see, for example, Ps. 40:3; 98:1; 149:1; Rev. 5:9; 14:3; D&C 84:98). Each time the song is one of praise. Such songs appear to be called *new* because they praise the Lord for *new* works of glory and blessing. The Lord commands the entire earth to sing a new song unto him.

*end of the earth.* To this phrase Isaiah adds *ye that go down to the sea,* the isles and their inhabitants, the wilderness and its cities, villages of Kedar, *inhabitants of the rock,* and *islands.* All peoples and creatures on the earth and in the sea are called to sing praises to the Lord, because he comes in power and glory to destroy the wicked and establish his reign.

**42:11** *the wilderness and the cities thereof/villages that Kedar doth inhabit.* These phrases refer to the gentile nations who will sing praises to the Lord (regarding *Kedar,* see commentary on 21:6–7).

*top of the mountains.* This phrase often refers to temples, holy places, or other places of worship. It is from this location that the inhabitants of Zion, like the gentile nations, will sing a "new song" to God.

**42:13** *mighty man/man of war.* Isaiah describes the Lord as a mighty man, a man of war, one who will *go forth, stir up, cry, roar,* and *prevail against his enemies.*

*stir up jealousy.* "Jealousy" here should read "zeal" (NIV) or "fury" (JB).

*roar.* The Lord will prevail against his enemies with the power of a lion (31:4).

**42:14** *I have . . . refrained myself.* For a long time the Lord held his peace, he has been still, and he has refrained himself from destroying the wicked (64:12; D&C 121:1–6).

*cry like a travailing woman.* The Lord cries out like a woman in labor, perhaps similarly pained because of the wicked acts of humanity or perhaps because he, in pain, is bringing forth a great work.

*I will destroy and devour. Devour* (like a lion) recalls *roar* in 42:13. The Lord destroys the wicked (D&C 105:15).

**42:15** *I will make the rivers islands.* Isaiah prophesies a great drought that will make the rivers into islands. Twice in this verse he uses the expression *dry up.*

**42:16** *I will bring the blind by a way.* The Lord now leads us, the spiritually blind, down the gospel paths and into his marvelous light.

*make darkness light.* The Lord will bring his people out of spiritual darkness and into the light of the gospel (2 Ne. 3:5). He will *not forsake them.*

*crooked things straight. Crooked* represents the disorderly, dishonest ways of men, and *straight* represents the order of God (40:4; see also Luke 3:5).

**42:17** *They shall be turned back . . . that trust in graven images.* In the Day of Judgment, those who said to their idols and images, *Ye are our gods,* will be turned away from receiving inheritance in the kingdom of God, and they will reap shame instead of glory.

## THE SERVANT TO THE BLIND (42:18–25)

Isaiah makes numerous references to Israel's sinful state—her people are spiritually deaf and blind (mentioned four times), they have sinned, they did not walk in God's ways, and they were disobedient to his law. Therefore, the Lord permitted them to be robbed, spoiled, snared, thrown in prison, and burned—all these having reference to Israel's captivity by other nations.

After Isaiah declares the blindness of Israel, he provides hope by prophesying that Jesus Christ, who is the servant and messenger, will "open the eyes of the blind," so that "they shall be made perfect notwithstanding their blindness, if they will hearken unto" the Lord. This prophecy may also find fulfillment in those who go forth as Christ's servants—including Isaiah and others—bringing the light of truth to the world.

*Isaiah 42:18–25*

> *Hear,* ye <u>deaf</u>;
> and *look,* ye <u>blind,</u>
> that ye may see. (42:18)

> [For I will send my *servant* unto you who are blind;
> yea, a *messenger* to <u>open the eyes of the blind,</u>
> and <u>unstop the ears of the deaf;</u>
> And they shall be <u>made perfect</u> notwithstanding their blindness,
> if they will hearken unto the *messenger,* the *Lord's servant*].[6] (42:19)

> [Thou art a people,] *seeing* many things, but thou <u>observest not</u>;
> *opening the ears* [*to hear*], but [thou] <u>hear[est]</u>[7] <u>not</u>. (42:20)

> The Lord is [not] well pleased [with such a people, but][8] for his righteousness'
> sake;

---

[6] JST Isa. 42:19–20. The "blind" and "deaf" here are clearly not "he that is perfect" or "the Lord's servant" (as the KJV implies) but rather the same people spoken of in v. 18.
[7] All bracketed changes in this verse come from JST Isa. 42:21. The emphasis of this verse turns again toward the children of Israel who lack teachableness, and not the Lord's servant.
[8] All bracketed changes in this verse come from JST Isa. 42:22.

he will *magnify* the law,
and *make* it *honorable.* (42:21)

[Thou art] a *people* robbed and spoiled;
[thine enemies, all of them, have snared *thee*] in holes,

and *they* [have hid thee] in prison houses;
*they* [have taken thee][9]

for a *prey,* and none delivereth;
for a *spoil,* and none saith, Restore. (42:22)

Who among [them] will *give ear* [unto thee,
or] *hearken and hear* [thee] for the time to come?

[and] who gave *Jacob* for a spoil,
and *Israel* to the robbers?
did not the Lord, he against whom [they] have sinned? (42:23–24a)

[For they *would not walk* in his ways,
*neither were they obedient* unto his law;]

therefore he hath poured upon him the fury of his anger,
and the strength of battle;

and [they have] *set* [*them*] *on fire* round about, yet [they] knew not;
and it *burned* [*them*], yet [they][10] laid it not to heart. (42:24b-25)

## NOTES AND COMMENTARY

**42:18** *Hear, ye deaf/look, ye blind.* The Lord commands the spiritually blind and deaf children of Israel (6:9–10) to hear and see the truth. This passage may also apply to Jesus Christ's mortal ministry, when he healed the blind, the sick, and others with infirmities related to mortality.

**42:19** *send my servant/messenger.* Jesus Christ is God's primary servant and messenger. One aspect of the Lord's mortal mission was to open the eyes of the children of Israel to the truth of the everlasting covenant and to extend that truth to the Gentiles. (Prophets, including Isaiah, also serve God in this capacity.) By abiding by the everlasting covenant and receiving all the blessings of the Atonement, men are *made perfect* despite their blindness. Concerning this prophecy Elder Bruce R. McConkie wrote: "Truly this is what has been and is transpiring in this day. The scattered remnants of Israel, hearing again the voice of their Shepherd, are believing his gospel, accepting baptism at the hands of his servants, . . . taking upon themselves his name, and once again becoming his sons and his daughters."[11]

---

[9] All bracketed changes in this verse come from JST Isa. 42:23.
[10] All bracketed changes in this verse come from JST Isa. 42:24–25.
[11] *Promised Messiah,* 359.

**42:20** *seeing many things, but thou observest not.* Many truths were revealed to the house of Israel, but they did not observe them, showing their lack of obedience. Many of us find ourselves in a similar situation.

**42:21** *not well pleased with such a people.* Denying or ignoring the truths of the Lord always brings his displeasure.

*righteousness' sake.* Although the Lord is not pleased with the disobedient, because of his goodness "he will magnify the law and make it honorable" (NIV translates this phrase as the Lord will "make his law great and glorious"), meaning he will make the gospel great in the eyes of the world. Despite the unfaithful and hypocritical nature of some of the house of Israel, the honest in heart accept Christ because of the greatness of his law.

**42:22** *Thou art a people robbed and spoiled.* Because of their wickedness, Israel was temporarily *robbed* of her political freedom and her inheritance in Palestine. She was caught like prey in the "snare" (24:18) of her wicked neighbors, taken captive, and put *in prison houses.* Her possessions were "spoiled," or taken or destroyed in war.

*none delivereth/none saith, Restore.* Because Israel turned her back on God, no one is left to fight for her cause and restore her inheritance.

**42:23–24a** *Who among them will give ear unto thee.* Isaiah asks, "Who among Israel's enemies will hear the cries of the people of Israel and free them?"

*who gave Jacob for a spoil.* Isaiah asks, "Who delivered Israel to be robbed and spoiled [looted]?" Then he answers his own question, *Did not the Lord, he against whom [Israel] have sinned?*

**42:24b-25** *would not walk in his ways.* Isaiah lists two ways in which the people of Israel sinned against the Lord: they would not walk in his ways (meaning, adhere to the ordinances), and they were disobedient unto his law (the commandments).

*fury of his anger/strength of battle.* Because of the Israelites' rebellion, the Lord's anger was poured out upon them in the form of war and captivity.

*set them on fire/burned.* Again, because of the Israelites' rebellion, the Lord destroyed them with burning and fire; yet, Israel did not recognize the full meaning of the destruction and did not take to heart the warnings of the Lord.

# ISAIAH 43

## LIKENING ISAIAH 43 UNTO OURSELVES

*The Lord has done many things in our behalf. He provides us with safety as we pass through dangerous territory, whether physical or spiritual. Even as ancient Israel passed safely through the waters of the Red Sea, with the Egyptian armies in pursuit, so will we pass unharmed through our own difficult waters. God promises, "When thou passest through the waters, I will be with thee; and through the rivers, they shall not overflow thee" (43:2). Also, as Shadrach, Meshach, and Abednego came out of Nebuchadnezzar's fiery furnace with not "an hair of their head singed, neither were their coats changed, nor the smell of fire had passed on them" (Dan. 3:26–27), so God promises us, "When thou walkest through the fires thou shalt not be burned; neither shall the flame kindle upon thee" (43:2).*

## PROPHECY OF REDEMPTION (43:1–7)

As Isaiah emphasized Israel's punishment in the previous section, so his focus now is on Israel's redemption (43:1). The Lord provides us, members of the house of Israel, with great comfort and many promises. We, like ancient Israel, are promised safety as we pass through waters and rivers, fire and flames (43:2). We are comforted to know that Jehovah created us for his glory (43:1, 7)—we are not upon this earth by chance. We are also comforted to know that the Lord has redeemed us (43:1) and that he is our "God" and our "Savior" (43:3). We are told that others have given their lives in our behalf, because we are "precious" to the Lord (43:4). Finally, the Lord promises to gather Israel's scattered seed from the "ends of the earth" (43:6).

*Isaiah 43:1–7*

But now thus saith the *Lord that created thee,* O Jacob,
and *he that formed thee,* O Israel,

Fear not: for *I have redeemed* thee,
*I have called* thee by thy name; thou art mine. (43:1)

When thou passest through the *waters,* I will be with thee;
and through the *rivers,* they shall not overflow thee:

when thou walkest through the *fire,* thou shalt not be burned;
neither shall the *flame* kindle upon thee. (43:2)

For I am the *Lord thy God,*
the *Holy One of Israel,*
thy *Savior:*

I gave *Egypt* for thy ransom,
*Ethiopia and Seba* for thee. (43:3)

Since *thou* wast precious in my sight,
*thou* hast been [honored],[1]
and I have loved *thee:*

therefore will I give *men* for thee,
and *people* for thy life. (43:4)

Fear not: for I am with thee:
I will *bring* thy seed from the east,
and *gather* thee from the west; (43:5)

I will say to the north, *Give up;*
and to the south, *Keep not back:*

*bring* my sons from far,
and my daughters from the ends of the earth; (43:6)

Even every one that is called by my name:
for *I have* created him for my glory,
*I have* formed him;
yea, *I have* made him. (43:7)

## Notes and Commentary

**43:1** *created thee/formed thee.* The Lord *created* the people of Israel, just as he created all other people on the face of the earth, but he also *formed* (molded) them as a covenant, chosen people.

*redeemed.* Jesus Christ is the Redeemer who purchased Israel with his own blood.

---

[1] NIV Isa. 43:4.

*I have called thee by thy name.* The Lord gave Jacob the new name *Israel* to set him apart as His servant. We continue to bear his name, which sets us apart from other people.

*thou art mine.* We belong to God's family; we are his children, "spiritually begotten" of Christ (Mosiah 5:7).

**43:2** *passest through the waters/rivers . . . not overflow thee.* Isaiah recalls the exodus of ancient Israel from Egypt by mentioning her miraculous passage through the Red Sea (Ex. 14:21–22) and the Jordan River (Josh. 3:13–17). The gathering of modern Israel calls to mind the exodus from Egypt, and modern Israel will likewise be safely guided through the hardships and dangers of the world.

*when thou walkest through the fire, thou shalt not be burned.* This statement refers to the Lord's judgments that fall upon Israel (42:25) and the world (24:6) because of wickedness, with specific application to Shadrach, Meshach, and Abednego (Dan. 3:27). It also applies to the last days, when the wicked are destroyed by the burning that will accompany the Lord's coming, while the righteous of Israel remain unscathed.

**43:3** *Holy One of Israel.* See commentary on 1:4.

*Savior.* Jesus is our Savior, who delivers us from sin and death.

*I gave Egypt for thy ransom, Ethiopia and Seba for thee.* The meaning here is unclear, but the sense of this statement seems to be that Israel was so precious to the Lord that he was willing to give away kingdoms to deliver her. Of course, God has power over all and need not make such sacrifices. But the intent seems to be emotional rather than literal: *Thou wast precious in my sight,* the Lord says (43:4), and he will spare no cost to rescue us.

**43:4** *thou wast precious in my sight.* Because the people of Israel had been chosen by the Lord as *his* people (43:1), they were precious to him. He honored them by calling (Eph. 1:18) them to serve him (Ex. 19:4–6), and he loved them.

*I have loved thee.* The New International Version places this phrase in the present tense, "I love you" (see 63:9).

*therefore will I give men for thee, and people for thy life.* Many people lost their lives for the benefit and salvation of the Lord's people. These include the firstborn of Egypt (43:3), the Canaanite nations that were destroyed by Joshua and the Israelites, the prophets who were martyred while prophesying and bearing witness, and most important, Jesus Christ, who gave his own life to bring salvation to his people.

**43:5** *I will . . . gather thee.* The Lord promises to gather the posterity of the children of Israel from the four corners of the earth.

**43:5–6** *east/west/north/south.* The directions encompass the entire earth, and for emphasis the Lord adds, "from far" and "from the ends of the earth."

**43:7** *called by my name.* To be called by the Lord's name is to accept the covenants and ordinances, such as baptism and temple work. By accepting these covenants and ordinances, we will be gathered by the Lord in the last days (43:5–6).

*created/formed.* Compare 43:1, which also uses the terms *created* and *formed.*

*my glory.* Moses 1:39 explains God's glory—"to bring to pass the immortality and eternal life of man."

## WE ARE TO WITNESS THAT JEHOVAH IS GOD (43:8–13)

Twice the Lord tells us, "Ye are my witnesses" (43:10, 12). We are to witness and bear testimony to "all the nations" (43:9) that Jehovah is "God" (43:12) and "Savior" (43:11). Note Jehovah's repeated self-testimony—"I am he" (43:10), "before me there was no God formed, neither shall there be after me," "I, even I, am the Lord," "beside me there is no savior," "I am God," "I am he" (43:13).

*Isaiah 43:8–13*

Bring forth the *blind* people that have <u>eyes</u>,
and the *deaf* that have <u>ears</u>. (43:8)

*Let all the nations* be <u>gathered together,</u>
and *let the people* be <u>assembled:</u>

who among them can *declare* this, and [*show*]² us former things?
let them *bring forth their witnesses,* that they may be <u>justified:</u>
or let them *hear,* and *say,* It is <u>truth</u>. (43:9)

*Ye are my witnesses,* saith <u>the Lord,</u>
and *my servant* whom <u>I</u> have chosen:

that *ye* may *know* and <u>believe me,</u>
and *understand* that <u>I am he</u>:

before *me* <u>there was no God formed, neither shall there be</u> after *me*. (43:10)
*I, even I, am the Lord;* and beside me <u>there is no savior</u>. (43:11)

*I* have <u>declared,</u>
and have <u>saved,</u>
and *I* have [<u>shown</u>],

when there was no strange god among you:
therefore ye are my witnesses, saith the Lord, that I am God. (43:12)

Yea, before the day was³ I am he;

---

²We have replaced the archaic KJV *shew.*

³Literally, "also from a day."

and there is none that can deliver out of mine hand:
I will work, and who shall [prevent][4] it? (43:13)

NOTES AND COMMENTARY

**43:8** *blind people that have eyes.* This passage may refer to the people of the house of Israel (6:9–10), who have the ability to see and comprehend spiritual truths and yet do not (42:16). They are brought before the nations of the earth to witness that Jehovah, or Jesus Christ, is God (42:10).

**43:9** *Let all the nations be gathered together.* The Lord symbolically gathers the nations and peoples together and challenges them to "bring forth their witnesses," such as false prophets or gods, to show that they have, in the past, prophesied of something that has come to pass. If they do so, they will "be justified," or proved right. Otherwise, let them "hear" God's witnesses (our prophets, apostles, and missionaries) and agree that they speak the truth ("It is truth").

**43:10** *Ye are my witnesses.* This phrase is repeated in 43:12. The children of Israel were chosen to be witnesses of Jehovah and bear testimony of him to the world. Sometimes Israel has failed to do so, because her people were spiritually blind. In our own day we, the house of Israel (especially Ephraim and Manasseh), are instructed to bear witness of our God, as modern-day prophets have explained.[5]

*know and believe me/understand.* We are told to seek knowledge of the Lord's nature and character so we are able to understand who he is and can bear a stronger witness of him (D&C 19:23).

*I am he.* This clear statement answers the question asked in 43:9: "Who among them can declare this?" The expression also recalls Jehovah's title—*I Am* (Ex. 3:14).

*before me there was no God formed, neither shall there be after me.* In Isaiah's great discussion of false gods and idols (chapters 40–46), he assures both ancient and modern Israel that Jehovah is God.

**43:11** *beside me there is no savior.* Jehovah, who is Jesus Christ, is the Savior of the world. There is no other Savior.

**43:12** *I have declared, and have saved, and I have shown.* Jehovah has spoken his word; he has performed the acts of salvation; he has shown the truth to the world. We, having received these things, witness that he is "God."

*when there was no strange god among you.* Jehovah was Israel's God before they worshiped false deities.

---

[4] The KJV "let" is more correctly rendered "prevent" in modern English.
[5] *Teachings of the Prophet Joseph Smith,* 265; see also D&C 58:6; McConkie, *Promised Messiah,* 17.

**43:13** *before the day was.* Jehovah existed before the first day of Creation.

*I will work, and who shall [prevent] it.* The New International Version reads, "When I act, who can reverse it?" Jehovah will perform the works he has promised, and no one can hinder him from accomplishing what he has determined to do.

## JEHOVAH PROVIDES WATER FOR US (43:14–21)

God destroyed Babylon for the sake of ancient Israel, and for our sake he will destroy modern Babylon, or the world (43:14). As we travel through this telestial world, the Lord provides for us a "way," which is the gospel with its ordinances; and "rivers" and "waters" (43:19–20), which refer to spiritual drink. In return, we are required to "shew forth [the Lord's] praise" (43:21), or to witness to the world that Jehovah is our God.

Isaiah uses several titles that describe God's relationship to us: *Lord* (Hebrew *Yahweh*), *Redeemer, Holy One of Israel, Holy One,* and *King.*

*Isaiah 43:14–21*

Thus saith the *Lord,*
your *redeemer,*
the *Holy One of Israel;*

For your sake I have sent to *Babylon,* and have brought down all their nobles,
and the *Chaldeans,* whose cry is in the ships. (43:14)

I am the *Lord,* your Holy One,
the *creator of Israel,* your King. (43:15)

Thus saith the Lord, which maketh a *way* in the sea,
and a *path* in the mighty waters; (43:16)

Which bringeth forth *the chariot* and *horse,*
the *army* and *the power;*

*they* shall lie down together,
*they* shall not rise:

*they* are extinct,
*they* are quenched as tow. (43:17)

*Remember* ye not the former things,
neither *consider* the things of old. (43:18)

Behold, I will do a new thing;
now it shall spring forth; shall ye not know it?
I will even make a *way* in the wilderness,
and *rivers* in the desert. (43:19)

The *beast* of the field shall honor me,
the *[jackals]*[6] and the *owls:*

---

[6] Hebrew *taniym.* Brown, Driver, and Briggs, *Hebrew and English Lexicon,* 1072.

because I give *waters* <u>in the wilderness,</u>
and *rivers* <u>in the desert,</u>

to give *drink* to <u>my people,</u>
<u>my chosen.</u> (43:20)

This people have I formed for myself;
they shall [show] forth my praise. (43:21)

## NOTES AND COMMENTARY

**43:14** *redeemer.* See commentary on 41:14.

*Holy One of Israel.* See commentary on 1:4.

*I have sent to Babylon, and have brought down all their nobles.* The Lord sent powerful armies (including Assyria) to ancient Babylon to destroy her and her powerful and affluent citizens (*nobles*). She was *brought down.* In the future, the wicked world, or spiritual Babylon (D&C 1:16) will be destroyed by Jesus Christ at his second coming.

*Chaldeans.* The *Chaldeans* is another name for the Babylonians; in some periods the Chaldeans appear to have been the scholarly segment of the Babylonians (Dan. 2:2-10).

*cry is in the ships.* The Babylonians were active in trading and shipping at this time. They gloried in their prosperity, but they will *cry* out in pain from their *ships* at their destruction.

**43:15** *creator of Israel, your King.* The Lord, who brought Israel into being both as a people and as a nation (see commentary on 43:1) is her rightful King (6:5; 9:6; Ps. 10:16).

**43:16** *the Lord . . . maketh a way in the sea/a path in the mighty waters.* This passage seems to refer to the exodus of Israel from Egypt through the Red Sea and her entry into the promised land through the Jordan River. These events from the past exemplify how the Lord provides for his people in their time of need.

**43:17** *chariot/horse/army.* These three words are mentioned in connection with Pharaoh—Pharaoh's army, chariots, and horses were destroyed at the Red Sea; not one survived (Ex. 14:16-28), for they were "quenched as tow," meaning they were extinguished as one puts out a wick. Just as the Lord has fought Israel's battles in the past, he will continue to fight our battles now and in the future.

**43:18** *Remember ye not the former things.* In comparison with historical religious events, such as the destruction of Pharaoh's armies by God, the Lord declares that he is going to do new and greater things.

**43:19** *I will do a new thing; now it shall spring forth.* The *new thing* that will *spring forth* is "a way in the wilderness, and rivers in the desert." In other words, the new thing appears to be the restoration of the gospel in the last days (in the midst of the wilderness of sin and the desert of apostasy) and the establishment of Zion prior to the Lord's millennial reign.

*way in the wilderness.* The description of the "new thing" here compares with the "former things" described in 43:18. *Way* echoes "way in the sea," and *rivers* echoes "waters" (43:16). That is to say, God formerly provided a *way* in the Red Sea for Israel to escape from Egypt's Pharaoh, armies, and wickedness, and God's new thing includes a *way* for us (modern Israel) to escape through the wilderness, or the telestial nature of this world. Formerly, the way was an actual path, but now the way is a spiritual path. The *way in the wilderness* is the gospel of Jesus Christ.

*rivers.* Not only does the Lord provide a way in the wilderness but he also provides rivers in the desert for his people to drink from as they travel through forsaken territory. Christ himself is the living water in the wilderness of mortality.

**43:20** *beast of the field/jackals/owls.* The wild beasts and desert creatures probably represent the nations that have not been "tamed" by the gospel and that thirst for the living water. They will yet come to that water (the gospel) and will therefore have cause to honor the Lord.

*waters in the wilderness/rivers in the desert.* These *waters* are provided to God's people for drink. They are the *waters* that bring spiritual life (41:18; 35:1, 7; 51:3).

*my people, my chosen.* The covenant children of Israel (43:1, 5–7) not only anciently but in our own day.

**43:21** *This people have I formed for myself.* See commentary on 43:1.

*show forth my praise.* We *show forth* God's praise as we bear testimony and spread the gospel throughout the world.

## ISRAEL HAS FORGOTTEN THE LORD (43:22–28)

Israel ceased worshiping the Lord through prayer and temple sacrifices (43:22–24), but the Lord promised to forgive her (43:25) if her people would repent and remember him. We repeat history if we fail to pray sincerely and regularly and to worship at the temple.

*Isaiah 43:22–28*

> But thou hast not *called upon me,* O <u>Jacob</u>;
> but thou hast *been weary of me,* O <u>Israel</u>. (43:22)
>
> Thou hast not *brought me* the small cattle of thy <u>burnt offerings</u>;
> neither hast thou *honored me* with thy <u>sacrifices</u>.

I have not *caused thee* to serve with an <u>offering</u>,
nor *wearied thee* with <u>incense</u>. (43:23)

Thou hast *bought me* no <u>sweet cane</u> with money,
neither hast thou *filled me* with the <u>fat</u> of thy sacrifices:

but thou hast *made me to serve* with thy <u>sins</u>,
thou hast *wearied me* with thine <u>iniquities</u>. (43:24)

I, even I, am he that *blotteth out* thy <u>transgressions</u> for mine own sake,
and *will not remember* thy <u>sins</u>.[7] (43:25)

Put me in remembrance: let us plead together:
declare thou, that thou mayest be justified. (43:26)

Thy *first father* hath <u>sinned</u>,
and thy *teachers* have <u>transgressed</u> against me. (43:27)

Therefore I have *profaned* the <u>princes of the sanctuary</u>,
and have given <u>Jacob</u> to the *curse,*
and <u>Israel</u> to *reproaches*. (43:28)

## NOTES AND COMMENTARY

**43:22** *not called upon me/weary of me.* Israel did not pray to the Lord with a true heart, and she had become weary of the commandments and rituals required by God (1:10–15).

**43:23** *Thou hast not brought me . . . burnt offerings.* The children of Israel had ceased to honor the Lord with their sacrifices. They did not bring the best of their flocks to him (43:24; Mal. 1:6–7), and some neglected to offer a sacrifice at all, denying themselves purification from sin.

*I have not . . . wearied thee with incense.* The offerings and incense were meant not to weary the Lord's people but to strengthen them.

**43:24** *bought me no sweet cane.* Sweet cane is fragrant calamus (Ex. 30:23–25; Jer. 6:20–25), used with other spices to make the holy anointing oil. The priests and people of Israel had ceased to purchase the items required to purify the Lord's house; hence it was unclean.

*filled me . . . fat of thy sacrifices.* Israel had not *filled* (satisfied) the Lord by bringing the fat of their sacrifices, or the Lord's designated portion (Lev. 3:16–17) before him in repentance.

*thy sins/thine iniquities.* Instead of serving the Lord in righteousness, the children of Israel wanted him to serve them in their sins. And as Israel grew weary of righteousness, they had wearied the Lord in their sins. The New International Version

---

[7] DSS Isa. Scroll adds *more* to the end of the verse.

further clarifies this phrase by saying, "You have burdened me with your sins and wearied me with your offenses."

**43:25** *blotteth out thy transgressions.* The Lord reminds his people that he is capable of forgiving and forgetting their sins (6:7; 55:6–7). This beautiful promise also applies to us.

*will not remember thy sins.* A latter-day revelation reads similarly, "Behold, he who has repented of his sins, the same is forgiven, and I, the Lord, remember them no more" (D&C 58:42). Isaiah 43:25–26 corresponds with Isaiah 1:18.

*for mine own sake.* The Lord is glorified by the purification and salvation of his people. Note in Moses 1:39 the Lord's words: "This is *my* work and *my* glory—to bring to pass the immortality and eternal life of man" (emphasis added). Note also Isaiah 48:11, in which the words "For mine own sake" are found twice.

**43:26** *Put me in remembrance.* The Lord pleads with his people to remember him—perhaps he is asking them to live true to the baptismal and sacramental covenant to "always remember him" (D&C 20:77).

*let us plead together.* This phrase parallels "let us reason together" (1:18). See commentary there.

**43:27** *Thy first father hath sinned.* This statement seems to refer to Adam and his transgression (Gen. 3:17–19; 2 Ne. 2:22).

*thy teachers have transgressed.* The leaders (*teachers*) of the people of Israel were steeped in wickedness, and the people of Israel followed their example.

**43:28** *I have profaned the princes of the sanctuary.* The heads (*princes*) of the priestly families were no longer holy or temple worthy. Therefore, the Lord "profanes" them, meaning he removes their authority to act in his name. Likewise, the people of Judah will be "curse[d]" if they do not repent.

---

# ISAIAH 44;
# 45:1-6

### *LIKENING ISAIAH 44 UNTO OURSELVES*

*Isaiah's words remind us that it is a privilege to be a descendant of that great patriarch Israel and a recipient of the blessings attendant on that heritage (44:3). Isaiah prophesies that the Lord's Spirit will be poured out upon Israel's seed abundantly, as "floods upon the dry ground." We who are of Israel will be pleased to say, "I am the Lord's." We will be happy to proclaim, "I have the name of Jacob," or "my surname is Israel."*

*In ancient days, Israel was in bondage to an earthly conqueror, but God called up a deliverer (Cyrus) to rescue his people. We also are in bondage, but our enslavement is to the powers of sin, tradition, and death. In his great power, God has sent us a deliverer in Jesus Christ. He has the power to liberate us from our bondage and to set us free spiritually, if we will but turn to him and hearken with honest hearts. But to receive his blessing, we must be willing to submit to him, even as the clay does to the potter.*

---

## ISRAEL RECEIVES A MULTITUDE OF BLESSINGS IN THE LAST DAYS (44:1–8)

This prophecy sets forth Jehovah's relationship to us, members of the house of Israel. Jehovah is represented by the words *Lord* (Hebrew *Yahweh*), *King of Israel, redeemer, Lord of hosts, first, last, God, Rock,* and the personal pronouns *I* and *me*. We (Israel) are represented by the words *Jacob, servant* (twice), *chosen* (twice), *Israel, Jesurun, thirsty, dry ground, willows, ancient people,* and several pronouns.

Members of the house of Israel are spiritually thirsty, and Jehovah promises to provide them with water, refreshing floods, and water courses, all of which represent the Lord and his Spirit and accompanying blessings.

*Isaiah 44:1–8*

> Yet now hear, O *Jacob* my <u>servant</u>;
> and *Israel,* <u>whom I have chosen</u>: (44:1)

> Thus saith the Lord that *made thee,*
> and *formed thee* from the womb,

> which will help thee; Fear not, O *Jacob,* <u>my servant</u>;
> and thou, *Jesurun,* <u>whom I have chosen</u>. (44:2)

> For I will pour *water* upon him that is <u>thirsty,</u>
> and *floods* upon the <u>dry ground</u>:

> I will pour *my spirit* upon <u>thy seed,</u>
> and *my blessing* upon <u>thine offspring</u>: (44:3)

> And *they shall spring up* as <u>among the grass,</u>
> *as willows* by <u>the water courses</u>. (44:4)

> One shall say, *I am the Lord's;* and another shall <u>call himself by the name of Jacob</u>;
> and another shall *subscribe with his hand unto the Lord,* and <u>surname himself by the name of Israel</u>. (44:5)

> Thus saith the *Lord* the <u>King of Israel,</u>
> and his *redeemer* the <u>Lord of hosts</u>.[1]

> *I* am <u>the first,</u>
> and *I* am <u>the last</u>; and beside me there is no God. (44:6)

> And who, as I, shall *call,*
> and shall <u>declare</u> it,
> and *set it in order* for me,

> since I appointed the ancient people?
> and the things that are coming,
> and shall come,
> let them [show][2] unto them. (44:7)

> *Fear* ye *not,*
> *neither be afraid:*

> have not <u>I told thee</u>
> from that time, and have <u>declared it</u>?

> ye are even my witnesses.
> Is there a God beside me?
> yea, there is no God;
> I know not any. (44:8)

---

[1] DSS Isa. Scroll adds *is his name.*
[2] *Shew* is an archaic form of *show.*

NOTES AND COMMENTARY

**44:1** *servant/chosen.* This prophecy is directed to us (the opening words say "hear"), members of the house of Israel, who are the Lord's *servant,* his *chosen.* As such, we are his witnesses and need to bear our testimonies to the world of his divine work (see commentary on 43:10). *Servant* and *chosen* are repeated in 44:2 for emphasis.

**44:2** *formed thee from the womb.* Before the nation of Israel was born, the Lord covenanted with Abraham that his seed would be a chosen people and a great nation (Abr. 2:8–11). Before that, it is likely that things pertaining to Israel were decided in premortal councils.

*Jesurun.* This name, which means "righteous," was given to the house of Israel (Deut. 32:15; 33:5, 26). It reminds us of our calling as a holy nation and our status as the Lord's covenant people.

**44:3** *I will pour water upon him that is thirsty.* These are the living waters of Jesus Christ and his Spirit (12:3; 55:1; John 4:7–14). The *thirsty* are those who thirst not for actual water but for the spiritual salvation that only Jesus Christ can provide.

*floods.* God is generous with salvation; he will send floods, not simply a canteen full of water upon us to quench our thirst.

*dry ground.* This term refers to Israel's offspring who, upon receiving the spiritual water and floods, will spring up like willows (44:4). They will recognize the source of their spiritual light and will say, "I am the Lord's" (44:5).

*I will pour my spirit upon thy seed.* This phrase parallels *I will pour water upon him that is thirsty,* for the words *I will pour* and *upon* are found in both phrases. The Lord promises to pour his Spirit on Israel's seed (which includes us) as one pours water on the thirsty (32:15; Ezek. 39:29). This prophecy was partially fulfilled when the Spirit descended upon many of Christ's followers after Christ was resurrected (Acts 2:1–4); however, Peter indicated that the fulness of this prophecy would "come to pass in the last days" (Acts 2:17; see D&C 95:4).

**44:4** *grass/willows. Grass* represents humanity or all flesh (37:27; 40:6–7), and the *willows* are members of the house of Israel who will grow or *spring up* among the grass by the water courses nourished by the power of Jesus Christ. As willows stand apart from grass and are far fewer in number; so will it be with members of the house of Israel. Note that willows grow quickly when they have sufficient water.

*water courses.* This phrase corresponds with "water" and "floods" above.

**44:5** *One shall say/another shall call/another shall subscribe.* These three are not opposed to each other; they are not in different camps. Instead, Isaiah is showing three different ways that people appropriately declare their allegiance to the true God.

*I am the Lord's.* Those who partake of the water (44:3) will become part of Jehovah's spiritual family and accept his covenants (*subscribe with his hand*).

*call himself by the name of Jacob.* Those who partake of the water (44:3) will become members of the house of Israel. This phrase parallels "surname himself by the name of Israel" (44:5).

*subscribe with his hand.* The upraised hand, both anciently and today, represents one's taking the name of the Lord upon himself by covenant. It is frequently connected to ordinances, such as baptism and those performed in the temple. The righteous will "write (*subscribe*) on their hand" the phrase "the Lord's" as a constant reminder that they belong to him (NIV, RSV, JB, NEB). This writing is not literal but symbolic, pointing to sacred ordinances, where we pledge with the hand.

*surname himself by the name of Israel.* Those who accept the gospel and receive the gift of the Spirit become the "seed of Abraham"[3] and members of the house of Israel.

**44:6** *Lord/King of Israel/redeemer/Lord of hosts/the first . . . and the last.* These titles of Jehovah describe his relationship with his people (41:14; 43:15).

**44:7** *who, as I, shall call.* The New International Version reads, "Who then is like me?" The Lord once again (41:21–24) challenges all to do the great and marvelous things he has done, including calling a chosen people, setting the kingdom in order, and prophesying ("declare") of things that are to come (43:10–13; Moses 1:6). Jehovah's challenge goes unanswered, because no one is his equal: "Beside [him] there is no God" (44:6).

*ancient people.* The nation of Israel is God's *ancient people.*

**44:8** *Fear ye not, neither be afraid.* The Lord instructs Israel not to fear the idols and graven images, which are identified in Isaiah 44:9–20. Then the Lord asks, "Is there a God beside me? yea, there is no God; I know not any" (44:8), implying that Israel must fear God and none other.

*witnesses.* The people of Israel are again reminded of their calling as the Lord's witnesses.

*Rock.* Christ, or Jehovah, is the *Rock,* representing permanence, stability, and eternality (see commentary on 2:21; 8:14).

---

[3] *Teachings of the Prophet Joseph Smith,* 150.

## THE FOOLISHNESS OF IDOLATRY (44:9–20)

Isaiah illustrates the foolishness of those who worship false gods. Such are extremely vain, and one day they will be ashamed for their abominations. Those who cut down a tree and use one piece of the wood for cooking and another piece to fashion a god "have not known nor understood: . . . they cannot see . . . they cannot understand" (44:18). They will not find salvation (44:20).

Although Isaiah speaks specifically of idols made from wood, he refers to false gods of any type, including money, worldly possessions, and power.

### *Isaiah 44:9–20*

They that make a *graven image* are all of them vanity;
and [*the things in which they delight*]⁴ shall not profit;

and they are their own witnesses;
they see not, nor know; that they may be ashamed. (44:9)

Who hath *formed* a god,
or *molten* a graven image
that is profitable for nothing? (44:10)

Behold, all his fellows shall be ashamed:
and the workmen, they are of men:

*let them* all be gathered together,
*let them* stand up;

yet *they* shall fear,
and *they* shall be ashamed together. (44:11)

The smith with the tongs both *worketh* in the coals,
and *fashioneth* it with hammers,
and *worketh* it with the strength of his arms:

yea, he is *hungry,* and his strength faileth:
he *drinketh no water,* and is faint. (44:12)

The *carpenter* stretcheth out his rule;
*he* marketh it out with a line;
*he* fitteth it with planes,
and *he* marketh it out with the compass,
and *he* maketh it after the figure of a man,
according to the beauty of a man;
that it may remain in the house. (44:13)

He *heweth him* down cedars,
and *taketh* the cypress and the oak,

which he *strengtheneth* for himself among the trees of the forest:

---

⁴ From Hebrew *chamad*, meaning "desire, take pleasure in." Brown, Driver, and Briggs, *Hebrew and English Lexicon,* 326. MT has *their delectable things.*

he *planteth* an <u>ash</u>,
and the rain doth nourish it. (44:14)

Then shall it be for a man to *burn:* for he will take thereof, and <u>warm himself</u>;
yea, he *kindleth it,* and <u>baketh bread</u>;

yea, he maketh a *god,* and <u>worshippeth</u> it;
he maketh it a *graven image,* and <u>falleth down thereto</u>. (44:15)

He burneth part thereof in the fire; with part thereof he eateth flesh;
he *roasteth roast,* and is <u>satisfied</u>:
yea, he *warmeth himself,* and saith, <u>Aha, I am warm</u>, I have seen the fire: (44:16)

And the residue thereof he *maketh* <u>a god</u>, even his graven image:
he *falleth down* unto <u>it</u>,
and *worshippeth* <u>it</u>,
and *prayeth* unto <u>it</u>,
and saith, *Deliver me;* for <u>thou art my god</u>. (44:17)

They have not known nor understood: for [they have][5] shut *their eyes,* that they
<u>cannot see</u>;
and *their hearts,* that they <u>cannot understand</u>. (44:18)

And none considereth in his heart,
neither is there knowledge nor understanding to say,

I have *burned* <u>part</u> of it in the fire;
yea, also I have *baked* <u>bread</u> upon the coals thereof;
I have *roasted* <u>flesh</u>, and eaten it:

and shall I *make* the residue thereof an <u>abomination</u>?
shall I *fall down* to the <u>stock of a tree</u>? (44:19)

He feedeth on ashes:
a deceived heart hath turned him aside, that he cannot deliver his soul,
nor say, Is there not a lie in my right hand? (44:20)

## NOTES AND COMMENTARY

**44:9** *vanity.* The root of the word *vanity* (Hebrew *tohu*) means "emptiness, or nothingness"[6] (24:10; in 41:29 the KJV translates this word as "confusion"). Those who create or worship idols will be empty and as "nothing"—without an eternal inheritance and without eternal increase. The gods "in which they delight" will not benefit ("shall not profit") them.

*they are their own witnesses.* As the followers of the Lord serve as his witnesses (see 44:8), so the makers of idols are derided as witnesses of their idols. The idol makers are not credible witnesses, however, because they are "vanity," "they see not, nor know" the truth.

---

[5] This is the sense of a number of other translations, including JB, NAB, NIV, and NRSV.
[6] Brown, Driver, and Briggs, *Hebrew and English Lexicon,* 1062.

*they may be ashamed. Ashamed* is used three times in 44:9 and 44:11. Shame is an awareness of a loss of honor and glory. Isaiah says that he who "formed a god" along with his worshiping companions ("his fellows") will "be ashamed together," probably at the Day of Judgment.

**44:11** *the workmen, they are of men.* The *workmen* who form the idols are mere mortals, incapable of giving life to their creations.

**44:12** *The smith . . . is hungry, and his strength faileth.* The smith, who works with his tools to fashion an idol "with the strength of his arms," grows weak with hunger and faint with thirst. Ironically, it is upon the smith's tools, talent, and skillful arm that the god's existence depends, and yet the smith cannot maintain his own strength without outside assistance. How can a supernatural being be created by a frail mortal? (40:19; Jer. 10:3–4).

**44:13** *carpenter.* Like the smith, the woodworker uses his tools and imagination to create an idol, making it in the form ("figure") of a man and adorning it with the things men find beautiful so that it will be placed in a house (temple) of a god.

**44:14–17** *heweth him down cedars . . . he maketh a god, even his graven image.* Isaiah points out the contradiction of creating and worshiping idols. The same tree a man uses for fuel to keep himself warm ("he warmeth himself, and saith, Aha, I am warm"; 44:16) and to cook meals ("baketh bread"; 44:15; "he roasteth roast"; 44:16) is used to make an idol—*and the residue [of the tree] he maketh a god, even his graven image.* The man takes a piece of the wood that was not used for fuel, and he takes his tools (ruler, marker, chisel, and compasses; 44:13) and carefully fashions a god. He then worships and prays to it, the work of his own hands, saying, "Save me, you are my god" (NIV 44:17).

**44:18** *shut their eyes, that they cannot see.* The idolaters have shut their eyes and closed their hearts to the truth by worshiping man-made idols (Ps. 115:4–8) rather than the living God.

**44:19** *none considereth in his heart.* Those who create and worship false gods do not consider their folly, which is this: "'I have burned part' of the tree and used its coals to bake bread and roast flesh, 'and shall I make the residue thereof an abomination [false god]?' Shall I worship a tree trunk?"

**44:20** *feedeth on ashes.* The soul that looks for spiritual nourishment from false gods partakes of nothing but the ashes that remain after the wooden idol is burned. Contrast that with those who feed on the living water and bread of eternal life.

*he cannot deliver his soul.* His heart "deceived" by idolatry and his soul unable to receive the spiritual nourishment it requires, the idol worshiper cannot find the

Lord and thereby deliver his soul from the gates of hell (D&C 76:81–86). In other words, even if the idolater can create his own god, he still cannot save himself.

*Is there not a lie in my right hand? Right hand* here speaks of covenant making. An individual blinded by idolatry cannot recognize that covenants made with idols are nothing more than lies (Ps. 144:8). This also means that by creating his god with his own (right) hand, the idolater relies on his own hand ("the arm of flesh") for salvation, which is a lie.

## THE LORD HAS REDEEMED ISRAEL (44:21–23)

The Lord reminds the children of Israel of their preferred status as his servants (44:21), adding that he will forgive them and forget their sins if they will return to him. Indeed, the Atonement has already been firmly decreed, and mankind's sins can be blotted out by the Redeemer (44:22). Because of this great gift of redemption, all of God's creations sing praises to him (44:23).

*Isaiah 44:21–23*

> Remember these, O Jacob and Israel; for thou art my servant:
> I have formed thee; thou art my servant:
> O Israel, thou shalt not be forgotten of me. (44:21)

> I have blotted out, as a *thick cloud,* thy <u>transgressions,</u>
> and, as a *cloud,* thy <u>sins</u>: return unto me; for I have redeemed thee. (44:22)

> *Sing,* O ye <u>heavens</u>; for the Lord hath done it:
> *shout,* ye <u>lower parts of the earth</u>:
> *break forth into singing,* ye <u>mountains</u>, O <u>forest</u>, and <u>every tree</u> therein:

> for the *Lord hath redeemed* <u>Jacob,</u>
> and *glorified himself* in <u>Israel</u>. (44:23)

NOTES AND COMMENTARY

**44:21** *Remember these.* We, members of the house of Israel, are commanded to remember the idolaters spoken of in the last section. In other words, the Lord is saying, "Don't forget the idolaters and their foolishness—remember them so you don't become like them."

*thou art my servant . . . thou shalt not be forgotten.* This passage refers also to us, the children of Israel who live in this dispensation (3 Ne. 16:11–12). We are to take comfort that we are still the Lord's servants (44:1; 48:20)—he has not forgotten us.

**44:22** *blotted out, as a thick cloud. As a thick cloud* blots out the sky, the Lord will blot out and remove our sins from his memory (Heb. 10:16–17; D&C 58:42).

*return unto me.* In Hebrew, to *return* (*shub*) is to repent.

*I have redeemed thee.* This statement refers to Christ's atonement, wrought on our behalf.

**44:23** *Sing, O ye heavens . . . break forth into singing, ye mountains.* All the Lord's creations sing praises to the Lord because he redeemed Israel (49:13; 55:12; D&C 128:22–23).

*shout, ye lower parts of the earth.* This passage may refer to those who dwell in the spirit world (see commentary on 8:21–22).

*O forest, and every tree.* These may represent people who *break forth into singing* (see commentary on 2:13).

*glorified himself in Israel.* The obedience of the righteous Saints in all ages brings glory to the Lord himself (Moses 1:39).

## CYRUS, THE LORD'S ANOINTED (44:24–28; 45:1–6)

The Lord who created all things (44:24) addresses Cyrus (who has not yet been born), calling him by name (45:4) and appointing him to serve as a deliverer of captive Israel (45:1–2). Cyrus was a type of Christ, the preeminent Anointed One who delivered us from our captivity of sin and death. The Lord prepared the way for Cyrus to conquer Babylon by opening doors and making rough places smooth (45:1–2). In the same way, the Lord will open doors and prepare the way for us to come to Zion. The result of the Lord's power in all these cases (the sending forth of Cyrus, the coming of Christ, and the establishment of Zion) is that all the world may know that Jehovah is the true God, greater than all others (45:5–6).

*Isaiah 44:24–28; 45:1–6*

> Thus saith the *Lord,* thy *redeemer,*
> and he that formed thee from the womb,
> I am the *Lord* that maketh all things;
>
> that *stretcheth* forth the heavens alone;
> that *spreadeth* abroad the earth by myself; (44:24)
>
> That *frustrateth* the tokens of the liars,
> and *maketh* diviners *mad;*
>
> that *turneth* wise men *backward,*
> and *maketh* their knowledge *foolish;* (44:25)
>
> That *confirmeth the word* of his servant,
> and *performeth the counsel* of his messengers;

that saith to *Jerusalem,* Thou shalt be inhabited;
and to the cities of *Judah,* Ye shall be built,
and I will raise up the decayed places *thereof:* (44:26)

That saith to the *deep,* Be dry,
and I will dry up thy *rivers:* (44:27)

That saith of Cyrus, He is my shepherd, and shall perform all my pleasure:
even saying to *Jerusalem,* Thou shalt be built;
and to the *temple,* Thy foundation shall be laid. (44:28)

Thus saith the Lord to his anointed, to Cyrus,

whose *right hand* I have [strengthened],[7] to subdue nations before him;
and I will loose the *loins* of kings,

to *open* before him the two leaved gates:[8]
and the gates shall *not be shut;* (45:1)

I will go before thee,

and *make* the crooked places *straight:*
I will *break in pieces* the gates of brass,
and *cut* [*asunder*][9] the bars of iron: (45:2)

And I will give thee the *treasures* of darkness,
and hidden *riches* of secret places,

that thou mayest know that I, the Lord, which call thee by thy name, am the God
of Israel. (45:3)

For *Jacob* my servant's sake,
and *Israel* mine elect,

*I have* even called thee by thy name:
*I have* surnamed thee, though thou hast not known me. (45:4)

*I am the Lord,* and there is none else,
there is no God *beside me:*

*I girded thee,* though thou hast not known me: (45:5)

That *they may know*
from the rising of the sun,
and from the west,

that there is none *beside me.*
*I am the Lord,* and there is none else. (45:6)

## NOTES AND COMMENTARY

**44:24** *redeemer.* See commentary on 41:14.

*formed thee from the womb.* See commentary on 44:2; see also 1 Ne. 21:5.

---

[7] Footnote *c* to 45:1 in the LDS edition of the Bible suggests *strengthened* as a substitute for *holden.*
[8] Or *double doors.* See footnote *e* to 45:1 in the LDS edition of the Bible.
[9] This replaces the KJV *in sunder.*

*I am the Lord that maketh all things.* By reminding us that he made all things and that by himself he "stretcheth forth the heavens" and "spreadeth abroad the earth," the Lord gives us confidence in his ability to raise up Cyrus to deliver the Jews from Babylonian captivity and to raise up Jesus Christ to deliver all of us from death and sin.

**44:25** *frustrateth the tokens of the liars.* The Lord alone knows the future. He is able, therefore, to frustrate (make ineffectual) the tokens, signs, and omens of the false prophets, priests, and diviners.

*turneth wise men backward/maketh their knowledge foolish.* The diviners and *wise men* who counsel the kings of the ancient Middle East believe they have access to supernatural counsel, but their knowledge and promises are useless, for only God's true servants and messengers are able to confirm God's word. The wise men here refer to those who are "learned" and "think they are wise," but "they hearken not unto the counsel of God, for they set it aside, supposing they know of themselves" (2 Ne. 9:28).

**44:26** *confirmeth the word of his servant.* The Lord fulfills every prophecy made by his servants, the prophets (Luke 24:44; 2 Ne. 10:17; D&C 1:38).

*Jerusalem, Thou shalt be inhabited/cities of Judah, Ye shall be built.* This prophecy was to be fulfilled at least twice: once when Cyrus permitted the exiled Jews to return to their homeland, and again when the Jews return to their homeland in this dispensation. This latter fulfillment is occurring at the present time.

**44:27** *That saith to the deep, Be dry.* The great seas are often referred to by the prophets as *the deep* (D&C 133:20; 2 Ne. 4:20). By pointing out that the Lord can command the deep (and the rivers; 44:27) to dry up (Hel. 12:16; Jer. 51:36) Isaiah implies that restoring Judah to their lands is, by comparison, much more simple.

**44:28** *Cyrus/shepherd.* This is the first time Cyrus is mentioned by name in Isaiah's prophecy. He is called *my shepherd,* a common title of kings (Ezek. 34). Shepherd is one of the names of Christ, who is the King of Israel (43:15) and of whom Cyrus was a type.

Cyrus was the king who freed the people of Israel from political bondage and provided a way for them to return to their homeland. Christ is the King who frees all people from the bondage of death—and the repentant from spiritual death—and provides a way for us to return to our original home in God's presence. This temporal appointment was given to Cyrus, as it was to Peter, "according to the foreknowledge of God the Father" (1 Pet. 1:2). This prophecy concerning Cyrus was given by Isaiah approximately two hundred years before Cyrus ruled Babylon.

*shall perform all my pleasure.* Cyrus will do all the Lord asks of him; specifically, he will allow both Jerusalem and the temple to be rebuilt.

*saying to Jerusalem, Thou shalt be built.* See commentary on 44:26.

*saying . . . to the temple, Thy foundation shall be laid.* All that the Lord promised concerning Cyrus was accomplished, including the rebuilding of Jerusalem and the establishment of the temple (46:10; 2 Chr. 36:23; Ezra 1:1–2). The rebuilding of the temple by Jews who returned to their homeland in Cyrus' day anticipates a future time when the temple will again be built in Jerusalem.

**45:1** *his anointed.* The kings of Israel were known as "the anointed of Jehovah"; they were anointed with oil at their coronation. Cyrus was made king, or leader, over God's people (1 Sam. 10:1; 16:13; 1 Kgs. 1:39; 2 Kgs. 9: 3, 6). But there may be a second meaning here: the Hebrew word *anointed* becomes *Messiah* in English and *Christ* in Greek. By calling Cyrus *his anointed,* the Lord may be pointing out that Cyrus is a type of Christ. In addition, the *anointed* may be interpreted to mean any of God's servants who are anointed to do his work.

*Cyrus.* Cyrus was a historical ruler and conqueror who was also a type of Christ.

Biblical scholar John D. W. Watts commented on Isaiah's prophecy about Cyrus: "This description [in Isaiah 45] fits Cyrus's career. He had profited from many circumstances other than his military strength. He had gained the following of all the Persian tribes with singular ease. . . . Two successive Median armies that were sent against him decided to join forces with him instead. . . . He marched without opposition into Armenia and won a surprise victory over the Lydians when their horses were frightened by the smell of Persian camels. And now Babylon, the world's most heavily fortified city, opens its gates to him without a fight. . . . Truly *doors* and *gates* had been opened for Cyrus."[10]

*right hand.* Grasping another by the right hand indicates friendship, acceptance, guidance, and protection (41:13). It was the practice of the Babylonian ruler to take the hand of the idol Bel in the New Year's festival as a sign of union between him and Bel. Here Jehovah, the true God, indicates that Cyrus can have union, not with a false idol, but with God himself.

*subdue nations.* The role of conqueror is one of the roles of David (Ps. 21, 110). By acting in this role, Cyrus becomes a type of David who is a type of Christ. The collective strength of nations would not be able to resist Cyrus, nor would individual kings.

---

[10] *Isaiah 34–66,* 156.

*subdue/loose/open . . . gates/not be shut.* All these words suggest the great power the Lord would vest in Cyrus. Nothing would be able to stand in his way.

*loose the loins of kings.* To ungird their loins means to strip them of their weapons, making it impossible for them to fight. This verse not only tells how God will aid Cyrus but also proclaims God's power.

*two leaved gates.* These are not single doors but rather the wide, main, double doors (*two leaved*) of the city. The *gates* both grant and bar entrance. This passage seems to say the Lord will open cities to Cyrus as conqueror; in the same way, the Lord will remove barriers for his anointed ones in any age.

**45:2** *I will go before thee.* This promise is the same one the Lord gave to Israel as she prepared to make her exodus out of Egypt (Ex. 23:20; 32:34); it is the promise he gives us as we come to Zion (D&C 103:17–20). The Lord attends those who do his will, blessing them on their way (Mosiah 24:17; Eth. 1:42; D&C 39:12).

*make the crooked places straight.* The Lord will remove obstacles in Cyrus's way or in the way of any of his anointed ones. This expression is also used in prophecies concerning the first coming of the Lord (40:4; 42:16; Eccl. 7:13; Luke 3:4–5).

*break . . . brass/cut . . . iron.* God will exercise his power to break even the most imposing barriers in Cyrus's way. In a similar manner, God will exercise power to remove the barriers that prevent us from doing his will, if we will trust in him.

*bars of iron.* Iron gates, or the bars that help secure the gates (Deut. 3:5; Neh. 7:3; Ps. 107:15–16; Jer. 51:58; Nahum 3:13).

**45:3** *treasures/darkness/hidden riches.* Cyrus will be given the spoils of war, even though they be hidden in dark places. Another possible interpretation is that God will give his true servants the hidden treasures of revelation.

*call . . . by thy name.* God's word to Cyrus was specifically directed to him. That it was a personal call is reemphasized in the next verse. So also does God call us (40:26; 43:1).

**45:4** *my servant's sake.* Cyrus was not given victory or spoils for his own benefit. God called him to his work for the benefit of Israel so that ultimately the world would come to the knowledge of God (45:6). The same principle holds when we receive divine calls: we are not called just for our own benefit. Joseph Smith taught: "That we may learn still further that God calls or elects particular men to perform particular works, or on whom to confer special blessings, we read, . . . 'For Jacob my servant's sake, and Israel mine elect, I have even called thee [Cyrus] by thy name,' to be a deliverer to my people Israel, and help to plant them on my holy mountain."[11]

---

[11] *History of the Church,* 4:257.

*mine elect.* The elect are those who "hear my voice and harden not their hearts" (D&C 29:7). They are "holy and beloved" (Col. 3:12). They are people of faith (Titus 1:1; D&C 84:33–34). The elect are those who are righteous, who love the Lord with all their hearts, and, in the ultimate sense, have made their calling and election sure (2 Pet. 1:10).

*surnamed thee.* The Hebrew word here *(kanᵉak)* can mean either a surname or an honorary title. Perhaps the Lord gave Cyrus the surname of Israel, adopting him into the chosen people (44:5), or perhaps the Lord was honoring Cyrus's own name for the work Cyrus would do.

**45:5** *I am the Lord.* Jehovah declares himself to his people (43:10–11; 46:9; D&C 76:1).

*I girded thee.* The Lord equipped Cyrus with the means to win in battle, in contrast to the kings in 45:1, who were stripped of their weapons. The Lord will equip his servant (see 49:1, 3; 50:4–9; 52:13–15; and 53:1–12 for discussions on the identity of the Lord's servant), of whom Cyrus is a type, in spiritual battle, girding him with power from on high. Some translations give this as "I will strengthen you" (NEB, NIV).

*thou hast not known me.* Even though Cyrus was unacquainted with the true God, he did God's work. Contrast this statement with the blessing to those who benefit from the labors of Cyrus: "That they may know . . . that there is none beside me" (45:6). The real fulfillment of this promise would come through the labor of God's anointed servant, Jesus Christ, of whom Cyrus was a type. The promises Cyrus receives are similar to those given to David, another type of Christ, in Psalm 2:8–10 and 72:8–10.

Interestingly, the Jewish historian Josephus, who wrote only a few years after the crucifixion of Christ, recorded that Cyrus may have learned something of the true God:

"In the first year of the reign of Cyrus [539 B.C.], which was the seventieth from the day that our people were removed out of their own land into Babylon, God commiserated the captivity and calamity of these poor people, . . . for he stirred up the mind of Cyrus, and made him write this throughout all Asia:—'Thus saith Cyrus the King:—Since God Almighty hath appointed me to be king of the habitable earth, I believe that he is that God which the nation of the Israelites worship; for indeed he foretold my name by the prophets, and that I should build him a house at Jerusalem, in the country of Judea.'

"This was known to Cyrus by his reading the book which Isaiah left behind him of his prophecies; for this prophet said that God had spoken thus to him in a secret vision:—'My will is, that Cyrus, whom I have appointed to be king over many and great nations, send back my people to their own land, and build my temple.' This was foretold by Isaiah one hundred and forty years before the temple was demolished. Accordingly, when Cyrus read this, and admired the divine power, an earnest desire and ambition seized upon him to fulfil what was so written."[12]

It may be that Cyrus read the prophecy in which he was named and that he acknowledged Jehovah as the true God—but at the same time he "played both sides of the field" by also giving credit to the Babylonian god Marduk and other gods. Thus he did not truly know Jehovah as God, exactly as Isaiah prophesied.

**45:6** *rising of the sun/west.* These two lines denote that Jehovah is the God of the whole earth and will yet be known as such. Revealing Jehovah to all nations is part of the peculiar mission of Israel (42:1–4, 6–8), and we of the Church are latter-day Israel. This prophecy is similar to the one made by Malachi: "For from the rising of the sun even unto the going down of the same my name shall be great among the Gentiles; . . . for my name shall be great among the heathen, saith the Lord of hosts" (Mal. 1:11).

---

[12] Josephus, *Antiquities of the Jews,* 11.1.1–2.

# ISAIAH 45:7-25

### LIKENING ISAIAH 45 UNTO OURSELVES

*The Lord has great power over all his creations. He can bring light or darkness, peace or misfortune. Isaiah compares God to a potter and us to the pots; he compares God to a parent and us to a little child. The Lord has created earth and man, and he stands at the head of all the armies of heaven. Even the heathen will come to recognize his supremacy. With such power, the Lord can direct the events of earth as he desires—and we would be wise to submit ourselves to his will.*

## THE LORD'S POWER AND DOMINION (45:7–13)

There is opposition in all things—light and darkness, peace and evil (or trouble)—yet the Lord has power over all (45:7). Those who question the Lord in his works are as foolish as a pot would be to question the work of its potter; they are as foolish as an infant would be to question its parents (45:9–10). The Lord commands all the host of heaven (45:12), and he can raise up a deliverer unto Israel (45:13).

*Isaiah 45:7–13*

> I *form* the <u>light</u>,
> and *create* <u>darkness</u>:
>
> I *make* <u>peace</u>,
> and *create* <u>evil</u>: I the Lord do all these things. (45:7)
>
> *Drop down*, ye <u>heavens</u>, from above,
> and let the <u>skies</u> *pour down* righteousness:
> let the <u>earth</u> *open*,
>
> and let them *bring forth* <u>salvation</u>,
> and let <u>righteousness</u> *spring up* together; I the Lord have created it. (45:8)

Woe unto him that striveth with his Maker!
Let the [fragment of pottery][1] strive with the [pottery fragments][2] of the earth.

Shall the *clay* say to him that fashioneth it, <u>What makest thou</u>?
or thy *work,* <u>He hath no hands</u>? (45:9)

Woe unto him that saith unto his *father,* <u>What begettest thou</u>?
or to the *woman,* <u>What hast thou brought forth</u>? (45:10)

Thus saith the *Lord,*
the *Holy One of Israel,*
and his *Maker,*

*Ask me* of things to come <u>concerning my sons</u>,
and <u>concerning the work of my hands</u> *command ye me.* (45:11)

I have *made the earth,* and <u>created man</u> upon it:
I, even my hands, have *stretched out the*
*heavens,* and all <u>their host</u> have I commanded. (45:12)

*I have raised* <u>him up</u> in righteousness,
and *I will direct* <u>all his ways</u>:

*he shall* <u>build my city,</u>
and *he shall* <u>let go my captives,</u>

not for *price*
nor *reward,*

saith the Lord of hosts. (45:13)

## NOTES AND COMMENTARY

**45:7** *light . . . darkness.* This phrase echoes the account of the Creation: "And God said, Let there be light: and there was light. And . . . God divided the light from the darkness" (Gen. 1:3–4). Jehovah says he is above both light and darkness, having created them (Ezek. 32:8).

   *create evil.* Certainly the Lord is not the originator of evil; that is made clear in Moroni 7:12: "That which is evil cometh of the devil." But *evil* can also mean "ill fortune, trial, or difficulty." As the New International Version says, "I bring prosperity and create disaster." Job gave expression to this idea of the duality of God's power when he said, "Shall we receive good at the hand of God, and shall we not receive evil?" (Job 2:10). As the New International Version puts it: "Shall we accept good from God, and not trouble?" The point of 45:6–7 seems to be that God is in charge: he has power over all things and directs the affairs of men to their ultimate good.

---

[1] This replaces the KJV *potsherd.*
[2] This replaces the KJV *potsherds.*

**45:8** *Drop down, ye heavens . . . righteousness.* Instead of the sky dropping rain, it is dropping down righteousness. Perhaps this phrase refers to revelation, which comes down from the heavens and enables us to come to righteousness.

*earth open.* This expression has at least two meanings. One is to receive the righteousness (and revelation) from above, even as the earth receives the rain. Another, according to Elder Orson Pratt and others of the early Brethren of this dispensation, is to prophesy of the coming forth of the Book of Mormon.[3]

*bring forth/spring up.* This sweet prayer is a blessing the Lord pronounces on us, that righteousness, like plants, will spring forth on the earth. As Creator, the Lord implies, he has the power to bring about such a blessing (26:19). With our agency, we can choose to participate in this blessing. This passage may also refer to the coming of the Messiah, whose name is Son of Righteousness (3 Ne. 25:2).

*salvation.* The Hebrew word used here, *yesha*—also meaning "deliverance"—comes from the same root as the names *Isaiah* and *Joshua.* In the Greek New Testament the name became *Jesus.* Could Isaiah be saying in a symbolic way, "Let the heavens and the earth bring forth Jesus, our deliverer"?

**45:9** *Woe unto him that striveth with his Maker.* Here the Lord warns those who will not accept his will and his plan. In particular, the people of Israel seem to have questioned the Lord's plan to use a gentile conqueror (Cyrus) to liberate them from their oppressors. Their logic told them that replacing one heathen ruler with another was not the way to freedom and self-rule. But the Lord, in his wisdom, sought to direct the affairs of his people in the way that would most bless them. Like those of ancient Israel, too often the Lord's people in our day doubt and question him: "What makest thou? . . . What begettest thou? . . . What hast thou brought forth?" We have no more right to question the work of the Lord than a pot has to question the potter who fashioned it. Instead, we should trust the Lord, whose foreknowledge is perfect: "Ask me of things to come" (45:11). His power is supreme: "I have made the earth, and . . . all their host have I commanded" (45:12). In addition, we should accept any servants the Lord raises "up in righteousness," for the Lord's true servants allow him to "direct all [their] ways" (45:13). We should accept the Lord's divinely ordained and revealed plans, even when we cannot understand how they could work.

*Let the fragment of pottery strive with the pottery fragments of the earth.* We are as a fragment of pottery, the Lord being the potter. If we must strive or question, let it be with other human beings, certainly not with the Lord, who is our Maker.

[3] *Divine Authenticity of the Book of Mormon,* 96.

*clay/him that fashioneth it.* The Lord uses the image of the clay and the potter in other places as well (29:16; Jer. 18:1–6; Rom. 9:20–21). The clay, of course, is man, and the potter is God. This image is also reminiscent of God's forming the body of Adam from the clay of the earth (Gen. 2:7; Job 33:6).

*no hands.* It is foolishness for a created thing to say that its creator has no hands. Yet that is what man does when he says that God has no power to do his work. Contrast *no hands* in this verse with 45:12: "I, even my hands, have stretched out the heavens."

**45:10** *him/father.* Just as it is improper for us to question our parents concerning our begetting, so it is improper for us to question our Heavenly Father, in a spirit of doubt, concerning his works and his motivations.

**45:11** *the Holy One of Israel.* This term refers to Jehovah, who is holy indeed (29:23; 57:15; Lev. 11:45; see also commentary on 1:4).

*Ask me of things to come.* The Lord is willing to prophesy to us if we will ask.

*Ask/command.* It is improper to question the Lord in a spirit of doubt (45:9–10), but the Lord is willing to tell us much if we ask in humility and meekness. As footnote 11c in the LDS edition of the Bible says, "This invites one to tell the Lord what one wants to know." The New International Version gives an alternative reading, putting this verse as a continuation of the questions asked in verses 9 and 10: "Concerning things to come, do you question me about my children, or give me orders about the work of my hands?"

*my sons.* The true followers of Christ are born again as his sons and his daughters.

*hands.* God is the one whose hands made the heaven and the earth.

**45:12–13** *made the earth/stretched out the heavens/host . . . commanded.* These expressions demonstrate the power of God (40:26; 42:5; 44:24). He created the earth, he constantly extends his dominion, and he commands all his children.

*host.* Those who dwell in the heavens, meaning gods and angels.

*I have made/my hands/I commanded/I have raised/I will direct/my city/my captives.* The Lord's repeated use of the first person seems to emphasize that he is God and that it is he who works through his servant (see commentary on 45:13).

**45:13** *raised him up.* As the Lord has exercised power over the elements to create the heavens and the earth, so also has he exercised power over the affairs of men by raising up a deliverer. The person referred to here could be either Cyrus or Christ; the verse probably has a dual meaning and thus may refer to both. In fact, the description of the Lord's servant in this verse can apply to any righteous man or woman of God who hearkens to the Lord and helps to free those in bondage to sin (see D&C 101:80 for another instance of the Lord raising up men to do his work).

*my city.* This city may be Jerusalem or the great city of Zion, or the New Jerusalem (Heb. 12:22; 3 Ne. 21:23; Ether 13:8). Modern revelation further clarifies that it is the righteous of Israel who will build the Lord's city (D&C 109:58). This may indicate that righteous Israel as a body is the servant mentioned in this passage, or the servant could be Cyrus or another leader of Israel. Joseph Smith described this city of Zion as "the city of righteousness . . . where the people shall be of one heart and one mind, when the Savior comes; yea, where the people shall walk with God like Enoch, and be free from sin."[4]

*captives.* This term has three possible meanings, all of them true: Israel, who has been in bondage to a foreign nation; the Lord's people on earth, who have been in bondage to sin; and the prisoners in the spirit world (42:7; 49:9; Zech. 9:11–12).

*not for price/reward.* Captives traditionally became property for the captor to use or sell as slaves or to trade for ransom. But Israel's deliverance from bondage (through Cyrus or at any other time) would not come because Israel made any payment; it would come as a gift from God (53:6). In the same way, our deliverance from the bondage of sin does not come because we pay a price, but because Christ has paid in our behalf, so it also is a gift of God (52:3). Salvation is free to those who accept and follow Christ (55:1; 2 Ne. 9:50; 2 Ne. 26:25; Alma 5:34).

This phrase may also have another meaning. The deliverer performed his work to bless the people and to please the Lord, not because of any price or reward he himself would receive.

*Lord of hosts.* The Lord is a God who rules multitudes, even the hosts of heaven.

## THE HEATHEN WILL ACKNOWLEDGE THE LORD (45:14–17)

Israel has been in bondage, subject as slaves to the will of foreign oppressors. But through the deliverance that God will send, she will yet receive the wealth ("labour," "merchandise") and respect ("fall down unto thee," "make supplication") of many nations (45:14). The peoples of these nations will confess the true God ("Surely God is in thee," 45:14), while those who make and worship idols will be "ashamed" and "confounded" (45:16). But Israel "shall not be ashamed nor confounded world

---

[4] *History of the Church,* 2:358.

without end" (45:17). We are all in bondage to sin, but if we qualify, the Lord will give us rich blessings and will stand by us eternally.

*Isaiah 45:14–17*

> Thus saith the Lord,
>
> The *labour* of <u>Egypt</u>,
> and *merchandise* of <u>Ethiopia</u> and of the <u>Sabeans</u>,
>
> *men of stature,* shall <u>come over unto thee,</u>
> and *they* shall <u>be thine</u>:
>
> *they* shall <u>come after thee;</u>
> in chains *they* shall <u>come over,</u>
>
> and *they* shall <u>fall down unto thee,</u>
> *they* shall <u>make supplication unto thee</u>, saying,
>
> Surely God is in thee; and *there is* <u>none else,</u>
> *there is* <u>no God</u>. (45:14)
>
> Verily thou art a God that hidest thyself,
>
> O *God of Israel,*
> the *Saviour.* (45:15)
>
> *They* shall be <u>ashamed,</u>
> and also <u>confounded,</u> all of *them:*
> *they* shall go to <u>confusion</u> together that are makers of idols. (45:16)
>
> But Israel shall be *saved* in the Lord
> with an everlasting *salvation:*
>
> ye shall *not be ashamed*
> *nor confounded* world without end. (45:17)

## NOTES AND COMMENTARY

**45:14** *labour/merchandise.* The gentile nations, bringing their wealth with them, will help to build Zion (18:7; 23:18; 60:3–14).

*Egypt/Ethiopia/Sabeans.* These nations, which formerly had oppressed Israel (43:3), will now submit themselves to the Lord's people. In a broader sense, this may refer to all gentile nations (14:1; 60:14).

*men of stature.* This represents those who are important in the eyes of the world.

*come over unto thee/be thine/fall down/make supplication.* The Gentiles will come unto Israel and acknowledge that the true God is with them.

*chains.* They come as slaves, not free men. These chains most likely are spiritual chains, binding the people in spiritual bondage.

*there is no God.* That is, the Gentiles acknowledge that there is no other God besides Jehovah.

**45:15** *hidest thyself.* God remains hidden to the disobedient and unbeliever. Sometimes he also remains hidden to the righteous, to try their faith (8:17; Ps. 10:1; 44:23–24; 88:14; D&C 101:89; 121:1; 123:6). The expression can also mean that he does his work through others and remains unseen.

**45:16–17** *ashamed/confounded/not be ashamed nor confounded.* The wicked idolaters will be ashamed of their works and be confounded (meaning disgraced, confused, or destroyed), while the righteous are justified in their course and will be saved (41:11; 50:7; 54:4; Ps. 70:2; 2 Ne. 6:7, 13; D&C 109:29).

**45:17** *everlasting salvation.* Eternal life is *everlasting salvation* (Mosiah 5:15; D&C 43:25).

*world without end.* This phrase means through all eternity (Eph. 3:21; D&C 76:112).

## THE LORD IS GOD OF THE WHOLE EARTH (45:18–25)

This passage illustrates some of the roles and attributes of God: He is the Creator ("created the heavens; . . . formed the earth"), the Revealer ("I have not spoken in secret"), and the "Savior" (45:18, 19, 21). He is "just" (45:21) and gives us power to do righteousness ("in the Lord have I righteousness and strength"; 45:24). He is a God of truth and equity ("I . . . speak righteousness"; 45:19). He is the source of true prophecy, as contrasted with false gods ("Who hath declared this from ancient time? . . . have not I the Lord?"; 45:21). He is the only true God ("no God else beside me"; 45:21). He is the God of the whole earth ("look unto me, and be ye saved, all the ends of the earth"; 45:22). Eventually, all must acknowledge him ("every knee shall bow, every tongue shall swear"; 45:23). In him, the faithful will be "justified" and have cause to "glory" (45:25). All this stands in contrast to the gods of the heathen, which "cannot save" (45:20). It also stands in contrast to the things of our day that we embrace in place of the one true God.

*Isaiah 45:18–25*

> For thus saith the *Lord* that created the heavens;
> *God* himself that formed the earth
> and made it;
> *he* hath established it,
> *he* created it not in vain,
> *he* formed it to be inhabited: I am the Lord; and there is none else. (45:18)
>
> I have *not spoken* in secret,
> in a dark place of the earth: *I said not* unto the seed of Jacob,

Seek ye me in vain:

*I the Lord* <u>speak righteousness,</u>
*I* <u>declare</u> things that are *right.* (45:19)

*Assemble* yourselves and <u>come;</u>
*draw near together,* ye that are <u>escaped</u> of the nations:

they have no knowledge that *set up* the wood of their <u>graven image,</u>
and *pray* unto a <u>god</u> that cannot save. (45:20)

Tell ye, and bring them near; yea, let them take counsel together:

who *hath declared* this from <u>ancient time</u>?
who *hath told* it from <u>that time</u>?

have not *I the Lord?* and there is <u>no God else beside me;</u>
*a just God and a Saviour;* there is <u>none beside me.</u> (45:21)
Look unto me, and be ye saved, all the ends of the earth:
for *I am God,* and <u>there is none else.</u> (45:22)

I have *sworn* by <u>myself,</u>
the *word is gone out* of <u>my mouth</u> in righteousness, and shall not return,

That unto me every *knee* shall <u>bow,</u>
every *tongue* shall <u>swear.</u> (45:23)

Surely, shall one say, in the Lord have I righteousness and strength:
even to him shall men come;

and *all that are incensed* against him <u>shall be ashamed</u>. (45:24)
In the Lord shall *all the seed of Israel* be justified, and <u>shall glory</u>. (45:25)

## Notes and Commentary

**45:18** *established it.* The Lord set it (the earth) in place.

*created it not in vain.* The Lord has a purpose for the earth, which purpose will be fulfilled.

**45:19** *secret . . . a dark place.* Although the Lord is hidden to the unbeliever (45:15), he speaks openly, not in hiding, to those who will hear (43:10; 44:8). This phrase may also refer to the common practice of seeking revelations among the dead, which was often done "in secret, in a dark place of the earth" (1 Sam. 28:13). The oracles at Delphi, for example, prophesied in secret and then took credit in public for having foretold whatever happened.

*seed of Jacob.* The *seed of Jacob* are the literal or spiritual descendants of Jacob or Israel, the heirs of the covenant (3 Ne. 5:24–25; Morm. 7:10; D&C 103:17).

**45:20** *Assemble yourselves and come.* The call for Israel to gather represents the work of gathering in our day, which is accomplished through missionary work.

*escaped of the nations.* These are the righteous who are gathered to Zion, leaving the nations of the world.

**45:21** *counsel together.* Those who make and worship idols are to ask if they can find any evidence that the idols have been able to prophesy accurately, as the Lord has done.

*declared this from ancient time.* The Lord has declared his sovereignty and dominion from the beginning, whereas the idols have consistently shown themselves to possess neither.

*no God else beside me.* This idea is repeated three times in this verse and the next. The nations may worship many gods, but there is only one true God, with power to declare and to bring to pass. That God is Jehovah.

**45:22** *all the ends of the earth.* Every part of the earth. This phrase is repeated more than sixty times in the scriptures.

*Look unto me/be ye saved.* The idols (45:20) have no power to save. It is Christ and the power of his atonement that save.

**45:23** *sworn by myself.* Christ has taken an oath upon his own name. As God is unchanging and infallible, so is that which he promises.

*word . . . shall not return.* His oath is final and irrevocable: "Though the heavens and the earth pass away, my word shall not pass away, but shall all be fulfilled" (D&C 1:38).

*every knee shall bow, every tongue shall swear.* All people will acknowledge the Lord's supremacy with physical obeisance and verbal testimony. In Mosiah 16:1–2, Abinadi indicates that this prophecy will be fulfilled at the time of the Second Coming, "when all shall see the salvation of the Lord." President Joseph Fielding Smith taught that those who so bow are not necessarily candidates for celestial glory but also include those who will inherit a terrestrial and telestial glory[5] (Rom. 14:10–12; Mosiah 27:31; D&C 76:110–11; 88:104).

**45:24** *in the Lord have I righteousness and strength/to him shall men come.* It is by coming to Christ that we are able to develop righteousness and spiritual strength. As Moroni said, "Come unto Christ, and be perfected in him" (Moro. 10:32), suggesting that perfection (or righteousness and strength) comes only by coming to the Savior and receiving of the blessings of his atonement.

*incensed.* Being *incensed* means being deeply angered.

**45:25** *seed of Israel.* See commentary on 41:8.

*justified.* One who is *justified* is judged and found worthy.

*glory.* In this context, *glory* means having cause to rejoice and give praise to God.

---

[5] *Doctrines of Salvation,* 2:30–31.

⸺◦⟋◦⟋◦⸺

# ISAIAH 46

*LIKENING ISAIAH 46 UNTO OURSELVES*

*The idols of ancient nations had no power to help themselves against the encroach-ments of enemies. They were carried away on the backs of beasts and could not prevent it; they were equally powerless to help the people who worshiped them. So also are our material accumulations and our temporal pursuits unable to help us in times of need.*

*In contrast, the Lord not only has power to help but he carries us through our times of trial. He will support us from beginning to end. Even time and space are no obstacles to him. Whatever he decides to do, he will accomplish.*

---

## IDOLS HAVE NO POWER (46:1–7)

Bel and Nebo, two chief pagan gods, are carried away on the backs of beasts into captivity (46:1–2). In other words, the idols are carried by those who made them (46:7). In contrast, Jehovah has carried his people on his own back "from the womb," and he will continue to carry them "even to your old age" (46:3–4). While the idols have no power to deliver even themselves, Jehovah will deliver his people (46:2, 4). The idol worshipers may spend a fortune in making their images, but idols cannot help them in their time of "trouble" (46:6–7). Jehovah, who made us (46:4), will help us through every difficulty (D&C 3:8).

*Isaiah 46:1–7*

> *Bel* boweth down,
> *Nebo* stoopeth,
>
> their idols were *upon the beasts,*
> and *upon the cattle:*

[ 4 0 1 ]

your *carriages* were heavy laden;
*they* are a burden to the weary beast. (46:1)

They *stoop,*
they *bow down* together;

*they* could not deliver the burden,
but *themselves* are gone into captivity. (46:2)

Hearken unto me, O *house of Jacob,*
and all the remnant of the *house of Israel,*

which are *borne* by me from the belly,
which are *carried* from the womb: (46:3)

And even to your *old age* I am he;
and even to [grey]¹ *hairs* will I carry you:

*I* have made,
and *I* will bear;
even *I* will carry,
and will deliver you. (46:4)

To whom will ye *liken* me, and make me equal,
and *compare* me, that we may be like? (46:5)

They *lavish gold* out of the bag,
and *weigh silver* in the balance,

and *hire* a goldsmith;
and he *maketh* it a god:

they *fall down,*
yea, they *worship.* (46:6)

*They* bear him upon the shoulder,
*they* carry him,

and *set* him in his place,
and he *standeth;* from his place shall he not remove:

yea, one shall *cry unto him,*
yet can *he not answer,* nor save him out of his trouble. (46:7)

## Notes and Commentary

**46:1** *Bel/Nebo.* In the belief system of the Assyrians and Babylonians, *Bel* was the chief god, the father of all other gods. Nebo was the god of learning and wisdom. Bel seems to have been the pagan equivalent of God the Father or of Jehovah; *Nebo* was the pagan equivalent of the Holy Ghost. These idols should be seen as symbolic of all things in our lives that we love more than God and obedience to his will.

---

¹This word replaces the KJV *hoar.* This change is suggested in the LDS edition of the Bible, footnote *b* to 46:4.

**46:1-2** *boweth down/stoopeth/stoop/bow.* The idols are brought low into captivity.

**46:2** *captivity.* The pagan gods (idols) are literally carried away by the enemy, just as their worshipers are made captive to sin.

**46:3** *house of Jacob/Israel.* This phrase refers both to the literal descendants of Jacob, or Israel, and to those who become heir to the Abrahamic promise by obedience to the gospel covenant.

*remnant.* The surviving descendants of Jacob, both literally and spiritually, are the *remnant* (10:20–21; Micah 5:7–8; Alma 46:23–24; 3 Ne. 5:24; D&C 52:2).

*borne by me from the belly/carried from the womb.* Israel was carried, or protected, by God as a mother carries her unborn child, in a perfect protective and nourishing position, in contrast to the idol gods that had to be borne by their worshipers (44:2, 24). God likewise carries and protects his faithful ones of all ages.

**46:3–4** *womb/old age.* The Lord will support and help us from the beginning of our lives to the end (Ps. 71:16–18, 21).

**46:5** *liken me/equal/compare me.* No god or any other person or thing can be compared to the Lord; all else is nothing compared to him (40:25).

**46:6** *lavish gold/weigh silver.* Though the idol gods are made of precious materials, they still have no power (44:15–17).

**46:7** *bear him/carry him.* When we turn to other people or things in place of God, they become in the end only burdens for us to carry rather than blessings to help in time of trouble. This emphasizes again that these are man-made gods that have no power of their own.

## The Lord Will Accomplish All His Purposes (46:8–13)

God commands us to remember his power, to remember his dealings in earlier times, such as when he delivered Israel from Egypt ("the former things of old"; 46:9). "I am God, and there is none else," he says. "There is none like me" (46:9). He has power to declare events before they happen (46:10). He has power to do whatever he pleases (46:10). He can call helpers from faraway places ("ravenous bird," "man that executeth my counsel"; 46:11). Those who are stubborn ("stouthearted") and wicked ("far from righteousness") need to take heed, for the Lord will be victor and Zion and righteous Israel will triumph with him (46:12–13).

*Isaiah 46:8–13*

> *Remember* this, and [show]² yourselves <u>men</u>:
> *bring it again to mind,* O ye <u>transgressors</u>. (46:8)

> Remember the former things of old:

> for *I am God,* and <u>there is none else</u>;
> *I am God,* and <u>there is none like me</u>, (46:9)

> Declaring the *end* from the <u>beginning</u>,
> and from *ancient times* the things that are <u>not yet done</u>,

> saying, My counsel shall stand, and I will do all my pleasure: (46:10)

> Calling a *ravenous bird* from the <u>east</u>,
> *the man* that executeth my counsel from a <u>far country</u>:

> yea, I have *spoken it,* I will also <u>bring it to pass</u>;
> I have *purposed it,* I will also <u>do it</u>. (46:11)

> Hearken unto me, ye *stouthearted,*
> that are *far from righteousness:* (46:12)

> I *bring near* my <u>righteousness</u>;
> <u>it</u> shall *not be far off,*

> and my *salvation* shall *not tarry:*
> and I *will place salvation* in Zion for Israel my glory. (46:13)

## NOTES AND COMMENTARY

**46:8** *show yourselves men.* Demonstrate that you are people of integrity and honor.

**46:9** *former things of old.* Remember the historical evidences, including the Exodus and Israel's conquest of Canaan (43:18), that the Lord is a God of power.

**46:11** *ravenous bird from the east.* This image may refer to Cyrus, who came from the east (Persia) to deliver Israel from bondage (Ezek. 17:3). But more completely, it may refer to the second coming of Christ, who will come from the east to execute God's judgment (41:2; Rev. 7:2).

*executeth my counsel.* This statement refers to obedience to God's direction.

*far country.* Cyrus came from a far country (Persia) to deliver Israel, just as Christ will return from afar, at his second coming, to bring deliverance.

*purposed it.* The sense here is that God willed it, or established it as one of his purposes (14:24–27; Jer. 4:28).

**46:12** *stouthearted.* This word means hard-hearted, stubborn, or rebellious, rather than courageous (as we more often think of it).

---

²This word replaces the archaic KJV *shew.*

**46:12–13** *righteousness.* In this context, *righteousness* is rectitude, or right action. The rebellious resist righteousness, but God will bring his own righteousness (or salvation) to bless those of Zion. As Paul taught, our diligent efforts to be righteous help us come unto Christ, who then blesses us with salvation (Rom. 3:20–24; 5:19). Some versions of the Bible use the word *victory* instead of righteousness (JB, NEB, TEV). The Lord brings victory over sin and death, which is his salvation.

**46:13** *salvation.* In the immediate sense, this word refers to deliverance from Israel's enemies; in a more complete sense, it signifies deliverance from sin and death. These blessings accompany the gathering to Zion, the union of true Saints in the last days.

———ᴏ∕ᴏ∕ᴏ———

# ISAIAH 47

### LIKENING ISAIAH 47 UNTO OURSELVES

*Babylon is not only an ancient, powerful nation but a symbol of the wicked world in all ages. In our time, the last days, she reigns supreme, and many swear allegiance to her, loving the praise and comforts and riches of the worldly life. Ancient Babylon thought she was invincible, as does the modern incarnation. But suddenly, without warning, the Babylon of the last days will be thrown down, as was ancient Babylon, and all those who ally themselves to her will be destroyed with the world they loved so much.*

*This is a prophecy many of us may see come to pass in our time, some in horror and some in gratitude. The destruction of powerful Babylon can be a reminder to us to trust in the Lord and in nothing else. The Lord will be patient. He will refine us in the furnace of affliction. And he will give us prophets, to guide us and teach us truth. Those who hearken will enjoy unceasing peace and righteousness and will receive of the blessings of Abraham. To come to such peace, we must repent and flee from Babylon— the world and its pride and sinfulness.*

*The prophecies in this chapter apply both to the fall of the ancient kingdom of Babylon and to the fall of the wicked world in the last days.*

---

## BABYLON SHALL BE DESTROYED (47:1–15)

These verses have a dual meaning, referring both to the ancient kingdom of Babylon and to the wicked kingdom of the world. As Babylon was thrown down by God's power anciently, so will the world be destroyed in the end. Babylon's fate will take the people of Babylon (both the temporal and the spiritual Babylon) by surprise: "Thou saidst, I shall be a lady for ever" (47:7). The destruction will come suddenly, "in a moment in one day," and it will be complete—"they shall come upon thee in their perfection" (47:9). And what are Babylon's sins? She is "given to pleasures"

(47:8); she has "trusted in [her] wickedness" (47:10); she has been "perverted" by her "wisdom" and "knowledge" (47:10); and she has rejected the true God, saying in her heart, "I am, and none else beside me" (47:8, 10).

When the day of destruction comes, Babylon turns to her "enchantments," "sorceries," and "astrologers" for help (47:12–13)—the wisdom and power of the devil and his deceptions—but they will all fail her (47:14, 15).

It is interesting to note here that Babylon is consistently depicted as feminine— Lady Babylon, the embodiment of all evil—in direct opposition to Lady Zion, the embodiment of all that is good. Many terms in this passage present Babylon as feminine: "virgin" (47:1), "daughter" (47:1, 5), "tender and delicate" (47:1), "locks" (47:2), "lady" (47:5, 7), "widow" (47:8, 9). Compare these with the depiction of Lady Babylon in Revelation, who is called "whore" (17:1, 15, 16), "woman" (17:3, 4, 6, 7, 9, 18), "mother of harlots" (17:5), "queen" (18:7), and "widow" (18:7).

Why does the Lord use feminine symbols in this way? Perhaps it is because he regards righteous woman as the epitome of his creation, which makes the corrupted woman more abhorrent by contrast. Also, the holy woman, as partner in the process of procreation, is essential for the perpetuation of God's plan. The evil woman not only brings herself to destruction but also frustrates the plan itself.

## Isaiah 47:1–15

Come down, and *sit in the dust*, O virgin <u>daughter of Babylon</u>,
*sit on the ground*: there is no throne, O <u>daughter of the Chaldeans</u>:

for thou shalt no more be called *tender* and *delicate*. (47:1)

Take the millstones,
and grind meal:

*uncover* <u>thy locks</u>, make *bare* <u>the leg</u>,
*uncover* <u>the thigh</u>, pass over the rivers. (47:2)

Thy *nakedness* <u>shall be uncovered</u>,
yea, thy *shame* <u>shall be seen</u>:

I will take vengeance, and I will not meet thee as a man. (47:3)

As for our *redeemer*,
the *Lord of hosts* is his name,
the *Holy One of Israel*. (47:4)

Sit thou <u>silent</u>, and get thee into darkness, O *daughter of the Chaldeans*:
for thou shalt <u>no more be called</u>, The *lady of kingdoms*. (47:5)

*I was wroth* with <u>my people</u>,
*I have polluted* <u>mine inheritance</u>, and given them into thine hand:

thou didst [show]¹ them *no mercy*;
upon the ancient hast thou very *heavily laid thy yoke*. (47:6)

And thou saidst, I shall be a lady for ever:
so that thou *didst not lay* these things *to thy heart,*
*neither didst remember* the latter end of it. (47:7)

Therefore hear now this, thou that art *given to pleasures,*
that *dwellest carelessly,*

that sayest in thine heart,
*I am,*
and *none else beside me*;

*I shall not sit* as a widow,
*neither shall I know* the loss of children: (47:8)

But these *two things* shall come to thee in a moment in one day,
the *loss of children*, and *widowhood*:

they shall come upon thee in their perfection for the *multitude* of thy sorceries,
and for the *great abundance* of thine enchantments. (47:9)

For thou hast trusted in thy wickedness: *thou hast said*, None seeth me.
Thy wisdom and thy knowledge, it hath perverted thee;
and *thou hast said* in thine heart, I am, and none else beside me. (47:10)

Therefore shall *evil* come upon thee; *thou shalt not know* from whence it riseth:
and *mischief* shall fall upon thee; *thou shalt not be able* to put it off:
and *desolation* shall come upon thee suddenly, which *thou shalt not know*. (47:11)

Stand now with *thine* enchantments,
and with the multitude of *thy* sorceries, wherein thou hast laboured from thy
youth;

if so be *thou* shalt be able to profit,
if so be *thou* mayest prevail. (47:12)

Thou art wearied in the multitude of thy *counsels*.
Let now the *astrologers*, the *stargazers*, the monthly *prognosticators*, stand up,
and save thee from these things that shall come upon thee. (47:13)

Behold, *they* shall be as stubble;
the fire shall burn *them*;

they shall not deliver themselves from the power of the *flame*:
there shall not be a *coal* to warm at,
nor *fire* to sit before it. (47:14)

Thus shall they be unto thee with whom thou hast laboured, even thy merchants,
from thy youth: they shall wander every one to his quarter; none shall save thee.
(47:15)

## NOTES AND COMMENTARY

**47:1** *sit in the dust.* Those who sat *in the dust* to do their work were the slaves.
As a slave, Babylon is forced to grind meal with hand stones, to remove her veil and

---

¹ This word replaces the archaic KJV *shew.*

expose herself to public view, to immodestly "make bare the leg" (47:2) so that her skirts don't obstruct her work, and so forth. It is also likely that slaves were poorly dressed and thus inadequately covered. Sitting in the dust was also a sign of mourning (3:26; Lam. 2:10; Ezek. 26:15–17). This passage refers both to the captivity of the literal Babylon and Chaldea (seen through the eyes of prophecy) and to the loss of freedom and power suffered by those who belong to spiritual Babylon, which is the wicked world (contrast with 52:2).

*virgin daughter.* This term characterizes the offspring of Lady Babylon (the world). Even those who are young and seemingly innocent in Babylon will suffer the consequences of Babylon's downfall.

*Babylon. Babylon* is the world of wickedness, meaning those who live by a telestial law (Jer. 51:33–58; Zech. 2:7–9).

*no throne.* Those who had ruled on thrones in the wicked world are now slaves. This phrase may be symbolic: those who were the leaders of society in the wicked world are thrown down.

*Chaldeans.* The *Chaldeans* were the learned class of Babylon, the magicians and sorcerers (see commentary on 43:14).

*tender/delicate.* Those in the wicked world led pampered lives (Deut. 28:56).

**47:2** *millstones/grind meal.* This work of slaves (Judges 16:21; Lam. 5:11–13) symbolizes the servitude into which Babylon (the wicked world) will be forced, as well as the end of a life of ease and opulence. In a literal sense, Babylon was forced to serve her masters when she fell. In a symbolic sense, the wicked (Babylon) serve their master, Satan. Satan promises the wicked a life of pleasure but delivers only bondage and pain. Only righteousness brings lasting rewards.

*pass over the rivers.* The conquered of Babylon will be sent into exile. Passing over rivers may represent passing over borders into other lands, or it may symbolize moving from one state of being to another.

**47:2–3** *uncover/Thy nakedness shall be uncovered.* Perhaps ancient Babylonian women would be sexually abused in the fall of their empire. Those who belong to spiritual Babylon (the world of wickedness) will be exposed, meaning their sins will be seen by all.

*will not meet thee as a man.* The Lord will treat the wicked not as peers or equals but as subordinates or slaves. The Lord will not be Babylon's bridegroom, as he will be for Israel.

**47:4** *the Lord of hosts . . . the Holy One of Israel.* See commentary on 1:4, 9.

**47:5** *Sit thou silent/get thee into darkness.* This passage describes the silence and darkness of grief, sorrow, or humiliation (42:7; 50:10).

*Chaldeans.* See commentary on 47:1.

*The lady of kingdoms.* The wicked will no longer have this title, which may suggest the Saints as the bride of Christ.

**47:6** *I have polluted mine inheritance.* The Lord's inheritance is his people, those who will carry on his work and his name. Because of their agency, they have chosen to pollute themselves; as a result, they have been given into the hand of an enemy (43:28), who, ultimately, is Satan. Perhaps this phrase means that the Lord has disinherited them.

*upon the ancient . . . laid thy yoke.* Aged people, who should be given honor, instead are burdened by slavery or servitude. The yoke may also represent the yoke of sin, which all those who ally themselves with the world receive.

**47:7** *I shall be a lady for ever.* Babylon thought she would rule in royal supremacy forever. Likewise, some Church members mistakenly think they will always receive the blessings of the covenant, despite their lack of righteousness.

*lay these things to thy heart.* The heart is the seat of true belief. Lady Babylon did not believe the prophecies of the judgments and destruction that would come if she did not repent.

*latter end.* This phrase means the final result.

**47:8** *given to pleasures.* This term represents those who are more concerned with selfish and sensual desires than with the needs of others or with God (Luke 8:14; 2 Tim. 3:4).

*carelessly.* This word means without care for what God desires or requires (Ezek. 39:6).

*I am, and none else beside me.* This statement is something God says of himself (45:5–6, 18, 21–22; Ex. 3:13–14). Now Babylon (or the wicked world) is saying it of herself, suggesting she needs no God and is independent and self-sufficient (Zeph. 2:15). By saying "I am," Babylon is also saying, "I am God."

*not sit as a widow/neither shall I know the loss of children.* Babylon feels secure: she is convinced she will never lose her source of strength (husband) or continuance (children; see Rev. 18:7–8). Similarly, the loss of husband (bridegroom) and children symbolize the loss of the Abrahamic covenant. Some self-sufficient but unworthy Church members feel they are exempt from God's judgments.

**47:9** *in one day.* The events will occur suddenly, all at once.

*perfection. Perfection* means completion, wholeness, fulness.

*sorceries/enchantments*. These are the world's attempts to gain power and dominion without righteousness; such things come from Satan, whether the practitioner of them acknowledges it or not (Lev. 19:31; 2 Chr. 33:6; Rev. 18:23; Alma 1:32).

**47:10** *thou hast trusted in thy wickedness*. Babylon (the wicked world) thought her way of life was sufficient to fulfill all her needs—in short, that it would save her. As Hugh Nibley wrote, "Babylon is firm in the conviction that her system is a permanent one. . . . In such possession of power, she can get away with anything and keep power indefinitely by crooked means, concealing her acts."[2]

*wisdom/knowledge/perverted thee*. The wisdom and the knowledge that pervert are the learning and the philosophies of men, in contrast with those of God.

**47:11** *evil*. This evil is not wickedness—Babylon is already steeped in that—but tragedy. The New International Version uses the word *disaster*. "Babylon is always reserved for the burning . . . her fate is to be overthrown, violently, suddenly, unexpectedly, and completely by the direct intervention of God."[3]

*thou shalt not know from whence it riseth*. The destruction of the world will come suddenly and unexpectedly, and it will come from the Lord, in whom the world does not believe.

*mischief*. Other translations interpret this as "calamity" (NIV) or "disaster" (RSV).

*desolation/thou shalt not know*. No one could have anticipated such a "catastrophe" (NIV) or "ruin" (RSV).

**47:12** *enchantments/sorceries*. See commentary on 47:9.

*laboured from thy youth*. This phrase suggests that the world has used sorceries almost from the beginning.

*profit/prevail*. The wicked can seek to succeed or conquer through the powers given them by Satan, if they so choose, though of course they will ultimately fail.

**47:13** *wearied/multitude of thy counsels*. Lady Babylon's counselors have given so much advice that those listening have grown tired of it. The counsels likely come from astrologers, stargazers, monthly prognosticators (all of which are synonyms), from whom people foolishly still seek counsel in the latter days.

**47:14** *stubble*. Farmers burn their land to clear and cleanse it. The Lord will do the same at the end of the world. After he has harvested the wheat (the righteous), he

---

[2] Nibley, *Approaching Zion*, 325.

[3] Nibley, *Approaching Zion*, 31.

will burn the remainder (the chaff, or the wicked) with the fire of his coming (33:11–12; Mal. 4:1; 1 Ne. 22:15; 2 Ne. 26:4–6; D&C 64:24).

*coal/fire.* The fire of the Lord's coming will not be the comfortable fire of the hearth but a fire that devours all before it.

**47:15** *merchants/wander every one to his quarter.* The merchants who built the wealth of Babylon (the world) will desert the wicked at the end, being unable to save them (Rev. 18:15).

# ISAIAH 48

*LIKENING ISAIAH 48 UNTO OURSELVES*

*Isaiah 48 very much speaks to people of our day, particularly members of The Church of Jesus Christ of Latter-day Saints. In it, the Lord addresses those who have come up out of the waters of baptism—those who have joined themselves to the covenant but who are not true to their covenants and do not submit themselves to God. They have become stubborn and slow to hear the counsel of the Lord.*

## THE LORD DEALS WITH A STUBBORN COVENANT PEOPLE (48:1–16)

This chapter of Isaiah is the first one quoted in the Book of Mormon. Nephi gives his purpose in quoting it: "I speak unto all the house of Israel. . . . that I might more fully persuade them to believe in the Lord their Redeemer I did read unto them that which was written by the prophet Isaiah" (1 Ne. 19:19, 23).

In Isaiah 48 the Lord speaks to members of the Church, those who have come "out of the waters of baptism" (48:1). He is angry at those Church members who "swear by the name of the Lord" but "swear not in truth, nor in righteousness" (48:1). They are "obstinate" (48:4); they are prone to give credit to their "idol" or "graven image" for the works that God has done (48:5); and they are transgressors "from the womb" (48:8). But because of his goodness ("for my name's sake"; 48:9), the Lord will "defer" his anger, and not "cut thee . . . off" (48:9). Israel has been "refined" and "chosen . . . in the furnace of affliction" (48:10). The Lord will punish her enemies (48:14), and he will continue to send prophets to teach and bless those who will listen ("I have called him to declare"; 48:15). Of this passage and its greater context, commentary in the Jerusalem Bible says:

"The hardening of Israel is a familiar theme of the prophets and the historical books. Israel has 'stiffened his neck' (Exod. 32:9; Deut. 9:13[–24]; 2 Kgs. 17:14; Jer. 7:26[–28]), has made himself blind and deaf (Isa. 6:9–10 . . . ; 2:19–20; 43:8) by refusing to serve God, by breaking the yoke of his Law (Jer. 2:20; 5:5); his punishment is to bend his neck to the yoke of a foreign nation (Deut. 28:48; see Jer. 27:8, 11; 28; 30:8; Isa. 9:3; 10:27). But Yahweh, true to himself, has not rejected his people (vv. 9–11), and the light of his salvation will pierce the eyes of the blind who had rebelled (42:7, 16, 18; 43:8 . . . )."[1]

*Isaiah 48:1–16*

> [*Hearken* and]
> *hear* . . . this,
> O *house of Jacob,*
> [who] are called by the name of *Israel,*
>
> and are *come forth out* of the <u>waters of Judah,</u>
> [or *out* of the <u>waters of baptism,</u>]
>
> [who] *swear* by the name of the <u>Lord,</u>
> and *make mention* of the <u>God of Israel,</u>
>
> [yet they swear] *not in truth,*
> *nor in righteousness.*[2] (48:1)
>
> [Nevertheless,] *they call themselves* of the <u>holy city,</u>
> [but *they do not] stay themselves* upon the <u>God of Israel,</u>
>
> [who is the *Lord of Hosts;*
> yea,] The *Lord of Hosts* is his name.[3] (48:2)
>
> [Behold,] *I have declared* the <u>former things from the beginning;</u>
> and <u>they</u> *went forth out of my mouth,*
> and *I* [*showed*] <u>them;</u>
>
> *I did* [*show*] <u>them</u> suddenly. . . .[4] (48:3)
>
> [And I did it][5] because I knew that *thou* art <u>obstinate,</u>
> and *thy neck* is an <u>iron sinew,</u>
> and *thy brow* <u>brass;</u> (48:4)
>
> [And] *I* have even from the beginning <u>declared . . . to thee;</u>
> before it came to pass *I* [<u>showed them</u>] thee:
> [and *I* <u>showed them</u> for fear]

---

[1] The New Jerusalem Bible, 1265.
[2] 1 Ne. 20:1 makes several changes in this verse, including the addition of the explanatory phrase *or out of the waters of baptism.*
[3] The changes in this verse are from 1 Ne. 20:2.
[4] The changes in this verse are from 1 Ne. 20:3.
[5] These words are found in 1 Ne. 20:4.

lest thou shouldest say—
*Mine idol* hath done them, and *my graven image,*
and *my molten image,* hath commanded them.[6] (48:5)

*Thou hast [seen and] heard* . . . all this; and will [ye not] declare [them]?
[And that] I have *showed thee* new things from this time, even hidden things,
and thou didst not know them.[7] (48:6)

They are created now, and not from the beginning; even before the day when thou
heardest them not [they were declared unto thee];[8] lest thou shouldest say, Behold,
I knew them. (48:7)

Yea, [and] *thou* heardest not;
yea, *thou* knewest not;
yea, from that time . . . *thine ear* was not opened:

for I knew that thou wouldest *deal very treacherously,*
and wast called a *transgressor* from the womb.[9] (48:8)

[Nevertheless,][10] *for my name's sake* will I defer mine anger,
and for my praise will I refrain for thee, that I cut thee not off. (48:9)

[For] behold, *I have* refined thee, . . . [11]
*I have* chosen thee in the furnace of affliction. (48:10)

For *mine own sake,*
[yea,] for *mine own sake* will I do [this],

for [*I will not suffer*] my name [to] be polluted,
and *I will not give* my glory unto another.[12] (48:11)

Hearken unto me, O *Jacob*[,]
*and Israel* . . . my called;[13]

[for] *I* am he;
*I* am the first, [and]
*I* [am also] the last.[14] (48:12)

*Mine hand* [hath also] laid the foundation of the earth,
and *my right hand* hath spanned the heavens.

. . . I call unto them [and] they stand up together.[15] (48:13)

---

[6] The changes in this verse are from 1 Ne. 20:5.

[7] The changes in this verse are from 1 Ne. 20:6.

[8] 1 Ne. 20:7 includes this expression, which is missing from the KJV.

[9] The changes in this verse are from 1 Ne. 20:8.

[10] 1 Ne. 20:9 includes this word, which is not found in the KJV.

[11] 1 Ne. 20:10 drops the KJV expression *but not with silver.*

[12] The changes in this verse are from 1 Ne. 20:11.

[13] 1 Ne. 20:12 changes the punctuation in the KJV phrase *O Jacob and Israel, my called.* We can't be certain why this punctuation is different in the Book of Mormon. Of course, Jacob and Israel are two names for the same person; perhaps the Book of Mormon is emphasizing that Israel is the name God gave to Jacob when he called him and renewed the Abrahamic covenant with him (Gen. 32:28).

[14] The changes in this verse are from 1 Ne. 20:12.

[15] The changes in this verse are from 1 Ne. 20:13.

All ye, assemble yourselves, and hear; [who] among them hath declared these things [unto them]? The Lord hath loved him:

[yea, and *he* will fulfill his word which he hath declared by them; and] *he* will do his pleasure on Babylon, and his *arm* shall [come upon] the Chaldeans.[16] (48:14)

[Also, saith *the Lord*]
I [*the Lord,* yea],
 . . . *I* have spoken;
yea, *I* have called him [to declare,]
*I* have brought him,

and he shall make his way prosperous.[17] (48:15)

Come ye near unto me, . . .

*I have not spoken* in secret from the beginning; from the time that it was [declared *have I spoken*]:

and . . . the *Lord God,* and *his Spirit,* hath sent me.[18] (48:16)

## NOTES AND COMMENTARY

**48:1** *house of Jacob.* In a broad sense, the house of Jacob consists of all who, through baptism, partake of the covenant the Lord made with Abraham, Isaac, and Jacob.

*waters of baptism.* This wording found in 1 Nephi makes clear that those addressed are those who have been baptized, that is, those who are members of the Church.

*swear not in truth.* These Church members make oaths and covenants in the Lord's name, but they do so in hypocrisy rather than righteousness (Deut. 6:13; Lev. 19:12).

**48:2** *holy city.* Jerusalem (Neh. 11:1; Ether 13:5) or the New Jerusalem (Ether 13:8; D&C 109:58; 133:56) is the *holy city.* These members claim to be part of the Lord's people, part of the Church, and part of Zion (1:21).

*not stay themselves upon the God of Israel.* Despite their covenants, these Church members do not lean upon or take hold of the Lord.

**48:3** *former things.* God has power to foretell things to come, as he has in the past. Specifically, he foretold the miraculous deliverance of Israel under the leadership of Moses (42:9; 43:9; 46:9).

---

[16] The changes in this verse are from 1 Ne. 20:14.
[17] The changes in this verse are from 1 Ne. 20:15.
[18] The changes in this verse are from 1 Ne. 20:16.

*my mouth.* The Lord speaks directly to his prophets and to all who will hearken. When he speaks to us through the prophets, it is as if he has spoken directly to each of us (D&C 1:38).

*showed them.* He made his purposes manifest through his prophets.

**48:4** *obstinate.* The Lord knew that many Church members would be stubborn, unyielding, hard of heart (Ezek. 3:7–9).

*neck is an iron sinew.* This term describes Church members who will not bow before the Lord (Deut. 9:6; 31:27).

*brow brass.* This phrase describes Church members who will not give their mind or thoughts to the Lord (Ezek. 3:9).

**48:5** *from the beginning.* The Lord has shown his knowledge and power from the beginning of time. He desires that we love and revere him above all, that we might be able to partake of the blessings of his atonement.

**48:6** *new things.* This term represents the prophecy concerning Israel's deliverance through Cyrus (42:9; 43:9) or anything given by the Lord, who is a God of continuing revelation.

*hidden things.* Such things are known only by revelation. Hidden things might include the mysteries of godliness that are revealed in the temple.

**48:7** *created now.* The God of the present does indeed bring things to pass in all ages. Within the constraints of eternal law, he directs the destiny of the world continually.

**48:8** *ear was not opened.* Even though the Lord has demonstrated his foreknowledge, and even though he is speaking to members of his Church, they are unwilling to hear and obey his word (Jer. 7:24–26).

*deal very treacherously.* This phrase characterizes Church members who will be betrayers.

*transgressor from the womb.* This phrase describes Church members who will be known as sinners from the very beginning.

**48:9** *for my name's sake/defer mine anger/cut thee not off.* God's name represents who he is. Because of his goodness and mercy, he will defer his anger and will not immediately cut off these Church members from their covenant inheritance with Abraham and their fellowship with God.

**48:10** *refined/furnace of affliction.* In the process of refining metals, intense heat is used to burn off the grosser elements and impurities. The initial *furnace of affliction* for Israel was her servitude in Egypt (Deut. 4:20; 1 Kgs. 8:51). In all eras, the Saints are to be *refined* and made like Christ through affliction as metal is refined in the burning furnace. Though affliction is the furnace in which we will be refined, Christ is the refiner (Zech. 13:9; Mal. 3:2–3), cleansing our hearts and souls so that we can enter the Father's kingdom (3 Ne. 27:19–20). Those who are so refined are then chosen.

*chosen.* Israel (the covenant people) is given a mission and the authority to carry the gospel and its blessings to the world. In 48:12 the Lord refers to Israel as "my called." The combination of the words *called* and *chosen* appears repeatedly in the scriptures (41:9; Matt. 22:14; 1 Pet. 2:9; Rev. 17:14; D&C 95:5; 121:34–40).

Elder Bruce R. McConkie asked, "Called to what? Chosen for what?" and then answered, "Called in to the Church, . . . but chosen to be sealed up unto eternal life and to have one's calling and election made sure."[19]

Though Israel—specifically, members of the Church—has been rebellious, the Lord has pledged he would not cast her off. If she will be true to her calling, the Lord will choose her to receive the promised blessings.

**48:11** *my name/polluted.* We pollute God's name when we use it to join in covenant with him and then violate the covenant or when we participate unworthily in sacred ordinances (Jer. 34:16; Mal. 1:6–7).

*will not give my glory unto another.* Though these Church members have been rebellious, the Lord knows they will be refined through affliction and thus will continue to qualify to receive his glory.

**48:12** *my called.* See commentary on 48:10, *chosen.*

*first/last.* These words express the eternal nature of the Lord Jesus Christ (41:4; 44:6; Rev. 22:13; Alma 11:39; D&C 110:4). Jesus was the first to be born in the spirit. He is the first in position and dominion. He is the last in that he will continue as God, preeminent over all, through all eternity. Jesus is also the first and the last in that he is both the "author and finisher of our faith" (Heb. 12:2).

**48:13** *hand/right hand.* The *right hand* is the hand of authority. It is also the "covenant hand," or the hand we use to covenant with the Lord.

*laid the foundation of the earth/spanned the heavens.* God is the Creator, who has all power both in our sphere (earth) and in all other spheres (heavens; see Ps. 102:25; D&C 45:1; Moses 6:44).

*I call/they stand up.* Both earth and heaven obey God's command.

**48:14** *who among them hath declared these things.* God has sent forth a servant to declare his word unto his covenant people. That servant may be Isaiah, Jesus, another prophet, or perhaps several prophets, each in turn.

---

[19] *Doctrinal New Testament Commentary,* 3:349.

*he will fulfill his word/declared by them/pleasure/arm.* The prophecies and promises the Lord gives through his prophets will all be fulfilled. Specifically, he will punish the wicked and the oppressors by the power of his *arm.* His *pleasure* is what he chooses to do.

*Babylon/Chaldeans.* These terms symbolize all who reject God for other interests, desires, and focuses, both the wicked world as a whole (Babylon) and the learned people of the world (Chaldeans).

**48:15** *called him/brought him.* This phrase refers to the servant called to proclaim the Lord's word to his covenant people (48:14).

*make his way prosperous.* The Lord will enable his servant to do his work well and successfully.

**48:16** *Come ye near unto me.* Joseph Smith said: "We know not what we shall be called to pass through before Zion is delivered and established; therefore, we have great need to live near to God, and always to be in strict obedience to all His commandments, that we may have a conscience void of offense toward God and man."[20]

*not spoken in secret.* The Lord prophesies not in secret but openly, and the same is true of his servants (see commentary on 45:19). This verse ends with the words *hath sent me,* suggesting that the voice has changed from the Lord in verse 15 to that of the servant here.

## BLESSINGS GOD DESIRED FOR ISRAEL (48:17–19)

God has sent his servant to teach and lead us (48:17). That prophet may be Isaiah, Jesus, another prophet, or several prophets, each in turn. If we, as members of the Lord's Church, hearken to his servants, we will have peace and righteousness as steady and consistent as a river and as the waves of a sea (48:18). We will be heirs to the Abrahamic promises: we will have descendants as numerous as the sands of the seashore, and an everlasting name before God (48:19).

*Isaiah 48:17–19*

> [And] thus saith the *Lord,*
> thy *Redeemer,*
> the *Holy One of Israel;* [I have sent him,]
> . . . the *Lord* thy *God*

---

[20] *History of the Church,* 1:450.

*[who] teacheth thee to profit,*
*[who] leadeth thee by the way* . . . thou shouldst *go,* [hath done it].²¹ (48:17)

O that thou hadst hearkened to my commandments!

then had *thy peace* been as a river,
and *thy righteousness* as the waves of the sea: (48:18)

Thy *seed* also had been as the sand,
. . . ²² the *offspring* of thy bowels like the gravel thereof;

his name should *not* have been *cut off*
nor *destroyed* from before me. (48:19)

## NOTES AND COMMENTARY

**48:17** *Holy One of Israel.* See commentary on 1:4.

*who teacheth thee.* Called "Rabbi" (the Jewish title for a teacher) throughout his mortal ministry, Jesus Christ has always been the Master Teacher. Jehovah, the premortal Christ, presents himself as a teacher, as we see in this passage (2:3).

**48:18** *thy peace been as a river.* Peace of conscience and peace of spirit are gifts God gives to those who are obedient (26:3; Ps. 37:37; 119:165; Rom. 8:6; 14:17–19; Philip. 4:7). That kind of peace comes from the Holy Spirit and is made available through the power of Christ and his atonement (John 14:27; 16:33). God's peace is not offered for this world alone. The peace spoken of here continues with us into celestial glory (D&C 59:23) and will be consistent, ever flowing (66:12).

*righteousness/waves.* When we obey the Lord's commandments our *righteousness* will be unstoppable, as waves are. Also, our righteousness will truly be subject to the pull of the heavens, as the *waves* are subject to the moon.

**48:19** *seed/as the sand.* If errant Church members had been obedient, they could have enjoyed a renewal of the promise to Abraham (Gen. 22:17–18; D&C 132:30).

*name/not . . . cut off.* When our names are written in the Lord's book of life, we are not cut off but are recorded as being among the saved (Rev. 3:5; D&C 88:2). We have eternal life, with a continuation of seed forever, as opposed to having no heirs (48:9; 56:5).

---

²¹ 1 Ne. 20:17 introduces the words *I have sent him,* which clarifies that this verse refers to the servant mentioned in 48:14 and 16.
²² The change in this verse is from 1 Ne. 20:19. It is not apparent why the Book of Mormon version eliminates the "and" found in KJV.

## SONG OF THE FLIGHT FROM BABYLON (48:20–22)

Speaking to those who belong to his true Church (48:1 addresses those who have come "out of the waters of baptism"), the Lord calls us to "go ye forth of Babylon" (48:20). We are to leave the things of the world and then, "with a voice of singing" (48:20), proclaim the blessings of the Lord in redeeming Jacob and all who have become heir to his promises. The Lord blessed them with temporal salvation (literal water; 48:21) and "greater" things besides (spiritual salvation and living water; 48:22). "Go ye forth of Babylon," the Lord says, for "there is no peace . . . unto the wicked" (48:20, 22).

*Isaiah 48:20–22*

*Go ye forth* of <u>Babylon</u>,
*flee ye from* the <u>Chaldeans</u>,

with a voice of singing *declare ye,*
*tell* this,
*utter . . .* [23] to the end of the earth;
*say ye,* The Lord hath redeemed his servant Jacob. (48:20)

And they thirsted not; . . . [24] he led them through the deserts;

he caused the *waters to flow* out of the <u>rock</u> for them:
he clave the <u>rock</u> also and the *waters gushed out.* (48:21)

[And notwithstanding he hath done all this, and greater also,][25] there is no peace, saith the Lord, unto the wicked. (48:22)

### NOTES AND COMMENTARY

**48:20** *Go ye forth of Babylon/the Chaldeans.* The Lord promised ancient Israel that after seventy years of Babylonian captivity, Israel would be blessed to return to the land of her inheritance (Jer. 25:11; 29:10). A second meaning is to leave the carnal world for the spiritual. This command has great significance for our day: "When the lost and scattered sheep of Israel find place again in the fold of their Ancient Shepherd, they do so by forsaking the world and joining the true church. They leave the deserts of sin and lie down in the green pastures. They leave Babylon and return to Zion."[26]

---

[23] The change in this verse is from 1 Ne. 20:20. The Book of Mormon version omits words from the KJV, as noted by the ellipses.
[24] The change in this verse is from 1 Ne. 20:21. The Book of Mormon version omits words from the KJV, as noted by the ellipses.
[25] These words are found in 1 Ne. 20:22 but not in the KJV.
[26] McConkie, *New Witness for the Articles of Faith,* 536–37.

*voice of singing.* This phrase suggests an attitude of praise and rejoicing.

*end of the earth.* Every part of the earth will receive the Lord's message.

*redeemed/servant Jacob.* The righteous Saints are those who are redeemed, who have come unto Abraham's promise and are true servants.

**48:21** *thirsted not/led them through the deserts/caused the waters to flow/rock.* These statements refer to blessings the Lord gave to Israel in the wilderness (Num. 20:7–11; Deut. 8:15; Ps. 78:15–20; 2 Ne. 25:20). Likewise, the Lord will lead us through spiritual deserts and give us living waters to drink (41:18; 43:19; 44:3). The rock symbolizes Christ, the source of our living water (see commentary on 51:1; see also John 4:10–11; 7:38).

**48:22** *notwithstanding/no peace/unto the wicked.* Despite seeing great miracles of deliverance, some in Israel continue in wickedness. Miracles do not bring peace of soul to those who continue in sin (57:21; 1 Ne. 20:22; Alma 41:10).

— ❧ —

# ISAIAH 49

## LIKENING ISAIAH 49 UNTO OURSELVES

*We are of the house of Israel, and here the Lord calls us to hearken. He has sent a servant to testify of truth and to help restore Israel to her promised blessings. Through the efforts of such servants, the Lord will gather Israel from all parts of the earth. We in the latter days are privileged to help in this gathering work. As we stand as missionaries to our neighbors, inviting them to come and partake of the blessings of the gospel, we are joining the Lord's servant in his work and helping to bring to pass the prophecies about the deliverance and the gathering of Israel. Those who are so gathered will be greatly blessed. The Lord will open the way for them to return to him; he will lead and guide them and provide for their every spiritual need.*

*This passage has a wonderful message of comfort to all who suffer and feel lost in the world. "Can a woman forget her sucking child?" the Lord asks. "Yea, they may forget, yet will I not forget thee" (49:15)*

*In the gathering, the Lord will send many helpers: kings and queens will bring in their arms and on their shoulders those who have been lost.*

---

## SONG OF THE LORD'S SERVANT (49:1–7)

This passage introduces us to a servant of the Lord who has been called "from the womb" (49:1, 5), or from premortality. He has been hid and prepared of the Lord (49:2) and is promised glory (49:3). But the servant is discouraged, saying, "I have labored in vain" (49:4). The Lord reminds him of his mission and his promises: he is to help gather Israel and is to be a light to the Gentiles (49:6). Men despise the servant and nations abhor him, but kings and princes will yet give him respect and honor (49:7; the identity of this servant is discussed in the commentary on 49:1).

President Wilford Woodruff said of Isaiah 49: "The revelations that are in the Bible, the predictions of the Patriarchs and Prophets who saw by vision and revelation the last dispensation and fullness of times, plainly tell us what is to come to pass. The 49th chapter of Isaiah is having its fulfillment."[1]

*Isaiah 49:1–7*

[Hearken, O ye *house of Israel,*
all ye that are broken off and are driven out
because of the wickedness of the pastors of my people;
yea, <u>all ye that are broken off, that are scattered abroad</u>, who are of my people, O
*house of Israel.*][2]

*Listen,* O <u>isles</u>, unto me;
and *hearken,* ye <u>people, from far;</u>

The Lord *hath called me* from the <u>womb</u>;
from the [<u>womb</u>][3] of my mother hath *he made mention of my name.* (49:1)

And he hath made my mouth like a *sharp sword;* in the shadow of his hand hath
<u>he hid me</u>,
and made me a *polished shaft;* in his quiver hath <u>he hid me</u>; (49:2)

And said unto me, Thou art my servant, O Israel, in whom I will be glorified.
(49:3)

Then I said, I have *laboured* <u>in vain</u>,
I have *spent my strength* <u>for nought</u>, and <u>in vain</u>:

. . . [4] surely *my judgment* is <u>with the Lord</u>,
and *my work* <u>with my God.</u> (49:4)

And now, saith the Lord that formed me from the womb [that I should][5] be his servant,

*to bring* <u>Jacob</u> again to him—
Though <u>Israel</u> *be not gathered,*

yet shall I *be glorious* in the eyes of the <u>Lord</u>,
and my <u>God</u> shall *be my strength.* (49:5)

And he said, It is a light thing that thou shouldest be my servant

to *raise up* the <u>tribes of Jacob</u>,
and to *restore* the <u>preserved of Israel</u>:

I will also give *thee for a light* <u>to the Gentiles</u>,
that *thou mayest be my salvation* unto the <u>end of the earth</u>. (49:6)

Thus saith the *Lord,*

---

[1] *Collected Discourses,* 4 Oct. 1896, 5:187.
[2] The beginning lines of this verse are from 1 Ne. 21:1.
[3] The change in this verse is from 1 Ne. 21:1.
[4] The change in this verse is from 1 Ne. 21:4.
[5] The change in this verse is from 1 Ne. 21:5.

the *Redeemer of Israel,*
*. . . his Holy One,*

*to him* whom man despiseth,
*to him* whom the nation[s] abhorreth,

to . . . servant of rulers,
*Kings* shall see and arise,
*princes* also shall worship,

because of the Lord that is faithful. . . . [6] (49:7)

## NOTES AND COMMENTARY

**49:1** *broken off/driven out/scattered abroad.* Members of the house of Israel have been *broken off* from the main group, as a branch is broken off a tree, and *scattered* around the world.

*wickedness of the pastors.* The *pastors* who should have cared for Israel as spiritual leaders have instead led her astray.

*isles.* This word refers not only to islands but also to the continents of the earth (2 Ne. 10:20). It may also mean any place not immediately accessible to Israel by land.

*hath called me.* The one called is God's servant, Israel, as we learn in 49:3 (43:1; 48:12). The name *Israel,* however, may be symbolic for another servant (Jesus Christ, Isaiah, Joseph Smith, another prophet, the tribe of Ephraim, or each of these in turn).

*womb/womb of my mother.* This expression suggests foreordination, an experience similar to that of Jeremiah recorded in Jeremiah 1:4–5 (44:2, 24; 49:5).

*name.* The Lord knows us individually; he knows our names, thoughts, intents, and all our deeds. The Lord also knows us by the covenant names *Israel* and *Christ.* In addition, *he made mention of my name* could mean that, as well as being foreordained, the servant has been mentioned in prophecy.

**49:2** *mouth like a sharp sword.* This term refers to the power of the message brought by God's servant. It is an expression common in revelation (Heb. 4:12; Rev. 1:16; D&C 6:2, for example). Nephi spoke of the truth cutting people "to the very center" (1 Ne. 16:2).

*shadow of his hand.* A place of ultimate safety (51:16).

*in his quiver hath he hid me.* This phrase may refer to God's protection: God may have hidden the servant from the knowledge of the world, or He may have sheltered him from harm. Alternatively, the Lord's covenant with Abraham declares that

---

[6]The changes in this verse are from 1 Ne. 21:7.

even though Abraham's righteous seed were lost, or hid, from the world, both literally and figuratively (D&C 86:8–9), God knows where they are and protects them "in the shadow of his hand . . . in his quiver."

*sharp sword/polished shaft/quiver.* Through God's power, the servant is fully prepared and ready for the accomplishment of his mission. Though lacking sharpness of himself, he will be refined and "polished" by the Lord. Joseph Smith referred to this prophecy in relation to himself: "I am like a huge, rough stone rolling down from a high mountain; and the only polishing I get is when some corner gets rubbed off by coming in contact with something else, striking with accelerated force against religious bigotry, priestcraft, . . . corrupt men and women—all hell knocking off a corner here and a corner there. Thus I will become a smooth and polished shaft in the quiver of the Almighty."[7] Joseph Smith also applied phrases from this verse to his brother Hyrum,[8] and they could be applied to anyone who is polished to the point of having his or her calling and election made sure.

**49:3** *my servant . . . Israel.* This servant was introduced in 41:8–9 and 42:19. Israel comprises the literal and spiritual descendants of Abraham, specifically the members of the Church (D&C 103:17; 132:30–31). For more on the servant's identity, see commentary on 49:1, *hath called me.* For other references to Israel as God's servant, see 43:10; 44:1, 2, 21; 45:4; 48:20.

*I will be glorified.* God's glory or brightness increases when we come to the blessings of immortality and eternal life (Moses 1:39). Those who help to promote God's work contribute to God's glory.

**49:4** *laboured in vain/spent my strength for nought.* The servant laments that the people will not listen to him, but he acknowledges that God is his judge and ultimately it is He whom the servant must seek to please.

*judgment is with the Lord.* Perfect judgment is one of God's characteristics, and he reserves to himself the right to render judgment on the earth.

**49:5** *formed me from the womb.* See commentary on 49:1, *womb.*

*bring Jacob again.* This passage refers to the gathering, both physically and spiritually, of the descendants of Jacob.

*shall I be glorious.* We become glorious—bright and shining in righteousness—through the Lord, who shines through us (49:3). As we become glorious through him, we please him and become glorious in his eyes.

---

[7] *Teachings of the Prophet Joseph Smith,* 304.
[8] *History of the Church,* 1:466.

*God/my strength.* God is the source of our power and prosperity (Ps. 81:1; 84:5). Contrast this statement with 49:4, in which the servant says that he has spent his strength in vain.

**49:6** *a light thing.* This term means "a small matter." The New International Version clarifies the meaning of this verse: "It is too small a thing for you to be my servant to restore the tribes of Jacob and bring back those of Israel I have kept. I will also make you a light for the Gentiles, that you may bring my salvation to the ends of the earth." In other words, the Lord has a much greater work for the servant than to simply bless Israel—the servant is destined to bless the whole earth.

*raise up.* In this context *raise up* refers to bringing forth or lifting up through the covenant.

*tribes of Jacob.* The twelve tribes of Israel are also called the *tribes of Jacob*.

*preserved of Israel.* This term may refer to those who have remained true to God, who have been preserved in faith, or it may mean those in the last days who are delivered from spiritual bondage and restored to the blessings of the gospel covenant.

*light to the Gentiles.* God's servant not only will gather and restore the descendants of Abraham but will also reach out to the Gentiles. Thus salvation will reach "unto the end of the earth." The *light to the Gentiles* is variously defined in the scriptures as Jesus Christ (42:6–7; Luke 2:32), the priesthood (D&C 86:11), and Zion (60:3). If the servant referred to in this section is not the Messiah himself, he certainly will shine with the light of the Messiah.

*end of the earth.* "Every nation, and kindred, and tongue, and people" (Rev. 14:6; 1 Ne. 19:16; D&C 133:37).

**49:7** *him whom man despiseth/nations abhorreth/servant of rulers/Kings . . . arise/princes . . . worship.* In a great contrast, men despise the servant, showing their lack of respect for the Master (Luke 10:16), but kings will yet arise in respect to him (Judg. 3:20) and princes will worship him (49:23; 60:3, 11, 16). These may well be kings and princes (or priests) before God, having received the fulness of the priesthood in the temple.

*faithful.* The Lord keeps all his promises; he never fails.

## ISRAEL'S RETURN IN THE LAST DAYS (49:8–12)

Isaiah 49:8–12 describes the time of the gathering of Israel from her long dispersal. The gathering will take two forms: first, descendants of Abraham (both literal and adoptive) throughout the world will hear the gospel message and will enter into the Abrahamic covenant through baptism. Second, the covenant people (members of the Church and the Jews) will eventually gather to New and Old Jerusalem.

The gathering will come when the Lord hears the cries of scattered Israel (49:8). In that day ("a day of salvation"; 49:8) he will help them return to their land of promise, both spiritually and temporally. That day began with the opening of the last dispensation. Israel will receive again her ancient inheritance of land, which has become "desolate" because of the wars and judgments of the last days (49:8).

Israel has been in a form of spiritual prison ("darkness") because of the loss of the truth; her people have also often been in physical bondage to foreign nations (49:9). But on her return, they will go forth in the care of the Lord ("feed in the ways, . . . not hunger nor thirst: . . . he that hath mercy on them shall lead them"; 49:9–10). In gathering to Zion, Israel will receive of living water and the bread of life ("not hunger nor thirst," "springs of water"; 49:10). Israel will be led by the Lord ("he . . . shall lead them"; "[he] shall . . . guide them"; 49:10). Her people will receive the blessings of the temple ("high places," "mountains," "highways shall be exalted"; 49:9, 11).

The covenant people will be gathered from all parts of the earth: "from far," "from the north," "from the west," "from the land of Sinim" (49:12).

*Isaiah 49:8–12*

> Thus saith the Lord,
>
> In an *acceptable time* have <u>I heard thee,</u> [O isles of the sea,][9]
> and in a *day of salvation* have <u>I helped thee</u>:
>
> and *I will* <u>preserve thee,</u>
> and *give thee* [my servant] <u>for a covenant of the people,</u>[10]
>
> to *establish* the <u>earth,</u>
> to *cause to inherit* the <u>desolate heritages;</u> (49:8)
>
> That thou mayest say to the *prisoners,* <u>Go forth;</u>
> to *them that* [*sit*] *in darkness,* <u>[Show] yourselves.</u>[11]
>
> They shall *feed* in the <u>ways,</u>
> and their *pastures* shall be in all <u>high places.</u> (49:9)
>
> They shall not *hunger*
> nor *thirst;*
>
> neither shall the *heat*
> nor [the][12] *sun* smite them:

---

[9] The additional words *O isles of the sea* are in 1 Ne. 21:8.
[10] The additional words *my servant* are in 1 Ne. 21:8.
[11] The changes in this verse are from 1 Ne. 21:9.
[12] This additional word is in 1 Ne. 21:10.

for *he* that hath mercy on them shall <u>lead them,</u>
even by the springs of water shall *he* <u>guide them.</u> (49:10)

And I will make all my *mountains* a <u>way,</u>
and my *highways* shall be <u>exalted.</u> (49:11)

[And then, O house of Israel,][13] behold, *these* shall come <u>from far:</u>
and, lo, *these* <u>from the north</u>
and <u>from the west;</u>
and *these* <u>from the land of Sinim.</u> (49:12)

## NOTES AND COMMENTARY

**49:8** *acceptable time/day of salvation.* This phrase speaks of the period and the specific time when the Lord chooses to do his work. At least one fulfillment of this expression came in the meridian dispensation, when Paul wrote, "Behold, now is the accepted time; behold, now is the day of salvation" (2 Cor. 6:2). Another time of fulfillment appears to be the last days, when Israel is gathered.

*my servant for a covenant.* The existence and work of the servant is a sign that God is fulfilling his covenant with the people (42:6–7; see commentary on 49:1, *hath called me,* for the possible identity of the servant).

*establish the earth.* The New International Version and the Jerusalem Bible translate this phrase as "restore the land": Israel's rightful inheritance will be restored to her. The Lord's people—and his servant—will establish his kingdom in the earth.

*inherit the desolate heritages.* Israel will inherit her promised land, though it has been made desolate. *Desolate* often refers to the destruction of the temple—the blessings of which will be restored to the Lord's people.

**49:9** *prisoners/in darkness.* This term may refer to those in the spirit prison (D&C 128:22) or in spiritual bondage (42:22; 1 Ne. 22:12; see also Ps. 146:7–8).

*feed in the ways/pastures . . . in all high places.* Those who are physically gathered from lands of oppression will be cared for by the Lord. Those brought forth from spiritual prisons, on earth and in the spirit world, will be nourished with the word of life. *High places* signify barren hillsides—even these will provide sufficient sustenance for the Lord's flock. *High places* also signify temples, in which the faithful will find an abundance of spiritual food. He who has power to so bless his flock is the Savior. As the psalmist said: "The Lord is my shepherd; I shall not want. He maketh me to lie down in green pastures: he leadeth me beside the still waters" (Ps. 23:1–2).

---

[13] This addition is found in 1 Ne. 21:12.

**49:10** *not hunger nor thirst/neither shall the heat/sun smite them.* This passage refers to the Lord's blessings to those who are returning from exile, as well as to those returning from spiritual bondage. Whether in physical or spiritual captivity, they suffer both hunger and thirst, and the heat and sun threaten them; in their deliverance the Lord protects and nourishes them. In all circumstances, it is only through Christ that our spiritual hunger can be satisfied (John 6:35; Alma 31:38; 32:42; 3 Ne. 12:6; 20:8).

*springs of water.* This term symbolizes living water (35:6–7; 41:17–18; 43:19–20), or Jesus Christ.

**49:11** *mountains a way/highways shall be exalted.* The Lord will open the way for the return of the exiles from captivity, as well as the return of those who are captives to sin (35:8–10; 40:3; 62:10). A possible alternative meaning is that the mountain that is the temple will mark an exalted way for the Saints to walk.

**49:12** *come from far/north/west.* Israel was scattered to all parts of the earth, from whence she shall return (Luke 13:29; 3 Ne. 20:13).

*land of Sinim.* This phrase may refer to Syene, in southern Egypt, also known as Aswan, where there was a large Jewish colony after the Exile. Or it may refer to the desert of Sin, which is in the peninsula of Sinai. The point is that the Lord will gather his people from wherever they have been scattered. The same is true spiritually. The Lord will find us wherever we are and bring us back to our inheritance, if we will hearken to him and do our part.

## THE LORD COMFORTS HIS RETURNING CHILDREN (49:13–21)

The gathering of Israel will be an occasion of great joy for both heaven and earth ("Sing, O heavens; and be joyful, O earth"; 49:13) and a great blessing to those gathered ("smitten no more; for the Lord hath comforted his people, and will have mercy upon his afflicted"; 49:13).

Despite these promises, the people of Israel feel that they have been forgotten by the Lord (49:14). In tender expressions of love, the Lord assures them that he has not forgotten (49:15). He compares himself to a loving mother and says his love for his covenant people are found in the marks on his hands (49:16). Though a mother may forget her child, the Lord will hold his children in remembrance forever.

In the gathering, the descendants of Israel ("thy children"; 49:17) will come in great numbers (49:19–20). Though many may be lost through the dispersal and through apostasy, in the gathering, Zion will multiply with many inhabitants, so many that she will require more space to dwell in than before. Israel, who has felt abandoned and desolate, will be amazed to see so many descendants (49:21).

These prophecies have an application both for the Jews and for those who enter the Lord's covenant through baptism into The Church of Jesus Christ of Latter-day Saints. The Lord will never forget his promises to the Jews and will bring them back to the land of Palestine in great numbers. The Lord will also make good on his promises to other people throughout the world, sending forth missionaries and bringing into the fold all who will come.

## Isaiah 49:13–21

*Sing,* O heavens;
and be *joyful,* O earth;
[for the feet of those who are in the east shall be established;][14]
and *break forth into singing,* O mountains:
[for they shall be smitten no more;][15]

for the Lord hath *comforted* his people,
and will have *mercy* upon his afflicted. (49:13)

But, [behold,] Zion [hath] said, The *Lord* hath forsaken me,
and my *Lord* hath forgotten me[—but he will show that he hath not].[16] (49:14)

[For] can a *woman forget* her sucking child,
that *she should not have compassion* on the son of her womb?

Yea, *they* may forget,
yet will I not forget thee, [O house of Israel].[17] (49:15)

Behold, I have *graven thee* upon the palms of my hands;
thy *walls* are continually before me. (49:16)

Thy children shall *make haste [against]*[18] thy destroyers[;]
and they that made thee waste shall *go forth [from] thee.* (49:17)

*Lift up thine eyes* round about,
and *behold:*

*all these* gather themselves together,
and [*they* shall] come to thee.

[And] as I live, saith the Lord,

thou shalt surely *clothe thee* with them all, as with an ornament,

[14]This addition is found in 1 Ne. 21:13.
[15]This addition is found in 1 Ne. 21:13.
[16]The changes in this verse are from 1 Ne. 21:14.
[17]The changes in this verse are from 1 Ne. 21:15.
[18]1 Ne. 21:17 introduces *against* and the semicolon after *destroyers.* In the process, the meaning is changed and clarified. The KJV punctuation suggests that *thy children* shall make haste against both *the destroyers* and *they that made thee waste,* leaving *shall go forth of thee* as a confusing clause with uncertain meaning. With the Book of Mormon punctuation, the last clause is made separate and independent.

and *bind them* on [even] <u>as a bride</u> . . . [19] (49:18)

For thy *waste* and thy *desolate places,*
and the *land* of thy *destruction,*

shall even now be too narrow
by reason of the inhabitants, and they that swallowed thee up shall be far away.
(49:19)

The *children* [whom] <u>thou shalt have,</u>
after <u>thou hast lost</u> the *[first],* shall . . . again in thine ears [say],[20]

The *place* is too [constricting][21] for <u>me</u>:
give *place* to me that <u>I</u> may dwell. (49:20)

Then shalt thou say in thine heart,

Who hath *begotten* me <u>these,</u>
seeing I have *lost* my <u>children,</u>

and am *desolate,*
a *captive,* and removing to and fro?

and *who hath brought up these?*
Behold, I was left alone; these, *where had they been?* (49:21)

## NOTES AND COMMENTARY

**49:13** *Sing, O heavens/be joyful, O earth/break forth into singing, O mountains.*
The very creations of God will rejoice at the salvation he will send forth (44:23;
52:9–10; 55:12; D&C 128:22–23).

*those who are in the east/mountains. Those in the east* may be the Israelites in
Jerusalem; *mountains* may refer to Zion in America. The heavens and the earth shall
join in rejoicing when the Lord's people in both his capital cities are protected, comforted, and established.

*his people/his afflicted.* The Lord's people are afflicted because of their dispersion and long exile. They also are afflicted spiritually as a consequence of sin, but
through the Atonement the Lord will comfort and be merciful to the repentant, who
are truly the Lord's people.

**49:14** *Zion. Zion* can refer to the Lord's people or to a geographical location. In
this context it seems to refer to scattered Israel, who felt that God had forgotten her.

*The Lord hath forsaken me.* So many millennia have passed since the Lord made
his promises that the people of the covenant feel the Lord has turned his back on

---

[19] The changes in this verse are from 1 Ne. 21:18.
[20] The changes in this verse are from 1 Ne. 21:20.
[21] This word replaces the KJV *strait.*

them (compare Gideon's expression in Judges 6:13). When we as individuals have such feelings, we can lay claim to these same assurances.

**49:15** *woman forget her sucking child/son of her womb.* It seems unlikely that a loving mother would ever forget her precious baby, the *son of her womb.* Unfortunately, even such powerful love as that can be transitory. But the Lord's love is ever constant—he will never fail us (43:4; 44:21; 46:3–4).

**49:16** *graven thee/palms of my hands.* This phrase refers to the crucifixion of Christ, in which nails pierced his hands and left scars that remained after his resurrection (Luke 24:38–40; 3 Ne. 11:13–14). These nail marks are a sign to Israel—and to the world—that Christ has indeed fulfilled his mission as Savior (22:23, 25; John 20:25; 3 Ne. 11:14–15; D&C 6:37; 45:48–53). Marks in the palm of the hand are also a constant reminder to the Savior, who bears those marks and is always mindful of us.

*walls/before me.* The walls of Jerusalem are ever present in the consciousness of those who dwell in the city. In the same way, an awareness of Israel is ever present with the Lord (60:18).

**49:17** *Thy children shall make haste against thy destroyers.* The *children* are the descendants of ancient Israel. The *destroyers* are the nations that attacked and captured ancient Israel. In the days when Israel shall be restored to her former blessings, the descendants of ancient Israel will quickly turn against their ancient enemies. This passage may also refer to the success the faithful of Israel will have against those who would destroy them spiritually—including Satan and his followers.

*made thee waste/go forth.* Those who conquered and wasted Israel will depart.

**49:18** *clothe/ornament.* As additional souls are gathered unto Zion, they will add to the glory of those already there. As fine clothing or expensive jewelry are to a bride, so will the souls of those gathered be to the Church.

*bind/bride.* In Zion, we bind ourselves to others with a bond of charity. This binding, which brings us to union and oneness, is the very essence of Zion. Binding might also refer to the ordinance of sealing. In various scriptures, the bride is depicted as being the Saints (61:10), the Church (D&C 109:73–74), and the New Jerusalem (Rev. 21:2). In this verse, the bride represents those who join Zion.

**49:19** *waste/desolate places/narrow.* Israel's promised land has been laid waste and made empty, but when the gathering occurs, the available land will be too small for the great influx of those who are gathered (54:1–3). The waste places of Zion are symbolic of Israel's loss—both spiritual and physical—that shall be restored (58:12; D&C 101:75; 103:11–12). The restoration of the waste places thus brings joy and comfort (51:3; 52:9).

*they that swallowed thee . . . far away.* Israel's enemies, or our spiritual enemies, will be far from us.

**49:20** *children.* Those who come unto Zion are God's children.

*lost the first.* The first were the earlier generations of Israel; some of these fell away in apostasy, and others were carried away into captivity.

*constricting. Constricting* gives the sense of narrow, small, crowded, restricted.

**49:21** *lost my children.* This phrase may refer to Israel's captivity or to apostasy.

*desolate/captive.* Possible interpretations include Jerusalem's being made desolate and Israel taken captive; Jerusalem's losing her temple and becoming captive to spiritual death; and the world's becoming victim to spiritual desolation and captivity.

## GENTILES SHALL ASSIST RETURNING ISRAEL (49:22–26)

In the gathering, the Lord will provide loving caretakers to help Israel on her way. "The Gentiles . . . shall bring thy sons in their arms, . . . and kings shall be thy nursing fathers" (49:22–23). These people of power, rather than requiring that Israel bow down to them, "shall bow down" to Israel, giving great respect and honor to the returning children of Israel (49:23). These gentiles and kings and queens will "know that I am the Lord" (49:23) and that returning Israel is on the Lord's errand. Even those who are "captives" will come (49:24). The Lord will take them away from their captors, and he will "contend with him that contendeth with thee" (49:25). Captives might be those in bondage to political systems, to false religions, or to sin.

Apparently during this same time there will be great and devastating civil wars on the earth (49:26). As a result of God's judgments, all the earth will know that Jehovah is the Savior (49:26).

*Isaiah 49:22–26*

> Thus saith the Lord God,
>
> Behold, I will l*ift up mine hand* to the Gentiles,
> and *set up my standard* to the people:
>
> and they shall *bring thy sons* in their arms,
> and *thy daughters shall be carried* upon their shoulders. (49:22)
>
> And *kings* shall be thy nursing fathers,
> and their *queens* thy nursing mothers:
>
> they shall *bow down* to thee with their face[s] toward[s][22] the earth,
> and *lick up* the dust of thy feet;

[22] The changes in this verse are from 1 Ne. 21:23 and 2 Ne. 6:7.

and *thou shalt know* that I am the <u>Lord</u>:
for *they shall not be ashamed* that wait for <u>me</u>. (49:23)

[For] shall the *prey be taken* from the <u>mighty</u>,
or the <u>lawful captive[s]</u> *delivered?*[23] (49:24)

But thus saith the Lord,
Even the *captives* of the mighty shall be <u>taken away</u>,
and the *prey* of the terrible shall be <u>delivered</u>;

for [the Mighty God shall deliver his covenant people. For thus saith the Lord:] . . .
*I will contend* with him that contendeth with <u>thee</u>,
and *I will save* <u>thy children</u>.[24] (49:25)

And I will *feed them* that oppress thee <u>with their own flesh</u>;
and[25] *they shall be drunken* <u>with their own blood</u>, as with sweet wine:

and all flesh shall know that I the *Lord*
am thy *Saviour*
and thy *Redeemer,*
the *Mighty One of Jacob.* (49:26)

## NOTES AND COMMENTARY

**49:22** *lift up mine hand.* This phrase may signify the Lord's lifting his right arm in covenant, stretching forth his hand to accomplish his work, or perhaps reaching out to invite the Gentiles to come unto him (5:26; 13:2; see Gen. 14:22; Deut. 32:39–40).

*Gentiles. Gentiles* are all those who are not of Israel, with Israel being either the literal descendants of Jacob or those who have come spiritually unto the God of Jacob.

*standard.* A *standard* is a flag or ensign that serves as a rallying point around which people may gather. The scriptures define the *standard* as God's words (specifically, the Book of Mormon; 2 Ne. 29:2), the everlasting covenant (D&C 45:9), the great Zion of the last days (D&C 64:41–43), and the light of the righteous or the Church and its faithful members (D&C 115:3–5). Overall, the *standard* is the true gospel and church of Jesus Christ (5:26; 11:10–12; 62:10; Zech. 9:16).

**49:22–23** *thy sons/thy daughters/kings/queens.* Nephi comments on 49:22–23 in 1 Nephi 22:6–9, explaining that the Gentiles will bless his seed both temporally (meaning with physical nourishment) and spiritually (with spiritual nourishment, the gospel). Jacob casts a different light on this prophecy of Isaiah. In 2 Nephi 10:5–9 he explains that when the Jews come to believe in Christ, they will be "gathered in from

---

[23] The changes in this verse are from 1 Ne. 21:24 and 2 Ne. 6:16.
[24] In 1 Ne. 21:25, this verse appears without change from KJV. The changes shown in this verse appear in the JST and, in part, in 2 Ne. 6:17.
[25] 1 Ne. 21:26 omits this *and;* 2 Ne. 6:18, KJV, and JST all retain it.

their long dispersion, . . . and the nations of the Gentiles shall be great in the eyes of me, saith God, in carrying them forth to the lands of their inheritance. Yea, the kings of the Gentiles shall be nursing fathers unto them, and their queens shall become nursing mothers" (see also 45:14; 49:7; 60:4).

One interpretation of these words was given by Elder Spencer W. Kimball: "The brighter day has dawned. The scattering has been accomplished; the gathering is in process. May the Lord bless us all as we become nursing fathers and mothers (see Isa. 49:23 and 1 Nephi 21:23) unto our Lamanite brethren and hasten the fulfillment of the great promises made to them."[26] The kings and queens may well be the righteous men and women who have entered into the covenants of the fulness of the priesthood in the temple of God.

**49:23** *bow down/faces towards the earth/lick up the dust.* In the ancient Near East, these actions were signs of submission to a king or ruler (Gen. 42:6; 1 Sam. 24:8; Ps. 72:8–11; 2 Ne. 6:13). In times past, Israel was repeatedly conquered and forced to submit to the kings of the earth. But in the last days kings and queens will bow in obeisance and submission to the children of Israel.

*not be ashamed that wait for me.* Those who wait for the Lord are those who trust patiently in his plan. Their faith will be vindicated; they will not be ashamed that they believed, because all God's promises are fulfilled. The psalmist said, "O my God, I trust in thee: . . . let none that wait on thee be ashamed" (Ps. 25:2–3).

**49:24** *the prey/mighty/captives.* The context of 49:24 tells us that *prey/captives* refers to God's "covenant people," who are in bondage to the gentiles. The *mighty* (called "the terrible" in 49:25) could also refer to Satan, who makes us his captives when we sin. The prey shall indeed be "taken from the mighty," by God, who is mightier than all.

*lawful captives.* The description of being made captive by legal right may suggest that Israel was taken legitimately according to the rules of warfare, or that she is captive to Satan according to the law of justice. But, in his mercy, God's claim to his children supersedes the claims of all others.

**49:25** *captives/the prey.* See commentary on 49:24.

*thy children.* The descendants of the Israelites are *thy children.*

**49:26** *feed/own flesh/drunken/own blood.* In 1 Nephi 22:13, Nephi tells us that in the last days the great and abominable church "shall war among themselves, and the sword of their own hands shall fall upon their own heads, and they shall be drunken with their own blood." In the next verse, he explains that the same fate will befall

---

[26] Conference Report, Oct. 1965, 72.

"every nation which shall war against thee, O house of Israel"; they "shall be turned one against another, and they shall fall into the pit which they digged to ensnare the people of the Lord." Scriptural instances of kingdoms that have turned against themselves include Egypt (19:2), Babylon (Ezek. 38:21; Zech. 14:13), and, of course, the Jaredites (Ether 14–15).

*all flesh.* This term may refer to all human beings (Ezek. 21:4–5; D&C 63:5–6; 84:97–98) or even all members of the animal kingdom (Gen. 6:17, 19; Lev. 17:14). Perhaps the Lord's manifestation of power will be so great that all creatures will know he is God.

*Saviour/Redeemer/Mighty One of Jacob.* These three titles of Jehovah signify his power to rescue and succor us from death and sin (Savior), to ransom us and purchase us from the demands of justice (Redeemer), and to deliver us from all our enemies (Mighty One).

---

# ISAIAH 50

*LIKENING ISAIAH 50 UNTO OURSELVES*

*Even if we of the Church, as the bride of Christ, have not kept faith with the Lord, yet he will not cast us off or put us away. We are separated from God, but Isaiah promises that there is One who has the power of reconciliation. This restoration to a union with God is made possible by the atonement of Jesus Christ, who submitted himself to shame and pain, both physical and emotional, so that he could bless us. If we will fear the Lord and obey his servants, we will have his light.*

---

## ISRAEL IS FAITHLESS, DESPITE GOD'S POWER (50:1–3)

The Lord introduces the image of a marriage between God and Israel, with Israel (or the Church) being the bride and the Lord being the bridegroom (this metaphor is repeated in 62:4–5). The Lord speaks of the practice of a husband "put[ting] away" his wife by giving her a legal bill of divorcement (50:1). The law of Moses required that a husband give his wife such a "bill," or certificate, for a divorce to be valid (Deut. 24:1–4). But there is no such bill in this case. The Lord has not divorced Israel. He also speaks of Israel as his children, asking to which creditor he has sold them. In ancient Israel, a creditor could take a debtor's children and sell them into slavery to pay the debt (Ex. 21:7–8; 2 Kgs. 4:1; Neh. 5:1–5). The Lord assures Israel that he has not sold her (50:1).

But though the Lord (the husband) has been constant, Israel (the wife) has removed herself from his presence by sin (50:1). Because of this, "when [the Lord] came, there was no man" to meet him; and when he called, "there was none to answer" (50:2).

God has power to redeem and to deliver, just as he has all power over the elements (50:2–3). He will render both mercy and justice, according to our faith and our works.

Isaiah 50:2–3 are repeated, with changes, in Doctrine and Covenants 133:66–69, which puts this passage in the context of the Second Coming.

*Isaiah 50:1–3*

> [Yea, for thus saith the Lord:
> *Have I* put thee away,
> or *have I* cast thee off forever?
> For] thus saith the Lord,

> *Where* is the bill of your mother's divorcement?
> *[To] whom* [have I] put [thee] away,
> or *[to] which* of my creditors . . . [have I sold you?
> Yea,] *to whom* [have I] sold you?[1]

> Behold, *for your iniquities* have ye sold yourselves,
> and *for your transgressions* is your mother put away. (50:1)

> Wherefore, *when I came,* [there was] no man?
> *when I called,* [yea,] [there was] none to answer?

> [O house of Israel,] is *my hand shortened* at all, that it cannot redeem,
> or *have I no power* to deliver?

> Behold, at my rebuke *I* dry up the sea,
> *I* make [their] rivers a wilderness

> [and] their *fish [to] [stink],* because [the waters are dried up],
> and *[they die* because of] thirst.[2] (50:2)

> I *clothe* the heavens with blackness,
> and I make sackcloth their *covering.* (50:3)

NOTES AND COMMENTARY

**50:1** *put thee away/cast thee off.* Under Jewish law a husband separated from or divorced his wife by putting her away or casting her off. The Lord affirms that Israel had been *put away,* but it was Israel that turned away, not the Lord.

*bill of your mother's divorcement.* According to the law of Moses, a man could not divorce his wife without presenting her with a legal bill of divorcement (Deut. 24:1–4). At one point the Lord actually did separate himself from ancient Israel, as Jeremiah declared: "When for all the causes whereby backsliding Israel committed

---

[1] The changes in the first part of this verse appear in the JST and 2 Ne. 7:1.
[2] The many changes in this verse are found in both the JST and 2 Ne. 7:2. They are identical with only one exception: The 2 Ne. reading includes the *yea* on the second line; the JST does not.

adultery I had put her away, and given her a bill of divorce" (Jer. 3:8). Perhaps the Lord's reassurances here apply to latter-day Israel (54:6–8; see Hosea 2:4–9).

*creditors . . . have I sold you.* It was the custom in ancient Israel for some creditors to take the children of their debtors and sell them as slaves for payment of an overdue debt (Ex. 21:7–8; Neh. 5:1–5; Matt. 18:25). But the Lord has no creditors—he is in debt to no one—and he has not sold Israel into slavery. Ultimately, God and Israel are separated because of Israel's choices, not God's.

*sold yourselves/put away.* The children of Israel have sold themselves into the bondage of sin. And the mother has been set aside, or divorced, because of unfaithfulness. Perhaps the children here represent the sons and daughters of the covenant, and perhaps the mother represents the nation of Israel as a whole.

**50:2** *no man.* When Jehovah came to apostate Israel, there was no one to receive him. Unfortunately, in every generation there are few or even none to receive the Lord.

*I called/none to answer.* Too many of Israel were like Amulek before he repented: "I was called many times and I would not hear" (Alma 10:6).

*hand shortened.* The scriptures testify repeatedly of God stretching out his hand to deliver his people. His hand is indeed stretched out, not shortened (59:1–2; Num. 11:23), or inadequate to save.

**50:2–3** *dry up the sea/rivers a wilderness/fish to stink/waters are dried up/clothe the heavens with blackness.* The Lord uses these as examples of his power. These phrases may refer to drought and to the smoke of war (which, although perpetrated by man, can also be a judgment of God) that obscures the sky, and they remind us of the miracles of Moses in Egypt (Ex. 7:18–21; 10:21; 14:26–31). They may also refer not only to events of the past but also to the Second Coming, an event of the future (Rev. 6:12; 8:12; D&C 45:42; 133:66–69). The Lord gave the same prophecy through Jeremiah (Jer. 51:36). Just as the Lord has great power over the elements, so also does he have power to redeem and deliver.

**50:3** *heavens/blackness.* The dark sky heralds the coming judgments, as well as Christ's second coming. As the Lord said in Matthew 24: "Immediately after the tribulation of those days shall the sun be darkened, and the moon shall not give her light, and the stars shall fall from heaven, and the powers of the heavens shall be shaken: And then . . . they shall see the Son of man coming in the clouds of heaven with power and great glory" (Matt. 24:29–30; see D&C 29:11–14; 45:39–44). Perhaps earthquakes and volcanic activity in the last days will cover the heavens with blackness.

Elder Bruce R. McConkie gave another interpretation: "'I clothe the heavens with blackness' (Isa. 50:3), and there is no more revelation. . . . Thus saith our God. Such is his promise, spoken prophetically of our day. And here, given in modern times, is his announcement that as he spake, so has it come to pass: 'Verily, verily, I say unto you, darkness covereth the earth, and gross darkness the minds of the people, and all flesh has become corrupt before my face.' (D&C 112:23).'"[3]

*sackcloth. Sackcloth* is the clothing of mourning. Here, the darkness of the heavens may symbolize the mourning of the wicked at the second coming of Christ. Or it may symbolize the mourning of the righteous, and of the heavens and earth.

## PROPHECIES OF THE MESSIAH (50:4–9)

Isaiah 50:4–9 is known as a "servant song." (Other servant songs are found in 42:1–9; 49:1–7; 52:13–15; 53:1–12.) The servant in this case seems to be Christ in the meridian of time. As the headnote to this chapter in the LDS edition to the Bible says, "Isaiah speaks Messianically—Messiah shall have the tongue of the learned." These verses also apply to Isaiah or to any true servant of the Lord who obeys despite persecution.

The Lord enables the servant to speak and hear as a learned one does (50:4). This servant is faithful, "not rebellious" (50:5). He submits himself to the persecutions that come: "I gave my back to the smiter. . . . I hid not my face from shame and spitting" (50:6). He trusts in the Lord: "The Lord God will help me," he says (50:7, 9). He knows that his life and ministry please the Lord: "The Lord is near, and he justifieth me" (50:8). At the same time, the servant knows that his enemies will not stand: "I will smite him with the strength of my mouth . . . the moth shall eat them up" (50:8, 9).

This passage stands in contrast to earlier ones. Here, the servant receives the Lord's word (50:4); earlier, "no man" would listen (50:2). Here, the servant is confident in the Lord's help (50:7–9); earlier, the people doubted the Lord's love and power (49:14, 21). Here, the servant suffers because he is obedient (50:5–6); earlier, the people suffered because of their iniquities (50:1–3). Here, the servant is innocent of all charges (50:8–9), with the Lord supporting him; earlier, the Lord is an accuser and the people are guilty (50:1). Of course, we can and should be like the servant, rather than the sinful people; the servant is an example and model for us all.

---

[3] *Millennial Messiah,* 39.

*Isaiah 50:4–9*

The Lord God hath given *me* the <u>tongue of the learned</u>,
that *I* should know <u>how to speak</u> a word in season [unto thee, O house of Israel.

When ye are] weary
*he* [<u>waketh</u>] morning by morning.
*He* [<u>waketh</u>] mine ear to hear as the learned.[4] (50:4)

The Lord God hath appointed mine ears,[5]

and I was *not rebellious,*
*neither turned away back.* (50:5)

I gave my *back* to the [<u>smiter</u>],[6]
and my *cheeks* to <u>them that plucked off the hair</u>:
I hid not my *face* from *shame and spitting.* (50:6)

For the *Lord God will help* <u>me</u>;
therefore shall <u>I</u> *not be confounded:*

therefore have *I* set <u>my face like a flint</u>,
and I know that *I* shall <u>not be ashamed</u>. (50:7)

[And the *Lord*] *is near,* [*and he*] *justifieth me;* <u>who will contend with me</u>?
*Let us stand together.* <u>Who is mine adversary</u>?

Let *him* come near . . . <u>me</u>,
[and <u>I</u> will smite *him* with the strength of my mouth.][7] (50:8)

[For] the Lord God will help me.
[And all they who shall condemn me,

behold,] *they* all shall <u>wax old as a garment</u>
[and] the <u>moth shall eat</u> *them* <u>up</u>.[8] (50:9)

## NOTES AND COMMENTARY

**50:4** *tongue of the learned/know how to speak.* The Lord has blessed the servant with knowledge and eloquence. His speaking ability is in marked contrast to that of Enoch (Moses 6:31), Moses (Ex. 4:10), and Jeremiah (Jer. 1:6).

*speak a word in season.* The servant delivers the word of the Lord to those he serves. The Lord enables the servant to speak the right words at the right time.

*weary/waketh morning by morning.* Though Israel would rather slumber spiritually, the Lord repeatedly awakens her to his word of truth and righteousness. Or the *he* in this verse may refer to the servant rather than the Lord. As a contrasting

---

[4] This verse has been changed from the KJV in both the JST and 2 Ne. 7:4, though some punctuation differs between the two.

[5] The changes shown are found in the JST; 2 Ne. 7:5 reads the same as the KJV.

[6] 2 Ne. 7:6 changes the KJV *smiters* to singular *smiter.*

[7] The changes to this verse are from the JST and 2 Ne. 7:8.

[8] The changes in this verse are found in both the JST and 2 Ne. 7:9.

interpretation, then, the servant speaks to those who are weary because of the burdens of the world, offering daily comfort and blessings. Contrast these verses with Isaiah 28:11–12: "For with stammering lips and another tongue will he speak to this people. To whom he said, This is the rest wherewith ye may cause the weary to rest; and this is the refreshing."

*waketh mine ear.* The Lord speaks to the servant's responsive ear in continuing revelation.

*hear as the learned.* Those who know the most are most able to learn more. Through God's gift, the servant not only speaks as the learned do but hears (or learns) as the learned do as well.

**50:5** *appointed mine ears.* The Lord speaks to the servant by revelation (1 Sam. 9:15; Job 36:10, 15).

*turned away back.* The servant did not turn from his appointed mission, nor did he turn off the strait and narrow path.

**50:6** *back/smiter/cheeks/plucked off the hair.* The servant submitted himself to great insult for his testimony (Jer. 20:7–9). "The striking language calls to mind . . . the physical sufferings of our Lord (cf. Matt. 26:67ff; John 19:1ff). . . . Beating on the back would seem also to be the custom in [punishing] evil men (cf. Prov. 10:13; 19:29; 26:3; Ps. 129:3).

"In addition the servant gave his cheeks to those who pluck out the hair. . . . The Oriental regarded the beard as a sign of freedom and respect, and to pluck out the hair of the beard (for *cheek* in effect would refer to a beard) is to show utter contempt"[9] (Neh. 13:25; 2 Sam. 10:5.).

*hid not my face.* The servant did not try to hide or escape from persecution. As Nephi wrote regarding Christ: "And the world, because of their iniquity, shall judge him to be a thing of naught; wherefore they scourge him, and he suffereth it; and they smite him, and he suffereth it. Yea, they spit upon him, and he suffereth it, because of his loving kindness and his long-suffering towards the children of men" (1 Ne. 19:9).

**50:7** *God will help/not be confounded.* The servant knows that God will stand by him in his faithfulness (Jer. 1:18; Ezek. 3:8–9)—just as the Lord will stand by us, if we are faithful.

*set my face like a flint.* A sign of firmness or determination. Speaking of Jesus, Elder Bruce R. McConkie said: "The course of his life was toward the cross, and he was steadfast and immovable in his determination to follow this very course, one laid out for him by his Father. He had said of himself through the mouth of Isaiah, 'I set

---

[9] Young, *Book of Isaiah,* 3:300.

my face like a flint, and I know that I shall not be ashamed.' (Isa. 50:7.) Clearly, there was to be no turning back."[10]

**50:7–8** *not be ashamed/Lord . . . justifieth.* The servant knows that the Lord will bring his prophecies to pass and will validate all he has done in his ministry (62:1).

**50:8** *contend/stand together/adversary/come near.* In an ancient Middle Eastern civil court, the two opponents stood together to hear the judge's decision. In a criminal court, the accuser made the charge personally to the defendant. Here, the servant is persecuted from all sides, but "the Lord is near, and he justifieth me."

*strength of my mouth.* God's words, whether directly or through his servants, have great power, enabling the servant to overcome all his enemies (1 Ne. 17:26–31; Morm. 9:17; Ether 4:9; Moses 1:32; 6:47; 7:13).

**50:9** *wax old as a garment/moth shall eat them.* The servant's enemies will slowly but surely be destroyed, even as clothing is destroyed by time and pests (51:6–8; Job 13:28; Ps. 102:25–28).

## TRUST IN THE LORD (50:10–11)

Two classes of people are contrasted in these two verses. One class consists of those who fear the Lord and obey his servant (50:10). They will not walk in spiritual darkness but will have spiritual light (50:10). The other class consists of those who seek to be spiritually self-sufficient, relying on themselves instead of on God. They attempt to create their own light (50:11), but their efforts produce no more than sparks (50:11) when compared to the bright light that comes from God. Those in this group will eventually receive judgments from the Lord, resulting in sorrow (50:11).

*Isaiah 50:10–11*

> *Who* is among you that <u>feareth the Lord,</u>
> *that* <u>obeyeth the voice of his servant,</u>
>
> that walketh in *darkness,*
> and hath *no light?*[11] (50:10)
>
> Behold, *all ye that kindle . . . fire,*
> that *compass yourselves* about with <u>sparks,</u>
>
> walk in *the light* of <u>your fire,</u>
> and in *the sparks* [which][12] <u>ye have kindled.</u>

---

[10] *Doctrinal New Testament Commentary,* 1:439.
[11] This verse, which is quoted in 2 Ne. 7:10, omits the final phrase from the KJV reading.
[12] The changes to this verse are from the JST and 2 Ne. 7:11.

This shall ye have of mine hand—ye shall lie down in sorrow. (50:11)

## NOTES AND COMMENTARY

**50:10** *feareth the Lord/obeyeth . . . servant/walketh in darkness/no light.* Isaiah asks who fears the Lord and obeys God's servant, yet still walks in darkness. The answer is, No one. Therefore, since Israel is walking by her own light rather than God's, her people were obviously not fearing God and obeying his servant.

*walketh in darkness.* Being without spiritual light is walking *in darkness* (58:8–10; 59:9–10).

**50:11** *kindle . . . fire/sparks/walk in the light of your fire.* This expression refers to those who walk in their own way, according to their own will, rather than according to the will and direction of the Lord. The Lord's will comes to us through the Holy Ghost, which ministers truth as by fire (D&C 9:8). Speaking to the people of our dispensation, the Lord said, "They seek not the Lord to establish his righteousness, but every man walketh in his own way, and after the image of his own god" (D&C 1:16; 88:35).

Commenting on this chapter of Isaiah, Jacob said: "O that cunning plan of the evil one! O the vainness, and the frailties, and the foolishness of men! When they are learned they think they are wise, and they hearken not unto the counsel of God, for they set it aside, supposing they know of themselves, wherefore, their wisdom is foolishness and it profiteth them not. And they shall perish" (2 Nephi 9:28).

*have of mine hand.* This phrase refers to that which we receive from the Lord.

*lie down in sorrow. Lie down* probably means to die. Latter-day revelation gives us a valuable context for this passage, placing it in the last days at the time of the Second Coming: "Upon them that hearken not to the voice of the Lord shall be fulfilled that which was written by . . . the prophet Malachi: For, behold, the day cometh that shall burn as an oven, and all the proud, yea, and all that do wickedly, shall be stubble; and the day that cometh shall burn them up, saith the Lord of hosts, that it shall leave them neither root nor branch.

"Wherefore, this shall be the answer of the Lord unto them: In that day when I came unto mine own, no man among you received me, and you were driven out. When I called again there was none of you to answer; yet my arm was not shortened at all that I could not redeem, neither my power to deliver. Behold, at my rebuke I dry up the sea. I make the rivers a wilderness; their fish stink, and die for thirst. I clothe the heavens with blackness, and make sackcloth their covering [note that this passage draws from Isa. 50:2–3]. And *this shall ye have of my hand—ye shall lie down in sorrow.*

"Behold, and lo, there are none to deliver you; for ye obeyed not my voice when I called to you out of the heavens; ye believed not my servants, and when they were sent unto you ye received them not. Wherefore, they sealed up the testimony and bound up the law, and ye were delivered over unto darkness. These shall go away into outer darkness, where there is weeping, and wailing, and gnashing of teeth. Behold the Lord your God hath spoken it. Amen" (D&C 133:63–74; emphasis added. See Isa. 52:5, 8, 13).

# ISAIAH 51:1-16

## *LIKENING ISAIAH 51 UNTO OURSELVES*

*Again the Lord calls to members of the Church, asking them to hearken to his words. At the conclusion of the last days, as the Lord ushers in the Millennium, he will bring an end to the fallen condition of the earth. He will renew the earth and restore it to its Edenic state. The Lord will dwell among his people.*

*As the events of the last days unfold, the Lord assures us that if we are righteous, we need not fear the works of man. The Lord is greater than any man, and he will help us. He reminds us of his works of power in times past; by that same power he will bring Zion and fulfill all his promises to her.*

## A CALL TO SALVATION (51:1-8)

Isaiah 51 is a call to those who "follow after righteousness" (51:1). The call is repeated again and again: "Hearken" (51:1), "Look" (51:1, 2), "Hearken" (51:4), "Lift up your eyes" (51:6), and, again, "Hearken" (51:7).

The call reminds the righteous of their origins (Abraham and Sarah) and the blessings they received (51:1–2). Even as Abraham and Sarah received promises when fulfillment seemed beyond hope, so will the Lord fulfill his promises to comfort Zion (51:3). He will change the area of Palestine physically (51:3), and he will give the people a spirit of joy and gladness (51:3). The headnote to this chapter in the LDS edition of the Bible clearly places these events in the last days.

In the last days, then, Zion will be established and blessed (51:3). God's law will go forth from her (51:4), and his righteousness will dwell there (51:5). His judgment will punish the wicked and bless the righteous (51:4–5). When Christ comes, ushering in the Millennium, the heavens and the earth as we know them will be destroyed, as will the wicked, but the Lord's promises to the faithful will never end (51:6).

A recurring theme is the idea of *righteousness* and *salvation.* These two words appear eight times in this passage. In verses 1 and 7 the Lord indicates that he is speaking to those who seek righteousness. In verses 5, 6, and 8 he says that his righteousness is near, that it will not be abolished, and that it lasts forever (2 Ne. 1:19; Alma 26:8). Likewise, he tells us that his salvation has gone forth, that it is forever, and that it lasts from generation to generation (51:5, 6, 8). That seems to be a reminder of the principle of grace: our righteousness is insufficient, but if we will turn to the Lord, we can partake of his righteousness, which enables us to attain the blessings we seek (Rom. 10:3–4; 1 Cor. 1:27–31; Philip. 3:8–9).

Righteousness means to choose the good and godly way of life, to follow our God in all things. Salvation refers to deliverance from our enemies. In fact, deliverance from all our enemies is the very definition of salvation, according to the Prophet Joseph Smith.[1]

Elder Bruce R. McConkie has commented on verses 4 to 6 of this passage: "We hear a divine voice acclaim: 'Hearken unto me, my people,' and the Latter-day Saints are the Lord's people, 'and give ear unto me, O my nation: for a law shall proceed from me, and I will make my judgment to rest for a light of the people.' Thanks be to God, that law now has come; it is the fulness of his everlasting gospel; by it he will judge the world, and it now stands as a light for all men. 'My righteousness is near.' The millennial day is almost upon us. 'My salvation is gone forth.' The gospel is being preached to prepare a people for the coming day. . . . Hence, 'Lift up your eyes to the heavens,' O ye saints of the Most High, 'and look upon the earth beneath.' Read the signs of the times, the signs now being shown forth in the heavens above and in the earth beneath. 'For the heavens shall vanish away like smoke, and the earth shall wax old like a garment, and they that dwell therein shall die in like manner.' This old world shall die; there shall be a new heaven and a new earth; it will be a millennial earth. And 'my salvation shall be for ever, and my righteousness shall not be abolished,' saith the Lord (Isa. 51:4–6)."[2]

*Isaiah 51:1–8*

> Hearken [unto] me,
> ye that follow after righteousness, . . .

---

[1] *Teachings of the Prophet Joseph Smith,* 297.
[2] *Millennial Messiah,* 514–15.

Look unto *the rock* [from] whence ye [were][3] hewn,
and to the *hole of the pit* [from] whence ye are digged. (51:1)

Look unto *Abraham* your father,
and unto *Sarah,* [she] that bare you:

for I *called* him alone,
and *blessed* him.[4] (51:2)

For the *Lord shall comfort* Zion:
*he will comfort* all her waste places;

and *he will make her wilderness* like Eden,
and *her desert like* the garden of the Lord;

*joy* and *gladness* shall be found therein,
thanksgiving, and the *voice of melody.* (51:3)

*Hearken* unto me, my people;
and *give ear* unto me, O my nation:

for a *law* shall proceed from me,
and I will make my *judgment* to rest for a light [for][5] the people. (51:4)

*My righteousness* is near;
*my salvation* is gone forth,
and *mine arms* shall judge the people;

the *isles* shall wait upon me,
and on mine arm shall *they* trust. (51:5)

*Lift up your eyes* to the heavens,
and *look* upon the earth beneath:

for the *heavens* shall vanish away like smoke,
and the *earth* shall wax old like a garment,
and *they that dwell therein* shall die in like manner*:*

but *my salvation* shall be for ever,
and *my righteousness* shall not be abolished. (51:6)

Hearken unto me, *ye* that know righteousness,
the *people* in whose heart [I have written][6] my law;

*fear ye not* the reproach of men,
*neither be ye afraid* of their revilings. (51:7)

For the *moth* shall eat them up like a garment,
and the *worm* shall eat them like wool:

but my *righteousness* shall be for ever,
and my *salvation* from generation to generation. (51:8)

---

[3] The changes to this verse are from the JST and 2 Ne. 8:1.
[4] The changes to this verse are from 2 Ne. 8:2.
[5] The change to this verse is from 2 Ne. 8:4.
[6] The change to this verse is from 2 Ne. 8:7.

## NOTES AND COMMENTARY

**51:1** *rock/hewn/hole/digged.* Our origins, ancestry, or heritage. Our rock and quarry are Abraham and Sarah, from whom we descend. Ultimately, of course, the rock we come from is God the Father, and Christ, who is called the Rock at least thirty-four times in the scriptures.

**51:2** *Abraham/Sarah.* By looking to the great father and mother of our covenant (Gen. 12:2–3; 22:17), we can see that the Lord fulfills his promises even when it seems impossible, and we can look to them for an example of faithfulness.

*called him/blessed him.* See Genesis 12:1–5 for the initial calling and blessing of Abraham.

**51:3** *comfort Zion/waste places.* Jerusalem, which was wasted, will be blessed and restored (33:20; 44:26–28; 49:17–20; 52:8–10; Zech. 1:16–17). Zion, that is, the people and city of the Lord, will be built physically and spiritually. In Ezekiel 36:33 we learn that these events are millennial.

*wilderness like Eden/desert like the garden of the Lord.* The land of Israel, which has long been as desolate as a desert, will be made into a wonderful, fruitful garden (30:23; 35:1–2; Ezek. 36:35). This is representative of what will happen to the whole earth. As the tenth Article of Faith states, "The earth will be renewed and receive its paradisiacal glory." Also, when we truly come to Zion, which means a union with one another and with our God, the wilderness and desert areas of our souls will be renewed and blessed.

*joy/gladness/thanksgiving/melody.* These conditions contrast with the sorrow and misery suffered by the exiled Israelites and by those who have wandered in sin. When we return from any separation from the Lord or his promises, it is with much rejoicing (32:16–18; 35:10).

**51:4** *my people/my nation.* In a narrow sense this phrase refers to the people of Israel. In a broader sense, it is all those who come to the true God.

*give ear.* Listen.

*law.* "The Lord is our lawgiver" (33:22). "I will give thee tables of stone, and a law, and commandments which I have written," the Lord said to Moses (Ex. 24:12).

*judgment/light.* The Lord's judgment (or justice) is a light in that it is steady, reliable, and true. In addition, the Lord himself is a light for the people (42:4; Luke 2:30–32; Acts 26:23), as are his disciples (3 Ne. 15:12). In Doctrine and Covenants 45:9 the Lord says further that his "everlasting covenant" is also "a light to the world."

**51:5** *mine arms shall judge.* The Lord himself will be our judge: "He employeth no servant there" (2 Ne. 9:41). The Lord's arm of judgment (or justice) in this verse is the same as the arm on which we may trust (the arm of mercy).

*isles.* The uttermost areas of the Lord's kingdom on earth (42:4; 60:9).

*on mine arm shall they trust.* The Lord's arm represents the Lord himself. To trust in the arm of the Lord is to trust in the Lord. In contrast is the arm of flesh, or the ability of man (including ourselves), in which we must never trust (2 Ne. 4:34; 28:31; D&C 1:19). In a sense, the Lord's arm represents those who do his work with authority, specifically righteous priesthood holders.

**51:6** *Lift up your eyes . . . look.* If we will open our spiritual eyes and look, we will see signs in heaven and on earth. Joseph Smith assured us that when we begin to see signs, we may be confident that *all* that the Lord has prophesied will be fulfilled: "We see that perilous times have come, as was testified of. We may look, then, with most perfect assurance, for the fulfillment of all those things that have been written, and with more confidence than ever before, lift up our eyes to the luminary of day, and say in our hearts, Soon thou wilt veil thy blushing face."[7]

*heavens shall vanish.* Though the heavens and the earth as we know them seem permanent, both will vanish, or "pass away," when the Lord comes again in glory; they will be replaced by new heavens (2 Pet. 3:10; 3 Ne. 26:3; D&C 45:22) and a new earth. Though both heavens and earth will pass away, the Lord's salvation continues forever.

*like smoke.* Smoke is visible in the air only briefly and then vanishes (Ps. 37:20; 68:2; 102:3).

*earth shall wax old like a garment.* It is part of Latter-day Saint theology that the earth is a living being with a spirit and body and that it will die and then be resurrected.[8] Though heaven and earth will pass away, just as all clothing deteriorates and then disintegrates, the Lord and his righteousness continue forever (50:9; Ps. 102:25–27; Heb. 1:10–12; 2 Ne. 8:7–8).

**51:7** *heart I have written my law.* We are truly of God, not only when our acts reflect obedience to God's law but when our hearts—meaning our feelings, desires, attitudes, and intentions—are all turned to do his will. When we submit ourselves to God, he writes his law in our hearts even as he wrote the law on tablets of stone in Moses' day (Ps. 37:31; 40:8; 119:34).

---

[7] *History of the Church,* 3:291.
[8] See, for example, Smith, *Doctrines of Salvation,* 1:72–73.

*fear ye not the reproach of men.* Joseph Smith taught that persecution should not cause the Saints to falter: "I have reason to think that the Church is being purged. . . . So long as men are under the law of God, they have no fears."[9]

**51:8** *moth/garment/worm/wool.* All earth is transitory and subject to corruption and decay, as a garment is. But the Lord's righteousness never ends (2 Ne. 8:7–8).

*generation to generation.* This image gives the impression of never ending.

## ISRAEL APPEALS AND THE LORD ANSWERS (51:9–16)

The Lord has reminded Israel that all his promises will be fulfilled and that Zion will be established. Now the people who "follow after righteousness" cry unto the Lord for assurance that he will indeed bring the promised blessings. "Awake!" the people cry to the Lord, reminding him of the power he had shown forth in earlier days. He "wounded the dragon" and "dried the sea" (51:9–10). Just as he helped the children of Israel escape from Egypt through the Red Sea (51:10), they testify, so will he bring the latter-day redeemed ones back to Zion with songs of joy and gladness (51:11).

The Lord answers by reminding them of the weakness of man, who is "like unto grass" (51:12) and of the power of God, who "stretched forth the heavens" (51:13). The people of Zion have been fearful of their oppressors (51:13), forgetting that the Lord is God of all the armies (hosts) of heaven (51:15). Zion is "my people," and the Lord will care for them (51:16).

*Isaiah 51:9–16*

> *Awake, awake!* Put on <u>strength</u>,
> O <u>arm of the Lord</u>; *awake,*
>
> as in the ancient days. . . .
>
> *Art thou not* [*he*][10] that hath <u>cut Rahab</u>, and <u>wounded the dragon</u>? (51:9)
> *Art thou not* [*he who*][11] hath <u>dried the sea</u>, the <u>waters of the great deep</u>;
> that hath <u>made the depths of the sea a way</u> for the ransomed to pass over? (51:10)
>
> Therefore the *redeemed of the Lord* shall <u>return,</u>
> and <u>come</u> with singing unto *Zion;*

---

[9] *History of the Church,* 6:477.
[10] The changes in this verse are from 2 Ne. 8:9.
[11] The change in this verse is from 2 Ne. 8:10.

and *everlasting joy [and holiness]*[12] shall be <u>upon their head[s]</u>:[13]
[and]*[14] <u>they shall obtain</u> *gladness and joy;*

and *sorrow* and *mourning shall flee away.* (51:11)
<u>I [am he</u>;
yea,] <u>I am he</u> that *comforteth you.*

Behold, who art thou, that thou shouldst be afraid of . . . *man,* [who] <u>shall die,</u>
and of the *son of man,* [who] <u>shall be made [like unto] grass</u>?[15] (51:12)

And forgettest the Lord thy maker, that hath *stretched forth* <u>the heavens,</u>
and *laid* <u>the foundations of the earth;</u>

and hast feared continually every day because of *the fury of the oppressor,*
as if he were ready to destroy? And where is the *fury of the oppressor?* (51:13)

The *captive exile* hasteneth that he <u>may be loosed,</u>
and that *he* should <u>not die in the pit,</u>
<u>nor</u> that *his bread* <u>should fail.</u> (51:14)

But *I* am the <u>Lord thy God,</u> . . . [16]
whose waves roared: The <u>Lord of Hosts</u> is *[my]*[17] *name.* (51:15)

And I have put *my words* in <u>thy mouth,</u>
and . . . [18] have <u>covered thee</u> in the shadow of *mine hand,*

that I may *plant* the <u>heavens,</u>
and *lay the foundations* of the <u>earth,</u>

and say unto *Zion,*
[Behold,]*[19] thou art *my people.* (51:16)

## NOTES AND COMMENTARY

**51:9** *Awake.* This expression is also found in Isaiah 51:17 and 52:1. Here the Saints ask the Lord to *awake* from his seeming inactivity and fulfill his promises to Israel.

*Put on strength/arm of the Lord . . . ancient days.* This statement is reminiscent of the deliverance of Israel from Egypt, which came by the outstretched *arm of the Lord* (Ex. 6:6; 15:16). So also will he deliver his people in all ages.

*cut Rahab/wounded the dragon. Rahab* has several possible interpretations: Egypt, primordial chaos, or Satan. More important than the specific identification of

---

[12] This addition is found in the JST and in 2 Ne. 8:11.
[13] JST and 2 Ne. 8:11 makes plural the KJV *head.*
[14] This addition is found in 2 Ne. 8:11.
[15] 2 Ne. 8:12 makes several small changes in the KJV, some of which also appear in the JST.
[16] 2 Ne. 8:15 deletes the words *that divided the sea.*
[17] 2 Ne. 8:15 changes the KJV *his* to *my.*
[18] 2 Ne. 8:16 deletes the KJV *I.*
[19] This insertion is found in 2 Ne. 8:16 and the JST.

Rahab, however, is the understanding that God has power over all, even his mightiest enemies (27:1; Job 26:12; Ps. 74:13–17).

**51:10** *dried the sea/great deep/made . . . sea a way.* In this review of God's power, the speaker remembers that God made the sea and also dried it so the children of Israel could cross.

*ransomed.* Christ has "bought [us] with a price" (1 Cor. 7:23; see 1 Cor. 6:20). We were sold into sin (Rom. 7:14), but the Lord paid the price to set us free (35:10).

**51:11** *redeemed . . . return . . . with singing.* Those who will "return, and come with singing unto Zion" are the Latter-day Saints. Joseph Smith admonished us to work "diligently, spiritually and temporally for the redemption of Zion, that the pure in heart may return with songs of everlasting joy to build up her waste places, and meet the Lord when he comes in his glory."[20]

*upon their heads.* Blessings upon the head suggest priesthood ordinances, specifically the ordinances of the temple.

*gladness/joy/sorrow/mourning.* In the Zion of the Millennium, we will have much occasion to be glad, and none to be sorrowful. The plagues and wars and sin and bloodshed of the last days will be over. Death and sickness will have passed from the earth. The people will dwell in peace and unity. The Lord will be near, blessing all with his love and his light.

**51:12** *comforteth you.* Our merciful Lord comforts us in our trouble (Alma 31:31–32), not only with words but also with great blessings.

*man/son of man . . . like unto grass.* Grass withers quickly and dies easily—as does man (40:6–8). We need not fear man, who ultimately is very weak, but only the Lord.

**51:13** *stretched forth the heavens/laid the foundations of the earth.* In Genesis we read of God's creative powers, "In the beginning God created the heaven and the earth" (Gen. 1:1), dividing the light from the darkness. He laid the foundations of earth by causing dry land to appear and by bringing forth plants on the land (Gen. 1:9, 11–12). The God of creation would certainly also have power to fulfill his promises of deliverance and blessing to Zion.

*fury of the oppressor.* The enemy, both temporal and spiritual (Satan and his hosts), no matter how ferocious, is as nothing when compared to the Lord and his power.

---

[20] *Teachings of the Prophet Joseph Smith,* 77.

**51:14** *captive exile.* Those of Israel who have been carried away from the land of their inheritance, both temporally (in the scattering) and spiritually (through sin), shall be loosed from their captivity, leaving them free to return with the redeemed.

*pit.* This is a place of captivity, such as a dungeon. The *pit* may also be Sheol, the place of the dead (see commentary on 42:22).

*bread.* Bread represents that which maintains our physical life; spiritual bread, representing Christ and his word, symbolizes that which maintains spiritual life.

**51:15** *waves roared.* The Lord's control over the waves of the sea is another evidence of his great power.

*Lord of Hosts.* Jehovah is the Lord not only of the earth but also of the vast throngs of heavenly beings: the heavenly army of the righteous (D&C 45:1; 88:112).

**51:16** *put my words in thy mouth.* The Lord gives his servants inspiration on what to say, enabling them to speak by revelation and prophecy (49:2; 59:21; Jer. 1:9).

*shadow of mine hand.* The Lord protects and shelters his people (49:2).

*plant the heavens/lay the foundations of the earth.* As the Lord created the heaven and the earth originally, so will he create a new heaven and a new earth in the millennial day (65:17; 16:22).

*thou art my people.* Elder Bruce R. McConkie taught that such expressions as this one (63:18–19; Ps. 100:3; Jer. 14:9) "mean that the name of the Lord Jehovah (who is Christ) has been placed upon his people, and they, knowing the name by which they are called, are heirs of salvation."[21]

---

[21] *Promised Messiah,* 369.

# ISAIAH 51:17–23; 52

*LIKENING ISAIAH 51:17–23; 52 UNTO OURSELVES*

*Jerusalem is called to put on her beautiful garments; Zion is called to awaken, to remove the bonds of captivity that have held her bound. We, too, must awaken from spiritual slumbering, put off the chains of sin, and put on the "beautiful garments" of the priesthood. If we will come unto Christ, we can be redeemed without money.*

*In the last days the Lord will reach forth to bring again a Zion state among the righteous. His followers will lift up their voices with the good news of the gospel, going forth to all nations. We can participate in that work by seeking to establish Zion in our own homes and by joining our voices in bearing testimony of Christ and his gospel.*

*To be worthy to join the others of Zion, we must leave Babylon and no longer have contact with that which is unclean.*

## GOD'S WRATH ON JERUSALEM (51:17–23; 52:1–2)

The preceding passage began with Israel calling on the Lord to awaken and fulfill his promises. In this passage, the Lord calls on Jerusalem, or the people of Israel, to wake from their spiritual slumber and turn from the sins that have brought the Lord's fierce anger (51:17). The people have become so wicked that there is "none to guide her among all [her] sons" (51:18). But the Lord will send two sons to help her: two prophets will be raised up unto the Jews at the last day (51:19). They will come in a time of "desolation and destruction" by "famine and the sword" (51:19). Though all others among the Jews have failed her (51:20), these two will act in great power (51:10).

Israel has become drunken by partaking of the Lord's punishment for her sins, but the Lord will remove the cup of his fury from her, sparing her people in his mercy (51:22). That same cup will be given to "them that afflict thee" (51:23).

Again the Lord calls Jerusalem to awaken, to return to priesthood power ("thy strength") and temple covenants ("beautiful garments") and temple worthiness ("no more . . . the uncircumcised and the unclean"; 52:1). She is invited to arise from the dust and to sit down in a position of glory (52:2).

The Book of Mormon, in 2 Nephi 8, combines the first two verses of Isaiah 52 with the entirety of Isaiah 51. Isaiah 52:1–2 is quoted or paraphrased in three places in the Book of Mormon: by Jacob in 2 Nephi 8:24–25, by the Savior in 3 Nephi 20:36–37, and by Moroni in Moroni 10:31. Jesus explained that the fulfillment of these verses would come after the Jews were gathered to Jerusalem in the last days.

After reading Isaiah 51 and 52:1–2, Jacob said, "And now, my beloved brethren, I have read these things that ye might know concerning the covenants of the Lord that he has covenanted with all the house of Israel—That he has spoken unto the Jews, by the mouth of his holy prophets, even from the beginning down, from generation to generation, until the time comes that they shall be restored to the true church and fold of God; when they shall be gathered home to the lands of their inheritance, and shall be established in all their lands of promise. Behold, my beloved brethren, I speak unto you these things that ye may rejoice, and lift up your heads forever, because of the blessings which the Lord God shall bestow upon your children" (2 Ne. 9:1–3).

## Isaiah 51:17–23; 52:1–2

Awake, awake,
*stand up*, O Jerusalem,

which hast *drunk* at the hand of the Lord the <u>cup of his fury</u>;
thou hast *drunken* the dregs of the <u>cup of trembling</u> . . . wrung . . . out—[1] (51:17)

[And] . . . *none to guide her among all the sons* . . . <u>she hath brought forth;</u>
*neither . . . that taketh her by the hand, of all the sons* . . . <u>she hath brought up.</u>[2]
(51:18)

These two [sons] are come unto thee;

[they] *shall be sorry for thee*[—thy] <u>desolation and destruction,</u>
and the <u>famine and the sword</u> [—and] *by whom shall I comfort thee?*[3] (51:19)

---

[1] 2 Ne. 8:17 differs from the KJV, which reads *cup of trembling, and wrung them out.*
[2] 2 Ne. 8:18 changes this verse as shown.
[3] The changes in this verse are found in the JST and 2 Ne. 8:19.

Thy *sons have fainted*, [save these two],[4]
*they* lie at the head of all the streets[;]

as a wild bull in a net[,] they are full of the *fury* of the Lord,
the *rebuke* of thy God. (51:20)

Therefore hear now this, thou *afflicted*,
and *drunken*, [and][5] not with wine: (51:21)

Thus saith thy Lord, the Lord and thy God . . . pleadeth the cause of his people,

Behold, I have *taken out of thine hand* the cup of trembling, . . . [6]
the dregs of the cup of my fury; *thou shalt no more drink it* again. (51:22)

But I will put it into the hand of them that afflict thee; [who][7] have said to thy soul,

*Bow down*, that we may go over:
and thou hast *laid thy body as the ground*, and as the street, to them that went over. (51:23)

Awake, awake; *put on thy strength*, O Zion;
*put on thy beautiful garments*, O Jerusalem, the holy city:

for henceforth there shall no more come into thee the *uncircumcised* and the *unclean*. (52:1)

*Shake thyself from the dust;* arise, . . . [8] sit down, O Jerusalem:
*loose thyself from the bands* of thy neck, O captive daughter of Zion. (52:2)

## NOTES AND COMMENTARY

**51:17** *Awake.* The Jews are called to awaken from spiritual sleep.

*stand up.* Arise, as a prisoner arises in a courtroom to receive judgment. In God's court, the Lord himself "pleadeth the cause of his people" (51:22).

*Jerusalem.* The city symbolizes the people of Israel, particularly the Jews.

*hand of the Lord.* The Lord's hand represents the Lord himself, from whom Jerusalem and the Jews received judgment.

*cup of his fury/cup of trembling.* Elder James E. Talmage wrote: "Our Lord's frequent mention of His foreseen sufferings as the cup of which the Father would have Him drink (Matt. 26:39, 42; Mark 14:36; Luke 22:42; John 18:11; compare Matt. 20:22; Mark 10:38; 1 Cor. 10:21) is in line with Old Testament usage of the term 'cup' as a symbolic expression for a bitter or poisonous potion typifying experiences of suffering. See Psa. 11:6; 75:8; Isa. 51:17, 22; Jer. 25:15, 17; 49:12."[9]

---

[4] This important addition is found in both the JST and 2 Ne. 8:20, as are changes in punctuation in the verse.
[5] 2 Ne. 8:21 changes the KJV *but.*
[6] The changes in this verse are from 2 Ne. 8:22.
[7] 2 Ne. 8:23 changes the KJV *which.*
[8] The change in this verse is from 2 Ne. 8:25.
[9] *Jesus the Christ*, 620.

*dregs . . . wrung out.* The last drops of the cup of wrath will be wrung out for Israel to drink, including the sediment in the bottom of the cup which may symbolize the bitterest trials.

**51:18** *none to guide her.* Israel has lost both the priesthood and the gifts of the Spirit and thus has lost divine direction. This state of apostasy is described in 50:1–2.

*sons . . . brought forth.* None of the natural sons of Israel have sufficient light to guide her.

*taketh her by the hand.* This phrase symbolizes guidance and support.

**51:19** *two sons.* Because Israel has lost the gospel and its power to guide, direct, and lead to salvation, God has sent two priesthood holders to assist and bless her. These two are the two witnesses spoken of in Revelation 11:3–12, who will testify in Jerusalem for three and a half years, who will be killed and left dead in the streets, and who then will be resurrected and lifted up to meet Jesus Christ when he returns to make his appearance to the Jews.

*desolation and destruction.* Joseph Smith applied these words to the Latter-day Saints: "If we are not sanctified and gathered to the places God has appointed, . . . we must fall; we cannot stand; we cannot be saved; for God will gather out his Saints from the gentiles, and then comes desolation and destruction, and none can escape except the pure in heart who are gathered."[10]

**51:20** *sons have fainted/lie at the head of all the streets.* The Jews have lost spiritual strength and consciousness (Lam. 2:11, 19, 21).

*wild bull in a net.* A wild bull caught in a net may be captive but is still extremely dangerous. So it must be with these two prophets, who are "full of the fury of the Lord." Alternatively, this image may refer to the people rather than to the prophets. They are captured by their sins and are subjected to the fury and rebuke of the Lord.

*fury/rebuke.* God is filled with anger toward the wicked. His rebuke generally comes in the form of judgments.

**51:21** *afflicted.* The *afflicted* are those who are humbled and downtrodden.

*drunken, and not with wine.* Jeremiah casts further light on this phrase: "For thus saith the Lord . . . ; Take the wine cup of this fury at my hand, and cause all the nations, to whom I send thee, to drink it. And they shall drink, and be moved, and be mad, because of the sword that I will send among them. Then took I the cup at the Lord's hand, and made all the nations to drink, unto whom the Lord had sent me" (Jer. 25:15–17; see Ezek. 23:32–34). Jeremiah's words mark the beginning of the curse; Isaiah's words mark its removal in the last days.

---

[10] *Teachings of the Prophet Joseph Smith,* 71.

**51:22** *pleadeth the cause.* Christ is our Advocate, who pleads the cause of the repentant to the Father.

*taken out of thine hand/no more drink.* In time the Lord will remove his judgments from his people.

*cup of trembling/cup of my fury.* These phrases are descriptive of the judgments of God and their effects.

**51:23** *put it into the hand of them that afflict thee.* The judgments that Israel has suffered at the hands of the unrighteous will be brought upon the unrighteous.

*Bow down, that we may go over.* In some ancient societies, the vanquished were forced to lie on the ground while the victor walked over them (Josh. 10:24; Ps. 110:1).

*ground/street.* These terms symbolize the depths of humiliation.

**52:1** *awake.* See commentary on 51:17.

*put on thy strength.* Joseph Smith explained this expression by saying that Isaiah "had reference to those whom God should call in the last days, who should hold the power of priesthood to bring again Zion, and the redemption of Israel; and to put on her strength is to put on the authority of the priesthood, which she, Zion, has a right to by lineage; also to return to that power which she had lost" (D&C 113:8).

*Zion/Jerusalem.* Zion and Jerusalem are the two capital cities of the Lord's kingdom. They symbolize the covenant people.

*beautiful garments.* Israel is to replace her slave garments with beautiful garments, perhaps the garments of royalty or the holy garments of the temple. One of the ways in which Zion puts on her beautiful garments is through the law of consecration (D&C 82:14–20).

*uncircumcised/unclean.* These words refer to the disobedient, sinners, or disbelieving Gentiles. Such will not be found in Zion.

**52:2** *Shake thyself from the dust.* The Lord's people are to take action to rid themselves of the dust, which term represents sin, humiliation, and servitude.

*arise/sit down.* The Lord's people are instructed to get up from the dust, where slaves must sit, and sit instead in a place of honor, as on a throne. In contrast, Babylon has been cast from a throne into the dust (47:1).

*loose thyself . . . bands.* Joseph Smith wrote: "The scattered remnants are exhorted to return to the Lord from whence they have fallen; which if they do, the promise of the Lord is that he will speak to them, or give them revelation. . . . The bands of her neck are the curses of God upon her, or the remnants of Israel in their scattered condition among the Gentiles" (D&C 113:10). These are images of Israel coming forth from both physical and spiritual slavery.

*captive daughter of Zion.* The daughter of Zion, or Jerusalem, is captive not only to foreign oppressors but also to sin.

## DELIVERANCE OF CAPTIVE ISRAEL (52:3–12)

In 50:1, the Lord noted to Israel that "for your iniquities have ye sold yourselves." Here the Lord repeats that condemnation (52:3), but now he gives a promise of redemption: "Ye shall be redeemed without money" (52:3). This is not a transaction involving worldly means of exchange; their redemption shall come through the suffering of the Redeemer (53:4–5, 10–11).

The Lord's people have been "oppressed," "taken away," and made to "howl" (52:4–5). This passage may be read temporally, concerning oppressions by Egypt and Assyria, and spiritually, concerning the oppression of sin.

The Lord promises that his name will be known and his power seen (52:6, 9–10). He will comfort his people and redeem Jerusalem (52:9). He will "bring again Zion" (52:8). All nations will see what God has done to redeem and establish his people (52:10).

The testimonies of the Lord's work of redemption are "good tidings of good," which is a cause of joy and singing (52:7, 9). The watchmen of Israel—perhaps the leaders of the Church—will "lift up the voice" with the good news (52:8).

Those who come to Zion must depart from the world and its uncleanness (52:11). They will rely on the Lord, who shall attend them as they go (52:12).

An angel spoke of these things to Nephi, saying, "Blessed are they who shall seek to bring forth my Zion at that day, for they shall have the gift and the power of the Holy Ghost; . . . and whoso shall publish peace, yea, tidings of great joy, how beautiful upon the mountains shall they be" (1 Ne. 13:37).

Isaiah 52 is a chapter often quoted by the Lord's prophets. Jacob (brother of Nephi), Abinadi, Moroni, John the Revelator, Paul, and Joseph Smith all quoted from it—as did the Lord himself in his visit to the Nephites. When Jesus recited these writings, he rearranged the order of the verses, quoting them in this order: 8–10, 1–3, 6–7, 11–15 (3 Ne. 20:32–44). Verses 4 and 5 were not quoted at all.

The Lord verified that the events spoken of in Isaiah 52 will occur in the last days. He began his quotation by saying, "It shall come to pass that . . . when the fulness of my gospel shall be preached unto [the remnants of Israel]" (3 Ne. 20:30), which shall occur in the last days. The headnote to Isaiah 52 in the LDS edition of the Bible says, "In the last days, Zion shall return and Israel be redeemed."

In Mosiah 12:20–24, the wicked priests of King Noah asked Abinadi to explain the meaning of Isaiah 52:7–10. Abinadi answered by saying, the "holy prophets . . . are they who have published peace, who have brought good tidings of good" (Mosiah 15:13–14). So also are all those who have preached the gospel in all ages. In addition, "how beautiful upon the mountains are the feet of him that bringeth good tidings, that is the founder of peace, yea, even the Lord, who has redeemed his people" (Mosiah 15:18). In our dispensation, the Lord has applied this expression to those who go forth as missionaries (D&C 19:29; 31:3; 79:1).

Isaiah 52:8–10 is quoted four times in the Book of Mormon, twice by prophets and twice by the Savior himself (Mosiah 12:22–24; 15:29–31; 3 Ne. 16:18–20; 20:32–35). Abinadi used these verses as support for his teaching that "the salvation of the Lord shall be declared to every nation, kindred, tongue, and people" (Mosiah 15:28). Jesus taught that this prophecy would be fulfilled after the descendants of Lehi had again received the land of America as their inheritance (3 Ne. 16:16–18). He also taught that the fulfillment would come after the Jews had been restored to the land of their inheritance, Jerusalem, and had received Christ and his gospel (3 Ne. 20:29–32).

## Isaiah 52:3–12

> For thus saith the Lord,
>
> *Ye have sold* yourselves for <u>naught</u>;
> and *ye shall be redeemed* <u>without money</u>. (52:3)
>
> For thus saith the Lord God, *My people* went down aforetime into <u>Egypt</u> to sojourn there;
> and the <u>Assyrian</u> oppressed *them* without cause. (52:4)
>
> Now therefore, what have I here, saith the Lord, that my people is taken away for nought? they that rule over them make them to howl, saith the Lord; and my name continually every day is blasphemed] (52:5)
>
> [Verily, verily, I say unto you, that][11] therefore *my people* shall *know* <u>my name</u>:
> [yea, in that day][12] *they* shall *know* . . . that <u>I am he</u> that doth speak. . . . [13] (52:6)
>
> [And then shall they say:] How beautiful upon the mountains are the feet of him *that bringeth* <u>good tidings</u> [unto them],[14]

---

[11] The additional phrase is from 3 Ne. 20:39.
[12] The changes in this verse are from the JST.
[13] 3 Ne. 20:39 deletes the KJV words *behold, it is I.*
[14] These additions are found in the JST and 3 Ne. 20:40.

*that publisheth* <u>peace</u>;
*that bringeth* <u>good tidings of good,</u>
*that publisheth* <u>salvation</u>;
*that saith* unto Zion, <u>Thy God</u> <u>reigneth</u>! (52:7)

Thy *watchmen*[15] <u>shall lift up the voice</u>;
with the <u>voice</u> together shall *they* <u>sing</u>:
for they shall see eye to eye, when the Lord shall bring again Zion. (52:8)

Break forth into joy,
*sing* together, ye waste places of Jerusalem:

for the *Lord* hath <u>comforted his people,</u>
*he* hath <u>redeemed Jerusalem.</u> (52:9)

The *Lord* hath made bare his holy arm in the <u>eyes of all the nations</u>;
and <u>all the ends of the earth shall see</u> the salvation of our *God.* (52:10)

[And then shall a cry go forth:][16]
Depart ye,
depart ye,

*go ye out from thence,* <u>touch [not that which is] unclean</u> . . . ;[17]
*go ye out of the midst* of her; <u>be ye clean,</u> that bear the vessels of the Lord. (52:11)

For ye shall *not go out* <u>with haste,</u>
*nor go* <u>by flight</u>:

for the *Lord* will <u>go before you</u>;
and the *God of Israel* [shall] <u>be your [rearward].</u>[18] (52:12)

## NOTES AND COMMENTARY

**52:3** *sold yourselves for naught.* Israel gave herself away to sin and received nothing of value in return. Each of us has done the same when we have yielded to sin.

*redeemed without money.* Money buys the temporal things of the earth but not the spiritual things of heaven. In all ages we are redeemed by the atonement of Christ, not by the currency of earth (45:13; 2 Ne. 9:50–51; Alma 5:33–34).

**52:4** *My people.* This phrase refers to the covenant people, Jacob and his family (Gen. 46–47). In our day, the Lord's people are true Saints in The Church of Jesus Christ of Latter-day Saints.

*Egypt/Assyrian.* These are the two great oppressors of Israel, Egypt at the beginnings of Israel's history and Assyria in Isaiah's time. They symbolize the world and its oppression of the Saints, including Satan and the oppression of sin. Another way

---

[15] Mosiah 12:22 changes the KJV *watchmen* to *watchman.* Yet the Savior used *watchmen* (3 Ne. 16:18) or *their watchmen* (3 Ne. 20:32).
[16] This addition is found in 3 Ne. 20:41.
[17] 3 Ne. 20:41 changes the KJV *touch no unclean thing.*
[18] The changes in this verse are from 3 Ne. 20:42.

to read this passage is that the Father's children lowered themselves to the standards of the world and were oppressed by the enemies of the righteous.

*oppressed them without cause.* Israel did not provoke the oppression she received.

**52:5** *taken away for nought.* Physically, the enemies of Israel captured the Israelites and took them away without paying for them, as they would have done with legally held slaves. Spiritually, Satan took Israel captive and gave them nothing in return, as he continues to do with people of the covenant in our own day.

*they that rule over them.* Israel was in bondage to both earthly and spiritual powers.

*howl.* The oppressors cause them to cry out in agony.

*my name . . . blasphemed.* The name of God is often abused, which is why the Lord said, "Thou shalt not take the name of the Lord thy God in vain" (Ex. 20:7). It is uncertain here whether those in bondage blame the Lord for their plight, or whether the oppressors blaspheme God's name by mocking him and those they hold captive.

**52:7** *beautiful upon the mountains are the feet of him.* This expression is found six times in the scriptures (1 Ne. 13:37; Mosiah 12:21; 15:15–18; 3 Ne. 20:40; D&C 128:19). The singular pronoun *him* may refer specifically to Christ, the ultimate source of the gospel's good news. In addition, all those who preach the gospel are beautiful because of the wonderful message they take to others. By the Lord's definition, *mountains* describes the place where the gospel is preached, regardless of the actual physical location in the world. As we read in latter-day revelation: "Thou shalt declare glad tidings, yea, publish it upon the mountains, and upon every high place, and among every people that thou shalt be permitted to see" (D&C 19:29).

*feet.* The feet represent the whole body of those who travel about preaching the gospel (Rom. 10:14–15).

*bringeth good tidings/publisheth peace.* The good news of the gospel of Jesus Christ (D&C 76:40–43). The angel said to the shepherds on the night of Christ's nativity, "Behold, I bring you good tidings of great joy, which shall be to all people." Then a multitude of the heavenly host sang, "Glory to God in the highest, and on earth *peace,* good will toward men" (Luke 2:10, 14). God's peace is a gift of the Spirit to those who come unto Christ, the Prince of Peace (9:6; John 14:27).

*Zion. Zion* is either the people of Jerusalem, who finally receive the testimony of Christ, or the great Zion of the last days, centered in the New Jerusalem, where the people dwell in peace, harmony, and righteousness.

*Thy God reigneth.* Instead of having men as rulers, Zion will have God as her king (24:23; 43:15; Jer. 3:17; Zeph. 3:15; Zech. 14:9).

**52:8** *watchmen.* It was traditional in Palestine to place watchers, or guards, on the walls of the cities to observe those who approached. Symbolically, the watchmen are priesthood leaders who keep watch over the Church and call out the good news of redemption. Most likely they are the leaders of the Church, but also, in a sense, they are the missionaries of the Church.

*lift up the voice/with the voice . . . sing.* All shall join together in singing a new millennial song "when the Lord shall bring again Zion" (52:8). Doctrine and Covenants 84 gives us the words of the song:

> The Lord hath brought again Zion;
> The Lord hath redeemed his people, Israel,
> According to the election of grace,
> Which was brought to pass by the faith
> And covenant of their fathers.
>
> The Lord hath redeemed his people;
> And Satan is bound and time is no longer.
> The Lord hath gathered all things in one.
> The Lord hath brought down Zion from above.
> The Lord hath brought up Zion from beneath.
>
> The earth hath travailed and brought forth her strength;
> And truth is established in her bowels;
> And the heavens have smiled upon her;
> And she is clothed with the glory of her God;
> For he stands in the midst of his people.
>
> Glory, and honor, and power, and might,
> Be ascribed to our God; for he is full of mercy,
> Justice, grace and truth, and peace,
> Forever and ever, Amen.
>
> (D&C 84:99–102)

*eye to eye.* This metaphor represents being united in purpose and understanding (Mosiah 16:1; Alma 36:26; D&C 84:98). Unity is one of the key characteristics of Zion, as Moses recorded: "The Lord called his people Zion, because they were of one heart and one mind" (Moses 7:18). Joseph Smith declared, "What if all the world should embrace this Gospel? They would then see eye to eye, and the blessings of God would be poured out upon the people, which is the desire of my whole soul."[19]

*the Lord shall bring again Zion.* Zion was established in the time of Enoch (Moses 7:19) and then "was taken up into heaven" (Moses 7:23). In the last days, *the Lord shall bring again Zion* in two ways: The Zion of Enoch will return to earth (Moses 7:61–63); and the condition of Zion will be brought again to the earth in the last days (Moses 7:61–62, 64). Joseph Smith taught that the latter-day Zion would be centered in Jackson County, Missouri.[20]

**52:9** *Break forth/sing together.* This passage suggests that all the righteous will join in chorus.

*waste places.* This expression refers to the ruins of the city Jerusalem.

*comforted his people.* This comfort comes through the gospel, the Atonement, and the Holy Ghost. The comfort is that of redemption and a restoration to the Lord's promises.

*redeemed Jerusalem.* Jerusalem will be set free from captivity, both physical and spiritual. This image represents the city itself as well as the people of the covenant in the last days.

**52:10** *Lord hath made bare his holy arm.* In ancient times, men prepared for battle by throwing their cloak away from the shoulder of their fighting arm (Ps. 74:11). At the second coming of Christ, God will make bare his arm when he shows forth his power for all to see (D&C 133:2–3).

*eyes of all the nations.* All the world will know of the deliverance of God (40:5).

*ends of the earth shall see the salvation.* Every part of the earth will see and know the power of the Lord; all will see how he delivers those who turn to him. Joseph Smith promised the suffering Saints: "The days of tribulation are fast approaching, and the time to test the fidelity of the Saints has come. . . . but in these times of sore trial, let the Saints be patient and see the salvation of God. Those who cannot endure persecution, and stand in the day of affliction, cannot stand in the day when the Son of God shall burst the veil, and appear in all the glory of His Father, with all the holy angels."[21]

**52:11** *depart ye, go ye out from thence.* The place we are to depart from is Babylon, or "the midst of wickedness, which is spiritual Babylon" (D&C 133:5, 7, 14; 38:42). In his revelation, John the Beloved witnessed the same plea: "And I heard

---

[19] *History of the Church,* 5:259.
[20] *Teachings of the Prophet Joseph Smith,* 79–80.
[21] *History of the Church,* 1:468.

another voice from heaven, saying, Come out of her, my people, that ye be not partakers of her sins, and that ye receive not of her plagues" (Rev. 18:4).

*touch not that which is unclean.* We as the Lord's covenant people must not touch or be involved with idols or any other thing of Satan (2 Cor. 6:15–18).

*vessels.* This word refers to the sacred *vessels* of the temple (Ezra 1:7–11), which could be borne only by those who held the priesthood. Thus the Lord here is commanding priesthood holders to be clean (D&C 38:41–42; 133:5). The sacred vessels directly contrast with "that which is unclean."

**52:12** *not go out with haste/flight.* When Israel left Egypt, she did so in *haste* and in *flight* (Ex. 12:39; Deut. 16:3). When her people now go forth in the gathering to Zion, leaving Babylon, they will do so in peace and safety, with neither haste nor flight (D&C 133:14–15).

*Lord/God of Israel/go before/be your rearward.* God will lead those who return to Zion and will also protect them in the rear. The Hebrew makes it clear that Jehovah will lead them and the Father will come behind (58:8; D&C 49:27).

## THE SUFFERING OF THE SERVANT (52:13–15)

These verses begin another "servant song" (see others in 42:1–9; 49:1–7; and 50:4–9). The servant, we learn, will "deal prudently," or wisely, with others (52:13). He will be lifted up and praised (52:13). Many will be astonished at him (52:14). He will be marred in his physical appearance—more than other men (52:14). That "marring" suggests that the servant will experience great suffering. He will perform a work of gathering for many nations (52:15). His work will be so unexpected, kings will not know what to say about him (52:15).

These verses probably have at least a dual application. Most of the Christian world accepts these verses as applying to the mortal Jesus, and indeed the application fits. In fact, the LDS edition of the Bible says in the headnote to Isaiah 52: "Messiah shall deal prudently and be exalted." Yet Jesus himself indicated an additional application when he quoted these verses to the Nephites (3 Ne. 20:43–45) and then said, "I give unto you a sign, that ye may know the time when these things shall be about to take place" (3 Ne. 21:1). The sign was this: that the Book of Mormon would go forth unto the Gentiles and to the Lamanites (3 Ne. 21:1–7). At that time this servant would do his work.

Jesus spoke specifically of this servant when he said: "The life of my servant shall be in my hand; therefore they shall not hurt him, although he shall be marred because of them. Yet I will heal him, for I will show unto them that my wisdom is greater than the cunning of the devil. Therefore . . . whosoever will not believe in my words, who am Jesus Christ, which the Father shall . . . give unto him power that he shall bring . . . forth unto the Gentiles, . . . they shall be cut off from among my people who are of the covenant" (3 Ne. 21:10–11).

This prophecy seems to refer to Joseph Smith, who so marvelously brought the word of the Lord to the gentiles (3 Ne. 21:1–11). There is an interesting parallel in Doctrine and Covenants 10, which was revealed after the wicked had sought to mar the work of Joseph Smith by altering the words of the Book of Mormon manuscript Martin Harris had lost. The Lord said, "I will not suffer that they shall destroy my work; yea, I will show unto them that my wisdom is greater than the cunning of the devil" (D&C 10:43).

It is also possible that this servant is a prophet yet to come, who will be a type of Christ in the last days.

## Isaiah 52:13–15

Behold, my servant shall deal prudently,

he shall *be exalted* and *extolled,*
and *be very high.* (52:13)

As many were [astonished][22] at thee;

*his visage* was so marred <u>more than any man,</u>
and *his form* more <u>than the sons of men</u>: (52:14)

So shall he [gather][23] many nations; the kings shall shut their mouths at him:

for *that which had not been told* them shall <u>they see</u>;
and *that which they had not heard* shall <u>they consider</u>. (52:15)

### NOTES AND COMMENTARY

**52:13** *deal prudently.* The Lord's servant will have the knowledge and insight to understand exactly what to do, guaranteeing him success.

*exalted/extolled/very high.* These terms may represent the eternal destiny of the servant, or they may indicate the esteem and regard some will have for him.

**52:14** *astonished.* The life and work of the servant will be so unlike that of his fellows that many will be amazed. Other versions of the Bible give the words *dumbfounded* and *appalled.*

---

[22] 3 Ne. 20:44 changes the KJV *astonied.*
[23] The JST changes the KJV *sprinkle.*

*visage . . . marred/form.* The servant will be greatly disfigured by his sufferings, both in face and in body (Job 19:13–22). Certainly the pain that Jesus suffered in the Garden of Gethsemane was so great that it could be said that "his visage" would be "marred more than any man, and his form more than the sons of men."

Elder Bruce R. McConkie wrote: "Isaiah's prophecy about the marred servant is clearly Messianic and applies to Jesus who was crucified and rose from the dead to sprinkle the saving power of his blood in all nations. It is of him that kings shall shut their mouths as they ponder the marvel of his resurrection and all that he did. (Isa. 52:13–15.) But in this whole discourse [to the Nephites (3 Ne. 20:10–22:17)], Jesus is applying the prophetic word to the latter days, meaning that, as with many prophecies, the divine word has a dual fulfillment. In this setting we may properly say that Joseph Smith—whose voice declared the word for this dispensation—was marred, as his Lord had been, and yet should be healed, in the eternal sense, as was his Lord. And it may yet well be that there will be other latter-day servants to whom also it will apply."[24]

*more than the sons of men.* The marring or disfiguration of the "visage" of the servant will be to a greater degree than all other mortals. The Savior's suffering was more than we can comprehend.

**52:15** *gather many nations.* The servant will help bring people of many nations to the gospel.

*kings shall shut their mouths.* The kings represent those who stand at the head of the nations—even they will see and be amazed at the marvelous work of this servant. *Kings* may also represent Saints who are kings and priests as a result of having received the fulness of the priesthood in the temple. There may be some aspects of the work of the servant that even faithful members of the Church will be surprised to see and hear.

*that which had not been told them . . . see . . . consider.* The kings will see a work by the servant that they have never heard or considered before (Rom. 15:20–21; D&C 101:93–95).

---

[24] *Mortal Messiah,* 4:354.

---

✦᧞᧞᧞᧞

# ISAIAH 53

### LIKENING ISAIAH 53 UNTO OURSELVES

*Isaiah 53 is one of the greatest prophecies of the Messiah found in the Old Testament. It gives us great insight into the work of the mortal Jesus and the blessings he offers us. We learn from this chapter that he will bear our transgressions and iniquities, taking them upon himself so that we can be cleansed of them. He will also bear our grief and sorrow, our emotional pain and suffering. If we will turn to him, he will heal us of all these infirmities.*

*This chapter also bears testimony that Christ will die, not for his own transgressions but for the transgressions of the people. He will submit in all things to the will of the Father. His offering will bear wonderful fruit, for many will be justified by him. We can be among that number if we will receive him and his covenant and walk in righteousness.*

---

## SUFFERING AND TRIUMPH OF THE MESSIAH (53:1–12)

Isaiah 53 is often called the "Song of the Suffering Servant." Both Abinadi and Philip clearly tell us that the servant described here is Jesus Christ (Mosiah 15; Acts 8:26–35). Matthew, Peter, and Paul also understood that at least parts of this chapter referred to Jesus (Matt. 8:17; 1 Pet. 2:24–25; Rom. 4:25). The headnote to Isaiah 53 in the LDS edition of the Bible says, "Isaiah speaks Messianically—Messiah's humiliation and sufferings set forth—He makes his soul an offering for sin and makes intercession for transgressors." This passage has four recurring themes: the Messiah's sufferings, his assumption of our burdens and our sins, his death, and his reward.

First, the Messiah's sufferings: "He is despised and rejected of men" (53:3). "He is . . . a man of sorrows and acquainted with grief" (53:3). "He was despised, and we esteemed him not" (53:3). "We did esteem him stricken, smitten of God, and afflicted" (53:4). "He was wounded [and] bruised" (53:5). "He was oppressed, and he was afflicted" (53:7). "It pleased the Lord to bruise him; he hath put him to grief" (53:10). "He shall see the travail of his soul" (53:11).

Second, his assumption of our burdens and sins: "He hath borne our griefs, and carried our sorrows" (53:4). "He was wounded for our transgressions, he was bruised for our iniquities" (53:5). "The Lord hath laid on him the iniquities of us all" (53:6). "For the transgressions of my people was he stricken" (53:8). "He shall bear their iniquities" (53:11). "He bare the sin of many" (53:12).

Third, his death: "He is brought as a lamb to the slaughter" (53:7). "He was cut off out of the land of the living" (53:8). "He made his grave with the wicked, and with the rich in his death" (53:9). "He hath poured out his soul unto death" (53:12).

Fourth, his reward: "He shall see his seed" (53:10). "He shall prolong his days" (53:10). "The pleasure of the Lord shall prosper in his hand" (53:10). "He . . . shall be satisfied" (53:11). "Therefore will I divide him a portion with the great" (53:12). "He shall divide the spoil with the strong" (53:12).

## Isaiah 53:1–12

Who hath <u>believed</u> our report?
and to whom is the arm of the Lord <u>revealed</u>? (53:1)

For he shall grow up before him as a *tender plant,*
and as a *root out of . . .* [1] *dry ground:*

he hath *no form nor comeliness;* and when <u>we shall see him,</u>
there is *no beauty* that <u>we should desire him.</u> (53:2)

He is *despised*
and *rejected* of men;

a *man of sorrows,*
and *acquainted with grief:*

and *we hid as it were our faces* from <u>him;</u>
<u>he</u> was *despised,* and *we esteemed him not.* (53:3)

Surely he [has][2] *borne* <u>our griefs,</u>
and *carried* <u>our sorrows:</u>

yet we did esteem him *stricken,*
*smitten* of God,
and *afflicted.* (53:4)

But he was *wounded* <u>for our transgressions,</u>
he was *bruised* <u>for our iniquities:</u>

---

[1] This change is from Mosiah 14:2.
[2] This change is from Mosiah 14:4.

the *chastisement of our peace* was <u>upon him</u>;
and with <u>his stripes</u> *we are healed.* (53:5)

All *we* like sheep have <u>gone astray</u>;
*we* have <u>turned every one to his own way</u>;

and the Lord hath laid on him the [iniquities][3] of us all. (53:6)

*He was* <u>oppressed</u>,
and *he was* <u>afflicted</u>,

yet he *opened not his mouth:* he is brought as a <u>lamb to the slaughter</u>,
and as a <u>sheep before her shearers</u> is dumb, so he *[opened][4] not his mouth.* (53:7)

He was taken from prison and from judgment: and who shall declare his generation?
for *he* was <u>cut off out of the land of the living</u>:
for the transgression[s][5] of my people was *he* <u>stricken</u>. (53:8)

And he made his *grave* with the <u>wicked</u>,
and with the <u>rich</u> in his *death*;

because *he had* <u>done no [evil]</u>,[6]
<u>neither was any deceit</u> *in his mouth.* (53:9)

Yet it pleased the *Lord* to <u>bruise him</u>;
*he* hath <u>put him to grief</u>:

when thou shalt make his soul an offering for sin, *he* shall <u>see his seed</u>,
*he* shall <u>prolong his days</u>,
and the pleasure of the Lord shall <u>prosper</u> in *his hand.* (53:10)
*He* shall see . . . [7] the travail of his soul, and shall be <u>satisfied</u>:
by his knowledge shall *my righteous servant* <u>justify many</u>;

for he shall bear their iniquities. (53:11)

Therefore will I *divide* him a <u>portion with the great</u>,
and he shall *divide* the <u>spoil with the strong</u>;

because he hath poured out his soul unto death:

and he was *numbered* with the <u>transgressors</u>;
and he *bare* the <u>sin[s][8] of many</u>,
and *made intercession* for <u>the transgressors</u>. (53:12)

## NOTES AND COMMENTARY

**53:1** *report.* This term likely refers to the report of the prophets, or the revelation they have reported to the people about the life and mission of Christ. John observed that many did not believe the report about the works and mission of Christ: "Though

---

[3] Mosiah 14:6 changes the KJV *iniquity.*
[4] Mosiah 14:7 changes the KJV *openeth.*
[5] This change is from Mosiah 14:8.
[6] Mosiah 14:9 changes the KJV from *violence* to *evil.*
[7] Mosiah 14:11 deletes the KJV *of.*
[8] This change is from Mosiah 14:12.

he had done so many miracles before them, yet they believed not on him: That the saying of Esaias the prophet might be fulfilled, which he spake, Lord, who hath believed our report? and to whom hath the arm of the Lord been revealed? Therefore they could not believe, because that Esaias said again, He hath blinded their eyes, and hardened their heart; that they should not see with their eyes, nor understand with their heart, and be converted, and I should heal them. These things said Esaias, when he saw his glory, and spake of him" (John 12:37–41; Rom. 10:13–17).

*arm of the Lord revealed.* In Deuteronomy 7:18–19, the acts of the Lord's arm (which represents his power) were seen, but the arm itself remained unseen. In the birth and ministry of Christ, the Lord's arm is visibly revealed.

**53:2** *tender plant.* The Father would watch over the young Jesus as a careful gardener watches a tender plant. Luke records, "The child grew, and waxed strong in spirit, filled with wisdom: and the grace of God was upon him" (Luke 2:40).

*root.* The *root* here is Christ himself. Christ is the vine, or root, and we are the branches (John 15:5). He came forth not in a fertile land but in dry ground, both temporally and spiritually.

*dry ground.* The spiritual barrenness of the Jewish apostasy. The *dry ground* is the opposite of streams of water, which usually denotes temporal happiness and prosperity. Streams of water also represent the spiritual life brought by the gospel.

*no form nor comeliness/no beauty.* Scholars conjecture that this passage refers not to the Savior's physical appearance but to the fact that Jesus would not come in the glorious manner the Jews were expecting. President Joseph Fielding Smith interpreted these words to mean that Jesus would look like an ordinary man and thus the Jews would not recognize him as the Son of God.[9]

**53:3** *despised and rejected of men.* Jesus was rejected by his community and the Jewish nation as a whole (Mark 9:12; Luke 4:28–30; John 1:11; 5:18; 7:5; 1 Ne. 19:7–10).

"Jesus had come unto his own, and his own received him not!" wrote Elder Bruce R. McConkie. "The leaders of the people rejected his words when he preached in the temple at Passover time. The common people of Nazareth hardened their hearts against his words when he spoke to them in their synagogue. And so it would be throughout his whole ministry; save for a few believing souls, he was 'despised and rejected of men' (Isa. 53:3); and eventually *his own* would . . . [c]rucify him."[10]

---

[9] *Doctrines of Salvation,* 1:23.
[10] *Mortal Messiah,* 2:27; emphasis in original.

*hid . . . our faces.* The Living Bible says, "We turned our backs on him and looked the other way when he went by." A note in the Jerusalem Bible says that this "expression was used of lepers." In other words, not only did people refuse to follow him but they shunned him. Even though many people followed Christ for a time, in the end most turned from him. The same is true of people in all ages—most ("we") turn from a full and correct understanding of Jesus Christ and his gospel.

*despised/esteemed him not.* Though Christ had a few who followed him and remained faithful to the end, most viewed him as one of no worth.

**53:3–4** *man of sorrows/borne our griefs/carried our sorrows.* The mortal Jesus was surely filled with sorrow over the sin of the people of the world. He suffered sorrow in contemplating the fate of those who rejected him (Matt. 23:37–39). In addition, in the Garden of Gethsemane, he took upon himself our *griefs* and *sorrows,* as well as our sins. Through the atonement of Christ we can find peace in the midst of grief and trouble. It is because of the Atonement that the Comforter has power to accomplish his work of bringing solace to troubled souls. The word *sorrows* may also be translated *pains;* Christ carried our infirmities and sickness. As Matthew wrote, "[He] healed all that were sick: That it might be fulfilled which was spoken by Esaias the prophet, saying, Himself took our infirmities, and bare our sicknesses" (Matt. 8:14–17). These infirmities and sicknesses, are, of course, both physical and spiritual.

**53:4** *stricken.* This particular verb is used sixty times in Leviticus 13 and 14, always with the same meaning—that of suffering the emotional pain of having leprosy. The Servant will be viewed with the same disdain as the Jews viewed a leper.

*smitten of God/afflicted.* It has been common in many ages for people to assume that someone who suffers is being punished by God. Those who see the Servant consider that he is being punished for sin. Ironically, they are correct, but it is not his own sin that causes him to suffer; rather, it is ours.

**53:5** *wounded for our transgressions/bruised for our iniquities. Wounded* (Hebrew *chalal*) is better translated as "pierced fatally." *Bruised* (Hebrew *daka'*) is more correctly "crushed." The Servant suffered these pains because of what *we* had done. President Ezra Taft Benson wrote:

"He suffered the pains of all men, . . . He suffered as only God could suffer, bearing our griefs, carrying our sorrows, being wounded for our transgressions, voluntarily submitting Himself to the iniquity of us all, just as Isaiah prophesied. (See Isaiah 53:4–6.)

"It was in Gethsemane that Jesus took on Himself the sins of the world, in Gethsemane that His pain was equivalent to the cumulative burden of all men, in Gethsemane that He descended below all things so that all could repent and come to Him.

"The mortal mind fails to fathom, the tongue cannot express, the pen of man cannot describe the breadth, the depth, the height of the suffering of our Lord—nor His infinite love for us."[11]

*chastisement of our peace was upon him.* This passage might read, "He suffered the chastisement that brings us peace." The suffering of his atonement, which Christ bore, brings us peace as we partake of the blessings of that atonement.

*with his stripes we are healed.* When Jesus was scourged by Pilate's men, the whip left stripes on his back (Matt. 27:24–26). With prophetic sight, Isaiah apparently saw that event, which he then used as a symbol of Christ's atoning sacrifice. The symbol is a paradox: through the wounding of one person, another's wounds are healed. Jesus is healer of our physical and mental infirmities as well as of our spiritual sicknesses. The risen Lord, who rose "with healing in his wings" (2 Ne. 25:13), invited the Nephites to "return unto me, and repent of your sins, and be converted, that I may heal you" (3 Ne. 9:13). Peter interpreted the purpose and result of Isaiah 53:5–6 when he wrote: "Who his own self bare our sins in his own body on the tree, that we, being dead to sins, should live unto righteousness: by whose stripes ye were healed. For ye were as sheep going astray; but are now returned unto the Shepherd and Bishop of your souls" (1 Pet. 2:24–25).

**53:6** *All we like sheep have gone astray/own way.* Every one of us has gone astray from the strait and narrow path; every soul who has ever lived—except for Jesus—has sinned (Rom. 3:23; 1 Pet. 2:25; 1 Jn. 1:8, 10). Rather than walking the Lord's path, we walk our own way.

*laid on him the iniquities.* This passage harks back to the meaning of the ritual of the Day of Atonement (Lev. 16), when the high priest laid his hand on the head of the victim and, in essence, transferred to him the sins of the people. Jesus suffered "for our offences" (Rom. 4:25), not his own.

**53:7** *oppressed/afflicted.* Jesus was oppressed and afflicted throughout his ministry, as the Gospels record. But this passage seems to refer particularly to the legal trials he suffered immediately before his crucifixion (Matt. 26:67–68; 27:29–30).

*he opened not his mouth.* This prophecy was fulfilled when Jesus appeared before Herod, who "questioned with him in many words; but he answered him nothing" (Luke 23:9). When Jesus stood before Pilate, Mark records, "the chief priests

---

[11] Benson, *Come unto Christ,* 6–7.

accused him of many things: but he answered nothing. And Pilate asked him again, saying, Answerest thou nothing? behold how many things they witness against thee. But Jesus yet answered nothing" (Mark 15:3–5).

*lamb to the slaughter.* Not only is Christ the Good Shepherd (John 10:14) but he is also the sacrificial lamb, which went without protest or resistance to his death. This is in contrast to us, as the sheep of the previous verse, who willfully went astray. The sacrifice of an unblemished lamb under the law of Moses prefigured the atoning sacrifice of Christ (Gen. 22:7–8; Ex. 12:3; Lev. 5:7): the Atonement fulfills the symbolism of the lamb.

**53:8** *taken from prison/judgment.* He was taken by force (Hebrew *'utser*) and without justice (Hebrew *mishᶜpat*).

*who shall declare his generation?* The New International Version renders this phrase as "who can speak of his descendants?" implying that because he was "cut off from the land of the living" he had none. But Jesus did indeed have descendants, those who become his children through righteousness; see the commentary on 53:10, *he shall see his seed.*

*cut off.* He was *cut off,* or removed, from the land of the living.

*stricken.* This word repeats the word used in verse 4. There, he was considered stricken by those who would not recognize him. Here, he truly is stricken as he bears on himself the "transgressions of my people."

**53:9** *grave with the wicked.* This prophecy may have been fulfilled when Christ was crucified between two thieves (Matt. 27:38). It may also mean that his grave was with those who had sinned, unlike him, who had not sinned.

*with the rich.* This prophecy that Jesus would be buried with the rich was fulfilled when he was buried in the tomb of the wealthy Joseph of Arimathea (Matt. 27:57–60).

*he had done no evil/deceit.* Peter referred to Jesus as "[he] who did no sin, neither was guile found in his mouth" (1 Pet. 2:22). Jesus' life was perfect in deed and word. Even Jesus' judge, Pilate, declared he could find no fault in Jesus (Matt. 27:22–24; Luke 23:1–4, 13–24).

**53:10** *pleased the Lord to bruise him.* Certainly the Father took no pleasure from the suffering of his Son. But the Father was pleased that his Son would obediently offer such a sacrifice, meaning the sacrifice was according to the Father's wishes and his will. The Father was pleased further because of the love manifest by his Son and also because of the blessings that would come to the rest of his children.

*he shall see his seed.* Abinadi interpreted this expression in Mosiah 15:10–13, saying that the seed of Christ are the righteous who have heard the good word of salvation and believed and obeyed: "These are his seed, or they are the heirs of the kingdom of God. For these are they whose sins he has borne; these are they for whom he has died, to redeem them from their transgressions." Elsewhere we learn that the seed of Christ are those who are "spiritually begotten" as his sons and daughters (Mosiah 5:7), born of water and the Spirit (Moses 6:64–68). Beginning with this expression, we move from Isaiah's prophecy of the Lord's suffering to his prophecy of the Lord's triumph.

*prolong his days.* This expression means to lengthen his life. Isaiah has already written that Christ would be killed ("cut off out of the land of the living"); now he says Christ will have a long and prosperous life. This paradox contains a wonderful gospel truth: The righteous who die will enjoy a life of glory that never ends.

*pleasure of the Lord shall prosper in his hand.* Christ will exercise his agency to truly fulfill all the will of the Father.

**53:11** *travail of his soul.* Jesus suffered so mightily in the Garden of Gethsemane in the process of bearing our iniquities that he bled from every pore (Luke 22:44; Mosiah 3:7; D&C 19:18). The suffering that Christ will undergo in performing the Atonement—which will result in his "seeing his seed," or those spiritually reborn in Christ—is likened to the *travail,* the pain and suffering, of a woman which precedes her being able to see her own seed, or her newborn child.

*He . . . shall be satisfied.* It is unclear whether the pronoun *he* in this sentence refers to the Father or to the Son. But ultimately it does not matter: Both the Father and the Son were well satisfied by what Jesus had accomplished in the Garden of Gethsemane.

*his knowledge.* The Lord would have the knowledge he needed to perform the Atonement, something that is simply beyond comprehension to the rest of us. Some scholars recognize this phrase as "experience," "humiliation," "suffering," "affliction."

*righteous servant.* Christ the Lamb was a perfect and unblemished sacrifice.

*justify.* This word means accounted righteous, or judged, in a legal sense, to be innocent. We will not be justified, or accounted righteous, through our own merits but because of the sufferings of Christ. Paul wrote that by Christ "all that believe are justified from all things, from which ye could not be justified by the law of Moses" (Acts 13:38–39). Lehi taught, "The law is given unto men. And by the law no flesh is justified; or, by the law men are cut off. . . . Wherefore, redemption cometh in and through the Holy Messiah; for he is full of grace and truth" (2 Ne. 2:5–6).

*bear their iniquities.* Christ carries their sins metaphorically on his shoulders. This use of *bear* is the same as that in 53:4, "hath borne our griefs." The Israelite high priest symbolically bore the sins of Israel (Lev. 10:17), pointing forward to Christ's atonement.

**53:12** *divide him a portion/the spoil.* As conqueror, Christ has won the right to the rewards of his efforts. The portion he will receive is to be an heir of God, receiving all the Father hath. So also do all the righteous (D&C 84:37–38), but on Christ's merits, not their own.

*great/strong.* Christ's portion among the great and strong ones is the first and greatest.

*numbered with the transgressors.* Mark referred to this prophecy when he wrote: "And with him they crucify two thieves; the one on his right hand, and the other on his left. And the scripture was fulfilled, which saith, And he was numbered with the transgressors" (Mark 15:27–28; Luke 22:37).

*poured out his soul unto death.* The scriptures suggest that pouring out the soul is to experience great pain and sorrow (Job 30:16; Lam. 2:12), which Christ experienced unto death. Another interpretation may be based on the idea of pouring out the soul in prayer (1 Sam. 1:15; Enos 1:9; Alma 19:14; Hel. 7:14). When we pour out our souls in prayer, we express our deepest, most heartfelt desires to the Lord, holding nothing back. So it was with Christ—and as he poured out his soul unto his father, he also fully yielded to his will, even unto death.

*bare the sins.* See commentary on 53:11, *bear their iniquities.*

*made intercession for the transgressors.* Jesus Christ is the one who makes intercession for us. Paul wrote, "It is Christ that died, yea rather, that is risen again, who is even at the right hand of God, who also maketh intercession for us" (Rom. 8:34). Lehi said that Christ "shall make intercession for all the children of men; and they that believe in him shall be saved. And because of the intercession for all, all men come unto God; wherefore, they stand in the presence of him, to be judged of him" (2 Ne. 2:9–10). With the role and power of intercessor, Christ stands between us and the Father, seeking blessings in our behalf. He prays for us, mediates, petitions, and intercedes, requesting mercy for the repentant. Christ has this power because he took our sins upon himself in his great atoning sacrifice. Wonderful examples of Christ acting in his intercessory role are found in prayers he offered that are recorded in John 17 and 3 Nephi 19.

———◦◦◦——

# ISAIAH 54

*LIKENING ISAIAH 54 UNTO OURSELVES*

*In the last days, or the time in which we now live, the Lord will bring many people to Zion. They will be so many that they cannot all fit in one place. Rather than there being only one land of Zion, she will be established in many stakes.*

*The Lord tells us not to fear. He remembers all his promises to establish Zion in the latter days. The Saints may at times have cause to feel forsaken, but the Lord has not forgotten us, and he will have mercy on us. Even if the mountains were to flee, he would not forget his covenant, and his mercy would continue. He will establish the righteous in the beautiful city of New Jerusalem. All our enemies will be put down.*

*These promises give comfort to us as a people and as individuals. The Lord will not forget us in our trouble. He always reaches out to comfort and to bless. He will bring us, individually, to his precious promises, if we are worthy.*

---

## ZION SHALL BE ESTABLISHED (54:1–3)

This passage is an invitation for Zion to rejoice. Zion, who has heretofore not brought forth the desired children (54:1), will nevertheless have children "on the right hand and on the left" (54:3). The children are those who have gathered to the family of Christ as members of the Church. No longer will all the righteous fit in the existing "habitations" of Zion, so her tent will need to be enlarged (54:2). They will also "inherit the [lands of the] Gentiles" (54:3), and stakes of Zion will be established and strengthened (54:2).

The resurrected Jesus quoted this chapter during his visit to the Nephites, telling them it would come to pass after the work of the Father had commenced "among all nations" (3 Ne. 21:28). In 3 Nephi 20–21 Jesus told the Nephites some of the things that would transpire before the events recorded in Isaiah 54. Among them were the

[ 4 7 9 ]

following: the gospel would go forth to the Gentiles (20:27–28; 21:2), the Jews (20:29–31), the Lamanites (21:4–7), and the dispersed of Israel (20:13; 21:26–28); the remnants of Israel would gather to Zion (21:1); and the covenant people of the Lord would be restored to the lands of their inheritance (20:14, 22, 29, 33, 46; 21:26–28).

## Isaiah 54:1–3

*Sing,* O barren, <u>thou that didst not bear;</u>
*break forth into singing,* and *cry aloud,* <u>thou that didst not travail with child</u>:

for more are the *children* of the desolate
than the *children* of the married wife, saith the Lord. (54:1)

*Enlarge* <u>the place of thy tent,</u>
and let them *stretch forth* <u>the curtains of [thy]</u>[1] <u>habitations</u>:
spare not, *lengthen* <u>thy cords,</u>
and *strengthen* <u>thy stakes;</u> (54:2)

For thou shalt break forth on the *right hand* and on the *left;*

and *thy seed shall inherit* the Gentiles,
and make the desolate cities to *be inhabited.* (54:3)

## NOTES AND COMMENTARY

**54:1** *barren.* The barren woman seems to be Israel, who had not previously borne the promised fruit of her covenant with God. She has never travailed with child but will rejoice to have children (meaning the blessings of the covenant) as a result of another's travail, that of Christ (53:11).

*children of the desolate/married wife.* The married wife (or bride of Christ) appears to be both the Church and the New Jerusalem (Rev. 21:2, 9; D&C 109:73–74). The children of the married wife may be the members of the Church, or those who inhabit New Jerusalem. The children of the desolate may be the Israelites who are scattered around the earth. When Jesus was teaching the Nephites, he put this verse in the context of the New Jerusalem (3 Ne. 21:22–29; 22:1). Thus the children of the married wife appear to be those who first build up New Jerusalem, and the children of the desolate are those who are gathered later (62:4). It seems clear that the children of the desolate are greater in number.

Latter-day Saint scripture scholar Victor Ludlow has a different view: "The desolate woman and her relationship to the wife can be understood in two ways: (1) The desolate woman represents the gentiles, and the wife Israel; thus the gentiles will

---

[1] This change is from 3 Ne. 22:2.

bring forth greater spiritual fruits than Israel has delivered; (2) the desolate woman is Israel in her scattered condition, while the wife is those people remaining in the Holy land. Thus Israel will bring forth more children (both physically and spiritually) outside the land of her original inheritance than in it. (See Gal. 4:22–31; Rev. 12:1–6.) In either case, Isaiah uses these images to symbolize the relationship of the Lord to Israel; those who join with covenant Israel are the children of that relationship."[2]

**54:2** *tent/curtains/cords/stakes.* The *tent* is reminiscent of the tabernacle of Moses, a tent to which all Israel was invited to come. The word *stakes* here is the source of the latter-day ecclesiastical division of the Church called a stake. Tent stakes (or pegs) help hold up and enlarge the tent of Zion. Each stake must be strong to keep the tent stable. The five command forms in this verse—*enlarge, stretch forth, spare not, lengthen,* and *strengthen* (see also Moro. 10:31; D&C 133:9)—teach us what we should be doing to build Zion in these last days. One way that Zion will enlarge her tent and strengthen her stakes is to practice the law of consecration (D&C 82:12–15).

President Ezra Taft Benson wrote: "To members, the term *stake* is a symbolic expression. Picture in your mind a great tent held up by cords extended to many stakes that are firmly secured in the ground. The prophets likened latter-day Zion to a great tent encompassing the earth. That tent was supported by cords fastened to stakes [see 3 Ne. 22:2; Isa. 54:2]. Those stakes, of course, are various geographical organizations spread out over the earth. Presently Israel is being gathered to the various stakes of Zion."[3]

**54:3** *break forth on the right hand/left.* Israel will grow and expand in all directions. Other versions translate the idiom *break forth* as "burst out" (JB), "spread out" (NIV), or "spread abroad" (RSV).

*seed shall inherit the Gentiles.* This passage seems to mean that the Lord's people will dispossess the Gentiles of their lands and inheritances and that Israel will then inherit what has been vacated (Deut. 2:12, 21, 22).

*the desolate cities . . . inhabited.* The children of Israel will inherit the cities of the gentiles, which will have become desolate and empty, most likely because of the wars and upheavals of the last days (49:19). The New International Version says, "Your descendants will dispossess nations and settle in their desolate cities."

---

[2] *Isaiah,* 459.
[3] *Come unto Christ,* 101.

## GOD'S EVERLASTING KINDNESS (54:4–10)

The headnote to this chapter in the LDS edition of the Bible says, "Israel shall be gathered in mercy and tenderness." This passage is indeed one of tenderness and comfort. "Fear not," the Lord says to Israel (54:4). She shall not be confounded; she shall not be brought to shame; in her blessings she will even forget the shame of her past (54:4). "For a small moment have I forsaken thee; but with great mercies will I gather thee," the Lord says (54:7).

Like others, this passage is filled with references to Israel as a wife, clearly calling the Lord her "husband" (54:5). The Lord notes that she is a widow who will no longer remember her reproach (54:4), a woman who had been forsaken (54:6), a wife of youth who was refused (54:6). Though Israel has suffered much, the Lord will restore to her all blessings and will bring her unto himself.

Marriage represents the most intimate, most joyful, most fulfilling relationship on earth. That is the kind of relationship the Lord is inviting us to join with him. The union of the Saints in a Zion society (in which they are of one heart and one mind; Moses 7:18; John 17:11, 22) and the turning of the Saints' hearts to the Lord make such a relationship with the Lord possible. These blessings come through the Atonement (*at-one-ment*) of Christ, which was performed so that we might repent and return to God, becoming one with him as Christ is one with him (John 17:21, 23; 3 Ne. 19:23, 29).

To illustrate how serious he is about this covenant, the Lord reminds Israel of his promise after the great flood of Noah. Just as he promised that never again would there be such a flood, in the same way he promises that his anger against Israel will pass (54:9) and that then he will have mercy (54:8, 10). Even though the mountains and hills shall be moved from their seemingly everlasting foundations, the Lord will continue in his kindness (mentioned twice; 54:8, 10) and the "covenant" of his people (54:10).

*Isaiah 54:4–10*

> *Fear not;* for thou shalt <u>not be ashamed</u>:
> *neither be thou confounded;* for thou shalt <u>not be put to shame</u>:
>
> for *thou shalt forget* the <u>shame of thy youth,</u>
> and *shalt not remember* the <u>reproach of thy [youth,</u>
> and *shalt not remember* the <u>reproach of thy]</u>[4] <u>widowhood</u> any more. (54:4)

---

[4] This change is from 3 Ne. 22:4.

For thy *maker, . . . [thy] husband,* the *Lord of Hosts* is his name;
and thy *Redeemer,* the *Holy One of Israel*—the *God of the whole earth* shall he be
called.[5] (54:5)

For the Lord hath called thee as a *woman* forsaken and grieved in spirit,
and a *wife of youth,* when thou wast refused, saith thy God. (54:6)

For a *small* moment have I forsaken thee;
but with *great* mercies will I gather thee. (54:7)

In a *little wrath* I hid my face from thee for a moment;
but with *everlasting kindness* will I have mercy on thee,

saith the Lord thy Redeemer. (54:8)

For this, . . . the waters of Noah unto me,
for as *I have sworn* that the waters of Noah should no more go over the earth;
so *have I sworn* that I would not be wroth with thee. . . . [6] (54:9)

For the *mountains* shall depart,
and the *hills* be removed;

but *my kindness* shall not depart from thee,
neither shall the *covenant of my [people]*[7] be removed,

saith the Lord that hath mercy on thee. (54:10)

## NOTES AND COMMENTARY

**54:4** *shame of thy youth/reproach of thy widowhood.* From youth to widowhood covers the whole of life. Even though Israel has suffered shame and reproach, both in youth and in old age, in the latter days the Lord will cause these things to be put behind her in the midst of his blessings. *Youth* may refer to Israel's days of sin before the exile; *widowhood* may refer to the time of the exile itself, when Israel was separated from her land and her God. In the day of blessing, Israel will remember no more her days of trial.

**54:5** *thy husband.* Once again the Lord identifies himself as the husband of Israel, or the righteous (50:1; 62:5; Matt. 25:1–13; 2 Cor. 11:1–4; Rev. 19:7–9; D&C 33:17; 133:10, 19). When the Lord returns to redeem Zion, he will be as a loving and tender bridegroom coming to claim his beloved bride.

*Lord of Hosts.* See commentary on 1:9.

*God of the whole earth.* Idol worshipers felt that each of earth's many gods held jurisdiction over a limited area. But the true God rules over all. In truth, Jehovah is the God not only of the Israelites or the Latter-day Saints but of all creatures on the face of the earth (3 Ne. 11:14).

---

[5] 3 Ne. 22:5 makes some small but important clarifying changes in this verse.
[6] The changes in this verse are from 3 Ne. 22:9.
[7] The JST changes the KJV *peace* to *people.*

**54:6** *called thee.* The Lord calls latter-day Israel to gather unto Zion and unto him (54:7). To put it another way, he calls the righteous to join him in the marriage.

*woman forsaken/wife of youth . . . refused.* Israel has been cast off because of her sins, as a wife might be forsaken or refused. But the rejection is temporary, "for a small moment," and then the Lord will bless Israel "with great mercies" (54:7; 50:1; Prov. 5:18; Mal. 2:14).

*grieved in spirit.* Like a wife forsaken, Israel grieves because of her separation from her Lord.

**54:7** *small moment.* This term means *only a short time.* Joseph Smith also felt a degree of abandonment by the Lord and cried out, "O God, where art thou?" The Lord answered, "My son, peace be unto thy soul; thine adversity and thine afflictions shall be but a small moment" (D&C 121:1, 7). The Prophet promised the Saints that if they were faithful, their sufferings "will be but a little season, and all these afflictions will be turned away from us."[8]

*gather.* In the latter days, the Lord will gather Israel back into his fold as a shepherd gathers his sheep into the fold at night, or as a farmer gathers his crops into his barn at harvest time. The gathering will occur primarily through missionary work, as the Lord's servants range throughout the world seeking the honest in heart who will come unto Christ and his true Church. In addition to this gathering of hearts and souls, the Jews will gather to their land of promise in Palestine. It also appears that there will be a gathering of a large group of the ten tribes, who may return *en masse* from the land or lands of their exile (D&C 133:26–34).

**54:8** *hid my face.* The Lord turned away from his people because of their wickedness, but he will yet turn to them in kindness and mercy.

**54:9** *waters of Noah.* This metaphor symbolizes a great and terrible judgment for wickedness. But in the same way that the Lord swore never to flood the earth again, here he swears that in the end he will no longer be angry with Israel.

**54:10** *mountains shall depart/hills be removed. Mountains* and *hills* are symbols of stability (Ps. 36:6). For them to shake or move indicates significant changes in the earth, but there shall be no changes in the Lord's kindness, his mercy, or his covenant.

*my kindness.* The Revised Standard Version reads "my steadfast love."

*covenant of my people.* The Joseph Smith Translation changes the *peace* in this phrase to *people,* underscoring that the Lord's covenant is indeed with his children. The expression *my people* suggests a relationship and a bond between God and us.

---

[8] *History of the Church,* 5:141.

At the same time, 3 Nephi 22:10 retains the wording found in the King James Version: "covenant of my peace." With that reading, the phrase refers to the Lord's everlasting promise to give us peace (of heart, of soul) when we come unto him. The covenant of peace, and the covenant of "my people," is the covenant of the gospel (Lev. 26:3–6; Ps. 29:11; 85:8–10; Ezek. 37:26).

## New Jerusalem Shall Be Established (54:11–17)

The Lord continues his promises to latter-day Israel: He will establish her in righteousness and protect her from oppression (54:14). Those who seek to fight against her will fail (54:15, 17); those who speak against her will be condemned (54:17). Her city, the New Jerusalem, will be beautiful (54:11–12), and her children will "be taught of the Lord" and will have peace (54:13).

This passage promises rich blessings to the faithful: The promise of peace (54:14) fulfills the covenant spoken of in 54:10. The blessing of righteousness (54:14, 17) flows from Christ's atonement (54:11). Those now afflicted by life's storms (54:11) will yet be established on safe, firm foundations (54:11, 14). And the people "not comforted" (54:11) will be taught, protected, and blessed (54:13–17).

These things come to the faithful through right of inheritance (54:17). Though our diligent efforts are necessary to bring us to the Lord, ultimately it is his grace that enables us to receive his blessings: "their righteousness is of me, saith the Lord" (54:17).

*Isaiah 54:11–17*

O thou *afflicted*,
*tossed with tempest*,
and *not comforted!*

Behold, I will *lay thy stones* with <u>fair colours</u>,
and *lay thy foundations* with <u>sapphires</u>. (54:11)

And I will make *thy windows* <u>of agates</u>,
and *thy gates* <u>of carbuncles</u>,
and all *thy borders* <u>of pleasant stones</u>. (54:12)

And all *thy children* <u>shall be taught of the Lord</u>;
and <u>great shall be the peace</u> of *thy children*. (54:13)

In righteousness shalt thou be established:

thou shalt be far *from oppression;* for <u>thou shalt not fear</u>:
and *from terror;* for <u>it shall not come near thee</u>. (54:14)

Behold, *they shall surely gather together* [against thee], . . . not by me:[9]
*whosoever shall gather together* against thee shall fall for thy sake. (54:15)

Behold, I have created the *smith* that bloweth the coals in the fire,
and *that* bringeth forth an instrument for his work;
and I have created the waster to destroy. (54:16)

No *weapon that is formed* against thee shall prosper;
and *every tongue that shall [revile]*[10]against thee in judgment thou shalt condemn.

This is the heritage of the servants of the Lord, and their righteousness is of me,
saith the Lord. (54:17)

## NOTES AND COMMENTARY

**54:11** *afflicted/tossed with tempest.* The New English Bible reads, "O storm-battered city, distressed and disconsolate," referring to the troubled city of Jerusalem, which shall be given peace by the Lord. Jerusalem here stands as a symbol for the people of the covenant.

*stones with fair colours.* Some versions indicate that the stones will be laid with antimony, which women used as a cosmetic to enhance the color of their eyes (2 Kgs. 9:30; Jer. 4:30). In the same way, the mortar in the foundation and walls will help to set off the beauty of the precious stones. Jerusalem, which was once destroyed and left desolate, will be restored and beautified by the Lord in the form of a new Jerusalem.

**54:11–12** *foundations/windows/gates/borders.* These elements of the city's architecture symbolize the whole city. *Windows* is more correctly translated as *battlements* or *towers,* which are set atop walls and used for defense. *Borders* are the outer walls of the city. The precious stones that form the city's architecture symbolize the love and care the Lord will lavish on his people.

*sapphires/agates/carbuncles/pleasant stones.* These precious stones seem to symbolize the spiritual and temporal blessings the Lord will pour out on his people (60:17; Rev. 21:18–21). *Sapphires* were sparkling blue stones, but probably not the sapphires of today—they may have been lapis lazuli (NEB, NIV, NRSV); *agates* likely were what we know as rubies; *carbuncles* may have been clear crystals; *pleasant stones* can better be translated as "precious stones" (NKJV, NIV, JB).

**54:13** *taught of the Lord.* Jesus quoted these words in saying: "No man can come to me, except he doeth the will of my Father. . . . And this is the will of him who hath sent me, that ye receive the Son; . . . It is written in the prophets, And they shall be all

---

[9] The changes in this verse are from 3 Ne. 22:15 and, to a lesser extent, from the JST.
[10] 3 Ne. 22:17 changes the KJV *rise.*

taught of God. Every man therefore that hath heard, and hath learned of the Father, cometh unto me" (JST John 6:44–45). It is uncertain from the context whether this phrase means that the children will be taught *about* the Lord or that they will be taught *by* the Lord—perhaps both interpretations are correct. Virtually all other major English translations (including GNB, JB, NAB, NEB, NIV, NKJV, and NRSV) provide some variation of the reading, "All thy children shall be taught *by* the Lord."

**54:14** *oppression/terror.* The millennial Zion will not be troubled by unjust rulers who will oppress, neither by invasion of enemies (26:1–3; 32:17–18; 33:20–22).

**54:16** *I have created the smith/I have created the waster.* The Lord has created both the man who creates and the man who destroys. All are subject to God's power (for God as a destroyer, see Jer. 13:7–14; 18:4–17).

*instrument for his work.* The blacksmith seems to be creating a tool to help him in his work.

**54:17** *No weapon.* This promise was repeated in our dispensation (D&C 71:9; 109:25); ultimate triumph over enemies is the heritage of the Lord's people. Weapons, of course, may come in many forms, such as instruments of physical harm and destruction, lies and slanders, or efforts to harm another economically (D&C 122:4–7).

*every tongue that shall revile against thee in judgment.* The Lord's people will be able to stand against gossip, slander, and accusations in a court of law.

*heritage.* The servants of the Lord may look forward to and expect blessings that are theirs by right or inheritance or birthright, even as children may expect to share in their parents' estate.

*their righteousness is of me.* Ultimately, our righteousness is insufficient to save us. Though our obedience with broken hearts is required to bring us unto Christ, it is his righteousness that saves (2 Ne. 2:4–8).

# ISAIAH 55

### LIKENING ISAIAH 55 UNTO OURSELVES

*The Lord invites us, every one, to come unto him and partake of his living waters, of which we may drink freely. He offers us the sweet and powerful blessings of his atonement, which have no earthly cost. He invites us to seek him and call on him while we are able, to turn from our sins and turn toward God. As we do, we will find mercy. He promises to "abundantly pardon."*

## COME TO THE LIVING WATERS (55:1–3)

This short passage is a sweet invitation to come to the living waters of Christ and drink freely (55:1). The gospel and the blessings of the Atonement have no temporal cost (55:1–2). Why would we spend our time, effort, and money for that which has no lasting value? (55:2). Rather than spending money and labor on things that "cannot satisfy" (55:2), we can come unto the Lord and "feast" on things of eternal value, which never will perish (55:2). Such things are a delight to the soul (55:2). Come unto Christ, then, hearken to him, and live (55:2–3).

*Isaiah 55:1–3*

Ho, every one that thirsteth,

*come ye to the waters,* and he that hath <u>no money;</u> *come ye,* buy, and eat;
yea, *come,* buy wine and milk <u>without money and without price.</u>[1] (55:1)

Wherefore do [not] *spend money* for <u>that which is [of no worth,]</u>
nor your *labour* for <u>that which [cannot satisfy]</u>.

---

[1] Nephi gives a helpful paraphrase to this verse in 2 Ne. 25:26.

*Hearken* diligently <u>unto me</u>,
and [*remember* the <u>words which I have spoken</u>;
and *come* <u>unto the</u> <u>Holy One of Israel</u>,
and *feast* <u>upon that which perisheth not</u>, neither can be corrupted,]
and *let your soul delight* itself <u>in fatness</u>.[2] (55:2)

*Incline your ear,* and <u>come unto me</u>:
*hear,* and <u>your soul shall live</u>;

and I will make an everlasting covenant with you, even the sure mercies of David.
(55:3)

## NOTES AND COMMENTARY

**55:1** *Ho.* This interjection is an exclamation to capture attention. A modern-day equivalent might be "Hey!"

*thirsteth/waters.* These are the living *waters* of the gospel (John 4:10). This promise is echoed in the Gospel of John, in which the apostle recorded Jesus as saying, "If any man thirst, let him come unto me, and drink" (John 7:37; Rev. 21:6; 22:17). The living water is also the love of God (1 Ne. 11:25). Ultimately, it is also Jesus Christ and his atonement, the only true source of life eternal. One place where the water can be found, as deep in a well, is the "mysteries of [the] kingdom" (D&C 63:23; Rev. 22:17; D&C 133:29), a key to which is given in the temple.

*no money/buy, and eat/without money and without price.* We need pay no earthly price to receive the blessings of the gospel and the atonement of Christ. Yet there is a price that God requires: a broken heart and a contrite spirit (2 Ne. 2:7; 3 Ne. 9:20; D&C 59:8; see commentary on 52:3, *redeemed without money*).

*wine/milk.* Those who are thirsty are offered living water, and *wine* and *milk* besides. "The feast is one of love and forgiveness. The abundance and freeness of the water of refreshment (44:3), the wine of joy (25:6-8) and the milk of richness (Ex. 3:8) and supremacy (60:16) is figurative of the Lord's salvation."[3]

**55:2** *no worth/cannot satisfy.* The things of this world are transitory and, in an eternal sense, have *no worth.* They *cannot satisfy* our deepest and most vital needs.

*feast/delight . . . in fatness.* The very choicest of foods, especially those that nourish spiritually (25:6; Ps. 36:8; 65:11-13).

**55:3** *Incline your ear.* This statement is an invitation to listen.

*your soul shall live.* Those who "come unto me" and "hear" the Lord, obeying his command, shall have everlasting life.

*everlasting covenant.* See commentary on 24:5.

---

[2] The changes in this verse are from 2 Ne. 9:51.
[3] Motyer, *Prophecy of Isaiah,* 453.

*sure mercies of David.* Paul equates this phrase with the resurrection (Acts 13:34). David knew that the Lord would redeem him from endless death through the resurrection: "Thou wilt not leave my soul in hell," he wrote, "neither wilt thou suffer thine Holy One to see corruption" (Ps. 16:10). The Lord's mercy to David, which was a sure promise, is also given to all mankind through "an everlasting covenant." The Lord's promise is that if David—who had committed the two of the greatest sins (adultery and murder, through ordering Uriah's wrongful death)—will be resurrected, all may have that same hope.

## God's Witness to the People (55:4-5)

In the last days, the Lord will give Israel (meaning his people, or Zion) another leader who has the qualities of David: he will be a witness of the gospel to the people, he will lead them, and he will command their armies (55:4; David's roles as leader and commander are well-known; for passages on David as a witness of the gospel, see Ps. 9:11–12; 18:49–50; 57:9–12; 145:21). Other nations will be drawn to Israel and her king because of the blessings and goodness of her God (55:5; compare 49:7, which indicates that the Lord's servant will be a servant of rulers but at the same time will receive honor and respect from kings and princes). This latter-day David may be Christ himself; or it may be a king patterned after the King of kings.[4]

*Isaiah 55:4–5*

> Behold, I have given him for a *witness* <u>to the people,</u>
> a *leader* and *commander* <u>to the people.</u> (55:4)
>
> Behold, thou shalt call a *nation* that <u>thou knowest not,</u>
> and *nations* that <u>knew not thee</u> shall run unto thee
>
> because of the *Lord thy God,*
> and for the *Holy One of Israel;* for he hath glorified thee. (55:5)

### Notes and Commentary

**55:4** *a witness . . . , a leader and commander.* This phrase seems to refer primarily to the latter-day David (Ezek. 34:23–24; 37:24–25; Jer. 30:9; Hosea 3:5), who may be Christ, but it also likely refers to others who represent the Lord on earth.

**55:5** *thou/thee.* The Lord refers to his covenant people.

---

[4] For a discussion on the identity of the latter-day David, see Turner, "Two Davids," 240–60.

*call a nation that thou knowest not.* The covenant people will take the gospel to the Gentiles, who will help take the word throughout the world. Compare this phrase to Psalm 18:43: "Thou has made me the head of the heathen: a people whom I have not known shall serve me."

*glorified thee.* The New International Version renders this "endowed you with splendor."

## SEEK THE LORD, WHO IS MUCH GREATER THAN MAN (55:6–9)

The first passage of chapter 55 emphasizes the free gift of salvation, which is offered to all (55:1–3). This later passage (55:6–9) teaches us what we must do to receive the proffered gift:

Seek the Lord (55:6).

Call upon him (55:6).

Forsake our wicked way of living (55:7).

Forsake the thoughts and reasoning that lead to the wicked way of life (55:7).

Having turned *from* sin, now turn *to* the Lord (55:7).

In response, the Lord will experience a *feeling* of mercy and then take the *action* of granting us pardon (55:7). He will treat us with such loving-kindness because, in his perfection, his thoughts and ways are far above ours, as far as the "heavens are higher than the earth" (55:8–9).

*Isaiah 55:6–9*

> *Seek* ye *the Lord* while he may be found,
> *call ye upon him* while he is near: (55:6)

> Let the *wicked* forsake his way,
> and the *unrighteous man* his thoughts:

> and let him return *unto the Lord,* and he will have mercy upon him;
> and *to our God,* for he will abundantly pardon. (55:7)

> For *my thoughts* are not your thoughts,
> neither are your ways *my ways,* saith the Lord. (55:8)

> For as the *heavens* are higher than the earth,
> so are *my ways* higher than your ways,
> and *my thoughts* than your thoughts. (55:9)

NOTES AND COMMENTARY

**55:6** *Seek ye/call ye.* This passage evokes the familiar and well-beloved invitation from the Lord to his children: "Ask, and it shall be given you; seek, and ye shall find; knock, and it shall be opened unto you: For every one that asketh receiveth" (Matt. 7:7–8).

*found/near.* The Lord may be *found,* and he will be *near* as long as we desire to be near to him. As he said through Joseph Smith, "Draw near unto me and I will draw near unto you; seek me diligently and ye shall find me; ask, and ye shall receive" (D&C 88:63).

**55:7** *thoughts.* We must watch not only our words and actions but even our *thoughts* (Acts 8:18–24; 2 Cor. 10:5; Mosiah 4:30).

*return.* Repent and turn from wickedness. "But if ye will repent and return unto the Lord your God I will turn away mine anger, saith the Lord; yea, thus saith the Lord, blessed are they who will repent and turn unto me" (Hel. 13:11).

**55:8–9** *thoughts/ways.* The unrighteous man has his own thoughts (as noted in 55:7), but they are far inferior in both substance and understanding to the Lord's *thoughts.* Paul wrote, "For the wisdom of this world is foolishness with God" (1 Cor. 3:19; 2 Ne. 9:28).

## GOD'S WORD CANNOT FAIL (55:10–11)

The rain and the snow have but one purpose: to bless us with food, which in turn gives life (55:10). In the same way, God's word blesses us with the bread of life (44:3; 45:8). In fact, God's word is ultimately even more important than the physical bread that keeps us alive (Matt. 4:4). In contrast to the sweetness of the word portrayed here, Jeremiah 23:29 describes God's word as "a fire . . . and like a hammer that breaketh the rock in pieces."

This passage from Isaiah has some interesting parallels with Alma 32, in which Alma compares the word to a seed that sprouts and grows as we nourish it. And in the parable of the sower and the soils, Jesus also compares the word to a seed that falls on different types of ground (Matt. 13:3–9, 18–23).

*Isaiah 55:10–11*

> For as the *rain* <u>cometh down,</u>
> and the *snow* <u>from heaven,</u> and returneth not thither,
> but *watereth* the <u>earth,</u>

and *maketh* <u>it</u> *bring forth* and *bud,*

that it may *give seed* <u>to the sower,</u>
and *bread* <u>to the eater</u>: (55:10)

So shall *my word* be that <u>goeth forth</u> out of my mouth:
*it* shall <u>not return</u> unto me void,

but *it shall accomplish* <u>that which I please,</u>
and *it shall prosper* in the <u>thing whereto I sent it.</u> (55:11)

## NOTES AND COMMENTARY

**55:10** *bring forth and bud.* This phrase means to sprout and begin to grow.

*seed to the sower/bread to the eater.* The Lord's gifts provide for the needs both of the person who plants food (both physical and spiritual) and the person who partakes of it.

**55:11** *word/mouth.* God's *word* is his revelations, given from his own *mouth.*

*not return . . . void.* This emptiness refers to having failed in one's purpose.

*that which I please.* God's word helps to accomplish God's will.

*prosper.* To *prosper* means to have success, or to bring to pass abundantly that which God desired.

*the thing whereto I sent it.* God has a specific purpose in mind.

## ISRAEL SHALL RETURN WITH JOY (55:12–13)

When Israel is gathered, she will come forth in joy and peace (55:12). Even nature will join in the rejoicing as the children of Israel pass by (55:12). The land will produce pleasant plants instead of briers and thorns (55:12). These conditions appear to be the millennial reversal of the physical conditions of the Fall, a return to the paradisiacal earth. They may also be symbolic, meaning that all things will work together for the blessing of those who fully come unto Christ and his kingdom.

*Isaiah 55:12–13*

For ye shall *go out* <u>with joy,</u>
and be *led forth* <u>with peace</u>:

the *mountains and the hills* shall <u>break forth before you into singing,</u>
and all the *trees of the field* shall <u>clap their hands.</u> (55:12)

*Instead of the thorn* <u>shall come up the fir tree,</u>
and *instead of the brier* <u>shall come up the myrtle tree</u>:

and it shall be to the Lord for a *name,*
for an *everlasting sign* that shall not be cut off. (55:13)

NOTES AND COMMENTARY

**55:12** *go out with joy . . . peace.* The Good News Bible reads "You will leave Babylon with joy." This situation greatly contrasts to the going out from Egypt at the time of the Exodus, which was in fear and turmoil (Ex. 5–14; see also Isa. 52:12). *Joy* and *peace* are two of the most desired fruits of the Spirit (Rom. 14:17; Gal. 5:22). Joy and peace also are the two primary messages of the gospel: "Whoso shall publish peace, yea, tidings of great joy, how beautiful upon the mountains shall they be" (1 Ne. 13:37). Joy comes from "having received a remission of their sins" (Mosiah 4:3); peace comes from a clear conscience.

*mountains/hills/singing . . . trees/clap their hands.* All nature will join in rejoicing at the deliverance of the Lord's people (44:23; 49:13; 1 Chr. 16:33; D&C 128:22–23).

**55:13** *thorn/brier/fir tree/myrtle tree.* The *thorn* and *brier* are plants that grow in lands of desolation. When Zion is redeemed, they will be replaced with the vegetation of fertility: the *cypress* and the *myrtle* (7:23–25; 29:17; 32:15; 35:1–2). Likewise, in the Millennium, the long spiritual barrenness of the Lord's covenant people will be replaced with spiritual abundance.

*name/everlasting sign that shall not be cut off.* That which the Lord does to change the conditions of the earth and his people will forever be a sign of his power.

# ISAIAH 56:1-8

## LIKENING ISAIAH 56 UNTO OURSELVES

*Chapter 56 contains a powerful message on the meaning of the Sabbath. Sabbath worship is a key indicator of our obedience to the covenant. The Lord invites all to join with his people in proper observance of the Sabbath. Those who do so will be given great blessings, even the blessings of the temple.*

*We too may seek and receive these blessings. Even though we may have already joined ourselves to the covenant of the Lord through baptism, we can grow in his blessings and his grace by observing the Sabbath with full purpose of heart.*

## THE GENTILES ARE WELCOMED TO THE COVENANT (56:1–8)

"Keep my sabbaths," says the Lord, obey my commandments, and "take hold of my covenant" (56:4). "Love the name of the Lord" and "serve him" (56:6). Then, even though you may not be of the covenant race ("son of the stranger"), and though you once may have been excluded ("eunuch," representing those not allowed an inheritance under the law of Moses), you may receive the full blessings of the temple ("in mine house") and of exaltation ("an everlasting name") (56:3, 5). "All people" who come unto Christ will enjoy temple blessings (56:7).

A theme repeated in this passage is the temple: "mine house" and "within my walls" (56:5) and "my holy mountain," "my house of prayer," "mine altar," "mine house," and "an house of prayer" (55:7).

*Isaiah 56:1–8*

Thus saith the Lord,

*Keep* ye judgment,

and *do* justice:

for *my salvation* is near to come,
and *my righteousness* to be revealed. (56:1)

Blessed is the *man* that doeth this,
and the *son of man* that layeth hold on it;

that *keepeth the sabbath* from polluting it,
and *keepeth his hand* from doing any evil. (56:2)

*Neither let the son of the stranger,* that hath joined himself to the Lord, speak,
saying,
The Lord hath utterly separated me from his people:
*neither let the eunuch* say, Behold, I am a dry tree. (56:3)

For thus saith the Lord unto the eunuchs that keep my sabbaths,

and *choose* the things that please me,
and *take hold* of my covenant; (56:4)

Even unto them will I give in *mine house* and within *my walls*
a [hand][1] and a name better than of sons and of daughters:
I will give them an everlasting name, that shall not be cut off. (56:5)

Also the sons of the stranger, that *join themselves to the Lord,* to serve him,
and *to love the name of the Lord,* to be his servants,

every one that *keepeth the* sabbath from polluting it,
and *taketh hold of* my covenant; (56:6)

Even *them will I bring* to my holy mountain,
and *make them joyful* in my house of prayer:

their burnt *offerings* and their *sacrifices*
shall be accepted upon *mine altar;*

for mine *house* shall be called
an *house of prayer* for all people. (56:7)

The Lord God which *gathereth* the outcasts of Israel saith,
Yet will I *gather* others to him,
beside those that are *gathered* unto him. (56:8)

## NOTES AND COMMENTARY

**56:1** *Keep ye judgment/do justice.* Do what is lawful and fair.

*salvation. Salvation* brings deliverance, both temporal and spiritual.

*righteousness.* Goodness and righteousness are basic elements in the Lord's character. His *righteousness* will be shown forth to all who keep his Sabbath.

**56:2** *blessed.* The Hebrew word here, *'ash<sup>e</sup>rey,* means "happy," as does the word used by Jesus in the Beatitudes (Greek *makariŏs*).

*layeth hold.* This verb refers to making something part of one's life.

---

[1] The word *hand* is from the Hebrew *yad;* the KJV *place* is an incorrect translation.

*sabbath.* To the Israelites, a *Sabbath* was not only the holy day on which they worshiped once a week but also the periodic religious holidays they observed. Keeping a true Sabbath is symbolic of keeping the whole covenant (58:13; Ezek. 20:12–26; 22:8, 26).

*hand.* This term symbolizes the whole being. The person who keeps his hand from doing evil keeps his whole person from evil.

**56:3** *son of the stranger.* This phrase describes a foreigner. The Gentiles who come unto Christ are promised all the blessings of faithful members of the house of Israel.

*the eunuch.* A *eunuch* is a man who has been emasculated and therefore is physically unable to beget children. Under the law of Moses, eunuchs were denied full fellowship with the Israelites (Lev. 21:17–23; Deut. 23:1–2) and had no inheritance in Israel because they had no offspring. The Lord promises that they will receive full blessings in the gospel if they will receive and keep his laws. Among these blessings is the Abrahamic covenant, which includes a promise of endless seed.

*dry tree.* A *dry tree* is one that cannot bear fruit. In reference to a person, a *dry tree,* like a eunuch, is one that cannot have children.

**56:5** *mine house/within my walls.* Such terms refer to the temple (Matt. 21:12–13).

*a hand and a name better than of sons and of daughters/everlasting name.* The Lord promises those who come into "mine house," or his temple, *a hand and a name.* Hands and names are important parts of the temple covenants (D&C 88:119–21, 130–36; 130:11). The New English Bible may help clarify the meaning of this verse when it says, "[they] shall receive from me something better than sons and daughters, . . . I will give them an everlasting name, a name imperishable for all time." The name may be the new name given to those who are exalted (D&C 130:11), or it may be the name that King Benjamin gave to his people, which "never should be blotted out" (Mosiah 5:11)—that is, the name of Christ. Compare this usage of "everlasting name, that shall not be cut off" with the usage in 55:13.

**56:6** *polluting it.* Any activity counter to the sacred and holy purposes of the Sabbath pollutes it.

*taketh hold of my covenant.* This phrase refers to those who receive and honor the covenants of the gospel.

**56:7** *my holy mountain.* The temple (see commentary on 11:9).

*house of prayer.* When Jesus cleansed the temple in Jerusalem for the second time, he quoted this phrase from Isaiah, saying, "It is written, My house shall be called the house of prayer; but ye have made it a den of thieves" (Matt. 21:13; Mark 11:17; Luke 19:46).

The temple has ever been a house of prayer for the faithful. The Psalmist wrote, "One thing have I desired of the Lord, . . . that I may dwell in the house of the Lord all the days of my life, to behold the beauty of the Lord, and to enquire in his temple" (Ps. 27:4). In the latter days the Lord commanded, "Organize yourselves; . . . and establish a house, even a house of prayer, a house of fasting, . . . a house of God" (D&C 88:119; 109:16).

*all people.* The blessings of the covenant and the temple will be offered to everyone, regardless of race or physical imperfection (Alma 19:86; D&C 38:16).

*offerings/sacrifices. Offerings* and *sacrifices* are offered to the Lord in the temple, according to his command. The sacrifices and offerings of the faithful will be effective in helping us to draw nearer to him.

*mine altar.* The place of sacrifice in the temple is the *altar.*

**56:8** *gathereth the outcasts of Israel/gather others.* The Lord reaches out to all people, including those who have been judged unworthy or who have been scattered, both literally and spiritually (2 Ne. 26:33).

# ISAIAH 56:9–12; 57

## LIKENING ISAIAH 57 UNTO OURSELVES

*Isaiah 57 contains a description of gross idol worship and temple prostitution. Israel seemed to go out of her way to offend the Lord by participating in religious practices that not only rejected him but also caused them to commit the very sins that were most abhorrent to him.*

*One message of Isaiah seems to be a reminder of the first of the Ten Commandments: "Thou shalt have no other gods before me" (Ex. 20:3). It is not only the abhorrent that can turn our hearts. Even good things can take us away from God. We let other things become our God when we give them first place in our lives, whether the primary object of our affection is our family, work, money, recreation, sports, or a particular sin.*

*The Lord concludes by reminding us of his mercy when we repent. We will be gathered to Zion; he will heal us and comfort us and remove obstacles from our way.*

## ISRAEL'S WICKED LEADERS (56:9–12; 57:1–2)

In these verses, Israel's enemies are invited to come and destroy the Lord's people (56:9). The watchmen called to protect and care for Israel are slothful, selfish, and uncaring; having only contempt for their sacred stewardships, they look to their own interests while their charges perish or are enslaved (56:10–11).

The Lord's criticism of these unrighteous leaders is scathing. He calls them blind watchmen, "ignorant," "dumb dogs," "greedy dogs," "shepherds that cannot understand" (56:10–11). Despite the Lord's warnings, the watchmen will not listen, desiring only to "eat, drink, and be merry" (2 Ne. 28:7; Isa. 56:12). Even though the righteous perish from the land, those who remain appear indifferent (57:1). Yet the righteous who have perished will be blessed to pass "into peace" (57:2). These prophecies likely have a dual fulfillment, applying both to ancient Israel and to people of the last days.

*Isaiah 56:9–12; 57:1–2*

> *All ye beasts* of the field, come to devour,
> yea, *all ye beasts* in the forest. (56:9)

> His watchmen are *blind:*
> they are all *ignorant,*
> they are all *dumb* dogs,
> they *cannot bark;*

> sleeping,
> lying down,
> loving to *slumber.* (56:10)

> Yea, *they are greedy dogs* which can never have enough,
> and *they are shepherds* that cannot understand:

> *they* all look to their own way,
> *every one* for his gain, from his quarter. (56:11)

> Come ye, say they, *I will fetch* wine,
> and *we will fill ourselves* with strong drink;

> and tomorrow shall be as this day, and much more abundant. (56:12)

> The *righteous perisheth,* and no man layeth it to heart:
> and *merciful men are taken away,* none considering
> that the *righteous* is *taken away* from the evil to come. (57:1)

> *He* shall enter into peace:
> *they* shall rest in their beds, each one walking in his uprightness. (57:2)

## NOTES AND COMMENTARY

**56:9** *beasts of the field/forest.* These terms seem to refer to foreign nations that will invade Israel, both before the exile and perhaps also immediately before the Millennium (Jer. 12:9).

**56:10** *watchmen are blind/ignorant/sleeping.* Watchmen are those, particularly leaders, who have the gospel and are charged to protect it from apostasy. In this passage, the watchmen themselves have become apostates. In 56:11, they are referred to as shepherds who have turned from their care of the flock. Like watchdogs who have become lazy, blind, and incapacitated, or like shepherds who have lost sight of their calling and are no longer able to recognize the enemy, these watchmen have left off caring for their flock and have turned instead to caring for their own needs and desires (Jer. 6:17; Ezek. 3:17; 34:1–28).

Besides describing Israel's religious leaders in ancient times, this prophecy may also refer to leaders of apostate religions in our day (2 Ne. 28:3–9; Morm. 8:31–33, 37–39).

**56:10–11** *dumb dogs/greedy dogs.* Dumb dogs are watchdogs that cannot bay or bark, and thus they are incapable of sounding a warning (Ezek. 33:2–6). Greedy dogs, instead of selflessly protecting their flocks, feed themselves and perhaps even turn on the sheep to satisfy their own ravenous appetites (Ezek. 34:3, 10). Like dumb, greedy dogs, Israel's religious leaders lost the power to warn Israel of sin, selfishly thinking more of their own needs than of those of the people (5:13). That is also true of some religious leaders in all time periods.

*shepherds. Shepherds* are the leaders of the flock of God, in this case leaders who desire their own advancement and thus practice priestcrafts (2 Ne. 26:29).

*own way/his gain/his quarter.* The shepherds are charged with willfulness, seeking that which will bring profit to themselves rather than blessings to the people. Our purpose in life is to be tested and proved, "to see if [we] will do all things whatsoever the Lord [our] God shall command [us]" (Abr. 3:25). But like those in this passage, many seek their own will and their own desires, rather than the Father's (53:6; Judg. 17:6; 1 Cor. 13:5; Philip. 2:21; Mosiah 16:5; D&C 1:16). Even some of those who are called to be shepherds concentrate on worldly pursuits and pleasures, neglecting the flock. As in all things, Jesus Christ set the great example for us in these things, saying, "Not my will, but thine, be done" (Luke 22:42).

**56:12** *wine/strong drink.* Symbolic of revelry and seeking the unlawful pleasures of life, the wine here is contrasted to the offer of wine at the Lord's table in 55:1. Anything that dulls the senses also dulls one's commitment to God and his ways (Hosea 4:11), making it more difficult to detect the still, small voice of the Spirit. Those who persist in such a path will be given to drink of a different kind of wine, "the wine of the fierceness of his wrath" (Rev. 16:19).

**57:1** *The righteous perisheth/no man layeth it to heart.* The righteous generation passes away, yet the wicked take no notice, or, if they do, they are untroubled by it.

*righteous is taken away/evil to come.* God's judgments (evil) will come upon the wicked, because the righteous will have perished from the land.

**57:2** *He shall enter into peace/rest in their beds.* This statement refers to the righteous mentioned in 57:1. As the LDS edition of the Bible states in the headnote to

57, "When the righteous die they enter into peace" (57:2; Ps. 37:37; 119:165; Alma 40:12; D&C 45:46).

## ISRAEL'S GROSS WICKEDNESS (57:3–13A)

The ancient and abhorrent practice of temple prostitution, a practice engaged in even by the Jews, is described in this passage from Isaiah 57. This sinful practice was triply offensive to the Lord: it brought people into both immorality and idolatry, and it sometimes also involved human sacrifice. In doing so, of course, it took them far from their God.

Though temple prostitution is a thing of the past, among those who profess Christ there exists another form of spiritual adultery that is also damning. The scriptures make it clear that Christ is the bridegroom and that the Church is the bride. When the bride turns her affections from the Lord to someone or something that will lead her away from Christ, she is committing a form of spiritual adultery that will keep her from God and his blessings. For other powerful descriptions of spiritual adultery, see Ezekiel 16:1–63 and 23:1–49.

*Isaiah 57:3–13a*

But draw near hither, ye *sons* of the sorceress,
the *seed* of the adulterer and the whore. (57:3)

*Against whom* do ye sport yourselves?
*against whom* make ye a wide mouth, and draw out the tongue?

are ye not *children* of transgression,
a *seed* of falsehood, (57:4)

*Enflaming yourselves with idols* under every green tree,
*slaying the children in the valleys* under the clifts of the rocks? (57:5)

Among the *smooth stones* of the stream is thy portion;
they, *they* are thy lot:

even to them hast *thou* poured a drink offering,
*thou* hast offered a meat offering.

Should I receive comfort in these? (57:6)

*Upon a lofty and high mountain* hast thou set thy bed:
even thither wentest thou *up to* offer sacrifice. (57:7)

Behind the doors also and the posts hast *thou* set up thy remembrance:
for *thou* hast discovered thyself to another than me, and art gone up;

*thou* hast enlarged thy bed,
and made *thee* a covenant with them;
*thou* lovedst their bed where thou sawest it. (57:8)

And thou wentest to the king with ointment, and didst increase thy perfumes,
and didst send thy messengers far off, and didst debase thyself even unto hell.[1]
(57:9)

Thou art wearied in the greatness of thy way; yet saidst thou not, There is no
hope:
thou hast found the life of thine hand; therefore thou wast not grieved. (57:10)

And *of whom* hast thou been <u>afraid or feared</u>, that thou hast lied, and hast not
remembered me, nor laid it to thy heart? have not I held my peace even of old, and
thou <u>fearest</u> *me* not? (57:11)

I will declare *thy righteousness,*
and *thy works;* for they shall not profit thee. (57:12)

When thou criest, let thy companies deliver thee;

but the *wind* shall <u>carry them all away</u>;
*vanity* shall <u>take them</u>: (57:13a)

## NOTES AND COMMENTARY

**57:3** *sons of the sorceress/seed of the adulterer and the whore.* Lady Israel has
committed spiritual adultery, and her children no longer qualify for Jehovah's blessings (1:21; Jer. 3:1–20; Ezek. 16). This condemnation can be directed at many in our
day, as well as anciently.

**57:4** *sport yourselves make ye a wide mouth . . . tongue.* These are types of
mockery, or making fun of someone else. Against whom do they sport themselves?
Probably the prophet, but any who mock the prophet are also mocking God.

*children of transgression/seed of falsehood.* The New International Version says
"brood of rebels, the offspring of liars." The sin of Israel has become so pervasive
that it passes from generation to generation, ever perpetuating itself (1:2). *Children of
transgression*—those who follow the ways of the world and the whisperings of the
adversary—are called a variety of names in the scriptures: "children of this world"
(Luke 16:8; 20:34), "children of disobedience" (Eph. 2:2), "children of wrath" (Eph.
2:3), "children of the kingdom of the devil" (Alma 5:25), and "the children of them
which killed the prophets" (Matt. 23:31). Jesus said bluntly that they follow their
"father the devil" (John 8:44).

**57:5** *Enflaming yourselves/green tree/slaying the children/rocks.* This passage
refers to the evil fertility rites in groves and on high places, rites that often included
child sacrifice (Ezek. 23:38–39; Jer. 2:20; 7:31; 19:4–5). Some people in all ages
choose gross sin in the name of religion.

---

[1] In the JB the last line reads, *you send your envoys far afield, down to Sheol itself.* The note adds, *By sacrificing infants.*

**57:6** *stones.* These may have been stones that were set up for a male fertility deity (Jer. 32:35). Or perhaps these stones refer to the smooth stones from a stream that David used to slay Goliath (1 Sam. 17:40–50). The people here were choosing the smooth stones of the stream instead of the Rock who is their Redeemer (Ps. 78:35; Moses 7:53).

*stream.* The Hebrew word used here, *nachal,* can also mean "valley." The wicked reject the living waters for unholy streams.

*portion/lot.* The Lord should be the lot, portion, or inheritance for covenant Israel (Ps. 16:5; 119:57). But in rejecting him and turning to false gods, her inheritance is only what the false gods made of stone could give her (Ezek. 6:13). That is also true of us in the latter days, when we choose things of the world over God. Another interpretation is that the lot of idol worshipers is death and destruction, the just desserts of their sinfulness.

*drink offering/meat offering.* These are sacrifices that God required to be made in the temple (Lev. 6:14–18, 23); instead, they are given to idols. The greatest sacrifice, of course, is our hearts, but most people give their hearts to the wrong things.

**57:7** *mountain.* Mountains can be temples of the Lord. Here, a mountain serves as a pagan temple, which in turn symbolizes all false worship.

*set thy bed.* This metaphor represents the fertility couch of pagan religions. Instead of giving one's whole being to the true God, many people give themselves to worship of other gods and other things.

*thither.* This word suggests going to the bed of spiritual adultery.

**57:8** *doors/posts.* The New International Version translates, "Behind your doors and your doorposts, you have put your pagan symbols." Israel has made their false god an integral element of their homes and their lives. This stands in contrast to the Lord's command that Israel keep the law of the Lord written on their doorposts (Deut. 11:20) as a sign of dedication and for remembrance of the Lord.

*thy remembrance. Remembrance* means a memorial to an idol. The Jerusalem Bible identifies this as "a domestic idol standing by the threshold or over the door." Their false god is an integral element of their lives.

*discovered thyself/gone up/enlarged thy bed.* The New International Version renders this statement in painful plainness: "Forsaking me, you uncovered your bed, you climbed into it and opened it wide; you made a pact with those whose beds you love, and you looked on their nakedness." This phrase has a literal meaning, referring to the pagan practices of temple prostitution, and also a symbolic meaning, referring to the unfaithfulness of Lady Israel (in our age, as well as anciently) in joining herself to other gods after making a covenant with Jehovah.

**57:9** *wentest to the king.* The Hebrew suggests that the people may have gone to Molech, or Melech, the idol representing the terrible Canaanite god. (*Melech* is the Hebrew word for *king.*) Another possible meaning is that the Lord's people dishonored their covenants by seeking security in earthly powers instead of trusting in the Lord (see, for example, 2 Kgs. 16:7).

*ointment/perfumes.* These adornments are used to make oneself more attractive to a lover and symbolize the ways people seek to please false gods.

*messengers far off.* The Israelites looked to the gods of other nations (for example, the gods of Assyria and Tyre), rather than to their own true God (17:7–8; 30:1–2; 1 Sam. 28:13). The messengers may be those who are sent to look for new gods to worship in many places.

*debase thyself . . . unto hell.* The Revised Standard Version translates this as "sent down even to Sheol." Not only did apostate Israel send messengers afar seeking false gods but she even looked to the pagan god of Sheol, the underworld (28:14–15). Some today are so far removed from the truth that they seek in "far places" for spiritual fulfillment, forgetting the only true source of blessings.

**57:10** *wearied . . . greatness of thy way/saidst not . . . no hope.* Lady Israel's quest after other gods is a wearisome one (Jer. 2:25; 18:12). But despite the greatness of the undertaking, Israel (like apostates in all ages) continued in her false search.

*life of thine hand/not grieved.* According to the Revised Standard Version, "You found new life for your strength, and so you were not faint." Though Israel's quest after other gods seemed hopeless, she redoubled her efforts and continued on. Some people today do the same thing—they continue to seek fulfillment in the wrong places even though the desired happiness does not come.

**57:11** *afraid or feared/hast not remembered.* The Lord's people have become more fearful of displeasing false gods than the true God. The result: Israel has lied to God and has not remembered either him or his covenants. *Remembered* in this context means to turn to and obey.

*laid it to thy heart.* Israel has not let the Lord's displeasure trouble her. She has not taken it to heart.

*held my peace/fearest me not.* The Lord has chosen not to speak to Israel for a time, and in response Israel has forgotten him.

**57:12** *declare thy righteousness . . . works/shall not profit.* The Lord knows Israel's works and the level of her righteousness, and he knows that they are wanting. They are insufficient to gain the reward Israel seeks.

**57:13a** *When thou criest, let thy companies deliver.* Let your idols answer your prayers (2:20; 31:7), which, of course, they cannot do.

*wind . . . carry them all away.* The New International Version translates this passage as "the wind will carry all of them [the idols] off, a mere breath will blow them away." Those to whom apostate Israel looks for help are powerless and are quickly removed.

*vanity shall take them.* Trust in idols shall prove vain, or transitory and useless.

## BLESSINGS FOR THE CONTRITE (57:13B–21)

After condemning the wicked, the Lord now gives promises of blessings to the faithful:

If they put their trust in God, they will "possess the land" (57:13), meaning the land of their inheritance.

They will be gathered to Zion without stumbling blocks to hinder them (57:14).

If they are humble and contrite, the Lord will revive their flagging spirits and troubled hearts (57:15).

The Lord will remove his wrath from them (57:16).

The Lord will heal them (57:18, 19).

The Lord will lead them down life's paths (57:18).

The Lord will comfort them (57:18).

The Lord will give them peace, whether they are physically near or far (57:19).

The wicked, of course, receive no such promises. Instead, they are assured that they will have no peace but will be like troubled waters that cannot rest. Waters in constant motion continually stir up dirt and mire, and the wicked do the same (57:20–21).

*Isaiah 57:13b–21*

> but he that putteth his trust in me *shall possess* <u>the land</u>,
> and *shall inherit* <u>my holy mountain</u>; (57:13b)

> And shall say, *Cast ye* <u>up</u>,
> *cast ye* <u>up</u>,

> *prepare* the <u>way</u>,
> *take up the stumblingblock* out of the <u>way</u> of my people. (57:14)

For thus saith the high and lofty *One* that <u>inhabiteth eternity,</u>
whose name is *Holy;* I <u>dwell in the high and holy place,</u>

with him also that is of a *contrite* and <u>humble spirit,</u>
to revive the <u>spirit of the humble,</u> and to revive the heart of the *contrite* ones.
(57:15)

For *I* <u>will not contend for ever,</u>
<u>neither will</u> *I* <u>be always wroth:</u>

for the *spirit* should fail before <u>me,</u>
and the *souls* which <u>I</u> have made. (57:16)

For the *iniquity of his covetousness* <u>was I wroth,</u> and smote him:
I hid me, and <u>was wroth,</u> and he [continued willfully][2] in the *way of his heart.*
(57:17)

I have seen his ways, and will *heal* <u>him:</u>
I will *lead* <u>him</u> also, and *restore comforts* unto <u>him</u> and to his mourners. (57:18)
I create the fruit of the lips;

*Peace, peace to him* <u>that is far off,</u>
and *to him* <u>that is near,</u> saith the Lord;

and I will heal him. (57:19)

But the wicked are like the <u>troubled</u> *sea,*
when *it* <u>cannot rest,</u> whose *waters* <u>cast up mire and dirt.</u> (57:20)

There is no peace, saith my God, to the wicked. (57:21)

## NOTES AND COMMENTARY

**57:13b** *possess the land.* Those who trust in the Lord will be joint heirs to his promises with the rest of the righteous. *The land* symbolizes security and stability, as well as the blessing of having temporal needs met. Further, the land is where the temple is built; the two are often inextricably connected.[3]

*inherit my holy mountain.* Those who trust in the Lord will have a legitimate place in the temple and, by extension, in the presence of the Lord.

**57:14** *Cast ye up.* The righteous will join the call to build up the way whereby Israel may return from her long spiritual and physical dispersion.

*prepare the way.* This phrase has reference to the "highway of salvation" of 40:3 and 62:10. It often refers to the return of the ten tribes, but here it seems to have reference to preparing the way for a spiritual return to God.

*stumblingblock.* The righteous pray that the path on which we return to the Lord will have all obstacles removed from it, so that we do not stumble in our journey.

---

[2] A change from the archaic KJV *went on frowardly.*
[3] Davies, *Gospel and the Land,* 94, 153.

**57:15** *high and lofty One . . . name is Holy.* The Lord is high and lofty in that he dwells in the heavens and rules over all (6:1; D&C 88:13). The Lord is called Holy because his righteousness and purity are essential and eternal elements of his character.

*inhabiteth eternity.* The Lord inhabits eternity in the sense that he dwells in a state beyond time—past, present, and future are always before him (D&C 130:7). Joseph Smith taught: "When his commandments teach us, it is in view of eternity; for we are looked upon by God as though we were in eternity. God dwells in eternity, and does not view things as we do."[4]

*high and holy place.* In the ancient temples of Israel, the two most sacred, innermost rooms were called the *holy place,* which only the priests could enter, and "the most holy place," or "the holy of holies," which only the high priest could enter and even then only on the most holy day of the year (Day of Atonement). A *holy place* would be in the temple; a *high and holy place* would be the temple in heaven, the celestial kingdom.

*contrite and humble spirit.* Those who are sorrowful for their sins, repentant, and fully reliant on God have a *contrite and humble spirit.* These are they who will dwell in the house of the Lord forever; these are they who are invited to live with him in his "high and holy place" in the celestial world.

*revive the spirit/revive the heart.* Those who are humble and contrite will be given new life and energy in Christ, despite their own weakness (61:1–3; Ps. 51:10).

**57:16** *will not contend for ever.* The New International Version reads, "I will not accuse forever." The Lord will not forever accuse us of our sins if we are humble, contrite, and repentant.

*wroth.* The Lord will not always be angry with us if we are repentant.

*spirit . . . fail/and the souls.* God is our Father, having made our souls. If he were to remain ever angry at us, we would fail to attain any degree of glory, which would go contrary to his work and glory, which is to bring to pass our immortality and eternal life (Moses 1:39).

**57:17** *iniquity of his covetousness. Covetousness,* the sin of greed, is another form of idolatry, in which mankind worships wealth instead of the Lord (Col. 3:5). Joseph Smith said that "God had often sealed up the heavens because of covetousness in the Church."[5]

---

[4] *Teachings of the Prophet Joseph Smith,* 356.
[5] *Teachings of the Prophet Joseph Smith,* 9.

*was wroth, and smote him.* The Lord was deeply angry with the wicked and punished them.

*I hid me.* In his anger, the Lord removed himself from the wicked (54:8; Ps. 27:9; 88:14; 104:29).

*continued willfully in the way of his heart.* The wicked did what they wanted, following their own desires rather than the Lord's.

**57:18** *seen his ways.* The Lord knows all our wickedness, and he knows our repentance.

*heal him/lead him/restore comforts.* When we repent and turn to Christ, he will heal our spirits and give us his Comforter. This promise of healing, leading, and comforting is reminiscent of the spirit of the Twenty-third Psalm.

*his mourners.* Those who have mourned the ways of the wicked will be comforted when the wicked repent. This may also be an expression of the promise in Matthew 5:4, "Blessed are they that mourn: for they shall be comforted."

**57:19** *create the fruit of the lips.* The Lord gives us power to speak (Heb. 13:15). In this context, the Lord gives words to those who mourn because of the sin they see; these likely are words of prayer, praise, thanksgiving, and pleading for grace in behalf of the sinner.

*Peace.* The true source of *peace* is Christ, as Paul points out (Eph. 2:12–17). This cry of "peace, peace" may also be the Lord's greeting to those who are coming to Zion: "Shalom, Shalom!" (Ps. 37:11, 37; 119:165; Philip. 4:7; 2 Thes. 3:16).

*far off.* Israel has been scattered to distant places. Also, many are spiritually *far off*; those who "draw near to me with their lips, but their hearts are far from me" (JS–H 1:19; Isa. 29:13) may find peace through repentance.

**57:20** *troubled sea/waters cast up mire and dirt.* The wicked have not the peace promised in the previous verse; they toss like a *troubled sea,* and the result of their movement through life is *mire and dirt.* Elder Bruce McConkie has described a troubled sea: "The sea—a raging, restless sea—is a symbol of a sinful and wicked world. The beasts seen by Daniel in vision and used as types of worldly kingdoms came up out of the sea. . . . (Dan. 7.) And the Lord said to Isaiah: 'The wicked are like the troubled sea. . . . ' (Isa. 57:20–21)—leaving us to conclude that when Christ calms the seas of life, peace enters the hearts of men."[6]

**57:21** *no peace . . . to the wicked.* This statement is a repetition of 48:22, but here it forms a contrast to the peace offered to the repentant in 57:19. Peace is the reward for those who come unto Christ, but those who refuse receive no peace.

---

[6] *Mortal Messiah,* 2:278.

# ISAIAH 58

## LIKENING ISAIAH 58 UNTO OURSELVES

*This chapter outlines the true law of the fast. In our fasting we are to do far more than simply abstain from two meals, nor are we to put on an appearance of one who is making a sacrifice. In a true fast we seek to help and bless others. We remove heavy burdens from the shoulders of others. We share our substance. If we do these things, we will be blessed spiritually and temporally. Our portion of light will increase. Our health will be strengthened. The Lord will be our guide in all things.*

*The Lord speaks again of the Sabbath. He promises that if we will turn away from our own pleasures on the Sabbath and turn to the things that will delight the Lord, he will lift us up to spiritual richness and bestow on us all the blessings of Jacob.*

## THE TRUE LAW OF THE FAST (58:1–12)

As the headnote to Isaiah 58 in the LDS edition of the Bible reads, 58:1–2 gives us the "true law of the fast, with its attendant blessings." That fasting is more than going without food and drink for a period of time is made unmistakably clear.

The passage opens with the Lord instructing Isaiah to proclaim the sins of the house of Israel (58:1), the people of the covenant both then and now, with boldness. They appear to be righteous, the Lord observes, being prayerful and obeying the ordinances of the gospel (58:2). Yet, as we soon learn, their righteousness is that of outward obedience only and not of the heart.

Israel asks why the Lord has not blessed them for their sacrifice in fasting (58:3). The Lord answers that in their fasting they have not turned to him. They continue to seek pleasure and do business (58:3). They care more for the show of fasting—to afflict their soul, to bow the head, to sit on sackcloth and ashes (58:5)—than to attend to the true purposes of the fast: to help themselves and others to repent, to find respite

[ 5 1 0 ]

from the emotional burdens they carry, and to help others with their problems and afflictions (58:6, 9–10). True fasting involves sharing with the hungry, the poor, and the naked, including needy members of one's own family (58:7, 10).

Those who obey this law are promised great blessings, including spiritual light (58:8); physical health (58:8); increased righteousness (58:8); answers to prayer (58:9); continual guidance from the Lord (58:11); a plenitude of spiritual food and water, representing the full blessings of the Atonement, even when others lack (58:11); and a restoration of their lands of inheritance (58:12). This passage parallels 1:10–20, in which the Lord rebukes the people for outward obedience without a true yielding of the heart.

*Isaiah 58:1–12*

> *Cry* <u>aloud</u>, spare not,
> *lift up thy voice* <u>like a trumpet</u>,
>
> and *[show] my people* <u>their transgression</u>,
> and the *house of Jacob* <u>their sins</u>. (58:1)
>
> Yet they *seek* <u>me</u> daily,
> and *delight to know* <u>my ways</u>,
>
> as a nation that <u>did righteousness</u>,
> and <u>forsook not the ordinance of their God</u>:
>
> *they ask of me* the <u>ordinances of justice</u>;
> *they take delight* in <u>approaching to God</u>. (58:2)
>
> *Wherefore have we fasted,* say they, and <u>thou seest not</u>?
> *wherefore have we afflicted our soul,* and <u>thou takest no knowledge</u>?
>
> Behold, in the day of your fast ye find pleasure, and exact all your labours. (58:3)
>
> Behold, *ye fast* <u>for strife and debate</u>, and to smite with the fist of wickedness:
> *ye shall not fast* as <u>ye do this day</u>, to make your voice to be heard on high. (58:4)
>
> Is it such a fast that I have chosen?
>
> a day for a man to *afflict his soul?*
> is it to *bow down his head* as a bulrush,
> and to *spread sackcloth and ashes* under him?
>
> wilt thou call this *a fast,*
> and *an acceptable day* to the Lord? (58:5)
>
> Is not this the fast that I have chosen?
>
> to *loose* the <u>bands of wickedness</u>,
> to *undo* the <u>heavy burdens</u>,
>
> and to let the oppressed <u>go free</u>,
> and that *ye* <u>break every yoke</u>? (58:6)
>
> Is it not to *deal thy bread* to the <u>hungry</u>,
> and that *thou bring* the <u>poor</u> that are cast out to thy house?

when thou seest the naked, that *thou* <u>cover him</u>;
and that *thou* <u>hide not thyself</u> from thine own flesh? (58:7)

Then <u>shall</u> *thy light* <u>break forth</u> as the morning,
and *thine health* <u>shall spring forth</u> speedily:

and *thy righteousness* <u>shall go before thee</u>;
the *glory of the Lord* <u>shall be thy [rear guard]</u>.[1] (58:8)

Then *shalt thou call,* and <u>the Lord shall answer</u>;
*thou shalt cry,* and <u>he shall say, Here I am</u>.

If thou take away from the midst of thee the yoke, the putting forth of the finger,
and speaking vanity; (58:9)

And if thou *draw out thy soul* to <u>the hungry</u>,
and *satisfy* <u>the afflicted soul</u>;

then shall *thy light* rise in obscurity,
and *thy darkness* be as the noonday: (58:10)

And the Lord shall *guide* <u>thee</u> continually,
and *satisfy* <u>thy soul</u> in drought,
and *make fat* <u>thy bones</u>:

and thou shalt be <u>like a watered garden</u>,
and <u>like a spring of water</u>, whose waters fail not. (58:11)

And *they that shall be of thee shall build* the <u>old waste places</u>:
*thou shalt raise up* the <u>foundations</u> of many generations;

and thou shalt be called, *The repairer* <u>of the breach</u>,
*The restorer* <u>of paths to dwell in</u>. (58:12)

## NOTES AND COMMENTARY

**58:1** *voice like a trumpet.* Alma longed to speak with a voice like a trumpet, in loudness and clarity, when he cried out, "O that I were an angel, . . . that I might go forth and speak with the trump of God, with a voice to shake the earth. . . . Yea, I would declare unto every soul, as with the voice of thunder, repentance and the plan of redemption, that they should repent and come unto our God, that there might not be more sorrow upon all the face of the earth" (Alma 29:1–2).

**58:2** *ordinance of their God.* In this context, this expression refers to the laws of God.

*ordinances of justice.* This phrase may refer to righteous judgments, just laws, or ordinances that help to justify us before God.

**58:3** *Wherefore have we fasted.* Here the people ask why the Lord doesn't recognize their efforts to fast.

---

[1] Most modern translations use *rearward* or *rearguard* to replace the archaic KJV *rereward.*

*afflicted our soul.* Some have viewed fasting as a time to seek suffering or self-abasement (Lev. 16:29, 31; 23:27, 32). In 58:5, the Lord rebukes such attitudes, saying he has not commanded a fast wherein a person would "afflict his soul."

*ye find pleasure/exact all your labors.* Here the prophet explains why the people's fasting and prayers for deliverance went unheard. They were not sincere in their devotion, they turned to their own pleasures "in the day of [their] fast" instead of losing themselves in the Lord and his work, and they required others to work instead of allowing them to participate in the spirit of the fast.

*exact all your labours.* This phrase may mean "inflict travail on others." Though the Israelites themselves may not have been working on their fast days, they were requiring others to work, most likely hired laborers.

**58:4** *fast for strife and debate/smite with the fist of wickedness.* What should have been a religious observance that increased love and holiness led only to hunger and irritability, strife, debate, and physical fighting.

**58:5** *bow down his head as a bulrush.* This expression means hanging the head to give the appearance of suffering.

*sackcloth and ashes.* These signs of self-abasement and mourning (22:12; 1 Kgs. 21:17–29; Job 42:6) were parts of a true fast in ancient Israel. For example, Daniel said, "I set my face unto the Lord God, to seek by prayer and supplications, with fasting, and sackcloth, and ashes: And I prayed unto the Lord my God, and made my confession" (Dan. 9:3–4). But outward signs of fasting, when they are performed to be seen by men, do not fulfill the requirement of the true fast.

**58:6** *the fast that I have chosen.* To fast in the Lord's way, we must repent of our willful sins, our unkindnesses, and our selfishness (1:16–17).

*loose the bands of wickedness.* The *bands of wickedness* may be the chains or bonds of sin (2 Ne. 1:13, 23; 9:45). As President Spencer W. Kimball put it, "Sin [is] like handcuffs on the wrists, a ring in the nose, and slave bands around the neck."[2] The *bands of wickedness* may also refer to the bonds of slavery and oppression discussed below.

*undo the heavy burdens.* These burdens might be those a master would place on a servant, or they could refer to the emotional burdens people carry.

*let the oppressed go free.* People were oppressed under slavery or other forms of servitude. For instance, it was the practice in ancient times to take the property of the poor—even the clothes from their backs—as collateral for a debt. With no property, including clothing, the poor had no option but to stay in the servitude of their creditor

---

[2] *Miracle of Forgiveness*, 27.

(Job 22:6). The Lord urges mercy (Ezek. 18:7, 16), even to a removal of the debt (Deut. 24:12–13; Ex. 22:25–26).

*break every yoke.* Yokes are used to control beasts of burden to keep them in a straight path of servitude. The mentality and practice of using other human beings in this manner must be broken. Also, the bondage of sin is a yoke to the soul that fasting can help to break.

**58:7** *bread to the hungry/bring the poor/cover him.* These actions are the essence of pure religion (Matt. 25:31–46; James 1:27). Those who have done these things will receive God's blessings (Ezek. 18:7–9, 16–17): their fasting will be recognized and their prayers heard.

*hide not thyself.* When someone is in distress we must not pretend that we do not see or "[pass] by on the other side" (Luke 10:31–32) and refuse to help (Deut. 22:1–4). This injunction applies particularly to "thine own flesh," meaning members of our own families.

*thine own flesh.* Footnote *c* to 58:7 in the LDS edition of the Bible equates this phrase with "thy brother, or relative." In a broader sense, however, all men are children of the same God (Job 31:15) and should be treated as brothers.

**58:8** *light break forth as the morning.* Spiritual light in our lives brings happiness and joy (9:2; 60:1–3), and spiritual darkness brings misery (59:10). It is in turning from wickedness to righteousness that a spiritual dawning may occur (Job 11:13–17), as was promised here to Israel as a people.

*thine health shall spring forth speedily.* The word translated as *health* (or *healing,* in some versions) means the growth of new flesh in the place of the old wound. Those who fast properly will enjoy greater health and healing of spiritual wounds. In addition, the prophets use this figure in speaking of the restoration of Israel to her blessings (30:26; Jer. 8:22; 30:17; 33:6).

*righteousness . . . go before thee/glory of the Lord . . . thy rear guard.* As he did in 52:12, the prophet here refers to the pillar of light that went before the children of Israel during their exodus from Egypt (Ex. 13:21–22). Those who fast in a manner pleasing to the Lord will grow in righteousness and will have the glory of the Lord as a guide, presence, and protector in their lives.

**58:9** *call . . . answer/cry . . . Here I am.* The Lord will be near us and will readily grant that which we seek in righteous prayer.

*yoke.* See 58:6.

*putting forth of the finger.* This is a gesture of insult (Prov. 6:13). Isaiah 59:3 speaks of hands "defiled with blood" and fingers "with iniquity"; perhaps this expression refers to using the fingers (or hands) to harm another or steal his property.

*speaking vanity.* "Vain speaking" might include "malicious talk" (NIV), "spreading vicious rumors" (LB), "speaking wickedness" (RSV), and "lay[ing] false charges" (NEB). Avoiding these is part of the spirit of fasting.

**58:10** *draw out thy soul to the hungry.* This phrase means to let your heart and feelings be turned to those in need.

*satisfy the afflicted soul.* To *satisfy* means to give what is needed.

*thy light rise in obscurity/thy darkness be as the noonday.* This passage refers to the future glory of Israel (54:1–13; 55:13). Her humiliation and captivity are as the darkness just before daybreak. And just as her (and our) deliverance from slavery and oppression is as the dawn (v. 8), so the eventual state of Zion will be as the brightness of the sun at noon (Job 11:17). This also has an individual application: As we fast, we seek to become like the Bright and Morning Star (Rev. 22:16), the Dayspring (Luke 1:78), the Light of the World (John 8:12; Alma 38:9; D&C 11:28), Jesus Christ.

**58:11** *the Lord shall guide thee/satisfy thy soul in drought/make fat thy bones.* As a shepherd, the Lord leads his flock (which also includes us in the latter days), providing for their every need (Ps. 23:2–3). For those who become his sheep, he provides living water in times of spiritual drought. Bones were considered the gauge of the body's vitality—they become dry and brittle with age and illness but are moist and fresh with youth, health, and vigor (Job 21:24). Bones that are made fat are renewed and made strong (66:14). *Make fat thy bones* may also refer to the resurrection.

*like a watered garden/like a spring.* In a garden, the source of life, or water, comes from the outside. So shall it be with the righteous, who will receive sustenance from the Lord (51:3; Num. 24:5–6). This situation contrasts with the curse in 1:30: "For ye shall be as an oak whose leaf fadeth, and as a garden that hath no water." With a spring, the waters come from within rather than from without. Jesus said, "He that believeth on me, as the scripture hath said, out of his belly shall flow rivers of living water" (John 7:38). In this dispensation the Lord promised, "Unto him that keepeth my commandments I will give the mysteries of my kingdom, and the same shall be in him a well of living water, springing up unto everlasting life" (D&C 63:23).

**58:12** *they that shall be of thee.* This phrase refers to our descendants, or generations yet to come (Prov. 20:7). Those who hear our testimony and return to God may also be included.

*build the old waste places.* The old waste places were laid waste by the invasion of enemies. The descendants of ancient Israel will, however, be restored to their inheritance, with the means to repair and restore Israel. This expression could also have a spiritual application—the waste places might refer to Israel's sin and separation from God, which chasm the descendants will repair through repentance. (This verse is virtually repeated in 61:4; see also 44:26, 28.)

*raise up the foundations of many generations.* Israel will rebuild her cities on their ancient foundations. Symbolically, this expression may refer to the Lord's covenant to give Abraham countless offspring (Gen. 17:4, 6), or it may refer to the eternal increase of all the righteous.

*repairer of the breach/restorer of paths.* The New English Bible translates this expression as "You shall be called Rebuilder of broken walls, Restorer of houses in ruins." Symbolically, this passage may suggest that the righteous of Israel will help to repair broken relationships, especially the relationship between God and man, and broken homes, perhaps through the sealing power.

## BLESSINGS OF THE SABBATH (58:13-14)

Here we are given the true law of the Sabbath: Do not seek your own will or pleasure on the Lord's holy day but seek to do his will (58:13). In contrast to those who fast according to the law but not with purity of heart, we must keep the law of the Sabbath with "delight" (58:13). If we keep the Sabbath with such an attitude, we will "delight" ourselves in the Lord (58:14). The Lord will then give us high and lofty blessings, even those promised to "Jacob thy father" (58:14).

*Isaiah 58:13-14*

> If *thou turn away thy foot* from the sabbath,
> from *doing thy pleasure* on my holy day;
>
> and call the sabbath *a delight,*
> the *holy of the Lord,*
> *honourable;* and shalt honour him,
>
> *not doing* thine own ways,
> *nor finding* thine own pleasure,
> *nor speaking* thine own words: (58:13)

Then shalt thou delight thyself in the Lord;
and I will cause thee to ride upon the high places of the earth,
and feed thee with the heritage of Jacob thy father:
for the mouth of the Lord hath spoken it. (58:14)

## NOTES AND COMMENTARY

**58:13** *turn away thy foot from the sabbath/doing thy pleasure.* The New International Version renders this passage: "If you keep your feet from breaking the Sabbath and doing as you please on my holy day."

*honourable.* The Lord would have us consider the Sabbath worthy to be honored.

*not doing thine own ways/nor finding thine own pleasure.* On the Sabbath, only the Lord's work is to be accomplished. Yet even in the earliest days of Israel as a nation, some resented the Sabbath's interruption of their merchandising and worldly pursuits (Amos 8:5). Here the Lord challenges his people to do his will on the Sabbath, not their own.

*speaking thine own words.* This phrase means speaking idle words. The words we use in our lives matter, and the words we use on the Sabbath should reflect the sanctity of the day.

**58:14** *delight thyself in the Lord.* If we obey the Sabbath with pure hearts, not only will we find joy in our obedience but we will find joy in the Lord himself.

*high places of the earth.* The holy mount, or the temple, would be the high places on which the Lord treads (Deut. 33:29; Micah 1:2-3; Hab. 3:19). Thus, those mortals who "ride upon the high places" are those who are blessed to be where the Lord is. This verse compares very closely with Deuteronomy 32:13, which speaks of Israel's conquest of Canaan. Thus Isaiah's prophecy may refer to the renewal of the covenant between God and Israel and to the reconquest of the promised land.

*feed thee with the heritage of Jacob.* When we keep the Sabbath, the Lord will enable us to partake freely of the blessings promised to Jacob.

*the mouth of the Lord hath spoken it.* This passage testifies of the source of the promises in this passage. The same words are recorded in 1:20 and 40:5.

# ISAIAH 59

### LIKENING ISAIAH 59 UNTO OURSELVES

*When we feel lost from God, he has not lost his power to bless and help us, and he continues to hear our prayers. But our iniquities can separate us from him. The Lord here speaks plainly against those who give themselves to sin. Israel apparently is aware of her state, for she laments her darkness and blindness. The state of those who choose sin is truly a miserable one.*

*When the Lord comes again, he will come in vengeance, and he will punish the wicked for their sins. But he will also come in mercy and love, bringing blessings to the repentant in Zion. It is a regular duty of the Lord's people to search their hearts, always seeking to know if they are clean and worthy. When the Lord comes again, will we rejoice to see him? Or will we tremble and fear because of our unworthiness?*

## CONDEMNATION OF SIN (59:1–8)

Chapter 59 begins with a stern condemnation of Israel's sinful state. Their iniquities have separated them from God (59:2). They are so sinful that every part of their being is corrupted: hands, fingers, lips, tongue, feet, even their very thoughts (59:3, 7). Isaiah emphasizes this sinfulness again and again, using such words as *iniquities* (or *iniquity*, repeated four times), *sins, defiled with blood, lies* (repeated once), *perverseness, vanity, mischief, violence, evil, innocent blood, wasting, destruction, crooked paths*. The people care nothing for justice, truth, peace, or judgment. They are compared to such vile things as the cockatrice's eggs, spider's webs, and vipers (59:5). Their sins will turn to their own destruction, the Lord says (59:7), and they know no peace (59:8).

Isaiah 59:5–7 illustrates the justice of God: Those who sin (eat cockatrices', or serpents', eggs) bring punishment and destruction upon their own heads (die), and all their evil efforts will bring them nothing good or profitable (see Job 8:14).

Paul paraphrases some of these verses in Romans 3:12–18: "There is none that doeth good, no, not one. Their throat is an open sepulchre; with their tongues they have used deceit; the poison of asps is under their lips: Whose mouth is full of cursing and bitterness: Their feet are swift to shed blood: Destruction and misery are in their ways: And the way of peace have they not known: There is no fear of God before their eyes." Unfortunately, what Isaiah and Paul saw in their days, we can see in our own— even some who once were of the covenant have forgotten their God and have turned to wickedness.

Victor Ludlow observes: "In chapters 59 and 60, Isaiah describes a complete transformation of Israel as she moves from wickedness to righteousness through a sequence of changes: sin (59:1–8), repentance (59:9–15a), deliverance (59:15b–21), gathering (60:1–9), rebuilding (60:10–13), prosperity (60:14–18), and the presence of the Lord (60:19–22). . . . Isaiah portrays a pattern of progression as Israel rises from the depths of spiritual death to eternal life in God's presence."[1]

## Isaiah 59:1–8

Behold, the *Lord's hand* is not shortened,
that *it* cannot save;

neither *his ear* heavy,
that *it* cannot hear: (59:1)

But *your iniquities* have separated between you and your God,
and *your sins* have hid his face from you, that he will not hear. (59:2)

For *your hands* are defiled with blood,
and *your fingers* with iniquity;
*your lips* have spoken lies,
*your tongue* hath muttered perverseness. (59:3)

*None calleth* for justice,
*nor any pleadeth* for truth:

*they trust* in vanity,
and *speak* lies;
*they conceive* mischief,
and *bring forth* iniquity. (59:4)
*They hatch* cockatrice' eggs,
and *weave* the spider's web:

---

[1] *Isaiah,* 492.

he that eateth of their eggs dieth, and that which is crushed breaketh out into a viper. (59:5)

*Their webs* shall not become garments,
neither shall they cover themselves with *their works:*

*their works* are works of iniquity,
and the act of violence is in *their hands.* (59:6)

*Their feet run* to evil,
and *they make haste* to shed innocent blood:

*their thoughts* are thoughts of iniquity;
wasting and destruction are in *their paths.* (59:7)

*The way of peace* they know not;
and there is no judgment in *their goings:*

they have made them crooked paths:
whosoever goeth therein shall not know peace. (59:8)

## NOTES AND COMMENTARY

**59:1** *the Lord's hand is not shortened, that it cannot save.* The Lord does not lack strength or power to save his children (50:2; Num. 11:23).

*ear heavy/cannot hear.* The Lord does not lack the capacity or readiness to hear us and attend to our needs.

**59:2** *hid his face from you.* The Lord withholds his presence and other blessings when we remove ourselves from him through sin (8:17; 57:17).

**59:3** *hands are defiled with blood.* In a specific sense, this passage may refer to bloodshed; in general, it refers to wickedness and sin.

*hands/fingers/lips/tongue.* These parts of the human body express the agency to act and to do wickedly. A fifth body part leads the people to evil: the feet (59:7). The hands that people use to reach out in pleading to God are the same hands they use to injure their fellowman; the same lips and tongue used in prayer for deliverance and blessing are those that speak deception (1:15; 5:7; 58:9).

*perverseness.* The New International Version reads this as "wicked things."

**59:4** *None calleth for justice, nor any pleadeth for truth.* These phrases use legal imagery, the former representing a plaintiff and the latter a defendant in a suit (Job 9:15; 13:22).

*vanity.* The New International Version reads "empty arguments."

*mischief.* Wickedness abounds.

**59:5** *hatch.* Rather than *hatch*, the true meaning appears to be that the eggs are broken open for the purpose of eating the contents. Job 20:12–16 uses the same imagery to develop the idea that sin is like eating a seemingly delicious food, only to discover that one has swallowed poison.

*cockatrice/viper.* Most translations replace the word *cockatrice,* a legendary serpent,[2] with *adder,* a real one. The adder and the viper are particularly poisonous snakes. The people have sunk so low in their wickedness that they are killing themselves spiritually. The snakes probably represent Satan, and the spider's web, the bonds of sin.

**59:6** *webs . . . not . . . garments.* Their evil plans and sins (compared to webs) will not provide for their temporal or spiritual needs.

*act of violence is in their hands.* These wicked people are using their agency to choose violent, unrighteous behavior.

**59:7** *feet run to evil/make haste to shed innocent blood.* The people described are so wicked that they rush—*run, make haste*—to sin (Prov. 1:16; Rom. 3:15).

*wasting and destruction are in their paths.* These sinners leave a trail of trouble behind them. Their paths are in contrast to that of Proverbs 16:17, "the highway of the upright" which "depart[s] from evil."

**59:8** *The way of peace they know not.* The wicked cannot know peace because true peace is a gift of the Spirit, available only to the righteous. The fruits of hatching the works of Satan and weaving "spiders' webs" (59:6) are emptiness and futility, not peace and well-being.

*no judgment in their goings.* There is no equity or justice in their way of life. The wicked do not follow the path of justice toward God (Prov. 10:9) or to hear their fellowmen, nor do they feel that God has dealt justly with them (Job 27:8–10).

*crooked paths.* A twisted, perverted, unrighteous way of life is contrasted with the strait and narrow path. These are the same paths as in 59:7, which lead to waste and destruction.

## Confession of Iniquity (59:9–15a)

Those speaking in this passage are probably those once of the covenant who come to realize their spiritual plight. They walk in darkness (59:9), looking for justice and salvation but finding neither (59:11). They know they are in sin (59:12). They have transgressed against the Lord and lied to him, they oppress others, and their

---

[2] *Merriam-Webster's Collegiate Dictionary,* 220, defines *cockatrice* as "a legendary serpent that is hatched by a reptile from a cock's egg and that has a deadly glance."

society is so corrupt that justice, truth, and equity are far from them (59:14). In fact, those who seek to live righteously become "a prey" to all the others (59:15).

The repetition of certain words and concepts in this passage clearly shows the emphasis on Israel's sin and its consequences: There is no "judgment" (59:9, 11, 12), "justice" (59:9, 14), "salvation" (59:11), "truth," or "equity" (59:14–15). The people suffer "obscurity," "darkness," and "blindness" (59:9, 10); they "grope" and "stumble" (59:10). They "are in desolate places as dead men" (59:10), and they "roar" and "mourn sore" (59:11). They know their "transgressions" and "iniquities"; they know they have departed from God (59:12–13). They confess to "lying," "speaking oppression and revolt," and "uttering" falsehoods (59:13). All in all, it is a dismal picture of a people lost in sin, a people who know their sinfulness but who have not yet come to repentance.

*Isaiah 59:9–15a*

> Therefore is *judgment* far from us,
> neither doth *justice* overtake us:
>
> we wait for *light,* but behold <u>obscurity;</u>
> for *brightness,* but we walk in <u>darkness</u>. (59:9)
>
> *We grope* for the wall <u>like the blind,</u>
> and *we grope* <u>as if we had no eyes</u>:
>
> we stumble at noonday as in the night;
> we are in desolate places as dead men. (59:10)
>
> *We roar* all <u>like bears,</u>
> and *mourn sore* <u>like doves</u>:
>
> we look for *judgment,* but <u>there is none;</u>
> for *salvation,* but it is <u>far off from us</u>. (59:11)
>
> For *our transgressions* <u>are multiplied before thee,</u>
> and *our sins* <u>testify against us</u>:
> for *our transgressions* <u>are with us;</u>
> and as for *our iniquities,* <u>we know them</u>; (59:12)
>
> *In transgressing and lying* <u>against the Lord,</u>
> and *departing away* <u>from our God,</u>
>
> *speaking* <u>oppression and revolt,</u>
> *conceiving and uttering* from the heart <u>words of falsehood</u>. (59:13)
>
> And *judgment* is <u>turned away backward,</u>
> and *justice* <u>standeth afar off</u>:
> for *truth* is <u>fallen in the street,</u>
> and *equity* <u>cannot enter</u>. (59:14)
>
> Yea, truth faileth; and he that departeth from evil maketh himself a prey: (59:15a)

## NOTES AND COMMENTARY

**59:9** *Therefore.* This word ties the troubles of this passage with the wickedness of the previous passage; it establishes a cause-and-effect relationship.

*judgment far/neither . . . justice overtake us.* Because of their iniquity, the people receive neither God's judicial verdict in their favor (*mish°pat*) nor God's justice in their behalf, meaning his righteous (*ts°daqah*) power of deliverance.

*light/brightness/obscurity/darkness.* Israel seeks the *light* of deliverance but sees only the *darkness* of continuing bondage, both to sin and to foreign oppressors. Why can someone who looks for light not find it? Perhaps these people are those who draw near only with their lips, while, as the previous verses make clear, their hearts remain far from their God (Job 19:8; 30:26; Isa. 29:13; Matt. 15:8).

**59:10** *grope . . . like the blind/as if we had no eyes/stumble at noonday as in the night.* Those who have turned from the light, at least in their hearts, are unable to find their way through life. Not only are they like those who are blind, but even worse, it is as if they have no eyes at all. As a consequence, night and noon are the same to them; spiritual brightness and darkness are indistinguishable to those who have no spiritual eyes. This is the fulfillment of a curse pronounced on the wicked by the Lord in Deuteronomy (Deut. 28:28–29). The Lord has power to heal this blindness, if we will repent and return unto him.

*in desolate places as dead men.* Israel has become spiritually dead, lost in a desolate world without God.

**59:11** *We roar . . . like bears/mourn . . . like doves.* Sometimes Israel's anguished laments are loud like the angry roaring (or growling) of bears; sometimes they are soft and subdued, like the sad moaning of doves. The wickedness of Israel, and the fruits of that wickedness, makes them angry at the troubles of sin while at the same time giving them cause for true mourning (38:14; Ezek. 7:16).

*judgment/salvation.* These words repeat the idea expressed in 59:9.

**59:12** *transgressions/sins/iniquities.* The people have many sins, or rebellions, that condemn them. But they do not sin in ignorance—they are well aware of their sins.

**59:13** *lying against the Lord/speaking oppression and revolt/uttering . . . words of falsehood.* These are sins of expression, of lying and bearing false witness to the Lord himself. The New International Version puts the situation in an even more serious light: "We acknowledge our iniquities: rebellion and treachery against the Lord, . . . uttering lies our hearts have conceived."

**59:14** *judgment is turned away backward/justice standeth afar off.* This statement is another repetition of the idea expressed in 59:9 and 11.

*truth is fallen in the street.* Integrity has collapsed; it is not even to be found in
public (as the street is public), where people are inclined to put on their best appearance.

*equity cannot enter.* Justice, honesty, and integrity are not allowed as part of
Israel's life.

**59:15a** *truth faileth.* This expression echoes the idea found in 59:14.

*he that departeth from evil maketh himself a prey.* Those who repent and turn to
righteousness are at the mercy of those who have no moral sense. Those who choose
good are subject to being victimized by those who choose evil.

## SALVATION FOR THE RIGHTEOUS, VENGEANCE FOR THE WICKED (59:15B–21)

The Lord beholds the great wickedness described in the previous passage, and he
is much displeased (59:15). (The Jerusalem Bible reads "indignant" and the New
American Bible "aggrieved.") Even worse, there is no one to make intercession for
the few righteous in Zion (59:16). The Lord himself therefore brings salvation, sustained by the power of his own righteousness (59:16–17).

But in going forth as Savior, he goes also as Judge, bringing vengeance upon the
unrepentant (59:17), both at the time of the Second Coming and in all ages. He will
bring punishments according to their deeds (59:18), and all the wicked of the earth
will know of his judgments and shall fear (59:19). No enemy of Zion shall stand,
though they come in great multitudes, for the Lord will rise up against them (59:19).

Then he will come to his people in Zion and to all those of the house of Jacob
who have repentant hearts (59:20). This coming can properly be seen as the Second
Coming; it can also be understood to be the coming of the Lord to the hearts of the
faithful of all ages. When the Lord visits the faithful, he brings his covenant.

Finally, the Lord promises that his Spirit and his truths will continue with his
anointed servant and the seed of the servant forever (59:21).

*Isaiah 59:15b–21*

> and the Lord saw it, and it displeased him that there was no judgment. (59:15b)
>
> And he *saw* that there was <u>no man</u>,
> and *wondered* that there was <u>no intercessor</u>:

therefore his arm brought *salvation* unto him;
and his *righteousness,* it sustained him. (59:16)

For he put on *righteousness* as a breastplate,
and an helmet of *salvation* upon his head;

and he *put on* the garments of vengeance for clothing,
and *was clad* with zeal as a cloke. (59:17)

According to their deeds, accordingly *he will repay,* fury to his adversaries,
recompence to his enemies; to the islands *he will repay* recompence. (59:18)

So shall they fear the *name of the Lord* from the west,
and *his glory* from the rising of the sun.

When the enemy shall come in like a flood, the Spirit of the Lord shall lift up a
standard against him. (59:19)

And the *Redeemer* shall come to Zion,
and unto them that turn from transgression in Jacob, saith the *Lord.* (59:20)

As for me, this is my covenant with them, saith the Lord;

*My spirit* that is upon thee,
and *my words* which I have put in thy mouth,

shall not depart out of *thy* mouth,
nor out of the mouth of *thy seed,*
nor out of the mouth of *thy seed's seed,*

saith the Lord, from henceforth and for ever. (59:21)

## NOTES AND COMMENTARY

**59:15b** *Lord saw it.* The Lord is always aware of our sinfulness, both public and private.

*judgment.* There was no justice in the affairs of men.

**59:16** *no man.* No one could be an intercessor for Zion (63:5).

*wondered.* Several versions of the Bible render this word as "appalled" (NIV, NAB, NRSV). Perhaps the idea here is that the Lord desired to raise up some kind of intercessor among mortals and was troubled that there was none.

*no intercessor.* There was no one to intercede for the Lord's covenant people, no one to help them in their bondage. The context suggests that the intercession here may not be that of the Atonement but of the Second Coming.

*his arm brought salvation unto him.* The Lord himself became the intercessor. His arm, which symbolizes his power, became the force that brought salvation or deliverance to his people.

*his righteousness . . . sustained him.* The Lord was able to deliver Zion because of his personal righteousness.

**59:17** *breastplate/helmet.* The Saints have repeatedly been commanded to put on the "armour of God" (Eph. 6:13), including the "breastplate of righteousness" (Eph. 6:14), and the "helmet of salvation" (Eph. 6:17; 1 Thes. 5:8; D&C 27:15–18), but here the Lord tells us *he* will put on such armor to pour out vengeance on the wicked. In the Second Coming, he will fight Israel's battles (Israel being both the Jews and the Lord's Zion) and win her deliverance from her enemies (40:10; 42:13; 49:24–26; 52:10).

*garments of vengeance/zeal as a cloke.* As garments or a cloak cover a person, so is the Lord enveloped in his desire to exact punishment on the enemies of the latter-day Zion. The Revised Standard Version uses the word *fury* instead of *zeal.*

**59:18** *According to their deeds . . . he will repay.* The Lord, who is perfectly just, will bring the wrath of his judgments against those who deserve them.

*fury to his adversaries/recompence to his enemies.* The Lord's enemies are those who choose willfulness and sin (Luke 19:27). Even worse are those who fight against Zion and the prophets (D&C 101:43–62; 103:1–2). All such will receive their just reward, or *recompense,* the punishing wrath of God.

*the islands.* Islands symbolize the uttermost parts of the earth (11:11; 42:12). No nation, people, or individual will escape the just wrath of the Lord.

**59:19** *fear the name of the Lord . . . and his glory/the west/the rising of the sun.* Those who receive God's judgments will be afraid of both death and eternal punishment, and they will fear the Lord who brings both. When the Lord comes in his glory, "every knee shall bow, and every tongue shall confess, . . . saying: Fear God, and give glory to him" (D&C 88:104). These responses will occur from the west to the east, over the entire globe (40:5; 52:10).

*like a flood.* The enemies of the Lord's people will come with such power and in such numbers that they cannot be stopped or turned (8:6–8). But the Lord will stop them nonetheless.

*a standard against him.* Just as the Lord will lift a banner or ensign as a rallying point for the righteous, so will he lift a banner or ensign as a rallying point in the battle against evil (49:22; Alma 46:11–21, 36; 62:4–5).

**59:20** *Redeemer shall come to Zion.* When Christ comes again, before he appears in glory, he will first come to Zion, both to the temple and to the gathering at Adam-ondi-Ahman (Mal. 3:1).[3] Moroni gave a valuable context to this prophecy when he quoted it to Joseph Smith on 22 September 1823. He said that the Church would prosper and grow despite persecution, "increasing in knowledge till they shall

---

[3] *Teachings of the Prophet Joseph Smith,* 157.

be sanctified and receive an inheritance where the glory of God will rest upon them; and when this takes place, and all things are prepared, the ten tribes of Israel will be revealed in the north country, whither they have been for a long season; and when this is fulfilled will be brought to pass that saying of the prophet . . . [quotes 59:20]."[4]

Not only will Christ come to Zion but he will then go forth from Zion. Paul wrote: "Blindness in part is happened to Israel, until the fulness of the Gentiles be come in. And so all Israel shall be saved: as it is written, There shall come out of Sion the Deliverer, and shall turn away ungodliness from Jacob: for this is my covenant unto them, when I shall take away their sins" (Rom. 11:25–27). Elder Orson Pratt declared, "The Zion of the last days . . . is the Church and kingdom of God; and out of that Church or kingdom or Zion is to come a Deliverer, who will turn away ungodliness from Jacob after the times of the Gentiles are fulfilled."[5]

*them that turn from transgression in Jacob.* The Lord will "come to" the repentant among those who receive the Abrahamic covenant (66:5). This seems to refer to the Second Coming.

**59:21** *this is my covenant.* "There is an eternal decree, issued in heaven above by the Lord himself. It is that in the day of gathering, when for the last time he assembles the outcasts of Israel, he will never again forsake them. They and their seed forever shall remain steadfast to the truth. The gospel will never be given to another people, nor the kingdom placed in other hands. The Lord's work will roll forward until the conversion of the world is completed" (see also 54:10).[6]

*them/thee.* These pronouns refer to righteous Israel in the latter-day Zion. The Lord's promise to them is that his words and his Spirit will continue with them and their descendants forever. Paul cited this prophecy twice, both times indicating that it would come to pass when Israel was cleansed from sin (Rom. 11:26–27; Heb. 10:15–17). Alternatively, *them* may refer to the covenant people and *thee* may refer to one through whom the covenant is fulfilled—perhaps the Lord's servant. This servant could be the Messiah, all of righteous Israel, or perhaps a great prophet yet to come forth (see 49:1–10 and commentary).

*my words which I have put in thy mouth, shall not depart out of thy mouth.* The Lord's words will be treasured and not lost (51:16; Ezek. 36:26–27; Jer. 1:9). The Lord gives this promise to Zion and his servant, who will bless all the righteous in Israel.

---

[4] Cowdery, *Messenger and Advocate* (Oct. 1835): 199.
[5] *Journal of Discourses,* 14:64.
[6] McConkie, *New Witness for the Articles of Faith,* 571.

*mouth.* This expression suggests that Zion and the servant will be true to the Lord's word.

*thy seed/thy seed's seed.* The *seed* is the children and descendants of those in Zion or of the servant (53:10; Gen. 22:18). This also is part of the covenant to Abraham and his seed that the gospel (and its word) would continue among them in all ages (Abr. 2:10–11; D&C 132:30).

# ISAIAH 60

*Likening Isaiah 60 unto Ourselves*

*In the last days Zion will be established, shining like a light to the world. The glory of the Lord will be there, and many will seek to join themselves to her, bringing their wealth with them. Zion will be found in the beautiful city of New Jerusalem, which will be nothing less than a city of God. It will be a place of peace and righteousness, with no violence or war. These are blessings the Lord delights to bring us; we should earnestly seek to belong to that Zion.*

## THE GLORY OF NEW JERUSALEM (60:1–22)

The first part of Isaiah 60 deals with the New Jerusalem and the Zion condition that will be found there; the individual addressed is the personified New Jerusalem. The headnote to this chapter in the LDS edition of the Bible verifies that this passage speaks first of the last days and finally of the splendor of the celestial Zion.

The Lord invites the New Jerusalem to "arise, shine." The light and glory of the Lord have come to rest on her (60:1). In contrast to the light of the New Jerusalem is the darkness that covers the earth and its people (60:2). The light of God in Zion will be seen by outsiders, and the Gentiles will be attracted by it to join her (60:2–3). The Gentiles will add much wealth and strength to Israel, symbolized by such terms as "forces," "multitude of camels," "gold," "incense," "flocks of Kedar," "rams of Nebaioth," "ships of Tarshish," "silver," and "glory of Lebanon" (60:5–13). The many references to wealth may also refer to spiritual gifts and treasures.

The coming of the Gentiles is combined with the coming of the lost ones of Israel; many shall be gathered to New Jerusalem from all parts of the world. Verse after verse of this passage speaks of that gathering: "all they gather themselves together, . . . thy sons shall come from far" (60:4); "thou shalt . . . flow together, . . . and be enlarged" (60:5); "all they from Sheba shall come" (60:6); "all the flocks of Kedar shall be gathered" (60:7); "Who are these that fly as a cloud?" (60:8) "ships . . . to bring thy sons from far" (60:9); "men may bring unto thee the forces of the Gentiles" (60:11); "The glory of Lebanon shall come unto thee" (60:13); "The sons also of them that afflicted thee shall come bending unto thee" (60:14).

Another recurring theme is that of kings coming: kings will "come to" Zion's brightness (60:3); kings will "minister" to her (60:10); kings will be "brought" to her (60:12); and in Zion, Israel will be nourished by kings (60:16).

Conditions in the New Jerusalem will be peaceful and glorious: "the glory of the Lord is risen upon thee" (60:1); "the Lord shall arise upon thee" (60:2); "Gentiles shall come to thy light" (60:3); "I will glorify the house of my glory" (60:7); "he hath glorified thee" (60:9); "I will make the place of my feet glorious" (60:13); "I will make thee . . . a joy of many generations" (60:15); "I will also make thy officers peace" (60:17); "thou shalt call thy walls Salvation, and thy gates Praise" (60:18); "the Lord shall be unto thee an everlasting light, and thy God thy glory" (60:19); "Thy people also shall be all righteous" (60:21).

Part of the reason for Zion's glory is the temple in New Jerusalem. The gold and incense in 60:6 are a feature of the temple. The flocks and rams of 60:7 appear to be temple sacrifices "with acceptance on mine altar" in the "house of my glory." And 60:13 speaks of beautifying "the place of my sanctuary," which is the temple.

Joseph Smith's words about temples in general also apply to the temple in Zion, the New Jerusalem: "What was the object of gathering . . . the people of God in any age of the world? . . . The main object was to build unto the Lord a house whereby He could reveal unto His people the ordinances of His house and the glories of His kingdom, and teach the people the way of salvation; . . . It is for the same purpose that God gathers together His people in the last days."[1]

Joseph Smith recorded a vision similar to the one Isaiah describes here: "And with one heart and with one mind, gather up your riches that ye may purchase an inheritance which shall hereafter be appointed unto you. And it shall be called the New Jerusalem, a land of peace, a city of refuge, a place of safety for the saints of the Most High God; And the glory of the Lord shall be there, and the terror of the Lord also shall be there, insomuch that the wicked will not come unto it, and it shall be called Zion" (D&C 45:65–67; see also 45:68–71).

---

[1] *Teachings of the Prophet Joseph Smith,* 308.

Other scriptures give us many parallels to this prophecy.[2]

| Isaiah's Prophecy | Future Old Jerusalem | New Jerusalem |
|---|---|---|
| 60:1–2 | D&C 45:47–53; 133:20–21; Zech.14:4, 9 | Rev. 21:2–3; D&C 84:4–5 |
| 60:3–5; 66:19–20 | Zech. 14:6 | Rev. 21:24; D&C 133:12 |
| 60:6 | Zech. 14:14 | Rev. 21:10–11, 18–21; D&C 124:11 |
| 60:7 | Zech. 14:21 | D&C 128:24 |
| 60:10 | | 3 Ne. 21:23–24 |
| 60:11 | | Rev. 21:25 |
| 60:12 | Zech. 12:6, 9 | D&C 97:18–22 |
| 60:13 | Ezek. 37:25–27; 47:1–10 | D&C 57:1–3; 84:4 |
| 60:14 | Zech. 14:20 | D&C 45:66–67; 84:2; Moses 7:62 |
| 60:15; 62:4 | Ezek. 36:34–36 | D&C 45:70–71; 66:11 |
| 60:16 | Zech. 14:1–3, 12–15 | D&C 64:43 |
| 60:17–18 | Zech. 14:11 | D&C 45:66–71 |
| 60:19–20 | 3 Ne. 20:30–31 | Rev. 21:23; 22:5 |
| 60:21 | Ezek. 37:25; 2 Ne. 10:7 | 2 Ne. 10:10–12 |

*Isaiah 60:1–22*

Arise,
shine;

for thy *light* is come,
and the *glory of the Lord* is risen upon thee. (60:1)

For, behold, the *darkness* shall cover the earth,
and *gross darkness* the people:

---

[2]This chart is adapted from Ludlow, *Isaiah,* 499–500.

but the *Lord* shall <u>arise upon thee,</u>
and *his glory* shall <u>be seen upon thee.</u> (60:2)

And the *Gentiles* shall come to <u>thy light,</u>
and *kings* to the <u>brightness of thy rising.</u> (60:3)

*Lift up thine eyes* round about,
and *see:*

all *they* <u>gather themselves</u> together,
*they* <u>come</u> to thee:

*thy sons* shall come from far,
and *thy daughters* shall be nursed at thy side. (60:4)

Then *thou* <u>shalt see,</u> and *flow together,*
and *thine heart* <u>shall fear,</u> and *be enlarged*;

because the *abundance of the sea* shall be <u>converted unto thee,</u>
the *forces of the Gentiles* shall <u>come unto thee.</u> (60:5)

The multitude of *camels* <u>shall cover thee,</u>
the *dromedaries* of Midian and Ephah; all they from Sheba <u>shall</u> <u>come</u>:

*they* <u>shall bring</u> gold and incense;
and *they* <u>shall [show] forth</u> the praises of the Lord. (60:6)

All the *flocks* of Kedar shall be gathered together <u>unto thee,</u>
the *rams* of Nebaioth shall minister <u>unto thee</u>:

they shall come up with acceptance on *mine altar,*
and I will glorify the *house of my glory.* (60:7)

Who are these that *fly* as a cloud,
and as the *doves* to their windows? (60:8)

Surely the isles shall wait for me, and the ships of Tarshish first, to bring thy sons
from far, their silver and their gold with them,

unto the name of the *Lord thy God,*
and to the *Holy One of Israel,*

because he hath glorified thee. (60:9)

And the *sons of strangers* <u>shall build up thy walls,</u>
and their *kings* <u>shall minister unto thee</u>:

for *in my wrath* <u>I smote thee,</u>
but *in my favour* have <u>I had mercy on thee.</u> (60:10)

Therefore *thy gates* <u>shall be open continually;</u>
*they* <u>shall not be shut day nor night;</u>

that *men* <u>may bring</u> unto thee the forces of the Gentiles,
and that *their kings* <u>may be brought.</u> (60:11)

For the *nation and kingdom* that will not serve thee <u>shall perish;</u>
yea, those *nations* <u>shall be utterly wasted.</u> (60:12)

The *glory of Lebanon* shall come unto thee,
the *fir tree,* the *pine tree,*
and the *box* together,

to *beautify* the place of <u>my sanctuary</u>;
and I will make the <u>place of my feet</u> *glorious.* (60:13)

The *sons also of them that afflicted thee* shall come <u>bending unto thee</u>;
and all *they that despised thee* shall <u>bow themselves down at the soles of thy feet</u>;

and they shall call thee, The *city* <u>of the Lord,</u>
The *Zion* <u>of the Holy One of Israel</u>. (60:14)

Whereas *thou* hast been <u>forsaken and hated,</u>
so that <u>no man went through</u> *thee,*

I will make thee an *eternal excellency,*
a *joy* of many generations. (60:15)

Thou shalt also *suck* the <u>milk of the Gentiles,</u>
and shalt *suck* the <u>breast of kings</u>:

and thou shalt know that I the *Lord* am thy *Saviour*
and thy *Redeemer,* the *mighty One of Jacob.* (60:16)

For *brass* I will <u>bring gold,</u>
and for *iron* I will <u>bring silver,</u>

and for *wood* <u>brass,</u>
and for *stones* <u>iron</u>:

I will also make thy *officers* <u>peace,</u>
and thine *exactors* <u>righteousness</u>. (60:17)

*Violence* shall no more be heard <u>in thy land,</u>
*wasting nor destruction* <u>within thy borders</u>;
but thou shalt call *thy walls* <u>Salvation,</u>
and *thy gates* <u>Praise</u>. (60:18)

The *sun* shall be <u>no more thy light</u> by day;
<u>neither for brightness</u> shall the *moon* give light unto thee:

but the *Lord* shall be unto thee an <u>everlasting light,</u>
and thy *God* thy <u>glory</u>. (60:19)

Thy *sun* shall <u>no more go down</u>;
<u>neither</u> shall thy *moon* <u>withdraw itself</u>:

for the Lord shall be thine everlasting light, and the days of thy mourning shall be ended. (60:20)

Thy people also shall be all righteous: they shall inherit the land for ever,

the *branch* of <u>my planting,</u>
the *work* of <u>my hands,</u> that I may be glorified. (60:21)

A *little one* shall become <u>a thousand,</u>
and a *small one* <u>a strong nation</u>:

I the Lord will hasten it in [my][3] time. (60:22)

---

[3] The JST changes the KJV from *his* to *my.*

## NOTES AND COMMENTARY

**60:1** *Arise/shine/glory.* Elder Orson Pratt said that this verse "has reference to the latter-day Zion. . . . There is no one thing more fully revealed in the Scriptures of eternal truth, than the rise of the Zion of our God in the latter days, clothed upon with the glory of God from the heavens—a Zion that will attract the attention of all the nations and kindreds of the whole earth."[4] Verses 1 through 3 of this chapter contain a remarkable chiasm, which is quite clear in the King James Version but even clearer in a translation provided by Nils W. Lund[5]:

A. Arise,

B. Shine,

C. For thy light is come,

D. And the glory

E. Of Yahweh

F. Upon thee is risen.

G. For behold, darkness shall cover the earth,

G. And gross darkness the people.

F. But upon thee will arise

E. Yahweh,

D. And his glory upon thee be seen,

C. And nations shall come to thy light,

B. And kings to the brightness

A. Of thy rising.

*thy light is come.* Israel had been groping in the darkness (59:10), but now the promised light is about to shine (58:8, 10). That light is Christ himself. It is also the true gospel restored to the earth by Jesus Christ.[6]

**60:2** *darkness shall cover the earth.* Because of wickedness, hard-heartedness, false traditions, and apostasy from the true gospel, most of humanity has lost the spiritual light sent from the Lord. The Lord indicated in 1837 that such darkness prevailed on the earth at that time (D&C 112:23). Joseph Smith said:

"Consider for a moment, brethren, the fulfillment of the words of the prophet; for we behold that darkness covers the earth, and gross darkness the minds of the

---

[4] *Journal of Discourses,* 16:78.

[5] *Chiasmus,* 44.

[6] McConkie, *Doctrinal New Testament Commentary,* 1:452–53; McConkie, *Millennial Messiah,* 107.

inhabitants thereof—that crimes of every description are increasing among men—vices of great enormity are practiced— . . . intemperance, immorality, extravagance, pride, blindness of heart, idolatry, the loss of natural affection; the love of this world, and indifference toward the things of eternity increasing among those who profess a belief in the religion of heaven, and infidelity spreading itself in consequence of the same—men giving themselves up to commit acts of the foulest kind, and deeds of the blackest dye, blaspheming, defrauding, blasting the reputation of neighbors, stealing, robbing, murdering; advocating error and opposing the truth, forsaking the covenant of heaven, and denying the faith of Jesus."[7]

*Lord shall arise upon thee.* Even though darkness covers the earth and its people, there is one place where light will dawn: the latter-day Zion, God's dwelling place, which radiates his glory, or his goodness and peace. The contrast there between the worldly and the godly is clear for all to behold.

**60:3** *Gentiles shall come to thy light.* In Isaiah 55:1 an invitation went out to "every one that thirsteth" to "come . . . buy, and eat." In response to that invitation, the Gentiles will come. Many translations read "all nations" rather than "Gentiles," further cementing the idea that "every one" is attracted by Zion's glory (2:2).

*kings to . . . thy rising.* Some scholars believe that this prophecy was fulfilled when the wise men traveled from the east to worship the baby Jesus (Matt. 2:1–2). That may have been one fulfillment of the prophecy, but the context tells us that a more complete fulfillment will come in the latter days. *Light* and *brightness* here may refer to the spiritual light the Lord's covenant people will spread to the nations (42:6; 49:6). *Rising* suggests the rising sun; symbolically it may refer to the rising up, or restoration, of the gospel or of Israel. It also refers to the coming of the Lord, described in the same terms in 60:1, 2.

**60:4** *Lift up thine eyes.* Lady Zion here is depicted as a woman who sees her long-departed children returning (49:18, 22; see 43:5–7).

*thy sons shall come from far, and thy daughters.* All the children of Zion are coming home, regardless of the distance they must travel or how physically difficult it may be. The children are those who gather to the restored gospel.

*nursed at thy side.* Those who gather to Zion will be supported or held firm, as a nurse would assist a patient or even carry someone in the arms or on the hip, as one would do with a child (49:22; 66:12). The implication is that those who gather will be lovingly cared for and strengthened by those in Zion.

---

[7] *Teachings of the Prophet Joseph Smith,* 47.

**60:5** *flow together.* Those of Zion will come in unity, as waters join in one when they flow together.

*thine heart shall fear, and be enlarged.* An alternate reading from other versions is helpful: "Your heart shall thrill" (RSV) and "swell with joy" (NIV; Jer. 33:9; Hosea 3:5).

*abundance of the sea.* This phrase indicates that the riches of the seafaring nations will be brought to Zion. Moreover, Jesus compared the kingdom of heaven to a net cast into the sea, which then drew forth many fishes (Matt. 13:47–48). In this symbolism, the sea is the earth, and the fishes are those brought into the Lord's kingdom, or the *abundance of the sea.*

*forces of the Gentiles.* The riches or wealth or power of the nations will come to strengthen Zion (60:11). A multitude of souls from the nations will come.

**60:6** *multitude of camels.* The many camels symbolize much wealth that will be brought to Zion.

*cover thee.* This phrase is rendered by the New International Version as "cover your land."

*bring gold and incense.* Scholars often interpret this expression as a prophecy of the visit of the wise men to the baby Jesus, which may be a partial fulfillment. But the overall context is the latter days. Not only will the Gentiles gather to Zion but they will also carry many riches with them. The gifts they take to the Lord at the temple of Zion—gold, incense, praises—are similar to the gifts the wise men took to the Lord as a baby (Matt. 2:11).

**60:6–7** *Midian/Ephah/Sheba/Kedar/Nebaioth.* The Old Testament tribe of *Midian* dwelt east of Moab. *Ephah* was also a tribe of Midian (Gen. 25:4). *Sheba* was part of Arabia. *Kedar,* a group of nomadic Bedouins, was a branch of Ishmael (Gen. 25:13). *Nebaioth* was another branch of Ishmael, also nomadic. More important than the specific identity of these nations is Isaiah's purpose for including them here. The prophecy seems to say that people of many nations would come to the New Jerusalem, bringing their riches with them. Even such former enemies as Midian would come (see 60:14).

**60:7** *flocks/rams . . . shall minister.* The wealth of these tribes will be used in sacrifice to Jehovah (23:18).

*they shall come up with acceptance on mine altar.* The Gentiles who have been converted to the Lord are offering acceptable sacrifices on their own behalf.

*house of my glory.* The riches of the nations will be used to beautify the temple in New Jerusalem.

**60:8** *fly as a cloud . . . doves.* Some have interpreted this phrase as describing the airplanes to be used in the gathering of Israel. In the April 1964 general conference, Elder John Longdon said, "Is the airplane flying in the skies from one country to another a sign? The heavens are filled with them, and people are fulfilling the prophecy of Isaiah 60:8."[8] Another interpretation may be that the people who "flock in" from over the sea[9] to Zion travel as easily as a cloud travels through the sky, and they are so sure of their destination that they are like doves returning to their cotes.

**60:9** *isles shall wait for me.* *Isles* refers at least partly to the land of America, as we learn from 2 Nephi 10:20: "The Lord has made the sea our path, and we are upon an isle of the sea." *Isles* also represent the uttermost parts of the earth—in this context, the people around the world. *Wait for me* indicates a desire to obey and to patiently do God's will. The verb used here, *qavah,* also means "to gather."

*ships of Tarshish.* These were the merchant ships, often used to carry metals (including precious metals), from the Phoenician port of Tartessus (see commentary on 2:16; 23:1). The symbolism is that the Lord will provide means to enable the covenant people—and their wealth—to gather to Zion.

*first.* Some translations render this word as "as at first" or "as in former days." As the Lord provided means for Israel to come to the promised land anciently, so will he help the people of his covenant to come to Zion at the last.

**60:10** *sons of strangers/their kings.* This phrase represents the Gentiles. Strangers destroyed Jerusalem, and the sons of strangers will rebuild it (Zech. 6:15). The nations made servants of Israel, but now their kings will minister unto Israel and their children (49:7, 23; 61:4). To this prophecy of Isaiah, Joseph Smith added one of his own, giving an application for his generation: "I now deliver it as a prophecy, if the inhabitants of this state, with the people of the surrounding country, will turn unto the Lord with all their hearts, ten years will not roll around before the kings and queens of the earth will come unto Zion, and pay their respects to the leaders of this people; they shall come with their millions, and shall contribute of their abundance for the relief of the poor, and the building up and beautifying of Zion."[10] Unfortunately, the people did not meet the required condition and thus the prophecy could not be fulfilled.

**60:11** *gates . . . open continually.* John the Revelator saw the same thing in his vision: "And the gates of it shall not be shut at all by day: for there shall be no night

---

[8] Conference Report, Apr. 1964, 116.

[9] See note *a* to 60:8 in the LDS edition of the KJV.

[10] *Teachings of the Prophet Joseph Smith,* 227.

there" (Rev. 21:25). The practice in Jerusalem was to shut the gates at night for security, but there will be neither night nor need for security in the New Jerusalem, and thus the gates need never be shut. Through the open gates will come kings and the wealth and power of the Gentiles.[11]

*forces of the Gentiles.* See commentary on 60:5.

**60:12** *nation . . . serve thee.* In the last days, nations will either be converted and enter the safety of Zion to serve the true and living God, or they will remain outside and be destroyed (Zech. 14:16–19).

**60:13** *glory of Lebanon/fir tree/pine tree/box.* The glory of Lebanon is its trees. In the days of Solomon they were used to build the temple (1 Kgs. 5:5–6, 18); in the last days, the best woods will again be used to help build and beautify the temple in New Jerusalem (35:1–2).

*the place of my feet.* This place is where the Lord stands, walks, and dwells—in other words, the temple (Ezek. 43:7).

**60:14** *come bending/bow themselves down.* Whereas historically Israel had been the slaves, the former victors will come on their knees to Israel's Zion (45:14–15; 49:23), attracted by its glory.

*The city of the Lord/Zion.* These are names for the New Jerusalem, reflecting its state of being and role as the center point of Zion. Ezekiel gives another name for the city: "The Lord is there" (Ezek. 48:35). Isaiah spoke of Zion more often than any other Old Testament writer (forty-five times).

**60:15** *forsaken and hated.* Ezekiel 16 elaborates on this depiction of Lady Israel as a forsaken and hated woman. She was cast off and left in the street to die, but Jehovah, passing by, saw her, ministered to her, and treated her as royalty. She proved unfaithful to him and so was taken into exile and again treated with shame and disgust. But in the latter days Jehovah will again rescue her and return her to her former glory, renewing his covenant with her.

*no man went through thee.* The city of Jerusalem became so hated that no commerce or travel took place there (34:10; Ezek. 14:15; 33:28; Zeph. 3:6). This expression also symbolizes the people of Israel, who were shunned for centuries.

*eternal excellency/joy of many generations.* Whereas the city of Jerusalem was seen formerly as low and disgusting, it has now been transformed, becoming the royal city of the Lord and his people. Such it shall be for all time (eternal), becoming a source of joy to people from generation to generation. Again, the condition of the

---

[11] See note *b* to Isaiah 60:11 in the LDS edition of the KJV.

city stands as a symbol for the people who inherit it; they also will be transformed and be a source of joy to the Lord.

**60:16** *milk of the Gentiles/breast of kings.* Here Israel is compared to a child, one whom Jehovah treats as royalty, nourishing her with the milk of kings (49:23). *Milk* suggests rich, nourishing food, the first an infant is given. *Breast* speaks of that which is intimate and maternal, sustenance from the mother herself. *Gentiles* and *kings* are those who once sacked Israel and took from her all her wealth and goods. Now they provide her with all her needs in a loving and tender way. The underlying meaning is that the Lord will tenderly care for his people.

*thou shalt know.* All will recognize the Savior of the world (49:23), but the people of Zion shall know him particularly.

**60:17** *brass/gold/iron/silver.* These terms represent the wealth of restored Jerusalem compared to that of the original city. The meaning is clearer if the lines are rearranged, which may have been the order in Isaiah's original:

> For stones I will bring iron,
> and for iron I will bring silver,
> and for wood brass,
> and for brass gold.

*make thy officers peace/thine exactors righteousness.* In the past, Israel had been ruled by external authority in the form of foreign overseers and cruel taskmasters (exactors). But under Jehovah's millennial reign, peace will govern and righteousness will rule. For Zion's inhabitants, worldly evil and oppression will be replaced by inward peace and purity (32:16).

**60:18** *thou shalt call thy walls Salvation, and thy gates Praise.* In ancient Israel, the walls and gates of Jerusalem had names. In the New Jerusalem the names of the walls and gates will indicate the reign of Jehovah (Rev. 21:12, 14). Zion will not need walls of stone for protection, for the Lord himself will save her (26:1), and all who enter through the gates will do so for the purpose of praising him (26:1–2). *Salvation* is God's gift to his people; *praise* is what they bring in return.

**60:19** *the Lord shall be unto thee an everlasting light.* Former sources of light will no longer be necessary; in the new Jerusalem light will come from Christ himself (60:1).

**60:20** *sun/moon.* In the millennial New Jerusalem the Lord's light will be so consistent it will be as though both sun and moon are ever-present (Rev. 21:23; 22:5).

*the days of thy mourning shall be ended.* In the Millennium, Israel will no longer mourn over the past trials and sorrows caused by her oppressors. The individuals of Zion will no more mourn over their own sins, for they will have truly repented and received the Lord's forgiving and redeeming love (57:18; 61:1–3). During the Millennium, all sorrow will pass away, because there will be no sickness, death, or sin.

**60:21** *all righteous/inherit the land for ever.* Because of Zion's righteousness, her people will receive a fulfillment of all God's promises (32:16; 57:13; 58:14), including their promised land (Gen. 17:8). The promise of land is symbolic of the fulfillment of the Abrahamic covenant.

*the branch of my planting/work of my hands.* In the Millennium, Israel will return to her former status as the Lord's chosen vineyard (5:1–7; 27:2–3; 61:3), for which he will rejoice (44:23). As branches of the vine that is Christ (John 15:5), we are not the source of our own life or strength, but are the work of the hands of God.

*that I may be glorified.* Our righteousness brings us glory, but it also increases the glory of the Lord. "For behold, this is my work and my glory," he declares, to bring us to immortality and eternal life (Moses 1:39).

**60:22** *little one shall become . . . a strong nation.* The *little one* is the gathered house of Israel, which started very small but will grow until it becomes very powerful in the strength of the Lord. This promise to Israel is an extension of the Lord's promise to Abraham, the father of the house of Israel, wherein a little one (Abraham) became a strong nation (Gen. 12:2; 18:18; see D&C 133:57–58).

# ISAIAH 61

*LIKENING ISAIAH 61 UNTO OURSELVES*

*This chapter enumerates blessings to those who receive Christ: He will bring good tidings, healing to the brokenhearted, liberty to those who are in bondage to sin, and comfort to those who mourn the pain of death and sin. We will receive temporal support and the priesthood. The blessings we receive will be so apparent that the whole world will acknowledge them. The Lord will cherish us and bind us to himself as a loving husband does his bride.*

## THE MISSION OF THE MESSIAH (61:1–3)

When Jesus taught in the synagogue in Nazareth, he quoted all of 61:1 and the first line of 61:2, indicating that he was the fulfillment of this prophecy (Luke 4:16–21). The remainder of 61:2 is millennial and does not apply to Christ's first coming.

Isaiah 61:1–3 provides a powerful, compact description of the Savior's mission, both during his mortal ministry and as long as the earth shall last: Isaiah prophesies that Jesus will have the Spirit of God; he will be anointed by God; he will preach good tidings; he will be sent to bless the brokenhearted, the captives, and those who mourn (61:1–2).

Those in Zion will receive special blessings from the Messiah: a crown of beauty will replace the ashes of mourning, gladness will replace sorrow, praise and rejoicing will replace depression. As Christ is the tree of life, so will his children be trees of righteousness, given life by the Lord, to his glory and to theirs (Alma 13:23).

*Isaiah 61:1–3*

> The *Spirit* of the <u>Lord God</u> is upon me;
> because the <u>Lord</u> hath *anointed* me

*to preach good tidings* unto the <u>meek</u>;
he hath sent me *to bind up* the <u>brokenhearted</u>,
*to proclaim liberty* to the <u>captives</u>,
and *the opening* of the prison to <u>them that are bound</u>; (61:1)

*To proclaim the acceptable year* <u>of the Lord</u>,
and the *day of vengeance of our God;*

*to comfort* <u>all that mourn</u>; (61:2)
*To appoint* unto <u>them that mourn</u> in Zion,

to give unto them *beauty* for <u>ashes</u>,
the *oil of joy* for <u>mourning</u>,
the *garment of praise* for the <u>spirit of heaviness</u>;

that they might be called *trees* <u>of righteousness</u>,
the *planting* <u>of the Lord</u>,

that he might be glorified. (61:3)

## NOTES AND COMMENTARY

**61:1** *anointed me.* The very words *Messiah* (Hebrew *Mashiyach*) and *Christ* (Greek *Christos*) mean "anointed one."

*good tidings.* On an immediate level, *good tidings* refers to deliverance from bondage. Israel, in her slavery and oppression, believed the Lord had forgotten her (40:27; 49:14), but the Lord's deliverance is assured (40:1–2; 51:17; 52:1). On a broader level, the good tidings are that we can be delivered from sin and death—the message of the gospel, the "good tidings" of Jesus Christ (D&C 76:40–42).

*bind up the brokenhearted.* The Lord will *bind up* all emotional and spiritual wounds, personally healing each soul. We, as his agents, can seek to minister in the same way.[1]

*proclaim liberty/captives/prison.* As a nation, Israel received her liberty through Cyrus (45:13). *Proclaim liberty* is an Old Testament expression referring to the practice of setting free the slaves in Israel's jubilee year (Lev. 25:10; Jer. 34:8–9) in anticipation of the mission of Christ, who liberates all who are in bondage to sin (49:9). This phrase likely also applies to the freedom Christ grants those in spirit prison (42:7; 1 Pet. 3:18–19; D&C 128:22).

**61:2** *acceptable year of the Lord.* The New International Version reads "the year of the Lord's favor."

*day of vengeance of our God.* This day is the second coming of Christ, when he will cleanse the earth and intervene for his people Israel against their enemies (34:8; 49:8; 63:4). This cleansing applies to Israel herself, to her enemies, and to everyone

---

[1] *Teachings of the Prophet Joseph Smith,* 40, 76.

who is bound spiritually. The cleansing will be accomplished quickly, as in a day, when the deliverance will be complete and the time of favor will begin. *The acceptable year of the Lord* subtly emphasizes his mission of saving grace. It is a long period in which the righteous enjoy the "favor" of the Lord (NIV). *Day of vengeance* reminds us that the Lord brings judgment as well as salvation. "The contrast between *year* and *day* is important: grace is God's constant attitude toward men; vengeance is an occasional judgment necessary to remove obstacles to his grace."[2]

*comfort all that mourn.* The word *mourning* appears three times in this passage; the mourning is for physical and spiritual captivity, as well as for the pain of sin and death. See commentary on 60:20; see also 40:1–2; 50:4; 57:18.

**61:3** *appoint unto them that mourn.* The word *appoint* here means to give the blessing promised to those who mourn.

*beauty for ashes.* As a sign of mourning in Old Testament times, one experiencing great sorrow sprinkled ashes on his head or sat in a pile of ashes (Job 2:12). Putting ashes on the head signified self-abasement and humiliation (2 Sam. 13:19; Esther 4:3; Jer. 6:26). This practice was generally combined with the wearing of sackcloth, an uncomfortable, coarse fabric made of the hair of camels and goats. Sackcloth was intended to be used for sacks and bags rather than for clothing, but mourners wore it to show sorrow and humility (Gen. 37:34; Esth. 4:1–3; Jer. 6:26). For the faithful, the Lord will replace the ashes of mourning with a "crown of beauty" (NIV), meaning he will crown them as joint heirs of God with Christ.

*oil of joy.* It was the Israelite custom to anoint oneself with oil in preparation for festivities and in times of happiness and prosperity (Eccl. 9:8; Ps. 45:8). In times of sorrow and mourning, anointing oil was not used (2 Sam. 14:2). The Lord will bless the faithful that their sorrows will be replaced with joy.

*garment of praise.* A garment of praise was worn for festivals and times of rejoicing (52:1), in contrast to the sackcloth worn in times of mourning (3:24). The Lord will give the faithful cause to rejoice with praise instead of feeling discouraged or depressed.

*spirit of heaviness.* A spirit of heaviness is characterized by discouragement, despair, and weakness of spirit.

*that they might be called trees of righteousness, the planting of the Lord.* Men of faithfulness and of prosperity are likened to healthy trees (Ps. 1:3; Jer. 17:7–8), just as the Perfect Man is likened to the tree of life. In addition, as Isaiah declares, Israel is the Lord's chosen vineyard (5:7; 27:6; 60:21; Gen. 49:22; Ps. 80:8–11). When we

---

[2] *Interpreter's Bible*, 5:710.

are planted by the Lord, we submit our will to his, relying on him for strength and blessing.

## BLESSINGS TO RESTORED ISRAEL (61:4–9)

When scattered Israel returns to the covenant, entering the Lord's Church, they will be given great blessings:

They will be given their former inheritance of lands, which they will rebuild (61:4).

People of other nations will serve them (61:5); the Gentiles will bring their wealth (61:6).

The Lord's people will be given the priesthood (61:6).

Israel will be more than compensated for the loss suffered in their earlier captivity (61:7).

The descendants of these righteous ones will be known around the world; and all those that see them will acknowledge that they have been blessed by God (61:9).

*Isaiah 61:4–9*

And *they shall build* the old wastes,
*they shall raise up* the former desolations,
and *they shall repair* the waste cities, the desolations of many generations. (61:4)

And *strangers* shall stand and feed your flocks,
and the *sons of the alien* shall be your plowmen and your vinedressers. (61:5)

But *ye shall be named* the Priests of the Lord:
*men shall call you* the Ministers of our God:

*ye shall eat* the riches of the Gentiles,
and in their glory *shall ye boast yourselves.* (61:6)

*For your shame* ye shall have double;
and *for confusion* they shall rejoice in their portion:

therefore in their land *they* shall possess the double:
everlasting joy shall be unto *them.* (61:7)

For *I the Lord* love judgment,
*I* hate robbery for burnt offering;

and *I* will direct their work in truth,
and *I* will make an everlasting covenant with them. (61:8)

And *their seed* shall be known among the Gentiles,
and *their offspring* among the people:

*all that see* them *shall acknowledge* them,
that they are the seed *which the Lord hath blessed.* (61:9)

Notes and Commentary

**61:4** *build the old wastes.* For many generations the land and cities of Palestine have been wasted. In the last days Israel will be blessed to repair, restore, and reinhabit these lands (58:12; 60:10). Rebuilding the ancient ruins can also symbolize the Savior's healing of old wounds caused by sin and sorrow.

**61:5** *strangers/sons of the alien.* Strangers is a metaphor for Gentiles. Those who formerly were their oppressors—even the kings—will now be Israel's servants and aides (60:10). This metaphor may also have spiritual application—the converted Gentiles may help feed the flocks that are the members of the Church.

**61:6** *Priests of the Lord/Ministers of our God.* This prophetic phrase indicates that in the Restoration, the priesthood will be given to many, not just to the Levites. With the priesthood, the Lord's people will minister the ordinances of the gospel to the world. As the Lord promised in Exodus, "If ye will obey my voice indeed, and keep my covenant, . . . ye shall be unto me a kingdom of priests, and an holy nation" (Ex. 19:5–6).

*eat the riches of the Gentiles/in their glory shall ye boast.* The priests of ancient Israel received on behalf of the Lord offerings from the people. In the same way, latter-day Zion will receive tribute (glory or wealth) for God from the nations (60:5–11).

**61:7** *shame . . . double/confusion . . . rejoice in their portion.* This passage is rendered in the New International Version as "instead of their shame my people will receive a double portion, and instead of disgrace they will rejoice in their inheritance." For generations the people of God have been shamed by bondage to sin or to foreign conquerors. But in the last days, God's people not only will have their lost blessings restored to them but their blessings will be doubled. In ancient Jewish law, the double portion was allotted to the firstborn, thus indicating that restored Israel is in a favored position (Deut. 21:17).

*everlasting joy.* The inheritance of the faithful is never to be taken away again. Instead, they will have eternal *joy* in Christ (35:10; 51:11; D&C 45:71; Moses 7:53; Rom. 5:11).

**61:8** *hate robbery for burnt offering.* Other translations read, "I hate robbery and iniquity" or "robbery and wrong," without a reference to offerings. But the translation here is a reminder of Malachi's scathing "Will a man rob God? . . . In tithes and offerings" (Mal. 3:8). Certainly God would be displeased if we were to offer that which we had gained by theft. But giving to the Lord only part of what he is due is another form of robbery. With burnt offerings in ancient times, the sacrifice was total, with nothing held back. The Lord requires full obedience to his laws; only complete commitment merits the desired blessings.

*I will direct their work in truth.* The Lord is the head of his church and the director of the covenant people. As a God of truth, he leads his people to proceed in the spirit of truth and obedience in all they do for him.

*everlasting covenant.* The Lord will make the righteous his covenant people (55:3; 59:21). The *everlasting covenant* is the gospel with all its requirements of man and its promises from God.

**61:9** *seed shall be known . . . the seed which the Lord hath blessed.* This passage is a renewal of the promise made to Abraham (Gen. 12:1–2). Furthermore, in the future all the world will recognize the Lord's hand in the spiritual and temporal prosperity of his covenant people (60:3, 14).

## A PSALM OF REJOICING (61:10–11)

These verses are a psalm of praise to God, sung about the pending marriage between Jehovah and his bride, the Church (Rev. 19:7–9). The Church rejoices because the Lord has given her salvation and righteousness. Isaiah uses two analogies to demonstrate the blessings of the Lord. First, he compares the blessings of salvation and righteousness to the ornaments and jewels of a bridegroom and bride (61:10). Second, he compares the blessings of righteousness and praise to the buds and seeds that spring forth, without fail, from the garden after it has been sown (61:11).

*Isaiah 61:10–11*

> *I will greatly rejoice* in the Lord,
> *my soul shall be joyful* in my God;
>
> for *he hath clothed me* with the garments of salvation,
> *he hath covered me* with the robe of righteousness,
>
> *as a bridegroom decketh himself* with ornaments,
> and *as a bride adorneth herself* with her jewels. (61:10)
>
> For *as the earth bringeth forth* her bud,
> and *as the garden causeth* the things that are sown in it *to spring forth;*
> so *the Lord God will cause* righteousness and praise *to spring forth* before all the nations. (61:11)

## NOTES AND COMMENTARY

**61:10** *I will greatly rejoice.* This psalm is sung by the Saints in Zion. It may also be a song of Israel: how she has been saved, cleansed, and prepared for the fulfilling of her covenant.

*garments of salvation/robe of righteousness.* These garments are not the same as those of 61:3, which was clothing worn in celebration, but instead suggest the garments and robes of the priesthood, as found in the temple. These earthly garments and robes, when one is purified, will be exchanged for eternal robes of glory. Jacob compared the robe of righteousness to "being clothed with purity" (2 Ne. 9:14; Ps. 132:16; Isa. 22:21).

*bridegroom . . . ornaments/bride . . . jewels.* We will be adorned with the Lord's blessings as a bridegroom and bride are adorned with ornaments on their wedding day.

**61:11** *bud . . . garden . . . spring forth.* This image is the reason for Zion's rejoicing: Like the promise of a bud in a garden, the prophecies concerning Israel's deliverance and glory will be fulfilled. Her righteousness and favor before the Lord will blossom and become as a garden full of pleasant plants and flowers (42:9; 45:8).

*before all the nations.* All nations will see the marvelous works of the Lord (40:5; 52:10).

# ISAIAH 62

*LIKENING ISAIAH 62 UNTO OURSELVES*

*When we truly come to Christ, joining ourselves to one another with one heart and one mind, we help to establish Zion. Many in the world will see and know the righteousness of the people Zion, who will be known as a holy people. We will feel the love and approval of God for us. We can help to bring that day by calling on the Lord continually and by seeking to do our part through obedience and sacrifice, drawing near to the Lord as a bride draws near to her husband.*

## BLESSINGS FOR ZION (62:1–12)

In the last days, Zion will be established in her glory (62:2). Her righteousness will be like a light to the world, which the Gentiles will see and approach (62:1–2). No longer will she be called forsaken or desolate (meaning divorced or widowed), but she will be known as a married woman (62:4). Zion will be cherished by the Lord as a bride is cherished by her bridegroom (62:5).

The Lord counsels those who call on him to give him no rest until Jerusalem is restored and glorified (62:6–7). He promises that Israel will come to reap the rewards of her labors and that he will bring that blessing by the power of his arm (62:8–9). The way will be prepared for Israel to be gathered, and her people shall be called "The holy people, The redeemed of the Lord" (62:10–12).

This chapter has two matching sets of six themes, repeated in sequence:

A1 The Lord will not hold his peace (62:1).

    B1 The watchmen will not hold their peace (62:6).

A2 Zion will shine brightly, attracting Gentiles and "all kings" (62:1–2).

    B2 Zion will be praised throughout the earth (62:7).

A3  Zion will be given a new name, the rightful reward for her righteousness (62:2).

> B3  The people of Zion will be given food and drink, the rightful fruits of their labors (62:8).

A4  The people of Zion will be a royal crown and diadem in the Lord's hand (62:3).

> B4  The people of Zion will be honored in the royal courts of God's holiness (62:9).

A5  Zion will no longer be forsaken or desolate (62:4).

> B5  Zion will not be forsaken (62:12).

A6  The Lord will rejoice over Zion as a bridegroom rejoices over a bride (62:5).

> B6  The Lord promises salvation and reward (62:11).[1]

## Isaiah 62:1–12

*For Zion's sake* <u>will I not hold</u> my peace,
and *for Jerusalem's sake* <u>I will not rest</u>,

until *the righteousness thereof* go forth <u>as brightness</u>,
and *the salvation thereof* <u>as a lamp that burneth</u>. (62:1)

And *the Gentiles* shall see <u>thy righteousness</u>,
and *all kings* <u>thy glory</u>:

and thou shalt be *called* by a <u>new name</u>,
which the *mouth* of the Lord shall <u>name</u>. (62:2)

Thou shalt also be *a crown of glory in the hand of the Lord*,
and *a royal diadem in the hand of thy God*. (62:3)

Thou shalt *no more be termed* <u>Forsaken</u>;
*neither* shall thy land *any more be termed* <u>Desolate</u>:

but thou shalt be called [*Delightful*], and <u>thy land</u> [*Union*]:[2]
for the Lord *delighteth* in thee, and <u>thy land</u> shall be *married*. (62:4)

For as a *young man* <u>marrieth a virgin</u>,
so shall *thy* [*God*][3] <u>marry thee</u>:

and as the *bridegroom* <u>rejoiceth over the bride</u>,
so shall *thy God* <u>rejoice over thee</u>. (62:5)

I have set *watchmen* upon thy walls,
O Jerusalem, which shall <u>never hold their peace</u> day nor night:

*ye that make mention of the Lord,* <u>keep not silence</u>, (62:6)

---

[1] Ludlow pointed out these matching sets of themes in *Isaiah*, 508–9.

[2] The JST changes the KJV, which reads *thou shalt be called Hephzi-bah, and thy land Beulah.* In Hebrew, *Hephzi-bah* means "delightful" and *Beulah* means "married wife."

[3] The JST changes the KJV *sons* to *God*.

And give him no rest, *till he establish,*
and *till he make Jerusalem* a praise in the earth. (62:7)

The Lord hath sworn *by his right hand,*
and *by the arm of his strength,*

Surely I will no more give thy *corn* to be meat for <u>thine enemies</u>;
and the <u>sons of the stranger</u> shall not drink thy *wine,* for the which thou hast
laboured: (62:8)

But *they that have gathered it* <u>shall eat it</u>, and praise the Lord;
and *they that have brought it* together <u>shall drink it</u> in the courts of my holiness.
(62:9)

*Go through, go through* the gates; <u>prepare ye the way</u> of the people;
*cast up, cast up* the highway; <u>gather out the stones</u>; lift up a standard for the
people. (62:10)

*Behold,* the Lord hath proclaimed unto the end of the world,
Say ye to the daughter of Zion,
*Behold,* thy <u>salvation</u> cometh;
*behold,* his <u>reward</u> is with him, and his work before him. (62:11)

And they shall call them, *The holy people,*
*The redeemed of the Lord:*

and thou shalt be called, *Sought out,*
*A city not forsaken.* (62:12)

## NOTES AND COMMENTARY

**62:1** *the righteousness thereof.* The word *righteousness* here may perhaps more
accurately be translated "vindication." The Lord will not rest until Zion is established
and the covenant people receive all their promised blessings.

*brightness/lamp.* In the last days, the people of the Lord will shine before the
world as the sun does when it rises in the morning, or as the burning light of a torch
in a dark place (58:8; 60:1). Truly, his people will shine as a light to all nations
(60:3).

**62:2** *the Gentiles shall see thy righteousness.* Once viewed with scorn, Israel in
her glory will inspire awe and esteem in the eyes of the nations (61:11).

*new name.* Abram's name was changed to Abraham, Jacob's to Israel, and Saul's
to Paul—all to signify a new character, a new devotion, a new condition, a new life.
So it will be with Israel. The new name given to Israel may be The Church of Jesus
Christ of Latter-day Saints.[4] The name also, as given in this passage, is both *Delight-*
*ful* and *Union,* both of which are names of Zion. These names stand in contrast to the
old names of *Forsaken* and *Desolate.*

---

[4] McConkie, *Millennial Messiah,* 131.

In addition, those who come unto Zion will receive other names: "I will write upon him the name of my God, and the name of the city of my God, which is new Jerusalem, . . . and I will write upon him my new name" (Rev. 3:12).

**62:3** *crown of glory/a royal diadem in the hand of thy God.* Zion and her people, as heirs of God, will add to God's glory by their great righteousness (Moses 1:39). A similar prophecy is found in latter-day scripture. Concerning the return of the lost tribes of Israel, the Lord said, "They [shall] fall down and be crowned with glory, even in Zion, by the hands of the servants of the Lord" (D&C 133:32; see D&C 60:4).

**62:4** *Forsaken/Desolate/Delightful/Union.* Because the image of this passage is that of marriage, these adjectives represent the contrast between Israel in her exiled state and as the covenant wife (which is latter-day Zion) of Jehovah. Before her deliverance and redemption, she was seen as forsaken, abandoned by her husband, and desolate—deserted, barren, and without hope. But all that will be forgotten in her glorious future (54:1, 6–8; 60:14–15). Then she will be known as *Hephzi-bah* ("My delight is in her," or "Delightful") and *Beulah* ("married wife" or "Union").

*thy land shall be married.* The earth was divided into continents in the days of Peleg (Gen. 10:25), and it will be brought back to its original state in the last days (in Hebrew, the name *Peleg* means "divided"). The marriage of the land is symbolic, first, of the union found in Zion; and second, of the reunion of the souls of the righteous with their God, through the atonement of Christ. This remarkable event is prophesied to occur in conjunction with the return of Israel's lost tribes from the north countries (D&C 133:23–34; 3 Ne. 21:23–26).

**62:5** *so shall thy God marry thee.* As the continents, once separated, are rejoined, so will the people of God be joined to their God. The scriptures make clear that Christ is the bridegroom and the Church is the bride (54:5–6; Matt. 25:1–13; D&C 133:10, 19).

**62:6** *watchmen upon thy walls . . . never hold their peace.* Those who watch and pray for a fulfillment of the Lord's promises (52:8) are to continue day and night, and, like the importunate widow (Luke 18:2–7), "weary" the Lord (their just judge) with their pleas for the establishment of latter-day Zion.

**62:8** *sworn by his right hand/arm of his strength.* The Lord uses his greatest strength and power, his right arm, to accomplish his purposes. To swear by the right hand is to covenant unequivocally to fulfill one's promises (40:10; 41:10; 52:10).

**62:8–9** *no more give thy corn . . . for thine enemies . . . they that have gathered it shall eat it.* This statement is a reversal of the cursing Israel was threatened with in

Deuteronomy: "Thou shalt betroth a wife, and another man shall lie with her: thou shalt build an house, and thou shalt not dwell therein: thou shalt plant a vineyard, and shalt not gather the grapes thereof. . . . The fruit of thy land, and all thy labours, shall a nation which thou knowest not eat up" (Deut. 28:30, 33). That cursing was renewed by later prophets (Amos 5:11; Micah 6:15), but the Lord promises to bless the righteous. In the day of her salvation, Israel will enjoy the fruits of her labors.

**62:9** *in the courts of my holiness.* This expression refers to the temple. The people of Israel had been commanded to eat the firstfruits of their fields not in their homes but at the Lord's sanctuary as a token of their thanksgiving, rejoicing, and recognition of his blessings to them (Deut. 12:17–18; 14:23; 16:9–17). After millennia of being unable to do so, they will enjoy that privilege again. Faithful Latter-day Saints enjoy a feast of spiritual food in the Lord's house.

**62:10** *go through the gates/cast up the highway/gather out the stones.* Here the Lord says: Leave the city, clear a path for a highway, remove the stones from the path. Let my people be unhindered as they come to Zion (35:8; 40:1–5; 57:14).

*lift up a standard.* Give the people a signal: now is the time for the exiles to return (5:26; 18:3; 49:22; Zech. 9:16). The standard, which is a flag or an ensign, is variously given in the scriptures as the "root of Jesse" (11:10), the Book of Mormon (2 Ne. 29:2–3), the great Zion of the last days (D&C 64:41–43), and The Church of Jesus Christ of Latter-day Saints (D&C 115:4–5).

**62:11** *the Lord hath proclaimed . . . thy salvation cometh.* By conquering Israel's enemies, the Lord has proclaimed her freedom to all the world (40:5; 52:10). This freedom from oppression as well as from death and sin is a form of salvation.

*his reward . . . his work.* The Lord's reward and his work (or recompense, as some translations put it, such as NAB, NEB, NIV, and NRSV) are his people, his righteous seed, who will come with him when he returns in glory. The Lord will bring the faithful the reward they deserve; the righteousness of the faithful is his work (40:10).

**62:12** *holy people.* The sanctified ones, specifically those worthy of attending the temple, are the *holy people* (61:6).

*redeemed of the Lord.* Those for whom the Lord has paid the debt of justice for their sins are the *redeemed of the Lord* (35:10; 51:11).

*Sought out.* Zion is populated by those whom the Lord has sought out and gathered to himself (Ezek. 34:11; John 1:43; 9:35).

*not forsaken.* See commentary on 62:4.

# ISAIAH 63:1–14

*LIKENING ISAIAH 63 UNTO OURSELVES*

*The Lord has suffered greatly for us, as is symbolized by the blood-red color of his garments when he returns. He will come in fury and in anger to punish the wicked. Will we be among that group? Or will we be among those who feel his mercy and lovingkindness? With Isaiah, we can plead with the Lord for his mercy, asking him to return to earth with his deliverance.*

## THE LORD'S VENGEANCE IN THE SECOND COMING (63:1–6)

The opening verses of Isaiah 63 give two important questions and answers about the second coming of Christ. The first question is, "Who comes with dyed garments, . . . traveling in the greatness of his strength?" The answer: "The Righteous One, who is mighty to save" (63:1; see Rev. 19:13, 15; 14:20; D&C 133:46–48). The second question is, "Why are your garments red, as one who has been treading in the winefat?" The answer: "Because I have trodden the winepress alone, and I will trample the wicked and stain my garments with their blood" (63:2–3).

The second coming of the Lord will be a "day of vengeance," but it will result in "the year of my redeemed" (63:4). Doctrine and Covenants 133:50–53 quotes Isaiah 63:3–9 with a few slight changes. Isaiah 63:1–9 and 64:1–5 are both quoted in Doctrine and Covenants 133 but in reverse order.

*Isaiah 63:1–6*

*Who* is this that cometh <u>from Edom</u>,
*with dyed garments* <u>from Bozrah</u>?
this that is *glorious* <u>in his apparel</u>,
travelling in the *greatness* <u>of his strength</u>?

I that speak in righteousness, mighty to save. (63:1)

Wherefore art thou *red* in <u>thine apparel,</u>
and <u>thy garments</u> like him that *treadeth in the* [*winevat*][1]? (63:2)

*I* have trodden the winepress <u>alone;</u>
and of the *people* there was <u>none with me</u>:

for I will *tread* them in <u>mine anger,</u>
and *trample* them in <u>my fury;</u>

and their blood shall be *sprinkled* upon <u>my garments,</u>
and I will *stain* all <u>my raiment.</u> (63:3)

For the *day* <u>of vengeance</u> is in mine heart,
and the *year* <u>of my redeemed</u> is come. (63:4)

And *I looked,* and <u>there was none</u> to help;
and *I wondered* that <u>there was none</u> to uphold:

therefore *mine own arm* <u>brought salvation unto me</u>;
and *my fury,* it <u>upheld me.</u> (63:5)

And I will *tread down the people* in <u>mine anger,</u>
and *make them drunk* in <u>my fury,</u>

and I will bring down their strength to the earth. (63:6)

## NOTES AND COMMENTARY

**63:1** *Edom/Bozrah.* In Hebrew, the consonants of *Edom* are the same as those in the word translated as *red;* the consonants of *Bozrah* may be interpreted as one who takes part in processing grapes into wine. (As a rule, Hebrew is written without vowels.) This parallel of red apparel and wine making is made even plainer in 63:2, in which we have the repetition of *red* and *winevat.*

*Edom* is called *Idumea,* which the Lord equates with "the world" (D&C 1:36). In this sense, the Lord is coming from the world, referring, perhaps, to his atonement, in which he took upon himself the sins of the world, though he himself was without sin. *Edom* was also a land in the ancient Near East, of which *Bozrah* was the capital; both may symbolize worldliness. The Lord "descended below all things" (D&C 88:6) in performing the Atonement—we might say he went to the center and chief part of the world's wickedness. Having done so, he will return in fury to punish the unrepentant in the last days.

*dyed garments.* The Lord's garments are dyed red or stained a crimson color.

**63:2** *red in thine apparel.* When Christ returns, his garments will be red, as John saw: "And he was clothed with a vesture dipped in blood" (Rev. 19:13; D&C 133:48). The red clothing symbolizes at least three things: the blood Christ shed in

---

[1] This replaces the archaic KJV *winefat.*

performing the Atonement (Luke 22:44; D&C 19:18); the blood (or sins) of the wicked that he took upon himself (blood and sins are equated in Jacob 1:19; see also 1 Pet. 3:18; Alma 33:22; 3 Ne. 11:11); and the blood of the unrepentant wicked he has slain in his wrath (63:3; Lam. 1:15; D&C 133:48, 50–51). The blood symbolism is repeated here in the use of the words *Edom, dyed garments, garments like him . . . in the winevat, winepress, blood . . . upon my garments,* and *stain all my raiment.*

*treadeth . . . winevat.* The Jerusalem Bible reads, "Yahweh is represented as one who treads the grapes, his garments stained red. But what he has been treading are the nations, whose blood has spattered him, and who are represented by Edom. Some emend 'Edom' and 'Bozrah' and translate 'Who is this that comes all in red, in crimson garments like a wine-harvester?'"

**63:3** *have trodden the winepress alone.* When Christ offered the Atonement in the Garden of Gethsemane, his agony was so great that "his sweat was as it were great drops of blood" (Luke 22:44), which presumably stained his garments. In addition, the blood of our sins—the signs of our wickedness—will stain his garments. This blood of atonement is symbolized by the image of a man who treads red grapes in a winepress, staining his clothing with the juice. But, with Christ, not only his hem but his whole garment will be stained. His whole being was engaged in the work of atonement. He trod the winepress alone because he alone could and did perform the Atonement, kneeling alone in the Garden of Gethsemane, hanging alone on the cross. "I . . . have trodden the winepress alone, even the winepress of the fierceness of the wrath of Almighty God" (D&C 76:107; 88:106).

*will tread them in mine anger/trample them in my fury.* Christ has trodden the winepress in offering the Atonement in the Garden of Gethsemane; but he will yet tread the nations in vengeance, even as in the winepress one treads on the grapes to force out the juice. Both acts stain his garments with blood (34:6; Joel 3:13; Lam. 1:15).

**63:4** *day of vengeance/year of my redeemed.* The Lord is a God of both justice and mercy. Yet it appears that his blessings will continue far longer (*year*) than his punishments (*day*), at least in relation to this temporal earth (see commentary on 61:2). The "year of my redeemed" may refer to the jubilee year, when Israelite slaves were freed (Lev. 25:39–40; Ex. 21:2; Deut. 15:12). When the Lord comes, we will be freed from all the bonds of our enemies and oppressors.

**63:5** *there was none to help/mine own arm.* Jehovah is the only one who can bring about the redemption of Israel. His *arm* brings vengeance to the wicked, salvation to the righteous. This verse closely parallels 59:16.

**63:6** *make them drunk in my fury.* He will cause them to drink the cup of his wrath (51:17), just as he himself earlier had to drink the bitter cup of atonement (3 Ne. 11:11; D&C 19:18).

*bring down their strength.* Other translations read, "poured their lifeblood on the ground." The day of vengeance is finished.

## PSALM OF MERCY (63:7–14)

This passage is a beautiful psalm of the Lord's loving-kindness, great goodness, and mercy to the repentant (63:7). Isaiah notes that the Lord claims faithful Israel as his people and his children. He was not only a father but a Savior (63:8). He bore their afflictions; he redeemed them "in his love and in his pity"; he carried them in their time of need (63:9). "But they rebelled," making God their enemy, "and he fought against them" (63:10). Then they remembered his goodness to the people in the time of Moses. He had led them (an idea repeated three times in 63:11–13) and blessed them with his Spirit (63:14), and, by implication, so will he do again.

*Isaiah 63:7–14*

> I will mention the *lovingkindnesses* of the Lord,
> and the *praises* of the Lord,
>
> according to *all that the Lord hath bestowed* on us,
> and the *great goodness* toward the house of Israel,
>
> which he hath bestowed on them *according to* his mercies,
> and *according to* the multitude of his lovingkindnesses. (63:7)
>
> For he said, Surely *they are my people,*
> children that will not lie:
> so *he was their Saviour.* (63:8)
>
> *In all their affliction* he was afflicted, and the angel of his presence saved them:
> *in his love and in his pity* he redeemed them;
>
> and he *bare* them,
> and *carried* them all the days of old. (63:9)
>
> But they *rebelled,*
> and *vexed his holy Spirit:*
>
> therefore *he was turned* to be their enemy,
> and *he fought* against them. (63:10)
>
> Then he remembered the days of old, Moses, and his people, saying,
>
> *Where is he* that brought them up out of the sea with the shepherd of his flock?
> *where is he* that put his holy Spirit within him? (63:11)

That *led them* by the right hand of Moses with his glorious arm, dividing the water
before them, to make himself an <u>everlasting name</u>? (63:12)
That *led them* through the deep, as an horse in the wilderness, that they should not
stumble? (63:13)

As a beast goeth down into the valley, the Spirit of the Lord caused him to rest:
so didst thou *lead thy people,* to make thyself a <u>glorious name</u>. (63:14)

## NOTES AND COMMENTARY

**63:7** *lovingkindnesses of the Lord/praises/great goodness/mercies.* These words
refer particularly to Jehovah's goodness and kindness in delivering the children of
Israel from their Egyptian bondage (Ps. 89; 22:3–5; 44:1–7; Neh. 9:6–15). That
bondage—and the Lord's deliverance—are types of our spiritual bondage and our
deliverance through his loving-kindness, goodness, and mercy. Joseph Smith added
his testimony to Isaiah's by saying, "Our heavenly Father is more liberal in His
views, and boundless in His mercies and blessings, than we are ready to believe or
receive."[2]

**63:8** *Surely they are my people.* The Lord's people are not simply those
descended from Abraham but those who have broken hearts and contrite spirits
(2 Ne. 2:7).

*children that will not lie.* The Lord testifies that his true *children* will not deal
falsely with him. In other words, they will keep their covenants.

*he was their Saviour.* As people become the sons and daughters of Christ, he
becomes their Savior (Mosiah 5:7–8).

**63:9** *the angel of his presence saved them.* The Lord himself saved Israel (Ex.
33:12–15; Deut. 4:37); he is *the angel of his presence.* Moses proclaimed the same
blessing in Exodus 33:12–17 (see also D&C 133:52–53).

*in his love and in his pity he redeemed them.* Christ redeems us from the demands of justice, setting us free from the bonds of sin and death. He is motivated by
*love* for his Father and for us (John 15:9–10, 12–14; D&C 34:3).

*bare them/carried them.* God is always there to tenderly care for his people, as he
did in leading Israel forth from bondage in Egypt and caring for them in the desert
(Deut. 32:11; Isa. 46:3–4; Acts 13:17–18). Descriptions of bearing and carrying
another usually refer to a mother and her child. The Lord would have us see that he
cares for us as a mother cares for her newborn child.

*all the days of old.* This phrase means the time of Israel's exodus from Egypt and
her wanderings in the wilderness (63:11).

---

[2] *Teachings of the Prophet Joseph Smith,* 257.

**63:10** *But they rebelled.* Despite his love and mercy, Israel rebelled against her God (Deut. 32:15; Ps. 78:8; Neh. 9:16–18). Her people thus became enemies of God, as are all natural men and women (Mosiah 3:19).

*vexed his holy Spirit.* The Lord's people offended or grieved the Spirit (Eph. 4:30; D&C 121:37). When we make choices that turn us from the Spirit of God, that Spirit must leave us, and we, at the same time, become estranged from our Father and our God.

*their enemy/he fought against them.* The Lord punishes his people solely to motivate them to turn to him (Deut. 32:20–25; Judg. 2:14–15).

**63:11** *he remembered.* According to footnote *a* to 63:11 in the LDS edition of the Bible and the opinions of other scholars, this statement means "his people remembered." Specifically, they remembered the Lord's blessings to Moses and the people of old. The purpose of the Lord's chastisement of the people Israel, as always, is to cause them to turn back to him. When they do, he blesses and delivers them (Judg. 2:16; see Job 36:10–12).

*Where is he . . . ?* After remembering how Jehovah saved the people during the Exodus, the people now long for his saving presence in their lives, for his guidance, for his loving comfort and tenderness (Jer. 2:6).

*out of the sea.* The Lord delivered Israel by miraculous means, taking them through the Red Sea. He does the same with us, bringing us safely past seemingly impassable obstacles in our lives.

*shepherd of his flock.* Moses was the shepherd the Lord used to bring his flock (the Israelites) through the Red Sea to safety (Ps. 77:19–20; Micah 6:4). Ultimately, of course, the good shepherd for us all is Christ (John 10:14).

*put his holy Spirit within him.* The *him* used here seems to refer to Moses, the shepherd, rather than to Israel, the flock. Moses was blessed with the Spirit (Num. 11:17, 25).

**63:12** *right hand of Moses/his glorious arm.* "Moses stretched out his hand over the sea; and the Lord caused the sea to go back by a strong east wind all that night, and made the sea dry land, and the waters were divided" (Ex. 14:21). As we learn from Exodus, Moses used the priesthood to divide the waters of the Red Sea. The waters divided not by Moses' power but by the power of God, symbolized in the expression *his glorious arm.*

*everlasting name.* The Lord forever established his reputation as a God of supreme power when he led the children of Israel out of Egypt.

**63:13** *led them through the deep.* The Lord took Israel safely through the waters of the Red Sea.

*horse in the wilderness.* A horse in the wilderness is sure and steady of foot. In the same way, the Lord helped Israel to flee Egypt into the wilderness with steadiness, without faltering. Likewise he will help us flee our captivity to sin (Prov. 21:31).

**63:14** *beast . . . into the valley.* The valley represents a place where beasts find water and grass, the sustenance they need. In the same way, the Lord makes all his children to "lie down in green pastures" (Ps. 23:2).

*Spirit of the Lord caused him to rest.* The Lord gave ancient Israel rest from bondage, rest from care, peace of heart, and peace of conscience, which are gifts of the Spirit. So will he also do for all his children, in any age.

*make thyself a glorious name.* This statement is spoken in the same sense as the phrase "make himself an everlasting name" in 63:12. Through the Lord's mercy, goodness, and power, he has established his reputation as a God of such qualities forever.

# ISAIAH 63:15–19; 64

*LIKENING ISAIAH 63:15–19; 64 UNTO OURSELVES*

*In this chapter Isaiah offers a prayer to the Lord, pleading for him to return in his glory. Do we join him in such a prayer? Or do we hope that he will delay his coming, so that we might have longer to repent? Isaiah acknowledges our weakness and sinfulness, but he also knows—as we should—that if we will submit ourselves to him in all things, we can trust in his mercy. And, in the end, the Lord will bring with him blessings that exceed our greatest imaginings.*

## ISAIAH'S INTERCESSORY PRAYER (63:15–19; 64:1–12)

Isaiah pleads in behalf of his people, asking the Lord to look down from heaven in mercy (63:15). The Lord is their Father and Redeemer (63:16). The enemies of Israel have defiled the Lord's temple, and they do not acknowledge Jehovah as God. But Israel has been called by his name (63:18–19).

Come down in power and glory, Isaiah pleads. Let the Second Coming bring salvation to Israel (64:1–3). Bring the blessings promised, even those greater than ear has heard or eye seen (64:4). We know that thou dost rejoice over the righteous, bringing them salvation (64:5). We are unclean and unworthy (64:6)—we have forgotten our God and know we have angered thee (64:7). But we submit ourselves to thy hands as clay (64:8). "Thou art our father" (63:16; 64:8). Turn from thine anger for our sakes (64:9). Jerusalem has been laid waste (64:10). The temple has been destroyed (64:11). O Lord, avenge us and thyself of these wrongs (64:12).

The entire passage is a prayer, offered powerfully in poetry. Isaiah directly addresses the Lord eight times here ("O Lord," "O God," "thou art our father"). It is a prayer not only from those of old but from the hearts of God's covenant people in our time as well.

Doctrine and Covenants 133:40–45 quotes Isaiah 64:1–4 with changes and additions.

## Isaiah 63:15–19; 64:1–12

*Look down* from heaven,
and *behold* from the habitation of thy holiness and of thy glory:

where is *thy zeal* and *thy strength,*
the sounding of *thy bowels* and of *thy mercies* toward me?

are they restrained? (63:15)

Doubtless thou *art our father,* though Abraham be ignorant of us,
and Israel acknowledge us not: thou, O Lord, *art our father,* our redeemer;

thy name is from everlasting. (63:16)

O Lord, why hast thou *[suffered] us to err* from thy ways,
and *[to harden]*[1] *our heart* from thy fear?
Return for thy servants' sake, the tribes of thine inheritance. (63:17)

The people of thy holiness have possessed it but a little while: our adversaries have trodden down thy sanctuary. (63:18)
We are thine: thou never barest rule over them; they were not called by thy name. (63:19)

Oh *that thou wouldest* rend the heavens,
*that thou wouldest* come down,

that the mountains might flow down at thy presence, (64:1)

As when the *melting fire* burneth,
the *fire* causeth the waters to boil,

to make *thy name* known to thine adversaries,
that the nations may tremble at *thy presence!* (64:2)

When thou didst terrible things which we looked not for, thou camest down, the mountains flowed down at thy presence. (64:3)

For since the beginning of the world men have not heard,
*nor perceived* by the ear,
*neither hath* the eye seen,

O God, beside thee, what he hath prepared for him that waiteth for him. (64:4)

Thou *meetest him* that . . . worketh righteousness,
[and *rejoiceth him*] that remember[eth] thee in thy ways:

---

[1] The JST changes the KJV *made* to *suffered* and *and hardened our heart* to *to harden.* These changes place the responsibility for error where it belongs, on the people, who have the agency to choose good or evil.

[in righteousness there] is continuance, and [such] shall be saved.[2] (64:5)

But [we have sinned];[3] *we are all* as an <u>unclean thing</u>,
and *all our righteousnesses* are as <u>filthy rags</u>;

and *we all* do fade <u>as a leaf</u>;
and *our iniquities,* <u>like the wind</u>, have taken us away. (64:6)

And *there is none* that <u>calleth upon thy name</u>,
that *stirreth up himself* to <u>take hold of thee</u>:

for *thou hast hid thy face* <u>from us</u>,
and *hast consumed* <u>us</u>, because of our iniquities. (64:7)

But now, O Lord, *thou art our father;* <u>we are the clay</u>,
and *thou* our potter; and <u>we all are the work of thy hand</u>. (64:8)

*Be not wroth* very sore, O Lord,
*neither remember* iniquity for ever:

behold, see, we beseech thee, we are all thy people. (64:9)

Thy *holy cities* are a <u>wilderness</u>,
*Zion* is a <u>wilderness</u>,
*Jerusalem* a <u>desolation</u>. (64:10)

Our *holy and our beautiful house,* where our fathers praised thee, is <u>burned up
with fire</u>:
and *all our pleasant things* are <u>laid waste</u>. (64:11)

*Wilt thou* <u>refrain thyself</u> for these things, O Lord?
*wilt thou* <u>hold thy peace</u>, and afflict us very sore? (64:12)

## NOTES AND COMMENTARY

**63:15** *Look/behold.* Isaiah is asking the Lord to note the plight of his people. This could also be a prayer offered by the covenant people themselves.

*heaven/habitation of thy holiness and of thy glory.* The earthly temple is God's dwelling place on earth; the heavenly temple is his habitation in heaven (Rev. 7:15; 16:17).

*where is thy zeal and thy strength.* These phrases may be interpreted as meaning passion and power. Isaiah is asking the Lord if he has lost interest in his people—are his desires for them restrained or held back?

*sounding of thy bowels and of thy mercies.* "Your tenderness, the yearning of your heart, and compassion are withheld from us" (NIV, RSV). *To sound* can mean to measure the depth of, to probe, explore or examine; it can also mean to signal or proclaim, to make known. In Near Eastern thought, the *bowels* and the womb are the seat

---

[2] The changes in this verse are from the JST.
[3] This addition is in the JST.

of compassion, of tenderness and mercy (3 Ne. 17:6). God had in his displeasure hidden himself from his people. Isaiah here pleads for God's love and intervention.

**63:16** *thou art our father.* Abraham and Jacob were Israel's earthly ancestors, but they are long since dead and unable to help. Jehovah is their eternal Father, whose help will never fail.[4]

*redeemer.* The Lord pays the price to ransom us from sin and death. The term *redeemer* is used eighteen times in the Bible, thirteen of those in Isaiah (for example, 41:14; 43:14; 48:17; 54:8).

*thy name is from everlasting.* The Lord is God from all eternity to all eternity (63:12; Mosiah 3:5).

**63:17** *suffered us to err from thy ways, and to harden our heart.* Isaiah asks why the Lord allowed his people to sin (6:9–10).

*Return . . . the tribes of thine inheritance.* Because of their sins, the seed of Abraham (the twelve tribes of Israel) have been separated from their promised blessings. Isaiah asks the Lord to help them to return to their promised inheritance.

*for thy servants' sake.* This phrase means "for the sake of those who are faithful." Even though many of the covenant people have turned to sin, Isaiah asks that the Lord remember his promises to them because of the worthiness of a few. This is the same argument Abraham made when the Lord informed him of the pending destruction of Sodom and Gomorrah (Gen. 18:23–24, 26).

**63:18** *The people of thy holiness.* The people to whom the temple belongs are the *people of [God's] holiness.*

*trodden down thy sanctuary.* This phrase refers to the destruction of the temple in Jerusalem in 587 B.C.

**63:19** *We are thine.* Israel remembers that Jehovah is her God, her king, her Savior, and she desires a renewal of the covenant made in former times (Deut. 7:6). This statement also reminds us of Paul's expression that we belong to God, having been bought with a price (1 Cor. 6:19–20).

*thou never barest rule over them/not called by thy name.* Isaiah here sets up a difference between the chosen, covenant people, and their adversaries. The true people of God have been known to him by covenant; they have subjected themselves to him. Others have refused to humble themselves and receive the Lord as their God

---

[4] For an excellent and definitive discussion on the ways in which Jehovah, or Christ, can be called *Father,* see the doctrinal exposition by the First Presidency and the Quorum of the Twelve entitled "The Father and the Son," in Talmage, *Articles of Faith,* 465–73.

and their king. Through covenant and submissiveness, a people can become the Lord's people—"we are thine"—and, in turn, lay claim to his blessings.

**64:1** *rend the heavens/mountains . . . flow down at thy presence.* To rend the heavens is to tear open the veil, so that God can be seen. Additionally, trembling, moving, and melting of mountains are manifestations of the presence of God (Ex. 19:18; Ps. 18:6–8; D&C 133:40–41). Isaiah asks the Lord to come to the deliverance of his people, tearing open the veil and bringing the fervent heat of his glory, which will literally melt the mountains. These are images directly related to the Lord's second coming. This expression may have another meaning: The Lord has power over heaven and earth, and he has power over all other gods. In his coming, Jesus will throw down the mountains, which here may represent the temples of false gods.

**64:2** *melting fire.* This is a fire so hot that it will melt the very elements of the earth, causing the mountains to flow down and the oceans to boil. Speaking in our dispensation, the Lord said: "Every corruptible thing, . . . that dwells upon all the face of the earth, shall be consumed; and also that of element shall melt with fervent heat" (D&C 101:24–25).

*make thy name known to thine adversaries.* The Lord's friends know him by covenant, by obedience, and by the still small voice of the Spirit. But the Lord's adversaries, who refuse these blessings, shall know him only by the power of his judgments. Isaiah asks the Lord to come with his burning fire so that all nations will know him and tremble at his presence.

**64:3** *terrible things which we looked not for.* These are things of wonder and amazement, things beyond expectation, things fearful to God's enemies, such as those seen preceding the Exodus (Deut. 10:21; 2 Sam. 7:23; Ps. 106:22).

*thou camest down, the mountains flowed down.* These phrases reinforce the cause-and-effect relationship between the Lord's coming and the burning of the earth (64:1).

**64:4** *men have not heard.* The blessings the Lord will bring with him—including those of the millennial reign and celestial glory—are beyond the comprehension and imagination of man. There is no other who can save and bless as can Jehovah. His power and love can bring grace and mercy greater than we can even imagine (45:22; 43:11–12). As Paul wrote, "As it is written, Eye hath not seen, nor ear heard, neither have entered into the heart of man, the things which God hath prepared for them that love him" (1 Cor. 2:9).

*what he hath prepared.* The Lord's blessings are already in place for the righteous, though we must endure to the end to receive many of them.

*waiteth for him.* Those who wait faithfully for the coming of the Lord.

**64:5** *Thou meetest him that . . . worketh righteousness. Meetest* (Hebrew *paga'*) means "reaches out to" or "makes intercession for." The Lord will reach out to the righteous, making intercession for them. The New International Version gives this statement as "you come to the help of those who gladly do right."

*rejoiceth him that remembereth thee in thy ways.* The Lord blesses not only those who remember his ways (meaning, his commandments, the path he would have us walk) but also those who remember *him.* That, of course, is part of the covenant made by all members of the Church: "that they do always remember him" (D&C 20:79). As we remember the Lord, he will bring us to a state of rejoicing.

*in righteousness there is continuance. Continuance* (Hebrew *'olam*) means eternity, always, everlasting, perpetual, worlds without end. The righteous will be blessed with everlasting life, with blessed life for all eternity.

*such shall be saved.* Those who meet the requirements—work righteousness, remember the Lord, and remember his ways—will be saved, gaining exaltation in the celestial kingdom. When we combine 64:5 with 63:19, which implies that the chosen people have been "called by thy name," we have all three elements of the sacramental covenant: "they are willing to take upon them the name of thy Son, and always remember him and keep his commandments." Those who keep their covenants will "always have his Spirit to be with them" (D&C 20:77), which brings such blessings as those mentioned in this passage: the Lord reaches out to them, intercedes for them; he brings them the gift of joy and promises eternal life and blessings greater than man ever has or ever could imagine.

**64:6** *unclean thing/righteousnesses are as filthy rags.* Under the Mosaic law the term *unclean* often applied to those with a bodily discharge (whether male or female) or with leprosy. Commanded to live outside the bounds of normal society, such people symbolized those whose sins made them spiritually unclean and unfit to live with God and his holy ones. Filthy rags were those stained with menstrual blood, a reminder of our mortal, fallen state. The implication here is that even though we perform righteous acts, we are still fallen, imperfect, and unclean before the Lord. Because of our fallen nature, our righteousness is insufficient to save us. Only when our righteousness is combined with the righteousness of Christ can we receive exaltation (2 Ne. 15:23).

*fade as a leaf, iniquities, like the wind, have taken us away.* Sin saps our moral strength and leads us to spiritual death (see Ezek. 18:24; 33:12). Our desire for righteousness fades, and we are swept away as the wind blows the dried autumn leaves (17:13; 29:5; Ps. 1:4).

**64:7** *none that calleth upon thy name.* No one is praying to the Lord. By implication, no one is trusting or relying on the Lord and his mercy.

*stirreth up himself.* No one makes the effort to become worthy of the Lord's name or blessings. To stir ourselves up is to exercise our agency, to act—in this case, to come unto Christ.

*take hold of thee.* To *take hold of* is to grab onto, to cling to, to rely on for one's support. Israel has failed to take hold of the Lord and thus is left alone.

*hid thy face.* The people's sins have so clouded their spirits that they no longer recognize God's presence in their lives. They have completely turned away from him, but in their minds he has turned away from them and left them to their iniquitous lives (Rom. 6:16).

*hast consumed us, because of our iniquities.* The Hebrew reads, "melted us by the hand of our iniquities."

**64:8** *thou art our father.* This plaintive appeal is to a God who is also a Father, one who knows and loves his children. To paraphrase, "Even though we have sinned and fallen short of our potential as thy children, we know that thou art our father and we desire to repent and be worthy of thee" (63:8, 16).

*we are the clay/potter.* The people are acknowledging their true relationship to their creator; as clay, they are nothing without the creator, having no shape and no power to mold themselves. They are in all things subject to the potter. See also commentary on 45:9.

**64:9** *behold, see, we beseech thee.* Israel asks the Lord to notice that she is once again calling upon him.

*we are all thy people.* Israel, both anciently and in the present, represents the Lord's people by ownership and by covenant.

**64:9–10** *thy people/Thy holy cities.* The people plead with the Lord, arguing that he is being asked to save his own: his people who are enslaved, his land that is besieged, his city that lies wasted, his temple that has been defiled.

**64:10** *holy cities/wilderness/desolation.* The city of Jerusalem, which is the holy city, and all other *cities* of the land have been laid waste by Israel's enemies. They are empty of the Lord's people, and the Lord's promises do not seem to be fulfilled. When we sin and turn from God, our lives become a wilderness, and that which once was holy for us becomes common.

*Zion.* *Zion* can be a synonym for Jerusalem or for the state of true unity between the Saints and God. When we turn from God, we lose our claim on his promises of Zion.

**64:11** *Our holy . . . house . . . burned up.* This expression refers to the destruction of the temple in Jerusalem in 587 B.C. The loss of the temple meant the loss of Israel's ability to practice her religion. It meant the loss or postponement of the covenant and its promises.

*where our fathers praised thee.* The ancestors of Israel in Isaiah's time praised the Lord in their temple, until it was destroyed by enemies.

*all our pleasant things are laid waste.* One translation is "All that we treasured lies in ruins" (NIV), perhaps referring to the sacred vessels and other accoutrements of the temple, or possibly the temple itself. Other translations read, "All our pleasant places have become ruins" (RSV); and "All the things of beauty are destroyed" (LB).

**64:12** *Wilt thou refrain thyself for these things?* Isaiah asks the Lord whether after all the destruction and trouble our enemies have brought on us, he will hold back in avenging our loss and in restoring us.

*hold thy peace, and afflict us.* "You hold yourself back? Will you keep silent and punish us beyond measure?" (NIV). Now that the people acknowledge their unworthiness before him and seek his face, now that they and their land are in the direst of circumstances, will he still withhold his help and allow them to suffer more? Or will he reveal himself and come to their aid? According to the *Interpreter's Bible,* "This is an argument from man at his tenderest to the most loving God. It is the plea of heartbroken sinners to . . . a heartbroken God. Calvin, who shared their feeling of the inward filthiness, the total ruination, and the iron slavery of sin, [offers the] prayer: 'Lord, let the bottomless depth of thy mercy swallow up the bottomless depth of my sin.'"[5]

---

[5] *Interpreter's Bible,* 5:744.

# ISAIAH 65

*LIKENING ISAIAH 65 UNTO OURSELVES*

*The Lord promises that if we seek him we will find him, and if we ask of him we will receive. He also testifies that we will not find him if we do not seek. Unfortunately, as this chapter shows, the measure of iniquity in the world is full. The people willfully choose false forms of worship and provoke the Lord to anger. The Lord sends his servant to a nation that does not know him, as he sends many of us as missionaries to people who do not know us or the Lord.*

*Though the wicked may continue in their sin for a time, eventually the Lord will bring them to judgment. Then the righteous will be blessed in every way, and those who reject the Lord will be cursed. Which group will we belong to—those who accept the covenant in obedience, or those who go their own way? The culmination of the Lord's blessings will come in the Millennium, which day many of us might see.*

## THE INIQUITY OF ISRAEL (65:1–7)

Isaiah 65–66 seems to answer the plea in the prayer found in the previous passage. Isaiah has acknowledged Israel's unworthiness but nevertheless asks the Lord to come in his glory to deliver her (63:15–19; 64:1–12). In response to Isaiah's prayer, the Lord says that his people were rejected because they rejected him (65:1–7, 11–12; 66:4). But the repentant will be forgiven (65:8–10, 13–16; 66:1–2, 7–14), and the righteous will triumph at the Second Coming (66:14–21) and during the Millennium (65:17–25; 66:22–24).

The Lord says that those who seek him righteously will find him (65:1), and he has reached out in great long-suffering to us (65:2). But the covenant people have continually sought after evil, worshiping idols and choosing the way of wickedness instead of the way of God (65:2–5). The Lord will punish all such; they will receive according to their works (65:6–7).

Paul quoted Isaiah 65:1–2 in Romans 10:20–21: "But Esaias is very bold, and saith, I was found of them that sought me not; I was made manifest unto them that asked not after me. But to Israel [God] saith, All day long I have stretched forth my hands unto a disobedient and gainsaying people."

## Isaiah 65:1–7

[*I am found of them* who seek after me,
*I give unto all them* that ask of me;]

*I am [not] found* of them that sought me not,
[or that inquireth not after me.]

I said [unto my servant],
*Behold* me,
[*look upon* me;

*I will send you] unto* a nation that [is] not called [after] my name, [for][1] (65:1)
*I have spread out my hands all the day [to]* a . . . people [who] walketh [not] in [my ways],

[and *their works* are evil and] not good,
[and *they walk*] after their own thoughts;[2] (65:2)

A people that provoketh me to anger continually to my face;

that *sacrificeth* in gardens,
and *burneth incense* upon altars of brick; (65:3)

*Which remain* among the graves,
and *lodge* in the monuments,

which *eat* swine's flesh, and broth of abominable [beasts,
and *pollute*][3] their vessels; (65:4)

Which say, *Stand* by thyself,
*come* not near to me; for I am holier than thou.

These are a *smoke* in my nose,
a *fire that burneth* all the day. (65:5)

Behold, it is written before me: I will not keep silence, but will *recompense,*
even *recompense* into their bosom, (65:6)

*Your* iniquities, and the iniquities *of your fathers* together, saith the Lord,

which have *burned incense* upon the mountains,
and *blasphemed me* upon the hills:

therefore will I measure their former work into their bosom. (65:7)

---

[1] The changes in this verse are from the JST.
[2] The changes in this verse are from the JST.
[3] The changes in this verse are from the JST.

NOTES AND COMMENTARY

**65:1** *I am found/I am not found.* When we seek the Lord with honest hearts, we surely find him. When we ask, he grants according to what we seek in righteousness. The converse also is true: When we do not seek him, we do not find him.

*I said unto my servant . . . I will send you.* The Lord here calls a servant to go to a nation that is not joined to him by covenant. That servant could be Isaiah, Jesus Christ, Joseph Smith, or another prophet—or the prophecy could apply to any others who fit that circumstance.

*nation that is not called after my name.* We are called by Christ's name when we have joined his family through the baptism of water and of fire. Thus the prophet is called to warn people who do not know the Lord in their heart of hearts, though they may profess him with their lips.

**65:2** *spread out my hands all the day.* This gesture of appeal, of pleading and longing (Lam. 1:17), can also be a gesture of holy prayer. The Lord here uses this gesture to invite a wicked people to repent and come unto him, and he does so unceasingly. This gesture also suggests the position of Christ on the cross with his hands spread out in our behalf.

*walketh not in my ways.* The people are willful, walking in paths of wickedness rather than in the Lord's paths of righteousness.

*walk after their own thoughts.* Actions begin with thoughts. The wicked first give place to thoughts that are displeasing to the Lord, and then they let those thoughts lead them to actions of wickedness (55:8–9).

**65:3** *provoketh me to anger continually to my face.* The people of whom the Lord is speaking not only do evil but do it continually and willfully, flaunting their evil before the Lord to his face.

*sacrificeth in gardens.* Sacrificing in gardens, a practice often used in worshiping idols, was forbidden in the law of Moses (2 Kgs. 21:3–6; Ezek. 20:28). The expression means that the people have turned from the right way of worship.

*burneth incense.* The verb used here means "to make to smoke" and can be used in describing all burnt offerings, not just offerings of incense (Jer. 44:3–5).

*altars of brick.* According to the law of Moses, incense was to be burned only on altars of unhewn stone (Ex. 20:24–25; Deut. 27:5; Josh. 8:31). Burnt offerings to pagan gods may have been made on rooftops or in the streets (Jer. 19:13; 32:29), or in the case of incense offerings, bricks may have been heated and then incense sprinkled on the bricks.[4]

---

[4] Motyer, *Prophecy of Isaiah,* 524.

**65:4** *remain among the graves/monuments.* This statement may refer to an effort to communicate with the spirits of the dead, an action forbidden by the Mosaic law (Lev. 19:31; Deut. 18:10–12; Isa. 8:19).

*eat swine's flesh/abominable beasts.* This statement describes another clear violation of God's law as given through Moses (Lev. 11:7–8; Deut. 14:7–8).

*broth of abominable beasts.* The people are eating broth made from unclean animals or unclean sacrificial flesh (Lev. 7:18; 19:7).

*pollute their vessels.* By eating foods forbidden by the Lord, the people make their pots, pans, and dishes unclean. The people who partake of forbidden foods also pollute their bodies, which are vessels for their spirits.

**65:5** *Stand by thyself/come not near/holier than thou.* The idea is, Do not come too close—you'll defile me. Having rejected the Lord's requirements of holiness, the people invented their own, and they apparently felt they were superior to others and refused to associate with those who did not abide by their laws.

*smoke in my nose/a fire that burneth all the day.* The people's unfaithfulness was, to the Lord, like smoke in the nose: a constant irritant.

**65:6** *it is written.* Isaiah here seems to refer to a scripture that predated him, but his quotation is not readily identifiable, and the scripture may have been lost.

*I will not keep silence, but will recompense.* As prophesied ("it is written") the Lord would speak through his judgments and bring chastisements on the wicked (42:14; Jer. 16:18).

*into their bosom.* This image means close to their heart, where it hurts. The inside front of the garment was used as a pocket to keep money and personal items, and payments were kept there (Luke 6:38). The Lord promises to repay their sins in full.

**65:7** *Your iniquities.* Israel is guilty of many sins, but the Lord is particularly incensed by idolatry, which is a direct rejection of Jehovah himself. In the broad sense, idolatry involves any belief, feeling, or activity that puts something else before God.

*iniquities of your fathers.* The sins of Israel are added to the sins of her ancestors. Both ancestor and descendant are guilty of the same thing.

*burned incense upon the mountains/blasphemed me upon the hills.* These phrases are references to idol worship, which often occurred on mountains and hills. An elevated place was said to be more effective in attracting the attention of Baal; such worship of idols was a perversion and counterfeit of true temple worship, which also was performed on mountaintops (57:5, 7).

*measure their former work.* The Lord will give us in punishment the exact measure of what we have earned through our works.

*into their bosom.* See commentary on 65:6.

## Blessings for the Righteous, Cursings for the Sinful (65:8–16)

Israel deserves destruction, yet because she has a few righteous people, the Lord will "not destroy them all" (65:8). This response is a direct answer to Isaiah's plea in 63:17. The Lord will provide an inheritance for his elect (65:9), and a safe place for the righteous (65:10). Yet the Lord will send judgments upon the wicked, who chose their own way rather than the things the Lord delighted in (65:12). Because of Israel's wickedness, the Lord threatens to slay her people and make his covenant with another people (65:15).

The Lord contrasts the blessings of the righteous ("my servants") with the punishments of the wicked: the righteous will eat while the wicked go hungry; the righteous will drink while the wicked thirst; the righteous will rejoice while the wicked will be ashamed; the righteous will sing in joy while the wicked will cry in sorrow (65:13–14). These blessings and cursings have both temporal and spiritual applications: for example, the wicked will go hungry for the bread of life and thirsty for the living waters brought by Christ.

*Isaiah 65:8–16*

> Thus saith the Lord, As the *new wine* is found in the cluster, and one saith,
> Destroy it not; for a blessing is in *it*:
> so will I do for my servants' sakes, that I may not destroy them all. (65:8)

> And I will bring forth a *seed* out of Jacob,
> and out of Judah an *inheritor* of my mountains:

> and *mine elect* shall inherit it,
> and *my servants* shall dwell there. (65:9)

> And *Sharon* shall be a fold of flocks,
> and the *valley of Achor* a place for the herds to lie down in, for my people that
> have sought me. (65:10)

> But ye are they that *forsake* the Lord,
> that *forget* my holy mountain,[5]

---

[5] These words appear to be addressed to those who have come into the Church but have forgotten their covenants and promises.

that *prepare a table* for that troop,
and that *furnish the drink offering* unto that number. (65:11)

Therefore will *I number you* to the sword,
and *ye shall all bow down* to the slaughter:

because *when I called,* ye did not answer;
*when I spake,* ye did not hear;

but *did evil* before mine eyes,
and *did choose that* wherein I *delighted not.* (65:12)

Therefore thus saith the Lord God, Behold, *my servants shall eat,* but ye shall be hungry: behold, *my servants shall drink,* but ye shall be thirsty:

behold, *my servants* shall rejoice,
but *ye* shall be ashamed: (65:13)

Behold, *my servants* shall sing for joy of heart,
but *ye* shall cry for sorrow of heart, and shall howl for vexation of spirit. (65:14)

And *ye* shall leave your name for a curse unto my chosen: for the Lord God shall slay thee, and call *his servants* by another name: (65:15)

That he who *blesseth himself in the earth* shall bless himself in the God of truth;
and he that *sweareth in the earth* shall swear by the God of truth;

because the *former troubles* are forgotten,
and because *they* are hid from mine eyes. (65:16)

## NOTES AND COMMENTARY

**65:8** *new wine . . . in the cluster.* Israel is the Lord's vineyard (5:1; 27:2), which has produced mostly wild grapes useless for wine. But there have always been a few who remained faithful to Jehovah and his law. For the sake of these few good grapes he has refrained from altogether destroying the vineyard. In the end, though, only the good clusters will be saved, and the rest of the unfruitful people will be destroyed (1:9, 27–28; 4:3–4).

*Destroy it not; for a blessing is in it.* This expression may have been part of a vintage song (16:10; Jer. 25:30). The grape cluster should not be destroyed, they say, because of the good juice in it. This image symbolizes the Lord's treatment of Israel—he promises not to destroy the whole of Israel because of the good people who remain.

*for my servants' sakes.* Because of the goodness of a few, who are his servants, the Lord will not destroy the whole cluster (see commentary on 63:17).

**65:9** *a seed out of Jacob.* The word *seed* here refers to a remnant among the descendants of Jacob (6:13).

*inheritor of my mountains/inherit it/dwell there.* Even though the land of Israel had been promised to the descendants of Abraham, Isaac, and Jacob, they possessed it only a short time (63:18). But they are assured that the promise will indeed come to pass and that a seed of Jacob will inherit the mountains of Palestine (14:25; 57:13; 60:21). Because mountains often symbolize temples, this passage seems to indicate that the covenant people will receive the blessings of the temple.

*mine elect/my servants.* The elect of God are those Saints who are faithful and true (Col. 3:12–13; D&C 29:7; 33:6; 35:20–21). They are justified by Christ and will come to his glory (Rom. 8:28–30). *Mine elect* and *my servants* are synonymous (45:4). They will inherit the promised land.

**65:10** *Sharon/Achor. Sharon,* on the west, was the coastal plain from Carmel south to Joppa (33:9; 35:2) The Israelites marched through the valley of Achor (perhaps the Wadi Qelt), on the east, to get from Jericho to Judah (Josh. 7:24; 15:7). This expression means that the whole land from east to west will become a place of safety and refuge for the Lord's people (Hos. 2:15).

*a fold of flocks/a place for the herds.* The wars, contention, and slavery to which Israel was repeatedly subjected will be replaced with a peaceful, pastoral lifestyle in the Millennium. Those who seek the Lord are blessed to live in peace.

*my people that have sought me.* Those who turn to the Lord with their hearts and deeds will be brought into his fold. This is in contrast to those in 65:11, who "forsake the Lord" (see also 65:1 in JST).

**65:11** *they that forsake the Lord/table for that troop/drink offering unto that number.* The Lord addresses those who left the worship of Jehovah and turned to other gods: *troop* refers to the pagan god Gad, who was "an idol of fortune"; and *number* refers to the pagan god Meni, who was "an idol of fate" (footnotes *a* and *b* to 65:11, LDS edition of the Bible). In other words, the Israelites were trusting in pagan gods, as well as chance or luck, rather than in the Lord, who is ultimately in charge of the universe.

*my holy mountain.* In turning to other gods and their abominable practices upon hilltops, the Israelites had turned away from the true God and his holy rites in his temple. "They found no difficulty being religious; . . . in fact they would climb any mountain except the one where they might meet the holy God."[6]

**65:12** *number you to the sword/ye shall all bow down to the slaughter.* The word *number* refers to the god Meni, the god of destiny (see commentary on 65:11), and thus is a play on words. If Israel is going to turn to pagan gods, the Lord is saying, I will *destine* you to destruction by *sword.* And if Israel is going to bow down to pagan gods, the Lord says, I will yet cause you to *bow down* to be killed.

---

[6] Motyer, *Prophecy of Isaiah,* 527.

*bow down.* Those who do not choose the Lord will be destroyed, perhaps by bowing or kneeling for execution.

*when I called.* When the Lord called the people to repentance, they ignored him and chose a different way (50:2; 65:1–2). Such divine calls generally come through the prophets, through the whisperings of the Spirit, or through our consciences (or the light of Christ).

*did evil before mine eyes.* The Lord is underscoring the fact that all their evil doings, though they may have been done in secret, were done before him. Nothing can be hid from the Lord; he sees and knows all we do, both good and evil.

*did choose that wherein I delighted not.* This statement is an understatement. The Lord is speaking to a people who worship idols, who will not hearken to him, who "did evil before mine eyes." Not only did he not delight in their works but he truly hated them. Yet this phrase reminds us not to be lukewarm in our obedience to the Lord; we should seek to delight him by our choices.

**65:13** *my servants.* These servants are those who serve and worship God—as opposed to those who serve and worship idols—or those who, in apathy or lack of conviction, do neither.

*eat/drink/rejoice/hungry/thirsty/ashamed.* Those who eat, drink, and are merry in this life will eventually receive a reversal of their conditions, while those who cling to the Lord despite temporal privation will be rewarded with eternal rejoicing. These blessings and cursings also have a spiritual application, referring to the bread and waters of life.

**65:14** *sing for joy/cry for sorrow.* In the end the faithful will rejoice, whereas the wicked will know only sorrow.

*howl for vexation of spirit.* The wicked will feel great anguish for their sins and their punishments, described elsewhere as "weeping, wailing and gnashing of teeth" (D&C 19:5).

**65:15** *leave your name for a curse.* This statement is the opposite of the blessing Abraham received (Gen. 12:1–3). With Israel's old reputation of shame and sin (1:21–23), her name had been used only in cursing. Israel's newness of life will require a new name (62:2).

*my chosen.* Israel is the chosen people, as the Lord said through Moses: "The Lord thy God hath chosen thee to be a special people unto himself, above all people that [are] upon the face of the earth" (Deut. 7:6). Many are called to come unto Christ and receive his power and blessings, but few are chosen to receive all he offers (D&C

95:5; 121:34–40). Those who are chosen are the faithful (3 Ne. 19:20, 28), who come with broken and honest hearts.

*slay thee.* The Lord will destroy wicked Israel and replace her with a righteous people.

*another name.* Because of the wickedness of the covenant people, the Lord will no longer call the righteous by the name of Israel but will call them by another name. The new name might be *Christian* rather than *Israelite.* Or, in our dispensation, the name could be The Church of Jesus Christ of Latter-day Saints. To that name, as Israel increases in holiness and harmony, will be added another name, Zion (1:26–27).

**65:16** *he who blesseth . . . he that sweareth . . . by the God of truth.* In asking blessings and making covenants, we will invoke only the name of the true God; all other gods will have been forsaken and forgotten (10:20).

*in the earth.* The Revised Standard Version renders this "in the land."

*the God of truth.* God is a being who "cannot lie" (Titus 1:2; D&C 62:6) but in all things is a God of truth (Deut. 32:4; Ps. 31:5; Ether 3:12). The Hebrew reads "God of amen," meaning the God in whom one can trust, whose word is worthy of confidence. In Revelation we see that "Amen" is a name for Jesus Christ (Rev. 3:14; 2 Cor. 1:20).

*the former troubles.* Israel's punishments, sorrows, and exile will be forgotten because they will be replaced with joy, prosperity, and blessing.

*hid from mine eyes.* Not only are the former troubles forgotten by the people who suffered them but because of the people's repentance, they are forgotten by the Lord as well (43:25; Jer. 31:34; Heb. 10:16–17; D&C 58:42).

## THE MILLENNIAL EARTH (65:17–25)

These verses portray the wonderful blessings of the millennial world:

The earth will be renewed (65:17).

The people will be filled with rejoicing, with no cause of weeping (65:18–19).

Children will not die, and neither will adults before they are one hundred years old (65:20).

The people will enjoy the fruits of their labors (65:21–23).

Their prayers will be answered before they are even uttered (65:24).

All animals will dwell in peace together (65:25).

*Isaiah 65:17–25*

> For, behold, I create *new heavens*
> and a *new earth:*
> and the former shall *not* be remembered,
> *nor* come into mind. (65:17)

> But be ye *glad*
> and *rejoice* for ever in that which I create:
> for, behold, I create *Jerusalem* a rejoicing,
> and *her people* a joy. (65:18)

> And I will *rejoice* in Jerusalem,
> and *joy* in my people:
> and the *voice* of weeping shall be no more heard in her,
> nor the *voice* of crying. (65:19)

> [In those days] there shall be *no more thence an infant* of days,
> *nor an old man* that hath not filled his days:
> for the *child* shall [not] die, [but shall live to be] an hundred years old;
> but the *sinner,* [living to be] an hundred years old, shall be accursed.[7] (65:20)

> And *they shall build houses,* and inhabit them;
> and *they shall plant vineyards,* and eat the fruit of them. (65:21)
> *They shall not build,* and another inhabit;
> *they shall not plant,* and another eat:

> for as *the days* of a tree
> are *the days* of my people,
> and mine elect shall long enjoy the work of their hands. (65:22)[8]

> They shall not *labour* in vain,
> nor *bring forth* for trouble;

> for *they* are the seed of the blessed of the Lord,
> and their offspring with *them.* (65:23)

> And it shall come to pass, that *before they call,* I will answer;
> and *while they are yet speaking,* I will hear. (65:24)

> The *wolf and the lamb* shall feed together,
> and the *lion* shall eat straw like the *bullock:*
> and dust shall be the *serpent's* meat.
> They shall not hurt nor destroy in all my holy mountain, saith the Lord. (65:25)[9]

## NOTES AND COMMENTARY

**65:17** *new heavens/new earth.* The desolation of Israel can be seen as symbolic of the awful state of the whole earth (24:1–6; Jer. 4:23–31). In the same way, the restoration of Israel will usher in not only a symbolic but an actual renewal of the *earth.*

---

[7] The changes are from the JST; see also D&C 63:49–51; 101:27–31.

[8] The Lord paraphrased and applied vv. 21 and 22 in D&C 101:101.

[9] D&C 101:26 says, "In that day the enmity of man, and the enmity of beasts, yea, the enmity of all flesh, shall cease from before my face."

The context of this chapter tells us that this renewal refers not to the celestialized earth but to the millennial condition referred to in the tenth Article of Faith: "The earth will be renewed and receive its paradisiacal glory" (see also 2 Pet. 3:10–13; Rev. 21:1–4; D&C 101:23–25).

*former shall not be remembered.* The changes in the earth will be so significant and remarkable that they will essentially remove all thought of the premillennial world. This statement refers both to the earth itself, which will be transformed into a paradisiacal state, and to mortal conditions on the earth.

**65:18** *I create Jerusalem a rejoicing.* Other versions of the Bible agree that something is missing from this phrase. The New International Version, for instance, translates it as "I will create Jerusalem to be a delight," and the New American Bible says, "I create Jerusalem to be a joy."

*glad/rejoice/rejoicing . . . joy.* Doctrine and Covenants 101:27–29 describes the conditions that will bring such great rejoicing: we will receive everything we ask for; Satan will be bound, with no power to tempt any man; and there will be no death. These conditions are in direct contrast with the former sorrows (57:18; 60:15; 61:3–4).

*weeping/crying.* The people will no longer have cause to weep because of the state of peace and righteousness in which they will dwell.

**65:19** *I will rejoice in Jerusalem/the voice of weeping shall be no more.* The time of sorrow is over. The Lord and the people rejoice together over the newness and holiness of Jerusalem (30:19; 62:5; Deut. 30:9).

**65:20** *no more thence an infant of days, nor an old man that hath not filled his days.* All inhabitants of Zion, both young and old, will live out their lives completely, none succumbing prematurely. This blessing had particular significance for those in ancient Israel, who often believed that long life meant God's approval.

*child shall not die.* In the Millennium there will be no death as we now know it— no infant or child mortality—but when an individual reaches a hundred years old, he or she will be changed from mortality to immortality "in the twinkling of an eye" (D&C 101:30–31; 63:50–51).

*the sinner.* The Millennium will be a time of righteousness and peace; however, there will still be agency, and some will choose the terrestrial rather than the celestial way of life. Some also will sin against the greater light and will become sons of perdition.[10]

---

[10] See Smith, *Doctrines of Salvation,* 3:63–64.

*the sinner, living to be an hundred years old, shall be accursed.* The curse may be that the sinner, having lived out his years, will suffer for his lack of repentance in the flesh. Rather than having a period of time in the spirit world to meet the demands of justice for his sins, he will live to be one hundred years old and then will be resurrected. That would be a curse if a person needed more time to prepare himself for the judgment of God.

**65:21–22** *they shall build . . . and inhabit/They shall not build, and another inhabit . . . not plant, and another eat.* The people will enjoy the fruit of their own labors rather than have them confiscated by enemies as in the past (62:8–9). More symbolically, this statement is a pledge that the Lord will fulfill all his promises to his covenant people.

*the days of a tree.* The tree symbolizes strength, firmness, endurance, and long life (Ps. 92:12). In contrast is grass (40:6–8), which symbolizes the fragility of mortality (Ps. 102:11).

*elect . . . long enjoy . . . work of their hands.* This statement may refer to spiritual labors as well as temporal. The Lord's elect enjoy the results of their righteous work forever.

**65:23** *not . . . bring forth for trouble.* The New International Version renders this phrase as "bear children doomed to misfortune"; the Revised Standard Version, as "bear children for calamity." As Isaiah makes clear, these are challenges that will not come to those in the Millennium.

*seed of the blessed.* This expression seems to refer to the spiritual offspring of Abraham, Isaac, and Jacob, the heirs to the Abrahamic covenant. As the Revised Standard Version puts it, "They shall be the offspring of the blessed of the Lord."

*their offspring.* Not only shall the righteous seed of Abraham be blessed but so also shall their children in turn.

**65:24** *before they call, I will answer.* Because of Israel's rebellion and wickedness, their past prayers to Jehovah went unheeded. In their righteous and glorious future, he will intervene even before they have called on him in prayer (33:21–22). The Millennium will be a time of great revelation: "In that day whatsoever any man shall ask, it shall be given unto him. . . . In that day when the Lord shall come, he shall reveal all things—Things which have passed, and hidden things which no man knew" (D&C 101:27, 32–33). This statement directly contrasts with the statement in 66:4, in which the Lord called to Israel but no one would answer him.

**65:25** *The wolf and the lamb shall feed together/lion shall eat straw/They shall not hurt nor destroy.* Great harmony, even among the creatures of nature, will characterize the millennial period of the earth's history (11:6–9). "The enmity of beasts, yea, the enmity of all flesh, shall cease" (D&C 101:26). All animals will be vegetarians, as will man, partly because death of man and animals (in which body and spirit are separated) will cease.

*dust shall be the serpent's meat.* Interestingly, this was the curse placed on the serpent in the Garden of Eden (Gen. 3:14). Here, it seems to mean that the serpent will no longer pose any physical harm to man or beast.

*holy mountain.* The whole earth will be as a temple, where the Lord dwells in glorious holiness with his people.

# ISAIAH 66

*Likening Isaiah 66 unto Ourselves*

*We can do many works of obedience, but they are as naught if we do not give the Lord the sacrifice he really desires: a broken heart and a contrite spirit. Those of such a spirit are those who come to Zion. If we are so blessed, we will feel God's love and care as a child feels the love and care of his mother.*

*We are living in a day in which great prophecies are being fulfilled. We can see the Lord gathering his children from all parts of the world. Many of us may see the Lord come in his glory, though no man knows when that will be. Those who witness his coming will see the beginning of the millennial day, with the creation of a new heaven and a new earth. These are blessings to be sought in faith.*

## THE RIGHTEOUS SHALL BE JUSTIFIED, THE WICKED PUNISHED (66:1–6)

To the righteous the Lord says, in effect, "You can build me a temple, but that which I desire most is the person with a broken heart and a contrite spirit, a person who hearkens to my word (66:1–2). I will come to justify you in your righteousness, while your enemy will be ashamed" (66:5).

To the wicked the Lord seems to say, "Those who choose their own way, who will not hearken unto me, will have their worst fears come upon them (66:3–4). Those who persecute the righteous will be ashamed (66:5). I come in power to bring justice on my enemies" (66:6).

*Isaiah 66:1–6*

Thus saith the Lord, The *heaven* is <u>my throne</u>,
and the *earth* is <u>my footstool</u>:

*where is the house* that ye build <u>unto me</u>?
and *where is the place* of <u>my rest</u>? (66:1)

For all *those things* hath mine hand made,
and *those things* have been, saith the Lord:

but to *this man* will I look,
even *to him* that is poor and of a contrite spirit, and trembleth at my word. (66:2)

He that *killeth an ox* is <u>as if he slew a man</u>;
he that *sacrificeth a lamb,* <u>as if he cut off a dog's neck</u>;

he that *offereth an oblation,* <u>as if he offered swine's blood</u>;
he that *burneth incense,* <u>as if he blessed an idol</u>.

Yea, *they have chosen* <u>their own ways</u>,
and *their soul delighteth* in <u>their abominations</u>. (66:3)

I also *will choose* <u>their delusions</u>,
and *will bring* <u>their fears</u> upon them;

because *when I called,* <u>none did answer</u>;
*when I spake,* <u>they did not hear</u>:

but *they did evil* before <u>mine eyes</u>,
and *chose that in which* <u>I</u> *delighted not.* (66:4)

Hear the *word* <u>of the Lord</u>,
ye that tremble at <u>his</u> *word;*

*your brethren* that <u>hated you</u>,
*that* <u>cast you out</u> for my name's sake,

said, Let the Lord be glorified: but he shall appear to your <u>joy</u>,
and they shall be <u>ashamed</u>. (66:5)

A *voice* of noise <u>from the city</u>,
a *voice* <u>from the temple</u>,
a *voice* <u>of the Lord</u> that rendereth recompence to his enemies. (66:6)

## NOTES AND COMMENTARY

**66:1** *The heaven is my throne/the earth is my footstool.* The Lord rules over heaven and earth; all things in all places are subject to him. As the Lord said to Abraham, "I am the Lord thy God; I dwell in heaven; the earth is my footstool; I stretch my hand over the sea, and it obeys my voice; I cause the wind and the fire to be my chariot; I say to the mountains—Depart . . . and behold, they are taken away" (Abr. 2:7).

The throne represents the Lord's role as eternal king (D&C 128:23). All heaven is his throne in that it is from there that he rules. But, more particularly, the Lord dwells in the heavenly temple, which is heaven itself, and in that temple is his throne (Ps. 11:4; Rev. 4:2; 20:11).

The earth as a footstool suggests a position of complete submission. The Lord rules from his throne, but he puts the earth under his feet. People on earth, even those of great power and wealth, are as nothing compared to the Lord. Yet this image of the earth is not entirely negative. In the Sermon on the Mount, Jesus taught that we should not swear by the earth, because it belongs to the Lord (Matt. 5:34–35; 3 Ne. 12:34–35). When the Lord spoke in our day of the earth as his footstool, he did so saying he would yet stand on it again (D&C 38:17).

*where is the house that ye build unto me?* The Lord spoke to King David through the prophet Nathan, saying, "Shalt thou build me an house for me to dwell in? . . . I have not dwelt in any house since the time that I brought up the children of Israel out of Egypt, . . . but have walked in a tent and in a tabernacle" (2 Sam. 7:5–6). The Lord's question was asked anew by Solomon when he exclaimed upon completion of the temple: "But will God indeed dwell on the earth? behold, the heaven and heaven of heavens cannot contain thee; how much less this house that I have builded?" (1 Kgs. 8:27).

**66:2** *For all those things hath mine hand made, and those things have been.* The Lord created all things in heaven and on the earth. Other translations clarify the second phrase: "by my hand all those things have been."

*to this man will I look.* The Lord has power over all, but he looks to a few with joy; he looks to a few to help him with his work. Those few are the obedient and contrite.

*poor and of a contrite spirit.* "Blessed are the poor in spirit who come unto me," Jesus said, "for theirs is the kingdom of heaven" (3 Ne. 12:3). A contrite spirit is often given as one of the principal requirements for receiving the saving grace of Christ (2 Ne. 2:7; Hel. 8:15). A contrite spirit is penitent and sorrowful for sin. A *poor* spirit is a humble spirit. Those with a humble and a contrite spirit are those to whom the Lord will bring his greatest blessings.

*trembleth at my word.* The Lord is most pleased with those who desire to receive his word of revelation, both through his prophets and through the Holy Spirit, and who then are filled with awe, amazement, and reverence at that word. Those with such an attitude, of course, are those who love and obey the Lord's word with all their hearts.

**66:3** *killeth an ox/slew a man/sacrificeth a lamb/cut off a dog's neck.* This verse means that our sacrifices and oblations are not acceptable to God if at the same time we transgress his laws by our worship of other things or by hating our brethren. A man might sacrifice a lamb to the Lord, for example, but if he did so with an impure heart he might as well have cut through a dog's neck. A man might offer an oblation to the Lord, but if his heart was impure, he might as well have offered swine's blood, which would be abhorrent to the Lord. The parallels in this verse illustrate how men may outwardly appear to worship Jehovah while in reality continuing their sinful ways, whether outwardly or in their hearts (James 3:9–10). Certainly the Lord wants our sacrifices, the outward signs of our devotion. But he also wants us to understand that outward symbols are empty without the inward devotions: obedience, repentance, humility, gratitude (1:11–13).

*they have chosen their own ways.* Isaiah speaks frequently about the way of the Lord in contrast to the way of man (55:8–9). Those who are righteous live their lives according to the laws and covenants of the gospel and by the guidance of the Spirit of the Lord (2:3; 26:7; 48:17). Others choose their own way and are condemned by the Lord (53:6; 56:11; 59:8; 65:2).

*their soul delighteth in their abominations.* Not only do these people choose to do evil works but they find delight in them. In other words, they have no remorse.

**66:4** *I also will choose their delusions, and will bring their fears upon them.* For *delusions,* other versions read, "affliction" (RSV), "harsh treatment" (NIV), or "hardships" (JB). In turning to other gods, the Israelites sought to avoid judgment from Jehovah. But now their worst fears will be realized; they will learn that they cannot escape justice (65:6–7). The Lord will choose their afflictions and troubles; they will not choose them. As for the Lord deluding us, or causing us to be deluded, Joseph Smith said, "The devil could not compel mankind to do evil; all was voluntary. . . . God would not exert any compulsory means, and the devil could not."[1] In other words, we are deluded because of our choices and desires, not because of the works or actions of either the Lord or Satan.

*when I called/evil before mine eyes/chose that in which I delighted not.* The contrast between 65:3 and 65:4 demonstrates that the things that delight the people are exactly the things that do not delight the Lord. See commentary on 65:12.

**66:5** *tremble at his word.* See commentary on 66:2.

*your brethren that hated you, that cast you out.* This statement suggests division within Israel itself, wherein the wicked cast out the righteous (51:7). The verb in Hebrew means "to excommunicate" but also suggests "to cast down" or "to reject." Those who treated the righteous in this manner will eventually "be ashamed." The

---

[1] *Teachings of the Prophet Joseph Smith,* 187.

righteous here are being cast out "for my name's sake" or because of their fervent belief in the Lord. That is the lot of the righteous in all dispensations (Matt. 5:11–12).

*Let the Lord be glorified.* These are not the true followers speaking here, rejoicing in their Lord; rather, they are the errant Israelites mocking their believing brethren. The prophet had earlier declared, "The glory of the Lord shall be revealed" (40:5), and the unbelievers were using these same words to jeer and ridicule those who indeed looked forward to Jehovah's intervention on their behalf (5:19). The wicked may actually believe they are doing God's will in casting out the righteous. They may be deceived into seeing evil as good and good as evil (5:20; Mal. 2:17).

*he shall appear to your joy/they shall be ashamed.* When the Lord comes again, the righteous will be filled with joy and the wicked (including the persecutors mentioned above) with great shame.

**66:6** *A voice of noise.* Those who do not "tremble at [his] word" will tremble at the sound of his vengeance (Joel 3:16–17; Amos 1:2).

*from the city/from the temple.* The noise from the city may be the sound of the mourning of the wicked as they experience God's judgments, which may come forth from his temple. The word translated here as *temple* (Hebrew *heykal*) also means "palace," as in 39:7 and 13:22. Because the city is where the people live, and the palace where the rulers live, the meaning here may be that the destruction will reach into every dwelling place.

*the Lord that rendereth recompence to his enemies.* The Lord will bring the appropriate judgment upon all those who fight against him, according to their works.

## BLESSINGS TO ZION (66:7–14A)

Zion will come to the fulness of her being suddenly, as a woman who gives birth without any pains or travail (66:7). And just as surely as a woman comes to the point of delivery and gives birth, so surely will Zion come to her fruition when her time has come (66:8–9). Those who now mourn because Zion has not yet come will then rejoice and be glad (66:10). She will have peace from the Lord, and he will give her spiritual sustenance, comfort, and care, even as a mother cares for her infant child (66:11–14).

The repetition of the image of woman and mother here is notable. We have a woman bearing a child (66:7–9), Jerusalem as a female (66:10), a mother nourishing her children at her breast (66:11–12), and a mother giving comfort to her children

(66:13). By using these images, the Lord shows us how thoroughly the children of Zion, after their long trials, will be blessed and comforted.

### Isaiah 66:7–14a

*Before she travailed,* she <u>brought forth;</u>
*before her pain* came, she was<u> delivered</u> of a man child. (66:7)

Who hath *heard* such a thing?
who hath *seen* such things?

Shall the *earth* be made to <u>bring forth</u> in one day?
or shall a *nation* be <u>born</u> at once?

for as soon as *Zion* <u>travailed,</u>
*she* <u>brought forth her children.</u> (66:8)

*Shall I bring to the birth,* and <u>not cause to bring forth? saith the Lord:</u>
*shall I cause to bring forth,* and <u>shut the womb? saith thy God.</u> (66:9)

*Rejoice ye with Jerusalem,* and *be glad with her,* <u>all ye that love her:</u>
*rejoice for joy with her,* <u>all ye that mourn for her:</u> (66:10)

*That ye may suck,* and <u>be satisfied with the breasts of her consolations;</u>
*that ye may milk out,* and <u>be delighted with the abundance of her glory.</u> (66:11)

For thus saith the Lord, Behold, I will extend peace to her <u>like a river,</u>
and the glory of the Gentiles <u>like a flowing stream:</u>

then shall ye suck, ye shall *be borne* <u>upon her sides,</u>
and *be dandled* <u>upon her knees.</u> (66:12)

As one whom his *mother* <u>comforteth,</u>
so will *I* <u>comfort</u> you; and ye shall <u>be comforted</u> in Jerusalem. (66:13)

And when ye see this, *your heart* <u>shall rejoice,</u>
and *your bones* <u>shall flourish like an herb:</u> (66:14a)

### NOTES AND COMMENTARY

**66:7** *Before she travailed, she brought forth.* The Living Bible translates this passage as follows: "In one day, suddenly, a nation, Israel, shall be born, even before the birth pains come." Isaiah's words make it plain that the creation of Zion is a miracle, as miraculous as would be the painless, effortless birth of a child. Suddenly and miraculously, it seems, a whole new society or a holy nation—Zion—is born. In viewing this same event, John the Revelator saw that there was indeed travail as the woman (the perfected "church of God," or Zion) brought forth the man child ("the kingdom of our God and his Christ") (JST Rev. 12:1–7). By combining Isaiah and Revelation, we come to this possible reading: "Before Zion travailed to bring forth the multitude of her children, she travailed to bring forth the perfected kingdom of God, which will rule all nations with a rod of iron."

*delivered of a man child.* Elder Bruce R. McConkie interpreted this passage as meaning the birth of the kingdom of God, which accords with Joseph Smith's translation of Revelation 12:7.[2] The headnote to Isaiah 66 in the LDS edition of the Bible identifies the child as "Israel, as a nation," placing the event at the Second Coming.

**66:8** *bring forth in one day/nation be born at once.* Victor Ludlow gives this helpful commentary on this phrase: "In this prophecy, Isaiah apparently promises that shortly after Zion is established in Jackson County, great numbers of unexpected peoples, including the Ten Tribes and other Israelite remnants, will join with Zion to prepare the earth for the Millennium. These verses convey the feeling of suddenness and surprise at Zion's rapid growth."[3]

*brought forth her children.* The children of the woman are the people of Zion, who are of one heart and one mind, prepared to greet the Lord at his coming.

**66:9** *bring to the birth . . . shut the womb.* In the natural world, once a woman comes to the point of travail, where labor has begun and the baby is ready to be born, the baby is indeed brought forth. The Lord does not at that point "shut the womb." In the same way, he will not cause Zion to come to the point of giving birth to her children of righteousness and then shut the womb. The birth of the children of Zion is as certain as the birth of any infant.

There is also another possible way to understand this phrase. Anciently, the birth of infants was not always certain. A woman could come to the point of delivery and yet because of complications (such as the cord being around the baby's neck or the baby being in an unworkable position), she would find her womb, in effect, to be "shut," and both she and the baby could die without delivery. The Lord says, however, that what he brings to delivery will indeed come forth.

**66:10** *Rejoice/be glad/rejoice for joy.* The cause of the rejoicing is the fulfillment of the Lord's promises: Zion shall be established, her children shall be born, and Jerusalem will be restored to her promised blessings.

*ye that love her/ye that mourn for her.* These are they who continue to trust in Jehovah's promises, not those who forgot him and forsook Zion, as in 65:11. These faithful ones have had cause to mourn for Jerusalem—she has been destroyed and her children scattered—but in the last days the Lord will give them abundant cause to rejoice. The loss of Jerusalem symbolizes the loss or postponement of the blessing of the covenant, but in the last days, both Jerusalem and the covenant will be restored.

---

[2] See McConkie, *Doctrinal New Testament Commentary,* 3:516.
[3] Ludlow, *Isaiah,* 535.

**66:11** *That ye may suck, and be satisfied.* The righteous will be like a child who is returned to its mother (49:15–17; 60:16). They will receive both nourishment and comfort from the mother, who is Zion (symbolized by Jerusalem).

*breasts of her consolations.* The inhabitants of Zion will be safe and at peace, content and satisfied.

*ye may milk out.* The children of Zion will be blessed with spiritual nourishment and emotional comfort (at the breast of their mother, Zion) without limit.

*delighted with the abundance of her glory.* The children of Zion will rejoice to receive of the blessings of Zion's glory, which will be available in great abundance.

**66:12** *peace . . . like a river.* The Hebrew word here (*shalom*), usually translated *peace,* could more correctly be translated "prosperity." See commentary on 48:18.

*the glory of the Gentiles like a flowing stream.* The word *glory* (Hebrew *kabod*) may be translated "wealth." The wealth of the gentiles, both spiritual and temporal, will flow like a stream unto Zion. See commentary on 60:5; 61:6.

*borne upon her sides.* See commentary on 60:4.

*dandled upon her knees.* To *dandle* is to play with affectionately. The Lord is telling us that the people of Zion will be comfortable and happy.

**66:13** *As one whom his mother comforteth, so will I comfort you.* After all the trials and tribulations of their history, the people of the Lord will come to a place of peace and safety in Zion, and there they will be comforted, even as a child is comforted by *his mother.*

**66:14a** *your heart shall rejoice, and your bones shall flourish like an herb.* Simply put, the righteous in Zion will be both happy and healthy. In old age and illness, bones are considered dry and brittle (Ps. 31:10; Lam. 1:13), but in youth and health they are thought of as fresh and moist (Job 21:24; Prov. 15:30). Herbs, like all other healthy green plants, grow readily and easily.

## THE LORD SHALL RETURN IN POWER AND GLORY (66:14B–18A)

When the Lord comes in his glory, he will come with fire and the sword, bringing judgments on the wicked. The idea of fire is repeated five times in three verses: "fire" (three times), "flames," and "consumed" (66:15–17). The idea of the anger of the Lord is repeated four times in two verses with such words as *indignation, anger, fury,* and *rebuke* (66:14–15). Through the fire and the sword, many will die (66:16). None of the wicked will escape (66:17–18). These things are sent by way of deliverance to the Lord's servants but as a judgment against his enemies (66:14). Psalm 18:6–17 gives us an interesting parallel description of this same event.

## Isaiah 66:14b–18a

and the *hand of the Lord* shall be known <u>toward his servants</u>,
and *his indignation* <u>toward his enemies</u>. (66:14b)

For, behold, *the Lord* will come <u>with fire</u>,
and with *his chariots* <u>like a whirlwind</u>,

to render *his anger* <u>with fury</u>,
and *his rebuke* <u>with flames of fire</u>. (66:15)

For by fire and by his sword will the Lord plead with all flesh:
and the slain of the Lord shall be many. (66:16)

They that *sanctify* <u>themselves</u>,
and *purify* <u>themselves</u> in the gardens behind one tree in the midst,

eating *swine's flesh,*
and the *abomination,*
and the *mouse,*

shall be consumed together, saith the Lord. (66:17)

For I know their works and their thoughts: (66:18a)

## NOTES AND COMMENTARY

**66:14b** *hand of the Lord shall be known.* When the Lord comes again, he will bring terrible judgments and destructions on the wicked (his enemies). But those same judgments will serve to bless and deliver the righteous (his servants) from the wicked world.

*his indignation toward his enemies.* The enemies of God are all those who persist, unrepentant, in their ways as natural men and women (Mosiah 3:19). Further, God's enemies are those who participate in the grosser sins, who encourage others in sin, and who fight against the right. God's indignation, meaning anger or wrath, will be known toward all such.

**66:15** *the Lord will come with fire/chariots/whirlwind/flames of fire.* When the Lord returns he will bring with him a devouring *fire,* which shall burn the wicked as stubble and cleanse the world with flame (Mal. 4:1; D&C 29:9). Fire and flames of fire also symbolize God's glory and unapproachable holiness (30:27; Ex. 3:2). Chariots and the whirlwind symbolize God's power in bringing justice; the whirlwind also suggests the swiftness with which the Lord comes to destroy the wicked (19:1; Jer. 4:13; Ps. 104:3; Abr. 2:7).

*anger/fury/rebuke.* The Lord has reached out to the wicked in long-suffering and patience for many generations. When he returns in his second coming, the time for patience will have passed, and the time for judgments will have arrived.

**66:16** *by fire and by his sword.* Jehovah comes as a warrior to mete out justice. The wicked will be destroyed by the terrible wars of the last days (D&C 87:2–6) as well as by the fire of the Lord's coming (27:1; 30:30–33; 31:8; 33:12).

*plead with all flesh.* The Lord's judgments are designed to plead with us—everyone on the earth—to come to repentance. Other versions read "execute judgment" (see, for example, RSV, NIV).

*slain of the Lord shall be many.* "I will call for a sword upon all the inhabitants of the earth, saith the Lord of hosts. . . . And the slain of the Lord shall be at that day from one end of the earth even unto the other end of the earth" (Jer. 25:29, 33). "And the number of the army of the horsemen were two hundred thousand thousand: . . . And thus . . . was the third part of men killed" (Rev. 9:16–18).

**66:17** *They that sanctify themselves, and purify themselves in the gardens behind one tree.* The Lord's anger is aroused at idol worshipers who seek to cleanse and purify themselves in pagan rites. *One tree* may refer to a rite performed under the direction of one leader (57:5; 65:3; Ezek. 8:11).

*eating swine's flesh/abomination/mouse. Abomination* refers to all unclean animals (Lev. 7:21; Isa. 65:4; 66:3). Swine and mice were both forbidden as food for the Lord's covenant people under the law of Moses (Lev. 11:7, 29).

*consumed together.* All the wicked will be destroyed at the time of the coming of the Lord (JST Matt. 13:41–51).

**66:18a** *I know their works and their thoughts.* God knows all things (Morm. 8:17). He knows and judges us by our words, our thoughts, our works, even the intents of our hearts (Heb. 4:12; Alma 12:14; 18:32).

## GATHERING FROM ALL NATIONS (66:18B–21)

In preparation for the Second Coming and the Millennium, the Lord will gather the righteous from all nations (66:18). Missionaries will go forth to declare his glory among the Gentiles, even to far-off places that do not know the true God (66:19). The missionaries will bring the gentile converts to the temple (holy mountain), as an offering unto the Lord (66:20). The Gentiles will be granted the privilege of holding the priesthood and of participating in temple worship (66:21).

## Isaiah 66:18b–21

it <u>shall come</u>, that I will gather all nations and tongues;
and *they* <u>shall come</u>, and see my glory. (66:18b)

And I will set a sign among them, and I will send those that escape of them unto the *nations,* to *Tarshish, Pul,* and *Lud,* that draw the bow, to *Tubal,* and *Javan,* to the isles afar off,

that *have not heard* <u>my fame,</u>
*neither have seen* <u>my glory;</u>
and they shall declare my glory among the Gentiles. (66:19)

And *they shall bring* all your brethren for an <u>offering</u> unto the Lord out of all nations *upon horses,*
and *in chariots,*
and *in litters,*
and *upon mules,*
and *upon swift beasts,*
to my *holy mountain* Jerusalem, saith the Lord,
as the *children of Israel bring* an <u>offering</u> in a clean vessel into the *house of the Lord.* (66:20)

And I will also take of them for priests and for Levites, saith the Lord. (66:21)

### NOTES AND COMMENTARY

**66:18b** *I will gather all nations and tongues.* The gathering of Israel was prophesied by Moses (Deut. 30:3). The Lord allowed the dispersion of Israel because of her wickedness; but he also promised her return (11:12; 43:5; 49:18). The gathering involves bringing souls unto the gospel covenant; it also involves a physical gathering of people to the land and city of Zion.

*they shall come, and see my glory.* When the righteous gather to Zion, they will behold the glory of the Lord. This statement may refer to standing in the presence of the Lord in the New Jerusalem, where "the Lord shall be unto thee an everlasting light, and thy God thy glory" (60:19; 60:3; 62:2; Rev. 21:23–24). The righteous may also behold the glory of the Lord in his temple.

**66:19** *a sign.* Elder Orson Pratt taught that this *sign* was the Book of Mormon.[4] It may also be known as an ensign, whose purpose is to stand as a beacon to draw people to Zion.

*I will send those that escape of them unto the nations . . . Tarshish, Pul, and Lud, . . . Tubal . . . Javan.* Those that escape may be the Lord's faithful who do not perish in the latter-day destruction sent by Jehovah (see also 45:20). They may also be those who escape the bondage of sin. It will be their mission to tell the nations of the

---

[4] Pratt, *Journal of Discourses,* 18:16–17.

power, love, and glory of Jehovah. The place names were the extent of the known earth in ancient times, symbolizing the truth that the Lord will reach unto the ends of the earth.

*Tarshish* may have been in Spain (60:8–9); *Pul* and *Lud* are both probably in northern Africa (Gen. 10:6, 13; Jer. 46:9; Ezek. 30:5); *Tubal* is probably in Asia Minor near the Black Sea (Ezek. 32:26; 38:2; 39:1); and *Javan* is Greece (Ezek. 27:13).[5]

*that draw the bow.* Perhaps the missionaries will be called to places where their lives may be in danger. Or this expression may simply refer to a nation famous for its archers.

*to the isles afar off/not heard my fame/neither have seen my glory.* In the scriptures, even continents are sometimes referred to as *isles* (1 Ne. 22:4; 2 Ne. 10:8, 20). The isles (or continents) to which the missionaries are sent do not know the true God, having neither heard of his fame nor seen his glory.

**66:20** *they shall bring all your brethren for an offering. They,* the missionaries, will bring *your brethren,* the gentile converts, to Zion. Those who had been known as Gentiles now join the gathering as brothers (49:22; 56:8; 60:9–10; John 11:52).

The New International Version and Revised Standard Version interpret the offering as a grain or cereal offering, symbolizing the fruits of their labors. More likely, the missionaries sent to the nations (in 66:19) will bring their converts as their gift to Jehovah.

*out of all nations.* The missionaries will find converts among every nation of the world.

*horses/chariots/litters/mules/swift beasts.* The new converts will use whatever means of transport they can find to travel to Zion. Chariots, which are used for war, will be transformed into conveyances of peace. Litters will be used to carry the weak or infirm. Horses, mules, and swift beasts will be used by those who have access to them. Using all forms of transportation, the converts go to the Lord's holy mountain, his temple.

*holy mountain.* The *holy mountain* is the Lord's temple. See commentary on 65:25.

*children of Israel.* Specifically, the missionaries of the Church are the *children of Israel.*

*an offering in a clean vessel.* This phrase refers to an offering under the law of Moses. The offering may be the souls of converts, with the clean vessel being their pure bodies, or the offering may be the names of the dead we bring to the temple for vicarious ordinance work (D&C 128:24). Motyer sheds additional light: "The only

---

[5] Dummelow, *Commentary on the Holy Bible,* 453.

offering brought in a container was the firstfruits (Dt. 26:2). The converts of the nations come as the firstfruits of the harvest of the world."[6]

## BLESSINGS OF THE MILLENNIAL DAY (66:22–24)

In the Millennium, the Lord will make new heavens and a new earth, as promised in the previous chapter. Here he tells us that the new heavens and new earth will endure forever, as will the seed and name of the righteous (66:22).

In that millennial earth, all people will know the Lord and faithfully worship him (66:23). But they will have a reminder of the fate of the wicked, for they will see the carcasses of those who transgressed against God, which will be disgusting to all who remain (66:24). Further, the righteous will know that though the bodies of the wicked will eventually rot away and disappear, their spiritual punishment will continue forever (66:24).

### Isaiah 66:22–24

For as the *new heavens and the new earth,* which I will make, <u>shall remain</u> before me, saith the Lord, so shall *your seed and your name* <u>remain</u>. (66:22)

And it shall come to pass, that from *one new moon to another,*
and from *one sabbath to another,*
shall all flesh come to worship before me, saith the Lord. (66:23)

And they shall go forth, and look upon the carcases of the men that have transgressed against me:

for *their worm* shall <u>not die,</u>
<u>neither</u> shall *their fire* <u>be quenched</u>;

and they shall be an abhorring unto all flesh. (66:24)

### NOTES AND COMMENTARY

**66:22** *new heavens/new earth.* The Lord here promises that the new heavens and new earth will not be transitory, but will remain (see commentary on 65:17).

*your seed and your name remain.* The seed of the righteous is the eternal increase the Lord has promised to all who gain exaltation. Their name is the name of Christ, because they have become his sons and his daughters. As King Benjamin said, that is the name that will never be blotted out (Mosiah 5:10–11). The Lord here promises that the seed and the name of the righteous will remain as long as the new heavens and the new earth will remain, which is forever (see commentary on 62:2).

---

[6] Motyer, *Prophecy of Isaiah,* 542.

**66:23** *new moon/sabbath.* One of Israel's greatest sins was her corruption of the Lord's ordained feasts and holy days (1:13), two of which are alluded to here, "in the sabbaths, in the new moons" (1 Chr. 23:31; Isa. 58:13–14). In the millennial Zion, these feasts will regain their intended respect and will be kept perfectly, symbolizing the perfect worship that will be found in Zion.

*all flesh come to worship before me.* All the nations, even those that formerly oppressed Israel, will worship the Lord in the temple together (Zech. 14:16). This continues the promise of verses 19–20, where the nations became "your brethren." According to the *Interpreter's Bible,* "These two verses form a fitting conclusion to a great prophetic book. . . . Israel is the nation of priests, but chosen [so] that along with her all flesh may pay homage to the God of the whole earth. It is in worship that the unity of the nations is realized—*before me.*"[7]

**66:24** *they shall go forth, and look upon the carcases.* In the last of the last days, those who are slain by war and pestilence will be so numerous that they cannot be buried (Jer. 7:30–8:2). Jeremiah 7:32 refers to one location that will be called "the valley of slaughter: for they shall bury [there], till there be no place" (see also Ezek. 39:11–15). Those who go out into the land will see the dead bodies of those slain in the destruction of the wicked (Jer. 7:32–33). Motyer argues that inhabitants of Zion will deliberately "compel themselves to face the consequences of the last battle." They do so "to be repelled. To see and constantly refresh the memory that these are the consequences of rebellion, and so to turn in revulsion from such a thing and to be newly motivated to obedience by seeing that the wages of sin are indeed death."[8]

*their worm shall not die, neither shall their fire be quenched.* The torments of the wicked will last forever. The *worm* represents the worms that eat the bodies of the dead. But here the body is never consumed and the worm will never die; the punishment will never end. The *fire* may refer to the terrible burning of a guilty conscience, which fire will never be put out (Alma 15:3–5). This scriptural terminology seems to refer to two different groups: those who are in hell and those who become sons of perdition (Mark 9:44–48; Luke 16:24; D&C 76:43–48).

*an abhorring unto all flesh.* The carcasses strewn around the ground will be abhorrent in two ways: First, because the sight and the stench will be so horrible; and second, because it was offensive to an ancient Israelite not to care properly for the dead. For *an abhorring,* other versions have "loathsome" (NIV, JB), "disgusting" (TEV), and "a spectacle" (LXX).

---

[7] *Interpreter's Bible,* 5:772.
[8] Motyer, *Prophecy of Isaiah,* 544.

# NAMES, TITLES, AND SYMBOLS OF CHRIST IN THE BOOK OF ISAIAH

Isaiah provides numerous names, titles, and symbols of Jesus Christ in his writings, many of them more than once. The names *Holy One of Israel, God, Lord, Lord God, Lord of hosts,* and *Redeemer,* for instance, each appear a dozen or more times in the book of Isaiah. Truly, Isaiah's writings are centered in Christ. Following is a representative list of His names, titles, and symbols together with a reference from Isaiah.

Advocate (3:13)

Almighty (13:6)

Beloved (5:1)

Branch (11:1)

Bread (33:16)

Child (9:6)

Covert (32:2)

Creator (40:28)

Cyrus (45:1–5)

Elect (42:1)

Everlasting Father (9:6)

Everlasting God (40:28)

Everlasting Light (60:19)

First (41:4)

First and Last (48:12)

Gin (8:14)

God (54:5)

God of Israel (37:16)

God of Jacob (2:3)

God of Judgment (30:18)

God of the whole earth (54:5)

God of thy salvation (17:10)

God of truth (65:16)

God the Lord (42:5)

Great Light (9:2)

Hiding Place (32:2)

Holy One (12:6)

Holy One of Israel (1:4)

Holy One of Jacob (29:23)

Husband (54:5)

Immanuel (7:14)

Jehovah (12:2)

Judge (33:22)

King (6:5)

King of Jacob (41:21)

King of Israel (44:6)

Lamb (53:7)

Lawgiver (33:22)

Light (42:6)

Light of Israel (10:17)

Light to the Gentiles (49:6)

Lord (66:9)

Lord the Creator (40:28)

Lord God (30:15)

Lord God of Hosts (22:5)

Lord God of Israel (37:21)

Lord Jehovah (26:4)

Lord of hosts (22:25)

Lord the God of David (38:5)

Maher-shalal-hash-baz (8:1–4)

Maker (54:5)

Mighty God (9:6)

Mighty One of Israel (1:24)

Mighty One of Jacob (49:26)

Maker (54:5)

Man (32:2)

Man of Sorrows (53:3)

Master (1:3)

Messenger (42:19)

Mighty God (9:6)

Most High (14:14)

Owner (1:3)

Prince of Peace (9:6)

Redeemer (41:15)

Redeemer of Israel (49:7)

Refuge (25:4)

Righteous Man (41:2)

Righteous Servant (53:11)

Rivers (43:19)

Rivers of water (32:2)

Rock of offence (8:14)

Rock of thy strength (17:10)

Root (53:2)

Salvation (12:2)

Sanctuary (8:14)

Servant (42:1)

Savior (43:3)

Shadow (25:4)

Shepherd (40:11)

Snare (8:14)

Son (9:6)

Song (12:2)

Springs of Water (49:10)

Stem of Jesse (11:1)

Stone (28:16)

Stone of stumbling (8:14)

Strength (12:2)

Sure Foundation (28:16)

Teacher (48:17)

Tender Plant (53:2)

Water (44:3)

Waters (8:6)

Well-beloved (5:1)

Wells of salvation (12:3)

Wonderful Counselor (9:6)

# APPENDIX 2

# QUOTATIONS AND PARAPHRASES FROM ISAIAH IN THE BOOK OF MORMON

**Direct quotations**

| | |
|---|---|
| Isaiah 2–14 | 2 Nephi 12–24 |
| Isaiah 48–49 | 1 Nephi 20–21 |
| Isaiah 52:8–10 | 3 Nephi 16:18–20 |
| Isaiah 54 | 3 Nephi 22:1–17 |

**Paraphrases**

| | |
|---|---|
| Isaiah 9:12–13 | 2 Nephi 28:32 |
| Isaiah 11:4–9 | 2 Nephi 30:9, 12–15 |
| Isaiah 11:11; 29:14 | 2 Nephi 25:17 |
| Isaiah 28:10, 13 | 2 Nephi 28:30a |
| Isaiah 29:3–5 | 2 Nephi 26:15–16, 18 |
| Isaiah 29:4, 11 | 2 Nephi 27:6–9 |
| Isaiah 29:6 | 2 Nephi 6:15 |
| Isaiah 29:6–10 | 2 Nephi 27:2–5 |
| Isaiah 29:13b, 15 | 2 Nephi 28:9 |
| Isaiah 29:13–24 | 2 Nephi 27:25–35 |
| Isaiah 29:14 | 1 Nephi 14:7 |
| Isaiah 29:14; 11:11 | 2 Nephi 29:1; cf. 25:11 |
| Isaiah 29:21 | 2 Nephi 28:16a |
| Isaiah 40:3 | 1 Nephi 10:8 |
| Isaiah 45:18 | 1 Nephi 17:36 |

| | |
|---|---|
| Isaiah 49:22 | 1 Nephi 22:6 |
| Isaiah 49:22–23; 29:14 | 1 Nephi 22:8 |
| Isaiah 49:22–23 | 2 Nephi 6:6b–7, 16–18 |
| Isaiah 49:24–52:2 | 2 Nephi 6:16–8:25 |
| Isaiah 52:1; 54:2 | Moroni 10:31 |
| Isaiah 52:1–3, 6–7, 11–15 | 3 Nephi 20:36b–46 |
| Isaiah 52:7 | 1 Nephi 13:47; Mosiah 15:14–18 |
| Isaiah 52:7–10 | Mosiah 12:21–24 |
| Isaiah 52:8–10 | Mosiah 15:29–31; 3 Nephi 20:32–35 |
| Isaiah 52:10 | 1 Nephi 22:10–11 |
| Isaiah 52:12 | 3 Nephi 21:29 |
| Isaiah 52:15b | 3 Nephi 21:8b |
| Isaiah 53 | Mosiah 14:1–12 |
| Isaiah 53:10 | Mosiah 15:10 |
| Isaiah 55:1 | 2 Nephi 26:25 |
| Isaiah 55:1–2 | 2 Nephi 9:50–51 |

—*∾*—

# PROPHETIC SPEECH FORMS

An important literary device found in Isaiah's writings is prophetic speech forms, which is part of "the manner of prophesying among the Jews" (2 Ne. 25:1). These forms are also found often in the writings of Hosea, Ezekiel, Moses, Nephi, Alma, and Joseph Smith. Prophetic speech forms are brief revelatory statements that follow a set formula. They frequently contain the name of God, are often located at the beginning or the end of a revelation, and indicate prophetic authority. Those who are not prophets may not appropriately use these forms, for the authority attached to them originates from God. We know of two false prophets in the Old Testament who used the form "Thus saith the Lord" (Zedekiah, son of Chenaanah, and Hananiah) but they did so without authority from God, and one was destroyed by God for his presumption (1 Kgs. 22:11; 2 Chr. 18:10; Jer. 28:10–11, 15–17).

The first of these speech forms, "Thus saith the Lord," is called the messenger formula. This formula is found forty-six times in the writings of Isaiah. Its purpose is to set forth both the divine authority and the origin of the revelation.

The revelation formula, which is similar to the messenger formula, follows this format: "The word that Isaiah, son of Amoz, saw," or "the Lord spake also unto me again, saying. . . ." This form likewise indicates prophetic authority and the source of the revelation.

A third form, "Hearken unto me" or "Hear the word of the Lord," is called the proclamation formula. Its primary function is to call the people to attention, so that they can hear what the Lord would say to them through his prophet.

Another formula, the oath formula, reads "As the Lord liveth" or "The Lord of Hosts has sworn" (see 14:24). With this declaration the Lord essentially says, "As surely as I live, so surely will these prophecies come to pass," or "This will happen because I say it will, and I never lie."

A final prophetic speech formula is the woe oracle. (*Oracle* means essentially words of revelation from God.) This form can easily be recognized by the use of the word *woe* one or more times within the oracle. The characteristic woe oracle consists of the accusation ("wo" or "woe"), the person or group addressed ("Wo unto the kingdom of Moab," or "Wo unto Assyria," or "woe unto" other groups), the intent of the accusation ("Wo unto Moab because . . . ," or "Wo unto Judah because . . ."), and the promise of judgment ("Wo unto Moab because they have sinned against me, and they will be destroyed").[1]

Of course, revelations may lack such a formula and still have power and authority from God, but it aids our understanding to know what the prophetic speech forms are and to know that Isaiah wrote according to an ancient pattern given by the Lord.

---

[1] For examples of the woe oracle from the Book of Mormon, see Parry, "'Thus Saith the Lord,'" 182.

# THE PROPHETIC PERFECT TENSE
# IN ISAIAH

A powerful example of the prophetic nature of the book of Isaiah is Isaiah's use of the "prophetic perfect" verb tense.[1] With the prophetic perfect, the prophet may speak in verbs that are past, present, or future, yet in every case he may be speaking of things that are yet to come. An example is found in Isaiah 53:

Future: "For he *shall* grow up . . . when we *shall* see him" (53:2).

Present: "He *is* despised and rejected of men" (53:3).

Past: "We *hid* as it were our faces from him; he *was* despised" (53:3).

This juxtaposition of different verb tenses continues throughout the chapter and much of the book. Some people may be confused by the prophet's use of verbs, but he is simply using the "prophetic perfect" tense.

Through his prophecies, Isaiah shows clearly that God is in control of the world at all times. He is the God who creates history; and he organizes the history of the world with his elect people, the house of Israel, in mind, while ever viewing the needs of the Gentiles. He orders history by sending prophets to proclaim his word, judgments against wicked nations and peoples, blessings to the righteous, and by preparing Zion-like communities among those who follow him. He raises up an Isaiah, an Alma, or a Joseph Smith to teach the word of God to a generation, to prophesy, testify, and warn. He moves upon the leaders of an Assyria or a Babylon to lead their armies against others. The people of God can see God's hand in history, performing, as one author said, "a notable balancing of divine and human agency."[2] Of course,

---

[1] See Ricks, "I Have a Question," 28.
[2] Motyer, *Prophecy of Isaiah*, 136.

Isaiah also deals with the present and the near future. Sometimes the same prophecy has multiple applications, each one true.

—⟨∿⟩—

# ISAIAH'S POETRY

Isaiah consistently wrote in a form called poetic parallelism. In poetic parallelism, the prophet makes a statement in a line, a phrase, or a sentence and then restates it, so that the second line, phrase, or sentence echoes or mirrors the first. There are approximately eleven hundred of these short poetic units in the book of Isaiah. Understanding parallelisms is an important part of understanding Isaiah's message.

Isaiah 2:2, often quoted by latter-day Church leaders, is one well-known example. Isaiah prophesies that in the last days "the mountain of the Lord's house shall be established in the top of the mountains and shall be exalted above the hills." Notice the repetition:

[Line 1:] "Shall be *established* in the top of the *mountains,*

[Line 2:] and shall be *exalted* above the *hills.*"

*Shall be* parallels *shall be; established* is parallel to *exalted; in the top* parallels *above;* and *mountains* parallels *hills.*

Following is another example from Isaiah 2:

[Line 1:] "And all *nations shall flow* unto it.

[Line 2:] And many *people shall go . . .*"

Both lines 1 and 2 begin with the conjunction *and. All* parallels *many; nations* parallels *people;* and *shall flow* parallels *shall go.*

———

# SYMBOLISM AND ISAIAH

An important aspect of the manner of prophesying among the Jews is the use of symbols and symbolic language. The Lord said through Hosea, "I have also spoken by the prophets, and I have multiplied visions, and used similitudes" (Hosea 12:10). Symbols and types are so important that Nephi wrote, "My soul delighteth in proving unto my people the truth of the coming of Christ; . . . and all things which have been given of God from the beginning of the world, unto man, are the typifying of him" (2 Ne. 11:4). Symbolism is a key element of Isaiah's text; it appears to be part of every single revelation. Through revelation, Isaiah drew upon his social, cultural, religious, and political background to produce hundreds of different symbols. He used items that deal with common aspects of everyday life to illustrate prophecy and eternal truths.

As we seek to understand Isaiah and his use of symbolism, it is helpful to recognize that symbolic speech is a greater part of our own culture than we may realize. One example, the concept of *heart,* will illustrate this. Here are some of the ways that we use the heart symbolically:

"Change of heart" deals with a change in our affections, a change of mind, a change of feelings, or all of these.

"Eat one's heart out," a very different expression, means to feel frustration or unhappiness.

" From the bottom of my heart" means to be very sincere.

"Have a heart" means to be kind or sympathetic.

"He has his heart in the right place" means he is well-intentioned.

"She works with heart and soul" means she performs her work with great enthusiasm.

"He has his heart set on the riches of the world" means that riches were what he most desired.

"She stole his heart away" means that she caused him to love her deeply.

"Take heart" means to have courage, or to be encouraged.

"With all your heart" means to do something with all your emotional or physical power.

These are common idioms in our culture, each one symbolic. We all know that a person's heart is the muscle that pumps blood through our systems, but these expressions refer to something besides the physical heart in our bodies.

In the same way, much of what Isaiah says is symbolic, referring not to actual bears, cedars, or barley but to something else represented by each of these. We have to work harder to understand his symbols and idioms than we do those that are familiar to us, but through study, accompanied by the Spirit of the Lord, we can come to a true understanding of each.

The kinds of symbols Isaiah used seem to come from all aspects of life. Following are twenty-one major categories of Isaiah's symbols, with a few examples in each:

Actions
> Common actions: drinking, eating, falling down, fornicating, shaving hair, singing, sitting
> Sacred actions: anointings, ordinations, sacrifices, spreading forth hands

Animals/insects—asses, bear, beast, bee, bird, bittern, bullock, calf, camels, cattle, crane

Architectural elements—bulwarks, foundation, gate, house, pillar, wall, watchtower, windows

Armor and weaponry—armor, arrow, bow, shield, sword, weapon

Astronomical elements—cloud, constellations, heaven, moon, stars, sun

Atmospheric conditions—earthquake, flood, hail, storm, tempest, whirlwinds, wind

Colors—crimson, red, scarlet, white

Ecclesiastical offices—priests, prophet

Elements/rocks/minerals—ashes, clay, clods, dirt, gold, iron, rock, silver, tin

Family and social relationships—bridegroom, brother, children, daughter, father, firstborn, handmaids

Foods—barley, berries, bread, butter, corn, fruit, grapes, honey, milk, wheat, wine

Geography—brook, cities, deep, desert, dry ground, field, highways, hill, mountain, river

Human anatomy—arm, beard, belly, blood, bones, cheeks, ear, eye, face, feet, finger, heart

Names and titles
    Of Deity: Immanuel, Jehovah, Wonderful
    Of persons: Beulah, Cyrus, Lucifer

Numbers—thousand

Objects
    Common objects: ax, bed, bill of divorcement, book, chains, chariots, cup, idol
    Sacred objects: altar, drink offering, incense, temple

Occupations—carpenter, creditors, fishermen, harvester, king, officers, seller, servant

Persons—Abraham, Cyrus, David, Jesse, Sarah

Places—Ariel, Assyria, Babylon, Egypt, Jerusalem, Sodom, Tarshish

Plants—cedars, fig tree, flower, grass, groves, leaf, oak, olive tree, orchard, root, seed

Time—day, daytime, night, noonday, summer, winter

This list of symbols is representative only, for Isaiah used literally hundreds of symbols in his writings. As we study Isaiah's symbolic expressions, we will more fully appreciate his message to us.

———

# THE SPIRIT OF PROPHECY

A key to understanding Isaiah is to have the spirit of prophecy. Those who live righteously have claim to the Holy Spirit of God, which gives them, as a gift, the spirit of prophecy. Nephi taught that "the words of Isaiah . . . are plain unto all those that are filled with the spirit of prophecy" (2 Ne. 25:4). This is a vital and essential key to understanding the writings of Isaiah. In our opinion it is the most important key, although, of course, it depends on the key of righteousness.

It seems reasonable that the reader would be required to possess the spirit of prophecy to understand Isaiah's words, because Isaiah needed that same spirit of prophecy to receive revelation. Nephi explained to his brethren that the prophecies of Isaiah "were manifest unto the prophet [Isaiah] by the voice of the Spirit; for by the Spirit are all things made known unto the prophets, which shall come upon the children of men according to the flesh." (1 Ne. 22:2.)

The expression *the spirit of prophecy* belongs almost exclusively to the Book of Mormon, being used there more than twenty times. Contrast that number with the one instance in the Bible, found in Revelation 19:10. The definition of the phrase, as presented in scripture, refers to the testimony of Jesus. Joseph Smith understood this well, as he explained on one occasion: "Salvation cannot come without revelation; it is in vain for anyone to minister without it. No man is a minister of Jesus Christ without being a Prophet. No man can be a minister of Jesus Christ except he has the testimony of Jesus; and this is the spirit of prophecy. Whenever salvation has been administered, it has been by testimony."[1]

---

[1] *History of the Church,* 3:389–90.

President John Taylor taught, "The testimony of Jesus was the very principle, essence, and power of the spirit of prophecy whereby the ancient prophets were inspired."[2] Thus those who have a deep and true testimony of Christ have already experienced the spirit of prophecy. Those who have received the spiritual message, or testimony, that Jesus is the Christ have received a vital spiritual communication from on high. The spirit of prophecy is but another manifestation of that same Spirit.

Several ancient prophets have connected the spirit of prophecy to the Holy Ghost. Modern prophets have seen a virtual equivalency between the spirit of prophecy and the Holy Ghost. Elder Wilford Woodruff wrote that "it is the privilege of every man and woman in this kingdom to enjoy the spirit of prophecy, which is the Spirit of God."[3] Elder Delbert L. Stapley said that "the Holy Ghost is the spirit of prophecy."[4]

The formula for receiving the spirit of prophecy is presented in Alma 17:2–3. The key requirements appear to be diligent search of the scriptures, much fasting, and much prayer: "Now these sons of Mosiah . . . had waxed strong in the knowledge of the truth; for they were men of a sound understanding and they had searched the scriptures diligently, that they might know the word of God. But this is not all; they had given themselves to much prayer, and fasting; therefore they had the spirit of prophecy, and the spirit of revelation."

*Revelation* and *the spirit of prophecy* are terms commonly found together in scripture. Of twenty-six instances of the term *spirit of prophecy* in the scriptures, fourteen also refer to *revelation* or *revelations.*

---

[2] Taylor, *Gospel Kingdom,* 120.
[3] *Discourses of Wilford Woodruff,* 61.
[4] Conference Report, Oct. 1966, 113.

━◦◉◦━

# Sources Consulted

Benson, Ezra Taft. *Come unto Christ.* Salt Lake City: Bookcraft, 1983.

———. "Cleansing the Inner Vessel." *Ensign,* May 1986, 4–6.

———. "The Book of Mormon—Keystone of Our Religion." *Ensign,* November 1986, 4–7.

*Biblia Hebraica Stuttgartensia.* Stuttgart: Deutsche Bibelgesellschaft, 1990.

Brown, Francis, S. R. Driver, and Charles A. Briggs. *A Hebrew and English Lexicon of the Old Testament.* Trans. Edward Robinson. Oxford: Clarendon, 1977.

Cloward, Robert A. "Isaiah 29 and the Book of Mormon." In *Isaiah in the Book of Mormon.* Ed. Donald W. Parry and John W. Welch. Provo: Foundation for Ancient Research and Mormon Studies, 1988, 191–247.

Davies, W. D. *The Gospel and the Land: Early Christianity and Jewish Territorial Doctrine.* Sheffield, England: Journal for the Study of the Old Testament [JSOT] Press, 1994.

Dead Sea Scrolls.

Dummelow, J. R. *A Commentary on the Holy Bible.* New York: Macmillan, 1908.

Farley, S. Brent. "Nephi, Isaiah, and the Latter-day Restoration." In *The Book of Mormon: Second Nephi, The Doctrinal Structure,* ed. Monte S. Nyman and Charles D. Tate Jr., 227–39. Provo: BYU Religious Studies Center, 1989.

"The Father and the Son: A Doctrinal Exposition by the First Presidency and the Twelve." In James E. Talmage, *Articles of Faith.* Salt Lake City: Deseret Book, 1977.

Gentry, Leland H. "God Will Fulfill His Covenants with the House of Israel." In *The Book of Mormon: Second Nephi, The Doctrinal Structure,* ed. Monte S. Nyman and Charles D. Tate Jr., 159–76. Provo: BYU Religious Studies Center, 1989.

———. "Why So Much Isaiah in the Book of Mormon?" In *A Symposium on the Book of Mormon,* 45–47. Salt Lake City: The Church of Jesus Christ of Latter-day Saints, 1979.

Ginzberg, Louis. *Legends of the Jews.* 7 vols. Philadelphia: Jewish Publication Society, 1909–38.

*Good News Bible: The Bible in Today's English Version.* New York: American Bible Society, 1976.

Hailey, Homer. *A Commentary on Isaiah.* Grand Rapids, Mich.: Baker, 1985.

Haran, Menahem. *Temples and Temple-Service in Ancient Israel.* Winona Lake, Ind.: Eisenbrauns, 1985.

Holland, Jeffrey R. *Christ and the New Covenant: The Messianic Message of the Book of Mormon.* Salt Lake City: Deseret Book, 1997.

The Holy Bible. Authorized King James Version. Salt Lake City: The Church of Jesus Christ of Latter-day Saints, 1979.

Holy Bible. New King James Version. New York: American Bible Society, 1990.

Holy Bible. New Revised Standard Version. New York: Oxford University Press, 1989.

Holy Bible. Revised Standard Version. New York: Nelson, 1946, 1952.

The Holy Scriptures according to the Masoretic Text. Philadelphia: Jewish Publication Society of America, 1965.

*Hymns of The Church of Jesus Christ of Latter-day Saints.* Salt Lake City: The Church of Jesus Christ of Latter-day Saints, 1985.

*The Interpreter's Bible.* 12 vols. New York: Abingdon, 1956.

Jackson, Kent P. "Nephi and Isaiah." In *1 Nephi to Alma 29,* ed. Kent P. Jackson, 131–45. Studies in Scripture Series, vol. 7. Salt Lake City: Deseret Book, 1987.

Jessee, Dean C., ed. *The Papers of Joseph Smith: Autobiographical and Historical Writings.* Vol. 1. Salt Lake City: Deseret Book, 1989.

Jerusalem Bible. Reader's Edition. Garden City, N. Y.: Doubleday, 1968.

Jewish Bible. Philadelphia: Jewish Publication Society, 1985.

Josephus, Flavius. *Antiquities of the Jews.* Trans. William Whiston. Grand Rapids, Mich.: Kregel, 1981.

Joseph Smith's "New Translation" of the Bible. Independence, Mo.: Herald, 1970.

*Journal of Discourses.* 26 vols. London: Latter-day Saints' Book Depot, 1854–86.

Kaiser, Otto. *Isaiah 1–12: A Commentary.* Philadelphia: Westminster, 1983.

Keil, C. F., and F. Delitzsch. *Commentary on the Old Testament.* 10 vols. Reprint. Grand Rapids, Mich.: Eerdmans, 1975.

Kimball, Spencer W. *The Miracle of Forgiveness.* Salt Lake City: Bookcraft, 1969.

———. Conference Report, October 1965, 65–72.

Kissane, Edward J. *The Book of Isaiah.* Dublin: Browne and Nolan, 1941.

Koehler, Ludwig, and Walter Baumgartner. *Lexicon in Veteris Testamenti Libros.* Leiden: Brill, 1953.

Kutscher, E. Y. *The Language and Linguistic Background of the Isaiah Scroll.* Leiden: Brill, 1974.

Lee, Harold B. "The Way to Eternal Life." *Ensign,* November 1971, 9–17.

Living Bible. Wheaton, Ill.: Tyndale, 1976.

Longdon, John. Conference Report, April 1964, 115–17.

Ludlow, Victor L. *Isaiah: Prophet, Seer, and Poet.* Salt Lake City: Deseret Book, 1982.

Lund, Nils W. *Chiasmus in the New Testament.* Peabody, Mass.: Hendrickson, 1970.

Lundquist, John M. "What Is a Temple? A Preliminary Typology." In *Temples of the Ancient World: Ritual and Symbolism,* ed. Donald W. Parry, 83–117. Salt Lake City: Deseret Book and FARMS, 1994.

Matthews, Robert J. *"A Plainer Translation": Joseph Smith's Translation of the Bible.* Provo: Brigham Young University Press, 1975.

Maxwell, Neal A. *Meek and Lowly.* Salt Lake City: Deseret Book, 1987.

McConkie, Bruce R. *Doctrinal New Testament Commentary.* 3 vols. Salt Lake City: Bookcraft, 1965–73.

———. *A New Witness for the Articles of Faith.* Salt Lake City: Deseret Book, 1985.

———. *The Millennial Messiah.* Salt Lake City: Deseret Book, 1982.

———. *The Mortal Messiah.* 4 vols. Salt Lake City: Deseret Book, 1979–81.

———. *The Promised Messiah.* Salt Lake City: Deseret Book, 1978.

McConkie, Joseph Fielding, and Robert L. Millet. *Doctrinal Commentary on the Book of Mormon.* 4 vols. Salt Lake City: Bookcraft, 1987–92.

McConkie, Joseph Fielding, and Donald W. Parry. *A Guide to Scriptural Symbols.* Salt Lake City: Bookcraft, 1990.

*Merriam Webster's Collegiate Dictionary.* 10th ed. Springfield, Mass.: Merriam-Webster, 1993.

*[Latter-day Saints'] Messenger and Advocate.* Kirtland, Ohio, 1834–37.

Motyer, J. Alec. *The Prophecy of Isaiah: An Introduction and Commentary.* Downer's Grove, Ill.: InterVarsity, 1993.

*New Bible Dictionary.* Ed. J. D. Douglas. Leicester, England: InterVarsity, 1988.

New American Bible. Nashville: Nelson, 1987.

New English Bible. Oxford: Oxford University Press, 1961.

New International Version of the Holy Bible. Grand Rapids, Mich.: Zondervan, 1986.

New Jerusalem Bible. Garden City, N. Y.: Doubleday, 1985.

*The New Layman's Bible Commentary in One Volume.* Ed. George C. D. Howley, Frederick F. Bruce, and Henry L. Ellison. Grand Rapids, Mich.: Zondervan, 1979.

Nibley, Hugh W. *Approaching Zion.* Salt Lake City: Deseret Book and FARMS, 1989.

Nyman, Monte S. "Abinadi's Commentary on Isaiah." In *The Book of Mormon: Mosiah, Salvation Only through Christ,* ed. Monte S. Nyman and Charles D. Tate Jr. Provo: BYU Religious Studies Center, 1991, 161–86.

Nyman, Monte S. *Great Are the Words of Isaiah.* Salt Lake City: Bookcraft, 1980.

Ogden, D. Kelly. "Jerusalem." In *Encyclopedia of Mormonism,* ed. Daniel H. Ludlow, 2:722–23. 4 vols. New York: Macmillan, 1992.

Oswalt, John N. *The Book of Isaiah: Chapters 1–39.* Grand Rapids, Mich.: Eerdmans, 1986.

Parry, Donald W. "Garden of Eden: Prototype Sanctuary." In *Temples of the Ancient World: Ritual and Symbolism,* ed. Donald W. Parry, 126–51. Salt Lake City: Deseret Book and FARMS, 1994.

———. "'Thus Saith the Lord': Prophetic Language in Samuel's Speech." *Journal of Book of Mormon Studies,* vol. 1, no. 1 (1992): 181–83.

Parry, Donald W., and Elisha Qimron. *The Great Isaiah Scroll: Transcription and Photographs.* Forthcoming.

Parry, Donald W., and John W. Welch, eds. *Isaiah in the Book of Mormon.* Provo: Foundation for Ancient Research and Mormon Studies, 1998.

Parsons, Robert E. "The Prophecies of the Prophets." In *The Book of Mormon: First Nephi, The Doctrinal Foundation,* ed. Monte S. Nyman and Charles D. Tate Jr., 271–81. Provo: BYU Religious Studies Center, 1988.

Petersen, Mark E. Conference Report, October 1965, 59–63.

Pratt, Orson. *Orson Pratt's Works on the Doctrines of the Gospel.* Salt Lake City: Deseret News Press, 1945.

———. *Divine Authenticity of the Book of Mormon.* No. 6. Pamphlet. Liverpool, 1851.

Richards, LeGrand. *A Marvelous Work and a Wonder.* Salt Lake City: Deseret Book, 1950.

Ricks, Stephen D. "I Have a Question." *Ensign,* August 1988, 28.

Ricks, Stephen D., and John J. Sroka. "King, Coronation, and Temple: Enthronement Ceremonies in History." In *Temples of the Ancient World: Ritual and Symbolism,* ed. Donald W. Parry, 236–71. Salt Lake City: Deseret Book and FARMS, 1994.

Satterfield, Bruce. "Isaiah 2–4: Bringing the Real to the Ideal." Paper presented at the Sidney B. Sperry Symposium, Brigham Young University, Provo, October 1997.

Scanlin, Harold. *The Dead Sea Scrolls and Modern Translations of the Old Testament.* Wheaton, Ill.: Tyndale, 1993.

*Septuaginta.* Stuttgart: Deutsche Bibelgesellschaft, 1979.

Smith, Joseph. *History of The Church of Jesus Christ of Latter-day Saints.* Ed. B. H. Roberts. 2d ed., rev. 7 vols. Salt Lake City: The Church of Jesus Christ of Latter-day Saints, 1980.

———. *Lectures on Faith.* Comp. N. B. Lundwall. Salt Lake City: N. B. Lundwall, n.d.

———. *Teachings of the Prophet Joseph Smith.* Sel. Joseph Fielding Smith. Salt Lake City: Deseret Book, 1976.

Smith, Joseph Fielding. *Answers to Gospel Questions.* 5 vols. Salt Lake City: Deseret Book, 1957–66.

———. *Doctrines of Salvation.* 3 vols. Comp. Bruce R. McConkie. Salt Lake City: Bookcraft, 1954–66.

———. *The Signs of the Times.* Salt Lake City: Deseret Book, 1974.

———. Conference Report, April 1966, 101–3.

Sperry, Sidney B. *The Old Testament Prophets.* Salt Lake City: Deseret Sunday School Union, 1965.

———. *The Voice of Israel's Prophets.* Salt Lake City: Deseret Book, 1952.

Stapley, Delbert L. Conference Report. October 1966, 111–14.

Talmage, James E. *Articles of Faith.* Salt Lake City: Deseret Book, 1977.

———. *Jesus the Christ.* Salt Lake City: Deseret Book, 1970.

Taylor, John. *The Gospel Kingdom.* Ed. G. Homer Durham. Salt Lake City: Bookcraft, 1943.

*Times and Seasons.* Nauvoo, Ill., 1839–46.

Turner, Rodney. "The Two Davids." In *A Witness of Jesus Christ: The 1989 Sperry Symposium on the Old Testament.* Salt Lake City: Deseret Book, 1990.

Tvedtnes, John A. "The Isaiah Variants in the Book of Mormon." In *Isaiah and the Prophets: Inspired Voices from the Old Testament,* ed. Monte S. Nyman and Charles D. Tate Jr., 165–77. Provo: BYU Religious Studies Center, 1984.

Watts, John D. W. *Isaiah 1–33.* Waco, Tex.: Word Books, 1985.

———. *Isaiah 34–66.* Waco, Tex.: Word Books, 1987.

Wildberger, Hans. *Isaiah 1–12: A Commentary.* Minneapolis, Minn.: Fortress, 1991.

Woodruff, Wilford. *The Discourses of Wilford Woodruff.* Comp. G. Homer Durham. Salt Lake City: Bookcraft, 1969.

———. In *Collected Discourses Delivered by President Wilford Woodruff, His Two Counselors, the Twelve Apostles, and Others.* Comp. and ed. Brian H. Stuy. 5 vols. Burbank, Calif.: B. H. S. Publishing, 1992.

Young, Edward J. *The Book of Isaiah.* 3 vols. Grand Rapids, Mich.: Eerdmans, 1965.

# SCRIPTURE INDEX

—〰—

# S U B J E C T  I N D E X

—◆—